Lecture Notes in Artificial Intelligence 8758

Subseries of Lecture Notes in Computer Science

Fabiano Dalpiaz Jürgen Dix
M. Birna van Riemsdijk (Eds.)

Engineering Multi-Agent Systems

Second International Workshop, EMAS 2014
Paris, France, May 5-6, 2014
Revised Selected Papers

Volume Editors

Fabiano Dalpiaz
Utrecht University
The Netherlands
E-mail: f.dalpiaz@uu.nl

Jürgen Dix
Clausthal University of Technology
Clausthal-Zellerfeld, Germany
E-mail: dix@tu-clausthal.de

M. Birna van Riemsdijk
Delft University of Technology
The Netherlands
E-mail: m.b.vanriemsdijk@tudelft.nl

ISSN 0302-9743 e-ISSN 1611-3349
ISBN 978-3-319-14483-2 e-ISBN 978-3-319-14484-9
DOI 10.1007/978-3-319-14484-9
Springer Cham Heidelberg New York Dordrecht London

Library of Congress Control Number: 2014958993

LNCS Sublibrary: SL 7 – Artificial Intelligence

Typesetting: Camera-ready by author, data conversion by Scientific Publishing Services, Chennai, India

Printed on acid-free paper

Springer is part of Springer Science+Business Media (www.springer.com)

Preface

The engineering of multi-agent systems (MAS) is a complex activity: Such systems consist of multiple autonomous and heterogeneous agents, and their proper functioning depends on the effective interaction between these agents. While MAS have been used to some extent in industry, we feel that a wider adoption is hindered by the fact that the underlying engineering techniques are not as mature as those in mainstream software and systems engineering. Numerous challenges have to be addressed, including:

Design and software engineering: how to effectively *design* agents and their interactions?
Implementation: how to *implement* multi-agent coordination or organizations *efficiently*?
Verification: how to *formally verify* (un-) desired properties of individual agents and MAS?

We believe that these challenges can be tackled more effectively when considered within the discipline of MAS engineering. As an example, design artefacts (e.g., agents or MAS models) can be used to support and assist with debugging and testing. Other examples are the following: (1) the development of agent-oriented programming languages that result in programs that are more readily verifiable, (2) the use of declarative techniques that span design and implementation.

The International Workshop on Engineering Multi-Agent Systems (EMAS) is meant to be an ideal venue for papers that relate to all aspects of agent and MAS engineering. EMAS was created in 2013 as a merger of three separate workshops (with overlapping communities) that focused on software engineering aspects (AOSE), programming aspects (ProMAS), and the application of declarative techniques to design, programming, and verification (DALT).

The EMAS workshop series[1] explicitly pursues three goals:

To progress and further develop the understanding of how to engineer multi-agent systems.
To bring together the communities that are concerned with different aspects of engineering MAS, and by doing so, allow for better interchange of ideas between the communities, thus exploiting the synergies discussed above.
To provide a venue for workshop papers that report on experiences and lessons

[1] `http://emas.in.tu-clausthal.de`

learned from innovative applications of MAS, and have these lessons influence further research in the field.

To guide the authors in preparing their submissions and to establish a consistent set of expectations in the review process, all authors were asked to self-identify their papers with one or more of the categories (adapted from the ICSE 2014 guidelines[2]) listed below. In this way, we hope to foster the diversity of approaches for addressing challenges in engineering MAS.

Analytical: A paper in which the main contribution relies on new mathematical theory or algorithms. Examples include new logics and semantics for agent programming languages, algorithms for agent reasoning, algorithms for the efficient implementation of MAS languages.
Empirical: A paper in which the main contribution is the empirical study of an MAS engineering technology or phenomenon. This includes studies of the use of (existing or novel) MAS engineering techniques in practice, such as (industrial) experience reports, controlled experiments, and case studies, using qualitative and/or quantitative data analysis. This also concerns empirical evaluations of algorithms and performance of MAS platforms.
Technological: A paper in which the main contribution is of a technological nature. This includes novel tools, environments, testbeds, modeling languages, infrastructures, and other technologies.
Methodological: A paper in which the main contribution is a coherent system of broad principles and practices to interpret or solve a problem. This includes novel requirements elicitation methods, process models, design methods, development approaches, programming paradigms, and other methodologies.

EMAS 2014 received 41 submissions. Each paper was reviewed by three reviewers, and we accepted 22 papers for presentation at the workshop. These were distributed across the paper categories as follows: technological: 17; methodological: 14; analytical: 6; empirical: 4. The authors of accepted papers were invited to submit a revised version of their paper for the Springer LNAI proceedings, which underwent another round of reviewing. The result is this volume, containing 21 regular papers and an additional paper from one of the invited speakers at the workshop.

The EMAS 2014 chairs would like to acknowledge the great review work done by members of the Program Committee. Reviews were in general detailed (and, we hope, useful to the authors), and were followed by extensive discussion among Program Committee members and chairs to finally decide on the acceptance of the papers.

[2] `http://2014.icse-conferences.org/research`

We hope the reader of this volume finds the papers useful to get an idea about this exciting area.

October 2014

Fabiano Dalpiaz
Jürgen Dix
M. Birna van Riemsdijk

Organization

Workshop Chairs

Fabiano Dalpiaz	Utrecht University, The Netherlands
Jürgen Dix	Clausthal University of Technology, Germany
M. Birna van Riemsdijk	Delft University of Technology, The Netherlands

Steering Committee

EMAS is overseen by a (merged) Steering Committee from the three "parent" workshops (original Steering Committee indicated in parentheses).

Matteo Baldoni	DALT; Italy
Rafael Bordini	ProMAS; Brazil
Mehdi Dastani	ProMAS; The Netherlands
Jürgen Dix	ProMAS; Germany
Amal El Fallah Seghrouchni	ProMAS; France
Paolo Giorgini	AOSE; Italy
Jörg Müller	AOSE; Germany
M. Birna Van Riemsdijk	DALT; The Netherlands
Tran Cao Son	DALT; USA
Gerhard Weiss	AOSE; The Netherlands
Danny Weyns	AOSE; Sweden
Michael Winikoff	DALT/AOSE; New Zealand

Program Committee

Natasha Alechina	University of Nottingham, UK
Matteo Baldoni	University of Turin, Italy
Cristina Baroglio	University of Turin, Italy
Jeremy Baxter	QinetiQ, UK
Olivier Boissier	ENS Mines Saint-Etienne, France
Rafael H. Bordini	FACIN-PUCRS, Brazil
Lars Braubach	University of Hamburg, Germany
Rem Collier	University College Dublin, Ireland
Massimo Cossentino	National Research Council of Italy, Italy
Fabiano Dalpiaz	Utrecht University, The Netherlands
Mehdi Dastani	Utrecht University, The Netherlands
Scott A. Deloach	Kansas State University, USA
Louise Dennis	University of Liverpool, UK
Virginia Dignum	Delft University of Technology, The Netherlands

Jürgen Dix	TU Clausthal, Germany
Paolo Giorgini	University of Trento, Italy
Adriana Giret	Technical University of Valencia, Spain
Jorge Gomez-Sanz	Universidad Complutense de Madrid, Spain
Christian Guttmann	IBM, Australia
James Harland	RMIT University, Australia
Vincent Hilaire	UTBM/IRTES-SET, France
Benjamin Hirsch	EBTIC / Khalifa University, United Arab Emirates
Tom Holvoet	KU Leuven, Belgium
Jomi Fred Hubner	Federal University of Santa Catarina, Brazil
Yves Lespérance	York University, Canada
Brian Logan	University of Nottingham, UK
Viviana Mascardi	University of Genova, Italy
Philippe Mathieu	University of Lille 1, France
Frederic Migeon	IRIT, France
Ambra Molesini	University of Bologna, Italy
Pavlos Moraitis	Paris Descartes University, France
Jörg P. Müller	TU Clausthal, Germany
Peter Novák	Delft University of Technology, The Netherlands
Alexander Pokahr	University of Hamburg, Germany
Enrico Pontelli	New Mexico State University, USA
Alessandro Ricci	University of Bologna, Italy
Chiaki Sakama	Wakayama University, Japan
Guillermo Ricardo Simari	Universidad Nacional del Sur, Brazil
Tran Cao Son	New Mexico State University, USA
Bas Steunebrink	IDSIA, Switzerland
Pankaj Telang	CISCO Systems, USA
Paolo Torroni	University of Bologna, Italy
Birna van Riemsdijk	Delft University of Technology, The Netherlands
Wamberto Vasconcelos	University of Aberdeen, UK
Jørgen Villadsen	Technical University of Denmark, Denmark
Michael Winikoff	University of Otago, New Zealand
Wayne Wobcke	University of New South Wales, Australia
Neil Yorke-Smith	American University of Beirut, Lebanon

Additional Reviewers

Thomas Christopher King
Thomas Kennerth
Arman Noroozian
Patrizia Ribino
Yann Secq

Table of Contents

The Shaping of the Agent-Oriented Mindset: Twenty Years of Engineering MAS 1
Koen V. Hindriks

Keeping a Clear Separation between Goals and Plans 15
Costin Caval, Amal El Fallah Seghrouchni, and Patrick Taillibert

A Stepwise Refinement Based Development of Self-Organizing Multi-Agent Systems: Application to the Foraging Ants 40
Zeineb Graja, Frédéric Migeon, Christine Maurel, Marie-Pierre Gleizes, and Ahmed Hadj Kacem

Improving the Design and Modularity of BDI Agents with Capability Relationships 58
Ingrid Nunes

A Scalable Runtime Platform for Multiagent-Based Simulation 81
Tobias Ahlbrecht, Jürgen Dix, Michael Köster, Philipp Kraus, and Jörg P. Müller

Security Games in the Field: Deployments on a Transit System 103
Francesco M. Delle Fave, Matthew Brown, Chao Zhang, Eric Shieh, Albert Xin Jiang, Heather Rosoff, Milind Tambe, and John P. Sullivan

The AORTA Architecture: Integrating Organizational Reasoning in *Jason* 127
Andreas Schmidt Jensen, Virginia Dignum, and Jørgen Villadsen

Keep Improving MAS Method Fragments: A Medee-Based Case Study for MOISE+ 146
Sara Casare, Anarosa Alves Franco Brandao, and Jaime Sichman

Towards Process-Oriented Modelling and Creation of Multi-Agent Systems 163
Tobias Küster, Axel Heßler, and Sahin Albayrak

Environments and Organizations in Multi-Agent Systems: From Modelling to Code 181
Daniela Maria Uez and Jomi Fred Hübner

From Multi-Agent Programming to Object Oriented Design Patterns ... 204
Mehdi Dastani and Bas Testerink

CaFé: A Group Process to Rationalize Technologies in Hybrid AAMAS Systems ... 227
H. Van Dyke Parunak, Marcus Huber, Randolph Jones, Michael Quist, and Jack Zaientz

Efficient Verification of MASs with Projections ... 246
Davide Ancona, Daniela Briola, Amal El Fallah Seghrouchni, Viviana Mascardi, and Patrick Taillibert

Infinite States Verification in Game-Theoretic Logics: Case Studies and Implementation ... 271
Slawomir Kmiec and Yves Lespérance

Side Effects of Agents Are Not Just Random ... 291
Bruno Mermet and Gaële Simon

Mutation Testing for Jason Agents ... 309
Zhan Huang, Rob Alexander, and John Clark

Tractable Reasoning about Group Beliefs ... 328
Barbara Dunin-Kęplicz, Andrzej Szałas, and Rineke Verbrugge

Semantic Representations of Agent Plans and Planning Problem Domains ... 351
Artur Freitas, Daniela Schmidt, Alison Panisson, Felipe Meneguzzi, Renata Vieira, and Rafael H. Bordini

N-Jason: Run-Time Norm Compliance in AgentSpeak(L) ... 367
JeeHang Lee, Julian Padget, Brian Logan, Daniela Dybalova, and Natasha Alechina

Typing Multi-Agent Systems via Commitments ... 388
Matteo Baldoni, Cristina Baroglio, and Federico Capuzzimati

Robust Collaboration: Enriching Decisions with Abstract Preferences ... 406
Loïs Vanhée, Frank Dignum, and Jacques Ferber

The Interaction as an Integration Component for the JaCaMo Platform ... 431
Maicon Rafael Zatelli and Jomi Fred Hübner

Author Index ... 451

The Shaping of the Agent-Oriented Mindset
Twenty Years of Engineering MAS

Koen V. Hindriks

Delft University of Technology, EEMCS, The Netherlands

Abstract. In the past twenty years we have seen an enormous growth and development of new techniques, technologies, and tools that support the engineering of Multi-Agent Systems (MAS). The 1990s perhaps are best characterized as the period in which the foundations were laid and the more theoretical underpinnings of the MAS field were explored. Besides a continuation of this foundational work, since 2000 the agent-based community has also been increasingly able to demonstrate the great potential for applying the MAS technology that has been developed in a very broad and diverse range of application domains.

In this paper, I will trace the shaping of the agent-oriented mindset from the mid 90s on as it evolved in the work presented in the international workshops ProMAS, AOSE, and DALT that recently merged into the EMAS workshop. For this reason the focus of this overview will be in particular on *cognitive agents* as it seems fair to say that most work reported in ProMAS, AOSE, and DALT has taken its inspiration from Belief-Desire-Intention (BDI) agents.

1 Introduction

In a recent survey of applications of MAS technology [44], mature applications are reported in such diverse areas as Logistics and Manufacturing, Telecommunication, Aerospace, E-commerce, and Defense. The authors conclude that "dedicated agent platforms actually can make a difference regarding business success". They also write that "more recent platforms [...] may take some more time to mature". It was found, for example, that quite a few mature applications were built using one of the older and well-known agent platforms JADE [6]. In order to continue these successes, it is important to identify what is needed to advance more recently developed technologies for engineering MAS to a level that they can be used to engineer mature applications.

In this paper, we will focus in particular on *cognitive agent technology* as it seems fair to say that most work reported in the international workshops ProMAS, AOSE, and DALT that recently merged into the EMAS workshop has taken its inspiration from so-called Belief-Desire-Intention (BDI) agents. Arguably, the step to mature applications for technologies that support the engineering of cognitive agents and MAS is bigger than that of more general purpose frameworks for engineering agents such as JADE. One reason, moreover, why a broader uptake and the application of cognitive agent technologies has been

F. Dalpiaz et al. (Eds.): EMAS 2014, LNAI 8758, pp. 1–14, 2014.

somewhat slow perhaps, may be that this work originally has had a strong conceptual focus, aiming, for example, to relate agent frameworks to formal theories of rational agents.

To move forward it is important to learn from past successes and failures and to take stock of where we are today. To this end, the aim is to trace and to provide an overview of the agent-oriented mind-set by revisiting some of the results discussed and proposed in the past 20 years on Engineering MAS (EMAS). I will only be able here to provide a high-level overview of the past twenty years of developments related to engineering MAS and this overview thus will necessarily be far from complete and will only include some of what I consider to be its highlights. In the remainder, some of the core concepts, research goals, and achievements of twenty years of EMAS will be presented, followed by a brief perspective on future research of engineering MAS.

2 The Agent-Oriented Mindset

One perspective on what we as a research community are trying to achieve is that we are *shaping the agent-oriented mind-set.* This mind-set, among others, consists of key concepts that we use to design a multi-agent system. A lot of research has gone into clarifying and refining concepts associated with agent-based systems. In addition, to support the design and engineering of MAS using this mind-set, we have developed corresponding agent-oriented tools, techniques, and methodologies.

The agent-oriented mindset is well-established by now and it is not hard to answer the question what is part of that mind-set. A short interaction with the audience at EMAS yielded the concepts that are common and familiar by now to most MAS developers, including:

- *autonomy*,
- *environment*, *event*, *reactive*,
- *rational*, *goal-directedness*, *intentional stance*
- *decentralization*, *interaction*, and *social.*

To summarize and paraphrase a well-known definition [71], apart from being *autonomous*, an agent is *reactive*, *proactive*, and *interactive* (also known as a *weak* notion of agency).

Another defining notion in our field of research has been the notion of a *Belief-Desire-Intention (BDI) agent* [56]. The notion of a BDI agent is about the internal, cognitive structure of an agent that consists, among others, of an agent's *beliefs* and can be viewed as a refinement of a *pro-active* agent to an agent that has a *motivational state* that consists of, e.g., *desires*, *goals*, and/or *intentions.* The idea is that an agent aims at achieving something it wants and [56] therefore emphasises the *rationality* of agents instead of their autonomy. The cognitive state of an agent should, moreover, satisfy basic *rationality constraints*, e.g., goals should be compatible with the agent's beliefs, intentions should be compatible with goals, and agents should not procrastinate with respect to their intentions.

That is, agent should be *committed* to achieving their goals but should not do so blindly. Another very influential paper [55] proposed an agent programming language called AgentSpeak(L) derived from the notion of a BDI agent but which also added the concept of a *plan*. An agent in AgentSpeak(L) has a *plan library* that should provide an agent with the means to achieve its goals (see also Figure 1). Mental states have been identified by some as the essential ingredient of Agent-Oriented Programming (AOP) [13].

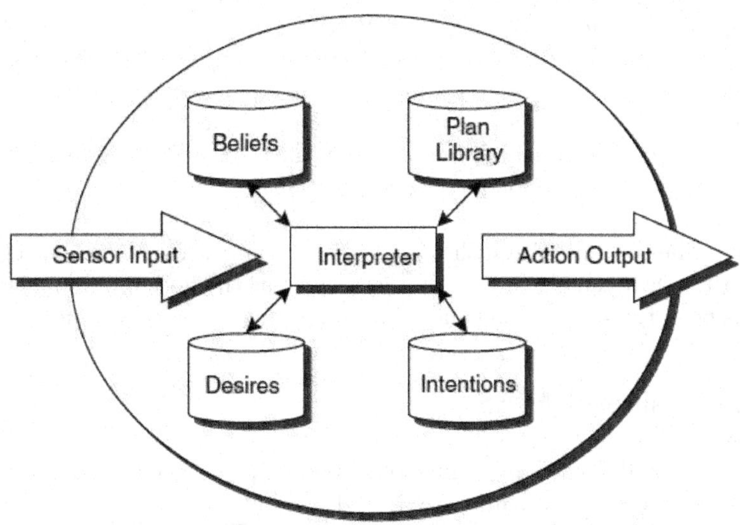

Fig. 1. Interpreter for BDI Agent

Models that formalized the notion of an agent have typically been based on some form of logic and throughout "the declarative paradigm" has been promoted within the community (and less so game theoretic models). Especially the work reported in the DALT workshop has contributed to implementation models and refinements or extensions of the notion of a BDI agent. Just to mention two examples, [2] introduced a cooperative BDI model *Coo-BDI*, and [1] presents an efficient (linear time) *belief contraction operation*.

Agents are distinctly different from other software entities such as objects because they are intrinsically motivated: agents are pro-active and aim to achieve their goals in order to meet their design objectives. It thus is not surprising to see that quite some work has focussed on the notion of a *goal*. For example, [66] studies the *dynamics of declarative goals*, [17] introduced a mechanism for *goal generation*, [38] presents an account of *goal change* that is able to handle prioritized goals and subgoals and their dynamics, whereas [70] has investigated the *interactions between goals* and provides a framework for reasoning about such interactions. Various goal types were distinguished in this work, including most importantly *achievement*, *maintenance*, and *perform* goals (see also [67]).

Important results were also obtained on the *life cycle of goals*: [12,61,67] discuss various states in different life cycle models which include, for example, the *suspension* and *abortion* of goals.

Right from the start it was recognized that agents that are part of a MAS should be somehow *organized*. An important aspect of this organization concerns the modelling of agent interaction. New models for interaction based on the notion of *commitment* rather than that of a speech act have been introduced with corresponding methods for verification based on the notion of compliance [3,7,15]. Another means to regulate the behaviour of agents is to introduce *norms* that agents should obey or comply with. Various works have looked at the notion of an *institution* with associated norms, including, for example, [68] which proposes a definition of norms for electronic institutions for synthesising *norm-aware agents*, [28] which introduces a social layer for MAS in which normative positions are explicitly represented and managed, and [27] which presents a model of norms for specifying, amongst others, *sanctions*.

Summary. The concept within the agent-oriented mindset that has been refined most over the years has been that of a *goal* whereas the notion of a *norm-aware* agent has been the most significant extension of the notion of a cognitive agent.

3 The Design of MAS

In Agent-Oriented Software Engineering (AOSE), agent interaction, not the agent's environment, was emphasized, at least initially, as a key characteristic of complex software that calls for new methods. The agent metaphor defines a new software engineering paradigm and agent metaphors and technologies are adopted to harness and govern the *complexity* of software systems. The basic idea was that the growing complexity of systems calls for new models and technologies that promote system predictability and MAS can provide a solution to this problem.

Although other methodologies were also proposed at the time (e.g., [51]), the multi-agent software engineering methodology MaSE is an early representative of work on design methodologies that is still being further developed [41]. The MaSE methodology is based on several key concepts that have remained important in AOSE, including *requirements*, *goal hierarchy*, *use cases or scenarios*, *roles*, *agents* and their *conversations*. MaSE has evolved into O-MaSE [40]. Another early well-known methodology for agent-oriented software engineering methodologies is Gaia [72]. The Gaia methodology proposed several design artifacts that the methodology required from a design of a MAS. The methodology supports the analysis and design life cycle phases but did not provide any tooling to support the design process. MASDK is an extension of Gaia [30].

The main life cycle phases that have been distinguished in the design process of a MAS include the *requirements* phase, *analysis* phase, *design* phase (sometimes a distinction is made between the architectural and detailed design phase), the *implementation* phase, and the *testing* phase. State of the art methodologies such as O-MaSE [40], Prometheus [52], and Tropos [29] cover and provide support for all of these phases by means of design tools. These methodologies are compared with each other using a conference management case study in [53]. See [60] for a recent overview of agent-oriented methodologies.

An important contribution of work on AOSE has been the introduction of graphical notations for design specifications of agent systems. UML [8] has been taken as a starting point because it is easier to develop an agent-based extension based on the object-oriented notation, and it is relatively easy to provide high-quality tools by extending existing object-oriented tools [4,48]. Typically, however, each methodology has introduced its own notation. Some effort has been done to unify notations again [54]. It is also worthwhile to mention some of the work on *design patterns* in this context (see, e.g., [50,20]).

Several methodologies also provide dedicated support for organizational modelling. A well-known model is the AGR model [26] which stands for Agent-Group-Role. The notion of a role refers to the *constraints* (obligations, requirements, skills) that an agent needs to have to obtain a role, the *benefits* (abilities, authorization, profits) that an agent will receive in playing the role, and the *responsibilities* associated to the role. A basic assumption of the AGR approach is that the organizational model does not make any assumptions about the cognitive capabilities of the agents within the organization. The notion of a *group* is used to partition agents into units in which they can freely interact whereas different groups are assumed to be opaque to each other. Several other organizational meta-models have been proposed, including MOISE+ [34], TEAMS [36], ISLANDER [24], and OperA [49].

A topic that has gained more attention recently is *testing*. Some initial work on providing a testing framework for MAS development, including SUNIT [63] and a framework integrated with Tropos [46]. [74] provides a technique for unit testing of plan based agent systems, with a focus on the automated generation and execution of test cases.

Summary. Much has been achieved with respect to design methodologies for MAS that provide useful graphical notation for the specification of a MAS and cover all design life cycle phases, where in particular the testing phase has gained more attention only recently. In particular the concept within the agent-oriented mindset that has been refined most over the years has been that of an *organization.*

4 Programming Languages for Cognitive Agents

Various programming languages have been proposed that facilitate the implementation of MAS based on cognitive agents. We have already mentioned the AgentSpeak(L) language [55] above. Programming languages are also needed for bridging the gap between analysis and design, which yields an agent-oriented system design, and implementation of a MAS. Agent programming languages aim to provide support for a rather direct implementation of the core concepts that are part of the agent-oriented mind-set.

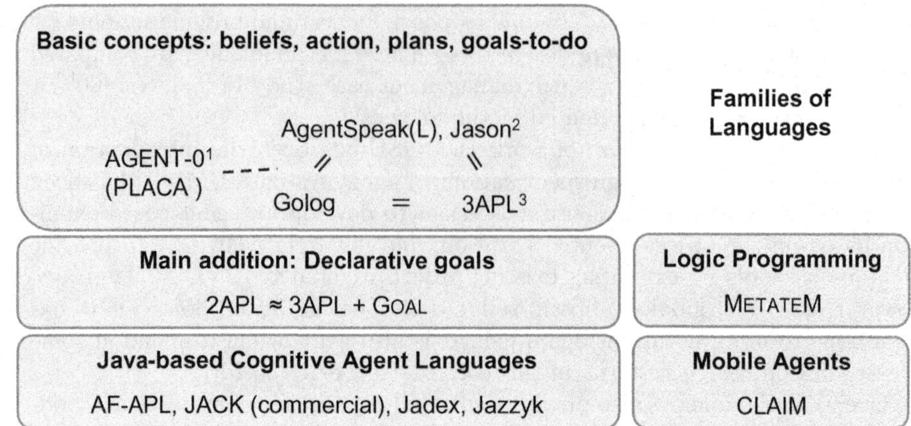

Fig. 2. Families of Agent Programming Languages

The community has been particularly productive in the area of programming frameworks for agent systems. Figure 2 provides an overview of the landscape of languages and highlights the distinction between *Java-based* and *logic-based* languages. Java-based languages stay closer to the well-known and familiar object-oriented paradigm whereas logic-based languages provide more powerful reasoning engines for reasoning about the beliefs and goals of an agent.

Early work introduced the JACK^{TM} language as an implementation of the Belief/Desire/Intention model of rational agency in Java with extensions to support the design and execution of agent systems [25] and the CLAIM language that supports the design of *mobile agents* [23]. Three other frameworks that were introduced and built on top of Java are Jadex [12], which was motivated by extending JADE with BDI agents, AF-APL [58], which was motivated by the need for a practical programming language for agent systems, and JIAC [37,42], which has been motivated by the desire to be able to meet requirements imposed by modern industrial projects. Finally, [47] presents the language Jazzyk which is motivated by the need for a clean separation between the knowledge representational and the behavioural level of an agent program. The work [19] incorporates the notion of a *declarative goal* into the agent programming language 3APL [33].

An important contribution of work on agent programming languages has been the introduction of *modules* that support modular design of agent programs. In [11] a module concept is presented that is based on the capability concept for structuring BDI agents in functional clusters introduced before [14] that supports a higher degree of *reusability*. In [31] and [43], respectively, the logic-based agent languages GOAL [32] and *Jason* [9] are extended with modules. Another approach for adding structure to a MAS program based on the notion of an *organization* is introduced in [62].

Substantial work has also been done in the area of *debugging MAS*. The Tracing method proposed in [39] assists a programmer in debugging agents by explaining the actual agent behaviour in the implemented system. The method logs actual agent behaviour from which it derives interpretations in terms of, e.g., the beliefs, goals, and intentions of an agent. [10] proposes the use of data mining to assist during the debugging of MAS. [16] describes how debugging has been supported for the Agent Factory Agent Programming Language (AF-APL). [18] proposes an assertion language for specifying the cognitive and temporal behaviour of an agent program as support for debugging.

The integration of sophisticated AI techniques into agent systems has mainly been looked at in the context of agent-oriented programming. A *planner* is integrated into Jadex for providing dynamic plans at runtime [69]. The integration approach used is one where the cognitive agent takes responsibility for plan monitoring and re-planning and only the responsibility for the creation of plans is delegated to the planner. Recently also work on integrating *learning* into the agent programming language GOAL has been reported in [59]. The focus in this paper is on improving action selection in rule-based agent programming languages using a reinforcement learning mechanism under the hood.

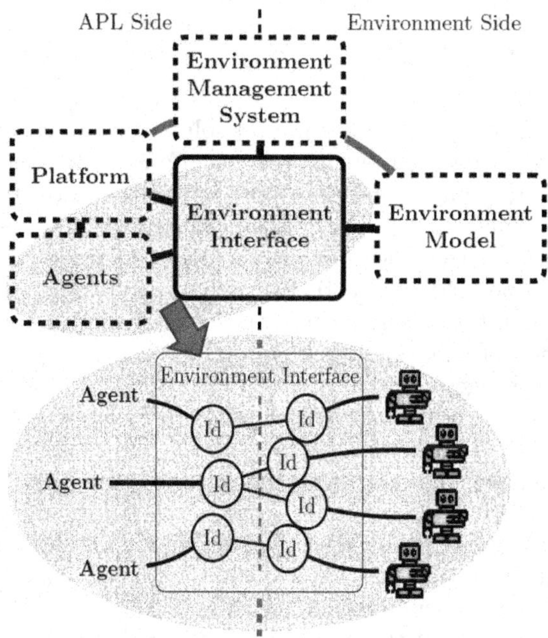

Fig. 3. Environment Interface for Agent Interaction with Environments

One important feature of agent systems has not yet been discussed: agent systems are embedded in and agent systems *interact with an environment.* Various models that support the interaction between agents and their environments have been proposed. The Agents and Artifacts (A&A) model of environments is based on the idea that an environment is composed of different sorts of artifacts that are shared and used by agents to support their activities[57].

The PRESAGE model introduced in [45] proposes the use of environments as a rapid prototyping tool for agent societies. The CIGA middleware proposed in [64] aims at facilitating the coupling between a MAS and a game engine. Finally, the Environment Interface Standard (EIS) introduced in [5] provides support for connecting agent platforms to environments such as games (see also [22] for a range of environment implementations that have been made available). The EIS interface provides generic functionality for executing actions and for perceiving changes in an agent's environment and also provides support for managing an environment, e.g., for starting, pausing and terminating it (see also Figure 3).

Summary. Various programming language that support the agent-oriented paradigm have been proposed. Several extensions such as the notion of modular programming have made these languages more useful in practice. Work on debugging agent programs has also contributed to this end. An important contribution has also been the development of several models that support the interaction of an agent with its environment.

5 Conclusion

Cognitive agent technology offers a powerful solution for developing the next generation autonomous decision-making systems. To make this happen it is important to continue to promote and contribute to the agent-oriented mindset. It also continues to be important to justify the need for a paradigm shift from existing paradigms such as the object- or service-oriented paradigms to the agent-oriented paradigm ([60]; see also [35]). In particular, it would be useful to be able to perform quantitative assessments and comparisons of the agent-based paradigm with other paradigms ([73]; see also [21]).

We also want to suggest that it is time to start paying more attention to the kind of support that a MAS developer needs to facilitate him or her when engineering future MAS applications (see also [21,65]). It is important to identify the needs of a developer and make sure that a developer is provided with the right tools for engineering MAS. For the same reason we should focus more on issues related to *ease of use*, *scalability and performance*, and *testing*. As we have seen, work on techniques and tools that support the testing phase has only quite recently produced more concrete results (see also [60]).

There are also promises of the agent-oriented paradigm that are still to be realized. As argued in [35], "agents are the right abstraction to (re-)integrate various AI sub-disciplines together again". Robots should come to mind here. Can we provide tools and techniques that facilitate the integration of sophisticated AI techniques into agents? As a community, we can provide an important contribution by focusing on understanding how to provide programmers with easy access to such techniques. We have seen that already some proposals have been made to re-integrated planning and learning. Similarly, it remains to be shown that agent-orientation can solve key concurrency and distributed computing issues. If agents are advocated as the next generation model for engineering complex, distributed systems, we should be able to demonstrate the added value of agent systems.

Finally, it seems particularly worthwhile to put more effort into integrating agent-based methodologies and programming languages. There are several areas of clear overlap where both can reinforce and improve their respective results, e.g., in the area of testing and the area of organizational modelling. In any case, to stimulate the adoption of cognitive agent technology and MAS, we need to provide methods and tools that jointly support the agent-oriented mindset.

References

1. Alechina, N., Jago, M., Logan, B.: Resource-bounded belief revision and contraction. In: Baldoni, M., Endriss, U., Omicini, A., Torroni, P. (eds.) DALT 2005. LNCS (LNAI), vol. 3904, pp. 141–154. Springer, Heidelberg (2006)
2. Ancona, D., Mascardi, V.: Coo-BDI: Extending the BDI model with cooperativity. In: Leite, J., Omicini, A., Sterling, L., Torroni, P. (eds.) DALT 2003. LNCS (LNAI), vol. 2990, pp. 109–134. Springer, Heidelberg (2004)
3. Baldoni, M., Baroglio, C., Marengo, E.: Commitment-Based Protocols with Behavioral Rules and Correctness Properties of MAS. In: Omicini, A., Sardina, S., Vasconcelos, W. (eds.) DALT 2010. LNCS (LNAI), vol. 6619, pp. 60–77. Springer, Heidelberg (2011)
4. Bauer, B., Müller, J.P., Odell, J.J.: Agent UML: A Formalism for Specifying Multiagent Software Systems. In: Ciancarini, P., Wooldridge, M.J. (eds.) AOSE 2000. LNCS, vol. 1957, pp. 91–103. Springer, Heidelberg (2001)
5. Behrens, T.M., Hindriks, K.V., Dix, J.: Towards an environment interface standard for agent platforms. Annals of Mathematics and Artificial Intelligence 61(4), 261–295 (2011)
6. Bellifemine, F.L., Caire, G., Greenwood, D.: Developing Multi-Agent Systems with JADE. Wiley (2007)
7. Bentahar, J., Moulin, B., Meyer, J.-J.C.: A tableau method for verifying dialogue game protocols for agent communication. In: Baldoni, M., Endriss, U., Omicini, A., Torroni, P. (eds.) DALT 2005. LNCS (LNAI), vol. 3904, pp. 223–244. Springer, Heidelberg (2006)
8. Booch, G., Rumbaugh, J., Jacobson, I.: The Unified Modeling Language User Guide. Addison Wesley Longman Publishing Co., Inc., Redwood City (1999)
9. Bordini, R.H., Hübner, J.F., Wooldridge, M.J.: Programming multi-agent systems in AgentSpeak using Jason, vol. 8. John Wiley & Sons (2007)
10. Botía, J.A., Hernansáez, J.M., Gómez-Skarmeta, A.F.: On the application of clustering techniques to support debugging large-scale multi-agent systems. In: Bordini, R.H., Dastani, M., Dix, J., El Fallah Seghrouchni, A. (eds.) PROMAS 2006. LNCS (LNAI), vol. 4411, pp. 217–227. Springer, Heidelberg (2007)
11. Braubach, L., Pokahr, A., Lamersdorf, W.: Extending the capability concept for flexible bdi agent modularization. In: Bordini, R.H., Dastani, M. M., Dix, J., El Fallah Seghrouchni, A. (eds.) PROMAS 2005. LNCS (LNAI), vol. 3862, pp. 139–155. Springer, Heidelberg (2006)
12. Braubach, L., Pokahr, A., Moldt, D., Lamersdorf, W.: Goal Representation for BDI Agent Systems. In: Bordini, R.H., Dastani, M., Dix, J., El Fallah Seghrouchni, A. (eds.) PROMAS 2004. LNCS (LNAI), vol. 3346, pp. 44–65. Springer, Heidelberg (2005)

13. Burkhard, H.-D.: Agent-oriented programming for open systems. In: Wooldridge, M.J., Jennings, N.R. (eds.) ECAI/ATAL 1994. LNCS, vol. 890, pp. 291–306. Springer, Heidelberg (1995)
14. Busetta, P., Howden, N., Rönnquist, R., Hodgson, A.: Structuring BDI Agents in Functional Clusters. In: Jennings, N.R. (ed.) Intelligent Agents VI. LNCS (LNAI), vol. 1757, pp. 277–289. Springer, Heidelberg (2000)
15. Chopra, A.K., Singh, M.P.: Producing compliant interactions: Conformance, coverage, and interoperability. In: Baldoni, M., Endriss, U. (eds.) DALT 2006. LNCS (LNAI), vol. 4327, pp. 1–15. Springer, Heidelberg (2006)
16. Collier, R.: Debugging agents in agent factory. In: Bordini, R.H., Dastani, M., Dix, J., El Fallah Seghrouchni, A. (eds.) ProMAS 2006. LNCS (LNAI), vol. 4411, pp. 229–248. Springer, Heidelberg (2007)
17. da Costa Pereira, C., Tettamanzi, A.G.B.: Goal Generation from Possibilistic Beliefs Based on Trust and Distrust. In: Baldoni, M., Bentahar, J., van Riemsdijk, M.B., Lloyd, J. (eds.) DALT 2009. LNCS (LNAI), vol. 5948, pp. 35–50. Springer, Heidelberg (2010)
18. Dastani, M., Brandsema, J., Dubel, A., Meyer, J.-J.C.: Debugging BDI-Based Multi-Agent Programs. In: Braubach, L., Briot, J.-P., Thangarajah, J. (eds.) ProMAS 2009. LNCS (LNAI), vol. 5919, pp. 151–169. Springer, Heidelberg (2010)
19. Dastani, M., van Riemsdijk, M.B., Dignum, F., Meyer, J.-J.C.: A Programming Language for Cognitive Agents Goal Directed 3APL. In: Dastani, M., Dix, J., El Fallah-Seghrouchni, A. (eds.) PROMAS 2003. LNCS (LNAI), vol. 3067, pp. 111–130. Springer, Heidelberg (2004)
20. De Wolf, T., Holvoet, T.: Design patterns for decentralised coordination in self-organising emergent systems. In: Brueckner, S.A., Hassas, S., Jelasity, M., Yamins, D. (eds.) ESOA 2006. LNCS (LNAI), vol. 4335, pp. 28–49. Springer, Heidelberg (2007)
21. Dix, J., Hindriks, K.V., Logan, B., Wobcke, W.: Engineering Multi-Agent Systems (Dagstuhl Seminar 12342). Dagstuhl Reports 2(8), 74–98 (2012)
22. The Environment Interface (September 2014), `https://github.com/eishub`
23. El Fallah-Seghrouchni, A., Suna, A.: CLAIM: A computational language for autonomous, intelligent and mobile agents. In: Dastani, M., Dix, J., El Fallah-Seghrouchni, A. (eds.) PROMAS 2003. LNCS (LNAI), vol. 3067, pp. 90–110. Springer, Heidelberg (2004)
24. Esteva, M., De La Cruz, D., Sierra, C.: ISLANDER: An electronic institutions editor. In: Proceedings of the First International Joint Conference on Autonomous Agents and Multiagent Systems: part 3, pp. 1045–1052. ACM (2002)
25. Evertsz, R., Fletcher, M., Frongillo, R., Jarvis, J., Brusey, J., Dance, S.: Implementing industrial multi-agent systems using JACK^{TM}. In: Dastani, M., Dix, J., El Fallah-Seghrouchni, A. (eds.) PROMAS 2003. LNCS (LNAI), vol. 3067, pp. 18–48. Springer, Heidelberg (2004)
26. Ferber, J., Gutknecht, O., Michel, F.: From agents to organizations: An organizational view of multi-agent systems. In: Giorgini, P., Müller, J.P., Odell, J.J. (eds.) AOSE 2003. LNCS, vol. 2935, pp. 214–230. Springer, Heidelberg (2004)
27. Fornara, N., Colombetti, M.: Specifying and enforcing norms in artificial institutions: A retrospective review. In: Sakama, C., Sardina, S., Vasconcelos, W., Winikoff, M. (eds.) DALT 2011. LNCS (LNAI), vol. 7169, pp. 117–119. Springer, Heidelberg (2012)

28. García-Camino, A., Rodríguez-Aguilar, J.-A., Sierra, C., Vasconcelos, W.: A distributed architecture for norm-aware agent societies. In: Baldoni, M., Endriss, U., Omicini, A., Torroni, P. (eds.) DALT 2005. LNCS (LNAI), vol. 3904, pp. 89–105. Springer, Heidelberg (2006)
29. Giorgini, P., Mylopoulos, J., Perini, A., Susi, A.: The Tropos methodology and software development environment. In: Social Modeling for Requirements Engineering, pp. 405–423 (2010)
30. Gorodetsky, V., Karsaev, O., Samoylov, V., Konushy, V.: Support for Analysis, Design, and Implementation Stages with MASDK. In: Luck, M., Gomez-Sanz, J.J. (eds.) AOSE 2008. LNCS, vol. 5386, pp. 272–287. Springer, Heidelberg (2009)
31. Hindriks, K.V.: Modules as Policy-Based Intentions: Modular Agent Programming in GOAL. In: Dastani, M., El Fallah Seghrouchni, A., Ricci, A., Winikoff, M. (eds.) ProMAS 2007. LNCS (LNAI), vol. 4908, pp. 156–171. Springer, Heidelberg (2008)
32. Hindriks, K.V.: Programming Rational Agents in GOAL. In: El Fallah Seghrouchni, A., Dix, J., Dastani, M., Bordini, R.H. (eds.) Multi-Agent Programming, pp. 119–157. Springer US (2009)
33. Hindriks, K.V., De Boer, F.S., Van der Hoek, W., Meyer, J.-J.C.: Meyer. Agent Programming in 3APL. Autonomous Agents and Multi-Agent Systems 2(4), 357–401 (1999)
34. Hübner, J.F., Sichman, J.S., Boissier, O.: Developing Organised Multiagent Systems Using the MOISE+ Model: Programming Issues at the System and Agent Levels. Int. J. Agent-Oriented Softw. Eng. 1(3/4), 370–395 (2007)
35. Jennings, N.R.: Agent-oriented software engineering. In: Imam, I., Kodratoff, Y., El-Dessouki, A., Ali, M. (eds.) IEA/AIE 1999. LNCS (LNAI), vol. 1611, pp. 4–10. Springer, Heidelberg (1999)
36. Kaminka, G.A., Pynadath, D.V., Tambe, M.: Monitoring teams by overhearing: A multi-agent plan-recognition approach. Journal of Artificial Intelligence Research 17(1), 83–135 (2002)
37. Keiser, J., Hirsch, B., Albayrak, Ş.: Agents do it for money - accounting features in agents. In: Dastani, M., El Fallah Seghrouchni, A., Ricci, A., Winikoff, M. (eds.) ProMAS 2007. LNCS (LNAI), vol. 4908, pp. 42–56. Springer, Heidelberg (2008)
38. Khan, S.M., Lespérance, Y.: Prioritized goals and subgoals in a logical account of goal change: A preliminary report. In: Baldoni, M., Bentahar, J., van Riemsdijk, M.B., Lloyd, J. (eds.) DALT 2009. LNCS (LNAI), vol. 5948, pp. 119–136. Springer, Heidelberg (2010)
39. Lam, D.N., Barber, K.S.: Debugging agent behavior in an implemented agent system. In: Bordini, R.H., Dastani, M., Dix, J., El Fallah Seghrouchni, A. (eds.) PROMAS 2004. LNCS (LNAI), vol. 3346, pp. 104–125. Springer, Heidelberg (2005)
40. De Loach, S.A., Garcia-Ojeda, J.C.: O-MaSE: A customisable approach to designing and building complex, adaptive multi-agent systems. International Journal of Agent-Oriented Software Engineering 4(3), 244–280 (2010)
41. De Loach, S.A., Wood, M.: Developing Multiagent Systems with agentTool. In: Castelfranchi, C., Lespérance, Y. (eds.) Intelligent Agents VII. LNCS (LNAI), vol. 1986, pp. 46–60. Springer, Heidelberg (2001)
42. Lützenberger, M., Küster, T., Konnerth, T., Thiele, A., Masuch, N., Heßler, A., Keiser, J., Burkhardt, M., Kaiser, S., Albayrak, S.: JIAC V: A MAS Framework for Industrial Applications. In: Proceedings of the 2013 International Conference on Autonomous Agents and Multi-agent Systems, AAMAS 2013, Richland, SC, pp. 1189–1190. International Foundation for Autonomous Agents and Multiagent Systems (2013)

43. Madden, N., Logan, B.: Modularity and Compositionality in Jason. In: Braubach, L., Briot, J.-P., Thangarajah, J. (eds.) ProMAS 2009. LNCS (LNAI), vol. 5919, pp. 237–253. Springer, Heidelberg (2010)
44. Müller, J.P., Fischer, K.: Application Impact of Multi-Agent Systems and Technologies: A Survey. In: Agent-Oriented Software Engineering: Reflections on Architectures, Methodologies, Languages, and Frameworks. Springer (2014)
45. Neville, B., Pitt, J.: PRESAGE: A Programming Environment for the Simulation of Agent Societies. In: Hindriks, K.V., Pokahr, A., Sardina, S. (eds.) ProMAS 2008. LNCS (LNAI), vol. 5442, pp. 88–103. Springer, Heidelberg (2009)
46. Nguyen, D.C., Perini, A., Tonella, P.: A Goal-Oriented Software Testing Methodology. In: Luck, M., Padgham, L. (eds.) AOSE 2007. LNCS, vol. 4951, pp. 58–72. Springer, Heidelberg (2008)
47. Novák, P.: Jazzyk: A Programming Language for Hybrid Agents with Heterogeneous Knowledge Representations. In: Hindriks, K.V., Pokahr, A., Sardina, S. (eds.) ProMAS 2008. LNCS (LNAI), vol. 5442, pp. 72–87. Springer, Heidelberg (2009)
48. Odell, J.J., Van Dyke Parunak, H., Bauer, B.: Representing agent interaction protocols in UML. In: Ciancarini, P., Wooldridge, M.J. (eds.) AOSE 2000. LNCS, vol. 1957, pp. 121–140. Springer, Heidelberg (2001)
49. Okouya, D., Dignum, V.: OperettA: A Prototype Tool for the Design, Analysis and Development of Multi-agent Organizations. In: Proceedings of the 7th International Joint Conference on Autonomous Agents and Multiagent Systems: Demo Papers, AAMAS 2008, Richland, SC, pp. 1677–1678. International Foundation for Autonomous Agents and Multiagent Systems (2008)
50. Oluyomi, A., Karunasekera, S., Sterling, L.: An agent design pattern classification scheme: Capturing the notions of agency in agent design patterns. In: 11th Asia-Pacific on Software Engineering Conference, pp. 456–463 (November 2004)
51. Omicini, A.: SODA: Societies and Infrastructures in the Analysis and Design of Agent-Based Systems. In: Ciancarini, P., Wooldridge, M.J. (eds.) AOSE 2000. LNCS, vol. 1957, pp. 185–193. Springer, Heidelberg (2001)
52. Padgham, L., Luck, M.: Prometheus: A practical agent-oriented methodology. In: Henderson-Sellers, B., Giorgini, P. (eds.) Agent-oriented Methodologies, pp. 107–135. Idea Group Inc., Hershey (2005)
53. Padgham, L., Luck, M.: Introduction to AOSE tools for the conference management system. In: Luck, M., Padgham, L. (eds.) AOSE 2007. LNCS, vol. 4951, pp. 164–167. Springer, Heidelberg (2008)
54. Padgham, L., Winikoff, M., DeLoach, S., Cossentino, M.: A Unified Graphical Notation for AOSE. In: Luck, M., Gomez-Sanz, J.J. (eds.) AOSE 2008. LNCS, vol. 5386, pp. 116–130. Springer, Heidelberg (2009)
55. Rao, A.S.: Agentspeak(l): BDI agents speak out in a logical computable language. In: Van de Velde, W., Perram, J. (eds.) MAAMAW 1996. LNCS, vol. 1038, pp. 42–55. Springer, Heidelberg (1996)
56. Rao, A.S., Georgeff, M.P.: Modeling Rational Agents within a BDI-Architecture. In: Proceedings of the 2nd International Conference on Principles of Knowledge Representation and Reasoning (KR 1991), Cambridge, MA, USA, April 22-25, pp. 473–484 (1991)
57. Ricci, A., Viroli, M., Omicini, A.: The A&A Programming Model and Technology for Developing Agent Environments in MAS. In: Dastani, M., El Fallah Seghrouchni, A., Ricci, A., Winikoff, M. (eds.) ProMAS 2007. LNCS (LNAI), vol. 4908, pp. 89–106. Springer, Heidelberg (2008)

58. Ross, R.J., Collier, R., O'Hare, G.M.P.: AF-APL: Bridging Principles and Practice in Agent Oriented Languages. In: Bordini, R.H., Dastani, M., Dix, J., El Fallah Seghrouchni, A. (eds.) PROMAS 2004. LNCS (LNAI), vol. 3346, pp. 66–88. Springer, Heidelberg (2005)
59. Singh, D., Hindriks, K.V.: Learning to Improve Agent Behaviours in GOAL. In: Dastani, M., Hübner, J.F., Logan, B. (eds.) ProMAS 2012. LNCS (LNAI), vol. 7837, pp. 158–173. Springer, Heidelberg (2013)
60. Sturm, A., Shehory, O.: The landscape of agent-oriented methodologies. In: Shehory, O., Sturm, A. (eds.) Agent-Oriented Software Engineering, pp. 137–154. Springer, Heidelberg (2014)
61. Thangarajah, J., Harland, J., Morley, D., Yorke-Smith, N.: Operational behaviour for executing, suspending, and aborting goals in bdi agent systems. In: Omicini, A., Sardina, S., Vasconcelos, W. (eds.) DALT 2010. LNCS (LNAI), vol. 6619, pp. 1–21. Springer, Heidelberg (2011)
62. Tinnemeier, N.A.M., Dastani, M., Meyer, J.-J.C.: Orwell's Nightmare for Agents? Programming Multi-agent Organisations. In: Hindriks, K.V., Pokahr, A., Sardina, S. (eds.) ProMAS 2008. LNCS (LNAI), vol. 5442, pp. 56–71. Springer, Heidelberg (2009)
63. Tiryaki, A.M., Öztuna, S., Dikenelli, O., Erdur, R.C.: SUNIT: A Unit Testing Framework for Test Driven Development of Multi-Agent Systems. In: Padgham, L., Zambonelli, F. (eds.) AOSE 2006. LNCS, vol. 4405, pp. 156–173. Springer, Heidelberg (2007)
64. van Oijen, J., La Poutré, H., Dignum, F.: Agent perception within CIGA: Performance optimizations and analysis. In: Müller, J.P., Cossentino, M. (eds.) AOSE 2012. LNCS, vol. 7852, pp. 99–117. Springer, Heidelberg (2013)
65. van Riemsdijk, M.B.: 20 Years of Agent-oriented Programming in Distributed AI: History and Outlook. In: Proceedings of the 2nd Edition on Programming Systems, Languages and Applications Based on Actors, Agents, and Decentralized Control Abstractions, AGERE! 2012, pp. 7–10. ACM, New York (2012)
66. van Riemsdijk, M.B., Dastani, M., Dignum, F.P.M., Meyer, J.-J.C.: Dynamics of Declarative Goals in Agent Programming. In: Leite, J., Omicini, A., Torroni, P., Yolum, p. (eds.) DALT 2004. LNCS (LNAI), vol. 3476, pp. 1–18. Springer, Heidelberg (2005)
67. van Riemsdijk, M.B., Dastani, M., Winikoff, M.: Goals in Agent Systems: A Unifying Framework. In: Proceedings of the 7th International Joint Conference on Autonomous Agents and Multiagent Systems, AAMAS 200, Richland, SC, vol. 2, pp. 713–720. International Foundation for Autonomous Agents and Multiagent Systems (2008)
68. Vasconcelos, W.W.: Norm verification and analysis of electronic institutions. In: Leite, J., Omicini, A., Torroni, P., Yolum, p. (eds.) DALT 2004. LNCS (LNAI), vol. 3476, pp. 166–182. Springer, Heidelberg (2005)
69. Walczak, A., Braubach, L., Pokahr, A., Lamersdorf, W.: Augmenting BDI Agents with Deliberative Planning Techniques. In: Bordini, R.H., Dastani, M., Dix, J., El Fallah Seghrouchni, A. (eds.) PROMAS 2006. LNCS (LNAI), vol. 4411, pp. 113–127. Springer, Heidelberg (2007)
70. Winikoff, M.: An Integrated Formal Framework for Reasoning about Goal Interactions. In: Sakama, C., Sardina, S., Vasconcelos, W., Winikoff, M. (eds.) DALT 2011. LNCS (LNAI), vol. 7169, pp. 16–32. Springer, Heidelberg (2012)
71. Wooldridge, M., Jennings, N.R.: Intelligent agents: Theory and practice. The Knowledge Engineering Review 10, 115–152 (1995)

72. Wooldridge, M., Jennings, N.R., Kinny, D.: The Gaia Methodology for Agent-Oriented Analysis and Design. Autonomous Agents and Multi-Agent Systems 3(3), 285–312 (2000)
73. Zambonelli, F., Omicini, A.: Challenges and research directions in agent-oriented software engineering. Autonomous Agents and Multi-Agent Systems 9(3), 253–283 (2004)
74. Zhang, Z., Thangarajah, J., Padgham, L.: Automated testing for intelligent agent systems. In: Gomez-Sanz, J.J. (ed.) AOSE 2009. LNCS, vol. 6038, pp. 66–79. Springer, Heidelberg (2011)

Keeping a Clear Separation between Goals and Plans

Costin Caval[1,2], Amal El Fallah Seghrouchni[1], and Patrick Taillibert[1]

[1] LIP6, Paris, France
{costin.caval,amal.elfallah,patrick.taillibert}@lip6.fr
[2] Thales Airborne Systems, Elancourt, France

Abstract. Many approaches to BDI agent modeling permit the agent developers to interweave the levels of plans and goals. This is possible through the adoption of new goals inside plans. These goals will have plans of their own, and the definition can extend on many levels. From a software development point of view, the resulting complexity can render the agents' behavior difficult to trace, due to the combination of elements from different abstraction levels, i.e., actions and goal adoptions. This has a negative effect on the development process when designing and debugging agents. In this paper we propose a change of approach that aims to provide a more comprehensible agent model with benefits for the ease of engineering and the fault tolerance of agent systems. This is achieved by imposing a clear separation between the reasoning and the acting levels of the agent. The use of goal adoptions and actions on the environment inside the same plan is therefore forbidden. The approach is illustrated using two theoretical scenarios as well as an agent-based maritime patrol application. We argue that by constraining the agent model we gain in clarity and traceability therefore benefiting the development process and encouraging the adoption of agent-based techniques in industrial contexts.

Keywords: goal directed agents, goal reasoning, goal-plan tree.

1 Introduction

In the field of intelligent agents, BDI agents are used extensively due to their proactivity, adaptability and similarity between their abstract representation and the human reasoning. These agents are enticed with *beliefs* to cover their view of the world, a reason for their behaviors in the form of *desires* or *goals*, and a description of the means to act, in the form of *plans* or *intentions*.

In the original BDI model proposed by Rao and Georgeff [1], the "matching" between goals and plans is assured through a cycle that considers the options for *desires*, deliberates on them to update the existing *intentions* and then executes the actual actions. In more practical approaches, automata are used to handle the life-cycle of goals from their adoption to the appropriate plan selection and execution [2,3].

F. Dalpiaz et al. (Eds.): EMAS 2014, LNAI 8758, pp. 15–39, 2014.

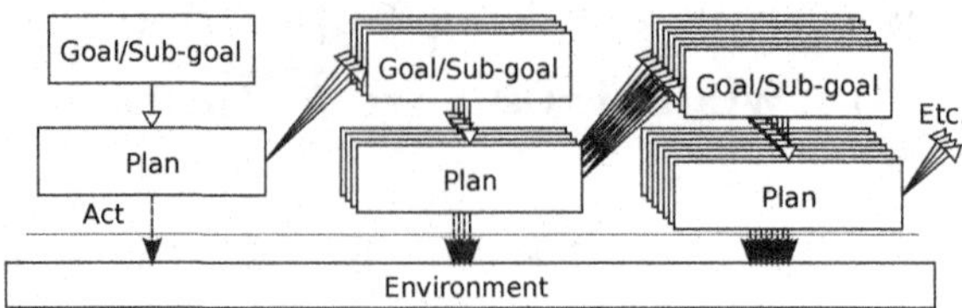

Fig. 1. Agent complexity when goals are adopted in plans acting on the environment

The purpose of an agent is usually to act on the environment, which is done through its plans. Actions can involve the use of actuators, but they also cover the sending of messages[1]. However, in practice, various works [3,4] and programming frameworks (Jason [5], Jadex [6] etc.) employ a model where plans can also adopt new goals, often termed *sub-goals*. A goal can thus have multiple possible plans, whose success depends on the achievement of their respective sub-goals and this can extend on many levels (Fig. 1). Note however that the successful completion of a plan does not necessarily guarantee the achievement of a goal, as goals can have success and failure conditions [7].

While it may be straightforward to design in this way, the fact that in a plan (1) actions on the environment – i.e., with effects "outside" of the agent – and (2) goal adoptions – i.e., with effects on the, possibly long-term, reasoning and behavior of the agent – are used together in the same structure can have adverse effects on the resulting agents: low intelligibility during design, difficult traceability during execution and poor reusability afterwards.

This recursive construction has the advantage of using already existing BDI building blocks and can help abstract certain aspects of an agent's behavior offering the possibility to define the agent in a top-down approach. However, it also creates a structure which is difficult to trace, especially when actions occur at any level, and whose depth may be unpredictable. Important aspects in the behavior of an agent might be hidden from the eyes of a developer or code reviewer due to this intricate design. One might always wonder whether the current plan is a terminal one or whether the model continues with further sub-goals. Given that the adoption of a goal usually implies a new reasoning process with an automaton and further plans, the goal adoption shouldn't be treated the same as an atomic action.

For a change of perspective, let us take the example of the army as a clear-cut multi-level organization. A soldier executes the orders (goals) given from "above" but cannot make high level decisions. Strategies and new objectives (goal adoptions) are decided by the higher ranks. This is due to the separation of responsibilities and competences, as well as the soldier's limited view of the situation. In a similar way, an agent's goals should not be mixed with the acting. This would also allow plans to have limited interdependencies, just as the soldier has a limited view of the situation, with benefits on complexity and fault confinement. A similar analogy can be made with other hierarchical human

[1] We do not consider belief revision to be an action.

organizations such as companies, where the management decides – either on a single or at multiple levels – before requiring the workers to perform the required tasks. Needs that can arise have to be discussed with the manager or managers, who can then decide to take new measures, just as an agent's reasoning would adopt new goals. While small companies with a "flatter" hierarchy can cope with certain issues faster, complex organizations have proven to benefit from this hierarchical composition[2].

Agent oriented development methodologies such as Tropos [8] and Prometheus [9] have top-down approaches where they start with system level characteristics to then "descend" towards agent goals before defining plans and other low level details. Implementing agent systems modeled using such methodologies would also be more natural if reasoning and acting were more clearly separated.

Several works [10,11,12,7] have argued for the interest of using declarative *goals-to-be* together with procedural *goals-to-do*, for decoupling goal achievement (the "to be" part) from plan execution (the "to do" part), giving the agents their *pro-activeness*, but also better flexibility and fault tolerance. Taking this delimitation a step further, we argue for the interest of separating a level where goal reasoning takes place – managing goal adoptions, dependencies, conflict resolution – from an action level where the agent interacts with its peers and environment.

While at runtime it is useful and even inevitable to alternate between reasoning and acting, we argue that these already conceptually distinct levels should be kept separate when designing agents.

To address these issues we propose a subtle change in the agent modeling that simplifies the agent representation by requiring the actions on the environment to be separated from the goal adoptions. We call the approach *Goal-Plan Separation*, or *GPS*. As shall be seen, the direct consequence of this separation is the structuring of the agent into two levels: one concerned with goals and one concerned with actions.

This paper is organized as follows. Section 2 presents the original approach of the paper which is illustrated on two examples. Section 3 discusses implementation issues and Sect. 4 some aspects of the goal execution. Section 5 presents an experimentation in the domain of maritime patrol. In Sect. 6 we discuss some fault tolerance issues with respect to the experimentation. Section 7 addresses the related work and Sect. 8 concludes the paper.

2 The Goal-Plan Separation

In this section we introduce a representation model from the literature which we use to illustrate our proposition through a first generic example. This allows us to discuss the consequence of the Goal-Plan Separation, followed by the more refined example of a Mars rover.

[2] Note: while we are presenting examples of organizations with many people, our scope remains the design of the reasoning of a single agent, which would thus correspond to the army or the company as a whole.

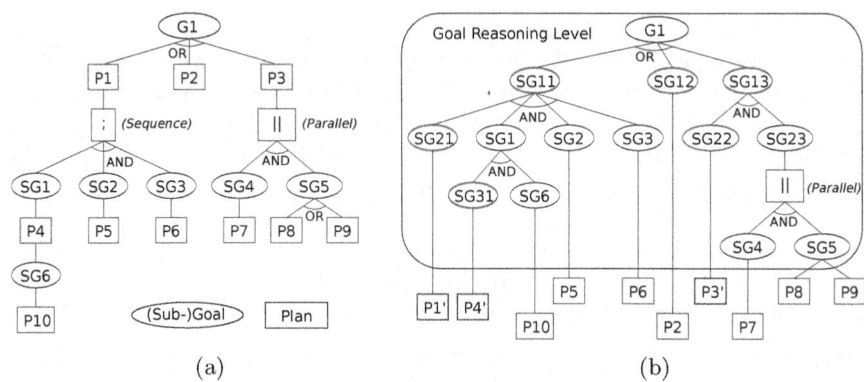

Fig. 2. An example of goal-plan tree (a) and a goal-plan separation of the same example (b)

2.1 Goal-Plan Trees to Goal-Plan Separation

Thangarajah [4,13] formalizes the representation of the agent model in the form of an AND-OR tree: the *goal-plan tree*, or *GPT*. Goals are *OR* nodes since their child nodes, the plans, offer alternative solutions and only one plan suffices for the achievement of a goal. Plans on the other hand are *AND* nodes in order to denote the obligation to achieve all the adopted sub-goals for a successful plan execution. Furthermore, two operators are added to the plan node, to indicate either that the goals have to be achieved in sequence (;) or in parallel (||). A generic example which illustrates all these is given in Fig. 2 (a). Here, the GPT using the two operators spreads in depth across several levels. Note that there can be more than one tree for a given agent, in other words more than one root goal. We chose this model because even if it is used more as an analysis than a development tool (see Related Work in Sect. 7), it shows well the issues we are addressing, in particular how the goal and plan levels alternate.

To illustrate the Goal-Plan Separation approach, the generic example was modified to obtain a possible goal-plan separation, as seen in Fig. 2 (b). The plans that are the most important here are *P1*, *P3* and *P4* as they are the ones that can contain both actions on the environment and goal adoptions. The new representation, which decomposes goals into sub-goals is an AND-OR tree (very similar to the one used in [14]) with only the leaf nodes having plans containing actions, but no goal adoptions. To save space, we consider that the default operator for the *AND* nodes is the sequence operator, unless stated otherwise, e.g., in the case of *SG23*. To preserve the original structure, goals are also allowed to be *OR* nodes, in order to depict cases where a goal or sub-goal can be achieved in more than one way. Similarly, goals that have more than one plan are *OR* nodes. While the original goals were preserved, the plans that were not leaves were replaced by sub-goals, e.g., *SG11*. To compensate, plan names of the form *P'* were used to indicate a variation of an original *P* plan which at least removes the goal adoptions. Note, however, that this exact transformation is not unique for the given example as it depends on the plan's specific features[3]. More examples can be seen in Sect. 2.3. *SG12* was introduced to avoid the existence of siblings of different types. This example shows that transforming an existing agent is possible. Nevertheless, as is the case with many such translations and as we discovered during the experimentation we describe in Sect. 5, a complete redesign of the agent produces a more appropriate result.

2.2 The *Goal Reasoning Level*

As can be seen in Fig. 2 (b), a direct consequence of the separation of goal adoptions from the actions on the environment is the appearance of two levels in the definition of the agent: a *goal reasoning level* and an *action level*.

The *goal reasoning level* is the part of the agent concerned with goal adoption, control, dependencies and interactions. In this paper, we are concerned mostly with the specification (by a programmer or designer) of dependencies between goals and issues related to the adoption and life-cycle control. For the purpose of the Goal-Plan Separation, no actions on the environment are present at this level. However, as will be discussed further on, other mechanisms can appear at this level, e.g., for handling perceptions, events or various types of goal dependencies.

2.3 Mars Rover Scenario

To further illustrate the GPS, let us consider a Mars rover example from [13]. Figure 3 (a) represents a goal-plan tree for a Mars rover's goal to analyze soil samples. The depth of the tree varies between *P7: ExpSoilByDelegationPlan* that is at a depth of one and *P6: TransmitTo(Lander)Plan*, at a depth of 5. While all leaf nodes are plans, there are also intermediary plans which adopt goals and can contain actions: *P1: ExpSoilBySelfPlan* and *P4: RecordResultsPlan*. If these two plans had no actions on the environment, the representation would be GPS-compliant as no unwanted action-goal adoption mix would be present. In this case, an alternative representation can also be obtained in the same manner as in the example in Sect. 2. As depicted in Fig. 3 (b), *P1* changes into a sub-goal and *P4* disappears completely as there is already *SG3* to regroup the corresponding sub-tree. For *P7*, a parent sub-goal *SG12* is created to avoid having two siblings of the *G1* node of different types, i.e., a goal and a plan. *SG12* also carries the precondition originally contained by *P7*.

Another approach would be to rewrite the Mars rover's behavior in a format similar to the goal diagram from Tropos [8], as in Fig. 3 (c). The representation can also be seen as a type of plan. It starts with a decision node that corresponds to *P7*'s precondition from the original scenario. The sequence operator is represented through the arrows that depict the dependencies between goals,

---

[3] E.g., a plan that *turns on a sensor*, adopts a goal to *retrieve data* and then *saves that data*. Such a plan would rather transform into a main goal with three sequential sub-goals, the first corresponding to the beginning of the original plan, and the last corresponding to its final part.

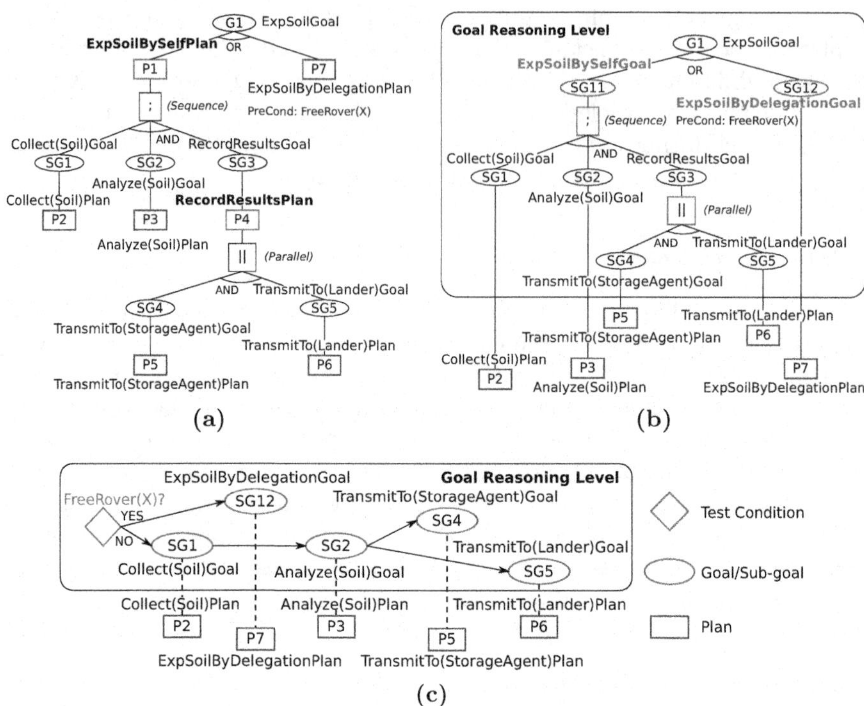

Fig. 3. (a) the goal-plan tree of a Mars rover from [13], (b) a translation of the Mars rover scenario in the form of a GPS-compliant AND-OR goal decomposition and (c) a modified representation of the scenario with a clear goal-plan separation

while the parallelism is implied through the fact that two arrows start from the same entity, in this case *SG2*.

If, however, *P1* and *P4* also contained actions on the environment, the transformation would become more complicated. Figure 4 shows only the sub-tree starting from *SG3* with three simple examples of possible cases: (1) actions in parallel with, (2) before or (3) after the goal adoptions. This shows the hidden complexity associated with the action-goal mix.

The examples in this section obey the GPS principle since in each case, the two levels, the goal reasoning level and the plan level, can be clearly distinguished. This shows the applicability of the Goal-Plan Separation is not restricted to a specific goal reasoning formalism.

3 GPS Method Implementation

Throughout the evolution of programming, languages and development tools often advanced by limiting the programmer's freedom to access lower level elements such as registers and pointers to data, and offering in exchange higher level tools and constructs such as variables and dynamically created references to

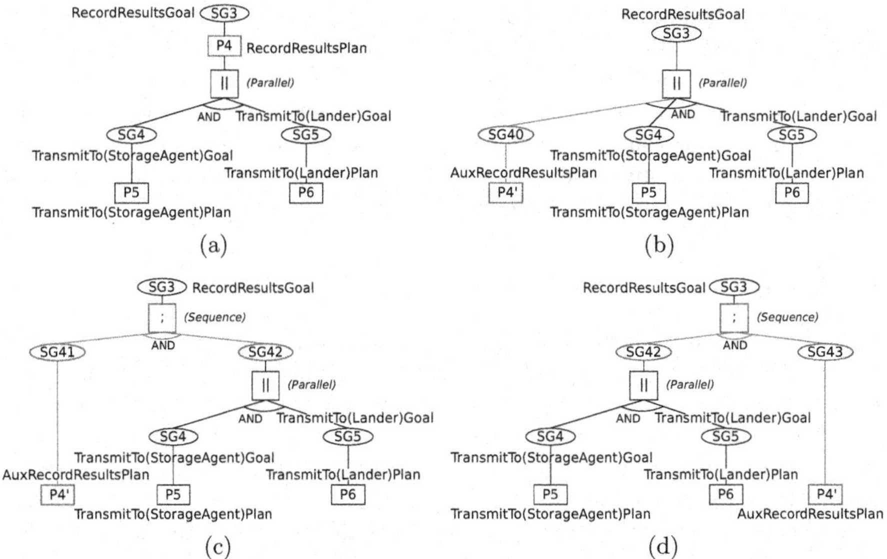

Fig. 4. Transformation of the *SG*3 sub-tree (a) from the Mars rover scenario (Fig. 3) into a GPS-compliant form, in some of the non trivial cases: *P*4 contains actions on the environment that happen in parallel with the goal adoption (b), *P*4 contains actions on the environment that happen before (c) or after (d) the goal adoption

data. These evolutions allowed for the creation of increasingly complex systems while decreasing the possibilities for coding errors. Similarly, we do not refrain from restraining the freedoms of the programmers and designers in the interest of clarity and reliability.

To achieve the goal-plan separation, rather than adopting sub-goals, at execution time an agent's action level (usually composed of action plans) would accomplish the necessary actions and then relinquish control to the higher level where the reasoning and possibly a following goal is adopted. This creates, as illustrated in the examples above, a distinct goal reasoning level where an agent's goals are chosen and their execution is managed.

As shall be discussed in this paper, the representation on multiple levels, either by using sub-goals or through other mechanisms, is important for the scalability and intelligibility of the resulting agents and therefore constitutes an important characteristic of the models that should be at least taken into consideration for the goal reasoning level.

In [15], GPTs are used as support for a study on plan coverage and overlap, with the hypothesis that the plan libraries discussed have no cycles. This is important to note as in the general case adopting goals inside plans may produce cycles, sometimes even with unwanted consequences similar to the infinite loops in classic programming. We, on the other hand, do not restrict cycles, as will be seen in the scenario in Sect. 5. However, the Goal-Plan Separation doesn't allow cycles created through plans that also have actions on the environment.

As the Goal-Plan Separation approach in its simplest form is the requirement to keep a clear distinction between the two abstraction levels, it is general enough so that it can be applied using any of the BDI frameworks that allow goal adoptions in plans. The important condition, however, is to make sure no goals are adopted in plans that act on the environment. Examples of representations that can be used are given next, followed by a more detailed description of a model based on what we call *goal plans* and that we use in Sect. 5.

3.1 Examples of Possible Models for the Goal Reasoning Level

Reasoning through Rules. Using goal trigger rules, an almost "reactive" agent can be created. The goal relationships are implicit but a dependency tree similar to the one seen in Fig. 3 (c) above can be constructed at runtime for tracing purposes. This reasoning model can be implemented in Jadex by simply specifying trigger conditions for each goal but without creating explicit connections between these goals. The advantage of this approach is that the representation can handle more complex systems that act in highly dynamic environments, with new goals added effortlessly. However, this model lacks *look-ahead* capabilities.

Reasoning Using a Planner. Rather than having goals simply triggered by rules, a planner can be used to select among available goals, as for example in CANPLAN [7]. The difference then from the reasoning model described above is that this time the reasoning allows the choice of goals to be prepared in advance starting form the current context. Another difference is that a planner would render the agent proactive, as it would not have to wait for events in order to act. The job of the planner would be to select, order and parallelize goals according to the current needs, and for this it could use certain operators [16]. The example in Sect. 5 does not correspond to this method as no planner is used and its *goal plan* (see below) is defined at design time. Our intuition is also that the GPS approach benefits this model as planning should be easier to perform only on goals, without the interference of details from actions.

3.2 Reasoning through a *Goal Plan*

Between the reactivity of the first model above, and the planning capabilities of the second, we propose here a middle solution that allows for a certain level of *look-ahead* owing to the use of pre-written goal dependencies, just as plan libraries can be used with BDI systems. As required by the GPS method, the goal reasoning level should be kept separate from the plans that handle action composition. Considering that relations between goals can be similar to those between actions, we can envisage using a modified plan language to represent the relations between goal adoptions. We call the resulting plans that handle goal composition *goal plans* and we oppose them to *action plans*.

$P = < N, E >$ // action plan
$N = A \cup O \cup T$ // nodes
$A = \{action \mid action \neq goalAdoption\}$
$O = \{o \mid o \in \{startNode, finishNode, AND, \ \|, wait(duration)\}\}$
$T = \{test(stateCond) \mid stateCond \in \{Beliefs, Events\}\}$ // conditions
$E = \{n_1 \rightarrow n_2 \mid n_1, n_2 \in N\}$ // edges

(a)

$GP = < N_g, E >$ // goal plan
$N_g = A_g \cup O \cup T$ // nodes
$A_g = \{adopt(G) \mid G \in Goals\}$
$O = \{o \mid o \in \{startNode, finishNode, AND, \ \|, wait(duration)\}\}$
$T = \{test(stateCond) \mid stateCond \in \{Beliefs, Events\}\}$ // conditions
$E = \{n_1 \rightarrow n_2 \mid n_1, n_2 \in N\}$ // edges

(b)

Fig. 5. Action plan (a) compared to goal plan (b). Only the action nodes differ.

As defined in Fig. 5, a *goal plan* is an oriented graph with three types of nodes:

- A_g, the *goal adoption nodes*, as the unique action allowed in the goal plan. Each node represents the invocation of an automaton associated with the goal. Note that this is the only distinction from the action plans which have $A = \{action \mid action \neq goalAdoption\}$.
- O, the *operator nodes*, with operations including a unique *start node* and at least one *finish node*. Different finish nodes can be used to indicate final states for a plan, e.g., "successful completion" or "partial failure". There is also an operator for branching parallel threads and one for the logical condition *AND* that can be used to synchronize threads or to indicate the obligation of two or more conditions to be all true, for example to require several goals to be achieved in order for the execution to continue.
- T, the *condition test nodes* that can handle state conditions for belief values and events such belief change and message arrival. They can either be used to test for a momentarily condition, or to wait for a condition to become true or for a message to arrive.

Edges indicate the succession of nodes in the goal plan and, as stated before, cycles are possible, for example to indicate a recurrent goal adoption.

The Mars rover scenario in Fig. 3 (c) with its inline goal dependencies can easily be transformed into a goal plan, as seen in Fig. 6. There are two possible finish nodes, with one for a successful mission where either *G7* or both *SG4* and *SG5* were achieved, and one to indicate all other cases as failures.

While implicit relations between entities (such as the rule-triggered goals above) may be enticing due to their ease of definition and generality, they are also difficult to follow and may hide unwanted interactions. The goal plans, however, favor the use of *explicit* specifications of dependencies between goals. If for example a Mars rover needs to perform an experiment at a location X and it has two goals for achieving this, one being G_1= *"move to X"* and the other G_2= *"drill"*,

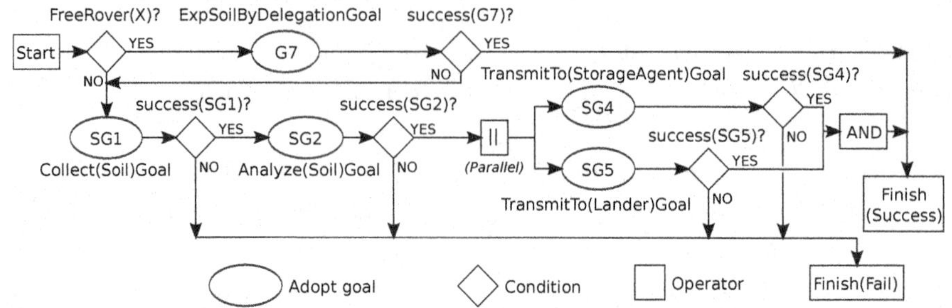

Fig. 6. A goal plan for the Mars rover scenario from Fig. 3

then it is clearer to link the adoption of G_2 to the successful achievement of G_1 rather than for example the belief that the rover is at location X.

In a framework like Jadex, this model can be implemented using a plan that is triggered at agent's birth. The plan would specify the dependencies between sub-goals and adopt them *without any other actions*.

In practice, this model can become difficult to manage as the agent grows in complexity. A solution to this problem is to group together parts of the goal plan and abstract them into *sub-goal plans*, that are to be expanded only when needed. In this way, the representation can still be conceptually on one level, while having the advantages, in particular the scalability, of a hierarchical representation.

This kind of reasoning is suitable for agent systems where the behavior can be thoroughly specified at design time so that all dependencies can be accurately included. Adding new goals and other modifications, however, are difficult to apply. The first implementation described in Sect. 5.2 corresponds to this approach.

3.3 Reasoning through Multiple Goal Plans

The method above has the advantage of providing a "big picture" of the agent's behavior but, as stated before, does not scale well to complex agents. Designing the behavior of an agent that can run for hours can for example create a large goal plan that is difficult to follow and which risks being too rigid in case of unforeseen events. The solution is then to decouple the sub-goal plans from their "parent" goal plans by using goals to manage the expansion, in other words, by allowing any goal not only to have action plans, but also goal plans. This means using the "classic" BDI mechanisms – i.e., goals, plans and automata – with just the subtle difference in the construction of plans: no goal adoption will be in the same plan as an action on the environment. Note, however, that in this case the states indicated through finish nodes do not necessarily reflect the achievement or failure of the parent goal, as the goal would normally have its own conditions for success and failure. Figure 7 (a) shows the Mars rover's behavior represented

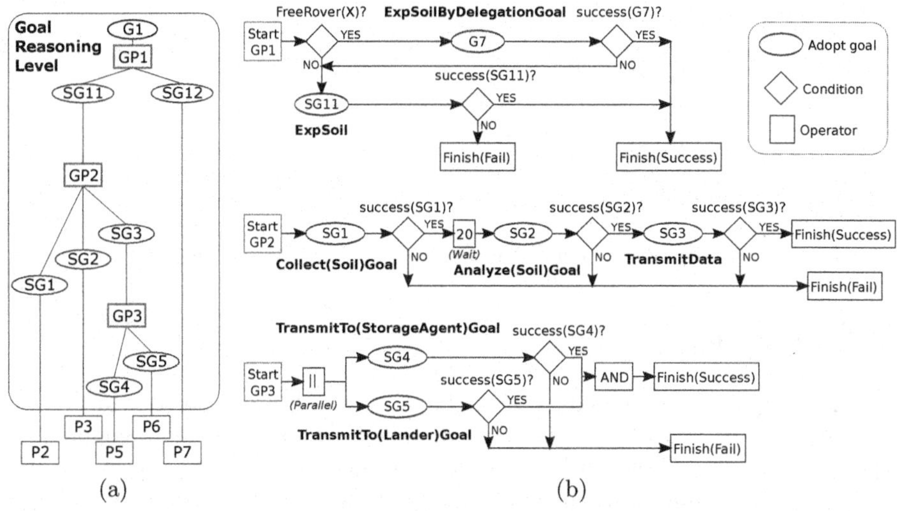

Fig. 7. A multiple level goal plan for the Mars rover scenario from Fig. 3, with (a) the resulting tree (similar to a goal-plan tree) representation and (b) the corresponding goal plans. Note the separation in (a) between the action plans, i.e., *P*2, *P*3, *P*5, *P*6 and *P*7, and the goal reasoning level comprising the goals and the three goal plans, i.e., *GP*1, *GP*2 and *GP*3.

with this model. The resulting model can be represented through a structure that is similar to the GPT as can be seen in the Fig. 7 (b), but this tree contains fewer details as more logic is included in the goal plans, while in the same time complying with the GPS approach.

There are many advantages of this multiple goal plan model. First of all, splitting the behavior into more levels of goals and sub-goals with the corresponding plans improves flexibility and fault tolerance – in case a plan fails, the BDI logics can require a retry using the same or a different plan, provided that such plan is available. Then, splitting the behavior into more manageable chunks leaves less room for hidden faults. The use of goal plans for managing goal dependencies allows for a more refined specification than what was available through the *AND*, *OR* and the operators in the GPT. For example, in Fig. 7, the suite of goal adoptions in *GP2* does represent the sequence that was originally in the GPT, but other operators – such as the *delay* in the example – can be added through this specification, and precise goal failures can be handled accordingly (while not present in the given example, one could add other goals to account for these specific sub-goal failures). This model is therefore preferred to the simple goal plans presented above, and is illustrated in the second implementation in Sect. 5.2.

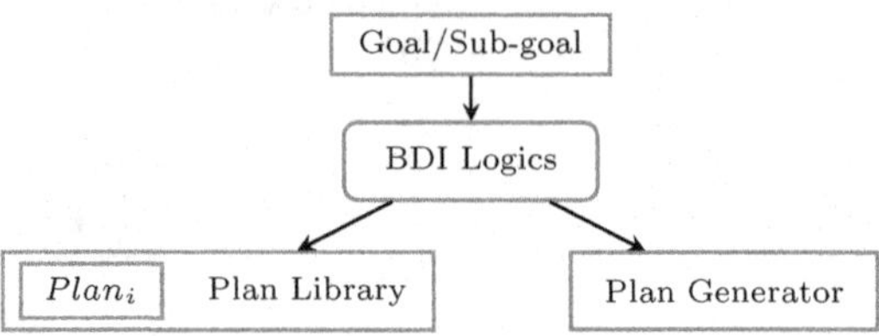

Fig. 8. BDI logics: handler of the goal-plan relation at runtime

4 Execution

While not explicitly presented in the GPT, as stated before and seen in Fig. 8, between the goal and plan levels there are the BDI logics or more commonly a goal automaton [2,3] which handles the goal life-cycle. This life-cycle usually starts with the adoption of the goal and includes the choice and execution of plans.

An example of a goal life-cycle for which an automaton is used is depicted in Fig. 9. It uses a series of beliefs for state changes, such as *desirable* (*des*) to indicate the presence in the automaton, *selected* (*sel*) to indicate the passage in an active state and *satisfaction* (*sat*) that indicates if the goal was achieved. We use these beliefs to control the execution of goals by linking them to other beliefs that justify them, for example the goal adoption conditions for *desirable.* In case any of these conditions is no longer valid, the belief is no longer justified so the automaton changes its state automatically, which in the case of the *desirable* belief means that the goal is aborted. If we take the example in Fig. 6, supposing that during the execution of *G7* the condition *FreeRover(X)* is contradicted by an observation, the adoption of the goal will no longer be justified and the goal will fail automatically. It is also important to note that as a higher level means of control, the goal reasoning level has precedence over the action level.

Beliefs can also be used to control the goal automaton from the higher level in a more straightforward manner, if for example we added another operator that causes a goal to abort its execution.

For the GPS approach the automaton is a black box that is given a goal to adopt and possible plans to execute and this is why we represent only goals and plans in our modeling examples. The execution can cause side effects such as belief changes that can lead the reasoning level to take actions with respect to current goal or even the adoption or execution of other goals. For example, this can cause the goal to be aborted in case it is estimated to take the agent in an unsafe state, or it can cause the adoption of a reparation or compensation goal to counter certain unwanted effects. Note that several automata can function at a given moment as parallelism is allowed in our method. While conflicts are normally treated at goal reasoning level and can even be explicitly handled in the goal plans, conflict management is not within the scope of this paper.

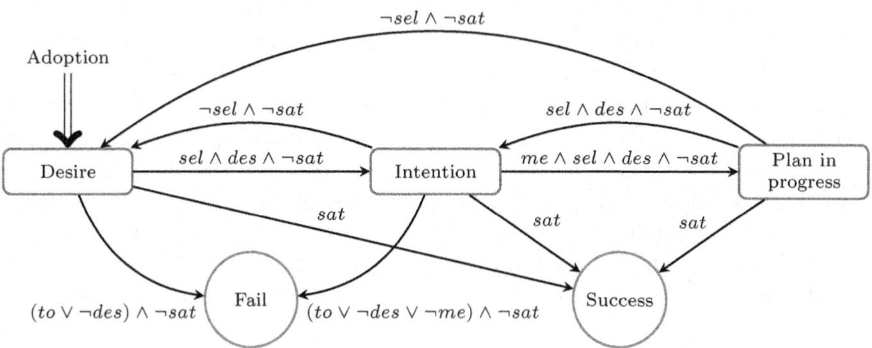

Fig. 9. Our generic goal life-cycle with transition conditions on state beliefs ($des = desirable$, $sel = selected$, $sat = satisfied$, $me = means$, $to = timeout$)

5 Experimenting with GPS

The GPS approach has been experimented in an industrial context at Thales Airborne Systems on an application designed for experimenting on AI in general and more precisely on Interval Constraints propagation and multi-agent systems (MAS). The purpose of this application, Interloc, is the localization of boats from a maritime patrol aircraft. It is implemented as a MAS and can contain dozens of agents implemented as Prolog processes.

Interloc was initially designed as a set of non goal-directed autonomous agents. This means that the agents had only one purpose that was achieved through a set of associated plans. Subsequently, it was redesigned in order to improve the level of autonomy of the agents by endowing them with goals. The pursuit of intelligibility brought along the idea of having a clear separation between the levels of abstraction of goals and plans.

A first implementation in the spirit of GPS used a goal plan formalism as the one described in Sect. 3.2. This meant designing a plan where the only possible action was goal adoption. For the ease of use, sub-goal plans – which anticipate the hierarchical approach later implemented – were also used, adding their activation to the goal adoption as the only possible "actions" in the goal plan. The intention of the designer (prior to the GPS methodology presented in the present paper) was to exhibit an abstract (goal) level describing the main features of the behavior of agents so that one would find it sufficient to only read the goal level description in order to understand the salient behavior of the agents. Agents were then implemented following the idea described in Sect. 3.3 as the flexibility and robustness of goals seemed preferable to the simple invocation of sub-goal plans.

In the pursuit of a more formal representation, we abstracted the goal plans into Time Petri Nets, TPNs [17], seen in Figs. 10 and 11 (b-e). We chose the TPNs because they present many advantages through their graphical and intuitive representation, as well as their expressive power (parallelism, sequence, synchronisation etc.). This extension over classic Petri nets gives the possibility of assigning firing time intervals to the transitions, which we used for representing waiting in the agent behavior. Furthermore, the TPNs allowed us to structurally verify the goal plans and ensure their correctness. We also used a type of Petri net that resemble the Recursive Petri Nets (already used for representing agent plans [18]) where we distinguished two types of transition: the elementary transitions to be fired according to the standard semantics of Petri nets and the abstract ones corresponding to the action of adoptiong a goal. However, the expansion of this action, the goal adoption, is not handled in this network, and its transition corresponds to a call to the associated automaton, e.g., the one in Fig. 9.

We first present the application itself, then the particular case of one of the main agents, the aircraft, in the two goal plan-based implementations mentioned above. This section concludes with a discussion on the advantages of the GPS approach in the specific case of the Interloc application.

5.1 Interloc

The main goal of the application is the localization of boats using a *goniometer*[4] on-board a maritime patrol aircraft. The sole use of a goniometer allows for a stealth detection, i.e., detect without being detected, of boats which is important for some missions such as gas-freeing prevention[5]. If the boats were steady, the problem would be simple. The fact that they move necessitates a reliance on non-linear regression methods, as is the case of existing commissioned implementations, or interval constraint propagation, in Interloc. Most of the agents, i.e., boats, the goniometer and the data visualization agent, were designed for the purpose of simulation. The main agent, the aircraft, must (1) follow all the boats visible from its location, (2) compute in real-time their position by accumulating bearings and interacting with computation agents (more precisely *artifacts* [19]) operating interval propagation, (3) adapt its trajectory to observations and contingencies and (4) transmit results to the visualization agent. For the patrol aircraft, boats may appear or vanish at any time. Several aircraft might be present at the same time, but so far they do not communicate with each other. Typically 20 to 30 agents or artifacts are active in the system at a given time.

5.2 The Aircraft Agent

Boats and aircraft have been designed following the GPS method. We present here the aircraft, which is the most complex agent type and hence the most interesting for illustrating the methodology.

Five goals corresponding to five main activities of the agent were identified:

[4] Tool which displays the direction towards the source of a signal, in this case a boat and its radar.

[5] Deterring tankers from polluting the environment by cleaning their fuel tanks at sea.

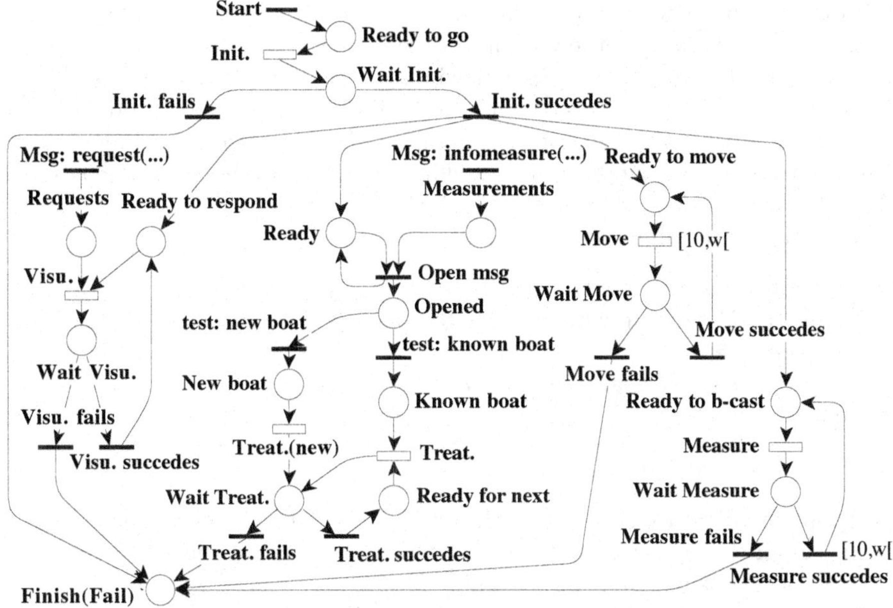

Fig. 10. Petri net representation of the goal plan for the aircraft agent with goal adoptions represented as hollow transitions. The *Treat.* (for "treatment") goal is adopted in two different contexts in order to insure that messages from each boat are treated sequentially, but in parallel with the other boats. Multiple instances of the goal with different beliefs are thus created.

- *Init.* (for "initialization") of the system: get data related to the aircraft trajectory (pre-defined, planned or human-guided) and various parameters characterising the simulation
- *Move*: execute one *step* forward
- *Measure*: initiate measurement of the bearing of all the visible boats
- *Treat.* (for "treatment"): process a received measurement
- *Visu.* (for "visualization"): process a single request from the visualization agent

The sole knowledge of the various goals present in the system is not sufficient to understand (and define) its behavior. One must also describe the way in which these goals are adopted and what happens when they are achieved, for example by specifying their chronology, conditions for becoming a desire, conditions for becoming an intention. This knowledge may be provided in different forms, corresponding to the different ways of applying the GPS approach.

Using a Single Goal Plan. For the first implementation we present here, the aircraft agent in Interloc was designed using a goal plan with four sub-plans to indicate the dependencies of the goals above. These dependencies correspond to the goal reasoning level in the GPS approach.

Informally, the goal plan is the following (a more formal description of this plan is given in Fig. 10 as a Petri net): the achievement goal Init. is adopted. If the goal is not achieved, the system is halted. Otherwise, four sub-branches implemented as sub-goal plans are activated in parallel: *main_move*, *main_measure*, *main_visualization* and *main_analyze*.

The *main_move* sub-plan:

- Wait for a *move_time_step* delay
- Adopt the Move goal, whose associated plans will compute and execute the next time step
- Wait for the Move goal achievement
- Loop

The *main_measure* sub-plan:

- Adopt the Measure goal, where the associated plans will measure the bearings of all the visible boats through interactions with the measurement artifact and the (simulated) boat agents
- Once achieved, the goal will be re-adopted after a given time delay

The *main_analyze* sub-plan:

- Wait for a measurement, in the form of a message that arrives randomly after a measurement request message is issued
- Record the newly present boats
- Adopt the Treat. goal, whose associated plan will generate a constraint to be added to the previously received measurements and send it to an interval constraint propagation artifact which will compute a more and more precise boat location
- Loop, in order to process waiting measurements

The *main_vizualization* sub-plan:

- Wait for a request from the visualization agent
- Adopt the Visu. goal in order to process the request
- Wait for the achievement
- Loop to process pending requests

Using the Multiple Levels of Goal Plans. When the pursuit for flexibility and robustness pushed us further and we separated the goal plans and their sub-goal plans through new goals, we obtained the tree structure seen in Fig. 11 (a). *GP1*, in Fig. 11 (b), guides the adoption of four intermediary goals that are internal to the goal reasoning level, i.e., they do not have action plans. *GP2*-*GP5* correspond roughly to the sub-goal plans described above and can easily be matched with the corresponding branches in the initial one-level goal plan (Fig. 10).

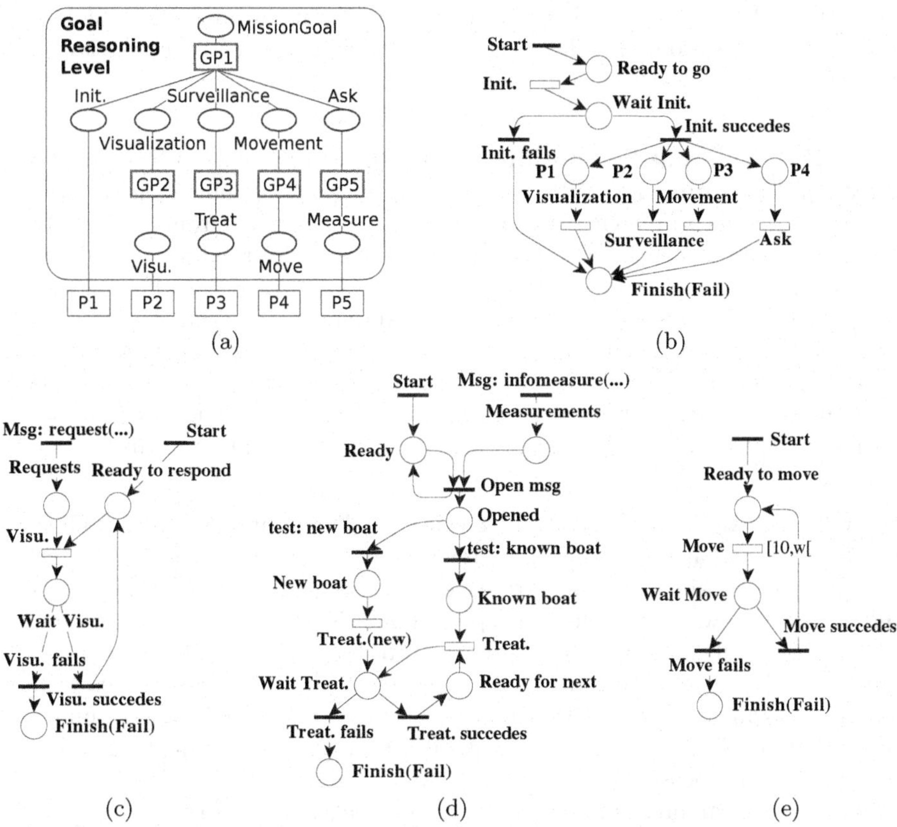

Fig. 11. (a) the goal-plan structure of the aircraft agent, (b-e) Petri net representations of the *GP1* (b), *GP2* (c), *GP3* (d) and *GP4* (e) goal plans. *GP5* is not presented because it is very similar to *GP4*, as can be deduced from Fig. 10. Goal adoptions are represented as hollow transitions.

5.3 Discussion

With GPS, Iterative and Timed Behaviors Appear at Goal Level: In the pre-GPS version of the application, the natural tendency was to incorporate dynamic aspects into the plans, making them fairly complex. For instance, the Move goal was not conceived as a single step as presented above, instead, it was charged with the complete management of the aircraft's trajectory, including the loop sequencing individual steps. This rather straightforward design would close the loop inside the plans and after the actions on the environment – e.g., the movement or broadcast of measure request messages – were performed. The *move time-step*, which is important for the global understanding of the behavior of the aircraft, was also "buried" in the plan pursuing the goal. In the GPS-compliant versions, deciding to rewrite the plan and change the scope of the goal to the achievement of a single movement step, created the need for the definition of the time-step and the iterative behavior at the goal reasoning level, leading to a clearer design. The fact that such details are at an upper level of abstraction emphasizes their importance and improves the understanding of the agent behavior.

With GPS, Relevant Perceptions of the Environment Are Required at the Goal Reasoning Level: It is the case of messages coming from the visualization or the measurement agents. Here again, it emanates from the fact that certain perceptions can be essential for the global understanding of the agent behavior. In Interloc, measurements trigger the adoption of a goal whose achievement is more or less secondary since other measurements can occur rapidly. That is the reason why it seems to be a good approach to handle these measurements at the upper level of abstraction. A perception filtering strategy, to avoid unnecessary inputs or even overloading the agent, can also appear in this goal plan, possibly by the adoption of a specific goal prior to the adoption of the Measure goal itself.

With GPS, Handling Errors Is Easier to Take into Account: This is because errors, whatever their cause, often manifest through the failure of goals. This provides an adequate range of exception mechanisms in the language in which plans are written. Hence, the programmer's effort with regard to fault tolerance is mainly to take into account the processing of non-achieved goals. Of course, this does not concern the goal plan itself, which has to be designed traditionally by explicitly introducing fault tolerance actions. However the amount of code regarding the classic plans is far greater than the amount of the goal plan code. In the Interloc application, no specific fault tolerance effort has been carried out but a clean processing of non-achieved goals in order to stop the system rather than have it crash. As a consequence, application debugging was greatly facilitated. For the same reasons, the GPS approach proved to facilitate the evolution of the multi-agent system. Thus, the aircraft agent was easily changed into a UAV (Unmanned Autonomous Vehicle), with a larger autonomy in the trajectory choice. Here again, the abstraction obtained by separating goals and plans seems to be the reason.

In Interloc, we used an in-house agent programming language (Alma) to implement the goal plans. All the required primitives were available, since a goal plan is a type of plan. Nonetheless, it appears that specific primitives could be introduced to facilitate the programming of the goal level. These concern mainly iterative and time-controlled behaviors.

6 Discussion on the Fault Tolerance with Goal Reasoning

In real life applications agents tend to have more refined representations than the ones discussed in Sect. 2. In particular, when it comes to handling errors, the specification easily grows in complexity as specific cases have to be taken into consideration [20]. Goals give agents a level of abstraction that is beneficial for a system's robustness as errors, exceptions, anomalies etc. usually occur during plan execution which, in a robust[6] system, only cause the plan to fail and the goal automaton to react normally and reattempt to achieve the goal. While there are studies that treat the more general case of partial goal satisfaction [21] (described below), if we only consider a binary goal definition, a goal's adoption has only two possible outcomes at reasoning level: the goal is either achieved or not. Requiring the programmer to specify not only the actions to take after the achievement of a goal, but also the actions to take in case the goal fails enhances the reliability of the agent without dramatically increasing its complexity.

In the Mars rover scenario represented in Fig. 6, the failure to delegate the task to another agent, i.e., the failure of *G7*, causes the rover to attempt to accomplish the mission by itself through the adoption of *SG1*. Similarly, in the aircraft specification of the Interloc application (Sect. 5), both the successful achievement and the failure of goals are represented in the Petri net and also in the implementation. However, for simplicity reasons, in our example, no special actions are taken and the only result of a goal failure is to ensure the agent does not reach unforeseen states. Also, the current format implies an infinite life for the agent, which is not necessarily desirable in a real application.

In the paper cited above [21], goal satisfaction is evaluated using a *progress metric*. Partial goal satisfaction could be integrated with our model by enforcing the coverage of the whole range of possible values for the progress metric used. For example for a Surveillance goal, instead of specifying success and fail behaviors, it could be interesting to estimate the percentage of the assigned area that was covered and to use thresholds for the desired behaviors: less than 30% would be considered a mission failure with the area announced as *unsafe*, a coverage between 30 and 80% would require a call for backup to finish the job, while a coverage of more than 80% would be considered a success. Note that this does not concern the intermediary stages such as those that are handled by the goal automata, but final goal failures, i.e., when all alternatives have been tried and no positive outcome resulted.

7 Related Work

The aspect of the Goal-Plan Separation that handles goal reasoning is situated at what Harland et al. [3] and Thangarajah et al. in earlier works [4,13] call *agent deliberation level*. This is where agent goals are *considered*, which constitutes the point where goals start their life-cycle. It is the same level where *top level commands* are issued to interfere with the goal life-cycle, e.g., when deciding to drop or suspend the goal. As the cited authors point out, goal deliberation can deal with issues such as goal prioritization, resource management and even user intervention. These aspects are beyond the scope of this paper but can be considered for future developments of our approach. We note, however, that in [3] changes in the goal state have preference over any executing plans, just as in

[6] In this case, we understand by *robust* an agent system in which an error or exception in a plan is caught and only causes that plan to fail, while the rest of the agent continues to function normally, i.e., does not cause the whole agent to fail.

the case of GPS, where the goal reasoning level takes precedence over the lower levels that it controls, i.e., the goal life-cycle automata and the plan execution.

The arguments for planning in BDI agents at goal level employed by Sardina and Padgham [7] offer more reasons for the existence of the goal reasoning level (be it hardcoded, created through planning or other means) that the GPS approach delimits: *"(a) important resources may be used in taking actions that do not lead to a successful outcome; (b) actions are not always reversible and may lead to states from which there is no successful outcome; (c) execution of actions take substantially longer than "thinking" (or planning); and (d) actions have side effects which are undesirable if they turn out not to be useful"*. All these advocate for an agent that behaves strategically and proactively rather than react based on a limited context, and it is at goal reasoning level that such a strategic reasoning is possible. The multi-level goal plan structure proposed in Sect. 3.3 allows for both complex "strategic" and simple "reactive" behaviors ($GP3$ vs. $GP2$ in Fig. 11).

While this paper discusses the goal reasoning level in the need to better organize the levels "below", i.e., the plans, Morandini et al. [14] approach the same level from a different perspective: the need to fill in the gap between goal based engineering and goal implementations. They propose a tool for transforming an agent designed using the Tropos methodology [8] into Jadex code, for which they introduce a formalism based on rules for the life-cycle of non-leaf goals in a goal hierarchy. This segregation between leaf and non-leaf goals creates a goal level that corresponds to our goal reasoning level and thus their work is consistent with the GPS approach. This further confirms our statement with respect to the utility of a goal-plan separation for the implementation of goal-based methodologies. Furthermore, our proposition of using goal plans on multiple levels means that even goals that are internal to the goal reasoning level will have the same life-cycles as goals that use action plans. A specific life-cycle, as proposed by Morandini et al. is therefore no longer needed, deeming the development process easier, as there are less types of goals to consider. One of the interesting aspects is that Morandini et al. take into account the fact that even if the sub-goals are achieved, the parent goal may still fail due to its own achievement condition, which is often not taken into consideration when discussing the goal-plan trees. While this formalism is rich and GPS-compliant, as our application example shows, our approach aims to provide a model that allows for a more refined representation, with more diverse goal relations, event-based goal reasoning and time constraints.

There are many parallels that can be drawn between our approach and the one employed by the Prometheus agent development methodology [9] in the detailed design phase. This is where functionalities identified in the previous phases of the methodology – system specification and architectural design – are used as a starting point for designing capabilities. A capability is a module within the agent that can contain further capabilities, and at the bottom level plans, events and data, e.g., capability C_1 uses data D or plan P_1 sends message to plan P_2. Internal messages are used to connect between different design artifacts, such as plans and capabilities. This functionality is assured by either beliefs or direct goal dependencies in our work. This nested structure of capabilities is similar to the sub-goal plans (Sect. 3.2) in its pursuit of *"understandable complexity at each level"*, and while semantically different, it does provide a very similar functionality to our goal reasoning level. Furthermore, the use of internal messages to indicate dependencies between internal artifacts (mostly capabilities and plans) creates a very similar structure to our goal plans where we explicit dependencies between goals, often guided by tests on beliefs and messages. In Prometheus, BDI goals at agent level can be represented through a specific type of event, because events can trigger plans. As events, i.e., goal events, but also messages, percepts and internal messages, can be produced in plans as well as in outside the agent, a clearly defined goal reasoning level in the GPS sense cannot be delimited in the current form of the methodology. The Goal-Plan Separation approach would, however, benefit from the integration with the first two phases of the Prometheus methodology: the system specification and the architectural design. Due to the fact that these two phases correspond to a top-down design approach, and also, as we showed above, the fact that there are already similarities in the current form of Prometheus, we feel that such an integration would be possible, resulting in a methodology tailored for goal-directed GPS agents.

In [22] Pokahr et al. address the issue of *goal deliberation*. This concept is not equivalent but rather included in our goal reasoning level as they consider only goals that have already been adopted. Their work focuses on the similar issue of goal interactions, i.e., when goals interfere positively or negatively with each other, and they base their proposed strategy on the extension of the definition of goals. They include for example inhibition arcs that block the adoption of a certain goal or type of goal when another goal is adopted. Such mechanisms can be integrated when specifying the goal reasoning level discussed in our approach.

The goal automaton proposed by Braubach et al. [2] presents a goal state labeled "New" with a "Creation condition" acting as a triggering condition for the goal before the adoption and the actual goal life-cycle. This state, together with the condition are at the level of our goal reasoning level. A goal that was defined for the agent is considered to be in the "New" state, as opposed to a goal that can for example be received from the exterior or generated through the agent reasoning. Only when such a goal is received does it pass into the "New" state. All the goals discussed in the examples in this paper are already in this state.

The goal-plan trees have been used in various works for representing agent specifications and as a basis for further treatments. In [4] GPTs are used to gather resource requirements called summary information and identify possible goal interactions. This is due to the hierarchical structure of the tree where summary information can be propagated upwards towards the root of the tree. Further works on the subject [3] reuse the model to illustrate their operational semantics for the goal life-cycle. Furthermore, Shaw et al. propose different approach for handling goal interactions using Petri Nets [23] and constraints [24] instead of GPTs. These, as well as other works that use GPTs, such as [25] on intention conflicts, can be used with GPS, and our intuition is that by separating the goal reasoning level, goal interactions can be managed more easily.

Singh et al. [26] use learning for plan selection in BDI agents. They also use GPTs to describe the agents and even note briefly that only *"leaf plans interact directly with the environment"*, which is consistent with the GPS approach. This allows for a representation where, given the results – i.e., *success* or *fail* – of the executions of all leaf nodes, the success or failure of the root node is decided by simply propagating these logic values in the AND-OR tree. This is a confirmation of the benefits of the GPS approach, for, if actions were included in intermediary plans, even if all sub-goals of a plan were achieved, the plan would not necessarily cause the achievement of its parent goal. The GPT is therefore already a simplification of the system, as it uses the rather strong hypothesis that there are no perturbations, such as the one in the afore-mentioned case, in the AND-OR tree. Another example of "perturbation" in the propagation of success values in the tree can be the use of specific achievement and failure conditions for each goals [7,14].

Note that, while we use the GPT representation to justify our approach, the GPS is concerned with more general agent models. Also, this paper does not argue against the GPT formalism, neither does it dispute the plethora of works that use it as a model, but rather discusses the more general issue of specifying agents with interwoven goal and action levels. The current paper complements the cited works on goal interactions as it concerns the agent specification rather than the runtime mechanisms that aim to improve the efficiency, proactivity, reactivity etc. of the agents.

Another representation used for resource handling is the *task expansion tree* described in [27]. This tree represents the decomposition of a task (a concept similar to goals in our work) into subtasks. The particularity is the introduction of special *composite tasks* that are used to compose other tasks in a functional manner. These include, besides the sequence and parallel operators present in the GPT model described in this paper, other tasks that allow other types of branching and tests. The use of these operators in a tree structure situates their model between classic goal hierarchies and our goal plan.

Clement et al. [28] champion the advantages of abstraction for solving various problems such as large scale planning and scheduling. They argue that by abstracting the less critical details in a large problem, the overall solution is easier to find, and can then be expanded to the actual detailed solution. This applies well to our Goal-Plan Separation approach, as well as to their approach on planning in a hierarchical way. They extend HTNs (hierarchical task networks) to take time into consideration and use summary information at higher levels in the HTN to identify possible interactions between plans while working with abstract actions (which are similar to the BDI concept of goal). HTNs are quite similar to goal hierarchies in that they too offer a gradual refinement for the behavior of an agent from the more abstract to the actual actions. The advantage of using goals instead of "abstract plans" is given by the flexibility and resilience offered through the goal life-cycles where a goal's achievement can be attempted through various plans, with different constraints etc. Nevertheless, our work does not exclude the possibility of using HTNs for plan selection, for example in a similar fashion with CANPLAN [7].

8 Conclusion and Future Work

In this paper, we argued that the separation of reasoning and acting is important for the specification and construction of BDI agents. It was shown that the possibility to mix actions on the environment with goal adoptions in various agent models and languages can have negative effects on the resulting representation and can hinder the development process. A series of examples illustrated what an agent would look like when complying with the *Goal-Plan Separation* approach, with emphasis on the two resulting levels: a *goal reasoning level* and an *action level*. As a possible representation for the former, *goal plans* were introduced. The GPS therefore imposes a constraint on agent design that does go against the reflex of adopting a goal in any place it is needed but produces a better-structured result. The GPS also results in agents that "step back and look at the overall picture" rather than react "rashly" to their current situation, making it suitable for "strategic", proactive and complex behaviors, without necessarily neglecting the reactive ones, e.g., *GP2* in Fig. 11. The importance of tidy agent representation lies with the ease of development, which can, in turn, facilitate the wide-scale adoption of the development model. Furthermore, a clean representation that helps diminish the number of design and development faults and also improves maintainability helps bring the overall project costs down.

As discussed in the paper, on the side of BDI agent modeling there are many studies on goal representations and goal life-cycles. However, the higher level that is placed above these automata is less examined in the literature and constitutes a point of this paper that we plan as a further study. For this, a more in-depth research on specifying the agent's goal reasoning will have to be undertaken. Among other primitives, the handling of temporal constraints is important for agent systems and should be taken into consideration. Furthermore, as stated above, there are fault tolerance aspects related to this direction in agent development that can be exploited. We are particularly interested in the use of GPS and goal-directed agents in general for designing multi-agent systems that can better cope with faults that were not foreseen at design. As presented in Sect. 5, we have already began the empirical evaluation of the approach and its advantages on agent design on a real time application. However, more evaluations will be necessary in order to extend and generalize the GPS approach. In the long run, the goal is to integrate this approach in an agent development methodology.

Acknowledgement. The authors would like to thank the anonymous reviewers for their insights on this work. The authors would also like to acknowledge the usefulness of the discussions at the the EMAS14 Workshop that helped refine and advance our research on this topic.

References

1. Rao, A.S., Georgeff, M.P.: BDI-agents: From theory to practice. In: Proceedings of the First International Conference on Multiagent Systems, pp. 312–319. AAAI Press, San Francisco (1995)
2. Braubach, L., Pokahr, A., Moldt, D., Lamersdorf, W.: Goal representation for BDI agent systems. In: Bordini, R.H., Dastani, M., Dix, J., El Fallah Seghrouchni, A. (eds.) PROMAS 2004. LNCS (LNAI), vol. 3346, pp. 44–65. Springer, Heidelberg (2005)
3. Harland, J., Morley, D.N., Thangarajah, J., Yorke-Smith, N.: An operational semantics for the goal life-cycle in BDI agents. Autonomous Agents and Multi-Agent Systems 28(4), 682–719 (2014)
4. Thangarajah, J., Padgham, L.: Computationally effective reasoning about goal interactions. Journal of Automated Reasoning 47(1), 17–56 (2011)
5. Bordini, R., Hübner, J., Vieira, R.: Jason and the golden fleece of agent-oriented programming. In: Bordini, R., Dastani, M., Dix, J., El Fallah Seghrouchni, A. (eds.) Multi-Agent Programming. Multiagent Systems, Artificial Societies, and Simulated Organizations, vol. 15, pp. 3–37. Springer US (2005)
6. Braubach, L., Pokahr, A., Lamersdorf, W.: Jadex: A short overview. In: Net.ObjectDays 2004: AgentExpo. (2004)
7. Sardina, S., Padgham, L.: A BDI agent programming language with failure handling, declarative goals, and planning. Autonomous Agents and Multi-Agent Systems 23(1), 18–70 (2011)
8. Giunchiglia, F., Mylopoulos, J., Perini, A.: The tropos software development methodology: Processes, models and diagrams. In: Giunchiglia, F., Odell, J.J., Weiß, G. (eds.) AOSE 2002. LNCS, vol. 2585, pp. 162–173. Springer, Heidelberg (2003)
9. Winikoff, M., Padgham, L.: Developing Intelligent Agent Systems: A Practical Guide. Wiley Series in Agent Technology. John Wiley and Sons (2004)
10. Hindriks, K.V., de Boer, F.S., van der Hoek, W., Meyer, J.-J.C.: Agent programming with declarative goals. In: Castelfranchi, C., Lespérance, Y. (eds.) Intelligent Agents VII. LNCS (LNAI), vol. 1986, pp. 228–243. Springer, Heidelberg (2001)
11. Winikoff, M., Padgham, L., Harland, J., Thangarajah, J.: Declarative and procedural goals in intelligent agent systems. In: Proceedings of the 8th International Conference on Principles of Knowledge Representation and Reasoning, pp. 470–481. Morgan Kaufman, Toulouse (2002)
12. Dastani, M., van Riemsdijk, M.B., Dignum, F., Meyer, J.-J.C.: A programming language for cognitive agents goal directed 3APL. In: Dastani, M. M., Dix, J., El Fallah Seghrouchni, A. (eds.) PROMAS 2003. LNCS (LNAI), vol. 3067, pp. 111–130. Springer, Heidelberg (2004)
13. Thangarajah, J.: Managing the Concurrent Execution of Goals in Intelligent Agents. PhD thesis, RMIT University, Melbourne, Australia (2005)
14. Morandini, M., Penserini, L., Perini, A.: Operational semantics of goal models in adaptive agents. In: Proceedings of the 8th International Conference on Autonomous Agents and Multiagent Systems, vol. 1, pp. 129–136. International Foundation for Autonomous Agents and Multiagent Systems, Budapest (2009)
15. Thangarajah, J., Sardina, S., Padgham, L.: Measuring plan coverage and overlap for agent reasoning. In: Proceedings of the 11th International Conference on Autonomous Agents and Multiagent Systems, vol. 2, pp. 1049–1056. International Foundation for Autonomous Agents and Multiagent Systems, Valencia (2012)

16. Chaouche, A.C., El Fallah Seghrouchni, A., Ilie, J.M., Sadouni, D.E.: A higher-order agent model for ambient systems. Procedia Computer Science 21(0), 156–163 (2013), The 4th International Conference on Emerging Ubiquitous Systems and Pervasive Networks and the 3rd International Conference on Current and Future Trends of Information and Communication Technologies in Healthcare
17. Berthomieu, B., Diaz, M.: Modeling and verification of time dependent systems using time petri nets. IEEE Transactions on Software Engineering 17(3), 259–273 (1991)
18. El Fallah Seghrouchni, A., Haddad, S.: A recursive model for distributed planning. In: Proceedings of the 2nd International Conference on Multi-Agent Systems, pp. 307–314. AAAI Press, Kyoto (1996)
19. Omicini, A., Ricci, A., Viroli, M.: Artifacts in the a&a meta-model for multi-agent systems. Autonomous Agents and Multi-Agent Systems 17(3), 432–456 (2008)
20. Torres-Pomales, W.: Software fault tolerance: A tutorial. Technical report, NASA Langley Research Center, Hampton, Virginia, USA (2000)
21. van Riemsdijk, M.B., Yorke-Smith, N.: Towards reasoning with partial goal satisfaction in intelligent agents. In: Collier, R., Dix, J., Novák, P. (eds.) ProMAS 2010. LNCS, vol. 6599, pp. 41–59. Springer, Heidelberg (2012)
22. Pokahr, A., Braubach, L., Lamersdorf, W.: A goal deliberation strategy for BDI agent systems. In: Eymann, T., Klügl, F., Lamersdorf, W., Klusch, M., Huhns, M.N. (eds.) MATES 2005. LNCS (LNAI), vol. 3550, pp. 82–93. Springer, Heidelberg (2005)
23. Shaw, P., Bordini, R.H.: Towards alternative approaches to reasoning about goals. In: Baldoni, M., Son, T.C., van Riemsdijk, M.B., Winikoff, M. (eds.) DALT 2007. LNCS (LNAI), vol. 4897, pp. 104–121. Springer, Heidelberg (2008)
24. Shaw, P., Bordini, R.H.: An alternative approach for reasoning about the goal-plan tree problem. In: Dastani, M., El Fallah Seghrouchni, A., Hübner, J., Leite, J. (eds.) LADS 2010. LNCS (LNAI), vol. 6822, pp. 115–135. Springer, Heidelberg (2011)
25. Shapiro, S., Sardina, S., Thangarajah, J., Cavedon, L., Padgham, L.: Revising conflicting intention sets in BDI agents. In: Proceedings of the 11th International Conference on Autonomous Agents and Multiagent Systems, vol. 2, pp. 1081–1088. International Foundation for Autonomous Agents and Multiagent Systems, Valencia (2012)
26. Singh, D., Sardina, S., Padgham, L., James, G.: Integrating learning into a BDI agent for environments with changing dynamics. In: Proceedings of the Twenty-Second International Joint Conference on Artificial Intelligence, vol. 3, pp. 2525–2530. AAAI Press, Barcelona (2011)
27. Morley, D.N., Myers, K.L., Yorke-Smith, N.: Continuous refinement of agent resource estimates. In: Proceedings of the Fifth International Joint Conference on Autonomous Agents and Multiagent Systems, pp. 858–865. ACM, Hakodate (2006)
28. Clement, B.J., Durfee, E.H., Barrett, A.C.: Abstract reasoning for planning and coordination. Journal of Artificial Intelligence Research 28(1), 453–515 (2007)

A Stepwise Refinement Based Development of Self-Organizing Multi-Agent Systems: Application to the Foraging Ants

Zeineb Graja[1,2], Frédéric Migeon[2], Christine Maurel[2], Marie-Pierre Gleizes[2], and Ahmed Hadj Kacem[1]

[1] Research on Development and Control of Distributed Applications Laboratory (ReDCAD)
Faculty of Economics and Management
University of Sfax, Tunisia
zeineb.graja@redcad.org, ahmed.hadjkacem@fsegs.rnu.tn

[2] Institute for Research in Computer Science in Toulouse (IRIT)
Paul Sabatier University
Toulouse, France
{graja,migeon,maurel,gleizes}@irit.fr

Abstract. This paper proposes a formal modeling for Self-Organizing Multi-Agent Systems (SOMAS) based on stepwise refinements, with the Event-B language and the Temporal Logic of Actions (TLA). This modeling allows to develop this kind of systems in a more structured manner. In addition, it enables to reason, in a rigorous way, about the correctness of the derived models both at the individual level and the global level. Our work is illustrated by the foraging ants case study.

Keywords: Self-organizing MAS, foraging ants, formal verification, refinement, Event-B, TLA.

1 Introduction

Self-Organizing Multi-Agent Systems (SOMAS) are made of a set of autonomous entities (called agents) interacting together and situated in an environment. Each agent has a limited knowledge about the environment and possesses its own goals. The global function of the overall system emerges from the interactions between the individual entities composing the system as well as interactions between the entities and the environment. Thanks to their self-organizing mechanisms, SOMAS are able to adjust their behavior and cope with the environment changes [14].

When designing this kind of systems, two levels of observation are generally distinguished: the micro-level which corresponds to the agents local behavior and the macro-level which describes the emergent global behavior.

One of the main challenges when engineering a SOMAS is about giving assurances and guarantees related to its correctness, robustness and resilience. Correctness refers to fulfillment of the different constraints related to the

F. Dalpiaz et al. (Eds.): EMAS 2014, LNAI 8758, pp. 40–57, 2014.

agents activities. Robustness ensures that the system is able to cope with changes and perturbations [5]. Whereas resilience informs about the capability of the system to adapt when robustness fails or a better performance is possible [2].

In order to promote the acceptance of SOMAS, it is essential to have effective tools and methods to give such assurances. Some works propose using test and simulation techniques [3], others define metrics for evaluating the resulting behavior of the system [9]. Our proposal to deal with SOMAS verification is to take advantage of formal methods. We propose a formal modeling for the local behavior of the agents based on stepwise refinement steps and the *Event-B* formalism [1]. Our refinement strategy guarantees the correctness of the system. In order to prove the desired global properties related to robustness and resilience, we make use of Lamport's Temporal Logic of Actions (TLA) and its fairness-based proof rules. The use of TLA was recently proposed in [8] in the context of population protocols to prove liveness and convergence properties and fits well with SOMAS. Our work is illustrated with the foraging ants case study.

This paper is organized as follows. Section 2 presents a background related to the *Event-B* language, the main principles on which it is based and TLA. In section 3, our refinement strategy of SOMAS is presented. An illustration of this strategy on the foraging ants is given in section 4. Section 5 presents a summary of related works dealing with verification of SOMAS. Section 6 concludes the paper and draws future perspectives.

2 Background

2.1 Event-B

The *Event-B* formalism was proposed by J.R. Abrial [1] as an evolution of the *B* language. It allows a correct-by-construction development for distributed and reactive systems. *Event-B* uses set theory as a modeling notation which enables, contrary to process algebra approaches, to support scalable solutions for system modeling. In order to make formal verification, *Event-B* is based on theorem proving. This technique avoids the problem of explosion in the number of the system states encountered with the model checkers.

The concept used to make a formal development is that of a *model*. A model is formed of components which can be of two types: *machine* and *context*. A context is the static part of the model and may include sets and constants defined by the user with their corresponding axioms. A machine is the dynamic part of the model and allows to describe the behavior of the designed system. It is composed by a collection of variables v and a set of events ev_i. The variables are constrained by conditions called *invariants*. The execution of the events must preserve these invariants. A machine may see one or more contexts, this will allow it to use all the elements defined in the seen context(s). The structures of a machine and an event in *Event-B* are described as follows.

```
Machine M
  SEES
    CM_i
  VARIABLES
    V_i
  INVARIANTS
    Inv(V_i)
  EVENT ev_1
  ...
  EVENT ev_i
END
```

```
EVENT ev_i
  ANY
    p
  WHERE
    grd_evi : G_evi(p, v)
  THEN
    act_evi : A_evi(p, v, v')
END
```

An event is defined by a set of parameters p, the guard $G\_evi(p, v)$ which gives the necessary conditions for its activation and the action $A\_evi(p, v, v')$ which describes how variables v are substituted in terms of their old values and the parameters values. The action may consist in several assignments which can be either deterministic or non-deterministic. A deterministic assignment, having the form $x := E(p, v)$, replaces values of variables x with the result obtained from the expression $E(p, v)$. A non-deterministic assignment can be of two forms: 1) $x :\in E(p, v)$ which arbitrarily chooses a value from the set $E(p, v)$ to assign to x and 2) $x : | \ Q(p, v, v')$ which arbitrarily chooses to assign to x a value that satisfies the predicate Q. Q is called a *before-after predicate* and expresses a relation between the previous values v (before the event execution) and the new ones v' (after the event execution).

Proof Obligations. Proof Obligations (POs) are associated with Event-B machines in order to prove that they satisfy certain properties. As an example, we mention the *Preservation Invariant* INV and the *Feasibility* FIS POs. INV PO is necessary to prove that invariants hold after the execution of each event. Proving (or discharging) FIS PO means that when an event guard holds, every action can be executed. This PO is generated when actions are non-deterministic.

Refinement. This technique, allowing a *correct by construction* design, consists in adding details gradually while preserving the original properties of the system. The refinement relates two machines, an *abstract* machine and a *concrete* one. Data refinement consists in replacing the abstract variables by the concrete ones. In this case, the refinement relation is defined by a particular invariant called *gluing invariant*. The refinement of an abstract event is performed by strengthening its guard and reducing non determinism in its action. The abstract parameters can also be refined. In this case, we need to use *witnesses* describing the relation between the abstract and the concrete parameters. The correctness of the refinement is guaranteed essentially by discharging POs GRD and SIM. GRD states that the concrete guard is stronger than the abstract one. SIM states that the abstract event can simulate the concrete one and preserves the gluing invariant. An abstract event can be refined by more than one event. In this case, we say that the concrete event is *split*. In the refinement process, new events can be introduced. In order to preserve the correctness of the model, we must prove that these new introduced events do not take the control for ever; i.e. they will *terminate* at a certain point or are *convergent*. This is ensured by the means of a *variant* –a numerical expression or a finite set– that should be decreased by each execution of the convergent events.

B-event is supported by the *Rodin* platform[1] which provides considerable assistance to developers by automating the generation and verification of all necessary POs.

2.2 Temporal Logic of Actions (TLA)

TLA combines temporal logic and logic of actions for specifying and reasoning about concurrent and reactive discrete systems [11]. Its syntax is based on four elements: 1) constants, and constant formulas - functions and predicates - over these, 2) state formulas for reasoning about states, expressed over variables as well as constants, 3) transition or action formulas for reasoning about (before-after) pairs of states, and 4) temporal predicates for reasoning about traces of states; these are constructed from the other elements and certain temporal operators [8]. In the remainder of this section, we give some concepts that will be used further in section 4.

Stuttering Step. A stuttering step on an action A under the vector variables f occurs when either the action A occurs or the variables in f are unchanged. We define the stuttering operator $[A]$ as: $[A]_f \mathrel{\widehat{=}} A \vee (f' = f)$. $\langle A \rangle$ asserts that A occurs and at least one variable in f changes.
$\langle A \rangle_f \mathrel{\widehat{=}} A \wedge (f' \neq f)$.

Fairness. Fairness asserts that if a certain action is enabled, then it will eventually be executed. Two types of fairness can be distinguished: 1) Weak Fairness for action A denoted $WF_f(A)$; which asserts that an operation must be executed if it remains possible to do so for a long enough time and 2) Strong Fairness for action A denoted $SF_f(A)$; asserts that an operation must be executed if it is often enough possible to do so [11]. Formally $WF_f(A)$ and $SF_f(A)$ are defined as follows.

$$WF_f(A) \mathrel{\widehat{=}} \Diamond\Box Enabled\langle A \rangle_f \Rightarrow \Box\Diamond\langle A \rangle_f$$
$$SF_f(A) \mathrel{\widehat{=}} \Box\Diamond Enabled\langle A \rangle_f \Rightarrow \Box\Diamond\langle A \rangle_f$$

$\Box$ and $\Diamond$ are temporal operators. $\Box P$ called *alwaysP* means that P is always true in a given sequence of states. $\Diamond P$ called *eventually* P means that P will hold in some state in the future.
$Enabled\langle A \rangle_f$ asserts that it is possible to execute the action $\langle A \rangle_f$. In addition, we define the *leads to* operator: $P \leadsto Q \mathrel{\widehat{=}} \Box(P \Rightarrow \Diamond Q)$, meaning that whenever P is true, Q will eventually become true.

Proof Rules for Simple TLA. We consider the two proof rules $WF1$ and $SF2$ given below. $WF1$ gives the conditions under which weak fairness assumption of action A is sufficient to prove $P \leadsto Q$. Condition $WF1.1$ describes a progress step where either state P or Q can be produced. Condition $WF1.2$ describes the inductive step where $\langle A \rangle_f$ produces state Q. Condition $WF1.3$ ensures that

[1] `http://www.event-b.org/`

$\langle A \rangle_f$ is always enabled. $SF1$ gives the necessary conditions to prove $P \rightsquigarrow Q$ under strong fairness assumption. The two first conditions are similar to $WF1$. The third condition ensures that $\langle A \rangle_f$ is eventually, rather than always, enabled.

$WF1$		$SF1$	
$WF1.1$	$P \wedge [N]_f \Rightarrow (P' \vee Q')$	$SF1.1$	$P \wedge [N]_f \Rightarrow (P' \vee Q')$
$WF1.2$	$P \wedge \langle N \wedge A \rangle_f \Rightarrow Q'$	$SF1.2$	$P \wedge \langle N \wedge A \rangle_f \Rightarrow Q'$
$WF1.3$	$P \Rightarrow Enabled\langle A \rangle_f$	$SF1.3$	$\Box P \wedge \Box[N]_f \Rightarrow \Diamond Enabled\langle A \rangle_f$
$\Box[N]_f \wedge WF_f(A) \Rightarrow P \rightsquigarrow Q$		$\Box[N]_f \wedge SF_f(A) \Rightarrow P \rightsquigarrow Q$	

3 Formal Modeling of Self-Organizing MAS

The formal modeling is based on two levels of abstraction; i.e. the micro level which corresponds to the local behavior of the agents and the macro level which describes the global behavior of the system. In this subsection, we identify the main properties that must be ensured when designing a SOMAS according to these levels. We give also a refinement strategy allowing to ensure the proof of these properties.

3.1 Formal Modeling of the Agents Local Behavior

The main concern at this level is the design of the behavior of the agents and their interactions. In a very abstract way, the behavior of each agent is composed by three steps: the agent senses information from the environment (perception step), makes a decision according to these perceptions (decision step) and finally performs the chosen action (action step). We refer to these steps as the *perceive – decide – act* cycle. Thus, an agent is characterized by the representations of the environment that it possesses (*rep*), a set of decision rules telling it which decisions to make (*decisions*), the set of actions it can perform (*actions*) and the set of operations (*perceptions*) allowing it to update its representations of the environment. Moreover, an agent is identified by its intrinsic characteristics such as the representations it has on itself (*prop*), its sensors (*sensors*) and its actuators (*actuators*). More formally, an agent is described by the following expression:

$$agent \triangleq < prop, rep, sensors, actuators, decisions, actions, perceptions >$$

In Event-B, the characteristics of agents, their representations of the environment, sensors and actuators are modeled by means of variables. Whereas their decisions, actions and update operations are formalized by events. Hence, a *before-after predicate* can be associated with each one of them. As a consequence, the decisions of each agent ag, belonging to the set of agents noted $Agents$, can be considered as a set of *before-after-predicates* denoted $Decide\_i(ag, d, d')$, where d is the set of variables corresponding to the properties and actuators of ag. Moreover, the actions of each agent ag can be considered as a set of *before-after predicates* having the form $Act\_i(ag, a, a')$, where a is the set of variables corresponding to the properties and sensors of ag. Indeed, an action event is responsible for getting the agent to the perception step. Since the actions of an agent can affect its local environment, the set a can also contain variables describing the environment state. Finally, *perceptions* is the event enabling an agent to update its perceptions. It is described by the *before-after predicate*: $Perceive(ag, rep, rep')$. The local agents behavior described earlier is said "correct", if the following properties are satisfied.

- LocProp1: the behavior of each agent is complied with the *perceive-decide-act* cycle.
- LocProp2: the agent must not be deadlocked in the decision step, i.e. the made decision must enable the agent to perform an action.

$$\begin{aligned} LocProp2 \triangleq\ & \forall ag \cdot ag \in Agents \wedge Decide\_i(ag, d, d') = TRUE \Rightarrow \\ & \exists Act\_i \cdot Act\_i \in actions \wedge G\_Act\_i(ag, a) = TRUE \end{aligned}$$

- LocProp3: the agent must not be deadlocked in the perception step; i.e. the updated representations should allow it to make a decision.

$$\begin{aligned} LocProp3 \triangleq\ & \forall ag \cdot ag \in Agents \wedge Perceive\_i(ag, rep, rep') = TRUE \Rightarrow \\ & \exists Decide\_i \cdot Decide\_i \in decisions \wedge G\_Decide\_i(ag, d) = TRUE \end{aligned}$$

3.2 Global Properties of the Macro-level

At the macro level, the main concern is to prove that the agents behavior, designed at the micro-level, will lead to the desired global properties. The aim is to discover, in the case of proof failure, design errors and thus make the necessary corrections at the micro-level. One of the most relevant global properties that should be proved, when designing self-organizing systems, is robustness. Serugendo ([5]) defines four attributes for the analysis of robustness:

- Convergence[2]: indicates the system ability to reach its goal,
- Stability: informs about the system capacity to maintain its goal once reached,
- Speed of convergence, and
- Scalability: shows if the system is affected by the number of agents.

Besides robustness, resilience represents another relevant property that should be analyzed for SOMAS. Resilience refers to the ability of the system to self-adapt when facing changes and perturbations. The analysis of resilience allows assessment of the aptitude of self-organizing mechanisms to recover from errors without explicitly detecting an error ([5],[2]).

In this paper, we only focus on proving the stability property. We give an example from the foraging ants case study and some guidelines to prove it in the next section. The formalization and proof of the remaining properties is still an ongoing work.

[2] Convergence here is different from the convergence of an event in Event-B, i.e. termination.

3.3 The Refinement Strategy

The formal development of SOMAS begins by a very abstract model representing the system as a set of agents operating according to the *Perceive-Decide-Act* cycle. This abstract model guarantees *LocProp*1. An overview of this machine is given in figure 1.

```
Machine Agents0
  SEES
    Context0
  VARIABLES
    stepAgent
  INVARIANTS
    defStepAg : stepAgent ∈ Agents → Steps
  EVENTS
  INITIALISATION
  THEN
    initStep : stepAgent := Agents × {perceive}
  END
  EVENT Perceive
  EVENT Decide
  EVENT Act
  ANY
    agent
  WHERE
    checkStep : agent ∈ Agents ∧ stepAgent(agent) = act
  THEN
    updStepAg : stepAgent(agent) := perceive
  END
END
```

Fig. 1. The *Agents*0 machine

The first refinement consists in identifying the different actions performed by the agents. Thus, the refinement of the machine *Agents*0 by *Agents*1 is achieved by splitting the *Act* event into the different actions an agent can perform. This refinement should ensure *LocProp*2. Figure 2 is an excerpt from the *Agents*1 machine modeling the actions of an agent.

In the second refinement step, we specify the events corresponding to the decisions that an agent can make. In addition, we describe the rules allowing the agent to decide. We also introduce the actuators of the agents. By using witness, we connect the actions introduced in the previous refinement with the corresponding decisions defined in this stage of refinement. Figure 3 describes how the decision and action events are refined.

In the third refinement, the perceptions of the agents and the necessary events to update them are identified. As a consequence the different events related to the decisions and actions are refined and property *LocProp*3 should be satisfied.

Figure 4 shows an excerpt from the *Agents*3 machine that refines the *Agents*2. The *gluInvSensorsPercept* invariant is a gluing invaraint making connection between the perception and the activation of the agent's sensors. In the context *Context*3, we define the ability *AbilityToPerceive* (used in the *Perceive* event in the figure 4 allowing the agent to determine the state of its local environment based on the global system state.

```
Machine Agents1
  SEES
    Context1
  EVENTS
...
  EVENT Act_Action_i
  REFINES Act
  ANY
    agent
    action
  WHERE
    checkStep : agent ∈ Agents ∧ stepAgent(agent) = act
    checkAction : action = Action_i
  THEN
    updStepAg : stepAgent(agent) := perceive
  END
END
```

Fig. 2. The refinement of the event *Act* in the *Agents*1 machine

```
EVENT Decide_Perform_Action_i
REFINES Decide
ANY
  agent
WHERE
  checkStep : agent ∈ Agents ∧ stepAgent(agent) = decide
THEN
  updStepAg : stepAgent(agent) := act
  updActAg : actuators(agent) := enabled
END
EVENT Act_Action_i
REFINES Act_Action_i
ANY
  agent
WHERE
  checkStep : agent ∈ Agents ∧ stepAgent(agent) = act
  checkActuator : actuators(agent) = enabled
WITH
  action : action =
  Act_Action_i ⇔ actuators(agent) = enabled
THEN
  updStepAg : stepAgent(agent) := perceive
END
```

Fig. 3. The refinement of the *Act* and *Decide* events in the *Agents*2 machine

4 Application to the Foraging Ants

The case study is a formalization of the behavior of a foraging ants colony. The system is composed of several ants moving and searching for food in an environment. Their main goal is to bring all the food placed in the environment to their nest. Ants do not have any information about the locations of the sources of food, but they are able to smell the food which is inside their perception field. The ants interact with one another via the environment by dropping a chemical substance called *pheromone*. In fact, when an ant discovers a source of food, it takes a part of it and comes back to the nest by depositing pheromone for marking food paths. The perturbations coming from the environment are mainly

```
Machine Agents3
  SEES
    Context3
  VARIABLES
    sensors
    rep
    ActualSysState
  INVARIANTS
    defSensorAg : sensors ∈ Agents → Activation
    defRepAg : rep ∈ Agents → Value
    defGlobalStateSys : ActualSysState ∈ SysStates
    gluInvSensorsPercept : ∀ag·ag ∈ Agents⇒
        (stepAgent(ag) = perceive
        ⇔sensors(ag) = enabled)
  EVENTS
  EVENT Perceive
  REFINES Perceive
  ANY
    agent
  WHERE
    grdAgent : agent ∈ Agents
    grdChekSensors : sensors(agent) = enabled
  THEN
    updStepAg : stepAgent(agent) := decide
    updRepAg : rep(agent) :=
AbilityToPerceive(ActualSysState)
    updSensorAg : sensors := disabled
  END
END
```

Fig. 4. Refinement of the *Perceive* event in the machine *Agents*3

pheromone evaporation and appearance of obstacles. The behavior of the system at the micro-level is described as follows. Initially, all ants are in the nest. When exploring the environment, the ant updates its representations in its perception field and decides to which location to move. When moving, the ant must avoid obstacles. According to its smells, three cases are possible:

1. the ant smells food: it decides to take the direction in which the smell of food is stronger (even if it smells some pheromone).
2. the ant smells only pheromone: it decides to move towards the direction in which the smell of pheromone is stronger.
3. the ant doesn't smell anything: it chooses its next location randomly.

When an ant reaches a source of food on a location, it collects it and comes back to the nest. If some food remains in this location, the ant drops pheromone when coming back. Arriving at the nest, the ant deposits the harvested food and begins another exploration. In addition to the properties *LocProp*1, *LocProp*2 and *LocProp*3 (described in section 3), the following properties should be verified at the micro-level.

- *LocInv*1: the ant should avoid obstacles
- *LocInv*2: a given location cannot contain both obstacle and food.

The main global properties associated with the foraging ants system are described in the following[3].

- $C1$: the ants are able to reach any source of food
- $C2$: the ants are able to bring all the food to the nest
- $S1$: when a source of food is detected, the ants are able to focus on its exploitation
- $R1$: the ants focusing on exploiting a source of food, are able to continue their foraging activity when this source of food suddenly disappear from the environment.

In the remainder of this section, we only focus on the properties related to the correctness (*LocProp*1, *LocProp*2, *LocProp*3, *LocInv*1 and *LocInv*2) and the stability ($S1$) of the system. The proofs of convergence and resilience are still an ongoing work. The next section illustrates the proposed refinement strategy.

4.1 Formalization of the Ants Local Behavior

Abstract Model: the initial machine *Ants*0 describes an agent (each agent is an ant) operating according to the *Perceive-Decide-Act* cycle. It contains three events *Perceive*, *Decide* and *Act* describing the agent behavioral rules in each step. At this very abstract level, these events are just responsible for switching an agent from one step to another. The current cycle step of each agent is depicted by the variable *stepAgent* defined as follows.

$$inv1 : stepAgent \in Ants \rightarrow Steps$$

where *Ants* defines the set of the agents and *Steps* is defined by the axiom *axm*1. The *partition* operator allows the enumeration of the different steps of an ant.

$$axm1 : partition(Steps, \{perceive\}, \{decide\}, \{act\})$$

As an example, we give below the event *Act* modeling the action step. The only action specified at this level is to switch the ant to the perception step.

```
EVENT Act
  ANY
    ant
  WHERE
    grd12 : ant ∈ Ants ∧ stepAgent(ant) = act
  THEN
    act1 : stepAgent(ant) := perceive
END
```

The proof obligations related to this machine concern essentially preservation of the invariant *inv*1 by the three events. All of them are generated and proved automatically under the Rodin platform.

First Refinement: In the first refinement *Ants*1, we add the variables *QuFood*, *Obstacles* modeling respectively the food and the obstacles distribution in the

[3] C refers to Convergence, S to Stability and R to Resilience.

environment, *currentLoc* and *load* which give respectively the current location and the quantity of food loaded of each ant. Invariants *inv*5 and *inv*3 guarantee the properties *LocInv*1 and *LocInv*2 respectively. The notation *dom* is the domain of a function. ⩥ denotes a range subtraction. Thus, $QuFood \rhd\!\!\!\!- \{0\}$ is a subset of the relation *QuFood* that contains all pairs whose second element is not equal to zero.

$inv1 : QuFood \in Locations \to \mathbb{N}$
$inv2 : Obstacles \subseteq Locations \setminus \{Nest\}$
$inv3 : Obstacles \cap dom(QuFood \rhd\!\!\!\!- \{0\}) = \varnothing$
$inv4 : currentLoc \in Ants \to Locations$
$inv5 : \forall ant \cdot ant \in Ants \Rightarrow currentLoc(ant) \notin Obstacles$
$inv6 : load \in Ants \to \mathbb{N}$

Moreover, the *Act* event is refined by the four following events:

1. *Act_Mov*: the ant moves in the environment
2. *Act_Mov_Drop_Phero*: the ant moves and drops pheromone when coming back to the nest
3. *Act_Harv_Food*: the ant picks up food
4. *Act_Drop_Food*: the ant drops of food at the nest

In the following, the event *Act_Mov* is presented as an action event example.

```
EVENT Act_Mov
REFINES Act
  ANY
    ant, loc, decideAct
  WHERE
    grd12 : ant ∈ Ants ∧ stepAgent(ant) = act
    grd34 : loc ∈ Next(currentLoc(ant)) ∧ decideAct = move
  THEN
    act12 : stepAgent(ant) := perceive||currentLoc(ant) := loc
END
```

The parameter *loc* is the next location to which the ant will move. It is the result of the decision process. This decision process will be modeled in the next refinement. The parameter *decideAct* is also an abstract parameter that will be refined in the next step. It indicates what type of decision can lead to the execution of the *Act_Mov* event.

The majority of the generated POs are related to proving the refinement correctness (the *SIM* PO) and the preservation of invariants. With the presented version of the *Act_Mov* event, it is impossible to discharge the *inv*5 preservation PO (*inv*5 states that an ant cannot be in a location containing obstacles). In fact, if *loc* belongs to the set *Obstacles*, *Act_Mov* will enable *ant* to move to a location containing an obstacle, which is forbidden by *inv*5. In order to discharge the *inv*5 preservation PO, we need to add the guard $grd5 : loc \notin Obstacles$ to *Act_Mov* event. Finally, in order to guarantee the property *LocProp*2 for the *Act_Mov* event, it is necessary to add another event *Act_Mov_Impossible* that refines *Act* and allows to take into account the situation where the move to *loc* is not possible because of obstacles. *Act_Mov_Impossible* will just allow *ant* to return to the perception step. The same reasoning is applied for

Act_Mov_Drop_Phero. For *Act_Harv_Food*, we should consider the case where the food disappears before that the ant takes it.
The Rodin tool generates 35 proof obligations for the correctness of the refinement. 85% of them are proved automatically and the rest has been proven using the interactive proof environment.

Second Refinement: The second refinement *Ants2* serves to create the links between the decision made and the corresponding action. We add the actuators of an ant: *paw*, *exocrinGland*, *mandible* as well as the ant's characteristic *nextLocation* which is updated when taking a decision. The *Decide* event is split into five events:

1. *Dec_Mov_Exp*: decide to move for exploring the environment
2. *Dec_Mov_Back*: decide to come back to the nest
3. *Dec_Mov_Drop_Back*: decide to come back wile dropping pheromone
4. *Dec_Harv_Food*: decide to take the food
5. *Dec_Drop_Food*: decide to drop food in the nest

As an example, we give the event *Dec_Mov_Exp* above.

```
EVENT Dec_Mov_Exp
REFINES Decide
  ANY
    ant, loc
  WHERE
    grd12 : ant ∈ Ants ∧ stepAgent(ant) = decide
    grd3 : loc ∈ Next(currentLoc(ant)) ∧ loc ≠ Nest
  THEN
    act123 : stepAgent(ant) := act||nextLocation(ant) := loc||paw(ant) := activate
END
```

As a result of event *Dec_Mov_Exp* execution, the ant chooses its next location and activates its paws. What is necessary now, is to link the activation of the paws with the triggering of the move action. Thus, we need to refine the event *Act_Mov* by adding a *Witness* relating the parameter *decideAct* in the event *Act_Mov* with the variable *paw*.

```
EVENT Act_Mov
REFINES Act_Mov
  ANY
    ant
  WHERE
    grd123 : ant ∈ Ants ∧ stepAgent(ant) = perceive ∧ loc ∈ Next(currentLoc(ant))
    grd4 : paw(ant) = activate
  WITNESSES
    decideAct : decideAct = Move ⇔ paw(ant) = activate
    loc : loc = nextLocation(ant)
  THEN
    act12 : stepAgentCycle(ant) := perceive||currentLoc(ant) := nextLocation(ant)
    act3 : paw(ant) := disabled
END
```

The Rodin tool generates 62 proof obligations for the correctness of the refinement. 79% of them are proved automatically and the rest has been proven using the interactive proof environment.

Third Refinement: At this level of refinement (*Ants*3), the ants representations about the environment are introduced . Every ant can sense food smell (*food*) as well as pheromone scent (*pheromone*). We introduce also the variable *DePhero* modeling the distribution of pheromone in the environment. The event *Perceive* (here above) is refined by adding the necessary event actions for updating the perceptions of an ant.

EVENT Perceive
REFINES Perceive
ANY
ant, loc, fp, php
WHERE
$grd123 : ant \in Ants \wedge stepAgent(ant) = perceive \wedge loc = currentLoc(ant)$
$grd45 : fp \in Locations \times Locations \nrightarrow \mathbb{N} \wedge fp = FPerc(QuFood)$
$grd67 : php \in Locations \times Locations \nrightarrow \mathbb{N} \wedge php = PhPerc(DePhero)$
THEN
$act1 : stepAgentCycle(ant) := decide$
$act2 : food(ant) := \{loc \mapsto fp(loc \mapsto dir) | dir \in Next(loc)\}$
$act3 : pheromone(ant) := \{loc \mapsto php(loc \mapsto dir) | dir \in Next(loc)\}$
END

FPerc (guard *grd*45) and *PhPerc* (guard *grd*67)[4] models the ability of an ant to smell respectively the food and the pheromone situated in its perception field. They are defined in the accompanying context of *Ants*3. After execution of the event *Perceive*, the ant acquires a knowledge about the food smell and pheromone scent for each direction from its current location. Moreover, we split the event *Dec_Mov_Exp* into three events:

1. *Dec_Mov_Rand*: decide to move to a location chosen randomly because no scent is smelt
2. *Dec_Mov_Fol_F*: decide to move towards the direction where the food smell is maximum
3. *Dec_Mov_Fol_Ph*: decide to move towards the direction in which the pheromone smell is maximum

This split guarantees the *LocProp*3 property for the decision concerning the move. The event *Act_Mov* is also refined in order to take into account these different decisions. The Rodin tool generates 59 proof obligations for the correctness of the refinement. 40% of them are proved automatically.

4.2 Formalization of the Ant Global Properties

The three refinement steps described in the last section have enabled us to specify a correct individual behavior for the ants. Let us now focus on the ability of the modeled behavior to reach the desired global properties. As we already mentioned, the focus of this paper is on the stability property ($S1$) which informs about the capability of ants to exploit entirely a source of food detected.

Recall in the machine *Ants*3, we have three events describing an exploration movement namely *Act_Mov_Fol_F*, *Act_Mov_Fol_Ph*, *Act_Mov_Rand*

[4] In the guards *grd*45 and *grd*67, $\nrightarrow$ denotes a partial function.

plus the event *Act_Harv_Food* corresponding to the action of picking up food. All these events are defined according to the parameter *loc* which refers to any location. In order to prove the stability property, we refine these events by instantiating the parameter *loc* with a precise location of food *loc*1. This refinement gives rise to the machine *Ants*4. Our aim is to prove that once *loc*1 is reached, the quantity of food in it will decrease until reaching zero. In *Event-B*, this kind of reasoning is possible by proving *convergence* (or *termination*) of the event responsible for decreasing this value, i.e. the event *Act_Harv_Food*. For carrying out the proof of termination in *Event-B*, we need to use a variant, i.e. a natural number expression or a finite set and prove that event *Act_Harv_Food* decreases it in each execution. Finding an implicit variant is trivial under weak fairness assumptions on the actions of this event ([8]). In our case, the non-determinism introduced by the movement actions makes such an assumption impossible. Indeed, *Act_Harv_Food* is not always enabled since once an ant reaches a source of food, the others can need time to reach this source.

For proving convergence, our work is inspired by the proofs done by D. Méry and M. Poppleton in [8] where they demonstrate how to prove convergence under fairness assumption by the use of the Temporal Logic of Actions (TLA) [11] and *Event-B*.

Let us consider the two states P and $Q_{Harvest}$ describing the quantity of food on *loc*1 and defined as follows:

$$P \mathrel{\widehat{=}} Inv_{Ants4} \wedge QuFood(loc1) = n+1, \; Q_{Harvest} \mathrel{\widehat{=}} Inv_{Ants4} \wedge QuFood(loc1) = n$$

Inv_{Ants4} denotes the conjunction of invariants of machine *Ants*4. Proving the termination of *Act_Harv_Food* is reformulated by the formula:

$P \leadsto Q_{Harvest}$.

We define N and $A_{Harvest}$ as follows.

$N \mathrel{\widehat{=}} Act\_Harv\_Food \vee Act\_Mov\_Fol\_F \vee Act\_Mov\_Fol\_Ph \vee Act\_Mov\_Rand$ and $A_{Harvest} \mathrel{\widehat{=}} Act\_Harv\_Food$.

By applying SF1, we prove $P \leadsto Q_{Harvest}$:

$SF1.1$	$P \wedge [N]_{QuFood(loc1)} \Rightarrow (P' \vee Q'_{Harvest})$
$SF1.2$	$P \wedge \langle N \wedge A_{Harvest} \rangle_{QuFood(loc1)} \Rightarrow Q'_{Harvest}$
$SF1.3$	$\Box P \wedge \Box [N]_{QuFood(loc1)} \Rightarrow \Diamond Enabled \langle A_{Harvest} \rangle_{QuFood(loc1)}$
$SF1.H$	$\Box [N]_{QuFood(loc1)} \wedge SF_{QuFood(loc1)}(A_{harvest}) \Rightarrow P \leadsto Q_{Harvest}$

Condition $SF1.1$ describes a progress step where either state P or $Q_{Harvest}$ can be produced.

Condition $SF1.2$ describes the inductive step where $\langle A_{Harvest} \rangle_{QuFood(loc1)}$ produces state $Q_{Harvest}$.

Condition $SF1.3$ ensures that $\langle A_{Harvest} \rangle_{QuFood(loc1)}$ will be *eventually* enabled. Note that both conditions $SF1.1$ and $SF1.2$ do not contain any temporal operator. As a consequence, they are expressible in Event-B. $SF1.3$ is a temporal formula that can be expressed in the *leads to* form. Thus, we can define SF1.31 as:

$$SF1.31 \mathrel{\widehat{=}} \Box[N]_{QuFood(loc1)} \Rightarrow P \leadsto \Diamond Enabled\langle A_{Harvest}\rangle_{QuFood(loc1)}$$

To demonstrate that condition $SF1.31$ is true, we need to prove that the formula $\Diamond Enabled\langle AHarvest\rangle_{QuFood(loc1)}$ holds.

Ants are able to reach food thanks to their movements for following food. Thus if we assume that once an ant smells food, it will be able to follow it (we do not consider case where food disappears suddenly), we can argue that the event *Act_Harv_Food* is always eventually *Enabled*. Consequently, we can prove $SF1.31$ under weak fairness assumption.
We consider:
$Q_{followFood} \mathrel{\widehat{=}} Enabled\langle A_{Harvest}\rangle_{QuFood(loc1)}$ and
$A_{FollowFood} \mathrel{\widehat{=}} Act\_Follow\_Food.$
We apply $WF1$:

$$\begin{array}{ll} WF1.311 & P \wedge [N]_{QuFood(loc1)} \Rightarrow (P' \vee Q'_{FollowFood}) \\ WF1.312 & P \wedge \langle N \wedge A_{FollowFood}\rangle_{QuFood(loc1)} \Rightarrow Q'_{FollowFood} \\ WF1.313 & P \Rightarrow Enabled\langle A_{FollowFood}\rangle_{QuFood(loc1)} \\ \hline WF1.31 & \Box[N]_{QuFood(loc1)} \wedge WF_{QuFood(loc1)}(A_{FollowFood}) \Rightarrow P \leadsto Q_{FollowFood} \end{array}$$

$WF1.311, WF1.312$ and $WF1.313$ do not contain any temporal operator, so that they are directly expressible in *Event-B*.

5 Related Work

Related work cited in this section deals in the first part, with the formal modeling and verification of self-organization. The second part is devoted to the presentation of works using *Event-B* for the development of adaptive systems.

Formal Modeling of Self-organizing Systems
In [6], *Gardelli* uses *stochastic Pi-Calculus* for modeling SOMAS for intrusion detection. This formalization was used to perform simulations using the $SPIM$ tool to assess the impact of certain parameters, such as the number of agents and frequency of inspections, on the system behavior. In [4], a hybrid approach for modeling and verifying self-organizing systems has been proposed. This approach uses stochastic simulations to model the system described as Markov chains and the technique of probabilistic model checking for verification. To avoid the state explosion problem, encountered with model-checkers, the authors propose to use approximate model-checking based on simulations. The approach was tested for the problem of collective sorting using the $PRISM$ tool. Konur and colleagues ([10]) use also the $PRISM$ tool and probabilistic model checking to verify the behavior of robot swarm, particularly foraging robots. The authors verify properties expressed by $PCTL$ logic (Probabilistic Computation Tree Logic) for several scenarios. These properties provide information, in particular, on the probability that the swarm acquires a certain amount of energy for a certain number of

agents and in a certain amount of time. Simulations were also used to show the correlation between the density of foraging robots in the arena and the amount of energy gained.

Most of the works exposed above use the model checking technique to evaluate the behavior of the system and adjust its parameters. Although they were able to overcome the state explosion problem and prove the effectiveness of their approaches, these works do not offer any guidance to help the designer to find the source of error in case of problems and to correct the local behavior at the micro level. For the purpose of giving more guidance for the designer, we find that the use of *Event-B* language and its principle of refinement are very useful.

Formal Modeling Using the Event-B Language

In [13], the authors propose a formal modeling framework for critical MAS, through a series of refinement step to derive a secure system implementation. Security is guaranteed by satisfying three properties: 1) an agent recovering from a failure cannot participate in a cooperative activity with others, 2) interactions can take place only between interconnected agents and 3) initiated cooperative activities should complete successfully. This framework is applied to model critical activities of an emergency. *Event-B* modeling for fault tolerant MAS was proposed in [12]. The authors propose a refinement strategy that starts by specifying the main purpose of the system, defines the necessary agents to accomplish it, then introduces the various failures of agents and ends by introducing the communication model and error recovery mechanisms. The refinement process ensures a set of properties, mainly 1) reachability of the main purpose of the system, 2) the integrity between agents local information and global information and 3) efficiency of cooperative activities for error recovery. The work of *Hoang* and *Abrial* in [7] was interested in checking liveness properties in the context of the nodes topology discovery in a network.

The proposed refinement strategy allows to prove the stability property, indicating that the system will reach a stable state when the environment remains inactive. The system is called stable if the local information about the topology in each node are consistent with the actual network topology.

These works based on the *correct by construction* approach, often providing a top-down formalization approach, have the particularity of being exempt from the combinatorial explosion problem found with the model checking techniques. They have the advantage of allowing the designer to discover the restrictions to be imposed to ensure the desired properties. We share the same goals as the works presented i.e. ensuring liveness properties and simplifying the development by the use of stepwise refinements. Our refinement strategy was used to guide the modeling of individual behaviors of agents, unlike the proposed refinement strategies that use a top-down development of the entire system. We made this choice to be as closely as possible to the bottom-up nature of self-organizing systems.

6 Conclusion

We have presented in this paper a formal modeling for SOMAS by means of *Event-B*. In our formalization, we consider the system in two abstraction levels: the micro and macro levels. This abstraction allows to focus the development efforts on a particular aspect of the system. We propose a stepwise refinement strategy to build a correct individual behavior. This refinement strategy is extended in order to prove global properties such as robustness and resilience. Our proposal was applied to the foraging ants case study. While the proof obligations were used to prove the correctness of the micro level models, it was necessary to turn to TLA in order to prove the stability property at the macro-level. We think that this combination of TLA and Event-B is very promising for formal reasoning about SOMAS.
Our ambitions for future works are summarized in the following four points:

- Reasoning about the convergence of SOMAS by means of TLA.
- Introduction of the self-organization mechanisms, based on the cooperation in particular, at the proposed refinement strategy of the local agents behavior and the analysis of the impact of these mechanisms on the resilience of the system. For the foraging ants, for example, the objective is to analyze the ability of the ants to improve the rapidity of reaching and exploiting food thanks to their cooperative attitude. To achieve this aim, we plan to use a probabilistic approach coupled with *Event-B*.
- Definition of design patterns for modeling and refinement of SOMAS and their application to real case studies.
- Integration of the proposed formal framework within SOMAS development methods in order to ensure formal proofs at the early stages of the system development. This integration will be made by using model-driven engineering techniques.

References

1. Abrial, J.R.: Modelling in Event-B. Cambridge University Press (2010)
2. Bankes, S.C.: Robustness, adaptivity, and resiliency analysis. In: AAAI Fall Symposium: Complex Adaptive Systems. AAAI Technical Report, vol. FS-10-03. AAAI (2010)
3. Bernon, C., Gleizes, M.-P., Picard, G.: Enhancing self-organising emergent systems design with simulation. In: O'Hare, G.M.P., Ricci, A., O'Grady, M.J., Dikenelli, O. (eds.) ESAW 2006. LNCS (LNAI), vol. 4457, pp. 284–299. Springer, Heidelberg (2007), http://dblp.uni-trier.de/db/conf/esaw/esaw2006.html#BernonGP06
4. Casadei, M., Viroli, M.: Using probabilistic model checking and simulation for designing self-organizing systems. In: SAC, pp. 2103–2104 (2009)
5. Serugendo, G.D.M.: Robustness and dependability of self-organizing systems - A safety engineering perspective. In: Guerraoui, R., Petit, F. (eds.) SSS 2009. LNCS, vol. 5873, pp. 254–268. Springer, Heidelberg (2009), http://dx.doi.org/10.1007/978-3-642-05118-0_18

6. Gardelli, L., Viroli, M., Omicini, A.: Exploring the dynamics of self-organising systems with stochastic π-calculus: Detecting abnormal behaviour in MAS. In: Trappl, R. (ed.) Cybernetics and Systems 2006, April 18-21, vol. 2, pp. 539–544. Austrian Society for Cybernetic Studies, Vienna (2006), 18th European Meeting on Cybernetics and Systems Research (EMCSR 2006), Proceedings of the 5th International Symposium "From Agent Theory to Theory Implementation" (AT2AI-5)
7. Hoang, T.S., Kuruma, H., Basin, D.A., Abrial, J.R.: Developing topology discovery in Event-B. Sci. Comput. Program. 74(11-12), 879–899 (2009)
8. Méry, D., Poppleton, M.: Formal modelling and verification of population protocols. In: Johnsen, E.B., Petre, L. (eds.) IFM 2013. LNCS, vol. 7940, pp. 208–222. Springer, Heidelberg (2013), http://dx.doi.org/10.1007/978-3-642-38613-8_15
9. Kaddoum, E., Raibulet, C., George, J.P., Picard, G., Gleizes, M.P.: Criteria for the evaluation of self-* systems. In: Workshop on Software Engineering for Adaptive and Self-Managing Systems (2010)
10. Konur, S., Clare, D., Fisher, M.: Analysing robot swarm behaviour via probabilistic model checking. Robot. Auton. Syst. 60(2), 199–213 (2012)
11. Lamport, L.: The temporal logic of actions. ACM Trans. Program. Lang. Syst. 16(3), 872–923 (1994)
12. Pereverzeva, I., Troubitsyna, E., Laibinis, L.: Development of fault tolerant MAS with cooperative error recovery by refinement in Event-B. CoRR abs/1210.7035 (2012)
13. Pereverzeva, I., Troubitsyna, E., Laibinis, L.: Formal development of critical multi-agent systems: A refinement approach. In: EDCC, pp. 156–161 (2012)
14. Serugendo, G.D.M., Gleizes, M.P., Karageorgos, A.: Self-organization in multi-agent systems. Knowledge Eng. Review (2005)

Improving the Design and Modularity of BDI Agents with Capability Relationships

Ingrid Nunes

Instituto de Informática
Universidade Federal do Rio Grande do Sul (UFRGS)
Porto Alegre Brazil
ingridnunes@inf.ufrgs.br

Abstract. The belief-desire-intention (BDI) architecture has been proposed to support the development of rational agents, integrating theoretical foundations of BDI agents, their implementation, and the building of large-scale multi-agent applications. However, the BDI architecture, as initially proposed, does not provide adequate concepts to produce intra-agent modular software components. The capability concept emerged to address this issue, but the relationships among capabilities have been insufficiently explored to support the development of BDI agents. We thus, in this paper, propose the use of three different types of relationships between capabilities in BDI agent development — namely association, composition and generalisation — which are widely used in object-oriented software development, and are fundamental to develop software components with low coupling and high cohesion. Our goal with this paper is to promote the exploitation of these and other mechanisms to develop large-scale modular multi-agent systems and discussion about this important issue of agent-oriented software engineering.

Keywords: Capability, Modularisation, BDI Architecture, Agent-oriented Development.

1 Introduction

The *belief-desire-intention* (BDI) architecture is perhaps the most adopted architecture to modelling and implementing rational agents. It has foundations in a model proposed by Bratman [3], which determines human action based on three mental attitudes: beliefs, desires and intentions. Based in this model, Rao and Georgeff [22] proposed the BDI architecture, integrating: (i) theoretical work on BDI agents; (ii) their implementation; and (iii) the building of *large-scale* applications based on BDI agents. Although their work has been widely used to model and implement BDI agents in theory and practice in academy, there is no real evidence that this approach scales up.

Much work on software engineering aims to deal with the complexity of large-scale enterprise software applications to support their development, and a keyword that drives this research is *modularity* [18]. Software developed with modular software components — i.e. components with high cohesion and low

F. Dalpiaz et al. (Eds.): EMAS 2014, LNAI 8758, pp. 58–80, 2014.

coupling properties — is more flexible and easier to reuse and maintain, and can be built in parallel by different software developers given specified interfaces of modules and components. Although modularity is highly investigated in the context of mainstream software engineering, it has been poorly addressed not only in work on BDI agents, but also by the agent-oriented software engineering community. Research in this context is limited to few approaches, for example, modularisation of crosscutting concerns in agent architectures with aspects [10,24] and the use of capabilities in BDI agent architectures [4,6].

We, in this paper, investigate the concept of *capability*, in order to allow the modular construction of BDI agents, with the aim of supporting the development of large-scale systems based on BDI agents (hereafter, agents). Capabilities are modules that are part of an agent, and they cluster a set of beliefs and plans that together are able to handle events or achieve goals. Therefore, it is a fundamental abstraction to modularise a particular functional behaviour that can be added to agents [13]. In particular, it was crucial and successfully used to modularise intra-agent features in multi-agent system product lines [15,16]. The capability concept is available in some of the BDI agent platforms, e.g. JACK [11], BDI4JADE [14], and Jadex [21]; however, there is divergence on its implementation, and therefore there is no standard structure for this concept. A communality shared by different capability implementations is the ability to include capabilities to another, but this relationship also varies in the different available implementations, as well as their implications in the agent reasoning cycle at runtime. Moreover, there is a single type of relationship between capabilities in each implementation. This differs from the object-oriented paradigm, which allows to establish many types of relationships between software objects, and each of which makes the nature of the relationship explicit in the design, using appropriate notations. Moreover, the relationship type also expresses semantic implications, which is the case of the aggregation and composition relationships between object classes.

We thus present an investigation of structures to improve the intra-agent modularity of BDI agents. We propose the use of different types of relationships that may occur between capabilities, specifically *association*, *composition* and *generalisation*. Using different relationship types allows one to understand the purpose of the relationship, its runtime implications, the intensity of coupling between two capabilities, and what is shared between related capabilities, by simply specifying the type of the relationship between the involved capabilities. This differs from existing approaches that require specifying the visibility of individual fine-grained BDI agent components. For each type of relationship, we describe both their structure and their implications at runtime, analysing how a pair of related capabilities work together in the context of the agent reasoning. These relationships may be used in combination to design and implement agents, and we show examples of this scenario. Moreover, we show a preliminary evaluation of our proposal, by comparing the design of agents composed of capabilities using our relationships and the most common approach to relate capabilities [4], implemented by Jack and Jadex. The presented relationships provide the basis

Table 1. Capability Specification [6]

PART	DEFINITION
Identifier	The capability identifier, i.e. a name.
Plans	A set of plans.
Beliefs	A set of beliefs representing a fragment of knowledge base and manipulated by the plans of the capability.
Belief Visibility Rules	Specification of which beliefs are restricted to the plans of the capability and which ones can be seen and manipulated from outside.
Exported Events	Specification of event types, generated as a consequence of the activity of the capability, that are visible outside its scope, and their processing algorithm.
Perceived events	Specification of event types, generated outside the capability, that are relevant to the capability.
Capabilities	Recursive inclusion of other capabilities.

for a discussion with respect to engineering aspects of agents, which support the construction agent-based systems. Our aim is to promote the exploitation of these and other mechanisms to develop large-scale modular multi-agent systems and discussion about this important issue of agent-oriented software engineering.

This paper is organised as follows. We first introduce work related to capabilities and their relationships in Section 2. Then, we describe the different capability relationships in Section 3, and exemplify their combined use in Section 4. We next present a preliminary evaluation of our approach in Section 5. We further analyse and compare these relationships and discuss relevant issues from object-orientation in Section 6. Finally, we conclude this paper in Section 7.

2 Background and Related Work

We begin by presenting work that has been done in the context of capabilities. We first introduce the concept of capability, and then discuss implementations of its relationships in existing BDI platforms.

2.1 The Capability Concept

The capability concept was introduced by Busetta et al. [6] and emerged from experiences with multi-agent system development with JACK [1,11], a BDI agent platform. The goal was to build modular structures, which could be reused across different agents. In Table 1, we detail the parts that comprise a capability according to this work. Some of which are specific to the JACK platform, such as the explicit specification of perceived events.

This work is the result of practical experience, so Padgham and Lambrix [17] formalised the capability concept, in order to bridge the gap between theory and practice. This formalisation included an indication of how capabilities can affect agent reasoning about its intentions. In order to integrate capabilities to the agent development process, Penserini et al. [19] proposed a tool-supported methodology, which goes from requirements to code. It identifies agent capabilities at the requirement specification phase, based on the analysis models of Tropos [5], and is able to eventually generate code for Jadex [21], another BDI agent platform.

Among the different available platforms to implement BDI agents, such as Jason[1] [2] and the 3APL Platform[2], three implement the capability concept: JACK[3] [11], Jadex[4] [4,21], and BDI4JADE[5] [14]. As we already discussed how JACK capabilities are implemented, we next detail the other two implementations.

A Jadex capability is composed of: (i) identifier; (ii) beliefs; (iii) goals; (iv) plans; (v) events; (vi) expressions; (vii) properties; (viii) configurations; and (iv) capabilities. Some of these parts are platform-specific, such as expressions, which are expressions written in a language that follows a Java-like syntax and are used for different purposes, e.g. goal parameters or belief values. The BDI4JADE capability, on the other hand, is composed of: (i) a belief base; (ii) a plan library; and (iii) other capabilities. These are the explicit capability associations with other BDI elements. As BDI4JADE is written in pure Java (no XML files), other properties may be obtained by manipulating the capability parts, besides the described components.

2.2 Capability Relationships in Existing BDI Platforms

Considering these three introduced BDI agent platforms that provide the capability concept, we will now discuss how each of these platforms provides capability relationships.

JACK. The JACK platform *explicitly* provides a single type of relationship: *inclusion*, allowing the construction of a hierarchical structure. When this relationship is declared, the visibility of the involved capabilities' components should also be specified. Beliefs may be imported (i.e. shared with its enclosing agent or capability), exported (i.e. accessible from its parent capability), or private (i.e. local to the capability). Events have the role of goals in JACK, and in this platform capabilities should explicitly declare the kinds of events that it is able to handle or post. When declaring this information, an `exports` modifier is used to indicate whether events are to be handled only within the scope of the capability or by any other capability.

Although these modifiers increase the flexibility of the platform, their use increases the possibility of breaking the code. When beliefs are exported, any other

[1] `http://jason.sourceforge.net/`
[2] `http://www.cs.uu.nl/3apl/`
[3] `http://aosgrp.com/products/jack/`
[4] `http://www.activecomponents.org`
[5] `http://www.inf.ufrgs.br/prosoft/bdi4jade/`

capability can access them, i.e. internal capability elements are accessible from outside, and consequently inconsistencies in the capability's beliefs may occur due to the modification on these beliefs by other capabilities. This goes against the principle of information hiding: it is equivalent to making attributes public in objects. Although in object-orientation attributes are sometimes exposed through getters and setters, this still preserves encapsulation, because a getter hides the actual implementation of the value being returned and setters control values to be assigned to an attribute.

Note that using solely capability inclusion results in limiting capabilities to be used as hierarchical structures.

Jadex. Jadex extended [4] the capability concept of JACK, providing a model in which the connection between an outer and an inner capability is established by a uniform visibility mechanism for contained components. The implemented relationship type is also inclusion, but it is more flexible by allowing the declaration of abstract and exported components.

In Jadex, any component (beliefs, goals, plans and so on) can be used only internally, if no modifier is specified. They can be exported, and thus accessed outside the capability scope. In addition, they may be declared as abstract, and be set up by an outer capability. For example, beliefs can be used only within the scope of the capability, exported to outside the capability scope, or abstract, meaning that a value of a belief outside the capability may be assigned to this abstract belief. This way of modelling capabilities is similar to that discussed above, and have the same issues.

Jadex was recently extended by changing its implementation based on XML files to an implementation based on pure Java, as BDI4JADE, making an extensive use of Java annotations. This new Jadex version, namely Jadex Active Components[6] [20], makes the implementation of capabilities more flexible, as all object-oriented features can be used.

BDI4JADE. BDI4JADE provides a flexible implementation as it is implemented in pure Java, allowing the customisation of its BDI model implementation without requiring to change how source code files are processed and compiled. Moreover, it allows the integration with frameworks that instantiate software objects by reflection. Goals are declared as Java classes, and therefore can be used in different capabilities. Moreover, Java modifiers can be used to limit goal visibility, for instance, by using a package visibility.

As the other two agent platforms discussed, it implements only the inclusion relationship. However, beliefs are always private to the capability, or accessible by its included capabilities. A goal is added to an agent within a plan with a specification of its scope. There are two possibilities: (i) it can be handled by any plan of any capability; or (ii) it can be handled by the capability whose plan added the goal, or any other included capability.

[6] `http://www.activecomponents.org/`

Although BDI4JADE does not intend to provide inheritance, it is possible to extend capabilities as they are Java classes — the same applies to other Java-based platforms. However, if the belief base or plan library of the parent capability is overridden by the child capability, the inheritance will loose its meaning.

As discussed above, all the implementations of the capability concept provide limited relationship types. Thus, we next introduce three different types of relationships between capabilities, which can simplify the design of BDI agents because, with a simple indication of the relationship type, it is possible to understand the coupling between capabilities.

3 Relationships between Capabilities

According to the object-oriented paradigm, a system is composed of software objects, which integrate state and behaviour. Such objects are building blocks to construct complex structures, and can be combined using different forms of relationships. Similarly, BDI agents have state, captured by beliefs, and behaviour, implemented by plans. A key difference is that a BDI agent is constantly running to achieve goals, and behaviour is not triggered by direct invocation, but the agent reasoning process chooses a plan that is adequate to achieve its goal. An agent can dynamically add goals to be achieved, i.e. they can *dispatch goals*, during its reasoning cycle or execution of its plans.

As BDI agents can be complex, it is essential to modularise its parts and, as introduced before, this is the main purpose of the capability abstraction. Agents A are an aggregation of capabilities C, which are in turn composed of a set of goals G (abstractions that represent a target to be pursued), a set of beliefs B (a piece of knowledge identified by a name and has a value of a certain type) and a set of plans P (which consist of actions to achieve a goal, identified by an id), i.e. $C = \langle G, B, P \rangle$. An isolated capability can: (i) dispatch only its own goals G during the execution of its plans; (ii) access only its own beliefs B; and (iii) its plans P are candidates to achieve only $g \in G$. In order to combine such capabilities, we describe and analyse three types of relationships between capabilities. These relationships are presented in Figure 1, which shows an abstract meta-model of BDI agents. Capabilities can relate to each other using: (i) association (Section 3.1), represented by the `Association` concept, when the `isComposition` attribute is `false`; (ii) composition (Section 3.2), represented by the `Association` concept, when the `isComposition` attribute is `true`; and (iii) inheritance (Section 3.3), represented by the `parent` attribute.

Throughout this section, to illustrate relationships, we will use a scenario in which we are developing two versions of an intelligent robot. The software infrastructure to be developed includes the ability to clean the floor (either with a sweep or with a vacuum cleaner) and to do laundry (regular and professional washes). In order to do so, the robot should also be able to move around. One version of the robot is to assist at home, and the other at professional laundries. Further details about this scenario will be given in the following sections to exemplify our relationships.

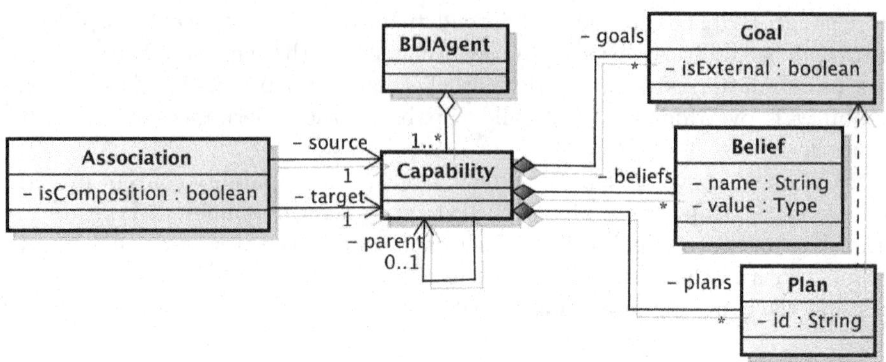

Fig. 1. BDI Agent Meta-model with Capability Relationships

3.1 Association

As said above, software objects encapsulate both state (represented by attributes) and behaviour (represented by methods). In order for a system to implement functionality, objects collaborate by invoking methods of other objects with which they are associated.

This collaboration is also needed for capabilities. Consider our scenario in which we are developing an intelligent robot, which is responsible for household duties, such as cleaning the floor and washing clothes. For both these duties, the robot has to move around and, while executing plans for cleaning the floor and washing clothes, the robot has to achieve a subgoal $move(x, y)$, i.e. move from a position x to a position y. In this case, our robot may have three modularised capabilities — `FloorCleaning`, `Laundry`, and `Transportation` capabilities — and both `FloorCleaning` and `Laundry` capabilities use the `Transportation` capability to achieve their goals.

How objects can collaborate with each other is specified through their *interface*, which is a collection of method signatures, which is inapplicable to capabilities. Similar to objects, capabilities implement some functionality, and have both state (represented by beliefs) and behaviour (represented by plans). However, while methods that are part of an object interface can be directly invoked by other objects, plans are invoked within the context of the agent reasoning cycle, and their execution are triggered by goals (or events, in some BDI models). As a consequence, in order for an agent behaviour to be the result of the interaction of more than one capability, an important question arises: *what is a capability interface?*

In a capability, beliefs are a piece of encapsulated knowledge, and are modified (added, removed, or updated) by the capability's plans. Consequently, following the principle of information hiding, the manipulation of beliefs are restricted to the capability. Plans, which correspond to methods, cannot be explicitly invoked, as explained before. Therefore, they are accessible only within the context of the capability, and are not part of the capability interface as well. Goals, on the

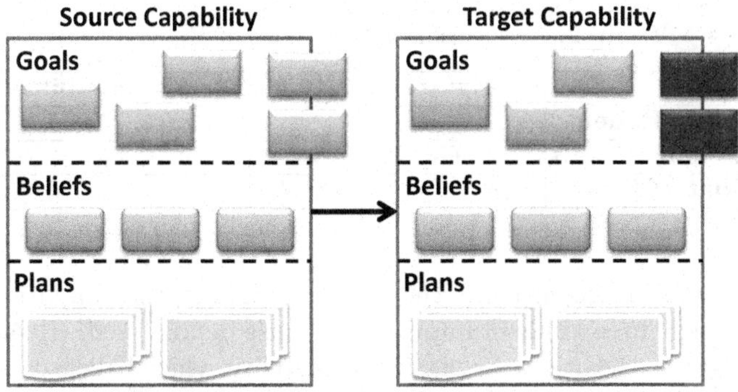

Fig. 2. Association: Structure and Element Visibility

other hand, indicate the objectives that a capability may achieve, and possibly there are different capability plans that can be used to achieve such goals. Therefore, goals represent services that a capability may provide to another, and thus comprise its interface. This definition of capability interface matches the goal-oriented agent modularisation approach proposed by van Riemsdijk et al. [23]. Capability interfaces are illustrated in capabilities of Figure 2, in which goals are in the border of the capabilities. Note, however, that there are goals used only internally, and are not part of the capability interface. Therefore, goals of a capability are split into two subsets $G = EG \cup IG$, where EG are external goals and IG are internal goals.

Given that we now have an interface for capabilities — specified in terms of a set of the external goals EG that a capability may achieve — we are able to associate capabilities so that they can collaborate. An *association* is a relation $Capability \times Capability$, where a source capability C_S uses a target capability C_T, by dispatching goals $g \in EG_{C_T}$, which will be handled and possibly achieved by C_T. The target capability, on the other hand, is not aware of the source capability. In the scenario described above, there are two association relationships: one from the `FloorCleaning` (source) to the `Transportation` capability (target), and another from the `Laundry` (source) to the same `Transportation` capability (target). The `Transportation` capability has an external goal $move(x, y)$, part of its interface.

An implication of any capability relationship is the accessibility of certain capability's components by other capability. In the case of association, such accessibility is shown in Figure 2. In this figure, and others similar presented throughout the paper, we show what the capability is composed of goals, beliefs and plans. These elements are in light gray when they can be accessed solely by the capability to which they belong. When they are in dark gray, it means that they can be accessed also by the other related capability, part of the relationship. Figure 2 shows that all components within the scope of the target capability are hidden and inaccessible by the source capability, except external goals, which are part of the target capability interface.

Table 2. Association: Implications at Runtime

	Source Capability C_S	**Target Capability C_T**
Accessible Beliefs	B_S	B_T
Dispatchable Goals	$G_S \cup EG_T$	G_T
Candidate Plans	P_S	P_T

During the runtime execution of the agent reasoning cycle, a relationship also has implications. Three kinds of implications must be analysed. (i) **Accessible Beliefs**: during the execution of a plan of a capability, which beliefs can accessed? (ii) **Dispatchable Goals**: which goals can be dispatched during the execution of a capability's plans? (iii) **Candidate Plans**: given a dispatched capability's goal, which plans are candidates to handle it? In Table 2, we detail the implications at runtime of the association relationship. This table shows, for instance, that during the execution of a plan of the source capability C_S it can access only its own beliefs B_S, and dispatch its own goals G_S and also external goals EG_T of the target capability C_T. But a goal $g \in EG_T$, dispatched possibly by C_S, can only be achieved by plans P_T of the capability C_T.

This described behaviour is similar to the notion of delegating a goal to another agent, but it has a key important difference. A multi-agent system is a multi-threaded system. Consequently, two agents mean two threads of execution, whereas two capabilities of one agent consist usually of a single thread of execution. Therefore, it is a design choice to use one approach or another.

The association relationship is directed, but it may be bidirectional. In order to better modularise an agent architecture, functionality associated with two different concerns may be split into two capabilities, and they may use each other to achieve their goals.

3.2 Composition

The association relationship allows us to modularise BDI concepts into two capabilities — composed of beliefs, goals, and plans — and each of which should address a different concern, thus having high cohesion. The connection between these capabilities is that the execution of at least one plan of the source capability requires achieving a goal that is part of and can be handled by the target capability. In this case, each capability uses the knowledge captured by their own beliefs to execute their plans.

However, there may be situations in which there should be shared knowledge between capabilities, that is, a capability uses the information stored in other capability's beliefs in the execution of its plans. This is the case when an agent is built by first developing functionality to achieve higher level goals, decomposing it into lower level goals. In this case, the composition relationship is used, which is also a relation $Capability \times Capability$, and expresses the notion of *containment*. This kind of relationship, illustrated in Figure 3, increases the coupling between the two involved capabilities when compared to association.

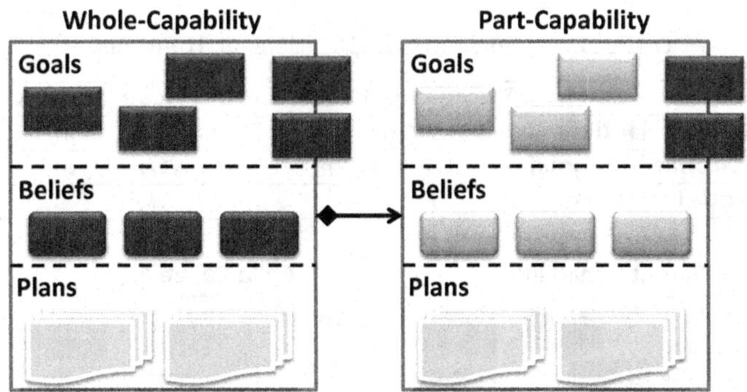

Fig. 3. Composition: Structure and Element Visibility

For example, the `FloorCleaning` capability of the robot agent must have goals, beliefs and plans to both sweep the floor and vacuum the dust, when there are carpets on the floor. As these are two different concerns, they may be modularised into two capabilities (`Sweeper` and `VacuumCleaner`), each being composed of the external goals related to their respective duty to be accomplished. The `FloorCleaning` capability, by having a composition relationship with the `Sweeper` and the `VacuumCleaner` capabilities, can thus dispatch external goals of these two capabilities — while executing a plan to clean a room, for instance. This can also be performed using the association relationship, but now there are three main differences.

First, the `FloorCleaning` capability may have knowledge stored in its beliefs, such as those related to the environment, and they need to be used both to sweep the floor and to vacuum the dust. So by composing the `FloorCleaning` capability with the other two, the `Sweeper` and `VacuumCleaner` capabilities may access the `FloorCleaning`'s beliefs in the execution of their plans. Second, these capabilities can also dispatch goals of the `FloorCleaning` capability. This is associated with the visibility of capability components involved in a composition relationship, namely the whole and the part, which is shown in Figure 3. The whole-capability is able to dispatch external goals of part-capability, but cannot access other components, while the part-capability can access both the beliefs and goals of the whole-capability.

Third, the `Sweeper` and the `VacuumCleaner` capabilities can have plans to handle `FloorCleaning`'s goals, so if goals are dispatched in plans of this capability, they may be achieved by plans of the composed capabilities. This is associated with the runtime implications of the composition relationship, which are detailed in Table 3.

The composition relationship is transitive, as containment is. Consider a capability C that is part of a capability B, which in turn is part of a capability A. C can access beliefs of both B and A in addition to its own beliefs (as C's whole consists of both A and B), in the same way that A's goals can be

Table 3. Composition: Implications at Runtime

	Whole-capability C_W	**Part-capability** C_P
Accessible Beliefs	B_W	$B_P \cup B_W$
Dispatchable Goals	$G_W \cup EG_P$	$G_P \cup G_W$
Candidate Plans	$P_W \cup P_P$	P_P

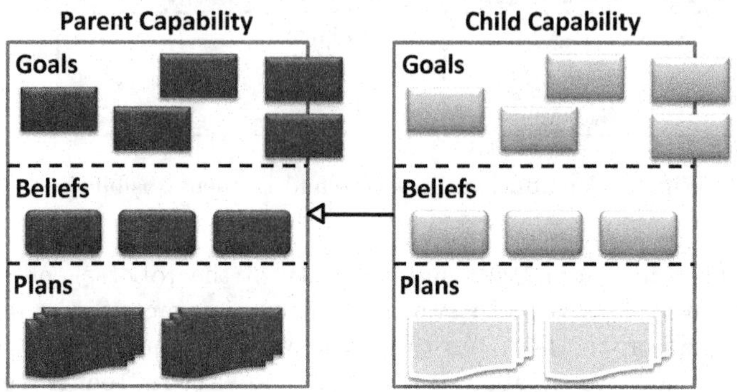

Fig. 4. Inheritance: Structure and Element Visibility

handled by plans of both B and C, in addition to its own plans. As a consequence, different compositions may be performed with capabilities that implement low level behaviour.

3.3 Inheritance

While the association and composition relationships focus on collaborating capabilities, the goal of the inheritance relationship — which will now be discussed — is mainly to promote reuse, by generalising common behaviour in a parent capability and specialising it in children capabilities. It consists of a partial function $parent : Capability \nrightarrow Capability$, which relates a capability to its parent capability, if it has one. This relationship increases the coupling between the involved capabilities, with respect to the other two types of relationships. It is also transitive, that is, a child capability inherits from its parent's parent.

The development of a multi-agent system may involve building agents that share a common behaviour, but have some particularities that distinguish one from another. In this case, we may need to design a capability with a set of beliefs, goals, and plans, to which other goals, beliefs and plans must be added to develop particularities. The inheritance relationship thus allows to connect this common behaviour to specialised variable behaviour. This relationship is illustrated in Figure 4.

When a capability extends another, it inherits all the components of the parent capability. Therefore, the components of a child capability can be seen as the union of its components — beliefs, goals, and plans — with its parent's

Table 4. Inheritance: Implications at Runtime

(a) Parent Capability Instance.

	Parent Capability C_P	**Child Capability C_C**
Accessible Beliefs	B_P	-
Dispatchable Goals	G_P	-
Candidate Plans	P_C	-

(b) Child Capability Instance.

	Parent Capability C_P	**Child Capability C_C**
Accessible Beliefs	B_P	$B_C \cup \{b \mid b \in B_P \wedge \nexists b' \in B_C.(name(b) = name(b'))\}$
Dispatchable Goals	G_P	$G_C \cup G_P$
Candidate Plans	$P_C \cup \{p \mid p \in P_P \wedge \nexists p' \in P_C.(id(p) = id(p'))\}$	

components. Such parent's components can be accessed within the scope of the child capability, that is, the child capability can: (i) dispatch both external and internal parent's goals; (ii) access and update parent's beliefs while executing its plans; (iii) have a goal handled and achieved by the parent's plans; and (iv) handle and achieve parent's goals. This full access to the parent capability's components by the child capability is shown in Figure 4. The parent capability, in turn, is not aware that there are capabilities that extend its behaviour.

In order to detail runtime implications of the inheritance relationship, we must highlight that this relationship has a significant difference with respect to the two previously presented relationships. When there are two capabilities related with association or composition, at runtime, there are two instantiated capabilities that are related to each other. In inheritance, we can either instantiate a parent capability, which has no relationship with the child capability at runtime, or instantiate a child capability, which inherits all parent capability's components. Therefore, at runtime, an instance of the parent capability access only its own components, as shown in Table 4a. The child capability, in turn, may handle both parent and child capabilities' dispatched goals, besides accessing all their beliefs and being able to dispatch all their goals, as detailed in Table 4b. Note that a child capability may modify the behaviour of a parent capability. For example, it may change values of beliefs, identified by a name, or the body of a plan identified by an id. In such cases, the child capability *overrides* components of a parent capability. Goals, on the other hand, are non-parameterised abstractions, and adding a goal to the child capability that was also added in the parent capability will produce the same effect as adding it just to the parent capability.

We will now illustrate a situation where inheritance may be used in the context of the development of our intelligent robot. As introduced before, we have physical robots, which are provided with some basic features, such as walking, moving arms, and so on, so that they are able to perform different household duties, depending on the software deployed on them. Moreover, some of these robots are developed for helping at home and and others for working on laundries. The `Laundry` capability should have plans to wash clothes in the wash machine and to hand washing, if the robot is for helping at home and, and if it will work on laundries, it should also have components to dry cleaning. Therefore, two capabilities may be designed: `Laundry` and `ProfessionalLaundry`. The latter extends the former, adding new beliefs, goals, and plans needed to provide the dry cleaning functionality.

4 Using Capability Relationships

Given that we presented the three capability relationships, we illustrate their use in this section. We gave examples of their individual use in the previous section within the same context, the intelligent robot example. In Section 4.1, we combine the examples previously given by providing a big picture of the design of our intelligent robot. In Section 4.2, we provide further examples of the use of capability relationships in the context of transportation.

4.1 Intelligent Robots

We provided many examples in the context of robot development, where the capability relationships may be applied to modularise agent concerns. We now present an integration of these different examples to show how relationships can be used together in the development of agents. An overview of the design of the intelligent robots example is presented in Figure 5. This is an overview, and therefore this figure does not correspond to the complete design of a system — many agent components are omitted.

We use a simple notation. Capabilities are represented with rectangles, split into four compartments: (i) capability name; (ii) goals; (iii) beliefs; and (iv) plans. For relating capabilities, we use the notation previously introduced. And we represent agents with ellipses, and an agent is an aggregation of capabilities.

The `Laundry` capability provides the basic functionality for washing clothes, and it is extended by the `ProfessionalLaundry` capability — an instance of the later adds the ability of dry washing to the former. The `Laundry` capability is associated with the `Transportation` capability, so that the `Laundry` capability can dispatch goals related to transportation. Note that, because the `ProfessionalLaundry` capability extends the `Laundry` capability, it also inherits the association.

The `FloorCleaning` capability has a goal (*clean*), which is not handled by any plan within this capability. It is, however, composed of two other capabilities, each having a plan that can achieve it, so that they can be selected to achieve the *clean* goal when appropriate (remember that capabilities have other omitted beliefs, goals and plans). The execution of plans of the `Sweeper` and `VacuumCleaner` capabilities also needs goals related to transportation to be achieved, thus both of them are associated with the `Transportation` capability.

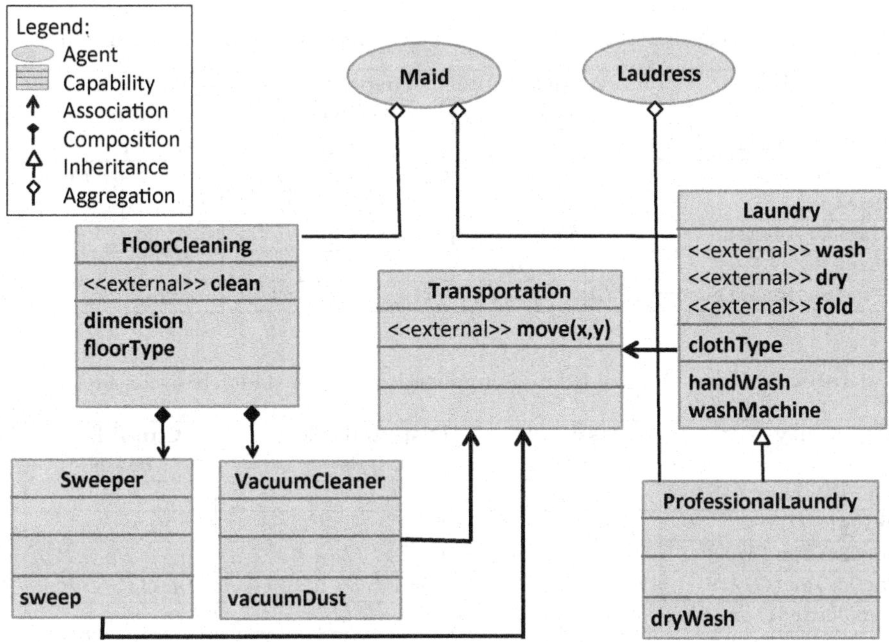

Fig. 5. Example: Intelligent Robots

The different types of relationships that relate the capabilities of our example causes different implications at the runtime execution of these capabilities, which are in accordance to the implications previously introduced. We summarise such implications in Table 5.

These capabilities are the building blocks to develop agents. A `Maid` agent (that is used to help at home) is an aggregation of both the `FloorCleaning` and `Laundry` capabilities, so that is can perform tasks related to them. The `Laudress` agent (who performs duties at laundries) must be able to perform other tasks related to washing clothes, therefore it is an aggregation of the `ProfessionalLaundry` capability, which in turn inherits the behaviour of its parent capability.

4.2 Driver Agents

We now will introduce a second example, which is in the transportation context. The objective is to design agents able to drive cars and motorcycles. As above, we will show an overview of the design, highlighting important parts of it, and omitting details. This example is illustrated in Figure 6, and runtime implications of capability relationships are described in Table 6.

The key functionalities associated with driving are implemented as part of the `Driver` capability, which has beliefs with respect to the current speed and location, an external goal $drive(x, y)$ that it is successfully achieved when the

Table 5. Intelligent Robots: Runtime Implications of Capability Relationships

Capability	Accessible Beliefs	Dispatchable Goals	Candidate Plans
`Transportation` (T)	B_T	G_T	P_T
`FloorCleaning` (FC)	B_{FC}	$G_{FC} \cup EG_S \cup EG_{VC}$	$P_{FC} \cup P_S \cup P_{VC}$
`Sweeper` (S)	$B_S \cup B_{FC}$	$G_S \cup G_{FC} \cup EG_T$	P_S
`VacuumCleaner` (VC)	$B_{VC} \cup B_{FC}$	$G_{VC} \cup G_{FC} \cup EG_T$	P_{VC}
`Laundry` (L)	B_L	$G_L \cup EG_T$	P_L
`ProfessionalLaundry` (PL)	$B_{PL} \cup B_L$	$G_{PL} \cup G_L \cup EG_T$	$P_{PL} \cup P_L$

Table 6. Driver Agents: Runtime Implications of Capability Relationships

Capability	Accessible Beliefs	Dispatchable Goals	Candidate Plans
`RoutePlanner` (RP)	B_{RP}	G_{RP}	P_{RP}
`Driver` (D)	B_D	$G_D \cup EG_{RP} \cup EG_{GC}$	$P_D \cup P_{GC}$
`MotoDriver` (MD)	$B_{MD} \cup B_D$	$G_{MD} \cup G_D \cup EG_{RP} \cup EG_{GC}$	$P_{MD} \cup P_D \cup P_{GC}$
`CarDriver` (CD)	$B_{CD} \cup B_D$	$G_{CD} \cup G_D \cup EG_{RP} \cup EG_{GC}$	$P_{CD} \cup P_D \cup P_{GC}$
`GearController` (GC)	$B_{GC} \cup B_D$	$G_{GC} \cup G_D$	P_{GC}

agent has driven from location x to location y, and internal goals dispatched by plans whose aim is to achieve the $drive(x, y)$ goal. There are two extensions of this capability: `MotoDriver` and `CarDriver`, which specialise the `Drive` capability to add behaviour specific to driving a motorcycle and a car, respectively. Besides other omitted details, each has its own plans to perform similar tasks, such as accelerating.

To drive from a location x to y, the `Driver` capability must first find a route between these two locations. This is modularised into the `RoutePlanner` capability, which has knowledge needed to calculate a route (maps, congestion zones, agent preferences, etc.), and different plans to find a route. To be able to find the route, the `Driver` capability has an association with the `RoutePlanner` capability, and consequently it can dispatch the $findRoute(x, y)$ goal.

Finally, there is a complicated part related to driving, which is the control of gears. This can be modularised in a separate capability, which needs specific beliefs, goals and plans to do so. However, it also needs the knowledge that is part of the `Driver` capability, and consequently there is a composition relationship between the `Driver` and `GearController` capabilities. In order to build agents able to drive a motorcycle or a car, an agent must aggregate the `MotoDriver` capability or `CarDriver` capability, respectively.

5 Preliminary Evaluation

Given that we have presented our capability relationships and examples of their combined use, we will now provide a preliminary evaluation of our approach.

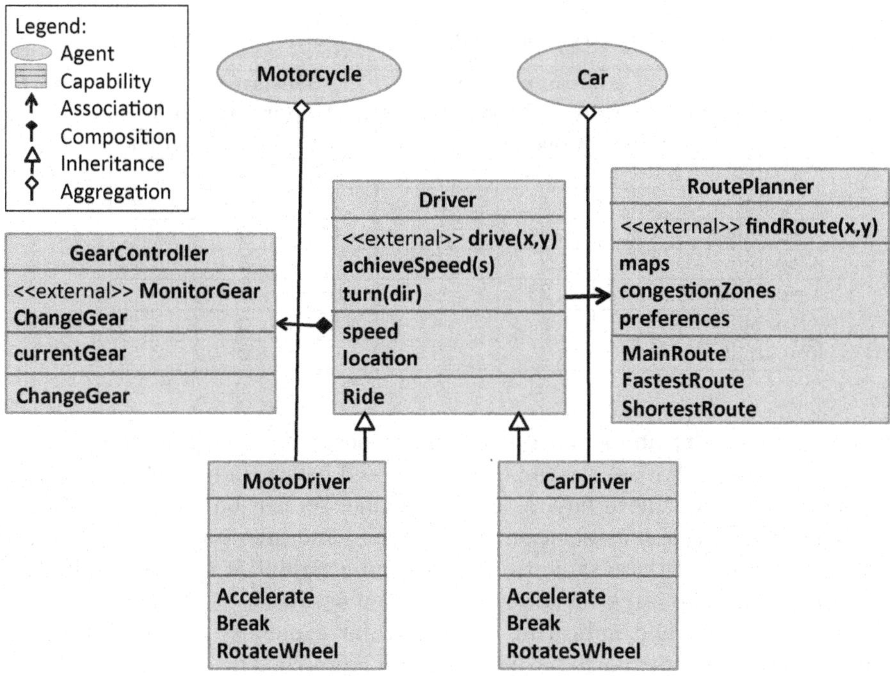

Fig. 6. Example: Driver Agents

If we compare our approach with the traditional BDI architecture, in which there is no capabilities, our approach makes improvements from a software engineering point of view. An agent, in the traditional BDI architecture, is composed of all beliefs, goals and plans, which in our approach are decomposed into capabilities. So, if we collect software metrics [7][7] — such as Lines of Code (LOC), Number of Attributes (NOF), Lack of Cohesion of Methods (LCOM) — to compare the design of this single agent with this agent decomposed into capabilities, the former would have much higher values for these metrics than the latter, indicating its poor design. However, the design improvement is not exclusively promoted by capability relationships, but also because of the use of the capability abstraction. Therefore, in order to make a fair comparison, we compare our approach with the most traditional way for relating capabilities: capabilities can be related using hierarchical composition, which allows to export and import capability components.

Our comparison is made using a hypothetical design of two agents — `AgentX` and `AgentY` — that are built using seven different capabilities. Each capability has its goals, beliefs and plans. Although this scenario is hypothetical, it is sufficient to show the impact of the two compared approaches in the design.

[7] We interpret traditional object-oriented metrics in the following way to be used in the context of BDI agents: beliefs and goals correspond to attributes, and plans correspond to methods.

Table 7. Comparison of Number of Capability Components

Capability	**Design with Capability Relationships**			**Design with Export/Import**		
	#Goals	#Beliefs	#Plans	#Goals	#Beliefs	#Plans
Capability A	4	3	6	4	3	6
Capability B	3	1	4	3	1	4
Capability C	2	3	3	**5**	**5**	3
Capability D	4	2	7	**10**	**5**	7
Capability E	3	2	4	**10**	**3**	4
Capability F	2	2	4	**5**	**3**	4
Capability G	3	2	5	**7**	2	5

The design of `AgentX` and `AgentY` using our proposed capability relationships is shown in Figure 7a. We use the same notation used before, indicating also which goal each plan can achieve beside the plan name. As can be seen, we use our three relationship types: association, composition, and inheritance.

A design model of these same two agents and capabilities that has a similar behaviour at runtime using the alternative design approach — i.e. using a single type of relationship and indicating the particular capability components that should be imported or exported — is shown in Figure 7b. The comparison of the two designs shows that, in terms of number of components, the second design model has much higher values, as detailed in Table 7. The high number of components of the second design model compromises the legibility of the code, and makes it harder to maintain. Moreover, some of the capability components must be kept consistent when evolving the code, which also compromises maintenance.

This comparison is a preliminar evaluation of our approach with the most common way of relating capabilities. Although the comparison uses a small and hypothetical scenario, it already indicates the potential that our approach has to improve the design of BDI agents. Moreover, it allowed us to identify limitations of the use of import/export to related capabilities. First, specifying access to particular beliefs is limited to beliefs specified at design time. If new beliefs are added to a capability, no other capability can access it. In our approach, the relationship specifies access to the set of beliefs of a capability, and if new beliefs are added to this capability, other capabilities, such that those involved in a composition relationship as part-capabilities, may access them. Second, the common way of relating capabilities considers a tree-like structure, where each capability has only one parent. However, there are situations, exemplified in this paper, that different capabilities must be related to the same capability (instance). And third, as can be seen in Figure 7b, modelling inheritance with this import/export approach is complicated, and it gets even more complicated when there are multiple levels in the hierarchy.

6 Discussion

In this section, we discuss relevant issues with respect to the described capability relationships. We first analyse them, pointing out their main differences and the impact of choosing one or another in Section 6.1. We next discuss in Section 6.2 other object-oriented concepts, and how they are related to the presented relationships.

6.1 Relationship Analysis and Comparison

We have presented three different kinds of relationships between capabilities, and understanding their differences in order to be able to choose one to be used in agent design is important. We thus in this section make this discussion.

First, a key difference among these relationships is their purpose. Associations should be used when different *independent* agent parts *collaborate* to achieve a higher level goal. This is similar to collaborations among agents, but capabilities are within the scope of a single agent, i.e. a single thread. Therefore, it is a design choice to develop two agents, each of which with one capability and collaborating through messages, or to develop a single agent with two capabilities, collaborating by dispatching goals to be achieved by other capability. Composition is adopted when the agent behaviour can be decomposed into modular structures, but parts *depend* on the whole, providing the notion of a *hierarchical* structure. And inheritance is used when there is a need for *reusing* a common set of beliefs, goals and plans, and then specialising it in different ways.

According to software engineering principles, the lower the coupling between capabilities, the better. Additionally, components of each capability should have high cohesion. These presented relationships have different degrees of coupling between the involved capabilities, so consequently relationships that reduce coupling should be preferred, when possible. We summarise this comparison of the relationships — discussed in the previous sections — in Table 8, which also indicates the visibility of components of capabilities involved in the relationships. For example, when there is a composition relationship, the whole-capability has access to the part-capability's external goals, while the part-capability has access to the whole-capability's beliefs, external goals and internal goals. We also emphasise the purpose of each relationship. Therefore, choosing a certain capability relationship is a design choice that not only implies restrictions over the visibility of the capability components, but also expresses the meaning of the relationship.

Now, we will focus on the impact at runtime of choosing different capability relationships. When a capability has access to components of another capability, it may use these components at runtime. The access to beliefs is already shown in Table 8, and this means that a capability can use and modify knowledge to which it has access. Besides accessing other capability's knowledge, a capability involved in a relationship may: (i) dispatch goals of another capability when one of its plans is executing; and (ii) execute a plan to achieve a goal of another capability. We show when these two possibilities can happen in Table 9, which

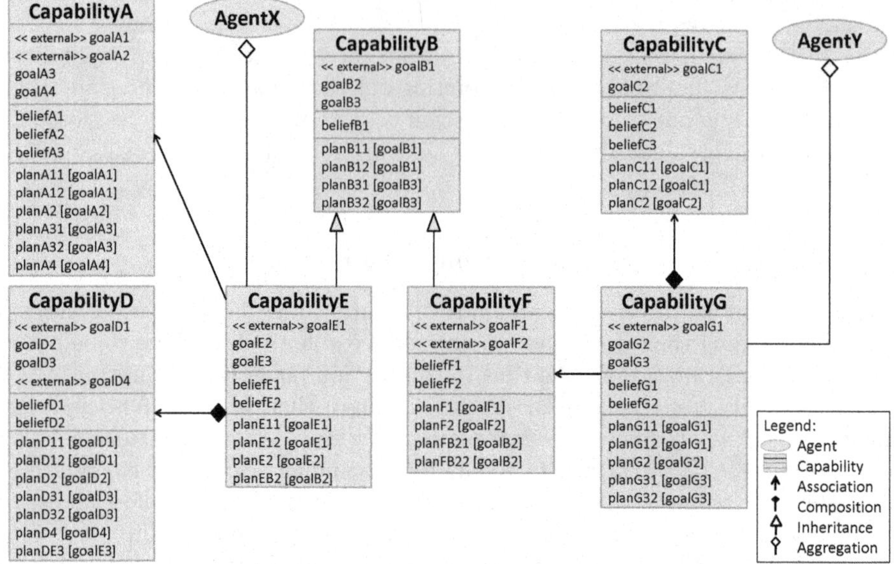

(a) Design with Capability Relationships.

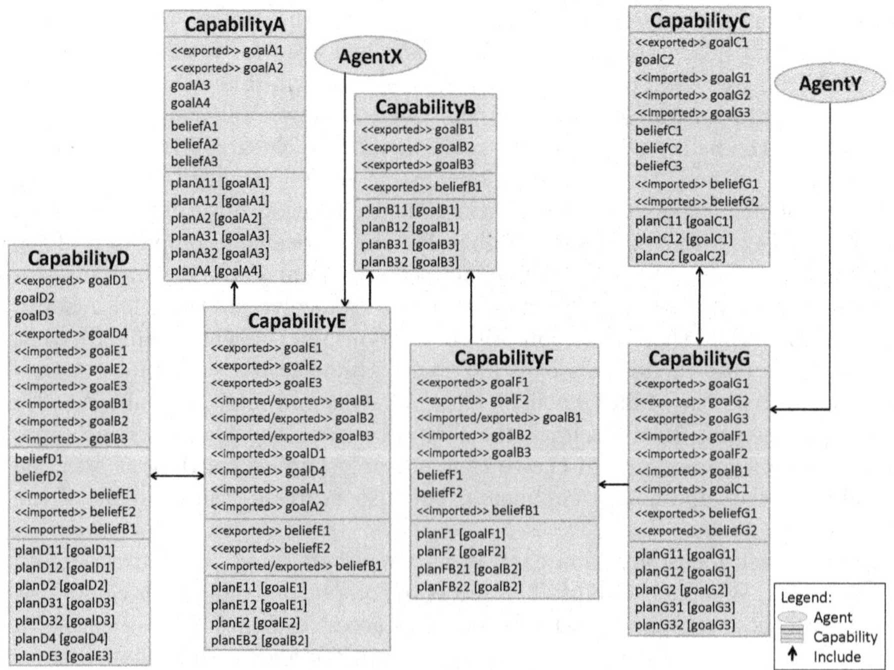

(b) Design with Export/Import.

Fig. 7. Capability Relationships vs. Export/Import

Table 8. Relationship Comparison (1)

			Association	Composition	Inheritance
Purpose			Collaboration	Decomposition	Extension
Coupling			+	++	+++
Visibility	Source/ Whole/ Parent	Beliefs		X	X
		External Goals		X	X
		Internal Goals		X	X
		Plans			X
	Target/ Part/ Child	Beliefs			
		External Goals	X	X	
		Internal Goals			
		Plans			

Table 9. Relationship Comparison (2)

		Whose goals can be dispatched within the scope of this capability?	Whose goals can be achieved by this capability's plans?
Association	Source	Source's goals Target's goals (external only)	Source's goals
	Target	Target's goals	Target's goals
Composition	Whole	Whole's goals Part's goals (external only)	Whole's goals
	Part	Part's goals Whole's goals	Part's goals Whole's goals
Inheritance	Parent	Parent's goals	Parent's goals
	Child	Child's goals Parent's goals	Child's goals Parent's goals

are associated with goal visibility. For example, if a whole-capability (of a composition relationship) dispatches one of its goals, this goal may be achieved by the execution of a whole-capability's plan or a plan of any the part-capabilities (and their parts).

6.2 Further OO Concepts

In this paper, we propose the use of relationships from object orientation to improve the modularity promoted by capabilities. This is just one of the object-oriented mechanisms that support the construction of high-quality software systems from a software engineering point of view. In this section, we discuss other mechanisms that may be adopted.

First, attributes and methods are always associated with an explicitly *specified visibility*, which can be private, protected, or public. JACK and Jadex, as previously discussed, provide similar concept using the `export` keyword. Here, we do not propose to use of visibility modifiers, except for goals, because exposing capability's beliefs goes against the principles of encapsulation and information hiding. In some situations, it is needed, and we provide mechanisms that explicitly show why there is a need for sharing beliefs, i.e. when there is a whole-part structure, and the parts involved. Nevertheless, visibility may be helpful to restrict the access of part or child capabilities to components of the whole or parent capabilities, respectively.

Associations between objects usually have a *cardinality* specified. If this is also applied to capabilities, it will allow capabilities to be associated with more than one instance of a capability. However, dispatching a goal of any of these capabilities will produce the same effect, unless their fragments of knowledge have different states, but this is unreasonable. We are not stating that any of these mechanisms (visibility or cardinality) should not be used, but they should be carefully analysed before being adopted in the context of capabilities, in order to evaluate their usefulness and their meaning.

Classes of objects can be *abstract*, when they cannot be instantiated and certain (abstract) methods must be implemented by subclasses. Although we do not address abstract capabilities in this paper, our examples shown in Figures 5 and 6 indicate that it would be useful to specify when capabilities are abstract. In the examples, the `FloorCleaning` and `Driver` capabilities have goals that they cannot handle, and are handled by child or part capabilities.

Finally, configurations of how capabilities are structured can be investigated, so as to form design patterns [9], or anti-patterns that should be avoided, such as object-oriented code-smells [8].

7 Final Considerations

Modularisation plays a key role in software engineering and is crucial for developing high-quality large-scale software. However, it has limited investigation in agent architectures, or more specifically BDI agents. Our previous studies have shown that there is a lack of mechanisms that allow modularising fine-grained variability in BDI agents [12].

Capabilities are one of the most important contributions to allow the construction of modularised BDI agent parts, increasing maintainability and promoting reuse. Nevertheless, this concept could be further explored to provide more sophisticated tools to increase the quality of BDI agents from a software engineering point of view, and supporting the construction of large-scale multi-agent systems. In this paper, we investigated the use of three types of relationships between capabilities, which are association, composition and inheritance. Each of which has a particular purpose, and indicates specific access to its components. We showed examples of their use, and discussed the implications of each relationship at runtime. Although some BDI agent platforms provide mechanisms to emulate most of these relationships, by means of the exportation of capability's components, they compromise maintenance, as shown in our preliminary evaluation. Keeping track of all shared beliefs and capabilities that can handle goals may become an error-prone task, thus making agents susceptible to faults.

The main goal of this paper is to promote the exploitation of capability relationships and other mechanisms to develop large-scale modular multi-agent systems and discussion about this important issue of agent-oriented software engineering. In this context, this work has left many *open issues* to be further discussed, with respect to capabilities and modularisation into agent architectures: (i) does it make sense to add visibility to all BDI agent components? (ii) is there any situation where there should be cardinality in the association relationship? and (iii) we specify the interface of a capability, but what is the interface of an agent? We are currently working on a new version of BDI4JADE, which will provide the capability relationships proposed in this paper, and it will soon be available for download.

Acknowledgements. I would like to thank the EMAS participants for the fruitful discussion on the subject of this paper during the workshop, in particular Michael Winikoff, Maarten Sierhuis and John Thangarajah. I also thank the anonymous reviewers for their time to read and review this paper, and their feedback. I am also grateful to Michael Luck for his useful feedback on the preparation of the revised version of this paper. FAPERGS and CAPES are acknowledged for their financial support.

References

1. Autonomous Decision-Making Software (AOS): Jack intelligent agents: Jack manual. Tech. Rep. 4.1, Agent Oriented Software Pvt. Ltd, Melbourne, Australia (2005)
2. Bordini, R.H., Wooldridge, M., Hübner, J.F.: Programming Multi-Agent Systems in AgentSpeak using Jason. John Wiley & Sons (2007)
3. Bratman, M.E.: Intention, Plans, and Practical Reason. Harvard University Press, Cambridge (1987)
4. Braubach, L., Pokahr, A., Lamersdorf, W.: Extending the capability concept for flexible BDI agent modularization. In: Bordini, R.H., Dastani, M., Dix, J., El Fallah Seghrouchni, A. (eds.) ProMAS 2005. LNCS (LNAI), vol. 3862, pp. 139–155. Springer, Heidelberg (2006)
5. Bresciani, P., Perini, A., Giorgini, P., Giunchiglia, F., Mylopoulos, J.: Tropos: An agent-oriented software development methodology. Autonomous Agents and Multi-Agent Systems 8(3), 203–236 (2004)
6. Busetta, P., Howden, N., Rönnquist, R., Hodgson, A.: Structuring BDI agents in functional clusters. In: Jennings, N.R. (ed.) Intelligent Agents VI. LNCS, vol. 1757, pp. 277–289. Springer, Heidelberg (2000)
7. Chidamber, S.R., Kemerer, C.F.: A metrics suite for object oriented design. IEEE Trans. Softw. Eng. 20(6), 476–493 (1994)
8. Fowler, M.: Refactoring: Improving the Design of Existing Code. Addison-Wesley Longman Publishing Co., Inc., Boston (1999)
9. Gamma, E., Helm, R., Johnson, R., Vlissides, J.: Design Patterns: Elements of Reusable Object-oriented Software. Addison-Wesley (1995)
10. Garcia, A., Lucena, C.: Taming heterogeneous agent architectures. Commun. ACM 51(5), 75–81 (2008)

11. Howden, N., Rönnquista, R., Hodgson, A., Lucas, A.: Jack intelligent agents^{TM}: Summary of an agent infrastructure. In: The Fifth International Conference on Autonomous Agents, Montreal, Canada (2001)
12. Nunes, I., Cirilo, E., Cowan, D., Lucena, C.: Fine-grained variability in the development of families of software agents. In: Sabater-Mir, J. (ed.) 7th European Workshop on Multi-Agent Systems (EUMAS 2009), Cyprus (December 2009)
13. Nunes, I., Cowan, D., Cirilo, E., de Lucena, C.J.P.: A case for new directions in agent-oriented software engineering. In: Weyns, D., Gleizes, M.-P. (eds.) AOSE 2010. LNCS, vol. 6788, pp. 37–61. Springer, Heidelberg (2011)
14. Nunes, I., Lucena, C., Luck, M.: Bdi4jade: a bdi layer on top of jade. In: ProMAS 2011, Taipei, Taiwan, pp. 88–103 (2011)
15. Nunes, I., de Lucena, C.J.P., Cowan, D., Alencar, P.: Building service-oriented user agents using a software product line approach. In: Edwards, S.H., Kulczycki, G. (eds.) ICSR 2009. LNCS, vol. 5791, pp. 236–245. Springer, Heidelberg (2009)
16. Nunes, I., Lucena, C.J.P.D., Cowan, D., Kulesza, U., Alencar, P., Nunes, C.: Developing multi-agent system product lines: from requirements to code. Int. J. Agent-Oriented Softw. Eng. 4(4), 353–389 (2011)
17. Padgham, L., Lambrix, P.: Formalisations of capabilities for bdi-agents. Autonomous Agents and Multi-Agent Systems 10(3), 249–271 (2005)
18. Parnas, D.L.: On the criteria to be used in decomposing systems into modules. Commun. ACM 15(12), 1053–1058 (1972)
19. Penserini, L., Perini, A., Susi, A., Mylopoulos, J.: From capability specifications to code for multi-agent software. In: 21st IEEE/ACM International Conference on Automated Software Engineering, ASE 2006, pp. 253–256. IEEE (2006)
20. Pokahr, A., Braubach, L., Haubeck, C., Ladiges, J.: Programming BDI agents with pure java. In: Müller, J.P., Weyrich, M., Bazzan, A.L.C. (eds.) MATES 2014. LNCS, vol. 8732, pp. 216–233. Springer, Heidelberg (2014)
21. Pokahr, A., Braubach, L., Lamersdorf, W.: Jadex: A bdi reasoning engine. In: Multi-Agent Programming, pp. 149–174. Springer (September 2005)
22. Rao, A.S., Georgeff, M.P.: BDI-agents: from theory to practice. In: Proceedings of the First Intl. Conference on Multiagent Systems, San Francisco (1995)
23. van Riemsdijk, M.B., Dastani, M., Meyer, J.J.C., de Boer, F.S.: Goal-oriented modularity in agent programming. In: Proceedings of the Fifth International Joint Conference on Autonomous Agents and Multiagent Systems, AAMAS 2006, pp. 1271–1278. ACM, New York (2006)
24. Sant'Anna, C., Lobato, C., Kulesza, U., Garcia, A., Chavez, C., Lucena, C.: On the modularity assessment of aspect-oriented multiagent architectures: A quantitative study. Int. J. Agent-Oriented Softw. Eng. 2(1), 34–61 (2008)

A Scalable Runtime Platform for Multiagent-Based Simulation

Tobias Ahlbrecht, Jürgen Dix, Michael Köster,
Philipp Kraus, and Jörg P. Müller

Department of Informatics, Clausthal University of Technology,
Julius-Albert-Str. 4, D-38678 Clausthal-Zellerfeld, Germany
firstname.lastname@tu-clausthal.de
http://www.in.tu-clausthal.de

Abstract. Using purely agent-based platforms for any kind of simulation requires to address the following challenges: (1) *scalability* (efficient scheduling of agent cycles is difficult), (2) *efficient memory management* (when and which data should be fetched, cached, or written to/from disk), and (3) *modelling* (no generally accepted meta-models exist: what are essential concepts, what just implementation details?). While dedicated professional simulation tools usually provide rich domain libraries and advanced visualisation techniques, and support the simulation of large scenarios, they do not allow for "agentization" of single components. We are trying to bridge this gap by developing a *distributed, scalable runtime platform for multiagent simulation*, *MASeRaTi*, addressing the three problems mentioned above. It allows to plug-in both dedicated simulation tools (for the *macro view*) as well as the agentization of certain components of the system (to allow a *micro view*). If no agent-related features are used, its performance should be as close as possible to the legacy system used.

Paper type: Technological or Methodological.

1 Introduction

In this paper, we describe ongoing work on a distributed runtime platform for multiagent simulation, *MASeRaTi*, that we are currently developing in a joint project (`http://simzentrum.de/en/projects/desim`). The idea for *MASeRaTi* evolved out of two projects, Planets and MAPC. In both projects, we implemented, completely independently, running systems for different purposes. One to simulate urban traffic management, the other to simulate arbitrary agent systems in one single platform.

Agent-Based Traffic Modelling and Simulation: We developed *ATSim*, a simulation architecture that integrates the commercial traffic simulation framework *AIMSuN* with the multiagent programming system *JADE* (implemented in JAVA): *ATSim* was realized within Planets, a project on cooperative traffic management (`http://www.tu-c.de/planets`).

F. Dalpiaz et al. (Eds.): EMAS 2014, LNAI 8758, pp. 81–102, 2014.

Agent-Based Simulation Platform: We implemented, in JAVA, an agent-based platform, *MASSim*, which allows several simulation scenarios to be plugged in. Remotely running teams of agents can connect to it and *play against each other* on the chosen scenario. *MASSim* has been developed since 2006 and is used to realise the MAPC, an annual contest for multiagent systems.

While the former system centers around a commercial traffic simulation platform (*AIMSuN*), the latter platform is purely agent-based and had been developed from scratch. Such an agent-based approach allows for maximal freedom in the implementation of arbitrary properties, preferences, and capabilities of the entities. We call this the *micro-level*: each agent can behave differently and interact with any other agent.

The traffic simulation platform *AIMSuN*, which easily runs tens of thousands of vehicles, however, does not support such a micro-level view. Often we can only make assumptions about the *throughput* or other *macro*-features. Therefore, with *ATSim*, we aimed at a hybrid approach to traffic modelling and integrated the *JADE* agent platform in order to describe vehicles and vehicle-to-X (V2X) communication within a multiagent-based paradigm. One of the lessons learned during the project was that it is extremely difficult to *agentize.*[1] certain entities (by, e.g. plugging in an agent platform) or to add agent-related features to *AIMSuN* in a scalable and natural way.

Before presenting the main idea in more details in Section 2, we point to related work (Section 1.1) and comment about the overall structure of this paper.

1.1 Related Work

In the past decade a multitude of simulation platforms for multiagent systems have been developed. We describe some of them with their main features and note why they are not the solution to our problem. The *Shell for Simulated Agent Systems (SeSAm) [22]* is an IDE that supports visual programming and facilitates the simulation of multiagent models. *SeSAm*'s main focus is on modelling and not on scalability.

GALATEA [9] is a general simulation platform for multiagent systems developed in Java and based on the High Level Architecture [24]. *PlaSMA* [14] was designed specifically for the logistics domain and builds upon JADE. *AnyLogic*(`http://www.anylogic.com/`) is a commercial simulation platform written in Java that allows to model and execute discrete event, system dynamics and agent-based simulations, e.g. using the included graphical modelling language. *MATSim*(`http://www.matsim.org/`) was developed for large-scale agent-based simulations in the traffic and transport area. It is open-source and implemented in Java. The open-source simulation platform *SUMO* [23] was designed to manage large-scale (city-sized) road networks. It is implemented in C++ and supports a microscopic view of the simulation while it is not especially agent-based.

[1] To agentize means *to transform given legacy code into an agent so that it belongs to a particular multiagent system (MAS)* This term was coined in [29]. In [28], Shoham used the term *agentification* for the same purpose.

Mason [26] is a general and flexible multiagent toolkit developed for simulations in Java. It allows for dynamically combining models, visualizers, and other mid-run modifications. It is open-source and runs as a single process. *NetLogo*[30] is a cross-platform multiagent modelling environment that is based on Java and employs a dialect of the Logo language for modelling. It is intended to be easily usable while maintaining the capability for complex modelling.

TerraME (`http://www.terrame.org/`) is a simulation and modelling framework for terrestrial systems which is based on finite, hybrid, cellular automata or *situated agents*. We are using a similar architecture (Section 3), but we add some features for parallelisation and try to define a more flexible model and architecture structure.

Most frameworks with IDE support are not separable, so the architecture cannot be split up into a simulation part (e.g., on a High Performance Computing (HPC) cluster) and a visualisation/modelling part for the UI. Therefore an enhancement with HPC structure produces a new design of large parts of the system. Known systems like *Repast HPC*(`http://repast.sourceforge.net/`) use the parallelisation structure of the message passing interface MPI (`http://www.mcs.anl.gov/research/projects/mpi/`), but the scenario source code must be compiled into platform specific code. Hence, the process of developing a working simulation requires a lot of knowledge about the system specifics.

Repast HPC represents a parallel agent simulation framework written in C++. It introduces local and non-local agents which can be distributed along with the environment among different processes. Technically, it uses Boost and Boost.MPI to create the communication between the processes. A dedicated scheduler defines the simulation cycle. A problem of *Repast HPC* is the "hard encoding" structure of the C++ classes, which requires good knowledge about the Repast interface structure. In our architecture, we separate the agent and scheduling structure into different parts, creating a better fit of the agent programming paradigm and the underlying scheduler algorithms.

Also, a number of meta models for multiagent-based simulation (MABS) have been developed so far. *AMASON* [21] represents a general meta-model that captures the basic structure and dynamics of a MABS model. It is an abstraction and does not provide any implementation. *MAIA* [15] takes a different approach by building the model on institutional concepts and analysis. The resulting meta-model is very detailed, focusing on social aspects of multiagent systems. *easyABMS* [13] provides an entire methodology to iteratively and visually develop models from which code for the *Repast Simphony* toolkit can be generated. The reference meta model for *easyABMS* is again very detailed making it possible to create models with minimal programming effort.

To summarize, we find that most platforms are either written in Java or are not scalable for other reasons. Many are only used in academia and simply not designed to run on a high performance computing cluster. Common challenges relate to agent runtime representation and communication performance.

1.2 Structure of the Paper

In Section 2 we discuss our past research (*ATSim* and *MASSim*), draw conclusions and show how it led to the new idea of a highly scalable runtime platform for simulation purposes. We also give a more detailed description of the main features of *MASeRaTi* and how they are to be realized. The main part of this paper is Section 3, where we describe in some detail our simulation platform, including the system meta-model and the platform architecture. Section 4 presents a small example on which we are testing our ideas and the scalability of the system as compared to *MASSim*, a purely agent-based approach implemented in Java. We conclude with Section 5 and give an outlook for the next steps to be taken.

2 Essential Concepts and Features of *MASeRaTi*

In this section, we first present our own research in developing the platforms *ATSim* (Subsection 2.1) and *MASSim* (Subsection 2.2). We elaborate on lessons learned and show how this resulted in the new idea of the scalable runtime platform *MASeRaTi* (Subsection 2.3).

2.1 Traffic Simulation (*ATSim*)

Most models for simulating today's traffic management policies and their effects are based on macroscopic physics-based paradigms, see e.g. [17]. These approaches are highly scalable and have proven their effectiveness in practice. However, they require the behaviour of traffic participants to be described in simple physical equations, which is not necessarily the case when considering urban traffic scenarios. Microscopic approaches have been successfully used for freeway traffic flow modelling and control [27], which is usually a simpler problem than urban traffic flow modelling and control, due to less dynamics and better predictability.

In [8], we presented the *ATSim* simulation architecture that integrates the commercial traffic simulation framework *AIMSuN* with the multiagent programming system *JADE*. *AIMSuN* is used to model and simulate traffic scenarios, whereas *JADE* is used to implement the informational and motivational states and the decisions of traffic participants (modelled as agents). Thus, all features of *AIMSuN* (e.g. rich GUI, tools for data collection and data analysis) are available in *ATSim*, while *ATSim* allows to simulate the overall behaviour of traffic, and traffic objects can be modelled as agents with goals, plans, and communication with others for local coordination and cooperation.

AIMSuN (Figure 1(a), left side) provides an API for external applications to access its traffic objects via Python or C/C++ programming languages. But the *JADE*-based MAS (right side of Figure 1(a)) is implemented in Java, which leads to problems with scalability. To enable *AIMSuN* and the MAS to work together in *ATSim*, we used CORBA as a middleware. Technically we implemented a CORBA service for the MAS and an external application using the

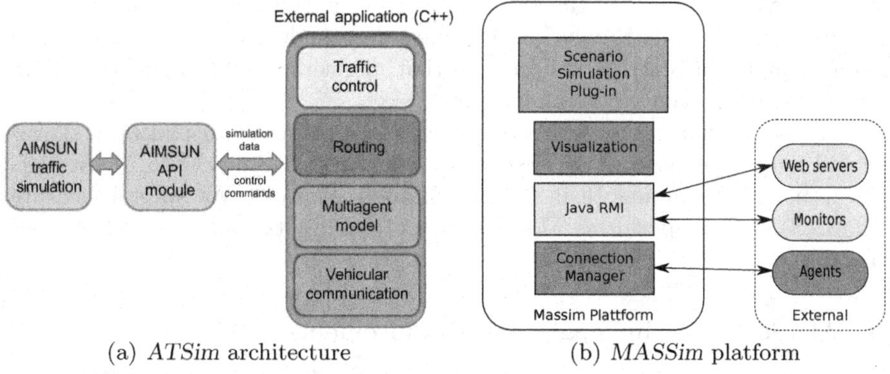

(a) *ATSim* architecture (b) *MASSim* platform

Fig. 1. Overview of the platforms

AIMSuN API to access the traffic objects simulated by *AIMSuN*. The CORBA service allows our external application to interact with the MAS directly via object references. For details on the integration architecture, we refer to [8]. Two application scenarios were modelled and evaluated on top of *ATSim*: The simulation of decentralized adaptive routing strategies, where vehicle agents learn local routing models based on traffic information [12], and cooperative routing based on vehicle group formation and platooning [16]. The overall system shown in Figure 1(a) was developed in a larger research project and contained additional components for realistic simulation of V2X communication (extending the OMNET++ simulator), and for formulating and deploying traffic control policies; see [11].

Our evaluation of the *ATSim* platform using a mid-sized scenario (rush hour traffic in Southern Hanover, one hour, approx. 30.000 routes, see [11]) showed that while the agent-based modelling approach is intuitive and suitable, our integration approach runs into scalability issues. Immediate causes identified for this were the computationally expensive representation of agents as Java threads in Jade and the XML-based inter-process communication between Jade and the *AIMSuN* simulator. In addition, system development and debugging proved difficult because two sets of models and runtime platforms needed to be maintained and synchronised.

2.2 Multi-Agent Programming Contest (MAPC)

The *MASSim* platform [5,4] is used as a simulation framework for the Multi-Agent Programming Contest (MAPC) [2](`http://multiagentcontest.org`). Agents are running remotely on different machines and are communicating in XML with the server over TCP/IP. The server computes the statistics, generates visual output and provides interfaces for the simulation data while the simulation is running.

A drawback of dividing the simulation in such a way is the latency of the network that can cause serious delays. Network communication becomes a bottleneck when scaling up; the slowest computer in the network is determining the overall speed of the simulation. Running the simulation in one Java virtual machine leads to a centralised approach that might impede an optimal run (in terms of execution time) of a simulation.

Figure 1(b) depicts the basic components of the *MASSim* platform. *MASSim* will mainly serve us as a reference to compare scalability with *MASeRaTi* right from the beginning (using the available scenarios). We want to ensure that *MASeRaTi* outperforms *MASSim* in both computation time and number of agents.

2.3 *MASeRaTi*: Challenges and Requirements

Our new simulation platform, *MASeRaTi* (`http://tu-c.de/maserati`), aims at combining the versatility of an agent-based approach (the *micro-view*) with the efficiency and scalability of dedicated simulation platforms (the *macro-view*). We reconsider the three challenges mentioned in the abstract for using a purely agent-based approach.

Scalability: Efficient scheduling of agent cycles is a difficult problem. In agent platforms, usually each agent has her own thread. Using e.g. Java, these threads are realised in the underlying operating system which puts an upper limit of approximate 5000 agents to the system. *These threads are handled by the internal scheduler and are therefore not real parallel processes.* In the *MASeRaTi* architecture we develop a micro-kernel where agents truly run in parallel. In this way, we reduce the overhead that comes with each thread significantly. We believe that this allows for a much better scalability than agent systems based on (any) programming language, where all processes are handled by the (black-box) operating system. Additionally, many simulation platforms use a verbose communication language (e.g., XML or FIPA-ACL) for the inter-agent communication that becomes a bottleneck when scaling up. We exploit the efficient synchronisation features of MPI instead.

Efficient Memory Management: Which data should when be fetched from disk (cached, written)? Most agent platforms are based on Java or similar interpreter languages. When using them we have no control over the prefetching or caching of data (agents need to access and reason about their belief state): this is done by the runtime mechanism of the language. We do not know in advance which available agent is active (random access), but we might be able to *learn* so during the simulation and thereby optimise the caching mechanism[1]. This is the reason why we are using the scripting language *Lua* in the way explained in the next section.

Modelling Support: As of now, no generally accepted meta-model for multiagent-based simulations exists. We would like to distinguish between essential concepts and implementation details. What are the agents in the simulation? Which agent features are important? We also want the modelling framework to assist a simulation developer in creating her scenario as well as hide the complexity of a parallelised simulation, while not being restrictive in terms of modelling capability.

So the main problem we are tackling is the following: *How can we develop a scalable simulation environment, where the individual agents can be suitably programmed and where one can abstract away from specific features?* We would like to reason about the macro view (usually supported by dedicated simulation tools) as well as zooming into the micro view when needed. The overhead for supporting the microview should not challenge overall system scalability:

(1) If no agents are needed (no micro-view), the performance of *MASeRaTi* should be as close to the legacy code (professional simulation tools) as possible.
(2) If no legacy code at all is used, *MASeRaTi* should still perform better or at least comparable to most of the existing agent platforms (and it should have similar functionality).

Due to general considerations (Amdahl's law[18]) and the fact that not all processes are completely parallelizable, it is not possible to achieve (1) perfectly (no agents: performance of *MASeRaTi* equals performance of legacy code).

In addition to a scalable platform we also provide a *meta-model* for multiagent-based simulations (MABS) in order to address the third challenge. The focus in this paper is on the first two challenges. The meta-model serves as a general starting point for the development of a MABS and ensures a certain structure of a simulation that is needed by the underlying platform in order to facilitate scalability. We have chosen *Lua* mainly because of its efficiency. It allows both object-oriented and functional programming styles and is implemented in native C. For details we refer to Section 3.2.

To conclude, we formulate these basic requirements for *MASeRaTi* that directly follow from the identified challenges: (1) the support of a macro and micro view of a simulation, (2) a scalable and efficient infrastructure, and (3) a multiagent-based simulation modelling framework that also supports non-agent components.

3 Overview of the System

The overall architecture of our framework is inspired by concepts from *game development*. The state of the art in developing massively multiplayer online role-playing games (MMORPGs) consists in using a client-server architecture where the clients are synchronised during game play [10] via a messaging system. Well-known games include Blizzards's *World of Warcraft* or EA's *SimCity 2013*, which supports multiplayer gaming with an "agent-based definition" in its own Glassbox engine(`http://andrewwillmott.com/talks/inside-glassbox`).

While a game architecture is a good starting point for our purposes, of course we cannot assume a server system with hundreds of hardware nodes, which is powerful enough to handle a MMORPG system. Also, for developing purposes, we need a system running on a single node (think of a common desktop PC). The source code (i.e. scenario) developed there must then be transferable to a HPC system, where the real simulation is executed.

Our underlying agent-oriented meta-model uses the well established concept of a BDI agent [28,31] in a variant inspired by the agent programming language Jason [7] combined with the idea of an entity [3] that evolved out of experiences gathered in the MAPC. However, the used concepts are completely exchangeable, due to the flexibility of Lua, and developers are not forced to use them. In our agent model, agents connect to these `entities` in the simulation world. Agents consist of a *body* and a *mind*: While the mind (being responsible for the deliberation cycle, the mental state etc.) does not have to be physically grounded, the entity has to be located in an area of the simulation. Thus, an entity is an object with attributes that an agent can control and that might be influenced by the actions of other agents or the overall simulation. Intuitively, an agent can be viewed as a puppet master that directs one (or more) entities.

3.1 Architecture

Our system is composed of three layers (Fig. 2):

Micro-Kernel (MK): The micro-kernel represents the technical backbone of the system. It is written in the C++ programming language to get the necessary performance and provides basic network parallelisation and scheduling algorithms. The layer defines the system's underlying structure containing interfaces e.g. for plug-ins, serialisation, Prolog for knowledge representation and reasoning, or statistical accumulation. In short, this bottom layer describes a meta-model for a generic parallel simulation (Section 3.2).

Agent-Model Layer (AML): The agent-model layer (Section 3.4) introduces agent-oriented concepts (e.g. agents, environments, artifacts etc.) to the system and thus describes a model of an agent-based simulation. It is implemented in the scripting language Lua(`http://www.lua.org/`) [20] to ensure maximum flexibility. Due to the multi-paradigm nature of Lua, pure object-oriented concepts are not supported by default. That is, Lua uses only simple data types and (meta-) tables. Fortunately, based on this, we can create an object-oriented structure in Lua itself. This allows us to work in a uniform fashion with UML models regarding the AML and the scenario layer.

Scenario Layer (SL): The third and topmost layer represents the instantiation of the AML with a concrete scenario, e.g., a traffic setting or the MAPC cow scenario (to be introduced later in Section 4). It is illustrated by dotted boxes in Fig. 2 to emphasise the distinction from the AML layer. Section 4 provides an example of a concrete scenario fitting this layer.

An important aspect is the linkage between the three layers, and in particular the connections between the micro-kernel and the AML (illustrated in Fig. 2) which is discussed further in the following sections.

3.2 Micro-kernel

The micro-kernel represents the technical side of the system and is split up into two main structures (Fig. 3(b)). The core part (below) contains the scheduler

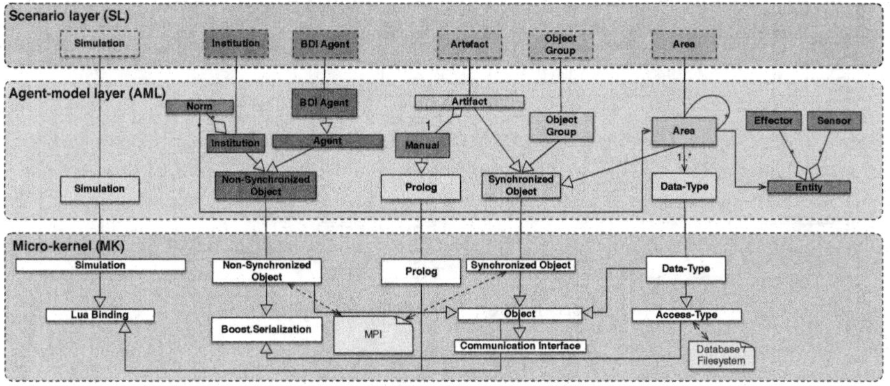

Fig. 2. *MASeRaTi* system architecture: UML class diagram

algorithms, the core and memory management, the network and operating system layers and the plug-in API together with a Prolog interpreter. Above these core utilities, the Lua interpreter (top) is defined and each class structure on the core can be bound to "Lua objects". The Lua runtime is instantiated for each process once, so there is no elaborated bootstrapping.

The choice of Lua was mainly motivated by the scaling structure and the game developing viewpoint. Lua, a multi paradigm language, has been used for game development for many years ([25]). An advantage of Lua is the small size of its interpreter (around 100 kBytes) and the implementation in native C with the enhancement to append its own data structures into the runtime interpreter with the binding frameworks. The multiparadigm definition of Lua, especially object-oriented and functional [20], can help us to create a flexible metamodel for our simulation model. Lua can also be used with a just-in-time compiler.

The kernel defines basic data structures and algorithms (Fig. 3(a)):

Simulation: A global singleton simulation object, which stores all global operations in the simulation e.g. creating agents or artifacts. It defines the initialization of each simulation; the constructor of the Simulation object must create the world object, agent objects, etc.

Object: Defines the basic structure of each object within the simulation. All objects have got a UUID (Universally Unique Identifier), a statistical map for evaluating statistical object data, the (pre-/post-)tick methods to run the object and the running time data, which counts the CPU cycles during computation (for optimisation).

Prolog: An interface for using Prolog calls within the simulation.

Each class is derived from the *Lua Binding* class, so the objects will be mapped into the AML.

The mapping between the micro-kernel and the AML is defined using a *language binding concept.* The Lua interpreter is written in native C. Based on this structure, a C function can be "pushed" into the Lua runtime. The function will

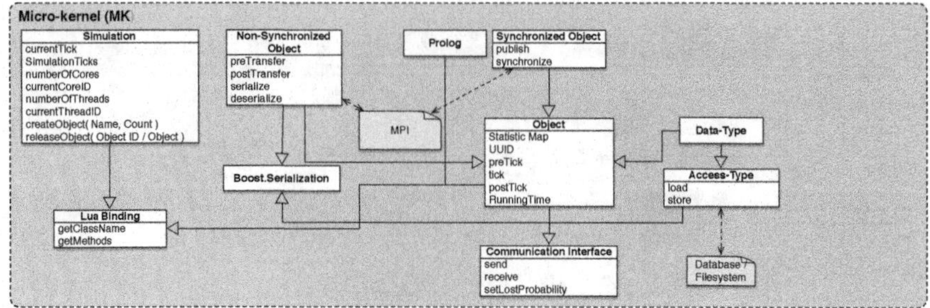

(a) Micro-kernel: UML class diagram

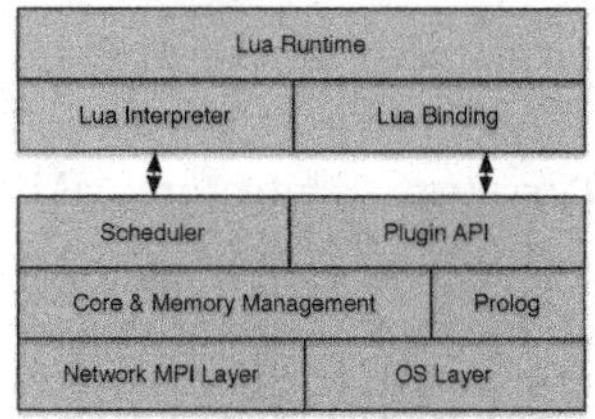

(b) Architecture

Fig. 3. Micro-kernel data model (a) and architecture (b)

be stored into a global Lua table; the underlying C function is used with a script function call.

Our concept defines the micro-kernel in UML; instantiated C++ objects are mapped into the runtime environment by a Lua binding framework (e.g. Lua Bridge (`https://github.com/vinniefalco/LuaBridge`) or Luabind (`http://www.rasterbar.com/products/luabind.html`)). Classes and objects in Lua are not completely separate things, as a class is a table with anonymous functions and properties. If a Lua script creates an object, it calls the constructor, which is defined by a meta-table function, the underlying C++ object will be also created and allocated on the heap. The destructor call to an object deterministically removes the Lua object and its corresponding C++ object. All C++ objects are heap-allocated and encapsulated by a "smart pointer", as this helps avoiding memory leaks. This concept allows consistent binding between the different programming languages and the layer architecture.

Each *Object* comes from the *Communication interface*, which allows an object to send any structured data to another object. Three subclasses inherit from the central *Object*. This structure is necessary for creating a distributed and scalable platform with optimisation possibility:

Synchronised Object: An object of this type is synchronised over all instances of the micro-kernel (thread and core synchronised). It exists also over all instances and needs a blocking communication. In the agent programming paradigm the world must be synchronised.

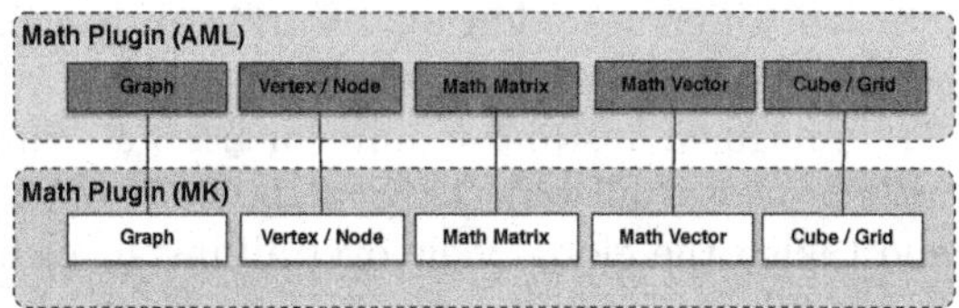

Fig. 4. Math plug-in architecture example

Non-synchronised Object: This object exists only on one instance of the micro-kernel and can be transferred between different instances of the micro kernel. It should be used e.g. for agents and norms, because the evaluation is independent from other objects. Using the "execution time" of the tick (time complexity), we can group such objects together.

Data-Type: This object represents a data structure, e.g. a multigraph for the traffic scenario with routing algorithms (Dijkstra, $A^\star$ and $D^\star$). The data types will be pushed into the micro-kernel with the plug-in API. The *Access-Type* creates the connection to the storing devices.

Synchronised and *non-synchronized* objects are implemented via Boost.MPI[2] structure, and the *Access-Type* defines the interface to a database or the filesystem for storing / loading object data. The access via the data interface will be defined by the Boost.Serialization library[2], so we can use a generic interface. Based on the *Data-Type* we can use the defined plug-in API for math datatypes, which allows e.g. to create a (multi-) graph interface for our traffic scenario, based on Boost-Graph[2]. A plug-in is defined in a two-layer structure (Fig. 4). The plug-in is written in C++ (the algorithm part) and based on the Lua binding structure mapped into the higher layers (the function invoking part). This two layer strucutre enables us to use a differential equation solver like OdeInt(`http://www.odeint.com/`) to simulate the macroscopic view in the simulation (e.g. a highway traffic model can be simulated with a differential equation while employing a microscopic agent-based view for an urban traffic area. The "glue" between these two types can be defined by a "sink / source data-type").

The plug-in interface is based on a native C implementation to avoid problems with name managing in the compiler and linker definition. Plug-ins are stored in a dynamic link library; they are loaded upon start of the kernel.

Design Tradeoffs. Next, we discuss alternatives and trade-offs when designing a runtime system to take a deeper look into that of *MASeRaTi*. During runtime we propose to ask which objects need to be defined as synchronised or non-synchronised datasets. The implementation of the FIPA-ACL definition, e.g., is a blocking operation, because we can update the object only after we have processed the input data, so each external data input creates a slower performance.

[2] `http://boost.org/doc/libs/release/libs/`

With the implementation we create additional workload, because parser, lexer and interpreter must also process the data.

One *MASeRaTi* runtime instance implements a thread-pool (see Subsection 3.3) which processes all objects. Scalability is obtained by looking at local instances and taking the global view over all instances into account.

3.3 Optimisation

In [32], Wooldridge describes some pitfalls in agent developing:

1. *"You forget that you are developing multithreaded software"*.
2. *"Your design does not exploit concurrency"*.
3. *"You have too few agents"*.

As discussed in Section 3.2 there are two disjoint sets of objects in our simulation: non-synchronised and synchronised objects. Taking the above three statements seriously, our aim is to design a scalable, multi-threaded and multi-core system which can handle a large number of agents that act concurrently. With the technical restrictions (memory and number of threads), we need another approach, which is inspired by the technical view of an MMORPG:

- We create a scheduler on its own to handle the agents. It is based on a thread pool.
- We measure the average of the calculation time of each agent when it is active (counting the CPU cycles).
- Based on this result, we optimise the number of agents between the micro-kernels with a thread-/core-stealing algorithm (in future work we aim to describe this with a stochastic process).

After having defined one discrete simulation step, we denote this step "tick" and the process definition of one step is as follows (Figure 5):

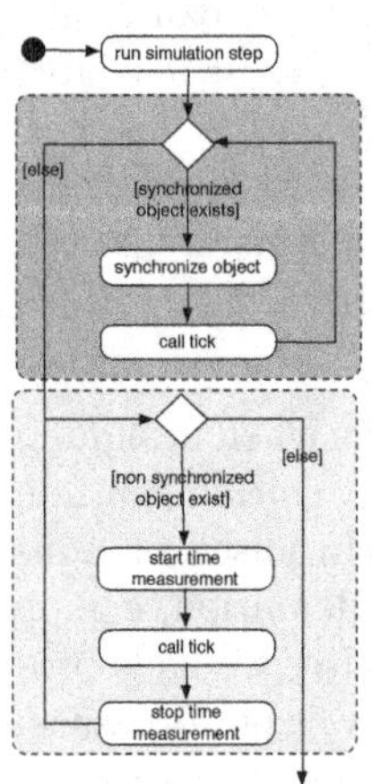


```
foreach simulation step
    foreach synchronized object
        synchronize object
        call tick
    wait for all threads are finished

    foreach non-synchronized object
        start object time measurement
        call tick
        stop object time measurement
    wait for all threads are finished
```

Fig. 5. Simulation tick

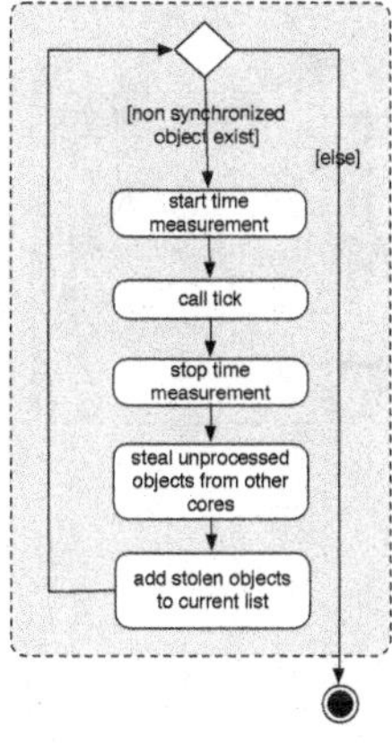


```
foreach unprocessed objects on each
   core

   foreach local non-sync. object
       start time measurement
       call tick
       stop time measurement

   steal unprocessed non-sync.
       objects from other cores
   push the stolen objects into the
       local working list

wait for all
```

Fig. 6. Stealing process on an instance

Each simulation object owns a tick method, which is called by the scheduler (pre/post tick calls are not shown here). There exist only two global blocking operations for synchronisation over all kernel instances. Each micro-kernel process runs the (global) synchronised objects first. After finishing, the simulation environment is synchronised on each kernel. In the next step, the kernel runs the non-synchronised objects. This second loop can be run in a fast way, e.g. the agents do nothing, so the micro-kernel idles, then the while-loop sends "steal requests" and gets objects from the other instances (Figure 6).

Figure 7 shows the stealing process (bullets are the agents, with different calculation times) over all running *MASeRaTi* instances

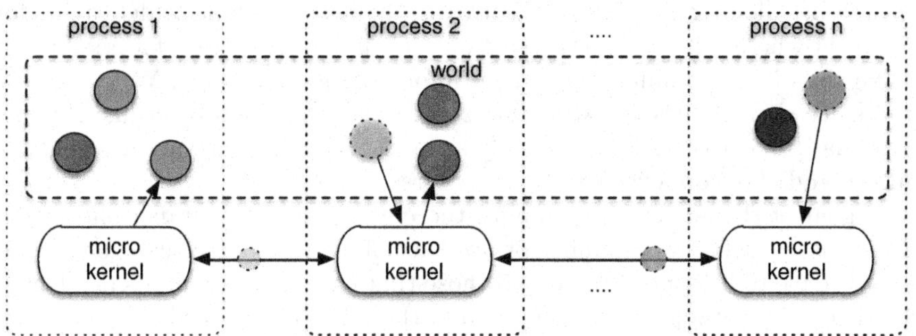

Fig. 7. Stealing process over all instances

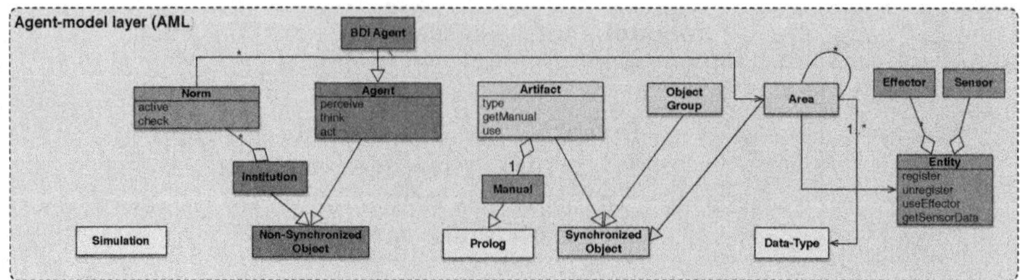

Fig. 8. Agent-model layer: UML class diagram

This idea allows the processing of a large number of agents with different (complex) plans and belief bases, because we can define the optimisation process with different targets and methods. The simulation consists of a finite number of discrete steps and objects, so we can describe the process with a discrete stochastic approach.

3.4 Agent-Model Layer

The agent-model layer (AML) (depicted in Fig. 8) defines a meta-model of an agent-based simulation. It provides the basic structure and serves as a starting point for an implementation. We start by explaining the structure, followed by the overall system behaviour; we end with a general description of the development process. Realization details (pseudo code) can be found in the appendix of [1].

Structure. The structure of the meta-model is heavily influenced by the goal of creating a simulation which can be distributed over several nodes or cores. In such a parallelised multiagent simulation, the developer has to determine for each object whether it has to be present on each and every core or if it is sufficient to have the object running independently on a single core only. We prefer the latter, since that implies *less execution time*. In contrast, an object like a global artifact has to be accessible by virtually any other object. Thus, it must be made available and therefore executed on each core.

The goal of the AML is to simplify the development of parallel multiagent simulations by defining a number of abstract objects or object categories that normally have to be synchronised and those that can usually run independently. Nevertheless, a developer can easily modify the AML to her needs, in particular redefining the synchronicity of objects.

Figure 8 illustrates the structure of the AML. Mainly, a simulation consists of a singleton `Simulation`, the non-synchronised object types `Agent`, `Norm`, and the synchronised classes `Area`, `Artifact`, `ObjectGroup`. While for the `Simulation` only one instance is allowed, the other objects can be instantiated several times. All instantiated objects are being executed in a step-based fashion and therefore implement a `tick` method that is called exactly once per simulation cycle.

Simulation: The `simulation` class in the AML is the Lua-based counterpart to the `simulation` class in the MK. It is responsible for the creation, initialisation and deletion of objects. Thus, it is in full control over the simulation.

Agent: As we aim to simulate as many agents as possible we have to ensure that this part of the model can run independently of the rest. Therefore we define two kinds of agents as non-synchronised objects: a generic agent based on [31] and a more sophisticated BDI agent [28] inspired by Jason [7]. The agent interacts with the environment through `entities` [3]. In general an agent can have random access to the simulation world. Therefore, we can only encapsulate some parts of the agent, namely the internal actions and functions like reasoning. But the effects on the environment have to be synchronised to make them known to all other objects. This is the reason for splitting the agent into two parts: the mind (the `agent`) and the body (the `entity`). The generic agent has three methods that are invoked in the following order: (1) `perceive`, (2) `think`, and (3) `act`. Inside these methods, those of the respective entity can be called directly while communication between objects has to be realised by a synchronised object (for instance by means of an `artifact`).

BDI Agent: The BDI agent is a little more sophisticated and consists of a `Belief Base` representing the current world view, a set of `Events` describing changes in the mental state, a set of plans `Plans`, and a set of `Intentions` describing the currently executed plans. Fig. 9 shows an overview of the agent cycle. Black (continuous) lines represent the activity flow while red (dashed) lines show the data flow. The agent cycle is executed from within the agent's `tick` method. In each `tick`, the agent first perceives the environment and checks for new messages. Based on this information, the belief base is updated and an event for each update is generated. From the set of events one particular event is selected and a plan that matches this event will be chosen and instantiated. During a simulation run this might result in multiple instantiated plans at the same time and allows the agent to pursue more than one goal in parallel. We decided to limit the agent to the execution of one external action (that affects the environment) but allow several internal actions per simulation `tick`. The next method selects the next action of an instantiated plan (i.e. the next action of an intention). In contrast to Jason, the agent cycle does not stop here if it was an internal action or a message, i.e., an action that does not affect the environment. Thus, the agent selects the next event (if possible) or next intention (if possible) until (1) it reaches a global timeout (set by the simulation) or (2) an external action is executed that forces a synchronisation, or (3) if the set of events and intentions are both empty.

Artifact: For all passive objects of a simulation we use the `artifact` methodology defined in [6]. Basically, each artifact has a `type`, a `manual` in Prolog (a description of the possible actions associated with it) and a `use` method that allows an agent to execute a particular action, i.e. make use of the artifact. Due to the generality of this approach the developer decides whether the actions are known by the agents beforehand or not. Additionally, since

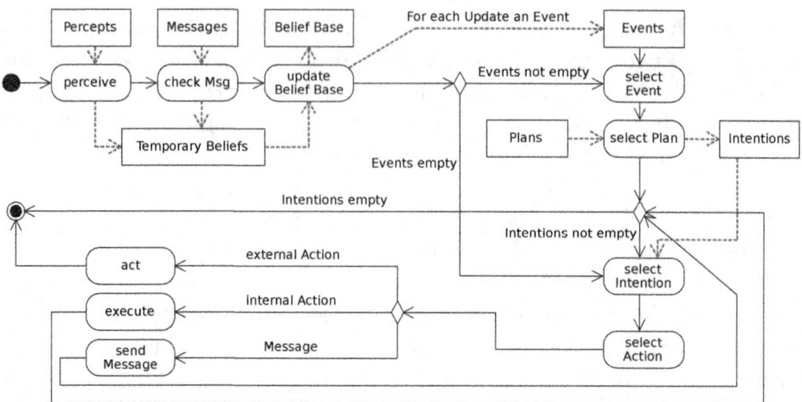

Fig. 9. BDI agent cycle: Activity diagram and data flow. Activity is red/dashed and data flow is black/solid.

the artifact is defined as a synchronous object, one can consider a variation of this object that implements a method for each of its offered capabilities and allows for direct method invocation.

Area: So far, we defined the main actors of a simulation but how are they connected among each other? An artifact does not have to be located inside a real simulation, i.e., it does not need a physical position (in contrast, most objects do need one). Therefore, we define an `area` as a logical or physical space (similar to the term *locality* introduced by [19]). There can be several areas, subareas, and overlapping areas. In the general case, agents can perform a random access on the environment, so the areas have to be synchronised and thus be available on all cores of the simulation platform. Within an area, we define some basic data structures and algorithms for path finding, etc. The most important issue, the connection of the non-synchronised agents with the synchronised areas is realised by the use of entities. Agents perceive the environment and execute actions by using the entities' sensors and effectors.

Entity: An entity can be seen as the physical body of an agent located inside an area. An agent can register to it, get the sensor data, and execute actions that possibly change the environment. The entity has some effectors and sensors that are easily replaceable by the simulation developer. Since such an entity represents the physical body of an agent and is meant to connect an agent with the environment, it has to be synchronised over all cores.

Institutions and Norms: For now, we provided a rudimentary model as a placeholder for future extension: An institution is an object that checks for norm violations and compliance. It operates as a monitor and is also responsible for sanctioning. But a developer can also decide to separate these two tasks. For the future, we are planning to focus only on three kinds of norms: obligations, permissions, and prohibitions. Additionally, we will focus on exogenous norms (events that occur in at least one area) and not on rules that affect the agent's mind, plans etc.

ObjectGroup: Finally, an `ObjectGroup` – as the name implies – defines a group of objects. It can be used to group agents, artifacts or other objects. Method calls on an `ObjectGroup` are forwarded to all group members, i.e., with a single method call, all corresponding methods (with the same type signature) of the group members are invoked. In order to reduce overhead and to avoid circular dependencies we only allow a flat list of members at the moment. However, if a hierarchy is needed, it can be easily implemented.

Agent-Model Layer Behaviour. So how does the overall behaviour look? Initially the simulation object creates a number of agents, areas, object groups, norms, etc., and changes the global properties in the three phases: `preTick`, `tick`, and `postTick`. It can delete and create new agents during runtime. But if the simulation developer decides to allow an agent to create another agent, this is consistent with the meta-model. The agent cycles are executed in each `tick` method. Also, the main procedures of artifacts, norms and areas are executed in this phase. The `preTick` is intended to be used as a preparation phase and the `postTick` phase for cleaning up.

Design Tradeoffs. As we have seen, the AML tries to facilitate the modelling of a parallel multiagent simulation by helping the developer deciding whether objects have to be synchronised or not. Of course, our classification might not fit each and every possible use case. But because of the flexibility of this layer, it is possible to easily adapt the AML to the specific domain.

Also, the layer cannot provide all of the concepts related to the agent-oriented paradigm. We tried to identify those which are of utmost importance and thus form something like the least common denominator of all agent-based simulations. If further concepts are needed, they can be easily added on demand or might be readily available if already implemented for another use case.

We mentioned that our BDI agent is restricted to perform at most one external action per simulation cycle, while it is allowed to perfom internal actions until it runs out of time. It will be easy to change this behaviour if it proves to be disadvantageous both in terms of agent or platform perfomance.

We provided a BDI agent in order to (1) show how to transfer an agent concept to the platform at this level of implementation and (2) ensure that the platform is easily usable if no specific kind of agent is needed. While our platform is open to use any agent concepts, it does not have to.

This section contains some heavy technical machinery and describes even some low level features that are usually not mentioned. But our main aim is to ensure scalability in an agent-based simulation system. In order to achieve that, we came up with some ideas (using Lua and how to combine it with BDI-like agents) that can only be understood and appreciated on the technical level that we have introduced in this section.

4 Evaluation: Cow Scenario

Scalability is an important requirement of the platform and therefore has to be evaluated early on. For that reason we chose the *cow scenario* from the MAPC as a first simulation that is realistic enough in the sense that it enforces the cooperation and coordination of agents. As it is already implemented for the *MASSim* platform, it can easily serve as a first benchmark.

In addition, we can test the suitability of the proposed meta-model and test a first implementation. Furthermore, the cow scenario contains already some elements of more complex scenarios (as in traffic simulation).

The cow scenario was used in MAPC from 2008 to 2010. The task for the agents is to herd cows to a corral. The simulated environment contains two corrals—one for each team—which serve as locations where cows should be directed to. It also contains fences that can be opened using switches. Agents only have a local view of their environment and can therefore only perceive the contents of the cells in a fixed vicinity around them. A screenshot of the visualisation as well as a short description of the scenario properties are depicted in Fig. 10. For a detailed description we refer to [4]. Using the proposed meta-model AML we can now implement the cow scenario in the following way.[3]

Fig. 11 shows how we derived the cow scenario classes from appropriate superclasses of the agent-model layer. The grid of the environment is implemented as an `Area`. Obstacles are defined by a matrix that blocks certain cells. The two corrals are subareas located inside the main area. Fences will become `Artifacts`. Similarly, we define a switch as an artifact that controls and changes the state (opened or closed) of a fence when getting activated. The cows are realised by a reactive agent that perceives the local environment and reacts upon it. For such a reactive agent the basic `Agent` definition together with an `entity` representing the cow are sufficient, while for the cowboy agents we need a more complex behaviour that facilitates coordination and cooperation. For this reason we use the `BDIAgent` (recall Fig. 9) class and create an `entity` for each cowboy agent. Furthermore, for each entity we create a simple `MoveEffector` that can be used by the entities to alter their position and a `ProximitySensor` providing the entities with their percepts. Additionally, we have to define the two teams by using the notion of an `ObjectGroup`. Finally, the `simulation` creates all agents and entities, assigns them to the two teams and creates the simulation world.

To conclude, this (very preliminary) evaluation shows that it is possible to express each aspect of the scenario using the predefined classes without the need to derive further ones from the synchronised or non-synchronised objects. (Nonetheless, doing so still remains a possibility). Regarding the suitability of Lua, it is an extremely flexible language that comes at the cost of a certain degree of usability: any newcomer needs some time to master it. But even then, having appropriate tools and methodologies that support the modelling process is a necessity to ensure an improved workflow and reduced error-proneness.

[3] The corresponding Lua code can be found in the appendix of [1].

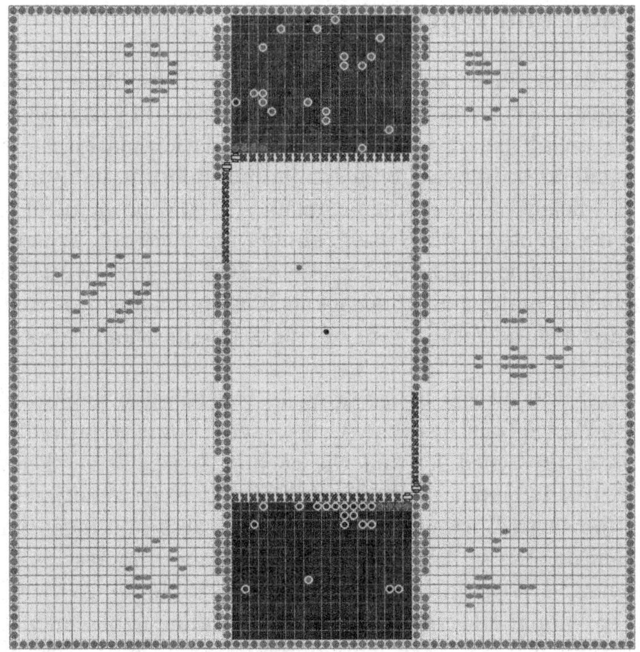

Fig. 10. The environment is a grid-like world. Agents (red (at top) and blue (at the bottom) circles) are steered by participants and can move between adjacent cells. Obstacles (green circles) block cells. Cows (brown circles) are steered by a flocking algorithm. Cows form herds on free areas, keeping distance to obstacles. If an agent approaches, cows get frightened and flee. Fences (x-shapes) can be opened by letting an agent stand on a reachable cell adjacent to the button (yellow rectangles). An agent cannot open a fence and then definitely go through it. Instead it needs help from an ally. Cows have to be pushed into the corrals (red and blue rectangles).

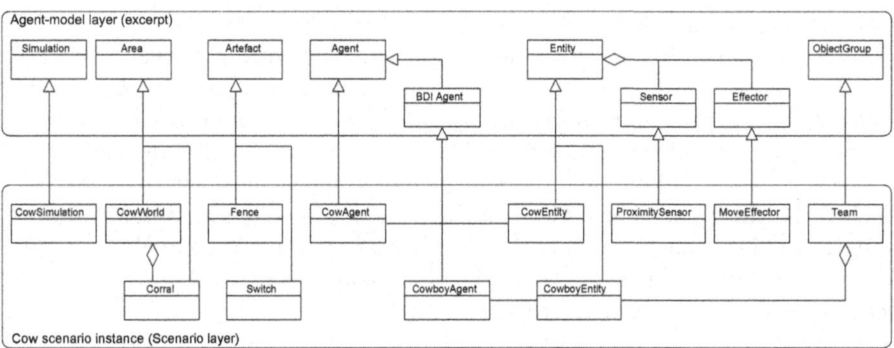

Fig. 11. Cow scenario: UML class diagram

5 Conclusion and Outlook

In this paper, we described ongoing work towards a distributed runtime platform for multiagent simulation. The main contributions of this paper are: (1) an analysis of the state of the art in agent-based simulation platforms, leading to a set of requirements to be imposed on a simulation platform, focusing on runtime scalability and efficient memory management; (2) the proposal of a novel architecture and design of the *MASeRaTi* simulation platform, bringing together a robust and highly efficient agent kernel (written in Lua) with a BDI agent interpreter including multiagent concepts such as communication and computational norms; and (3) an initial proof of concept realization featuring a simple application scenario.

The work presented in this paper provides the baseline for further research during which the *MASeRaTi* system will be extended and improved. Issues such as optimisation of the scheduler and the caching mechanisms sketched in the appendix of [1] will be explored in more detail. Also, systematic experimental evaluation will be carried out using more sophisticated and much larger traffic simulation scenarios. As the *ATSim* platform introduced in Section 2.1 can deal with a few thousand (vehicle) agents, we aim *MASeRaTi* to scale up to one million agents of comparable complexity (corresponding to the micro-simulation of multimodal traffic in a large city, including public transport, cars, pedestrians, city logistics, and infrastructure).

Simulation results obtained this way can be compared to the performance of other simulation frameworks using benchmark data; scalability can also be described by varying certain parameters (e.g. number / complexity of agents) and investigating the resulting degradation of performance. An idea for evaluating our optimisation approach (and in particular the adaptive mechanism for allocating agents to nodes of the runtime system) is the following: By modelling agents' preferences, capabilities, and interactions, a certain structure is imposed on the resulting MAS. We intend to evaluate the degree to which this structure can be mapped to the allocation of agents to the nodes of the distributed runtime system, by a (domain-independent!) entropy measure. We are also planning to consider different communication technologies like Bittorrent (`http://www.libtorrent.org/`) for the inter-object communication.

Given the three objectives in the abstract, our focus in this paper has been on the first two: scalability and efficient memory management, whereas we only touched the third, modelling. Here, one avenue of research is to develop appropriate modelling tools to support the *MASeRaTi* architecture. Finally, methodologies for simulation development will be explored, starting from established methodologies such as GAIA, Tropos, or ASPECS.

References

1. Ahlbrecht, T., Dix, J., Köster, M., Kraus, P., Müller, J.P.: A scalable runtime platform for multiagent-based simulation. Technical Report IfI-14-02, TU Clausthal (February 2014)

2. Ahlbrecht, T., Dix, J., Köster, M., Schlesinger, F.: Multi-Agent Programming Contest 2013. In: Cossentino, M., El Fallah Seghrouchni, A., Winikoff, M. (eds.) EMAS 2013. LNCS (LNAI), vol. 8245, pp. 292–318. Springer, Heidelberg (2013)
3. Behrens, T.: Towards Building Blocks for Agent-Oriented Programming. PhD thesis, Clausthal University of Technology (2012)
4. Behrens, T., Dastani, M., Dix, J., Köster, M., Novák, P.: The Multi-Agent Programming Contest from 2005-2010. Annals of Mathematics and Artificial Intelligence 59, 277–311 (2010)
5. Behrens, T.M., Dix, J., Dastani, M., Köster, M., Novák, P.: Technical Foundations of the Agent Contest 2008. Technical Report IfI-08-05, Clausthal University of Technology (December 2008)
6. Bordini, R.H., Dastani, M., Dix, J., El Fallah-Seghrouchni, A. (eds.): Multi-Agent Programming: Languages, Tools and Applications. Springer, Berlin (2009)
7. Bordini, R.H., Hübner, J.F., Wooldridge, M.: Programming multi-agent systems in AgentSpeak using Jason. Wiley & Sons (2007)
8. Chu, V.-H., Görmer, J., Müller, J.P.: ATSim: Combining AIMSUN and Jade for agent-based traffic simulation. In: Proceedings of the 14th Conference of the Spanish Association for Artificial Intelligence (CAEPIA), vol. 1, AEPIA (2011), Electronic Proceedings
9. Dávila, J., Uzcátegui, M.: Galatea: A multi-agent simulation platform. In: Proceedings of the International Conference on Modeling, Simulation and Neural Networks (2000)
10. Driel, M., Kraaijeveld, J., Shao, Z.K., van der Zon, R.: A Survey on MMOG System Architectures (2011)
11. Fiosins, M., Fiosina, J., Müller, J.P., Görmer, J.: Reconciling Strategic and Tactical Decision Making in Agent-oriented Simulation of Vehicles in Urban Traffic. In: Proceedings of the 4th International ICST Conference on Simulation Tools and Techniques, SIMUTools 2011, pp. 144–151. ICST (Institute for Computer Sciences, Social-Informatics and Telecommunications Engineering), Brussels (2011)
12. Fiosins, M., Fiosina, J., Müller, J.P., Görmer, J.: Agent-Based Integrated Decision Making for Autonomous Vehicles in Urban Traffic. In: Demazeau, Y., Pechoucek, M., Corchado, J.M., Perez, J.B. (eds.) Adv. on Prac. Appl. of Agents and Mult. Sys. AISC, vol. 88, pp. 173–178. Springer, Heidelberg (2011)
13. Garro, A., Russo, W.: easyABMS: A domain-expert oriented methodology for agent-based modeling and simulation. Simulation Modelling Practice and Theory 18(10), 1453–1467 (2010)
14. Gehrke, J.D., Ober-Blöbaum, C.: Multiagent-based Logistics Simulation with PlaSMA. In: Informatik 2007 - Informatik trifft Logistik, Band 1. Beiträge der 37. Jahrestagung der Gesellschaft für Informatik, pp. 416–419. Technologie-Zentrum Informatik (2007)
15. Ghorbani, A., Bots, P.W.G., Dignum, V., Dijkema, G.P.J.: MAIA: A Framework for Developing Agent-Based Social Simulations. J. Artificial Societies and Social Simulation 16(2) (2013)
16. Görmer, J., Müller, J.P.: Group Coordination for Agent-Oriented Urban Traffic Management. In: Demazeau, Y., Müller, J.P., Rodríguez, J.M.C., Pérez, J.B. (eds.) Advances on PAAMS. AISC, vol. 155, pp. 245–248. Springer, Heidelberg (2012)
17. Helbing, D., Hennecke, A., Shvetsov, V., Treiber, M.: MASTER: Macroscopic traffic simulation based on a gas-kinetic, non-local traffic model. Transportation Research Part B: Methodological 35(2), 183–211 (2001)
18. Hill, M.D., Marty, M.R.: Amdahl's Law in the Multicore Era. Computer 41(7), 33–38 (2008)

19. Huhn, M., Müller, J.P., Görmer, J., Homoceanu, G., Le, N.-T., Märtin, L., Mumme, C., Schulz, C., Pinkwart, N., Müller-Schloer, C.: Autonomous agents in organized localities regulated by institutions. In: 2011 Proceedings of the 5th IEEE International Conference on Digital Ecosystems and Technologies (DEST), pp. 54–61 (May 2011)
20. Ierusalimschy, R.: Programming with multiple paradigms in lua. In: Escobar, S. (ed.) WFLP 2009. LNCS, vol. 5979, pp. 1–12. Springer, Heidelberg (2010)
21. Klügl, F., Davidsson, P.: AMASON: Abstract Meta-model for Agent-Based SimulatiON. In: Klusch, M., Thimm, M., Paprzycki, M. (eds.) MATES 2013. LNCS, vol. 8076, pp. 101–114. Springer, Heidelberg (2013)
22. Klügl, F., Puppe, F.: The Multi-Agent Simulation Environment SeSAm. In: Kleine Büning, H. (ed.) Proceedings of Simulation in Knowledge-based Systems, Universität Paderborn, Reihe Informatik, Universität Paderborn, Universität Paderborn (April 1998)
23. Krajzewicz, D., Hertkorn, G., Rössel, C., Wagner, P.: Sumo (simulation of urban mobility). In: Proc. of the 4th Middle East Symposium on Simulation and Modelling, pp. 183–187 (2002)
24. Kuhl, F., Dahmann, J., Weatherly, R.: Creating computer simulation systems: An introduction to the high level architecture. Prentice Hall PTR Englewood Cliffs, Upper Saddle River (2000)
25. Ierusalimschy, R., de Figueiredo, L.H., Celes, W.: Lua Programming Gems. Roberto Ierusalimschy (2008)
26. Luke, S., Cioffi-Revilla, C., Panait, L., Sullivan, K.: Mason: A new multi-agent simulation toolkit. In: Proceedings of the 2004 SwarmFest Workshop, vol. 8 (2004)
27. Papageorgiou, M., Blosseville, J.-M., Hadj-Salem, H.: Modelling and real-time control of traffic flow on the southern part of Boulevard Peripherique in Paris: Part I: Modelling. Transportation Research Part A: General 24(5), 345–359 (1990)
28. Shoham, Y.: Agent-Oriented Programming. Artificial Intelligence 60(1), 51–92 (1993)
29. Subrahmanian, V.S., Bonatti, P., Dix, J., Eiter, T., Kraus, S., Özcan, F., Ross, R.: Heterogenous Active Agents. MIT Press (2000)
30. Tisue, S., Wilensky, U.: NetLogo: A simple environment for modeling complexity. In: International Conference on Complex Systems, pp. 16–21 (2004)
31. Weiss, G. (ed.): Multiagent systems. MIT-Press (2013)
32. Wooldridge, M.J.: An Introduction to MultiAgent Systems (2009)

Security Games in the Field: Deployments on a Transit System

Francesco M. Delle Fave[1], Matthew Brown[1], Chao Zhang[1], Eric Shieh[1], Albert Xin Jiang[1], Heather Rosoff[1], Milind Tambe[1], and John P. Sullivan[2]

[1] University of Southern California
CA 90049, Los Angeles, USA
{dellefav,matthew.a.brown,zhan661,eshieh,jiangx,rosoff,tambe}@usc.edu
http://teamcore.usc.edu/default.html

[2] Los Angeles County Sheriff's Department
CA 91754, Los Angeles, USA
jpsulliv@lasd.org

Abstract. This paper proposes the Multi-Operation Patrol Scheduling System (MOPSS), a new system to generate patrols for transit system. MOPSS is based on five contributions. First, MOPSS is the first system to use three fundamentally different adversary models for the threats of fare evasion, terrorism and crime, generating three significantly different types of patrol schedule. Second, to handle uncertain interruptions in the execution of patrol schedules, MOPSS uses Markov decision processes (MDPs) in its scheduling. Third, MOPSS is the first system to account for joint activities between multiple resources, by employing the well known SMART security game model that tackles coordination between defender's resources. Fourth, we are also the first to deploy a new *Opportunistic Security Game* model, where the adversary, a criminal, makes opportunistic decisions on when and where to commit crimes. Our fifth, and most important, contribution is the evaluation of MOPSS via real-world deployments, providing data from security games in the field.

Keywords: Security, Game-theory, Real-world deployment.

1 Introduction

Research in Stackelberg security games has led to several real-world deployments to aid security at ports, airports and air transportation [16]. Such systems generate unpredictable security allocations (e.g., patrols and checkpoints), while carefully weighing each potential target, considering the scarcity of defender resources and the adversary's response. In a Stackelberg security game, the defender (e.g., the security agency) commits to her strategy first, taking into

F. Dalpiaz et al. (Eds.): EMAS 2014, LNAI 8758, pp. 103–126, 2014.

account the attacker's (e.g., a terrorist's) ability to conduct surveillance before launching his attack [5,6].

Among the different applications of security games, the problem of patrolling a transit system has gathered significant interest [9,17]. Due to the large volume of people using it every day, a transit system is a key target for illegal activities such as fare evasion (FE), terrorism (CT) and crime (CR). The security of such a system then, poses a number of challenges. The first challenge is multi-operation patrolling. Whereas most previous work in security games has focused on single threats which could be represented with a single adversary model (e.g., PROTECT, TRUSTS and IRIS)[16], the comprehensive security of a transit system requires different specialized security responses against three threats (FE, CT and CR). The second challenge is execution uncertainty. Security resources are often interrupted during their patrols (e.g., to provide assistance or arrest a suspect). Thus, traditional patrol schedules are often difficult to complete. Current research in security games has proposed the use of Markov decision processes (MDPs) to plan patrols under uncertainty [9]. However, such schedules were not actually deployed in the field, therefore, their real effectiveness has yet to be verified in the real-world. The fourth challenge is accounting for joint activities. In CT patrolling, security resources, such as explosive detective canine (EK9) teams, often patrol train lines in cooperation with other resources. By doing so, their effectiveness is increased. Recently, [14] proposed a new security game model, SMART (*Security games with Multiple coordinated Activities and Resources that are Time-dependent*), that *explicitly* represents jointly coordinated activities between defender's resources. [14]. Yet, similarly to the work of [9] discussed earlier, this framework has still not been deployed in the real-world. The fourth challenge is crime. Literature in criminology describes criminals as opportunistic decision makers [15]. At a specific location, they decide whether to commit a crime based on available opportunities and on the presence (or lack thereof) of security officers. Thus far, this type of adversary—less strategic in planning and more flexible in executing multiple attackes— has not been addressed in previous work, which has focused on strategic single shot attackers [16].

The fifth and most important challenge is that, despite earlier attempts [13], the actual evaluation of the deployed security games applications in the field is still a major open challenge. The reasons are twofold. First, previous applications focused on counter-terrorism, therefore controlled experiments against real adversaries in the field were not feasible. Second, the number of practical constraints related to real-world deployments limited the ability of researchers to conduct head-to-head comparisons

To address these challenges, this paper introduces five major contributions. Our first contribution is MOPSS, the first Multi-Operation Patrol Scheduling System for patrolling a train line. MOPSS provides an important insight: the multiple threats (FE, CT and CR) in a transit system require such fundamentally different adversary models that they do not fit into state-of-the-art multi-objective or Bayesian security game models suggested earlier [18,4]. Instead, in MOPSS each of the three threats is modeled as a separate game with its own adversary model. These three game formulations provide security for the same transit system, require data from the same transit system as input, use smart-phones to display the schedules and share several algorithmic insights. Our second contribution addresses execution uncertainty. We deployed MDP-based patrol schedules in the field, and used sampling-based cross-validation to handle model uncertainty in such MDPs [8]. Similarly, our third contribution is the deployment of coordinated schedules for CT patrolling. We incorporate the framework in [14] to MOPSS, and use it to generate patrols for counter-terrorism. Fourth, we address crime patrolling. Our contribution is the first ever deployment of opportunistic security games (OSGs). We model criminals as opportunistic players who decide whether to commit a crime at a station based on two factors, the presence of defender resources and the opportunities for crime at the station.

Our fourth contribution is the real world evaluation of MOPSS. This evaluation constitutes the largest scale evaluation of security games in the field in terms of duration and number of security officials deployed. As far as we know, it constitutes the *first* evaluation of algorithmic game theory in the field at such a scale. We carefully evaluated each component of MOPSS (FE, CT and CR) by designing and running field experiments. In the context of fare evasion, we ran a 21-day experiment, where we compared schedules generated using MOPSS against competing schedules comprised of a random scheduler augmented with officers providing real-time knowledge of the current situation. Our results show that our schedules led to statistically significant improvements over the competing schedules, despite the fact that the latter were improved with real-time knowledge. For counter-terrorism, we organized a full-scale exercise (FSE), in which 80 security officers (divided into 14 teams) patrolled 10 stations of a metro line for 12 hours. The purpose of the exercise was a head-to-head comparison of the MOPSS game-theoretic scheduler against humans. The comparison was in terms of the schedule generation process, as well as provide a thorough evaluation of the performance of both schedules as conducted by a number of security experts. Our results show that MOPSS game-theoretic schedules were able to perform at least equivalently to (and in fact better than those) generated by human schedulers. Finally, we ran a two-day proof-of-concept experiment on crime where two teams of officers patrolled 14 stations of a train line for two hours. Our results validate our OSG model in the real world, thus showing its potential to combat crime.

2 Transit Line Patrolling

The Los Angeles Sheriff's Department (LASD), the security agency responsible for the security of the Los Angeles Metro System (LA Metro), requested a multi-operation patrol scheduling system to improve and facilitate the comprehensive security of each train line. This system should generate randomized schedules for three different operations each addressing a fundamentally different threat:

Fare Evasion Patrols (FE): This type of patrol covers both the trains and the stations of a train line. The purpose is to capture as many fare evaders as possible to improve the perception of order within an area. Thus, this type of patrolling should favor the locations with a large volume of riders because it would lead to a large number of fare evaders caught.

Counter-Terrorism Patrols (CT): This type of patrol covers the stations of a train line. Each station concentrates a large number of people at a specific place and time. In addition, in Los Angeles, several stations are located within key economic and cultural areas of the city (e.g., tourist locations, business and financial districts). Thus, the effects on society of any successful attack on the metro system would be catastrophic. Terrorists are then strategic adversaries who carefully study the weaknesses of a train line before committing an attack. To optimize security, this type of patrol should cover the different stations while favoring the stations either with large passenger volume and/or located in key areas.

Crime: This type of patrol covers the stations of a train line. Crimes can be of different types including robbery, assaults and drug dealing. Each of this crimes is a symptom that the train line's security is not sufficient. In addition, criminals behave differently than terrorists or fare evaders. They are opportunistic decision makers, they randomly traverse a train line, moving from station to station, seeking opportunities for crime (e.g., riders with smart-phones) [2,15]. The key purpose of crime patrolling is then to patrol each of these stations, while favoring the stations representing "hot-spots" for crime (i.e., the most attractive stations from a criminal's perspective).

Given the three operations defined above, the LASD computes patrol schedules, manually, on a daily basis. This task, however, introduces a significant cognitive burden for the human expert schedulers. Thus, to generate more effective schedules in a timely fashion, we introduce MOPSS, described in the next section.

3 MOPSS

MOPSS addresses the *global* security of a transit system. Hence, it presents two key advantages for the LASD. First, it can be used to generate specialized patrols for substantially different threats and second it concentrates *all* the information relevant to the comprehensive security of each transit line (e.g., crime and ridership statistics). MOPSS is comprised of a centralized planner and a smart-phone application (shown as a demonstration in [11]). The system is shown in Figure 1. The core of MOPSS consits of the three game modules. Each module generates patrols for one operation (FE, CT or CR). Each operation deals with a fundamentally different adversary model (fare evaders, terrorists or criminals), therefore each operation is modeled as a different two-player security game (the defender's resources represent the security officers). Each module takes as input the information about the requested patrol (i.e., the number of officers, the starting time and the duration) and connects to a database to get the data necessary

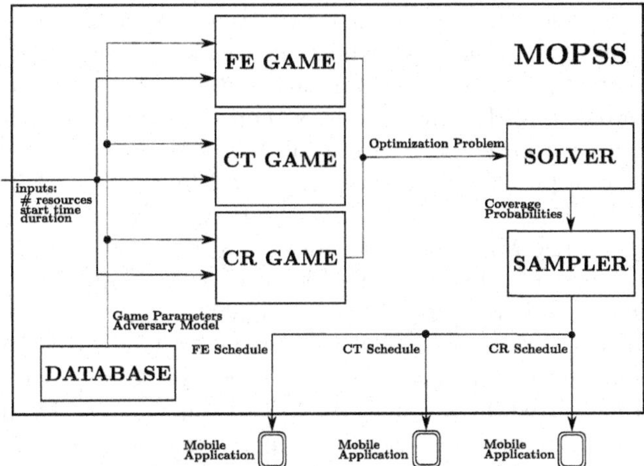

Fig. 1. The MOPSS system

to build the security game model. Each game is cast as an optimization problem and sent to the SOLVER which contains three algorithms, one for each game [14,20,9]. Once the game is solved, the defender's mixed strategy is sent to the SAMPLER to produce the schedule which is uploaded into the application.

3.1 Fare Evasion Module

This module aims to generate the defender's (i.e., security officers') mixed strategies against fare evaders [9]. The idea is to use such strategy to derive patrol schedules that randomly favor the trains and the stations with a large volume of riders. Fare evaders are modeled as daily riders based on statistics.

The key requirement of fare evasion patrolling is to be able to address execution uncertainty. To do so, in the FE module, the mixed strategy for each defender resource i is determined by an MDP denoted by a tuple $\langle S_i, A_i, T_i, R_i \rangle$ where: (i) S_i is a finite set of states ($s_i = (l, \tau)$ where l is a train or a station and τ is the time step); (ii) A_i is a set of two actions: perform a train or a station check (equivalently do a train or a station check) and (iii) $T_i(s_i, a_i, s_i')$ is the transition probability which can model execution uncertainty such as an officer being delayed while trying to conduct a fare check (e.g., due to arrests) and (iv) R_i is the immediate reward for transition (s_i, a_i, s_i'). Although this reward could potentially model more complex domains, it is unrelated to the game-theoretic payoffs, and is not considered in the remainder of this work.

The FE game is then represented as a two player Bayesian zero-sum game (see [9] for the definition of the linear program). Given a resource i and rider $\lambda \in \Lambda$ (i.e., defined by their daily itinerary in the train line), the objective is to maximize the expected utility of the defender, defined as $\max \sum_{\lambda \in \Lambda} p_\lambda u_\lambda$ where each utility u_λ is the defender's payoff against passenger type λ, which has a prior p_λ calculated using ridership statistics (calculated using ridership statistics). Each u_λ is calculated by the constraint $u_\lambda \leq \mathbf{x}^T U_\lambda \mathbf{e}_\alpha \forall \lambda, \alpha$ where each utility

$U_\lambda(s_i, a_i, s'_i, \alpha)$ represents the payoff that resource i will get for executing action a_i in state s_i and ending up in s'_i, while the attacker plays action α (defined by the base vector $\mathbf{e}_\alpha$) and $\mathbf{x}$ is the marginal probability that the resource will actually go from s_i to s'_i. In other words, $\mathbf{x}$ represents the probability that the officer will overlap with a fare evader of type λ playing action α.

The optimization problem defined above is used by the SOLVER module to produce a mixed strategy represented as a Markov policy π_i. The SAMPLER then generates a single MDP patrol schedule that is loaded onto the handheld smartphone. An example of such a schedule is shown in Figure 2(a). The figure shows the schedule as it is visualized by the mobile application. The schedule contains two actions: train checks and station checks. Given that there is now a full MDP policy on the smartphone, a schedule can be updated whenever a security officer is delayed, by pushing the ">" button shown in Figure 2(a).

We next turn to instantiating the parameters in this game model for deployment. Fortunately, given fixed train fares and penalties for fare evasion, populating the payoff matrices is straightforward. Furthermore, via observations, we were able to set the transition function T_i. However, the delay length, whenever an office was interrupted, seemed to vary significantly, and modeling this variability became important. A continuous-time MDP or modeling multiple fine-grained delays are both extremely expensive. As a practical compromise we use a model considering a single delay whose value is chosen via cross-validation [8]. First, we randomly generate N MDPs, each of which assumes that resource i can experience delays of five different lengths: 6, 12, 18, 24 and 30 minutes (any delay longer than 30 minutes is considered to be beyond repair and a new schedule is generated). Second, we solve each MDP and obtain N Markov policies π_i^k corresponding to each MDP^k which we cross validate by running 100000 Monte Carlo simulations. In each simulation, we sample one strategy for the defender and calculate the resulting expected utility against all N MDPs. Finally, we pick the policy that maximizes the minimum. If the officer gets into a state not directly represented in the MDP, we pick the next available state at their current action.

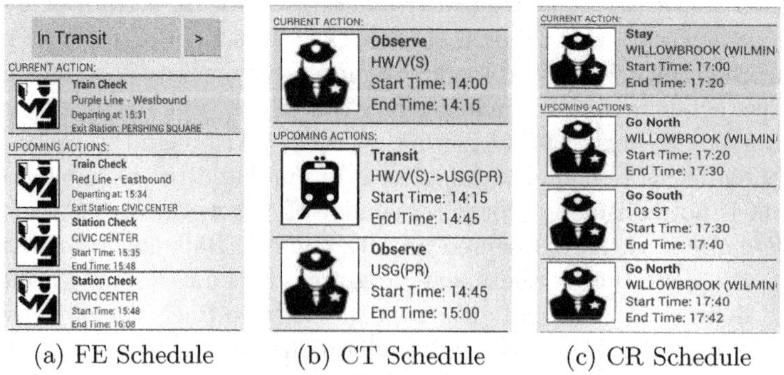

(a) FE Schedule (b) CT Schedule (c) CR Schedule

Fig. 2. Three schedules for each threat of a transit system

3.2 Counter Terrorism Module

The counter-terrorism module aims to generate a defender mixed strategy that can be used to produce schedules that deter terrorists from attacking the stations of a train line [14]. Since stations are often composed of multiple levels, these schedules should then randomly patrol each of these stations while taking the levels into account and while favoring the most important stations. Terrorists are modeled as strategic adversaries who carefully observe the security of a train line before executing an attack.

The key requirement of CT patrolling is to represent joint activities. We achieve this by incorporating the SMART problem framework defined in [14] in the CT component of MOPSS. A SMART problem is a Security Game [10] such that each target $t \in T$ is assigned a reward $U_d^c(t)$ and a penalty $U_d^u(t)$ if t is covered and uncovered by a defender's resource. Similarly, each target is assigned a reward $U_a^c(t)$ and a penalty $U_a^u(t)$ for the attacker. The defender has a set of R resources. Each resource chooses an activity from the set $\mathcal{A} = \{\alpha_1, \alpha_2, \ldots \alpha_K\}$ for each target $t \in T$. Each resource $r \in R$ is assigned a graph $G_r = (T, E_r)$, where the set of vertices T represents the set of targets to patrol and the set of edges E_r represents the connectivity between such targets. Each edge $e \in E_r$ is assigned a time value $\tau(e)$ representing the time that it takes to one defender resource r to traverse e.

The attacker's pure strategy space is the set of all targets, T. A pure strategy for the defender is a set of routes, one route X_i for each resource. Each route is defined as a sequence of activities α, conducted at a specific target t with specific duration γ. Joint activities are then represented when there exists two routes X_i and X_j such that $t_i = t_j$ and $|\gamma_i - \gamma_j| \leq W$, i.e. when two activities of two different resources overlap in space and time (within a time window W). For each activity α_i, $\texttt{eff}(\alpha_i)$ represents the individual effectiveness of the activity α_i, which ranges from 0% to 100%, and measures the probability that the defender will be able to successfully prevent an attack on target t. The effectiveness of the joint activity $\langle \alpha_i, \alpha_j \rangle$ is defined as $\texttt{eff}(\alpha_i, \alpha_j)$.

Given these parameters, the expected utilities $U_d(\mathbf{P}_i, t)$ and $U_a(\mathbf{P}_i, t)$ for both players, when the defender is conducting pure strategy $\mathbf{P}_i$ (defined as a joint pure strategy for multiple defender resources), and when the attacker chooses to attack target t is given as follows:

$$\omega_t(\mathbf{P}_i) = \max_{\substack{(t,\alpha,\gamma)\in\mathbf{P}_i \\ \{(t,\alpha_l,\gamma_l),(t,\alpha_m,\gamma_m)\}\subseteq\mathbf{P}_i, |\gamma_l-\gamma_m|\leq W}} \{\texttt{eff}(\alpha), \texttt{eff}(\alpha_l, \alpha_m)\} \tag{1}$$

$$U_d(\mathbf{P}_i, t) = \omega_t(\mathbf{P}_i) U_d^c(t) + (1 - \omega_t(\mathbf{P}_i)) U_d^u(t) \tag{2}$$

$$U_a(\mathbf{P}_i, t) = \omega_t(\mathbf{P}_i) U_a^c(t) + (1 - \omega_t(\mathbf{P}_i)) U_a^u(t) \tag{3}$$

Here $\omega_t(\mathbf{P}_i)$ defined in Equation (1) represents the *effective coverage* of the defender on target t when executing pure strategy $\mathbf{P}_i$.

To solve this problem, we use SMART$_H$, a branch-and-price, heuristic approach, which we incorporate in the SOLVER component of MOPSS. SMART$_H$ is based on a branch-and-price framework, it constructs a branch-and-bound tree, where for each leaf of the tree, the attacker's target is fixed to a different t'. Due to the exponential number of defender pure strategies, the best defender mixed strategy is determined using *column generation*, which is composed of a *master* and *slave* procedure, where the slave iteratively adds a new column (defender strategy) to the master. The objective of the pricing component is to find the best defender mixed strategy $\mathbf{x}$ at that leaf, such that *the best response of the attacker* to $\mathbf{x}$ is to attack target t'. The structure of the algorithm is illustrated in Figure 3. In the figure, the master solves the non-zero-sum game to get a defender mixed strategy over a small subset of joint patrol pure strategies. After solving the master problem, the duals are retrieved and used as inputs for the slave. The purpose of the slave is to generate a pure strategy which is then added to the master and the entire process is iterated until the optimal solution is found.

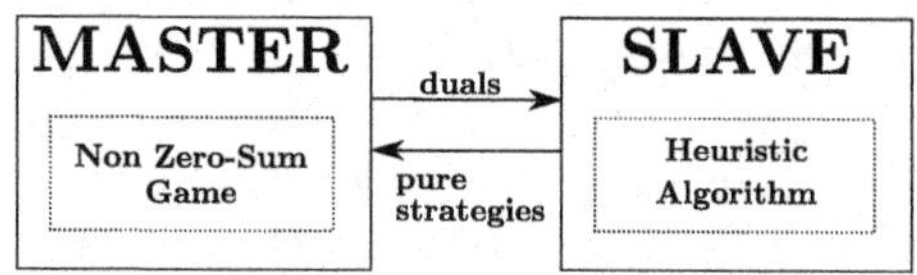

Fig. 3. The column generation algorithm

An example counter-terrorism schedule, as visualized by the mobile application, is shown in Figure 2(b). The schedule describes two actions, observe (patrol a station) and transit (go to a station) each with a specific time and duration. The key challenge to deploy CT schedules is to define an accurate SMART problem instance to accurately encompass the real-world problem. To achieve this, we had to define three types of features. First, we had to define the payoffs of the game[1]. We defined the payoffs for each target (32 in total) in discussions with security experts from the LASD. Each set of payoffs for each station was based on the number of people using the station every day and by the economic impact that losing this station would have on the city. The different levels of a single station had slightly different payoffs which were based on the number of persons present at each specific level of the station every weekday. Second, we had to define the defender different resources, i.e., the type of teams participating to the experiment, which we will refer to as type 1 to type 5[2]. Third, we had to define the single and joint effectiveness for both the observe and transit actions. All Transit actions were given a 0 effectiveness, since moving from one station to another (i.e., riding the trains or taking the car) will not have any effect on the security of the stations. Most teams were assigned the same positive individual effectiveness of 0.7, except one Type 3 which has a greater individual effectiveness because it is composed of officers from multiple agencies carrying

[1] We are not able to reveal the value of these payoffs due to an agreement with the LASD.

[2] The real name of each type is omitted as requested by the agencies participating to the FSE.

heavy weapons. Resources of types 1, 2 and 3 typically work alone. Hence, to define their effectiveness values, their individual effectiveness is positive while their joint effectiveness is null (any joint effectiveness value below 0.7 would induce the same type of behavior, but we chose 0 since it is a clear indicator of the type of behavior that we want to obtain). Resources of type 4 are assigned a joint effectiveness greater then their individual effectiveness because they can perform all type of activites, but, typically, they prefer joint over individual activities. In contrast, resources of type 5 typically work only in cooperation with other teams, therefore they are assigned a null individual effectiveness and a positive joint effectiveness of 0.75.

3.3 Crime Module

The crime module aims to generate a defender mixed strategy to prevent crime on a train line. The idea is to generate schedules that take criminal behavior into account and attempt to predict the stations that are more likely to be affected by crime. Crime statistics are used to characterize the behavior of criminals and the attractiveness that they attribute to each station of the train line. The key difference with the previous modules is that criminals behave differently than fare evaders and terrorists. They are less strategic in planning crimes and more flexible in committing them than is assumed in a Stackelberg game. They opportunistically and repeatedly seek targets and react to real-time information at execution-time, rather than strategically planning their crimes in advance.

Crime schedules are computed using an OSG [20]. An OSG is similar to a Stackelberg game in that the defender commits to a patrol strategy first, after which the criminal chooses the station(s) to attack given their belief about the defender's deployment. In an OSG, the defender's actions are computed using a Markov chain, which assigns probabilities for how the defender should move through the train line. The criminal's behavior is defined by a quantal-biased random walk, i.e., the next station to visit for potentially committing a crime is determined according the quantal response model [16]. This model takes as input information the attractiveness $Att(i)$ of each station i and the criminal's belief about the defender's strategy which is updated using real-time observations. Station attractiveness is a measure based on crime statistics about the availability of opportunities for committing crime as well as how likely criminals are to seize such opportunities. The behavior models for both the defender and the criminal are combined to form a Markov chain with transition matrix T_s, which along with the rewards to the defender, define an OSG that can be solved to generate an optimal defender strategy. To solve an OSG, we iteratively calculate the defender expected utility V_d over all the possible states of the Markov chain for a number of crime opportunities k as follows:

$$\begin{aligned} Obj &= \lim_{K \to \infty} \sum_{k=0}^{K} V_d(k+1) \\ &= \mathbf{r}_d \cdot (I - (1-\alpha)T_s)^{-1} \mathbf{X}_1, \end{aligned} \tag{4}$$

where R_d is a vector defining the utility of each state of the Markov chain in terms of the payoff u_d for the defender and the attractiveness $Att(i)$; I is the identity matrix; α is the probability of leaving the train line after an attack and X_1 is the initial coverage probability over all the possible states of the Markov chain. By maximizing Obj (i.e., minimizing the total amount of crime in the metro), we obtain a transition matrix T_s^*. This matrix is then used to compute the defender's Markov strategy π.

The maximization of Equation 4 is a nonlinear optimization problem. Therefore, to scale up to the number of states necessary to represent a real train line we use the Compact OPportunistic security game State algorithm (COPS) [20] in the SOLVER module. COPS returns a number of coverage probabilities for the different stations of the train line. These are then sent to the SAMPLER module which generates a schedule. An example of a schedule for crime patrolling is shown in Figure 2(c). It describes three actions, go north (i.e., take the next northbound train), go south (i.e., take the next southbound train) and stay (i.e., patrol a specific station).

To deploy crime schedules, two key challenges had to be addressed. The first challenge deals with defining of the attractiveness parameter. In our work, we define the attractiveness $Att(i)$ of station i following the statistical model presented in [15]. Formally, $Att(i) = 1 - \exp^{-aN(i)}$, where $N(i)$ is the number of past crimes at station i (based on actual crime statistics received from the LASD) and a is a weighting coefficient. The second challenge is the parameterization of the criminal behavior model, which consists of defining the quantal-biased random walk. In our crime tests (Section 4.3), we defined the criminal behavior in collaboration with both security agencies and criminologists.

4 Real World Evaluation

In collaboration with the Los Angeles Sheriff's Department (LASD), we designed three types of real world tests, one for each of the three operations defined in Section 2. Each of these tests allows us to evaluate different aspects of game-theoretic patrolling. This evaluation introduces the following novelties: (i) in fare evasion, we present the first real world deployment of game-theoretic schedules and analyze their performance against real adversaries (fare evaders); similarly, (ii) in counter-terrorism, we present the first real world head-to-head comparison between game-theoretic and human generated schedules. Finally, (iii) in crime, we introduce the first deployment of OSGs. The crime tests provide the first real world data showing the benefits of game-theoretic scheduling when facing opportunistic attackers.

4.1 Fare Evasion Experiment

This experiment took place over 21 days during the months of July and August 2013. The organization of the experiment (e.g., train the security officers, design and organize the experiment in collaboration with the LASD) required approximately two weeks. This experiment had two key purposes. The first was to validate the MDP model of the Fare Evasion module (Section 3.1) in the real world. The second was to run a head-to-head comparison between the game-theoretic approach calculated using MOPSS and a Markov policy that takes execution uncertainty into account, but that assign actions based on a uniform random probability. The uniform random Markov strategy (Markov UR) assigns, given a state $s \in S_i$ of the MDP defined in Section 3.1, a uniform probability to all the actions taken in s leading to another state $s \in S_i$. It was chosen because it constitutes is the approach that security agencies adopt when they are not using a game-theoretic approach for randomization. This section discusses the setup of the experiment and the results that we obtained.

Fig. 4. The map of the blue line of the LA Metro

Experiment Setup. The fare evasion experiment took place on the Blue line of the LA Metro system (see Figure 4 for the map of the metro line). Other lines could not be tested, because the LASD only allowed us to use our strategies on the Blue line during our real-world test. This line consists of 22 different stations and is one of the biggest lines in the LA Metro system. It was selected by the LASD, which helped to organize the experiment (e.g., assign security officers and patrol times).

Each day, a team of two security officers (see Figure 5), was randomly selected by the LASD, to patrol the line for a duration of at most 120 minutes. Patrols were run during both the morning and the afternoon. Some days the tests ended early due to the officers being reassigned. One of the two officers acted as the leader of the team: he was given the smartphone, he had to read the schedule

Fig. 5. Two security officers performing fare checks on a train

to the other officers, collect the data and eventually update it whenever a delay occurred. An update could be made either during a station-check, i.e., when checking riders at a station, or during a train-check, i.e., when checking riders on the coach of a train. In the latter case, the officers were required to leave the train at the next station to request an update. This was required because the Markov strategy is defined over each state of the MDP (i.e., station, time). Thus any new strategy has to be sampled from a specific state. Every week the team was provided with one of two types of schedules:

Game-theoretic schedules (GT): This type of schedule was generated using MOPSS' fare evasion component (Section 3.1).

Markov UR schedules (UR): This type of schedule was generated by modeling the problem as an MDP. However, the corresponding Markov strategy π_{s_i,a_i}, for each state s_i and action a_i was calculated assuming a uniform probability distribution.

The officers were not told which schedule they were using as not to bias their performance. Before the experiment, we anticipated that the officers might view some of the schedules as leading to low performance in terms of catching very few fare evaders. In such situation, the officers, in order to avoid poor performance, might end up voluntarily deviating from their given schedules to reach a better location because they were unsatisfied with the current one. In anticipation of such voluntary deviations, we augmented both the game-theoretic and UR schedules with the ability to perform updates. More specifically, we allowed the officers to request VOLUNTARY or INVOLUNTARY updates. VOLUNTARY updates consisted of the officers updating the current schedule because in their opinion, the current specified action was not fruitful as a venue to check fares. Officers were allowed to choose a new location that they considered more fruitful for catching fare evaders and request a new schedule from there. INVOLUNTARY updates consisted of the officers requesting a new schedule because they were delayed (e.g., from issuing citations or arresting a suspect) and were unable to perform the next action on their schedule. This type of update could be requested *anytime* an officer was delayed. As we will see below the officers used VOLUNTARY updates almost every day with the UR schedules, but never in the GT schedules.

Table 1. Patrol duration over each of the 21 days

	D1	D2	D3	D4	D5	D6	D7	D8	D9	D10	D11	total
GT	60	60	90	60	90	10	90	110	90	90	105	855
UR	60	60	60	60	60	75	100	100	100	90		765

Finally, it is important to notice that given the duration of our experiment, the game-theoretic schedules are essentially testing a maximin strategy. As discussed in Section 3.1, the fare evasion component computes a Stackelberg strategy, a strategy based on the assumption that the riders will conduct surveillance and observe the defender's mixed strategy. However, considering only 21 days of patrol whereby the officers could only patrol less than few hours per day, either in the morning or the afternoon, we cannot assume that the riders had sufficient time to conduct accurate surveillance, observe the mixed strategy and best respond to it. Nonetheless, the FE component in Section 3.1 solves a zero-sum game for which a Stackelberg equilibrium and the maximin strategy are known to be equivalent [19]. Thus, since the maximin strategy provides a guaranteed level of defender utility without making any assumption on the adversary's surveillance of the defender's mixed strategy, these experiments compare the benefit of using a maximin strategy against other (non-game-theoretic) approaches for generating patrol schedules.

Results. During the 21 weekdays of our experiments, we were able to run GT schedules for 11 days of testing while UR schedules were deployed for 10 days, resulting in 855 and 765 patrol minutes, respectively. The schedules were compared using two different metrics. First, we counted the number of passengers checked and the number of captures at the end of each patrol. The captures were defined as the sum of the number of warnings, citations, and arrests. Passengers without a valid ticket could be given a warning or cited for a violation on the discretion of the officer. This metric was chosen because it would allow us to measure the performance of each schedule in the real world. Second, we counted the number of times that the update function was used voluntarily and involuntarily. While involuntary updates helped determine the value of using MDPs as discussed below, voluntary updates measured the human (officer) perception of quality of the schedules – the more such voluntary updates, the more the officers were dissatisfied with their given action. Table 1 shows the duration of each day of patrol for both GT and UR schedules[3].

As shown in the table, the actual duration of a daily patrol was often different over the 21 days of the experiment, for both GT and UR schedules. For this reason, providing a comparison normalized over the days of the experiment was impossible. However, most of the days, we were able to collect data for multiples

[3] As shown in Table 1, each day of patrol correspond to a 2-day test where GT schedules were tested on the first day and UR schedules were tested on the second, both at identical times.

Table 2. Number of INVOLUNTARY (delays) deviations for each day of patrol

	D1	D2	D3	D4	D5	D6	D7	D8	D9	D10	D11	total
GT	0	1	3	1	1	0	2	2	4	2	1	18
UR	0	2	1	1	1	2	2	2	3	2		16

Table 3. Number of VOLUNTARY (updates) deviations for each day of patrol

	D1	D2	D3	D4	D5	D6	D7	D8	D9	D10	D11	total
GT	0	0	0	0	0	0	0	0	0	0	0	0
UR	1	0	1	1	1	0	1	1	1	1		8

of 30 minutes (e.g., 60, 90 minutes). Hence, to properly compare our results, we divided our data in 30 minutes segments. More specifically, we considered all the train and station checks within a time window of 30 minutes and collected the data resulting from these actions[4]. Having defined the data points, we can now proceed to analyze our results.

Validation of the MDP Model: As discussed at the beginning of this section Both GT and UR schedules were calculated by solving an MDP. For this reason both schedules could be updated to request a new schedule. Tables 2 and 3 then show, for each day of patrol, the number of VOLUNTARY and INVOLUNTARY deviations requested by the officers. In total, GT schedules were updated 18 times, all of which were *involuntary* deviations, i.e., delays. All these update requests confirm that the MDP model was able to provide schedules that could be updated whenever necessary.

All INVOLUNTARY deviations were due to the officers writing citations or helping people. The average delay length was of 12 minutes (the largest delay was of 20 minutes). In each case, as discussed at the beginning of this section, a new schedule was provided starting at the officers' current location and closest time. Finally, Table 3 shows that voluntary deviations were used only with UR schedules. This result strongly suggests that the officers were mostly satisfied with GT schedules. In addition, it means that GT schedules did not really compete against UR schedules only. Rather, the comparison was between UR schedules which were augmented with real-time human intelligence for most of the time (8 out of 10 days). We discuss the results of such comparison next.

Game-Theory vs. Uniform Random: The results that we obtained are shown in Figure 6 and in Table 4. Figure 6 shows eight boxplots depicting the

[4] In so doing, the segments are also statistically independent. Within each segment the officers will check different people who are unable to affect each other. Each segment corresponds to a sample of different train riders taken at different times and locations. Not only do the officers never check the same rider twice but most importantly, during 30 minutes, they will visit different locations by riding the trains (roughly, one train every 6 minutes in the blue line) and inspecting the stations (on-station operations last no longer than 20 minutes).

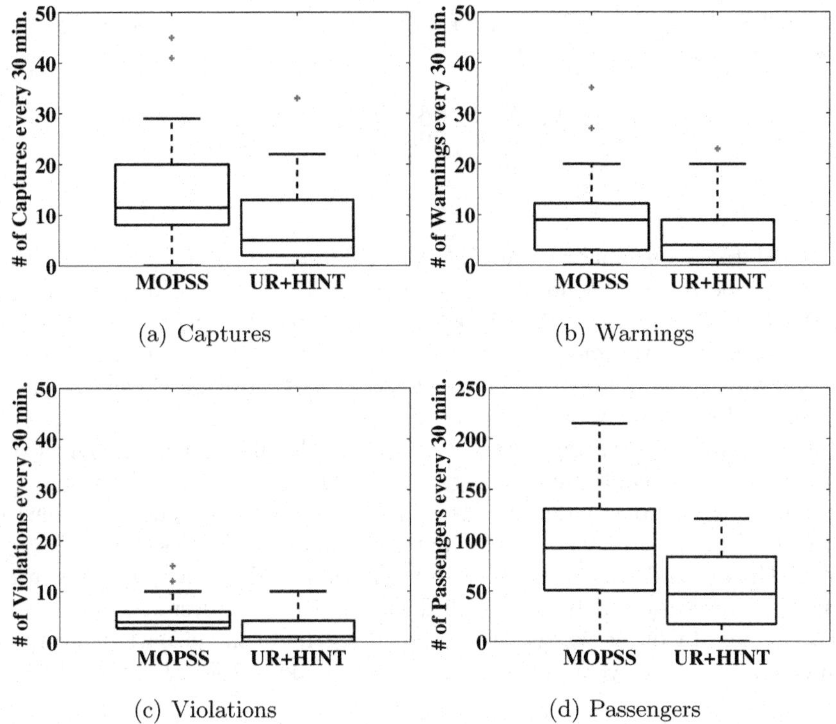

(a) Captures

(b) Warnings

(c) Violations

(d) Passengers

Fig. 6. Results of the Fare Evasion tests

data that we collected during each patrol, using both GT and UR schedules. Respectively, the four figures present data collected on captures (Figure 6(a)), warnings (Figure 6(b)), violations (Figure 6(c)), and passengers checked (Figure 6(d)) per 30 minutes of patrolling[5]. For each boxplot, the top and bottom of the box represent the 75th and 25th percentiles, respectively, while the middle line indicates the median of the collected data. The "+" data points indicate statistical outliers, while the whiskers show the most extreme non-outlier data points. Each of the four figures (captures, warnings, violations and passengers checked) shows that the data collected using GT schedules had higher values than the data collected using UR schedules. As shown in Table 4, on average, GT schedules led to, respectively 15.52 captures, 10.42 warnings and 5.03 violations issued every 30 minutes against, respectively against 9.55 captures, 6.48 warnings and 3.07 violations obtained using UR schedules. To confirm the statistical significance of these results, we ran a number of weighted unpaired student t-tests (p = 0.05) [7,1] and verified, for each metric, that the difference in the results was statistically significant. We used a weighted t-test because some data segments had a duration shorter than 30 minutes and we wanted to use all the

[5] GT schedules also led to two arrests on day 6. This is why the patrol only lasted 10 minutes.

Table 4. Average captures (C), warnings (W), violations (V) and passengers (P) based on the results obtained in Figure 6

	Days	avg. C	avg. W	avg. V	avg. P
GT	11	15.52	10.42	5.03	96.77
UR	10	9.55	6.48	3.07	60.85

available data for our analysis. As shown in Table 1, not all the patrol durations could be properly divided into a finite number of 30 minutes segments (e.g., UR: D6, D7, D8, D9 and GT: D6, D8, D11). Therefore, we calculated a weighted average for each of the metric defined above, whereby each segment was given a weight which was defined based on the segment's duration (longer segments corresponded to higher weights).

From a practical perspective, the magnitude of the difference between the two approaches is significant: cumulatively over a period of 21 days GT would capture a much larger total number of fare evaders. This result can be emphasized even further if we correlate it with the results shown in Tables 3 and 2. While running UR schedules the officers were requesting INVOLUNTARY deviations essentially every day, whereas no such deviations were requested while running GT schedules. In other words, they were using real-time situation awareness to augment the quality of the schedules, thus making the UR schedule more compelling.

The results in Table 4 also indicate that GT schedules led to 96.77 passengers checked every 30 minutes against 60.85 passengers checked by using UR schedules. As discussed in [9], GT schedules are generated by leveraging all the possible sequences of train and station checks and by taking into account key dimensions such as the train schedules, the officers' effectiveness and, most importantly the daily ridership statistics. This means that stations or trains with a higher presence of riders will be given a higher coverage probability since they are more likely to contain fare evaders. Hence, these results confirm the accuracy of the model as both Figure 6(d) and Table 4 show that GT schedules led the officers to check more passengers than UR schedules.

This raises the question of whether a static type of schedule, which only deploys the officers at the most crowded locations, would lead to similar or even better results than those obtained with GT. Given the limited amount of time that we had to conduct our experiments, we were unable to compare GT schedules against a static deployment – where the key weakness is predictability in the longer term. Indeed, effective randomization was one of the main reasons for LASD to collaborate on these experiments – security agencies know that static schedules become predictable in the long term[6]. After a certain amount of time, the passengers would know where the officers are located and could exploit this information to avoid paying the fare.

[6] [16] discusses the benefits of randomization in detail.

4.2 Counter-Terrorism Experiment

The purpose of this experiment is to run a head-to-head comparison between MOPSS and a manual allocation, the standard methodology adopted by several security agencies. Security agencies refer to this type of experiment as a mass transit full scale exercise (FSE). A FSE is a training exercise where multiple security agencies analyze the way their resources cooperate to secure a specific area while simulating a critical scenario. This scenario typically describes a "high level" threat, e.g., intelligence reports confirming that a terrorist attack might take place in the Los Angeles Metro System. The FSE consists of simulating the response to this threat, i.e., increasing the number of resources patrolling a train line on a daily basis to improve the quality of the security.

Setup: The FSE consisted of patrolling 10 stations of one train line of the LA Metro system for 12 hours. Each station on the train line is composed of three levels (street level, platform level and mezzanine) except station 1 which is composed of 5 levels (2 more platform levels). The exercise involved multiple security agencies, each participating with a number of resources. Overall, 80 security personnel were involved. These resources were divided into 14 teams, each with different abilities (see Section 3.2).

The exercise was divided into 3 different "sorties", each consisting of three hours of patrolling and one hour of debriefing. Human-generated schedules were used during the first sortie while MOPSS schedules were used during the second and the third sorties. The first two sorties were used to run the head-to-head comparison. Hence, the sorties were ran under the same settings: the same number of officers had to cover the 10 stations for a cumulative time of 450 minutes. The two sorties were ran during off-peak times (9h00 to 12h00 and 13h00 to 16h00, respectively), hence the type and the number of riders of the train lines could be considered to be, approximately, the same. The purpose of Sortie 3 was to test whether the officers were capable of following MOPSS schedules for a longer period (900 minutes instead of 450) and during peak time. We found out that the officers were actually able to follow the schedules. Thus, since the purpose of this Sortie was unrelated to our comparison, we will focus on Sorties 1 and 2 in the remainder of this section. Each type of schedule was generated as follows:

MOPSS schedules: The schedules were generated by (i) instantiating a CT game using the specifics of the FSE discussed earlier; (ii) solving this problem instance using the SOLVER and (iii) sampling a pure strategy in the SAMPLER to generate the patrol schedule for each of the different resources involved. Specifically, we ran the SMART_H in the SOLVER component, considering 14 resources and 32 targets. The algorithm produced a mixed strategy which was then sampled to generate a pure strategy in the SAMPLER. This pure strategy contains a schedule for each resource.

Manual Schedules: The schedules were generated by human expert schedulers of the LASD. They were generated using a two-step process. First, each station was assigned a coverage duration of 45 minutes (i.e., $\frac{1}{10}^{th}$ of the time). The idea was to have the officers perform *three observe* actions at each station. Second, the human expert schedulers assigned teams to each station so that each station was covered for exactly 45 minutes. Joint team activities were used 6 times in six different stations. This simple two-step process was adopted to avoid the cognitive burden involved with leveraging the effectiveness of each team to cover the different stations individually or while coordinating with other teams. Despite its simplicity, this process was difficult for the human expert schedulers. It involved several discussions and required one entire day of work.

Results: We first analyze the type of schedules generated as a result of using either MOPSS or manual scheduling. Then, we evaluate the results obtained by deploying the schedules during Sorties 1 and 2 and measuring their performance in the real-world.

Table 5. Count of Individual Activities

	S_1	S_2	S_3	S_4	S_5	S_6	S_7	S_8	S_9	S_{10}
Manual	3	3	3	2	3	2	2	2	2	2
MOPSS	2	2	3	3	2	2	2	3	3	2

Table 6. Count of Joint Activities

	S_1	S_2	S_3	S_4	S_5	S_6	S_7	S_8	S_9	S_{10}
Manual	0	0	0	1	0	1	1	1	1	1
MOPSS	1	0	0	0	0	2	0	1	1	1

The numbers of individual and joint activities for both the schedules generated during the FSE are shown in Tables 5 and 6. In both tables we can see that the number of individual (IA) and joint (JA) activities for both approaches are the same (IA: both 24; JA: both 6). All the joint activities in the MOPSS schedules are performed by CRM and EK9 teams, i.e., the teams with a positive joint effectiveness. This is similar to the behavior of the manual generated schedules, where joint activities are mostly performed by resources of types 4 and 5 (once by a team of resources of type 3). The remaining individual activities are performed by resources of type 1, 2 and 3.

There are two important differences between the two types of schedules. First, MOPSS sent the most effective type, type 3, to the most important stations because its individual effectiveness is greater than the effectiveness of other teams. This was not seen in the human schedule. Second, the schedules generated using MOPSS assigned the different teams to cover all the different levels of the different stations, whereas manual schedules did not specify such levels. The reason for this is that human schedulers were not able to reach this level of detail and thus they preferred to leave the decision of which level to patrol to the teams once they were deployed. In addition, the effort required to generate the schedules using MOPSS was much lower than the effort required to generate manual schedules, which required one day of work due to its significant cognitive burden. Since typically such patrols would be conducted day-in and day-out for several days in high-threat periods, the savings of human effort achieved by game-theoretic schedulers are thus very significant.

Each type of security allocation (either manual or game-theoretic based on MOPSS) was evaluated by security experts. A team of security experts (SEs) was placed at each station for the entire length of the exercise. Their task was to observe and evaluate the officers' patrolling activity during each sortie, and determine how their behavior was affecting the quality of the security within each station. In what follows, we report the conclusions of their analysis. The SEs did not know what type of schedules (so as to not bias their evaluation). To translate the observers' observations into a comparable value, each observer was asked to fill out a questionnaire every 30 minutes. The objective was to define a number of key sentences that could help to qualify the way in which the security officers had been patrolling the station in the last 30 minutes. Each questionnaire contained 11 *assertions* about the level of security within the station. The assertions were defined in collaboration with a team of SEs from the LASD and with social scientists. Each SE had to determine his level of agreement with each assertion, which was defined in the integer interval {0,6}, where 0 meant a strong disagreement, whereas 6 meant a strong agreement.

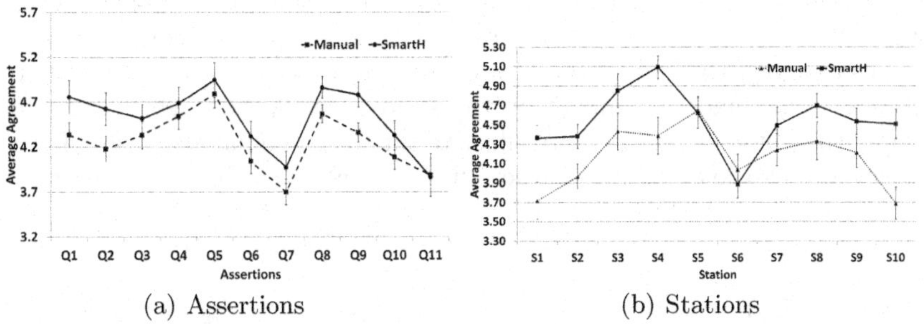

(a) Assertions (b) Stations

Fig. 7. Evaluation of the FSE: average agreement over the different questions and stations

Figures 7(a) and 7(b) show the results that we obtained. Figure 7(a) shows the weighted average agreement obtained for each assertion calculated over all the stations (the average was calculated considering each station's corresponding weight). Figure 7(b) shows the average agreement obtained for each station calculated over all the assertions. The error bars in both figures show the standard error of the mean calculated for each specific assertion (in Figure 7(a)) and station (in Figure 7(b)). As we can see the difference between some data points of the two approaches do not seem to be statistically significant. A student t-test confirmed this trend. This is expected, since we were only able to collect data for few hours of a single day. Nonetheless, we can still acquire some interesting information about the performance of game-theoretic schedules in the field, by analyzing the results that are statistically significant.

In Figure 7(a), we can see that MOPSS schedules seem to yield a higher level of agreement than manual schedules over all questions. As shown in the figure, the difference is significant only for assertions Q_1, Q_2, Q_8 and Q_9.These four assertions correspond to very general statements about the security at each station which address the efficiency of the schedules, their ability to provide a strong feeling of safety and to allow the officers to patrol each area as much as needed.

Similarly, in Figure 7(b), we can see that the average agreement is higher for MOPSS schedules over Manual schedules for stations S_1, S_2, S_3, S_4, S_8, S_9 and S_{10}. Some of these stations (S_1, S_8 and S_9) are the ones assigned a higher set of payoffs, as discussed above. Hence, they correspond to the ones given a higher coverage by MOPSS.

These results indicate that game-theoretic schedules were evaluated as more effective than manual schedules. By analyzing the differences between the schedules, we can infer that this happened for two key reasons. First, as discussed earlier, manual schedules were generated by leaving the decision of which level of a station to patrol to each deployed team. The officers then, were not able to properly coordinate over the different levels to patrol and therefore they ended up patrolling the same levels. Second, MOPSS produced a schedule which more effectively scheduled resources of type 3, i.e., the team with the highest effectiveness (0.8) for covering each target. More specifically, the resources of type 3 patrolled *all* the most important stations at key levels. In contrast, manual schedules assigned the same type of resources, without accounting for their effectiveness. This made an impact on the security evaluators, which considered the game-theoretic allocation more effective than the manual allocation, because it was leveraging the abilties of the resources in a way that human experts could not achieve.

4.3 Crime Experiment

Our crime experiment was designed to be a proof-of-concept of MOPSS crime component. As discussed in Section 3.3, OSGs are a new framework to represent opportunistic adversaries. The purpose of our experiment is then to validate this new framework in the real world to ascertain its ability to generate effective schedules against crime. The experiment was organized as follows:

Setup: We ran tests for two days with each test consisting of a two hours patrol involving two teams of two security officers. Each team had to patrol seven stations of a particular LA Metro train line using schedules generated using MOPSS. MOPSS generated the schedules by converting crime statistics into a set of coverage probabilities for the different stations. Figure 8 shows such probabilities and correlates them to the crime statistics for each of the 14 stations to patrol. In the figure, the x-axis enumerates the 14 stations to patrol. The bar graphs (y-axis on the right) show, for each station, the total number of crimes that happened during 2012 and 2013. Finally, the line graph shows the different coverage probabilities calculated for each station (y-axis on the left). In the figure, the stations with a larger coverage probability (stations 5 to 10) are either the stations with a large number of crimes (stations 5 and 8) or the adjacent stations (Stations 6, 7, 9 and 10). The latter stations are given a large coverage probability because the OSG model anticipates the possibility that criminals will choose stations 6, 7, 9 and 10 anticipating that stations 5 and 8 will be frequently patrolled by security officers [20]. Hence, these coverage probabilities show how game theory allows to build real world patrol schedules.

Results: During the tests, the officers were able to write 5 citations and make 2 arrests. In general, they were able to understand and follow the schedule easily. Overall, these tests indicate that the CR module in MOPSS can produce effective schedules that would work in the real world.

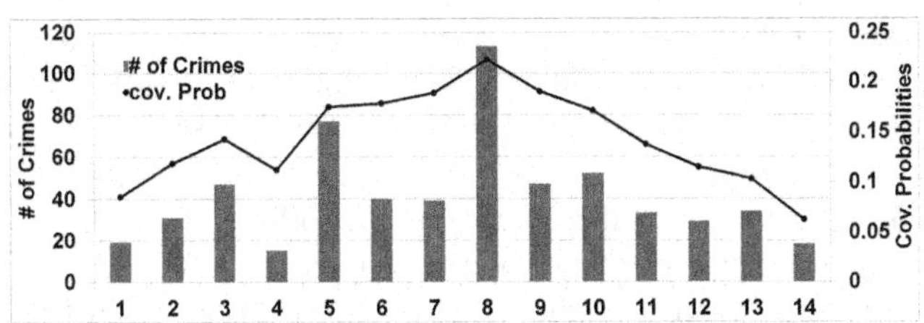

Fig. 8. Crime Statistics and Coverage Probabilities

5 Lessons Learned

The work presented in this paper is the result of a long term collaboration between university researchers and personnel from different security agencies including decision makers, planners and operators. To interact with such security agencies, we took inspiration from the lessons presented in [13]. We discussed the strengths and weaknesses of every aspect of MOPSS and emphasized the requirement of learning from the field to ascertain the performance of our system. In addition, The field experience allowed us to discover two new insights regarding real-world applied research in security games: (i) testing this research in the field requires a period of "immersion" and (ii) users are a key factor when when running field experiments.

The first insight is a key lesson for running field experiments. Any real world test of a security game based system will involve real security officers protecting a critical area for a long period of time. To succeed in such an experiment, researchers should immerse themselves in order to deeply understand the way officers and, more generally, a security agency operate every day. A period of "immersion", as we did for both the FE and the CT experiments, also ensures that the security agencies do not think researchers as ivory tower occupants leading to easier acceptance of technology. To test MOPSS, we spent several months observing the different security agencies patrolling the LA Metro to understand how they operate so as to set up effective field experiments.

The second insight comes from our interactions with the security personnel. These officers are the end users of our system. Thus, it is critical that they understand exactly the benefits of game-theoretic scheduling. Not doing this could severely affect the results of the evaluation. As an example, at the beginning of our FE tests (Section 4.1), the officers required a number of days to understand that their schedules could be updated without having to request a new allocation to the dispatch.

6 Summary

This paper steps beyond deployment to provide results on security games in the field, a challenge not addressed by existing literature in security games. Readers will notice that the paper does not contain any simulation results as all of our results are based on real world experiments. We presented MOPSS, a novel game-theoretic scheduling system for patrolling a train line. MOPSS introduced five contributions not addressed in previous applied systems, including both TRUSTS [18] and the system in [17].

The first contribution is multi-operation patrolling. Thus far, all existing game-theoretic scheduling systems [16] (in particular TRUSTS) and the system in [17] were focused on a single mission. In contrast, MOPSS is the *first deployed system* to use three significantly different adversary models to develop three different patrol schedules for the threats of fare evasion, terrorism and crime. In contrast with previous work suggesting such threats could be modeled as a multi-objective security game [4], A fundamental contribution of this paper is the insight that these different threat types lead to fundamentally different adversary models that cannot be folded into a single security game framework. MOPSS then is built upon these three adversary models. The second contribution deals with uncertain interruptions in the execution of patrol schedules. Existing systems, including TRUSTS [18], generated patrols that were often interrupted and left incomplete. This led to the use of MDPs for planning defender patrols in security games [9]. MOPSS exploits this idea to generate patrols for fare evasion. The third contribution is that MOPSS is the first system to generate patrols for counter-terrorism which accounts for joint coordinated activities between defender resources. This is achieved by incorporating the framework in [14] within both the SOLVER and the CT-Game in MOPSS. As a fourth contribution, MOPSS is the *first* system to deploy the *Opportunistic Security Game* model, where the adversary makes opportunistic decisions to commit crimes.

Finally, the fifth, and most important, contribution is the evaluation of MOPSS via real-world deployments. We ran three field experiments showing the benefits of game-theoretic scheduling in the real world. To the best of our knowledge, this evaluation constitutes the first evaluation of security games and, most importantly, the largest evalutation of *algorithmic* game theory, in the field. Existing literature on game theory in the field has focused on showing equilibrium concepts in the human and animal activities [12,3]. Our work shares their enthusiasm of taking game theory to the field, but fundamentally focuses on algorithmic deployments and the impact of such algorithms. Most importantly, our work opens the door of applied research in security games to the realm of field evaluation. Given the maturity that such research has acquired in the recent years and its strong connection with real world patrolling problems, we argue that field deployment should become a key area for future research in security games.

Acknowledgements. The authors would like to acknowledge their appreciation for the collaboration of the Los Angeles Sheriffs Department (LASD), the Booz-Allen Hamilton Company and the Transportation Security Administrations (TSA) Intermodal Security Training and Exercise Program (I-STEP). The LASD provided us with exceptional support and preparation which allowed us to organize our experiments with great detail and accuracy. Booz-Allen managed TSA s I-STEP Los Angeles Mass Transit Full-Scale Exercise, thus allowing us to run experiments and collect data in very realistic and practical conditions. This research was supported by the United States Department of Homeland Security (DHS) through the National Center for Risk and Economic Analysis of Terrorism Events (CREATE) at the University of Southern California (USC) under Basic Ordering Agreement HSHQDC-10-A-BOA19, Task Order No. HST02-12-J-MLS151. However, any opinions, findings, and conclusions or recommendations in this document are those of the authors and do not necessarily reflect views of the United States Department of Homeland Security, or the University of Southern California, or CREATE.

References

1. Bland, M.J., Kerry, S.M.: Weighted comparison of means. BMJ: British Medical Journal 316, 125–129 (1998)
2. Brantingham, P., Brantingham, P.: Criminality of place. European Journal on Criminal Policy and Research (1995)
3. Brown, A., Camerer, C.F., Lovallo, D.: To review or not to review? limited strategic thinking at the movie box office. American Economic Journal: Microeconomics 2 (2012)
4. Brown, M., An, B., Kiekintveld, C., Ordonez, F., Tambe, M.: An extended study on multi-objective security games. JAAMAS (2013)
5. Conitzer, V.: Computing game-theoretic solutions and applications to security. In: AAAI (2012)
6. Gatti, N.: Game theoretical insights in strategic patrolling: Model and algorithm in normal form. In: ECAI (2008)
7. Lisa, R., Goldberg, A.N.: Kercheval, and Kiseop Lee. t-statistics for weighted means in credit risk modeling. Journal of Risk Finance 6(4), 349–365 (2005)
8. Jaulmes, R., Pineau, J., Precup, D.: A formal framework for robot learning and control under model uncertainty. In: ICRA (2007)
9. Jiang, A.X., Yin, Z., Zhang, C., Tambe, M., Kraus, S.: Game-theoretic randomization for security patrolling with dynamic execution uncertainty. In: AAMAS (2013)

10. Kiekintveld, C., Jain, M., Tsai, J., Pita, J., Ordez, F., Tambe, M.: Computing optimal randomized resource allocations for massive security games. In: AAMAS, pp. 233–239 (2009)
11. Luber, S., Yin, Z., Delle Fave, F.M., Jiang, A.X., Tambe, M., Sullivan, J.P.: Game-theoretic patrol strategies for transit systems: The trusts system and its mobile app (demonstration). In: AAMAS (Demonstrations Track) (2013)
12. Ostling, R., Wang, J., Tao-yi, J., Chou, E.Y., Camerer, C.F.: Testing game theory in the field: Swedish lupi lottery games. American Economic Journal: Microeconomics (2011)
13. Shieh, E., An, B., Yang, R., Tambe, M., Baldwin, C., Di Renzo, J., Maule, B., Meyer, G.: Protect: A deployed game theoretic system to protect the ports of the united states. In: AAMAS (2012)
14. Shieh, E., Jain, M., Jiang, A.X., Tambe, M.: Effciently solving joint activity based security games. In: IJCAI (2013)
15. Short, M.B., D'Orsogna, M.R., Pasour, V.B., Tita, G.E., Brantingham, P.J., Bertozzi, A.L., Chayes, L.B.: A statistical model of criminal behavior. Mathematical Models and Methods in Applied Sciences (2008)
16. Tambe, M.: Security and Game Theory: Algorithms, Deployed Systems, Lessons Learned. Cambridge University Press (2011)
17. Varakantham, P., Lau, H.C., Yuan, Z.: Scalable randomized patrolling for securing rapid transit networks. In: IAAI (2013)
18. Yin, Z., Jiang, A., Johnson, M., Tambe, M., Kiekintveld, C., Leyton-Brown, K., Sandholm, T., Sullivan, J.: Trusts: Scheduling randomized patrols for fare inspection in transit systems. In: IAAI (2012)
19. Yin, Z., Tambe, M.: A unified method for handling discrete and continuous uncertainty in Bayesian stackelberg games. In: International Conference on Autonomous Agents and Multiagent Systems (AAMAS) (2012)
20. Zhang, C., Jiang, A.X., Short, M.B., Brantingham, J.P., Tambe, M.: Towards a game theoretic approach for defendingagainst crime diffusion. In: AAMAS (2014)

The AORTA Architecture: Integrating Organizational Reasoning in *Jason*

Andreas Schmidt Jensen[1], Virginia Dignum[2], and Jørgen Villadsen[1]

[1] Technical University of Denmark, Kongens Lyngby, Denmark
{ascje,jovi}@dtu.dk

[2] Delft University of Technology, Delft, The Netherlands
m.v.dignum@tudelft.nl

Abstract. Open systems are characterized by a diversity of heterogeneous and autonomous agents that act according to private goals, and with a behavior that is hard to predict. They can be regulated through organizations similar to human organizations, which regulate the agents' behavior space and describe the expected behavior of the agents. Agents need to be able to reason about the regulations, so that they can act within the expected boundaries and work towards the objectives of the organization. In this paper, we describe the AORTA (Adding Organizational Reasoning to Agents) architecture for making agents organization-aware. It is designed such that it provides organizational reasoning capabilities to agents implemented in existing agent programming languages without being tied to a specific organizational model. We show how it can be integrated in the *Jason* agent programming language, and discuss how the agents can coordinate their organizational tasks using AORTA.

1 Introduction

Open systems rely on organizational structures to guide and regulate agents, because these systems have no control over the internal architecture of the agents. This means that the agents must be able to reason about the organizational structures in order to know what to do in the system and how to do it. Regulations are often specified as organizational models, usually using roles that abstract away from specific agent implementations such that any agent will be able to enact a given role. Roles may restrict enacting agents' behavior space, such that it coincides with the expectations of the system.

Agents that can reason about organizations are *organization-aware* [20]. Organizational reasoning includes understanding the organizational specification, acting using organizational primitives, and cooperating with other agents in the organization to complete personal or organizational objectives. From the agent's perspective, there are two sides of organizational reasoning. First, how can it contribute to the objectives of the organization, and second, how can it take advantage of the organization, once it is a part of it.

From the organizational perspective, the system can be regulated, for example, by blocking certain actions (for example through a *middleware*, such as

F. Dalpiaz et al. (Eds.): EMAS 2014, LNAI 8758, pp. 127–145, 2014.

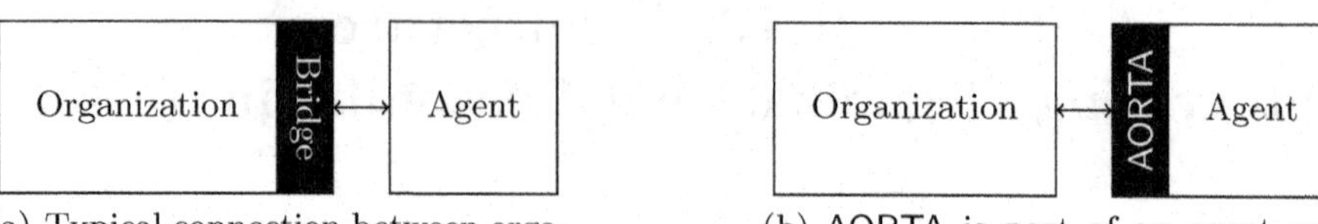

(a) Typical connection between organization and agent

(b) AORTA is part of an agent and provides it with an interface to the organization.

Fig. 1. How AORTA differs from other approaches to program agents that can participate in an organization

$\mathcal{S}$-$\mathcal{M}$OISE$^+$ [13], or governors in ISLANDER [10]), or by enabling the agents to reason about the expectations of the system. In these cases, agents are thus connected to the organizational entity via a *bridge*, as shown in figure 1(a). Here, everything related to the organization is controlled and regulated by the organization; the agent has little or no control over what happens.

AORTA (Adding Organizational Reasoning to Agents) [16] is an organizational reasoning component that can be integrated into the agent's reasoning mechanism, allowing it to reason about (and act upon) regulations specified by an organizational model using simple reasoning rules. AORTA assumes a preexisting organization, is independent from the agent, and focuses on reasoning rules that specify how the agent reasons about the specification. The organization is completely separated from the agent, as shown in figure 1(b), meaning that the architecture of the agent is independent from the organizational model, and the agent is free to decide on how to use AORTA in its reasoning. The separation is possible because AORTA is tailored based on an organizational metamodel, designed to support different organizational models.

In this paper, we describe the AORTA architecture for making agents organization-aware[1]. It is designed such that it can provide organizational reasoning capabilities to agents implemented for existing agent platforms. We present an integration of AORTA in the well-known agent platform *Jason* [2], and show how it lets *Jason*-agents decide how to use their capabilities to achieve their organizational objectives, and furthermore, how they are able to coordinate their tasks.

We consider software architecture as the highest level of abstraction of a software system. The AORTA architecture is designed as a component that can be integrated into existing agent platforms. Existing agents are extended with an AORTA component, which features an organizational reasoning cycle that performs organizational reasoning, providing the existing agent with organizational reasoning capabilities. Furthermore, the organizational reasoning is specified in an AORTA-program in which organizational actions and coordination mechanisms for each agent can be defined by the developer.

[1] The implementation of the AORTA architecture is available as open source at `http://www2.compute.dtu.dk/~ascje/AORTA/`.

The rest of the paper is organized as follows. We begin, in section 2, with a description of the organizational metamodel, and briefly discuss a simple scenario, which we later implement in AORTA and *Jason*. In section 3, we present the AORTA architecture. Section 4 describes the integration with *Jason*. We discuss related work in section 5 and conclude the paper in section 6.

2 Organizational Modeling

Organizational models are used in multi-agent systems to give agents an explicit representation of an organization. Similarly to [7] we use concepts from Organizational Theory (OT), which, even though it lacks formality, has been studied for years and has been applied successfully. OT defines an organization as an entity in which individuals have roles, and use these roles to accomplish collective goals. Organizations are furthermore defined with a purpose; individuals in the organization have intentions and objectives, which lead to the overall collective goals.

Different models are proposed in the literature (e.g. $\mathcal{M}$OISE$^+$[13], OperA [8], ISLANDER [9]). These models typically use concepts from OT as well, especially the notion of *roles*, abstracting implementation details away from expectations, and *objectives*, defining the desired outcome of the organization.

2.1 Organizational Metamodel

AORTA uses an organizational metamodel, which is based on roles and objectives.

Definition 1 (Organizational metamodel). *The organizational metamodel of AORTA is defined by the following predicates:*

$\mathsf{role}(r, O)$	*r is the role name, and O is a set of objectives.*
$\mathsf{objective}(o)$	*o is the name of an objective.*
$\mathsf{dependency}(r_1, r_2, o)$	*Role r_1 depends on role r_2 for completion of objective o.*
$\mathsf{order}(o_1, o_2)$	*Objective o_1 should be completed before objective o_2.*
$\mathsf{rea}(a, r)$	*Agent a enacts role r.*
$\mathsf{active}(o)$	*Objective o is currently active*[2].

Agents can reason about the organizational structure to make organizational decisions. For example, if an agent enters an organization with the purpose of completing a certain objective o_i, it can reason about which roles to enact based on that objective:

$$roles = \{r \mid \mathsf{role}(r, O) \wedge o_i \in O\}$$

Given such a set of possible roles, the agent can decide which role(s) to enact based on the organizational structure. In particular: what are the other objectives of a given role, do they coincide with the agent's own objectives and is the

[2] An objective is active if it has not yet been completed and all objectives it depends on have been completed.

role($medic$,{$injuredFound$,$injuredSaved$,$removeBlocker$}).
role($officer$,{$fightFound$,$fightStopped$}).

dependency($medic$,$officer$,$removeBlocker$).

order($injuredFound$,$injuredSaved$).
order($fightFound$,$fightStopped$).

objective($injuredFound$).
objective($injuredSaved$).
objective($removeBlocker$).
objective($fightFound$).
objective($fightStopped$).

Fig. 2. Organizational specification of the crisis response scenario

agent capable of completing them? Will the agent depend on other agents; or conversely, will other agents depend on this agent for completion of their objectives? Once a role is enacted it is furthermore useful to reason about the order of the objectives; it provides a starting point and enables the agent to "plan ahead" (e.g., after the completion of objective o_1, objective o_2 must be completed).

2.2 The First Responders Scenario

We consider a scenario of first responders at a fight between groups of people, some of them being injured and requiring medical attention.

> *After a match between two sports teams, fans are fighting and some of them are badly hurt. The authorities have been contacted, and a group number of medics and police officers (the first-responders) have arrived. The medics are supposed to help the injured, while the police officers are supposed to break up the fight. The fans may try to prevent medics from rescuing injured fans from the other team.*

The organizational specification is shown in figure 2. For this paper, we assume that the agents entering the organization are *cooperative*, that is, they will pursue organizational objectives and cooperate with the other agents in the organization. It is, however, simple enough to consider self-interested agents as well; they will just be more likely to pursue their personal objectives rather than those of the organization.

An agent entering the system will then need to decide which role(s) to enact, for example, by comparing role objectives to its own objectives and reasoning about the requirements of the role.

3 The AORTA Architecture

Agents are often based on the belief-desire-intention (BDI) model [18], where each agent has beliefs about the state of the world, desires are possible states of affairs that the agent might want to realize, and intentions are those states

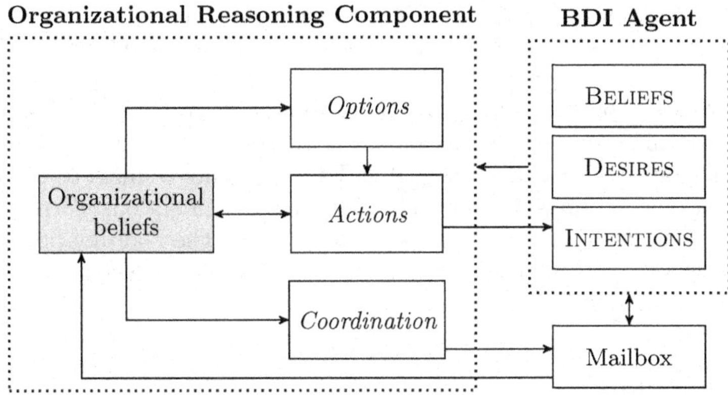

Fig. 3. The Organizational Reasoning Component of AORTA

of affairs that the agent has committed to (attempt to) realize. AORTA provides organizational reasoning capabilities to agents, and extends classical BDI reasoning, allowing the agents to reason about organizational matters. Organizational reasoning is divided into *organizational option generation*, *organizational action deliberation* and *organizational coordination*. An organizational option is something that the agent should consider, such as an active objective, or a role that can be enacted or deacted [15]. For instance, initially in the scenario, the medics will only search for injured people. When all areas have been searched, this objective has been completed and a new objective, rescuing the injured, will be possible. An organizational action is the execution of an organizational option: actually enacting a role or committing to an organizational objective. This creates the expectation (for the organization) that the agent should somehow believe it is able to (help) achieve it, either by itself, by cooperating with other agents, or by delegating it to one or more agents in the dependency relation of its role. Note that self-interested or deceitful agents might know that they cannot achieve an organizational objective, but will commit to it anyway to disturb the organization. Organizational coordination is organization-level coordination, which is based on the agent's mental state.

AORTA puts organizational reasoning into a separate *organizational reasoning component* inside the agent, which is connected to the mental state of the agent (see figure 3). The component lets the agent hold beliefs about the organization (its specification and instantiation) and can use that for reasoning about organizational objectives that are possible to achieve (or required to be achieved), roles that can be enacted, norms that are enforced, and so on. An integration of the organization within the agent makes the agent more likely to take both the organization and its own beliefs into account in its reasoning. Furthermore, by representing the organization as beliefs, the organizational structure can be changed, if necessary. For example, if the organization changes (reorganization), or if the agent finds out that it has wrong beliefs about the organization.

Based on the agent's mental state, AORTA can determine which organizational options to choose, and the organizational actions might change the mental state. For instance, in order to consider the available organizational options, AORTA uses the agent's capabilities and intentions. Furthermore, intentions may influence the reasoning, e.g., when the intention to coordinate a task requires use of the organizational model. Finally, AORTA lets agents commit to objectives: an organizational action leads to change in the agent's intentions, corresponding to the fact that the agent commits to the objective. The coordination component sends messages using the mailbox, and incoming messages can change the organizational structure.

3.1 Mental State

BDI agents usually have knowledge bases containing their beliefs and intentions. In this paper, we consider agents that contain an AORTA-component, which means that they not only have belief and intention bases, they also have knowledge bases for the organizational aspect. Each knowledge base will hold different kinds of formulas depending on their purpose.

Definition 2 (Knowledge bases). *The AORTA knowledge bases are based on a predicate language, $\mathcal{L}$, with typical formula ϕ and operators $\wedge, \neg, \forall$. The agent's belief base and intention base are denoted Σ_a and Γ_a, respectively. The language of the organization is denoted $\mathcal{L}^{\mathrm{org}}$, and $\mathcal{L}^{\mathrm{org}} \subseteq \mathcal{L}$. The organizational specification and options are denoted Σ_o and Γ_o, respectively. We then have the following knowledge bases:*

$$\Sigma_o, \Gamma_o \subseteq \mathcal{L}^{\mathrm{org}} \qquad \Sigma_a, \Gamma_a \subseteq \mathcal{L}$$

We define different kinds of formulas for each knowledge base, which allows us to target specific knowledge bases in different situations.

Definition 3 (Formulas). *AORTA uses reasoning formulas, $\mathcal{L}_R$, with typical element ρ, which are based on organizational formulas, option formulas, belief formulas and goal formulas.*

$$\rho ::= \top \mid \mathit{org}(\phi) \mid \mathit{opt}(\phi) \mid \mathit{bel}(\phi) \mid \mathit{goal}(\phi) \mid \neg\rho \mid \rho_1 \wedge \rho_2$$

Organizational formulas, $\mathsf{org}(\phi)$, queries the organizational specification, option formulas, $\mathsf{opt}(\phi)$, queries the options base, belief formulas, $\mathsf{bel}(\phi)$, queries the belief base and goal formulas, $\mathsf{goal}(\phi)$, queries the intention (or goal) base. We can use the formulas to specify things such as:

$$\mathsf{org}(\mathsf{objective}(\mathit{injuredFound})) \wedge \neg\mathsf{bel}(\mathit{injuredFound}),$$

where the first part of the conjunction queries the organizational specification, Σ_o, and the second part queries the agent's belief base, Σ_a. The formula queries whether there is an organizational objective (to find victims), which the agent currently does not believe it has achieved.

Definition 4 (Mental state). *The AORTA mental state MS is a tuple of knowledge bases:*

$$MS = \langle \Sigma_a, \Gamma_a, \Sigma_o, \Gamma_o \rangle.$$

The implementation of the mental state is based on tuProlog [6], which is a Java-based lightweight implementation of ISO-Prolog. We chose tuProlog because of its efficiency and straightforward interface in Java, allowing us to query a Prolog knowledge base without requiring any external system-dependent libraries. The AORTA component of each agent has its own instance of tuProlog, comprising its entire mental state. That is, all knowledge bases of an agent are implemented in a single Prolog instance by wrapping each rule in a predicate depending on its nature. For example, the reasoning formula $\mathsf{bel}(a \wedge b) \wedge \neg \mathsf{org}(c \wedge d)$ is converted to the following Prolog query:

```
bel(a), bel(b), \+ (org(c), org(d))
```

This translation makes querying straightforward, while still keeping the distinction between the different knowledge bases.

Note that the AORTA component contains its own copy of the agent's mental state, rather than integrating AORTA into the knowledge bases of the agent in an existing platform. This means that the belief base and goal base of AORTA must be synchronized with the agent, which could lead to pitfalls in an integration process (especially if the knowledge bases are not properly synchronized). However, our aim is to enable AORTA to be integrated with most of the existing agent platforms, and since it requires only that formulas must be converted between the language of AORTA and the agent platform in question, we find that it makes the implementation of AORTA simpler to understand.

3.2 Acting and Coordinating

At the center of agents in AORTA are the *organization-specific actions*. While the agent will have access to a number of domain-specific actions (such as a medic performing a life-saving action), the AORTA component will furthermore make it possible to consider certain organizational options (what happens by enacting a certain role, pursuing an objective), or performing organizational actions (enacting a role, committing to an objective).

Definition 5 (Organization-specific actions). *The set of options with typical element a_O is denoted Opt and the set of actions with typical element a_A is denoted Act.*

$$a_O ::= \mathit{consider}(\phi) \mid \mathit{disregard}(\phi)$$
$$a_A ::= \mathit{enact}(\rho) \mid \mathit{deact}(\rho) \mid \mathit{commit}(\phi) \mid \mathit{drop}(\phi)$$

Actions are executed using a transition function, $\mathcal{T}_O$ and $\mathcal{T}_A$, respectively. Each action is only applicable in certain states. For example, $\mathsf{consider}(\phi)$ can only be applied if $\Sigma_o \models \phi$ in the current state, and the effect is that ϕ is added to Γ_o.

Role enactment, $\mathsf{enact}(\rho)$, is applicable only when ρ is the name of a role and the agent does not currently enact that role. Committing to an objective, $\mathsf{commit}(\phi)$, is possible only if ϕ is an organizational objective and ϕ is not already a belief or a goal[3]. $\mathsf{disregard}(\phi)$, $\mathsf{deact}(\rho)$ and $\mathsf{drop}(\phi)$ simply remove the respective formula from the appropriate knowledge base.

Notice the correspondence between elements in Opt and Act: if the agent considers enacting a role, the enact action allows it to enact that role. However, once the role is enacted, the option is no longer an option. Since the agent now enacts the role, it seems appropriate to remove the option from Γ_o. This is done using an *option removal function*, O, which removes options, when they are no longer applicable (that is, when their respective organizational action would be undefined).

We are now in a position to introduce *organizational reasoning rules*: option and action rules. These rules enable the agent to decide which organization-specific actions to perform.

Definition 6 (Reasoning rules). *The sets of option rules $\mathcal{R}_O$ and action rules $\mathcal{R}_A$ are defined as follows.*

$$\mathcal{R}_O = \{\rho \implies a_O \mid \rho \in \mathcal{L}_R, a_O \in \mathsf{Opt}\}$$
$$\mathcal{R}_A = \{\rho \implies a_A \mid \rho \in \mathcal{L}_R, a_A \in \mathsf{Act}\}$$

Finally, since each agent has its own organizational state, they need to be able to coordinate and synchronize their organizational knowledge. While such coordination can happen in different ways, we choose to use *organizational messages.* In order to determine whether a message is intended for AORTA, organizational messages are wrapped in an organizational wrapper, om, which is an unary predicate with the message as a single term.

Definition 7 (Organizational messages). *An organizational message is defined as*

$$\text{msg}(\alpha, \mathsf{om}(M)),$$

where om *is the organizational wrapper, and M is the message. In* outgoing *messages, α corresponds to the set of recipient agents, and in* incoming *messages, α is the sender.*

Each agent can then specify how to coordinate using a set of *coordination rules*, which specifies certain criteria for *when* and with *whom* to coordinate.

Definition 8 (Coordination rules). *A coordination rule is a triple,*

$$(c, \phi, m),$$

where c is the trigger for coordination and is a set of positive or negative reasoning formulas, ϕ defines the set of agents to coordinate with, and m is the message.

[3] The correspondence between goals and beliefs is based on achievement goals in the GOAL agent programming language [11], which are defined such that ϕ is an achievement goal iff ϕ is a goal and ϕ is not currently believed.

The coordination trigger c can, e.g., be the set $\{\mathsf{bel}(\mathit{injuredFound})\}$, which will trigger at a point where $\Sigma_a \models \mathit{injuredFound}$ is true and $\Sigma_a \models \neg \mathit{injuredFound}$ was true in the previous state.

3.3 AORTA Reasoning Cycle

The configuration of the AORTA component consists of the agent's knowledge bases, a number of option, action and coordination rules, and a message box for incoming (inbox) and outgoing (outbox) organizational messages. The initial state consists of a set of initial beliefs and goals, and the organizational specification.

The agent has a number of *state transition rules* available, which can be used to change its state. A reasoning cycle in AORTA is executed using a *strategy* that decides which transition rules to execute.

The agent has transition rules for execution of option and action rules, called Opt and Act, a transition rule for external updates, Ext, and two rules for coordination, Coord and Chk.

Opt can be applied to an option rule in a given state, $\rho \implies a_O$, if ρ is entailed and the option transition function, $\mathcal{T}_O$, is defined for a_O.
Act can be applied to an action rule in a given state, $\rho \implies a_A$, if ρ is entailed and the action transition function, $\mathcal{T}_A$, is defined for a_A. The option removal function O is applied after a successful application of Act.
Ext changes the agent's mental state to accommodate updates from outside AORTA. For example, if the agent perceives something, Ext adds the percept to the belief base.
Coord is applied to coordination rules, (c, ϕ, m), when c is triggered by the state, and the set of agents entailed by ϕ is not empty. The message m is then sent to each agent.
Chk checks for new organizational messages by adding messages from the incoming message queue to the appropriate knowledge base[4].

For the purpose of this paper, we use a single linear strategy, which executes the state transition rules in a predefined order.

Definition 9 (Linear strategy). *The linear strategy is defined as follows:*

$$(\textsc{Chk})^*(\textsc{Ext})(\textsc{Opt})(\textsc{Act})(\textsc{Coord})^*,$$

where (Rule)* *denotes that* Rule *is executed until the agent's state no longer changes.*

The strategy executes each of the transition rules, as explained above, changing the agent's state. The linear strategy is rather simple, but it is possible to implement strategies, which e.g. allows the agent to explore different paths before choosing one.

[4] For simplicity, we assume that the agents will not consider whether a sender is trustworthy, and thus whether a message is reliable.

```
options {
  [org(role(R,Os)), bel(me(Me), member(O,Os), cap(O))] => consider(role(R,Os))
  [bel(me(Me)), org(role(R,Os), rea(Me,R), member(O,Os), objective(O), active(O))]
                                                      => consider(objective(O))
}
actions {
  [opt(role(R,_))] => enact(R)
  [opt(objective(O)), bel(me(Me)), org(role(R,Os), member(O,Os), rea(Me,R))] => commit(O)
}
coordination {
  [+bel(visited(R))] : [org(rea(A,medic))] => send(A,bel(visited(R)))
  [+goal(X)] : [bel(me(Me)), org(rea(Me,R1), dependency(R1,R2,X), rea(A,R2))]
                                                                => send(A, goal(X))
  [+bel(O)] : [org(role(R,Os), objective(O), member(O,Os), rea(A,R))] => send(A, bel(O))
  [+org(rea(A,R))] : [bel(agent(Ag))] => send(Ag, org(rea(A,R)))
}
```

Fig. 4. An example of an AORTA program

3.4 AORTA Programs

An AORTA program consists of three sections: *options*, *actions* and *coordination*. An example program, which can be used in the first responders scenario, is shown in figure 4.

Options and actions are of the form $[\phi]$ `=>` a, where ϕ consists of a comma-separated list of reasoning formulas. The content of each reasoning formula (i.e., the query) is Prolog code. For example, the action rule

```
[opt(role(R,_))] => enact(R),
```

states that if `role(R,_)` is an option (i.e. entailed by Γ_o), the agent should enact `R`. Note that this is a simplification of the reasoning process required by agents to decide whether or not to enact a role in an organization. It is, however, possible to incorporate more sophisticated reasoning, e.g., by using the notion of social power. For example, in [4], various forms of power agents may have over each other are identified and formalized as rules. These power relations can be used in the reasoning process by adding the rules to the agents' organizational state.

The coordination section consists of coordination triples, of the form $[c]$ `:` $[\phi]$ `=>` send(Ag, ψ), where c is a list of reasoning formulas, with either + or - in front of each, denoting that the trigger or its negation is now entailed by the agent's mental state. ϕ is identical to ϕ in option and action rules. Ag corresponds to a variable in ϕ or c, and ψ is the message to be sent. Thus, the following rule

```
[+org(rea(A,R))] : [bel(me(A),agent(Ag))] => send(Ag, org(rea(A,R)))
```

states that when the agent enacts a role, it should inform all other agents in the system.

The implementations of OPT and ACT are deterministic: the rules in each section are simply processed linearly, and the first matching rule is executed. COORD is implemented such that every triggered triple in a state will be executed in a single step.

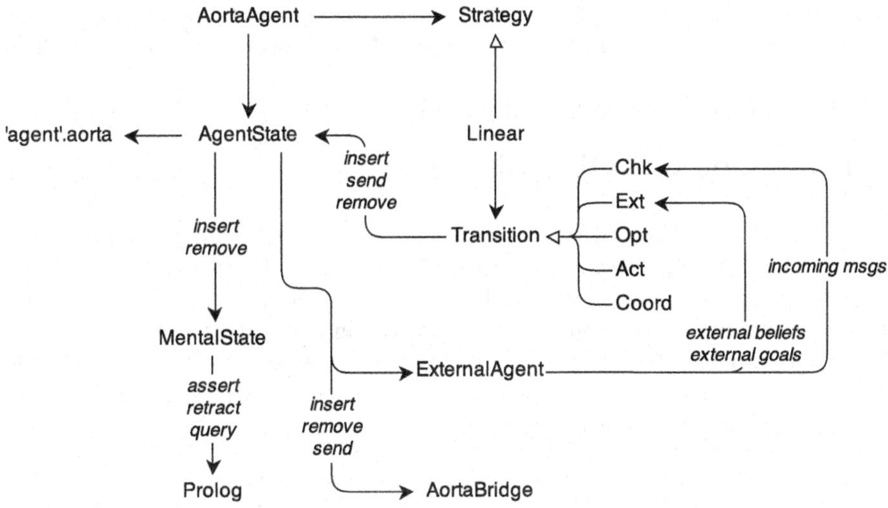

Fig. 5. Implementation overview with the most important components. A filled arrowhead indicates an association between components. An unfilled arrowhead indicates inheritance.

3.5 Implementation Overview

The architecture is depicted in figure 5. Each agent is associated with an instance of `AortaAgent`, which contains the agent's state, `AgentState`, and in which the reasoning cycle is implemented. The reasoning cycle performs two steps: executing the strategy and sending messages from the outbox.

3.6 Integration Considerations

The agent state contains the agent's the knowledge bases, rules and message boxes. Furthermore, it contains an `ExternalAgent` and an `AortaBridge`. The external agent corresponds to the message box and knowledge bases of the agent using AORTA. That is, whenever the agent commits to a new goal or updates its beliefs, these changes are propagated via the external agent into AORTA using Ext. The bridge lets AORTA manipulate the agent's mental state. For example, successful execution of commit(ϕ) will add ϕ to the agent's goal base using the bridge.

When integrating AORTA into an existing agent platform, there are thus three things to take care of.

Bridge. AORTA uses the bridge to send updates to the agent's goal and belief bases, so an agent platform-specific bridge should be implemented (by implementing the `AortaBridge` interface), such that the knowledge bases can be synchronized.

External agent. When the agent updates its goal or belief base, it should inform AORTA by invoking the appropriate methods of `ExternalAgent`.

Translation. AORTA makes use of tuProlog, so the contents of the agent's knowledge bases should be translated into Java objects supported by tuProlog.

4 Evaluation of AORTA in *Jason*

We now show how AORTA can be implemented in an existing agent platform, the *Jason* platform [2]. *Jason* is a Java-based interpreter for an extended version of AgentSpeak. *Jason* is based on the BDI model, is open source and highly extensible, making it a reasonable choice for the integration of AORTA.

The AgentSpeak language is a Prolog-like logic programming language, which allows the developer to create a plan library for each agent in a system. A plan in AgentSpeak is of the form

```
+triggering event : context <- body.
```

If an event matches a trigger, the context is matched with the current state of the agent. If the context matches the current state, the body is executed; otherwise the engine continues to match contexts of other plans with the same trigger. If no plan is applicable, the event fails. Triggering events can amongst other things be addition or deletion of beliefs (+l and -l) and addition or deletion of goals (+!l and -!l). The body contains a sequence of actions the agent should perform and goals to adopt. When adopting a goal in the body of a plan, the agent will attempt to achieve the new goal before continuing executing the current plan.

Note that when a plan for a goal has been completed, the goal is considered finished. This means that it will be removed from the agent's mental state. Since commit(ϕ) is only defined if ϕ is not already a goal and is not believed by the agent, the agent will be able to commit to a goal multiple times, until it believes it has been achieved.

4.1 *Jason*+AORTA

The AORTA integration in *Jason* is shown in figure 6. The integration consists of an extended agent architecture, which implements the actual integration with AORTA, and an infrastructure, which makes it possible to create an AORTA-project in *Jason* without having to deal with the specifics of the integration. This is done by specifying the infrastructure as follows:

```
MAS projectname {
   infrastructure: AORTA(organization(location, type))
   ...
}
```

The infrastructure takes two parameters: `location` refers to the location of the organizational specification, and `type` refers to the type of organizational model (currently, a generic organization based on the metamodel is supported).

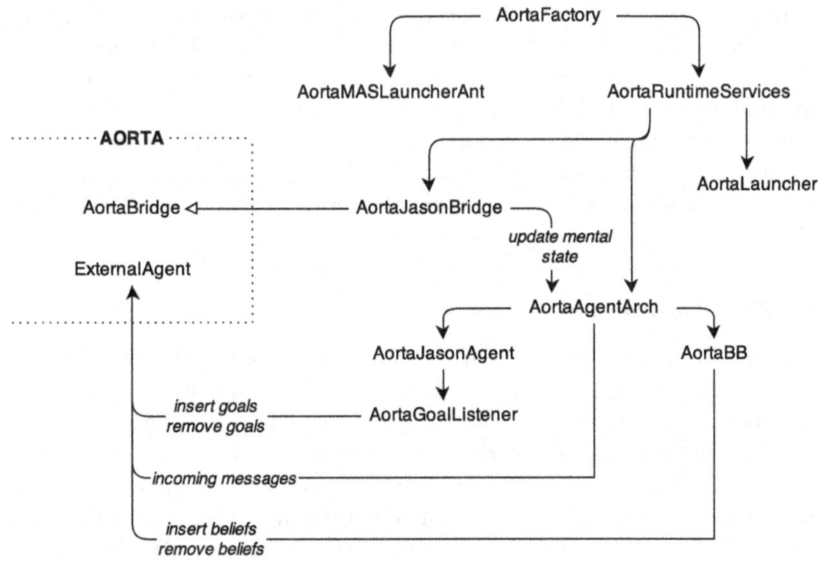

Fig. 6. *Jason*+AORTA. A filled arrowhead indicates an association between components. An unfilled arrowhead indicates inheritance.

AORTA does not make any changes to the *Jason* language, and any existing implementations of multi-agent systems in *Jason* should be compatible with *Jason*+AORTA. The integration does two things: (1) when the belief base or goal base in the AORTA component changes, these changes are propagated to the *Jason*-agent (via `AortaJasonBridge`), and an addition/deletion event is triggered and (2) when the *Jason*-agent's mental state changes, AORTA receives those changes (via the `ExternalAgent`). The *Jason*-agent is connected to the `ExternalAgent` in three places:

`AortaAgentArch` Organizational messages are filtered and sent to AORTA for processing. The normal procedure for checking an agent's mailbox is extended to check whether incoming messages are wrapped in the organizational wrapper.

`AortaBB` Whenever the *Jason*-agent's belief base is changed (i.e., a belief is added or removed), the changes are sent to AORTA to ensure synchrony between the mental states.

`AortaGoalListener` When a goal changes state (i.e., when a plan for it has started, failed, or stopped), the goal listener is responsible for sending the changes to AORTA.

Furthermore, *Jason* formulas are converted to AORTA formulas. Note that while *Jason* supports annotations on literals (e.g., denoting the source of a belief, `injuredFound[source(alice)]`), they are lost in conversion to AORTA formulas, since they are not supported. This should generally not be a problem, since formulas will not propagate back and forth between the systems. That is, if a belief originates from *Jason*, it will be sent to AORTA, which will not send it back to *Jason*, e.g. `+injuredFound[source(alice)]` $\rightarrow$ `bel(injuredFound)` $\rightarrow$ `+injuredFound` does not happen.

The AORTA reasoning cycle is executed in *Jason* via the method `reasoning-CycleStarted()` in `AortaAgentArch`, which is called in the beginning of a *Jason* reasoning cycle. This means that the agent will execute the AORTA reasoning strategy in the beginning of each cycle.

4.2 The First Responders Scenario

We now discuss how AORTA can be used to let agents participate in the first responders scenario. We use the Blocks World for Teams [17] testbed to simulate the first responders scenario by considering the drop zone being the ambulance, colored blocks being injured fans, and agents playing the roles of fans, medics and police officers. Fans are fighting just outside some of the rooms and they can stop the medic from rescuing injured fans by entering a room just before the medic does so. Police officers will look for areas where fans are standing, while medics will check the rooms to find injured fans.

Consider an agent, *Bob*, playing the role of a medic ($\Sigma_o \models \mathsf{rea}(bob, medic)$), using the program in figure 4. He is considering the objective *injuredFound* ($\Gamma_o \models \mathsf{objective}(injuredFound)$), to which he has not yet committed. The following action rule can then be executed.

```
[opt(objective(O)), bel(me(Me)),
 org(role(R,Os), member(O,Os), rea(Me,R))] => commit(O)
```

In the resulting state, *injuredFound* is added as a goal ($\Gamma_a \models injuredFound$), and is sent via the bridge to the *Jason*-agent. This will trigger an event, +!*injured-Found*, and if the agent has a plan matching this trigger, it will execute the body of the plan. *Bob* has the following simplified plan library, making him capable of searching for injured fans.

```
+!injuredFound : room(R) & not(visited(R)) <- !visited(R).
+!injuredFound <- +injuredFound.

+!visited(R) : in(R) <- +visited(R).
+!visited(R) : not(state(traveling)) <- goTo(R); !visited(R).
```

Bob is situated in an environment with a single room, *room1*. The flow of the execution is shown in figure 7. *Bob* commits to finding the injured, which leads to the subgoal of visiting *room1*. When he believes he has visited the room (when he is inside the room), both goals will finish, since !*injuredFound* waited on the completion of !*visited(room1)*. Since the main goal, *injuredFound*, has not yet been completed, *Bob* can execute the same action rule again, thus committing to the goal once more. Since there are no more rooms to visit, only the second plan is applicable, and he believes that all the injured fans have been found.

When *injuredFound* is achieved, several things happen. First, the following coordination mechanism is triggered:

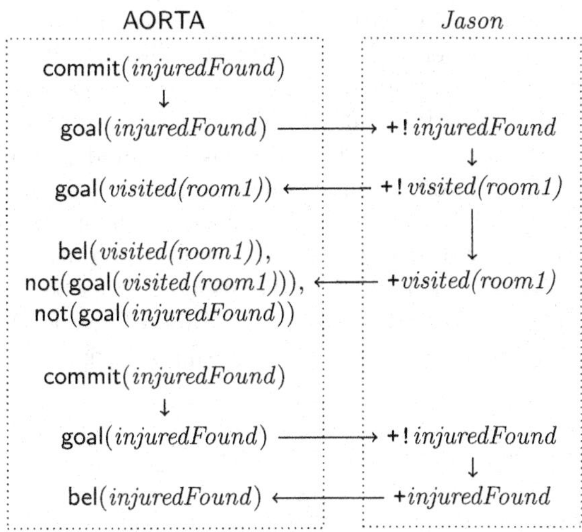

Fig. 7. The flow of execution starting when *Bob* performs the organizational action commit(*injuredFound*). not means that the formula is removed from the mental state.

```
[+bel(O)]
    : [org(role(R,Os), objective(O), member(O,Os), rea(A,R))]
    => send(A, bel(O))
```

Since bel(*injuredFound*) is added to the agent's mental state, and *injuredFound* is an objective, the agent will inform all agents responsible for that objective, that it has been completed. Second, the next objective, *injuredSaved*, becomes an option, and *Bob* will then commit to completing it. The flow of execution is similar to that of figure 7 and will not be described in detail.

If, during the rescue, a room is blocked by a fan, the agent may adopt a goal, *removeBlocker*, which will trigger the following coordination mechanism:

```
[+goal(X)]
    : [bel(me(Me)), org(rea(Me,R1), dependency(R1,R2,X), rea(A,R2))]
    => send(A, goal(X))
```

Since the agent commits to a goal for which there is a dependency, he sends a request to the agents enacting the role R2 (in this case the *officer* role). An officer should then commit to achieving the goal, and inform the medic when it has been done.

Notice that while it may seem like the agent is compelled to commit to the objectives given the organizational rules, it is important to emphasize that in the example this is the only rule. In other cases there will be more rules to choose between; rules that may influence the agent in different directions.

The agent can furthermore deliberately choose *not* to complete an objective. In *Jason*, the *intention selection function* can be changed to, e.g., prioritize the agent's own goals. This, of course, is only valid in the current integration; other frameworks may not have this possibility. However, the agent can deliberately skip parts of an objective, or even the entire objective, simply by marking the objective as done (i.e., a belief addition in *Jason*). This is a deliberate violation of the expectations of the role, but nothing prevents the agent from doing so.

Consider, for example, a different situation with two rooms, and in one of the rooms, the lights do not work. If the agent is scared of the dark, it may choose to simply skip that room, while convincing the organization that it has completed the objective. It is also possible that one of the medics is a fan of one of the soccer teams, and therefore deliberately chooses to only save injured fans from his own team. While this is in clear violation of the expectations from the organization, the agent is free to do so, since AORTA does not force the agent to perform certain actions, leading to, e.g., entering a dark room or saving fans from another team.

5 Related Work

There has been other work extending the BDI-architecture with organizational concepts, especially norms and obligations. This work differs from AORTA in that they modify the BDI-model, whereas AORTA extends the BDI reasoning with a component for the organizational reasoning. For example, the BOID architecture [3] imposes a strict ordering between beliefs, obligations, intentions and desires.

An abstract architecture for organizational reasoning is suggested in [20,1]. In this architecture, they suggest that organizational reasoning is done in a separate layer with a connection to the agent's cognitive layer (e.g., the BDI agent's beliefs and plans). The AORTA architecture is based on the same idea, that reasoning should be done within the agent, with a strong connection to the the cognitive layer of the agent. It is noted that several concrete architectures have been proposed that allow agents to understand and reason about organizations, e.g. [3,13,5].

The $\mathcal{M}$OISE$^+$ model is based on three organizational *dimensions*: the structural, functional and deontic dimensions [13]. Development of organized multi-agent systems using the $\mathcal{M}$OISE$^+$ model is separated into a system and an agent level. The system level, $\mathcal{S}$-$\mathcal{M}$OISE$^+$, provides an interface (a middleware) between the agents and the organization using a special agent, the OrgManager, to change the organizational state, ensuring organizational consistency. The agent level, $\mathcal{J}$-$\mathcal{M}$OISE$^+$, joins *Jason* and $\mathcal{M}$OISE$^+$, by making organizational actions available to agents, such that they can reason about (and change, using the OrgManager) an organization.

Similar to agents with an AORTA component, agents in $\mathcal{J}$-$\mathcal{M}$OISE$^+$ receive objectives (missions) that they can achieve using Jason plans. The main difference is that in $\mathcal{J}$-$\mathcal{M}$OISE$^+$, the organization-oriented reasoning is done as a part of the agent's normal reasoning process, whereas agents using AORTA perform the organizational reasoning inside the AORTA component, and then decides how to complete their objectives at a different level. The main advantage of keeping the reasoning apart in AORTA is that it allows agents on different agent platforms to perform the same kind of organizational reasoning without any extra development required.

The AMELI middleware for electronic institutions (EIs) specified in ISLANDER [9] *"mediates agents' interaction while enforcing institutional roles"* [10]. EIs specified in ISLANDER are based on dialogs; agents play *roles* in *scenes* in which they participate in interaction protocols to fulfill their goals (e.g., agents in an auction market use an interaction protocol for bidding on goods, where certain criterias decide whether the agent has bid on an item). The agents interact with the EI via a so-called *governor* using a predefined set of messages the governor will understand. These messages concern among other things entering the institution, moving to a scene, and say something in a scene. The governor can then agree to process the message (e.g. executing an action which can either succeed or fail) or refuse it. The governors of AMELI are similar to the middleware of $\mathcal{S}$-$\mathcal{M}$OISE$^+$; the control of the institution lays on the institution side. Our approach is to let the agents decide by themselves whether they can enter the institution or move to a different scene. Furthermore, if the agents want to utter something in a scene, they should be free to do so, even if it means unintentionally bidding for an item, or getting themselves kicked out.

The responsibility of deciding of whether an agent is allowed to enter an organization should not be put on the organizational entity but on the agents within that entity. In [19] it was shown that it is possible for agents to 1) reason about their own capabilities and 2) use this information to engage in an interaction with a gatekeeper in the organization (i.e. another agent) to determine whether the agent should be allowed to enter the organization. Such reasoning keeps the agents in control while still ensuring that the agents are capable of playing their roles in the organization.

Instead of putting mediators between the organization and the agents, or providing agents with a reasoning component, a third option is proposed in [12]: The ORA4MAS (Organizational Artifacts for Multi-Agent Systems) approach is another attempt to build a bridge between an organization and the agents in it. It is a general approach suitable for different kinds of organizational models, however in [12], $\mathcal{M}$OISE$^+$ is used as organizational model. They use artifacts, which they claim bring the control back to the agents (as compared to using a middleware), since the agents can, via their autonomy, choose whether to interact with the organizational artifacts of the system. We argue that the ultimate way of bringing the control back to the agents is to allow the agents *themselves* to perform the organizational reasoning. By integrating AORTA in agents, they are provided with organizational reasoning capabilities, but are still able to, e.g., decide not to commit to certain organizational objectives.

6 Conclusion and Future Work

We have described the AORTA architecture and have shown how it can be integrated in the *Jason* platform. The example shows how *Jason*-agents gain capabilities to reason about which organizational objectives to commit to, and how to coordinate completing them.

AORTA lets the developer focus on implementing the agents' domain-specific capabilities, while commitment to organizational objectives, coordination, and communication can be done entirely by AORTA. Furthermore, since AORTA can be integrated in different agent platforms, the same AORTA programs can be used for several different implementations in different agent programming languages. The use of the simple, generic language makes it possible to show how AORTA can be used to extend BDI-agents with organizational reasoning, however, the support of an existing, and more powerful, organizational language, such as $\mathcal{M}$OISE$^+$ or OperA, is a natural extension to the architecture, and would make it readily useful for more complex systems.

The decoupling of AORTA and the agent platform means that synchronization is required. However, the linear strategy makes sure that external changes are synchronized before options and actions are considered (via the EXT transition rule). As mentioned, the requirement is a translation between AORTA formulas and the formulas of the connected agent (e.g. AgentSpeak formulas). Furthermore, organizational reasoning is done in AORTA and is thus separated from the agent's normal reasoning. This is because the organizational state is only available to AORTA, as it is not shared with the agent. This means that the agent cannot reason about organizational matters, such as role enactment and organizational objectives without using the rules of AORTA. However, if necessary, in the case of *Jason*, it is possible to allow this kind of reasoning by introducing an *internal action*, e.g. `.org(Fml)` which succeeds if `Fml` can be translated to an AORTA formula and is entailed by the organizational state.

In the future, we plan to investigate other strategies that could improve the reasoning, such as a strategy that explores different paths of execution, and makes a decision based on this. Furthermore, since agents may have objectives that do not coincide with the organizational objectives, they need a way to decide which objectives to pursue, for example using a preference ordering [3] or individual agent preferences [14].

We are also investigating how to incorporate norms in the semantics, such that the agents are able to deliberately follow paths that violate the organization, while possibly being sanctioned by other agents in the organization. Finally, the scenario used in this paper was rather simple, so we are also working on evaluating the system on more advanced scenarios, and using other agent platforms (e.g. GOAL [11]) to show that the integration process is straightforward.

References

1. Boissier, O., van Riemsdijk, M.B.: Organisational Reasoning Agents. Agreement Technologies, 309–320 (2013)
2. Bordini, R.H., Hübner, J.F., Wooldridge, M.: Programming multi-agent systems in AgentSpeak using Jason. John Wiley & Sons (2007)
3. Broersen, J., Dastani, M., Hulstijn, J., Huang, Z., van der Torre, L.: The BOID architecture: Conflicts between beliefs, obligations, intentions and desires. In: Proceedings of the Fifth International Conference on Autonomous Agents, pp. 9–16 (2001)
4. Carabelea, C., Boissier, O., Castelfranchi, C.: Using Social Power to Enable Agents to Reason About Being Part of a Group. In: Gleizes, M.-P., Omicini, A., Zambonelli, F. (eds.) ESAW 2004. LNCS (LNAI), vol. 3451, pp. 166–177. Springer, Heidelberg (2005)

5. Castelfranchi, C., Dignum, F., Jonker, C.M., Treur, J.: Deliberate Normative Agents: Principles and Architecture. In: Jennings, N.R., Lespérance, Y. (eds.) Intelligent Agents VI. LNCS (LNAI), vol. 1757, pp. 364–378. Springer, Heidelberg (2000)
6. Denti, E., Omicini, A., Ricci, A.: *tu*Prolog: A light-weight Prolog for Internet applications and infrastructures. In: Ramakrishnan, I.V. (ed.) PADL 2001. LNCS, vol. 1990, pp. 184–198. Springer, Heidelberg (2001)
7. Dignum, V., Dignum, F.: A logic of agent organizations. Logic Journal of the IGPL 20(1), 283–316 (2011)
8. Dignum, V.: A model for organizational interaction: based on agents, founded in logic. PhD thesis, Utrecht University (2004)
9. Esteva, M., de la Cruz, D., Sierra, C.: Islander: An electronic institutions editor. In: Proc. AAMAS 2002 (2002)
10. Esteva, M., Rosell, B., Rodriguez-Aguilar, J.A., Arcos, J.L.: Ameli: An agent-based middleware for electronic institutions. In: Proceedings of the Third International Joint Conference on Autonomous Agents and Multiagent Systems, AAMAS 2004, vol. 1, pp. 236–243. IEEE Computer Society, Washington, DC
11. Hindriks, K.V.: Programming Rational Agents in GOAL. In: Multi-Agent Programming: Languages, Tools and Applications, pp. 119–157 (2009)
12. Hübner, J.F., Boissier, O., Kitio, R., Ricci, A.: Instrumenting multi-agent organisations with organisational artifacts and agents. Autonomous Agents and Multi-Agent Systems 20(3), 369–400 (2009)
13. Hübner, J.F., Sichman, J.S., Boissier, O.: Developing organised multiagent systems using the MOISE+ model: programming issues at the system and agent levels. International Journal of Agent-Oriented Software Engineering 1(3), 370–395 (2007)
14. Jensen, A.S.: Deciding between conflicting influences. In: Cossentino, M., El Fallah Seghrouchni, A., Winikoff, M. (eds.) EMAS 2013. LNCS (LNAI), vol. 8245, pp. 137–155. Springer, Heidelberg (2013)
15. Jensen, A.S., Aldewereld, H., Dignum, V.: Dimensions of organizational coordination. In: Proceedings of the 25th Benelux Conference on Artificial Intelligence, pp. 80–87. Delft University of Technology (2013)
16. Jensen, A.S., Dignum, V.: AORTA: Adding Organizational Reasoning to Agents. In: Proceedings of the 13th International Conference on Autonomous Agents and Multiagent Systems, pp. 1493–1494 (2014)
17. Johnson, M., Jonker, C., van Riemsdijk, B., Feltovich, P.J., Bradshaw, J.M.: Joint activity testbed: Blocks world for teams (BW4T). In: Aldewereld, H., Dignum, V., Picard, G. (eds.) ESAW 2009. LNCS, vol. 5881, pp. 254–256. Springer, Heidelberg (2009)
18. Rao, A.S., Georgeff, M.P.: BDI Agents: From Theory to Practice. In: Proc. ICMAS 1995 (1995)
19. van Riemsdijk, M.B., Dignum, V., Jonker, C.M., Aldewereld, H.: Programming Role Enactment through Reflection. In: 2011 IEEE/WIC/ACM International Conferences on Web Intelligence and Intelligent Agent Technology, vol. 2, pp. 133–140. IEEE Computer Society (August 2011)
20. van Riemsdijk, M.B., Hindriks, K., Jonker, C.: Programming organization-aware agents. In: Aldewereld, H., Dignum, V., Picard, G. (eds.) ESAW 2009. LNCS (LNAI), vol. 5881, pp. 98–112. Springer, Heidelberg (2009)

Keep Improving MAS Method Fragments: A Medee-Based Case Study for MOISE+

Sara Casare, Anarosa Alves Franco Brandao, and Jaime Sichman

Laboratório de Técnicas Inteligentes (LTI) – Escola Politécnica (EP)
Universidade de São Paulo (USP) - Brazil
sjcasare@uol.com.br,
{anarosa.brandao,jaime.sichman}@usp.br

Abstract. Continuous improvement is a procedure to improve products, services or processes. In the Software Engineering domain, software process improvement means understanding existing development processes and changing them to increase product quality and reduce development costs and time. In this paper, we present the Medee Improvement Cycle, which adopts this approach to improve development methods for Multiagent Systems (MAS). Such a cycle is anchored in the Medee Method Framework, which provides means for building methods through the combination of method fragments sourced from existing Agent-Oriented Software Engineering methods (AOSE methods) and Agent Organization models (AO models). The Medee Improvement Cycle allows to continuous evolving MAS methods and fragments, taking into account a set of quality attributes, such as understandability, visibility, supportability, acceptability and robustness. We have shown through the case study how to apply this cycle to evolve fragments through their usage, instead of assuming that we have already the definitive version of them from the beginning.

1 Introduction

Organization-centered multiagent systems (OC-MAS) are systems whose basic conceptual entity is the agent organization as a whole, composed of a set of goals, norms, and functionalities [18]. Such approach adopts a sociological and organizational vision for modeling MAS, involving organizations, teams and inter-agent relationships notions. Research in this area usually provides Agent Organization models (AO models) to support the specification of organizational aspects during MAS design and possibly changing them during MAS runtime, such as MOISE+ [16] and OperA [13]. Nevertheless, these models do not address a structured MAS development cycle in terms of phases, tasks, and work products, as extensively accepted by the software industry [19].

Moreover, although some existing Agent-Oriented Software Engineering (AOSE) methods, such as Gaia [25] and Ingenias [20], propose the development of MAS based on the notion of agent organization, they deal with organization specification at design time, preventing the modification of the organization core aspects during runtime.

F. Dalpiaz et al. (Eds.): EMAS 2014, LNAI 8758, pp. 146–162, 2014.

In order to fill this gap and provide reuse of existing AOSE methods and AO models, Casare et al [9] propose the Medee Method Framework (Medee for short), which allows the user to leverage advantages of both AOSE methods and AO models in order to develop OC-MAS, even though some AO models are not currently incorporated into AOSE methods. Such a method framework proposes the composition of MAS situational methods out of method fragments (i.e. small portions of methods) according to a given project situation, by applying the principles proposed by Situational Method Engineering [7] [14]. The proposed approach provides a high degree of reuse and flexibility, allowing the composition of new methods based on software industry standards for method description, such as SPEM [19].

Given that such situational methods are built on demand for immediate use and stored for further reuse, it is desirable that both methods and fragments could be improved in a continued way. Therefore, the definition of a cycle for guiding the continuous improvement of methods and fragments would reinforce the development of OC-MAS.

In this paper we present the Medee Improvement Cycle, a continuous cycle for evolving fragments and methods for MAS. The usage of such a cycle is illustrated in a case study conducted to improve fragments sourced from the MOISE+ agent organization model. The Medee Improvement Cycle is based on the idea that, although processes, methods, and tools are essential to the development of MAS, they should be underpinned by a continuous software process improvement in order to focus on product quality (e.g. OC-MAS applications quality) as well as on reducing development costs and time [21][22]. In brief, this cycle covers an entire improvement process for MAS method: (i) from tailoring a method according to the project characteristics (ii) to learning from the results how to evolve the method itself, in a way that lessons learned could give rise to method improvement.

Nevertheless, before explaining the Medee Improvement Cycle in details, which is done in Section 4, in Section 2 we briefly present the Medee Method Framework and in Section 3 we present the fragments sourced from MOISE+ that we have used. Our case study is presented in Section 5, and we discuss the advancements achieved with our approach in Section 6. Finally, we conclude the paper in Section 7.

2 Medee Method Framework

The Medee Method Framework supports the composition of MAS methods on demand, especially the ones for developing OC-MAS. In brief, it consists of a repository containing method fragments sourced from several AOSE methods and AO models, as well as a process for populating such a repository and a model for composing situational methods out of fragments according to a given MAS project situation. Therefore, this framework encompasses the following components: the Medee Method Repository, the Medee Delivery Process, and the Medee Composition Model. Together, these components cover most of a typical situational method procedure - from managing the method repository to building and publishing the situational method - in a seamless way, since they are based on the same conceptual model, i.e. the Medee Conceptual Model, as illustrated in Fig. 1. Moreover, this figure highlights that situational methods are published as HTML pages.

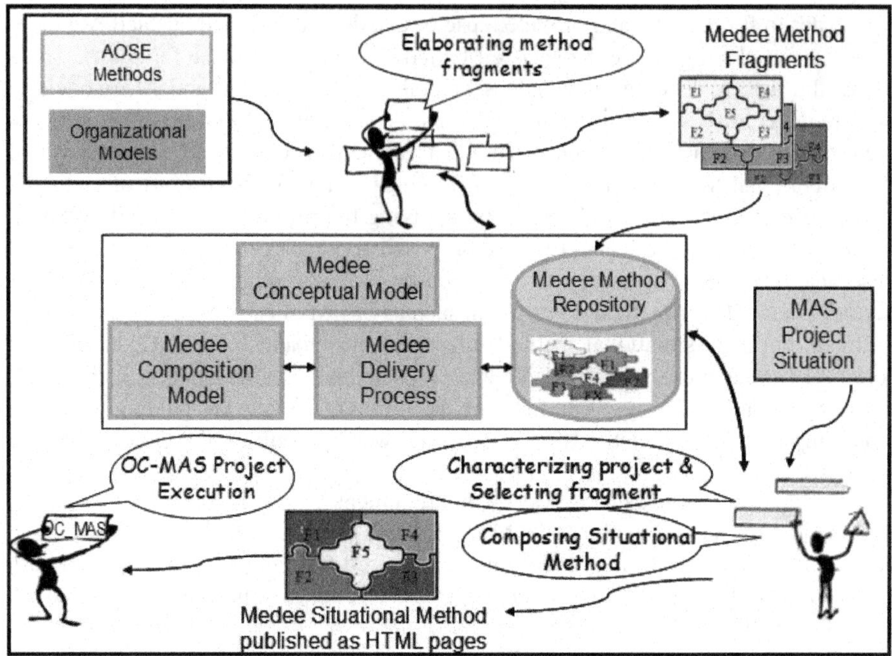

Fig. 1. The Medee Method Framework main components and functionalities

AOSE methods and AO models involve particular aspects, such as specific system architecture, development platform, design and programming languages. The Medee Method Framework takes these aspects into account in an integrated way, from the method repository management to the situational composition. Firstly, the Medee user can elaborate method fragments in a standard way, for instance by using common MAS development roles like MAS Developer and MAS Tester, as well as categorizing them according to the underpinned MAS component (e.g. agent, environment, organization), the MAS nature (e.g. open, closed), the design language (e.g. UML, AUML), and the programming language (e.g. Java, AgentSpeak), among other criteria provided by a semiotic taxonomy for MAS fragments.

Secondly, the Medee user can clearly state the project characteristics in terms of people, problem, product, and resource factors. Such characterization takes into account AOSE aspects, like the project team previous experience with developing MAS, the agent architecture to be used, like BDI, and the kind of product to be delivered, such as OC-MAS or agent-centered MAS. Finally, issues like how to proceed for elaborating fragments, characterizing the project, selecting fragments and putting them together in a situational method are described in great details in the Medee Delivery Process. This latter is published as a website and offers three phases: Method Element Capture, Method Fragment Elaboration, and Medee Method Composition phases.

A detailed description of the Medee Method Framework is available at the Medee website[1] and also at [9]. Currently, the Medee Method Repository stores 64 (sixty four) fragments sourced from AOSE methods such as Gaia, Tropos [6], PASSI [11], Ingenias, and from general-purpose development methods such as USDP (Unified Software Development Process) [17], as well as fragments sourced from AO models like MOISE+ and OperA. This repository can be easily extended with fragments sourced from other AOSE methods since the Medee Delivery Process provides step-by-step tasks for the method repository population. Moreover, new fragments can be categorized according to more than 25 semiotic criteria provided by the Medee Composition Model. Such functionalities allow the user to manage the method repository in a consistent and disciplined way, despite the number of stored fragments.

3 Method Fragments for MOISE+

MOISE+ is a well-established AO model tailored for specifying OC-MAS. It describes a MAS organization in terms of three dimensions: structural, functional and normative dimensions. For each one of these dimensions MOISE+ proposes one homonym specification.

The method fragments sourced from MOISE+ consisted of the smallest fragments that compose a MAS situational method. They contain tasks described in terms of steps, input and output work products, and development roles, as illustrated in Fig. 2 (right side). It should be noted that Fig. 2 shows a screenshot of the Medee website prior to the case study. Indeed, it depicts the fragment[2] MMF Analyze Organization with MOISE+, which was sourced from MOISE+ along with other four fragments: MMF Design Agent Organizational Behavior with MOISE+, MMF Design Organization with MOISE+, MMF Implement Agent with MOISE+, and MMF Implement Organization with MOISE+ (see Fig. 2, left side). These five fragments could take part in situational methods for developing OC-MAS projects.

It is important to observe that MOISE+ offers a conceptual framework and syntax to organizational specification, but it does not describe the work that should be done - as such activities, task or steps - to produce such specifications. Therefore, the fragments sourced from MOISE+ resulted from the analysis and interpretation made during a previous research presented in [8].

These fragments consisted of an important step towards the development of methods for OC-MAS. Nonetheless, they deserve to be improved through utilization. One way of doing that is using the Medee Improvement Cycle, as done during the case study presented in this paper.

---

[1] `http://medee.poli.usp.br/.`

[2] MMF stands for Medee Method Fragment, MPS stands for Medee work Product Slot, MTV stands for Medee Task Variability, MPV stands for Medee Product Variability.

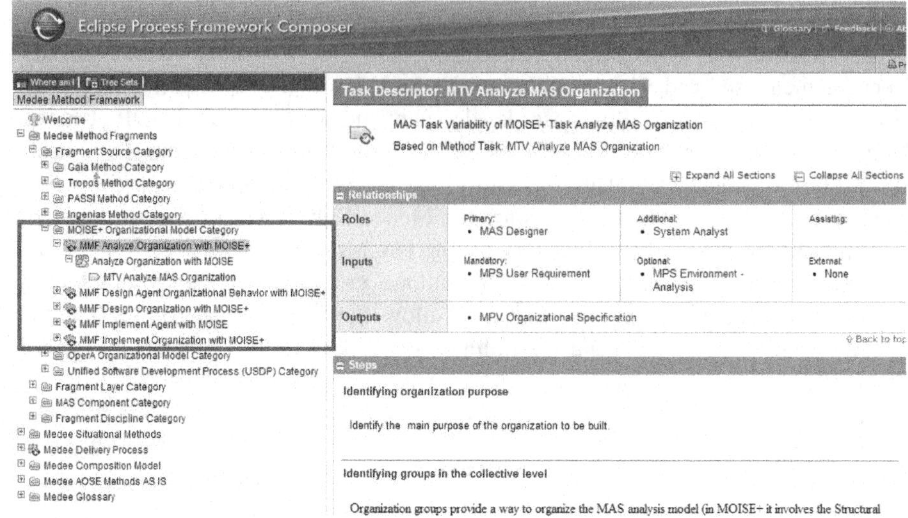

Fig. 2. Medee fragments sourced from MOISE+

4 Medee Improvement Cycle

The Medee improvement cycle is anchored in an empirical procedure for continuous evolving MAS methods and fragments based on previous project experience.

This cycle is built upon approaches proposed in Situational Method Engineering and Software Engineering areas: (i) an iterative procedure for building situational methods [7] [14], (ii) paradigms for software improvement through experimentation, namely Quality Improvement Paradigm (QIP) [1] [2] and Goal Question Metric (GQM) [3], and (iii) the method quality attributes proposed by Sommerville [22].

An iterative procedure for building situational methods usually encompasses the following steps: management of the method repository, characterization of the project situation, selection of method fragments, situational method building, and project execution. We have extended this set of steps by adopting those proposed by QIP, which is an evolutionary software quality process that provides a mechanism for software improvement through experimentation and reuse, based on project experience. Such a paradigm proposes to treat software development as empirical experiments in order to learn with them and thus improve the way to build software based on a goal-driven approach for collecting data around a particular experiment, the GQM paradigm. Given that method quality attributes (e.g. understandability, acceptability, reliability) may be used to drive method quality improvement [22], we have adopted these attributes in order to define the goals for improving methods and fragments.

Therefore, the Medee Improvement Cycle underpins seven steps that can be applied in two scenarios, depending on the improvement target: (i) a situational method, (ii) a method or some method fragments. Fig. 3 shows enclosed in solid bold line the five steps for improving fragments and methods, out of this rectangle, the other two steps involved on improving situational methods. The case study presented in Section 5 is concerned with fragments improvement and thus is based on the second scenario. Interested readers can find a case study involving the first scenario in [8]. The seven steps are described in the following.

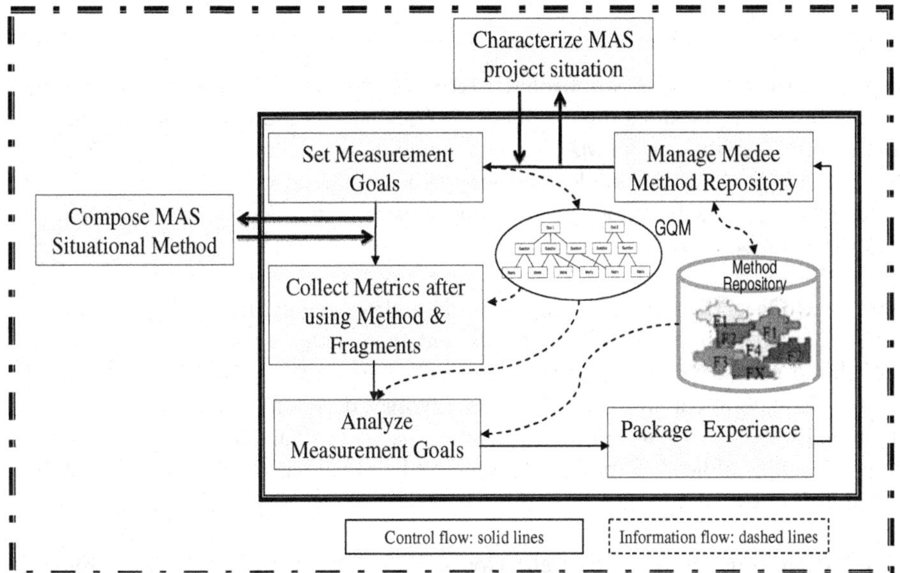

Fig. 3. Medee Improvement Cycle

Step 1 - Characterize MAS Project Situation using the Medee Composition Model. This step allows a Medee user to better understand and characterize the factors involved in the MAS project, mainly those related to AOSE aspects. Therefore, in this step s/he can clearly state project characteristics in terms of people, problem, product, and resource factors. Possible examples are: the project team has no previous experience of developing MAS, although having some skills related to agent-oriented methods and UML; the product to be delivered involves an organization-centered approach. This step is performed only while running the cycle for situational methods (first scenario).

Step 2 - Set MAS Measurement Goals. It consists of establishing a goal-driven model based on the GQM paradigm, according to the improvement targets selected for the empirical procedure. The method quality attributes proposed by Sommerville [22] were adopted as a backbone to define the measurement goals. Therefore, these goals are based on the following method and fragment issues: understandability, supportability, visibility, acceptability, reliability, robustness, rapidity, and maintainability. For instance, a goal related to fragment understandability could measure how easy it is to understand its elements (e.g. task, work product, roles), while another related to supportability could measure how easy it is to navigate in the website that describes methods and fragments. Although such quality attributes provide a steady basis for starting specifying measurement goals, they may be extended and refined according to a given set of method improvement targets. Section 5 presents the goal-driven model instantiated to measure the method fragments sourced from MOISE+ during the case study, involving goals concerned with understandability, supportability and visibility.

Step 3 - Compose MAS Situational Method. This step is performed only while running the cycle for situational methods. It consists of generating a situational method according to the current MAS project situation, by executing the Medee Method Composition phase of the Medee Delivery Process. Brandão et al [5] recently provided some automated support for selecting fragments in Medee in order to facilitate situational composition.

Step 4 - Collect Metrics after using method and fragments. It consists of applying methods or analyzing a set of fragments and then gathering the metrics specified through the goal-driven model. Every usage of fragments or methods will be considered as an experiment. Moreover, this step involves designing questionnaires that are filled out by the participants of the experiment, as well as validating data provided by them. Examples of how metrics can be collected and validated are presented and discussed in Section 5.

Step 5 - Analyze the Measurement Goals. It consists of identifying the strengths and weakness of methods or fragments, through the assessment of the previously collected questionnaires' answers. Examples of how to perform such analysis concerning MOISE+ fragments are presented in Section 5.

Step 6 - Package Experience to improve the Method Repository. It consists of capturing and describing the lessons learned during the experiment in terms of improvement opportunities, in such a way that it could be used to update fragments and/or methods, as well as other building blocks underpinned by the Method Repository itself, like the Medee Glossary. Lessons learned can give rise to improvement opportunities in several ways, such as: (i) understandability concerns can drive method fragment re-elaboration or the creation of new guidelines and examples; (ii) fragment acceptability or reliability concerns can drive method fragments re-classification, and (iii) rapidity concerns are related to the project required effort, can be captured as estimation consideration and associated either with the whole method or the corresponding fragments. Section 5 presents MOISE+ fragments' improvement identified during the case study.

Step 7 - Manage the Method Repository. It consists of populating the Medee Method Repository with new elements as well as modifying/updating already stored elements - like method fragments and Medee methods - based on lessons learned during an experiment, as illustrated in Section 5. This step is mainly underpinned by two phases of the Medee Delivery Process [9] - Method Element Capture and Method Fragment Elaboration phases - both described in great detail at the Medee website.

Finally, it should be observed that the Medee Improvement Cycle could be used to evolve the Medee Delivery Process itself, and not only fragments and situational methods. Examples of measurement goals and questions of interest that could be used in such an improvement scenario are:

Goal 1: Analyze the **Medee Delivery Process** for the purpose of evaluation with respect to the **usability**

Q1: How ease is it to create/modify method fragments?

Q2: How ease is it to compose the situational method out of fragments?

Goal2: Analyze the **Medee Delivery Process** for the purpose of evaluation with respect to its **rapidity/efficiency.**

Q3: How fast can the method engineer create a new fragment**?**

Q4: How fast can the method engineer compose a situational method?

Summing up, these seven steps embedded in the Medee Improvement Cycle offer a process for evolving both methods and fragments based on lessons learned. As described in the next section, lessons learned were packaged and integrated in the method repository for further use in a seamless way.

5 Case Study

The purpose of this case study was to investigate the use of the Medee Improvement Cycle for evolving fragments sourced from MOISE+. In a few words, it consisted of performing the step-by-step of such a cycle to improve MOISE+ fragments based on lessons learned.

Moreover, we investigated also how aware Medee users were about the improvements we have done. Therefore, some steps of the Medee cycle were performed twice namely, steps 2, 4, and 5.

This case study was conducted in 2013 and involved undergraduate students, MOISE+ authors and MAS researchers skilled in MOISE+ notions and method engineering, totalizing eight people.

The remainder of this section describes the five steps executed during this experiment, starting with Step 2 (Set measurement goals) and closing the cycle with Step 7 (Manage the method repository). It should be observed that evolving the fragments sourced from MOISE+ means also evolving the situational methods that include them as well as evolving the method repository as a whole.

5.1 Setting the Measurement Goals (Step 2)

This step consisted of defining a goal-driven model based on the GQM approach for evaluating the method fragments sourced from MOISE+ concerning three quality attributes: understandability, visibility, and supportability. Measurement goals were described in terms of the objects of study, issues, and viewpoints taken into account in this experiment, as well as detailed through questions of interest and metrics. Firstly, the five MOISE+ fragments presented in Section 3 were considered as objects of study. Second, the issues consisted of the quality attributes understandability, visibility, and supportability. Thirdly, the viewpoint entities encompassed MAS developers, MOISE+ experts and method engineers.

Finally, these goals were refined through eleven questions of interest and related metrics. Some questions of interest took into account the MAS developer viewpoint, while other considered the MOISE+ expert and Method Engineer viewpoints. In the following we present the three goals and the associate questions and metrics.

Goal 1: Analyze the MOISE+ Method fragment for the purpose of evaluation with respect to its **understandability**.

Q1: To what extent has the fragment facilitated the understanding of MOISE+ aspects (e.g. concepts, specifications, implementation)?

Metric 1: Ranging from 1 (not helpful at all) to 5 (very useful).

Q2: To what extent has the Medee Glossary helped to understand the elements encompassed in the fragment (e.g. tasks, work products, roles)?

Metric 2: From 1 (not helpful at all) to 5 (very useful).

Q3: How easy is it to understand the work that should be performed when adopting the fragment? In other words, is it easy to understand the task(s) and steps encompassed in the fragment?

Metric 3: From 1 (not easy at all) to 5 (very easy)

Q4: How easy is it to understand the work product encompassed in the fragment?

Metric 4: From 1 (not easy at all) to 5 (very easy).

Goal 2: Analyze the MOISE+ Method fragment for the purpose of evaluation with respect to its **visibility**.

Q5: To what extent the development phase (e.g. analysis, design) during which the fragment is expected to be used is clearly stated?

Metric 5: From 1 (unclear) to 5 (very clear).

Q6: To what extent the work product that should be generated by the fragment is clearly stated?

Metric 6: From 1 (unclear) to 5 (very clear)

Q7: To what extent the fragment inputs are clearly stated?

Metric 7: From 1 (unclear) to 5 (very clear).

Q8: To what extent the development role(s) assigned to the fragment are clearly stated?

Metric 8: From 1 (unclear) to 5 (very clear).

Q9: To what extent the MAS aspects involved in the fragment are clearly stated (e.g. MAS component, MAS nature)?

Metric 9: From 1 (unclear) to 5 (very clear).

Goal 3: Analyze the MOISE+ Method fragment for evaluation purposes with respect to **supportability**.

Q10: How easy is it to navigate in the website that describes the fragment?

Metric 10: From 1 (not easy at all) to 5 (very easy).

Q11: To what extent the guidance proposed by the fragment (e.g. examples, whitepapers, concepts) could help task execution and/or work product generation?

Metric 11: From 1 (not helpful at all) to 5 (very useful).

5.2 Collecting Metrics after Fragments Usage (Step 4)

Having defined the goal-driven model, a questionnaire was designed for each of the five MOISE+ fragments. Along with aforementioned goals, questions of interest and metrics, the designed questionnaires asked for additional comments.

Furthermore, the participants had inspected these fragments and analyzed them against the MOISE+ literature [15] [16]. Next, they filled out the five questionnaires. Questionnaires involving the Developer viewpoint were filled out by students, while those relating to the MOISE+ expert and Method Engineer viewpoints were filled out by MAS researchers.

Finally, to ensure completeness and consistency, the data provided in these questionnaires were validated through interviews with the students and researchers. The collected metrics are presented in Table 1.

5.3 Analyzing the Measurement Goals (Step 5)

This step consisted of analyzing the three measurement goals through the collected metrics. Table 1 (last row) shows a consolidated perspective of such metrics by the three goals, as well as perspectives broken by the five MOISE+ fragment (last column).

Table 1. Collected GQM metrics round 1

	Goal 1 Understandability	Goal 2 Visibility	Goal 3 Supportability	Total
Frag#1	4,3	4,4	4,6	4,4
Frag#2	4,3	4,2	4,3	4,3
Frag#3	4,0	4,4	4,5	4,3
Frag#4	4,8	4,7	4,6	4,7
Frag#5	4,2	4,1	4,6	4,3
Total	4,3	4,3	4,5	4,4

The metrics regarding Goal 1 – Understandability - have shown that MOISE+ fragments were quite easy to understand (4.3 points in a 1 to 5 scale). However, some comments stated that the two fragments related to the analysis and design of the organizational specification could be made more understandable if tasks and steps were more explicit about which of the three MOISE+ specifications they were concerned with (i.e. Structural, Functional, Deontic specifications).

Furthermore, this experiment showed that fragments' elements - like roles, input and output work products - had a quite well visibility (4.3 in a 1 to 5 scale). Nonetheless, some aspects related to Medee development roles were missing, such as role responsibility, while the work products could be more visible if they could also be accessed directly, besides embedded in tasks.

Finally, the metrics related to Goal 3 – Supportability - have shown that MOISE+ fragments offered a suitable collection of examples, whitepapers, and concepts, as well as an easy navigation through the Medee website (4.5 in a 1 to 5 scale). However, some comments suggested that fragments could provide definitions for concepts related to the agent-oriented paradigm to help newcomers.

5.4 Packaging Experience for Improving Fragments (Step 6)

This step consisted of describing improving opportunities in a way that such description could be used to manage fragments and/or the Method Repository itself, which is effectively done in the step 7.

Due to paper length limitations, this section describes only a couple of improvement opportunities related to the two fragments concerned with the analysis and design of OC-MAS, as well as some improvement related to the Method Repository as a whole.

Opportunities for Improving MAS Organization Analysis and Design

- Improve the comprehension about the work to be done, since tasks mixed up several MOISE+ concepts pertaining to different MOISE+ specification (functional, structural and deontic).
- State in a clear way each one of the MOISE+ specifications should be created or modified through the tasks/steps underpinned by the fragments.
- Recommend the use of MAS User Requirement specification during the design of the MOISE+ organization, as it is recommended during the organization analysis.

Opportunities for Improving the Method Repository

- Offer the definition of concepts related to the Agent-Oriented Paradigm.
- Make development roles characteristics more explicit.
- Make work products characteristics more explicit.

5.5 Managing the Method Repository (Step 7)

This step consisted of updating the Medee Method Repository according to the improvement opportunities previously identified. Such an update encompassed managing two MOISE+ fragments. Moreover, it involved managing some aspects related to the building blocks underpinned by the Method Repository itself, such as making more explicit the Medee development roles and work products, and expanding the Medee Glossary by including MAS concepts, as explained in the sequence.

Updating Fragments for MAS Organization Analysis and Design

It consisted of modifying two fragments, MMF Analyze MAS Organization with MOISE+ and MMF Design MAS Organization with MOISE+, by describing the work required to deal with MOISE+ specifications in a way that each task were focused on one single specification (i.e. Functional, Structural and Deontic). Therefore, the task called MTV Analyze MAS Organization was replaced by three new tasks: MTV Analyze MAS Functional Specification, MTV Analyze MAS Structural Specification and MTV Analyze MAS Deontic Specification.

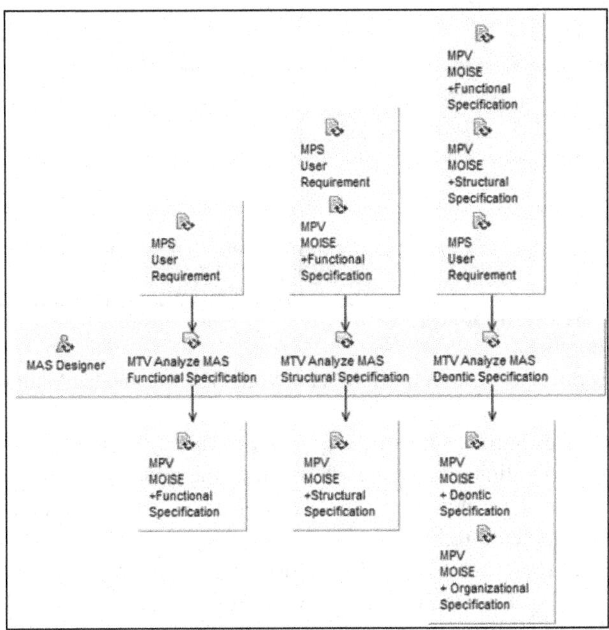

Fig. 4. Workflow for MMF Analyzing MAS Organization with MOISE+

As illustrated in Fig. 4, the new task in charge of analyzing the functional dimension of a MOISE+ organization takes a User Requirement (e.g. the one proposed by Tropos) as input and produces the MOISE+ Functional Specification as output. In a similar way, the new tasks in charge of analyzing structural and deontic MOISE+ dimensions produce the homonym MOISE+ specifications as outputs. Furthermore, the improved fragment for analyzing MOISE+ organization was built upon these new tasks and thus clearly states the specification created by each one of its tasks. Moreover, as illustrated in Fig. 4, as soon as a specification is available, it can be used as an input in the next task.

Such an approach promotes the coherence and consistence of the MOISE+ specifications generated by this fragment. A similar approach was adopted to update the MMF Design MAS Organization with MOISE+. Interested readers can find these new fragments in the Medee website (see Medee Method Fragments folder).

Updating the Method Repository Building Blocks

On one hand, it consisted of modifying the Method Repository navigation tree in order to present the Medee Development Roles and the Medee Work Product Framework in an explicit way, as illustrated in Fig. 5 (right side). In such a way, these elements can be accessed directly, and not only through method fragments.

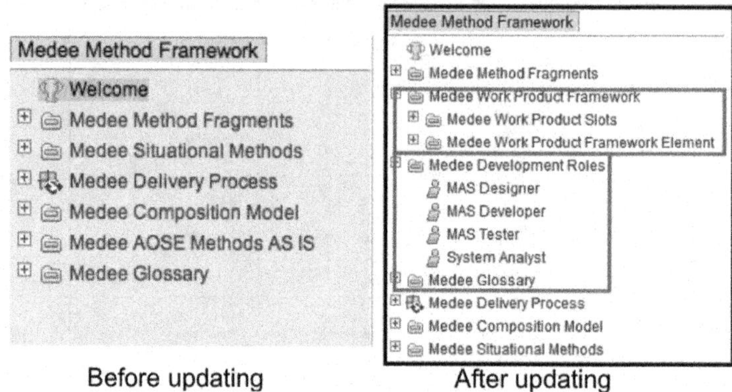

Fig. 5. Providing direct navigation for Roles and Work Products into the Method Repository

On the other hand, it consisted of extending the Medee Glossary by creating new concepts in order to facilitate the comprehension of the agent-oriented paradigm main notions. Examples of these new concepts are BDI agents, agent autonomy, and multiagent systems, as depicted in Fig. 6.

Therefore, after these modifications Medee users should better understand the agent-oriented paradigm, as well as easily discover the entire set of MAS development roles and MAS work products currently available in the Method Repository.

Summing up the Medee Method Repository Improvements

During this experiment we have improved several elements of the Medee Method Repository through modifications based on lessons learned. As illustrated in Figs. 4, 5 and 6, such modifications are ready for use since this repository has been updated and the Medee website related pages have been generated again as part of the method repository management procedure.

Therefore, from now on the Medee repository stores a glossary containing concepts that facilitate the comprehension of the agent-oriented paradigm, a navigation tree that presents in an explicit way the available MAS development roles and MAS work products, and method fragments that state in a clear way each one of the three MOISE+ specifications should be created/updated through the tasks and steps underpinned by them.

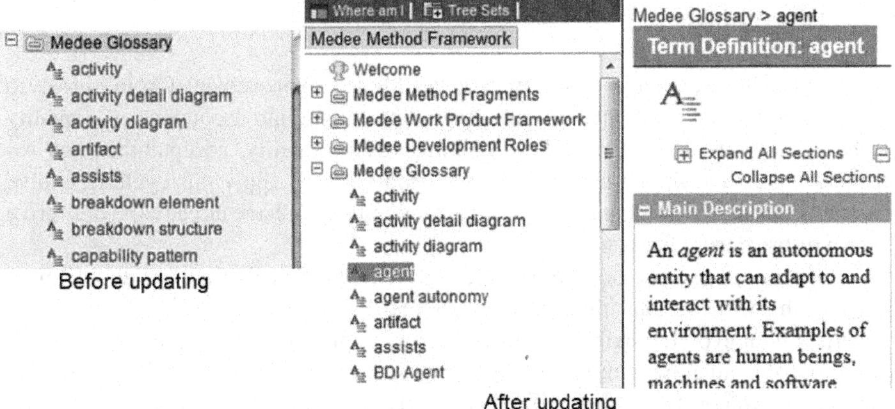

Fig. 6. Improving the Medee Glossary including MAS concepts

5.6 Repeating the Medee Improvement Cycle

As previously mentioned, we have performed twice some steps of the Medee Improvement Cycle to investigate in which extent the presented improvement were perceived by students and MAS researchers.

This second round took into account a narrower scope, since it concerned mainly the two improved MOISE+ fragments, those related to the analysis and design of organizations. Therefore, this round included the following steps: (i) Setting measurement goals, (ii) Collecting metrics after using method fragments, and (iii) Analyzing the measurement goals.

Table 2. Collected GQM metrics round 2

	Goal 1 Understandability	Goal 2 Visibility	Goal 3 Supportability	Total
Frag#1	4,6	4,6	4,8	4,6
Frag#2	4,8	4,6	4,8	4,7
	4,7	4,6	4,8	4,7

We have used a smaller version of the goal-driven model previously developed, by limiting the objects of study to the Fragments #1 and #2, respectively, MMF Analyze Organization with MOISE+ (Enhanced) and MMF Design Organization with MOISE+ (Enhanced). Thus, metrics were collected through two questionnaires involving the three goals and related questions of interest, and filled out by the same participants.

Table 2 presents a consolidated perspective of collected metrics by the three goals (last row), and perspectives broken by the two MOISE+ fragments (last column). Just by looking at the quantitative aspects one may think that improvement was marginal. Nevertheless, the comments were very important to evaluate the improvement perception. Participants said that their understanding about MOISE+ work products increased a lot, as well as the steps that must be followed to execute the tasks involved in their generation.

6 Discussion

As described in the course of this paper, the Medee Improvement Cycle allows to continuous evolving MAS methods and fragments, taking into account a set of quality attributes, such as understandability, visibility, supportability, acceptability and robustness. We have shown through the case study how to apply this cycle to evolve fragments through their usage, instead of assuming that we have already the definitive version of them from the beginning.

Furthermore, our approach encompasses several aspects that constitute advancements in the way we can improve methods and fragments for AOSE. Firstly, it is concerned with evolving both MAS methods and fragments based on lessons learned, and not only evaluating and comparing them, as proposed in [4] [10] [12] [23]. Our goal is to continuously improving method and fragments, instead of comparing them quantitatively.

Secondly, it provides an integrated approach to update fragments, methods, and other Method Repository building blocks, based on industry standards for describing methods [19]. As illustrated in the case study, fragment improvements were easily incorporated to the method repository for immediately reuse, which could involve composing new situational method or changing existing ones.

Although no one is able to ensure that has the best development method for a given project situation neither in traditional software engineering field in general nor in AOSE field, the Medee Improvement Cycle is an approach that could help pursuing such a goal.

To the best of our knowledge, in the AOSE field there is no currently such a broad approach for evolving methods, fragments, and method repository building blocks in an integrated way.

7 Conclusions

Having a set of well established MAS development methods would facilitate the adoption of the agent-oriented software engineering by the software industry . In such a context, method improvement is strongly desirable since it allows lessons learned from method usage to give rise to a continuous process for evolving method based on quality attributes, like understandability, supportability, visibility, and robustness, among others.

In this paper we have presented the Medee Improvement Cycle, a continuous process improvement approach to deal with MAS methods. Our approach may be applied for both whole methods or single fragments, and uses industry standards [19] for evolving them in a seamless manner. Moreover, it offers a controlled and disciplined way to learn from experience. Therefore, it can be used for reinforcing the development of MAS in the academy as well as in the software industry.

We show its applicability by presenting in which manners some fragments sourced from a well-established AO model, the MOISE+ model, could be improved towards a better understandability, visibility and supportability. In a few words, at the end of the improvement process we had facilitated the understanding of MOISE+ concepts as well as enhanced the visibility of the step-by-step in which MOISE+ specifications could be produced during the development of an OC-MAS project. Also, we have updated the Method Repository turning it easily to be navigated.

Acknowledgments. We would like to thank the participants of the experiment reported in this paper. Anarosa A. F. Brandão is partially supported by grant #010/2640-5, São Paulo Research Foundation (FAPESP). Jaime S. Sichman is partially supported by CNPq, Brazil. Sara Casare is partially supported by IBM Brasil.

References

1. Basili, V.: Learning through Applications: The Maturing of the QIP in the SEL. In: Oram, A., Wilson, G. (eds.) Making Software. O'Reilly (2011)
2. Basili, V.R.: The Experience Factory and its Relationship to Other Improvement Paradigms. In: Sommerville, I., Paul, M. (eds.) ESEC 1993. LNCS, vol. 717, pp. 68–83. Springer, Heidelberg (1993)
3. Basili, V., Weiss, D.: A Methodology for Collecting Valid Software Engineering Data. IEEE Transactions on Software Engineering 10(3), 728–738 (1984)
4. Bonjean, N., Gleizes, M.-P., Chella, A., Migeon, F., Cossentino, M., Seidita, V.: Metamodel-Based Metrics for Agent-Oriented Methodologies. In: Conitzer, Winikoff, Padgham, van der Hoek (eds.) Proceedings of the 11th International Conference on Autonomous Agents and Multiagent Systems (AAMAS 2012), Valencia, Spain, June 4-8 (2012), http://www.ifaamas.org/Proceedings/aamas2012/papers/
5. Brandão, A.A.F., Casare, S., França, D.I.: Towards automating method fragment selection for MAS. In: Proceedings of the IV Workshop on Autonomous Software Systems, AutoSoft 2013, pp. 32–40 (2013), http://cbsoft2013.unb.br/wp-content/uploads/2013/10/Autosoft-completo.pdf
6. Bresciani, P., Giorgini, P., Giunchiglia, F., Mylopoulos, J., Perini, A.: Tropos: An Agent-Oriented Software Development Methodology. Journal of Autonomous Agents and Multi-Agent Systems 8(3), 203–236 (2004)
7. Brinkkemper, S.: Method Engineering: Engineering of Information Systems Development Methods and Tools. Information and Software Technology 38(4), 275–280 (1996)
8. Casare, S.J.: Medee: A Method Framework for Multiagent Systems. PhD Thesis, Universidade de São Paulo, Brazil. (2012), http://www.teses.usp.br/teses/disponiveis/3/3141/tde-05032012-162517/en.php
9. Casare, S., Brandão, A.A.F., Guessoum, Z., Sichman, J.: Medee Method Framework: A Situational Approach for Organization-Centered MAS. Autonomous Agents and Multi-Agent Systems (June 2013), http://link.springer.com/article/10.1007%2Fs10458-013-9228-y
10. Cernuzzi, L., Rossi, G.: On the evaluation of agent oriented modeling methods. In: Proceedings of the Agent-Oriented Methodology Workshop, pp. 21–30 (2002)
11. Cossentino, M.: From Requirements to Code with the PASSI Methodology. In: Henderson-Sellers, B., Giorgini, P. (eds.) Agent-Oriented Methodologies, pp. 79–106. Idea Group Publishing (2005)

12. Dam, K.H., Winikoff, M.: Comparing Agent-Oriented Methodologies. In: Giorgini, P., Henderson-Sellers, B., Winikoff, M. (eds.) AOIS 2003. LNCS (LNAI), vol. 3030, pp. 78–93. Springer, Heidelberg (2004)
13. Dignum, V.: A model for organizational interaction:based on agents, founded in logic. Doctoral dissertation, Utrecht University, Utrecht (2004)
14. Harmsen, A.F.: Situational Method Engineering. Moret Ernst & Young (1997)
15. Hübner, J., Sichman, J., Boissier, O.: Developing organised multiagent systems using the MOISE+ model: Programming issues at the system and agent levels. International Journal of Agent-Oriented Software Engineering 1(3), 370–395 (2007)
16. Hübner, J.F., Sichman, J.S., Boissier, O.: Using the MOISE+ for a cooperative framework of MAS reorganization. In: Bazzan, A.L.C., Labidi, S. (eds.) SBIA 2004. LNCS (LNAI), vol. 3171, pp. 506–515. Springer, Heidelberg (2004)
17. Jacobson, B.G., Rumbaugh, J.: The Unified Software Development Process. Addison-Wesley (1999)
18. Lemaıtre, C., Excelente, C.B.: Multi-agent organization approach. In: The Second Iberoamerican Workshop on Distributed AI and MAS, Toledo, Espana (1998)
19. OMG. Object Management Group. Software & Systems Process Engineering Meta-Model Specification, version 2.0.2008. OMG document number: formal/2008-04-01, `http://www.omg.org/spec/SPEM/2.0/PDF`
20. Pavon, J., Gomez-Sanz, J., Fuentes, R.: The Ingenias Methodology and Tools. In: Henderson-Sellers, B., Giorgini, P. (eds.) Agent-Oriented Methodologies, pp. 236–276. Idea Group Publishing (2005)
21. Pressman, R.S.: Software Engineering: A practitioner's Approach, 7th edn. McGraw-Hill (2010)
22. Sommerville, I.: Software Engineering, 8th edn. Addison-Wesley (2007)
23. Sturm, A., Shehory, O.: A Framework for Evaluating Agent-Oriented Methodologies. In: Giorgini, P., Henderson-Sellers, B., Winikoff, M. (eds.) AOIS 2003. LNCS (LNAI), vol. 3030, pp. 94–109. Springer, Heidelberg (2004)
24. Uez, D., Hubner, J., Weber, C.: Método para modelagem de agentes, ambiente e organização de sistemas multiagentes. In: Proceedings of the IV Workshop on Autonomous Software Systems, AutoSoft 2013, pp. 41–50 (2013), `http://cbsoft2013.unb.br/wp-content/uploads/2013/10/Autosoft-completo.pdf`
25. Zambonelli, F., Jennings, N.R., Wooldridge, M.: Developing multiagent systems: The Gaia methodology. ACM Transaction on Software Engineering and Methodology 12(3), 417–470 (2003)

Towards Process-Oriented Modelling and Creation of Multi-Agent Systems

Tobias Küster, Axel Heßler, and Sahin Albayrak

DAI-Labor, Technische Universität Berlin, Germany
tobias.kuester@dai-labor.de

Abstract. Different ways of integrating business processes and agents have been proposed, but using restricted process models or targeting only single agents, none of them is truly convincing. Nevertheless, business processes have many notions in common with agents and would be well suited for modelling complex multi-agent systems. In this paper, we combine concepts of two existing approaches to a mapping from business process diagrams to readily executable agent components. The results are well-structured and extensible, and at the same time account for nearly the entire expressiveness of the process modelling notation.

Keywords: Technological, Methodological.

1 Introduction

In recent times, different approaches for modelling agents and multi-agent systems using business process diagrams and related notations have been introduced (e.g., [6], [10], [18]). However, none of these approaches is really compelling. Often, very simple workflow models are used, or if a more expressive process modelling notation is chosen, then only a limited subset of the language is covered. Furthermore, usually only single agents are targeted, while interactions between agents – which could very well be modelled using many process notations – are not regarded.

This is unfortunate, since process diagrams share many concepts and abstractions with multi-agent systems – in particular sophisticated notations such as the Business Process Model and Notation (BPMN) [22]. Those notations can be used for modelling the intertwined workflows of different participants in a process, as well as their interactions and communication, or their reactions to external events. The focus lies much more on *what* has to be done and less on *how* it is implemented. Thus, despite the shortcomings of existing approaches, BPMN and related notations appear to be very well suited for modelling agents and particularly multi-agent systems.

In this paper we take a look at some of the existing approaches – particularly the WADE extension to the JADE agent framework [10], and a mapping from BPMN to the agent-oriented scripting language JADL [18] – and combine the strong sides of both into a new approach. The result is a mapping from BPMN diagrams to behaviour components for the JIAC multi-agent framework [19].

F. Dalpiaz et al. (Eds.): EMAS 2014, LNAI 8758, pp. 163–180, 2014.

In this way, the core components of the agents can easily be modelled with and generated from BPMN process diagrams. Thus, we are helping to close the gap between design and implementation of multi-agent systems [8]. The resulting Java classes are similarly structured and as extensible as those of WADE, but they exhibit the expressiveness of BPMN, including communication between agents and event-handling, both as part of the workflow and for triggering the process.

The remainder of this paper is structured as follows: First, we discuss some related work, most notably the WADE framework and the mapping from BPMN to JADL, with their benefits and shortcomings. Then, in Section 3, we take a closer look at BPMN and the JIAC framework, and how they fit together, Thereafter, we describe how BPMN processes can be mapped to semantically equivalent JIAC Agent Beans (Section 4), and how the transformation was implemented (Section 5). In Section 6, the mapping is illustrated using an example, before we finally wrap up and discuss our results.

2 Related Work

Different approaches for combining process modelling and agent-oriented software development have been devised. Some using BPMN, others using simpler notations; some using code generations, others employing interpreting approaches. Each of those have their strengths and weaknesses.

In the following we discuss several works that are highly relevant to the approach described in this paper: The original mapping from BPMN to BPEL, a mapping from BPMN to JIAC's scripting language JADL, the WADE framework, mapping workflows to JADE behaviours, and GO-BPMN, a combination of BPMN and goal hierarchies.

2.1 Transformation from BPMN to BPEL

One of the motivations for developing BPMN was to provide a standardised graphical notation for *BPEL*, the Business Process Executable Language. Consequently, a mapping from BPMN to BPEL is part of the BPMN specification [22, Chapter 14], and a number of alternative or extended mappings have been proposed by various other authors (see for example [20], [23]).

In many aspects, the mapping is very straightforward: Each pool is mapped to a BPEL process (which can be deployed as a Web service), and the several events and activities within are mapped to the workflow of the process. The process is made up mostly of Web service calls, assignments and flow control, but can also contain, e.g., event handling based on timing and incoming messages. Given a sufficiently detailed BPMN diagram, the resulting BPEL process can be readily executable.

Still, there are enough elements in BPMN for which no mapping to BPEL is given. Thus, while BPMN was created with the mapping to BPEL in mind, it is not just a visualisation for BPEL but a distinct, self-contained language – and in fact more expressive than BPEL itself. Among the elements that are not mapped to BPEL are somewhat obscure elements such as the *ad-hoc* subprocess, or the complex gateway, but also many types of events and tasks.

2.2 Transformation from BPMN to JADL

In prior work of mapping BPMN to agents [14], JIAC's service-oriented scripting language *JADL* [15] was used as the target of the transformation.

Being conceptually close to BPEL, the mapping is similar, and the process can be mapped very directly to different language elements of JADL. For instance, like BPEL, JADL has dedicated language elements for complex actions such as invoking other services, or for sending and receiving messages, making the generated code compact and easy to comprehend.

Each pool in the BPMN process is mapped to a JADL service, and the service's input parameters and result types are derived from the pool's start- and end events [18]. Further, for each start event, a Drools rule is created, starting the respective JADL service on the occurrence of the given event (e.g., an incoming message, or a given time). Also, for each participant in the BPMN process, an agent configuration file is created, setting up the individual agents, each equipped with an Interpreter Bean and Rule Engine Bean, together with the generated JADL services and Drools rules.

Alternatively, the JADL services and rules created from the BPMN processes can be added to a running JIAC agent, thus dynamically changing its behaviour.

2.3 WADE: Workflows for JADE

A different approach, from which some of the concepts in this work have been drawn, is *WADE (Workflows and Agents Development Environment)*, which is an extension to the JADE multi-agent framework [3]. Using WADE, certain aspects of the behaviour of a JADE agent can be modelled using a simple workflow notation [10,9]. The workflows basically consist of only two elements: Activities and Transitions.

Using the *Wolf* tool [11], JADE behaviour classes can be generated from those workflow models. The generated Java classes show a clear distinction between the workflow (the order of the activities, together with conditions and guards) and the several activities. Each of them is mapped to an individual Java method that can either refer to existing functionalities or be implemented by the developer. Using this separation, generated workflows can safely be altered or extended.

However, the expressiveness of WADE is restricted by the simplistic workflow notation, which allows only the most basic workflows to be modelled. While the transitions can be annotated with guards (conditions), it seems impossible to model parallel execution and synchronisation, let alone more advanced concepts such as event handling or messaging. In fact, each workflow diagram covers only the behaviour of an isolated agent; to our knowledge, interactions between agents can not be modelled.

Later, WADE has been extended to provide better support for long-running business processes, event handling, user-interaction and Web-service integration [5,4] and as of today appears to be a very mature product used in many projects.

2.4 GO-BPMN and Go4Flex

In *GO-BPMN* (Goal-oriented BPMN), process models are combined with a goal-hierarchy and executed by agents [12]. The authors highlight the high flexibility of the system, and the prospects of parallelisation, but they also write that testing the system is difficult due to possible side-effects of the processes regarding other goals [7].

The individual processes (the "leafs" in the goal hierarchy) are described as BPMN processes; however, only a subset of BPMN is used. Particularly, each diagram shows only a single pool, and thus, as in the case of WADE, no communication and interaction can be modelled, but just the behaviour of a single agent. While using goals for connecting the individual processes is quite promising, in our opinion process diagrams can more efficiently be used at a higher level of abstraction, e.g., for providing an overview of the system as a whole, instead of for isolated behaviours of individual agents.

A similar approach is *Go4Flex*, or *GPMN* [6]. Like GO-BPMN, Go4Flex uses goal hierarchies with BPMN processes being the leafs. Both the goals and the processes are interpreted by Jadex agents [25]. The authors also present a mapping from FIPA/AUML interaction diagrams [2] to BPMN processes [24].

2.5 Other Approaches

While those are the works most similar to our own, there are of course other, slightly different approaches, that shall not go unmentioned.

Agent UML, or AUML as already mentioned above, extends the UML with several agent-specific diagram types, most prominently interaction diagrams [2]. However, while serving very well for describing the interactions among agents, interaction diagrams – following the principles of UML – show just this single aspect of multi-agent systems. BPMN diagrams, on the other hand, can be seen as a combination of AUML interaction and activity diagrams and thus seem to be better suited for conveying the whole picture of the behaviours and interactions.

In another approach, multi-agent systems are modelled as 'electronic institutions' [27], describing their common ontologies, roles, interactions and norms. Those norms are monitored and enforced by the agent runtime, facilitating the operation of open systems, where agents might try to break those rules. Similar to this, in 2COMM, interaction protocols are represented as artefacts, not only encapsulating the different roles and commitments involved in the interaction, but also providing for functionalities such as logging, auditing, etc. [1].

Finally, there are numerous agent development methodologies, many of which also make use of sophisticated graphical notations for one end or another. One of those is i^*, which is used in the TROPOS Methodology, among others [30].

The focus here lies particularly on modelling the *social* relationships of the several actors involved in the systems: Their goals, intentions, and mutual 'strategic dependencies'. While i^* itself is not used for modelling processes, it could well be used complementary to, e.g., BPMN to model the rationale behind the agents' behaviours and interactions.

3 A Closer Look at BPMN and JIAC

As we have seen, there are numerous approaches for combining process modelling and multi-agent system engineering, but to the best of our knowledge none of them makes full use of the expressiveness of BPMN or a similarly powerful process notation. This is unfortunate, since BPMN provides many notions that could very well be used for modelling high-level multi-agent behaviour.

In the following, we will take a closer look at the BPMN language and the JIAC agent framework, being the domain and co-domain of the mapping discussed in the next section of this paper.

3.1 BPMN

The *Business Process Model and Notation* [22] is a workflow representation that can be used both as a description language for real-world processes, and as a high-level modelling language for computer programs. It can be seen as a combination of UML's Activity Diagrams and Sequence Diagrams, depicting both the actors' internal processes and their interactions. An example diagram is shown in Figure 1.

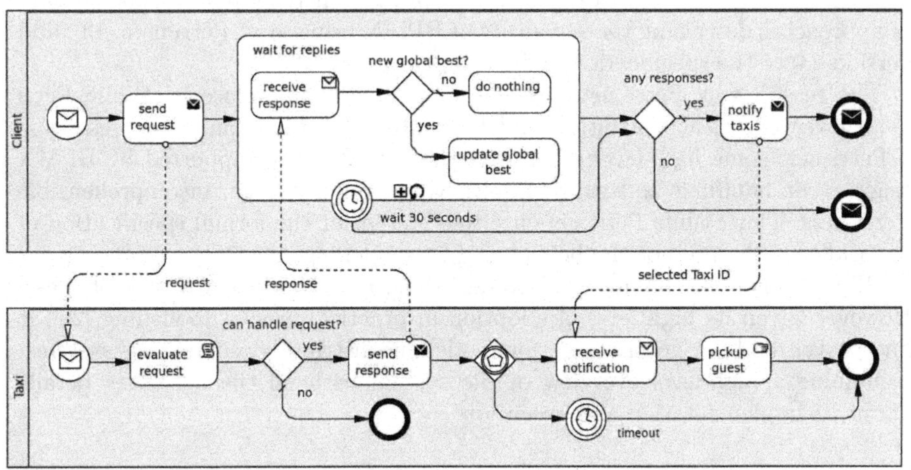

Fig. 1. Example BPMN Diagram: Taxi Request Service

BPMN diagrams can be understood at three levels of abstraction:

1. The diagrams are made up of a few easily recognisable elements, i.e. *events* (circles), *activities* (boxes) and *gateways* (diamonds), connected by *sequence-* and *message flows* and situated in one or more *pools*.
2. These basic elements are further distinguished using sets of marker icons, e.g., *message*, *timer*, and *error* events, or *parallel* and *exclusive* gateways.
3. Each element features a number of additional attributes that are hidden from the diagram and contain most of the information that is necessary for automated code generation, e.g., properties and assignments.

Consequently, the essence of a BPMN diagram is easily understood by all business partners, including those who have great knowledge in their domain but little understanding of programming and multi-agent systems. At the same time, BPMN diagrams provide enough information for the generation of executable programs.

A variety of notational elements make BPMN diagrams well suited for the design of distributed systems in general and multi-agent systems in particular. The process diagrams are subdivided into pools, each representing one participant in the process. Using message flows for communication between pools, even complex interaction protocols can be modelled clearly. Further, the notation supports features such as event- and error handling, compensation, transactions and *ad-hoc* behaviour.

In fact, one could argue that BPMN is *too* expressive, featuring many elements that are rarely used in practice [21] as well as redundancies w.r.t. how certain concepts can be modelled. Also, the semantics of some elements of BPMN – particularly those not covered in the official mapping from BPMN to BPEL [22, Chapter 14] – are not very clearly defined; however, there is an increasing number of approaches describing the semantics of BPMN using, e.g., Petri nets [13], and version 2.0 of the specification made things clearer, too.

The reason why Petri nets are not used in the first place is: While Petri nets have very clear semantics, and basically everything can be expressed as a Petri net, some high-level constructs that are directly supported by BPMN (e.g., event handling and cancellation) would require huge, incomprehensible Petri nets. Thus, while Petri nets are well suited for the formal specification of a workflow, they are not the best choice for modelling.

BPMN is neither the first process modelling notation, nor will it be the last. However, given its high level of adoption in practical process modelling [26], it has proven to be a good choice for modelling distributed computing systems, combining a high-level overview of the system with all the necessary details about its implementation and execution.

3.2 JIAC

JIAC V (Java-based Intelligent Agent Componentware, version 5) is a multi-agent development framework and runtime environment [19]. Among others,

JIAC features message-based inter-agent communication, tuple-space based agent memory, transparent distribution of agents and services, and provides support for dynamic reconfiguration in distributed environments, such as component exchange at runtime. Individual JIAC agents are situated within Agent Nodes, i.e. runtime containers, which also provide support for migration. The agents' behaviours and capabilities are defined in a number of so-called *Agent Beans* that are controlled by the agent's life cycle. The different structures and elements of a JIAC multi-agent system are shown in Figure 2.

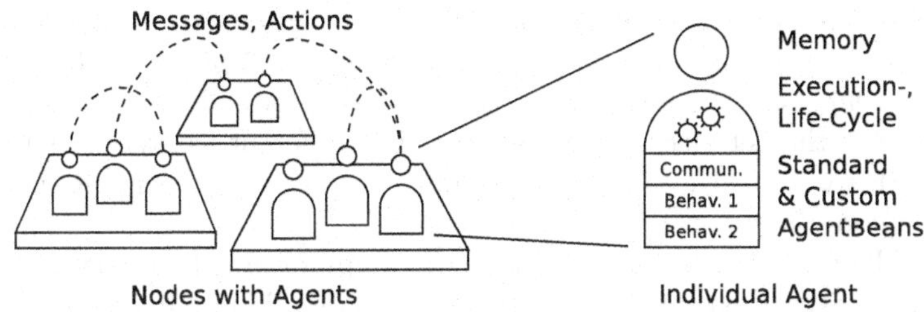

Fig. 2. Components of a JIAC multi-agent system and individual agents

Each JIAC agent is equipped with a *Communication Bean*, allowing agents to send and receive messages to and from other agents or groups of agents (multi-casting to message channels). The messages are not restricted to FIPA[1] messages and can have any serialisable data as payload. Other commonly used Agent Beans are the *Rule Engine Bean*, integrating a Drools[2] rule engine into the agent's memory for reactive behaviour, and the *Interpreter Bean*, providing an interpreter for the service-oriented scripting language JADL [15].

Besides these and other predefined Agent Beans, the developer is free to add application-specific Beans to the agent. Each such Agent Bean can:

- implement a number of *life-cycle* methods, which are executed when the agent changes its life-cycle state, such as initialized, or started,
- implement an *execute*-method, which is called automatically at regular intervals once the agent is running (i.e. cyclic behaviour),
- attach *observers* to the agent's memory, being called, e.g., each time the agent receives a message or its world model is updated, and
- contribute *action*-methods, or services, which are exposed to the directory and can be invoked by other agents or other Beans of the same agent.

Using these four mechanisms, it is possible to define all of the agents' capabilities and behaviours. For details on programming JIAC Agent Beans, we refer readers to the JIAC Programmers' Manual [16].

[1] Foundation for Intelligent Physical Agents: `http://www.fipa.org/`

[2] JBoss Drools: `http://www.jboss.org/drools/`

4 A Mapping from BPMN to JIAC Agent Beans

While the mapping from BPMN to JADL is well suited for modelling high-level behaviour or services, traditional JIAC Agent Beans were still advantageous – and often necessary – for defining the better part of the agent's behaviour, for instance when it comes to the integration with user interfaces or external libraries. Consequently, complementary to the mapping to JADL, a mapping to JIAC Agent Beans was developed [28].

The mapping is conceptually close to WADE: Each Pool in the BPMN diagram is mapped to one Agent Bean, i.e. a Java class, with one method for the workflow, and one method for each individual activity of the process.[3] The *workflow method* acts as an entry point to executing the process, while the several *activity methods* are invoked by the workflow method in accordance with the ordering of the activities in the process. The different workflow agent beans created in this way for the several pools representing one participant then make up the behaviour of the respective agent role.

Table 1 shows a high-level overview of the mapping. In the following, we will describe the several aspects of the mapping in detail. Finally, we will briefly illustrate how process modelling can be integrated into the overall development method.

Table 1. Overview of Mapping from BPMN to Agent Beans

BPMN Element	**Agent Concept**
participant	agent role (implicit, not created)
pool	workflow agent bean, holding all of the below
workflow	structured workflow method
start events	mechanisms to trigger workflow method
tasks	activity methods, doing the actual work
subprocess	nested class, same structure as workflow bean
boundary events	event handler threads, interrupting the activity
properties	variables, in appropriate scope

4.1 Workflow Method

The workflow method is made up of calls to several activity methods, being arranged into sequences, if-else statements and loops. While this requires the process to be structured properly (see Section 5), the result is structured and understandable, resembling manually written code, i.e. using conditions and loops instead of `goto`-like successor-relations. Thus, if necessary, the generated code can still be easily extended or altered by hand.

[3] In the following, we will use the term "workflow" for the order the individual activities are executed in the process, and the term "process" for the whole ensemble of activities and their ordering, events, variables, etc.

At the same time, BPMN allows for much more expressive workflows to be modelled, compared to the rather minimalistic workflow notation used in WADE. In particular, the following concepts of BPMN are covered by the mapping:

- Parallel execution (BPMN's AND-Gateway) is mapped to multiple threads being started and joined.
- Subprocesses (composite activities) are mapped to internal classes following the same schema as the main class, with workflow- and activity methods for the activities embedded into the subprocess.
- Event handler (intermediate events attached to an activity) are also mapped to threads, running concurrently to the thread executing the activity itself, and interrupting this thread in case the respective event occurs.
- The same pattern is applied to event-based XOR-gateways; in this case the main thread will wait until one of the events has been triggered.

4.2 Properties and Assignments

BPMN specifies a number of non-visual attributes, such as properties (i.e. variables) and assignments. Properties can be declared in the scope of whole processes or individual activities (both atomic tasks and composite subprocesses). When declared in the scope of a process or subprocess, the property is visible to all elements (transitively) contained therein.

Accordingly, properties are mapped to Java variables in different scopes in the Agent Bean, reflecting their visibility in the BPMN diagram. Properties of the process are mapped to variables in the scope of the Agent Bean class, properties of a subprocess to variables in the scope of the embedded subprocess class, and properties of an activity to local variables in the scope of the activity method.

Assignments are always bound to an activity or event, and are included in the respective activity method. In BPMN, assignments can have an *assign-time* of either 'before' or 'after', determining whether the assignment has to be applied before or after the actual activity is executed (see below).

4.3 Activity Methods

The several activity methods have neither parameters nor a return value and always follow the same schema:

1. *Properties*: First, for each property in the scope of the activity one Java variable is declared, using the respective data type.
2. *Start Assignments*: Then, assignments of the activity with assign-time 'before' are applied, e.g., for setting the input parameters of a service call.
3. *Activity Body*: Now, the code corresponding to the actual activity is carried out, e.g., invoking a service, sending a message, or executing a user-defined code-snippet.
4. *End Assignments*: Finally, assignments with assign-time 'after' are applied, e.g., for binding the return value of a service call to a local variable.

5. *Loop*: If the activity's *loop* attribute is set, the content of the activity method is repeated in a loop as long as a given condition is satisfied.

Similar to the mapping to JADL, we can make use of JIAC's communication infrastructure, by mapping *message* events and *send* and *receive* tasks to sending and receiving JIAC messages, while *service* tasks are mapped to the invocation of a JIAC action (i.e. a service). *Script* tasks allow the developer to attach a custom snippet of Java code to the task. Further, *timer* events are mapped to a temporary suspension of the execution.

There are more types of tasks and events in BPMN, for which no mapping has been devised yet, but these are the most common and important ones. Elements that will be covered in the near future include the *rule* event, evaluating a given Java condition, as well as the *user* task, presenting a generic input dialogue to the user.

4.4 Event Handler

As mentioned above, event handlers (i.e. intermediate events attached to an activity's boundary) are mapped to threads running in parallel to the actual activity, interrupting it in case the event has been triggered. To realise this behaviour, the activity itself is wrapped in another thread, and a reference is passed to the event handler thread, running in a loop and periodically checking whether the respective event has occurred (e.g., whether a message has arrived, or whether a given time has passed). If so, a marker flag is set and the activity thread is interrupted.

In the workflow method, both threads are started, and the activity thread is joined. Finally, when the activity has been completed or aborted, the event handler thread is stopped and the workflow is routed accordingly to whether the event handler has been triggered or not.

4.5 Start Events and Starter Rules

Finally, the processes' start events have to be mapped to mechanisms for starting the process on the occurrence of the respective events. In the mapping to JADL, a number of Drools rules are created for this purpose. Using Agent Beans, these 'starter rules' can be integrated directly into the code, making use of the mechanisms introduced in Section 3.2.

- If the process has a start event with unspecified type, or *none* type, then the workflow method is invoked in the Agent Bean's `doStart()` method (one of the *life-cycle* methods), being called when the agent is started.
- For a *timer* start event, the Agent Bean is given an `execute()` method, regularly checking the current time against the time the process was last started, invoking the workflow method at a given time or interval.
- A *message* start event results in a message observer being attached to the agent's memory when the Agent Bean is started, which will then invoke the workflow method every time a matching JIAC message is received.

- Finally, in case of a *service* start event, the workflow method is marked with the annotation `@Expose`, exposing the workflow method as a JIAC action to be discovered and invoked by other agents.[4]

Besides creating these mechanisms, a *service* start event also results in the workflow method's input parameters being updated to correspond to the specified service parameters. Analogously, a *service* end event results in the workflow method's return value being set accordingly.

4.6 Development Method

In previous work, we presented a method for integrating process modelling into the overall multi-agent system development cycle [18], as shown in Figure 3. While this was aimed at the mapping from BPMN to JADL, most of the ideas and concepts can be carried over to the mapping to JIAC Agent Beans as well.

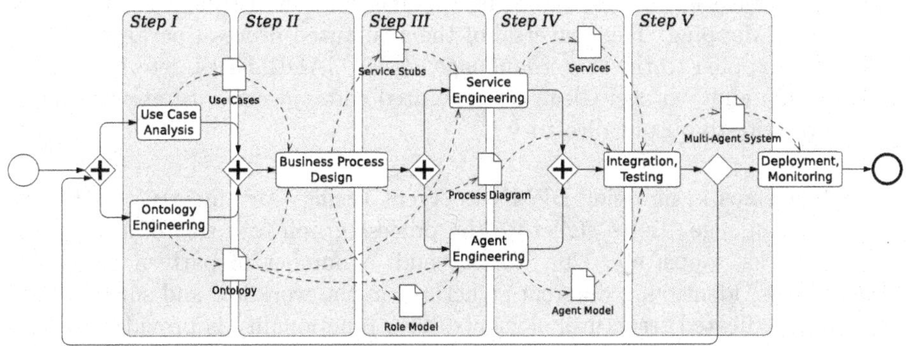

Fig. 3. Integration of process modelling into development method [18]

In a nutshell, we see process modelling as the next step after use case analysis. For each of the previously identified use case diagrams, one BPMN process diagram is created, holding one pool for each of the actors involved in the respective use case. Those diagrams should describe the behaviour and particularly the interaction of the several roles at a relatively high level of abstraction, illustrating the system behaviour without cluttering the diagrams with algorithmic details. The mapping then translates the pools to behaviours, encapsulated into Agent Beans, while each of the actors corresponds to a different agent role exhibiting those behaviours. Next, the generated JIAC Agent Beans can be extended with additional code not suited for inclusion in the process diagrams, and the agent roles are aggregated to concrete agents and the multi-agent system is set up.

[4] There is, as such, no *service* start event in BPMN. We use this term to distinguish *message* start events, where the message is in fact a service request.

5 Implementation

The first version of the mapping was implemented in the course of a diploma thesis [28] as an extension to the BPMN editor *VSDT (Visual Service Design Tool)*. The VSDT was developed with the goal in mind, to provide transformations from BPMN to diverse executable languages [17]. It also allows for the import of existing services, simulation/interpretation of process diagrams, and the generation of descriptive texts in written English from the process. Besides being a BPMN editor, it can also be used for creating the use case diagrams for connecting the different process diagrams that make up the entire system.

For exporting BPMN diagrams into different target languages, the VSDT uses a generic transformation framework [17]. The process can be subdivided into several stages, being executed one after the other:

1. Validation and Normalization: Check validity of BPMN diagrams and bring diagram into 'normalized' form to facilitate later stages.
2. Structure Mapping: Use pattern-matching to identify different structures, such as blocks and loops, and bring the diagram into a tree-like form.
3. Element Mapping: Tree-traversal of the structured process, performing the actual mapping to the target language (JIAC, JADL, BPEL, etc.)
4. Clean Up and Storage: Clean up generated code, merge with existing files, if any, write to output directory.

The first steps in mapping BPMN to Agent Beans – or any structured programming language – is to structure the process graph to a tree of sequences, decision blocks, loops, etc. [20]. To this end, a number of pattern matching rules are used, identifying different structures in the workflow and substituting them with dedicated structural elements. This functionality is provided by the VSDT's transformation framework and can be reused for the different target languages [17]. Thus, only the actual mapping of individual process elements to fragments of Java code, as specified in the previous section, had to be implemented.

This element mapping has been separated into two stages. First, the structured process model is translated to an intermediate model, being a high-level representation of the structure of a JIAC Agent Bean. This is done by traversing the process model, which now has a tree-structure, and thereby creating and assembling the respective elements of the Agent Bean model. Then, this model can be translated straightforwardly to executable Java code using a number of templates for the JET framework.[5] Using JET and JMerge, parts of the generated Agent Bean code can safely be modified and merged in case the process model changes and has to be re-generated.

[5] JET (Java Emitter Templates) is part of the Eclipse Model To Text (M2T) project: `http://www.eclipse.org/modeling/m2t/`

6 Example

In this section we will illustrate several aspects of the mapping by means of the simple example diagram from Section 3, shown in Figure 1.

The BPMN diagram consists of two pools, each representing an agent role: *Client*, and *Taxi*. The client's process is exposed and started as a service, expecting a customer ID, current location, desired destination and time of arrival, and returning the ID of the taxi selected for the tour, if any.

The interaction between the two starts by the client sending a request (customer ID, location, destination, desired time of arrival) to all available taxis, which evaluate the request and decide whether to accept it. If so, they send a response (taxi ID, estimated time of arrival, price) back to the client. Meanwhile, the client enters a looping subprocess, listening to responses and memorising the best response, until after 30 seconds the subprocess is interrupted by the attached timer event. The client then sends a notification to the selected taxi. The taxis listen to incoming message, either preparing to pick up the guest if the notification is received, or ending the process after waiting for a few more seconds. Note that the several properties (variables) and assignments are not visible in the diagram.

The resulting Agent Bean for the *Client* role is shown in Figure 4, along with the client's part of the process diagram for reference. The entire code was automatically generated and only slightly shortened to improve readability and to better fit into the figure. The full code also contains JavaDoc comments (not shown here) with descriptions of the bean class and each of the activity methods, taken from the *description* attribute of the respective BPMN elements.

As can be seen, the control-flow of the process is reflected in the `workflow()` method, which is also exposed as a JIAC action, or service. The workflow method is dominated by the threads for running the subprocess and the attached event handler, but also contains an if-else-statement for the gateway at the end of the process. The activities *send request* and *notify taxis* are mapped to two similar methods for sending JIAC messages to the specified message groups.

The code for, e.g., sending and receiving messages is quite extensive, and there are several components, such as the event handler classes, that are needed again and again for different workflows. Consequently, these parts are provided by the superclass `AbstractWorkflowBean`, allowing the generated code to be much more compact and readable.

The subprocess is mapped to the inner class `WaitForReplies_Sub`, also forming a new variable scope for its properties. The class follows the same schema as the outer workflow class. It features another workflow method (`run()` in this case) and three activity methods, most notably the `receiveResponse` method, where the client checks its memory for messages arriving at the specified message group channel. In accordance with the loop-condition of the original subprocess, the content of the workflow method is executed in an infinite loop. The subprocess itself is run in a thread, which will eventually be interrupted by the event handler thread, thus breaking out of the loop.

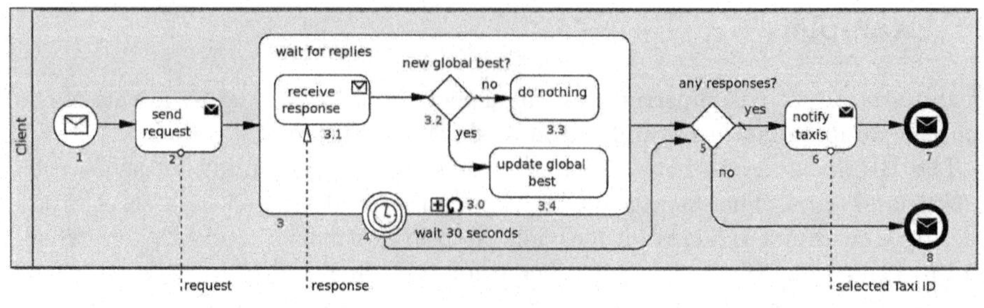


```
public class Client_requestTaxi extends AbstractWorkflowBean {
   protected TaxiResponse globalBest;
   protected Boolean noResponse;
   protected String appID;
   protected String location;
   protected String destination;

   public final static String ACTION_WORKFLOW = "requestTaxi";

   public void doStart() throws Exception {
      super.doStart();
      join("TaxiResponseTo"+appID+"");
   }

1  @Expose(name=ACTION_WORKFLOW, scope=ActionScope.GLOBAL)
   public Serializable[] workflow(String currentLoc, String currentDest) {
      location = currentLoc;
      destination = currentDest;
2     sendRequest();
3     Thread waitForReplies = new Thread(new WaitForReplies_Sub());
4     EventHandler wait30Seconds_timeout =
            new TimeoutEventHandler(waitForReplies, 30000);
      try {
         waitForReplies.start();
         wait30Seconds_timeout.start();
         waitForReplies.join();
         wait30Seconds_timeout.stopEventHandler();
      } catch (InterruptedException e) {
      }
5     if (noResponse) {
8        String taxiID = "none available";
         return new Serializable[] {taxiID};
      } else {
6        notifyTaxis();
7        String taxiID = globalBest.getTaxiID();
         return new Serializable[] {taxiID};
      }
   }

   // continued on right side

2  protected void sendRequest() {
      TaxiRequest request = new TaxiRequest(location, appID, destination);
      send("TaxiRequest", request);
   }

6  protected void notifyTaxis() {
      SelectedTaxi selectedTaxi = new SelectedTaxi(globalBest.getTaxiID());
      send("Notification", selectedTaxi);
   }

3  class WaitForReplies_Sub implements Runnable {
      protected TaxiResponse currentResponse;

      public void run() {
         noResponse = true;
3.0      while (true && ! checkInterrupted()) {
3.1         receiveResponse();
3.2         if (currentResponse.compareTo(globalBest) > 0) {
3.4            updateGlobalBest();
            } else {
3.3            doNothing();
            }
         }
      }

3.1   protected void receiveResponse() {
         TaxiResponse response = (TaxiResponse)
               receive("TaxiResponse", TaxiResponse.class, -1);
         noResponse = false;
         currentResponse = response;
      }

3.3   protected void doNothing() {
      }

3.4   protected void updateGlobalBest() {
         globalBest = currentResponse;
      }
   }
}
```

Fig. 4. Example: Taxi Request Service. Corresponding parts in the process diagram and the code are numbered correspondingly.

The Agent Bean for the *Taxi* role is similarly structured, and thus is not shown here. The main difference is that its workflow method is not exposed as an action, but is invoked by a memory observer listening for the request messages sent by the client role. The observer is attached to the agent's memory in the `doStart()` method (one of the life-cycle methods, which is started when the agent is started). The workflow method itself is rather straightforward, with an if-statement representing the first gateway, and an event-handler for the second. The logic for the *evaluate request* task can either be provided via the task's *script* attribute, or it can be implemented in the generated Java code.

6.1 Discussion

Using the domain-specific scripting language JADL, agent behaviours can be expressed in a very compact and readable way, but the overall expressiveness (e.g., the supported event types) is limited by the scripting language. JIAC Agent Beans, on the other hand, have the full expressiveness of the Java language at their disposal. Thus, basically everything that can be modelled in a BPMN diagram can be mapped to an Agent Bean.

While the resulting workflow method for complex processes can become somewhat bulky – particularly if event handling is used – its structured form as well as the separation into workflow methods and activity methods keeps the resulting code reasonably clear. Like in WADE, individual activity methods can be altered or extended without risk of losing the changes after the code is generated anew. The reason why this is important is that while BPMN is well suited for high-level behaviour, graphically modelling low-level algorithms and such would be too laborious. This way, those can be added to the generated code.

One potential problem might be raised by the extensive use of Java threads for event handling. We are currently investigating ways of integrating the event handling into the agent's main thread. Another alternative would be to move away from the current workflow methods towards a more interpreter-like approach, memorizing the current state of the process and executing one activity method in each step of the agent's execution cycle. Particularly for long-running processes this might be beneficial.

Regarding the high expressiveness of the generated Agent Beans and the good performance of compiled Java code when compared to the interpreted JADL scripts, the mapping from BPMN to JIAC Agent Beans is suited best for modelling and generating core components of the multi-agent system, while the mapping to JADL is of much use for creating dynamic behaviours and services to be deployed and changed at runtime.

7 Conclusion

In this paper, we have presented an approach for creating multi-agent systems from process models, combining the mapping from BPMN to JADL [18] with ideas borrowed from WADE [10]. The result is a transformation from BPMN process diagrams to JIAC Agent Beans, generating one method for the workflow as a whole, and one method for each individual activity. The resulting Agent Bean classes are highly expressive and at the same time well structured and readable. Being based on the wide-spread Business Process Model and Notation, the process diagrams are easy to understand and the mapping also supports important aspects such as communication and interaction and event handling, which are particularly suited for being modelled visually.

Comparing our approach with related works, our impression is that using a powerful yet high-level notation like BPMN provides for more expressive agent behaviours, in particular w.r.t. communication and event handling. On the other hand, we acknowledge that a simpler notation that is more streamlined to the requirements of agent engineering may be easier to learn, somewhat balancing the benefit of using an established industry standard.

Of course, it depends on the application to be developed whether process modelling in general and BPMN in particular are appropriate ways for designing the system: Particularly when intensive communication and event handling is involved, graphical process modelling notations have their benefits, but visually depicting every detail of a complex algorithm can become rather cumbersome.

Our work has not yet reached the maturity of some of the related approaches. Still, using the mapping proposed and exemplified in this paper, it is possible to model complex and distributed multi-agent systems by means of BPMN and to generate readily executable agent behaviours from the process diagrams. Also, while we decided to use JIAC in this work, the bulk of the mapping could be applied to other agent frameworks, as well.

7.1 Future Work

While the mapping can already be used for generating useful agent behaviours, it is not yet completed. First, there are still aspects of BPMN that are not covered by the mapping, such as some of the less common event types. Second, there are aspects of agents that can not yet be modelled adequately with BPMN.

One such issue that we want to tackle in the future is the modelling of goals and other kinds of dynamic behaviour by means of BPMN. Without those, the resulting agent systems, strictly following the process diagram, are rather procedural and inflexible. One promising approach is to use the *ad-hoc* subprocess for this task, executing a certain set of activities in no predefined order until a given *completion condition* is met. However, this is still work in progress.

Complementary to the transformation to JIAC code, we are currently working on a process interpreter agent bean. Similar to the JADL interpreter agent, this will allow to pass processes to the agent at runtime and to have that agent execute one or more of the roles in that process [29]. Without the additional layer of abstraction of the scripting language, this approach is expected to have the same expressive power as the generated JIAC bean while at the same time being more dynamic. Also, this will allow for monitoring and visualizing the current state of the running process by linking the process interpreting agent to the modelling tool.

The downside of the interpreter approach is that the entire behaviour has to be modelled in the process diagram or has to be made available as callable services, since there is no possibility to manually extend the generated code. Thus, we see the upcoming interpreter as a way to dynamically deploy very high-level processes to the running agent, while the core behaviours of the agent would still be created in a combination of process modelling, code generation, and manually extending and refining the generated code.

References

1. Baldoni, M., Baroglio, C., Capuzzimati, F.: 2COMM: A commitment-based MAS architecture. In: Cossentino, M., El Fallah Seghrouchni, A., Winikoff, M. (eds.) EMAS 2013. LNCS (LNAI), vol. 8245, pp. 38–57. Springer, Heidelberg (2013)
2. Bauer, B., Müller, J.P., Odell, J.: Agent UML: A formalism for specifying multiagent software systems. In: Ciancarini, P., Wooldridge, M.J. (eds.) AOSE 2000. LNCS, vol. 1957, pp. 91–103. Springer, Heidelberg (2001)

3. Bellifemine, F., Poggi, A., Rimassa, G.: JADE – a FIPA-compliant agent framework. Internal technical report, Telecom Italia (1999), part of this report has been also published in Proceedings of PAAM 1999, London, pp. 97–108 (April 1999)
4. Bergenti, F., Caire, G., Gotta, D.: Interactive workflows with WADE. In: 2012 IEEE 21st International Workshop on Enabling Technologies: Infrastructure for Collaborative Enterprises, pp. 10–15 (2012)
5. Bergenti, F., Caire, G., Gotta, D., Long, D., Sacchi, G.: Enacting BPM-oriented workflows with Wade. In: Proceedings of the 12th Workshop on Objects and Agents, Rende, CS, Italy, pp. 112–116 (July 2011)
6. Braubach, L., Pokahr, A., Jander, K., Lamersdorf, W., Burmeister, B.: Go4Flex: Goal-oriented process modelling. In: Essaaidi, M., Malgeri, M., Badica, C. (eds.) Intelligent Distributed Computing IV. SCI, vol. 315, pp. 77–87. Springer, Heidelberg (2010)
7. Burmeister, B., Arnold, M., Copaciu, F., Rimassa, G.: BDI-agents for agile goal-oriented business processes. In: Proc. of 7th Int. Conf. on Autonomous Agents and Multiagent Systems (AAMAS 2008), pp. 37–44. International Foundation for Autonomous Agents and Multiagent Systems, Richland (2008)
8. Cabri, G., Puviani, M., Quitadamo, R.: Connecting methodologies and infrastructures in the development of agent systems. In: Proceedings of the International Multiconference on Computer Science and Information Technology (IMCSIT 2008), pp. 17–23. IEEE, Wisla (2008)
9. Caire, G.: WADE User Guide, Version 2.6. Telecom Italia (July 2010), `http://jade.tilab.com/wade/doc/WADE-User-Guide.pdf`
10. Caire, G., Gotta, D., Banzi, M.: WADE: A software platform to develop mission critical applications exploiting agents and workflows. In: Berger, M., Burg, B., Nishiyama, S. (eds.) Proc. of 7th Int. Conf. on Autonomous Agents and Multiagent Systems (AAMAS 2008) – Industry and Applications Track, pp. 29–36 (May 2008)
11. Caire, G., Quarantotto, E., Porta, M., Sacchi, G.: WOLF – An Eclipse plug-in for WADE. In: Proceedings of the ACEC 2008 (2008)
12. Calisti, M., Greenwood, D.: Goal-oriented autonomic process modeling and execution for next generation networks. In: van der Meer, S., Burgess, M., Denazis, S. (eds.) MACE 2008. LNCS, vol. 5276, pp. 38–49. Springer, Heidelberg (2008)
13. Dijkman, R.M., Dumas, M., Ouyang, C.: Semantics and analysis of business process models in BPMN. Information & Software Technology 50(12), 1281–1294 (2008)
14. Endert, H., Küster, T., Hirsch, B., Albayrak, S.: Mapping BPMN to agents: An analysis. In: Baldoni, M., Baroglio, C., Mascardi, V. (eds.) Agents, Web-Services, and Ontologies Integrated Methodologies (AWESOME), pp. 43–58 (2007)
15. Hirsch, B., Konnerth, T., Burkhardt, M., Albayrak, S.: Programming service oriented agents. In: Calisti, M., Dignum, F.P., Kowalczyk, R., Leymann, F., Unland, R. (eds.) Service-Oriented Architecture and (Multi-)Agent Systems Technology. Dagstuhl Seminar Proceedings, vol. 10021, Schloss Dagstuhl – Leibniz-Zentrum für Informatik, Germany (2010)
16. JIAC Development Team: JIAC – Java Intelligent Agent Componentware, Version 5.1.5. DAI-Labor, TU Berlin (February 2014), `http://www.jiac.de`
17. Küster, T., Heßler, A.: Towards transformations from BPMN to heterogeneous systems. In: Ardagna, D., Mecella, M., Yang, J. (eds.) BPM 2008 Workshops. LNBIP, vol. 17, pp. 200–211. Springer, Heidelberg (2009)
18. Küster, T., Lützenberger, M., Heßler, A., Hirsch, B.: Integrating process modelling into multi-agent system engineering. Multiagent and Grid Systems 8(1), 105–124 (2012)

19. Lützenberger, M., et al.: A multi-agent approach to professional software engineering. In: Winikoff, M., El Fallah Seghrouchni, A., Winikoff, M. (eds.) EMAS 2013. LNCS (LNAI), vol. 8245, pp. 156–175. Springer, Heidelberg (2013)
20. Mendling, J., Lassen, K.B., Zdun, U.: Transformation strategies between blockoriented and graph-oriented process modelling languages (2005)
21. Muehlen, M.z., Recker, J.: How much language is enough? Theoretical and practical use of the business process modeling notation. In: Bellahsène, Z., Léonard, M. (eds.) CAiSE 2008. LNCS, vol. 5074, pp. 465–479. Springer, Heidelberg (2008)
22. Object Management Group: Business process model and notation (BPMN) version 2.0. Specification formal/2011-01-03, Object Management Group (August 2011)
23. Ouyang, C., Dumas, M., van der Aalst, W.M.P., ter Hofstede, A.H.M., Mendling, J.: From business process models to process-oriented software systems. ACM Transactions on Software Engineering and Methodology 19(1), 1–37 (2009)
24. Pokahr, A., Braubach, L.: Reusable interaction protocols for workflows. In: Workshop on Protocol Based Modelling of Business Interactions (2010)
25. Pokahr, A., Braubach, L., Jander, K.: Unifying agent and component concepts – Jadex active components. In: Dix, J., Witteveen, C. (eds.) MATES 2010. LNCS (LNAI), vol. 6251, pp. 100–112. Springer, Heidelberg (2010)
26. Recker, J.C.: BPMN modeling – who, where, how and why. BPTrends 5(3), 1–8 (2008)
27. Sierra, C., Rodríguez-Aguilar, J.A., Blanco-Vigil, P.N., Arcos-Rosell, J.L., Esteva-Vivancos, M.: Engineering multi-agent systems as electronic institutions. UPGRADE: European Journal for Informatics Professional V (4), 33–39 (2004)
28. Tan, P.S.: Automated Generation of JIAC AgentBeans from BPMN Diagrams. Diploma thesis, Technische Universität Berlin (November 2011)
29. Voß, M.: Orchestrating Multi-Agent Systems with BPMN by Implementing a Process Executing JIAC Agent Using the Visual Service Design Tool. Master thesis, Humboldt Universität Berlin, realized with support of DAI-Labor, TU Berlin (May 2014)
30. Yu, E.S.: Social modeling and *i**. In: Borgida, A.T., Chaudhri, V.K., Giorgini, P., Yu, E.S. (eds.) Conceptual Modeling: Foundations and Applications. LNCS, vol. 5600, pp. 99–121. Springer, Heidelberg (2009)

Environments and Organizations in Multi-Agent Systems: From Modelling to Code

Daniela Maria Uez and Jomi Fred Hübner

Department of Automation and Systems Engineering
Federal University of Santa Catarina
CP 476 - CEP 88040-900 - Florianópolis - SC - Brazil
daniela.uez@posgrad.ufsc.br, jomi.hubner@ufsc.br

Abstract. Although there are many agent oriented methods, organizational and environmental system dimensions have not been analysed nor implemented as first class entities. Due to the evolution of development platforms, we are able to consider these dimensions in all the development phases. In this paper we present Prometheus AEOlus method, that allows the integrated development of three systems dimensions: agent, environment and organization. This method was based on both Prometheus method and JaCaMo framework and aims to reduce the conceptual gap between the analysis and implementation phases.

Keywords: AOSE, Organization, Environment, Prometheus, JaCaMo, Code Generation.

1 Introduction

As proposed in [10], multi-agent system (MAS) can be formed by four dimensions: agents, environment, protocols of interaction, and organization. However, the methods.[1] provided by the agent oriented software engineering (AOSE) field focus essentially on the agent dimension. In these methods, some environment and organizational concepts are used mainly in the early stages to clarify the problem to be solved. Along the method, these concepts are analysed and, in the implementation phase, they disappear and are replaced by agent program primitives. For instance, methods like Prometheus [15] uses the organizational concept of role to describe part of the agent behaviour. During the analyses phase roles are grouped to give rise to the agents. However, the roles will not be properly coded, but the agents originated by a group of these roles will.

Thus, there is a gap problem between analysis and development during the phases of AOSE methods. One of the reasons for this gap is that the most used development platforms (i.e. Jade [1] and Jadex [4]) do not deal with organizational and environmental concepts as first class entities. However, we have now programming platforms that consider organization and environment as first class entities, like the JaCaMo [2] and Janus [11] frameworks, and thus this gap could

[1] We used method instead of methodology as suggested by [5].

F. Dalpiaz et al. (Eds.): EMAS 2014, LNAI 8758, pp. 181–203, 2014.

be reduced. Therefore AOSE methods which also deal with these concepts as first class entities can be improved.

Aiming the code generation for these four dimensions, we developed the Prometheus AEOlus method. Prometheus AEOlus is an extension to Prometheus method, in which we included concepts to improve the modelling and code generation of the environment and organization dimensions. In this paper we present the main concepts related to Prometheus AEOlus method. The paper is organized as follows: some AOSE methods are analysed and a state of the art discussion are introduced in Section 2; in Section 3, we present the technologies used to develop Prometheus AEOlus method; in Section 4 we present the concepts and the metamodel defined for Prometheus AEOlus; in Section 5 we present how these concepts are considered in the method; in Section 6 we present some guidelines used to translate these specifications into code; and in Section 7 we briefly discuss the experiments performed to test the method and some future works.

2 State of the Art

Given the existence of many methods, we selected some of them in order to identify how they deal with organizational and environmental concepts. The selected methods are well known, largely used by AOSE community and provide tools which allow code generation from the specification. We selected ASPECS [6], Ingenias [16], O-MaSe [9], PASSI [7], and Tropos [13].

As presented in Table 1, these methods basically deal with two organizational concepts: goals and roles. Goals are used to define the overall system behaviour. Roles are specified to achieve these systems goals, and each role defines a part of an agent behaviour. Some of them also use the group concept, that allows the roles to be structured in coherent sets.

Concerning the environment, excepting ASPECS that does not handle environmental concept, these methods deal with the concepts of actions, perceptions and two kinds of external entities: actors, which represent users or other systems; and resources, which are external objects or tools used by agents. Actions and perceptions are analysed by the agent point of view, i.e., we can specify an action performed from the agent without taking into account what this action changes the environment. In the same way, we specify a perception received by the agent without taking into account how this perception was generated. An actor is an external entity that can perform some operations in the system, and a resource is an external entity in which an agent can perform an action. In both cases, the method does not address how these events and actions are produced outside the agents.

Moreover, each method is supported by a tool that allows the translation from the specifications to code in a specific language. Essentially JADE, Jack and Jadex languages are used and, typically, most of the system functionality must be coded by the developer since they generate just a skeleton code in the target language. Furthermore, no target language allows environment and organization

Table 1. Organizational and environment concepts used by AOSE methods

Method	Organization	Environment	Tool	Platform
ASPECS	Role Group Goal		Janeiro	Janus
Ingenias	Role Group Goal	Resources Perceptions Actions	IDK	JADE
O-MaSe	Role Goal	External Entities Actions	AgentTool III	JADE
PASSI	Role	Actor Action	PTK	AgentFactory
Prometheus	Role Goal	Actor Resources Actions Perception	PDT	Jack
Tropos	Role Goal	Actor Action	TAM4E	Jack Jadex

implementation.[2] The Janus platform used by ASPECS is one exception that allows the implementation of some organizational concepts. Janus was indeed developed specifically to deal with the very concepts of ASPECS.

Thereby, environmental and organizational concepts are just used in these methods to support the agent analysis and not even the organizational ASPECS concepts are used considering more detailed models of these dimensions. Despite the existence of tools that allows the code generation, most used target platforms do not support these concepts implementation.

3 Background: Prometheus and JaCaMo

Two main technologies are used in Prometheus AEOlus development: the Prometheus method and the JaCaMo framework. Prometheus [19] is a method that proposes a detailed process for specifying and designing agent oriented software systems. Prometheus method defines a range of structured work products, graphical or textual, that are produced along three developments phases: system specification, architectural design and detailed design. The first phase, *system specification*, focus on identifying goals and basics functionalities of the system. The *architectural design* phase uses the work products produced in the previous phase to determine which agent types the system will contain and the interactions among them. The last phase, *detailed design*, focus on the internals of each agent to specify how they will accomplish their tasks. Due to its maturity

[2] Although Jack has a specific package with organizational concepts, the method do not use this package in the code generation process.

concerning the agent design and analysis, Prometheus was used as the starting point for the Prometheus AEOlus method, in which the environmental and organizational analyses and design are improved.

To improve these dimensions in Prometheus, we decided to use some concepts provided by JaCaMo framework. JaCaMo [2] is a framework for multi-agent programming that combines three separate technologies: the Jason language for programming autonomous agents; the CArtAgO framework for programming environment artifacts; and the $\mathcal{M}$oise organizational model for programming multi-agent organizations. JaCaMo allows the integrated development of these three dimensions (agent, environment and organization) using specific concepts and abstractions for each one.

In the agent dimension, JaCaMo uses abstractions inspired by the BDI architecture, and implemented in the Jason programming language. A Jason [3] agent is an entity composed of a set of *beliefs*, *goals*, and *plans*, and it is able to perform a set of *actions*. These can be *external actions*, which change the environment, or *internal actions*, which change only the internal state of the agent.

In the environment dimension, JaCaMo uses the CArtAgO [17] framework. CArtAgO is based on the Agents and Artifacts (A&A) model [18] and it allows the programming of software environments. Such environments are composed of one or more *workspaces*, which one composed of a set of *artifacts*. *Artifacts* are tools or resources and they provide *operations*, that can be used by the agents, *observable properties* and *observable events* that can be perceived by the agents. *Observable properties* can be updated by the *operation* execution likewise the *observable events* specified by it.

Finally, in the organizational dimension, JaCaMo uses the $\mathcal{M}$oise [12] organizational framework. $\mathcal{M}$oise specifies *i*) a structural specification, that points out the *roles* within the organization. *Roles* define the agent expected behaviour in the system and they can be arranged into *groups* and *subgroups*; *ii*) a functional specification, where the relation among organization's *goals*, called *social scheme*, and sets of goals the agents can commit to, called missions; *iii*) and the normative specification, that binds roles to missions through *norms*.

Since our objective are both to allow the code generation and to reduce the gap between the analyses and development stages, we decided to use JaCaMo concepts to improve the Prometheus development process to ensure that concepts used during the design and analysis stages will be used in the implementation stage. To the best of our knowledge, JaCaMo is the first approach that allows the integrated development of these three dimensions (agent, environment and organization).

4 Prometheus AEOlus Metamodel

We started the Prometheus AEOlus development by defining the concepts that are relevant for each dimension and how they relate to one another. These concepts were defined based on those used by both Prometheus and JaCaMo technologies. From such concepts, we defined a new metamodel, used by Prometheus

AEOlus method. In fact, a complete life cycle method uses different concepts during each phase, and one single metamodel can not cover all these phases. Considering that we focus on the code generation for agent, environment and organizational dimensions, we define the Prometheus AEOlus metamodel with concepts used during the implementation phase. As this phase is the closest to the code generation, the concepts must be closer to those used by the target platform, in order to reduce the conceptual gap.

To define the concepts used for each dimension and to generate the Prometheus AEOlus metamodel, we initially compared Prometheus [8] and JaCaMo [2] metamodels. It was not a straightforward process, since these technologies are developed in different projects with distinct objectives. Some concepts are present in both metamodels; some others have related meanings, but use different names; and still others have different meanings although they use the same name. We started this process with the existent concepts in the Prometheus metamodel and then we included, changed or removed concepts as needed for each dimension, based on those existent in the JaCaMo metamodel. As the result of these preliminary analysis, we defined a first metamodel, that integrated Prometheus and JaCaMo concepts, presented in Figure 1. It is important to note that in this preliminary metamodel some concepts used only in the analyses phase of the Prometheus method still remains.

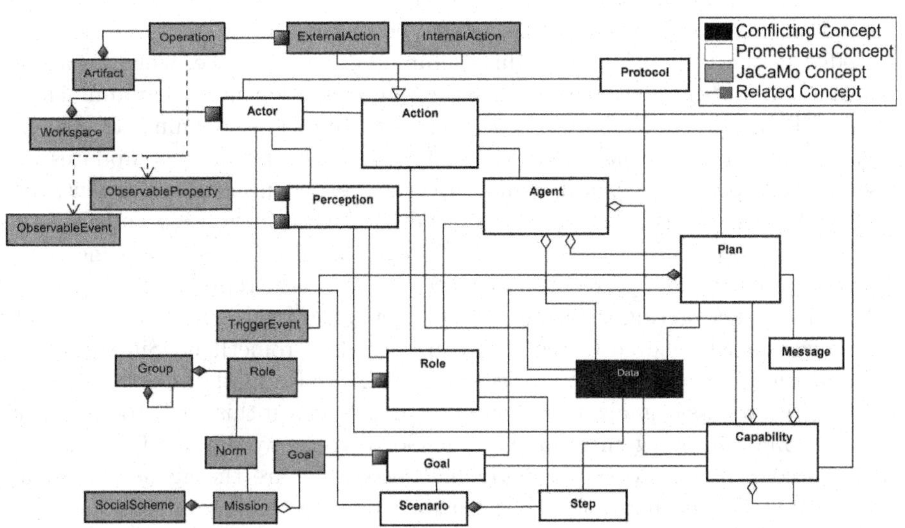

Fig. 1. Prometheus AEOlus preliminary metamodel

The environment dimension, in JaCaMo approach, is composed of a set of artifacts organized in workspaces. Each artifact provides a set of operations and each operation can generate observable events and change observable proprieties. In Prometheus approach, the environment dimension is described only by actors that interact with the system and resources used by the agents. Thus, we included in the metamodel the following concepts: *Workspace*, *Artifact*, *Operation*, *ObservableEvent*, and *ObservableProperty* to allow a more detailed description of the environmental dimension.

In Prometheus the role and goal organizational concepts are already considered. However, these role concepts are used as a part of the agent behaviour and the goal represents both, individual and organizational goals. In JaCaMo approach, however the organizational dimension includes the organizational goals that are arranged in missions, and the relation among these goals, called social scheme; roles that are arranged in groups and subgroups; and norms that bind roles to missions. To allow a more accurate description for the organizational dimension, we decided to include the following concepts from the JaCaMo approach: *Role*, *Group*, *Goal*, *Norm*, *Mission*, and *SocialScheme*.

At this point we realized that, despite the fact that the Prometheus metamodel provides most of the relevant concepts to describe the agent dimensions, some other concepts are important in order to best align the metamodels. Looking for the JaCaMo agent dimension, a plan is composed of a set of actions and by a trigger event. These actions can be performed in the internals of the agent or in the environment, called respectively internal and external actions. We decided to divide the Prometheus action concept in *ExternalAction* and *InternalAction*, and also include the *TriggerEvent* as a part of the agent plan.

The next step in our process was to identify related and conflicting concepts. Related concepts are concepts with similar meanings, hence only one of them is needed in the Prometheus AEOlus metamodel. For instance, when an agent performs an external action it is executing an operation in an environmental artifact. Thus, the *ExternalAction* concept has the same meaning as the environment concept *Operation*. In the same way, when an artifact updates an observable property or generates and observable event in the environment, the agent will receive it as a perception, and both *ObservableProperty* and *ObservableEvent* concepts are related to the *Percept* concept. The *Actor* concept is also related to the *Artifact* concept, since *Artifact* also represents all the external entities interacting with the system. The JaCaMo organizational concept of *Role* was clearly related to the *Role* concept from Prometheus. Similarly, the JaCaMo organizational *Goal* concept is related to the Prometheus *Goal* concept, that also represents organizational and personal goals. In this case, to allow the specification of both organizational and personal goals, we decided to specialize the *Goal* concept in two types: *IndividualGoals*, that are the agent's personal goals, and *OrganizationalGoals*, that are goals defined by the organization.

Conflicting concepts are those that do not share the same meaning in Prometheus and JaCaMo, like the Prometheus *Data* concept. The *Data* concept represents both agent's beliefs and environmental resources, which is already considered by the JaCaMo *Artifact* concept. Thus, we replaced the *Data* concept by the *Belief* concept, that only represents the agents beliefs.

Lastly, we removed from the metamodel the *Scenario* and *Step* Prometheus concepts. These concepts are used only in the analysis phase and are not in the implementation and code generation phases, thus they are not relevant to this Prometheus AEOlus implementation metamodel.

As a result of this analysis, we have the Prometheus AEOlus metamodel, presented in the Figure 2. In this Figure, white concepts came from Prometheus metamodel; gray concepts are from JaCaMo metamodel and black concepts are those existent in Prometheus that changed their meaning in the Prometheus AEOlus metamodel.

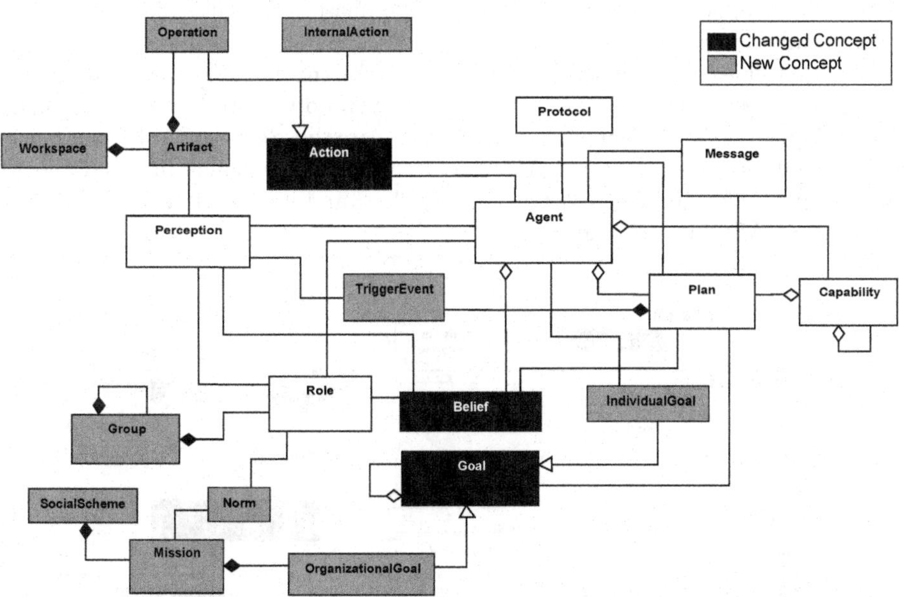

Fig. 2. Prometheus AEOlus metamodel

In the Prometheus AEOlus method *agents* can perform two types of actions: *InternalActions*, that only changes the agent's internals, and *Operations*, that is performed on an environmental *Artifact*. *Artifacts* are grouped in *Workspaces* and, when an *operation* is executed, they generate some *Perception* to the *Agents*. These *Perception* can become a new *Belief* in the agents beliefs base or a *TriggerEvent* that starts a *Plan*.

Agents have *Plans* to achieve their *Goals*. *Goals* can be composed of *Subgoals* and they can be either *IndividualGoals* or *OrganizationalGoals*. *OrganizationalGoals* are grouped in *Missions*, that structures the organization's *SocialScheme* and are assigned to the *Agent* by the *Role* it plays in the organization. *Missions* are bind to the *Roles* by a norm, that specify obligation or permissions to achieve a specific *OrganizationalGoal*. These *Roles* can be structured in *Groups* and *Subgroups*.

5 Prometheus AEOlus Method

The Prometheus AEOlus method uses an interactive incremental process based on the Prometheus process. Prometheus AEOlus starts with the three development phases used in Prometheus (system specification, architectural design and detailed design) and provides a fourth phase called implementation. During the system specification phase, a clearly and detailed system specification is created. Based on this specification, in the architectural design phase the overall system behaviour is defined, and in the detailed design phase the agent's plans are specified. Finally, in the implementation phase some entities defined in the previous phases are refined to allow the code generation for the JaCaMo framework.

Figure 3 presents all these phases and the work products produced in each one. In this Figure, work products presented in white are those existent in Prometheus method and used in Prometheus AEOlus as well; the ones existent in Prometheus but changed in Prometheus AEOlus are in black and new work defined only in Prometheus AEOlus are in grey.

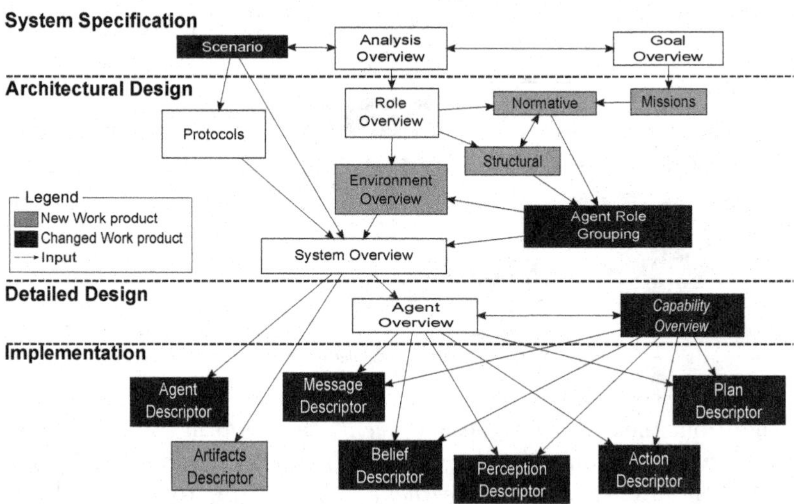

Fig. 3. Prometheus AEOlus overview

Although Prometheus AEOlus method considers most of the work products of Prometheus, we introduced four graphical work products in order to complement the environmental and organizational specifications. These work products, included in the architectural design phase of the Prometheus AEOlus method are the following: *structural*, *missions*, *normative* and *environment overview*. In the implementation phase, we produced some textual work product with a refined description of the entities required for the code generation. Most of these textual work product are also produced in Prometheus, along all its phases. In Prometheus AEOlus, however, these textual work product are produced only in the implementation phase. The *artifact descriptor* work product was introduced in this phase.

In this paper we present a brief description of the Prometheus AEOlus method based on the *Agents on Mars* scenario. In this scenario, two teams are competing to find the best water wells and occupy the Mars best zones. The environment is represented by a graph where each vertex has a number representing its value. A zone is a subgraph with at least two nodes and each zone has a value, determined by the sum of the vertices values. The main goal is to maximize the score, computed by summing up the values of the zones occupied by the team and its current money. The money is increased when the team executes some activities, like probe vertices, survey edges and attack enemies.

5.1 System Specification

To create a clear and detailed system definition, we started by defining use case scenarios as well as the system's goals. In this phase, the aim was to answer the question "What should the system do?". The *scenario description* started from the initial system description. This textual work product describes how things should happen in some particular circumstances. Each scenario shows a sequence of steps that take place within the system which were used to describe the expected behaviour during its normal running and also what was supposed to happen when something went wrong.

In the *goal overview* diagram we summarize all identified system's goals and subgoals, arranging them in an AND/OR tree that allows the definition of dependencies among these goals. The *Goal overview* diagram is also based on the initial system description. New goals can arise during the scenario description and new goals can originate new scenarios.

For example, in the *goal overview* for the *Agents on Mars* scenario, presented in Figure 4, the main system goal is *To Maximize Score* and it is decomposed in three subgoals: *Occupy good zones*, *Defend zones* and *Get Money*. All these subgoals can be pursuit at the same time since they are decomposed using an AND operator. The goal *Occupy good zones* is also decomposed using the AND operator with a precedence order, suggesting the sequence in which the subgoals must be pursuit. That is, first the *Figure out the map* subgoal is achieved, then *Define good zones* is achieved, and finally *Place the agents* is achieved. Likewise, the subgoal *Defend zones* is decomposed using the AND operator with a precedence order to be achieved. The goal *Get money* is decomposed using an OR operator and any of its subgoals (*Probe vertices*, *Attack enemies* and *Survey edges*) can be selected.

5.2 Architectural Design

This phase aims to define the overall system structure by the defining the system's elements (missions, roles, agents, artifacts) and the links between them. In this phase, the goals specified in the *goal overview* diagram are arranged in coherent sets called missions. Each mission is assigned to an agent by the role

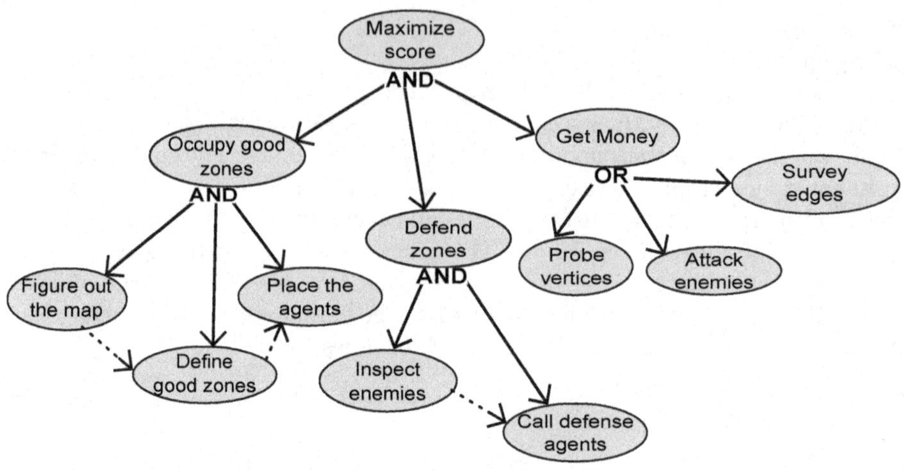

Fig. 4. Goal overview diagram

it plays in the system. Thus, a mission must be composed of a consistent set of goals, since the agent that assumes a mission should be able to achieve all its goals. These missions are presented in the *missions* diagram presented in Figure 5. This diagram is based on the *goal overview* diagram, and links missions to their goals. For example, the mission called *Occupy* is composed of *Define good zones* and *Place the agents* goals. Thus, the agent that assume this mission must achieve both goals.

Also in the architectural design phase, the *structural* diagram specifies the system's roles, how these roles are grouped, and the links among them. A role is defined when a specific behaviour is necessary in the system. These behaviours can be defined based on the *scenario diagram.* For example, in the description of *Agent on Mars*, we can identify five roles: *Sentinel*, *Inspector*, *Explorer*, *Repairer* and *Saboteur.* A sixth role, called *Leader*, is defined as a project choice, since this scenario uses a centralized approach for decision making. Figure 6 present the *structural* diagram for this example. In the Figure, the abstract role *TeamMember* is defined. This abstract role is used to simplify the specification by means of inheritance. No agent can directly play an abstract role and it is a "super-role" that all roles inherit characteristics.

A group is composed of a related set of roles. Each role is included in a group with its cardinality (min and max) that represents the number of agents that can play this role. A group can also contain some subgroups, each one with its cardinality. One group is labelled as "well formed" if all its cardinalities are satisfied. In the *Agent on Mars* example, we defined a main group called *Team.* This group is composed of two subgroups - *Conquest* and *Defense* - and one role called *Leader.* To be "well formed", exactly one instance of each subgroup should be created and one agent must play the role *Leader.* The subgroup *Defense* is composed of the roles *Repairer* and *Saboteur*, and the *Conquest* subgroup is composed of the roles *Sentinel*, *Inspector*, and *Explorer.* All these roles cardinalities

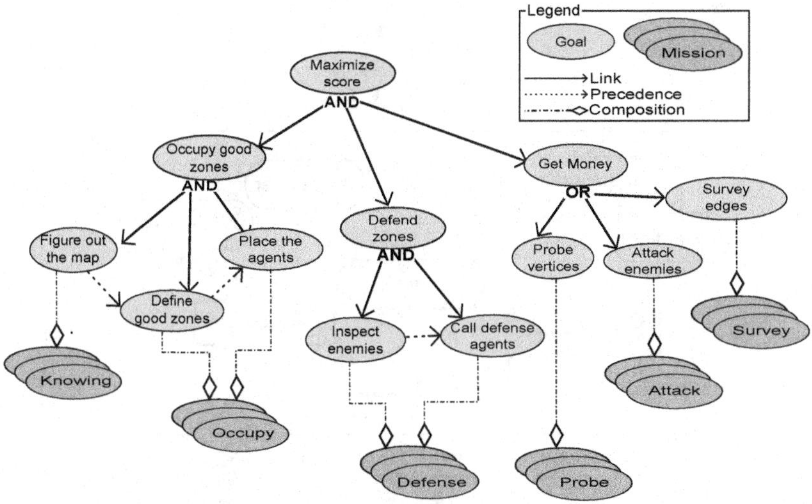

Fig. 5. Mission diagram

are four, that is, four agents have to play each role. The *Leader* is a role played by one agent that also plays the role *Explorer*. In a group, the roles are linked to represent acquaintance, authority, communication or compatibility among them. In the *Agents on Mars* example, presented in Figure 6, we used the abstract role *TeamMember* to define, by inheritance, compatibility and acquaintance among all other roles. Further, the role *Leader* has authority over the others and they can communicate with the *Leader*.

Based on these *missions* and *structural* diagrams, the *normative* diagram is defined. In this diagram the norms that link roles and missions are specified. Two kinds of norms are used: permission, used to state that an agent is allowed to commit to a mission, and obligations, to state that an agent ought to commit to a mission. It is important to note that if an agent is obligated to a mission it is also permitted to this mission. Figure 7 presents the *normative* diagram for the *Agents on Mars* example. In this Figure, some missions should be committed by more than one role, like the *Survey* mission that all agents have to commit to. Likewise, some roles are obliged/permitted to more than one mission, like the role *Explorer*, that is obligated to commit to the missions *Probe* and *Knowing* and is permitted to commit to the mission *Survey*. That implies that the agent playing *Explorer* must achieve the goals of all these missions.

The environmental artifacts are defined in the *environment overview* diagram. Each artifact encapsulates operations that represent functionalities or tools that can be used by agents. When an agent execute an artifact operation, it may provide some perceptions to the agent. Artifacts are grouped into workspaces and to execute operations or receive their perceptions the agent must enter this workspace. In the diagram, artifacts are presented with the actions and perceptions related to them. Artifacts can be defined based on the *scenario description*, when it is identified the need of a shared resource or a shared data among

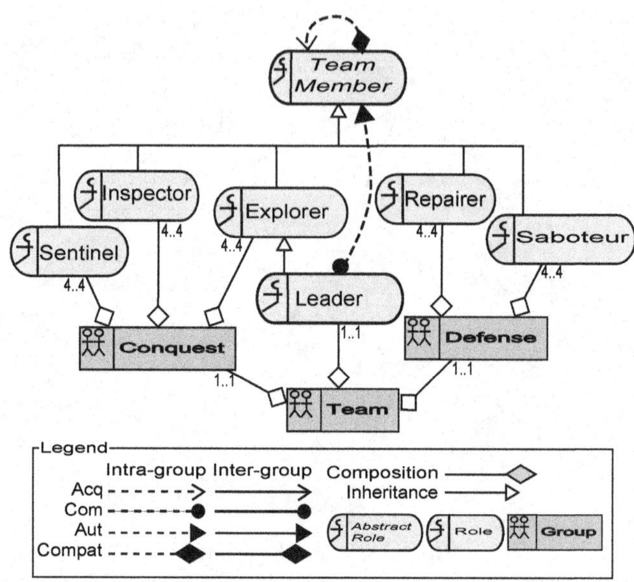

Fig. 6. Structural diagram

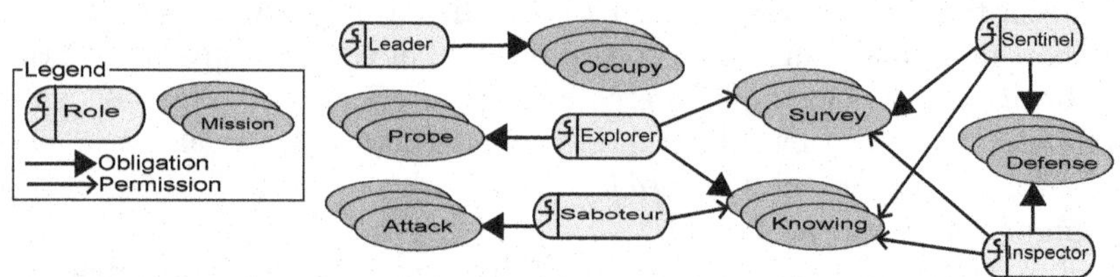

Fig. 7. Normative diagram

agents, or the need of an interface between the system and another external entity. For example, in the *environment overview* for the *Agents on Mars* example, presented in Figure 8, we used two artifacts in the same workspace called *Mars*. The artifact *Server* creates an interface between the system and the game server, and the artifact *Map* is used to share all agent informations about the scenario map. Furthermore, we can create artifacts to coordinate agents actions or to help the communication among them. In Figure 8, we also present some of the possible actions performed in each artifact (e.g. the *probe* action in the *Server* artifact and the *send_data* action in the *Map* artifact) and the perceptions provided them (e.g, the *position* perception from the *Server* artifact and the *new_zone* perception from the *Map* artifact).

The next step is to define the agents types that take part of the system. An agent type is defined when we identify that a specific role demand some specific characteristic or ability to be properly played. Thus, these agent types are defined based on the *scenario description*, the *structural*, and the *normative* diagrams previously created. An agent type can be defined to play one

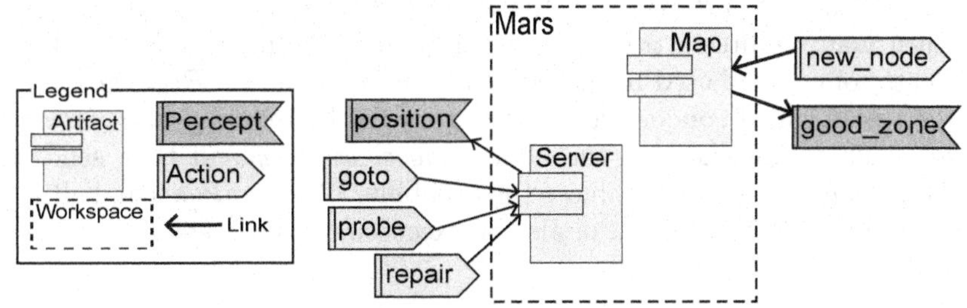

Fig. 8. Environment overview diagram

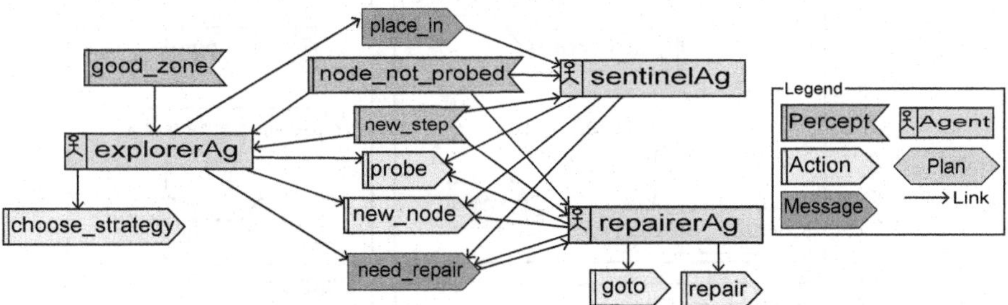

Fig. 9. System overview diagram

specific role or more than one role. These agents types are presented in the *system overview* diagram, in which the overall system structure is defined. The diagram also presents exchanged messages, perceptions and actions related to each agent. This diagram aims to provide an overview of elements and how they are related. Figure 9 presents a *system overview* diagram fragment for the *Agents on Mars* scenario. In this fragment three agent types are presented: *ExplorerAg*, *SentinelAg* and *RepairerAg*. This diagram also specifies some message exchange between the agents. The *ExplorerAg* sends a message *place_in* that is received by the *SentinelAg*; and all of them may send the message *need_repair* to the *RepairerAg*.

5.3 Detailed Design

This phase focus on the agent internals, that is, their plans, beliefs and capabilities. In this phase we assume that the agent uses the BDI architecture. In Prometheus AEOlus, like in Prometheus, a capability is conceived as a library that encompasses functionalities required in more than one single agent. A capability is described in the *capability overview* diagram while the agent uses the *agent overview* diagram. Both *agent overview* and *capability overview* diagram are used to describe the agents internals. A plan is described as a sequence of actions that can be performed by the agent to accomplish a goal or make a task. Each plan requires a trigger event that starts the plan execution. Figure 10 presents some plans used in the *Agents on Mars* scenario. *ExplorerAg* agent executes a plan called *conquer_zone*, that is started by receiving the perception *good_zone*. This plan executes the action *choose_strategy* and then sends the *place_in* message. This agent includes the capability *CommonPlans* and all plans detailed within this capability can also be executed by the agent.

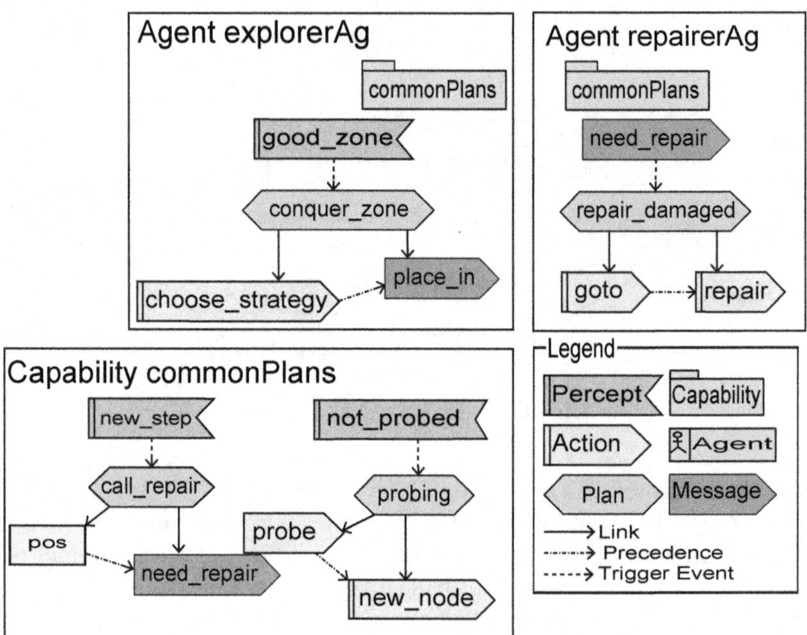

Fig. 10. Agent and capability overview diagrams

5.4 Implementation

The implementation phase is used to refine the entities including some relevant information used for the code generation phase. In this phase we assumed that the code is generated for the JaCaMo platform and we refine these entities based on JaCaMo characteristics. Each descriptor is a structured textual work product with specific information. In the *agent descriptor*, for example, we included information about how many agents are initialized during the system start; in the *message description* the performative and the content of the message is informed; and in the *artifact descriptor* we described the operations provided by each artifact, the parameters needed to instantiate it, and the observable properties and events provided by it. For the *Agents on Mars* example we present some descriptors in Table 2.

Table 2. Descriptors created in the implementation phase

(a) Agent descriptor

Agent explorerAg	
Description	Explorer agent is responsible for mapping the exploration zone and organize the defense zone
Cardinality	4

(b) Plan descriptor

Plan repair_damaged	
Description	Executed when a *need_repair* message is received, the repairer should have more than 3 points of health and it is not repairing another agent
Context	health(X) & X > 3 & free

(c) Message descriptor

Message need_repair	
Description	Sent by damaged agents. An agent is damaged if it has less than 3 points of health
Performative	achieve
Content	need_repair(Pos)

(d) Action descriptor

Action goto	
Description	Moves the agent to a specific vertex. Action provided by the Server artifact
Function	goto(Vertex)

(e) Artifact descriptor

Artifact Server	
Description	Used to interface the system and the server.
Operations	probe(Vertex) goto(Vertex) repair(AgentID)
Parameters	
Observable Properties	int[] position
Observable Events	

6 Code Generation

The Prometheus AEOlus method provides some guidelines to allow the assisted translation from the developed work products to code, using the JaCaMo framework as target platform; the code for the agent dimension is implemented in Jason; the organizational dimension is implemented in $\mathcal{M}$oise, using a XML file; and environment dimension is implemented in Java programming language using the CArtAgO framework.

6.1 Code Generation for the Agent Dimension

The code for the agent dimension starts with the generation of the Jason project file (that usually has the .mas2j extension) produced from *system overview* and

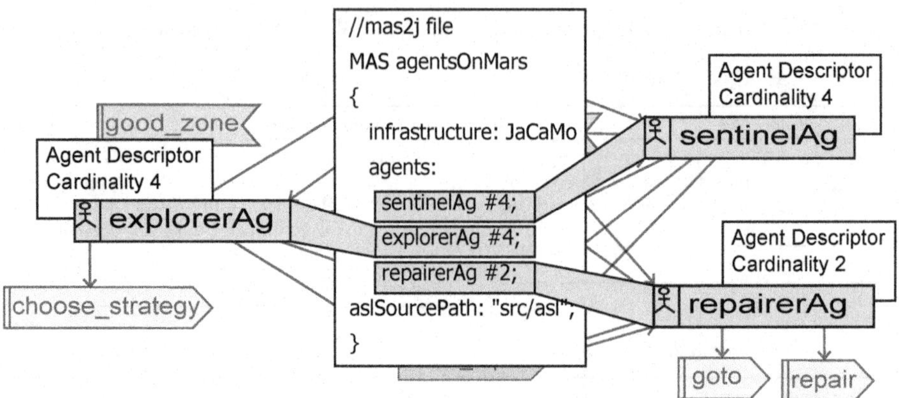

Fig. 11. Jason *.mas2j* file generated from system overview diagram

agent descriptor diagrams. Figure 11 presents the *.mas2j* file for the *Agents on Mars* scenario, a portion of the system overview diagram and the *agent descriptor* for each agent. This file includes some overall MAS characteristics. It defines that the infrastructure is *JaCaMo* and the location of the agents source code. This file also contains the agents that will take part in the system, i.e., their names and number of instances. These agents are defined based on the *system overview* diagram presented in Figure 9 and *agent descriptor* presented in Table 2a.

A Jason agent is coded in a file with the *.asl* extension. The file name is the agent name and the code is created based on the *agent overview* diagram. The agent code is composed of plans, beliefs and capabilities. A plan is composed of perceptions, messages and actions. All these entities have their own descriptor which are used to generate the code. Figure 12a presents the code for the agent *reapairerAg*, the *agent overview* diagram and the descriptors of each element. The plan has three parts: a trigger event, a context and a body. A trigger event can be a received message, like presented in the Figure, or a perception received from the environment and the body is a sequence of actions, messages and beliefs changes. Both are defined in the plan specification, presented in the *agent overview* diagram, while the context is defined in the plan descriptor. The *repairerAg* includes a capability called *commonPlans* and the include directive of Jason is thus used in the generated code. The *commonPlans* capability is also coded as an *.asl* file, named *commonPlans.asl.* A piece of the capability code is presented in the Figure 12b, with the *capability overview* diagram and the needed descriptors. This plan first executes a query in the belief base and then sends a message. In the *system overview* diagram we can see which agent will receive the message. In the example, the message *need_repair* is sent to the *repairerAg*.

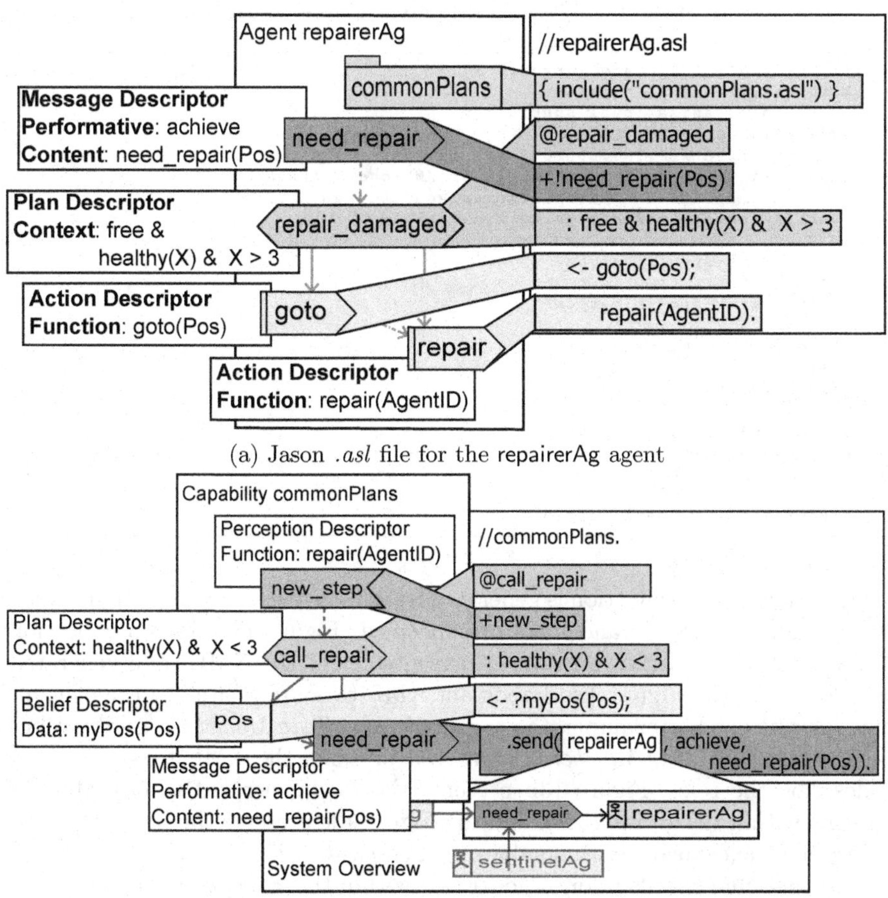

(a) Jason *.asl* file for the repairerAg agent

(b) Jason *.asl* file for the commonPlans capability

Fig. 12. Jason code generated for the agent dimension

6.2 Code Generation for the Organizational Dimension

The overall XML file structure to implement a $\mathcal{M}$oise code is presented in Listing 1.1. The organization is defined within the *<organizational_specification>* tag, where the code for structural, functional, and normative specifications will be included. For each specification one specific tag is used: *<structural_specification>*, to include the code for the organizational structure with their roles and groups; *<functional_specification>* tag, to include the code for the organizational goals and missions; and *<normative_specification>*, to include the code for the organizational norms. Each specification is detailed below.

Listing 1.1. Overall structure to $\mathcal{M}$oise *XML* file

```
<?xml version="1.0" encoding="UTF-8"?>
<organisational-specification
  id = "id_organizational_specification"
  os-version = "0.8"
  xmlns = 'http://moise.sourceforge.net/os'
  xmlns:xsi = 'http://www.w3.org/2001/XMLSchema-instance'
  xsi:schemaLocation = 'http://moise.sourceforge.net/os
    http://moise.sourceforge.net/xml/os.xsd' >

  <structural-specification>
    <!-- put structural specification here -->
  </structural-specification>

  <functional-specification>
    <!-- put functional specification here -->
  </functional-specification>

  <normative-specification>
    <!-- put normative specification here -->
  </normative-specification>

</organisational-specification>
```

The structural specification is generated from the *structural* diagram, in which all system roles, groups and links are specified. Figure 13 presents a portion of the *structural* diagram previously presented, and the XML code generated based on it. In the Figure, the important XML tags are related to the element that describes it. For example, the tag <*role id=“TeamMember”* / > describes the abstract role *TeamMember*. Figure 13a presents the XML tags generated to describe the roles; Figure 13b presents the tags generated to describe the elements within the group *Team*; and the Figure 13c presents the tags generated to describe the elements within subgroup *Conquest*.

The functional specification is generated within the <*scheme*> tag, based on the *missions* diagram. In Figure 14 a portion of the diagram for the *Agents on Mars* and its respective code is presented. Within this specification all systems goals and their hierarchy are coded. The *plan operator* tag as specified in Figure 14 indicates that the subgoals are achieved in sequence. The functional specification also includes all the missions and their goals.

The normative specification is generated based on the *normative* diagram. As presented in Figure 15, which presents a piece of the normative specification for the *Agents on Mars* example Generating the code for this specification is simple. Each *norm* tag is composed of an *id*, the name of the *role* for which this norm is applicable, the *type* of the norm (*permission* or *obligation*) and the *mission* that is related to the norm.

6.3 Code Generation for the Environmental Dimension

The code for the environmental dimension is implemented in Java programming language using the CArtAgO framework. A CArtAgO artifact is programmed directly by defining a Java class that extends the *cartago.Artifact* class. To create

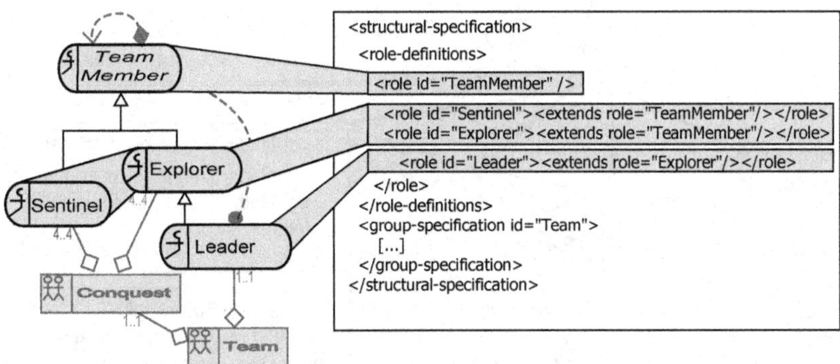

(a) XML code for the roles in the structural specification

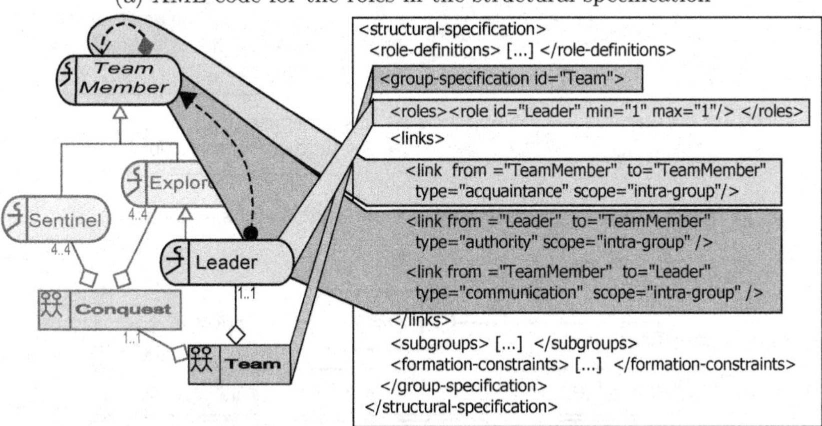

(b) XML code for the group *Team* in the structural specification

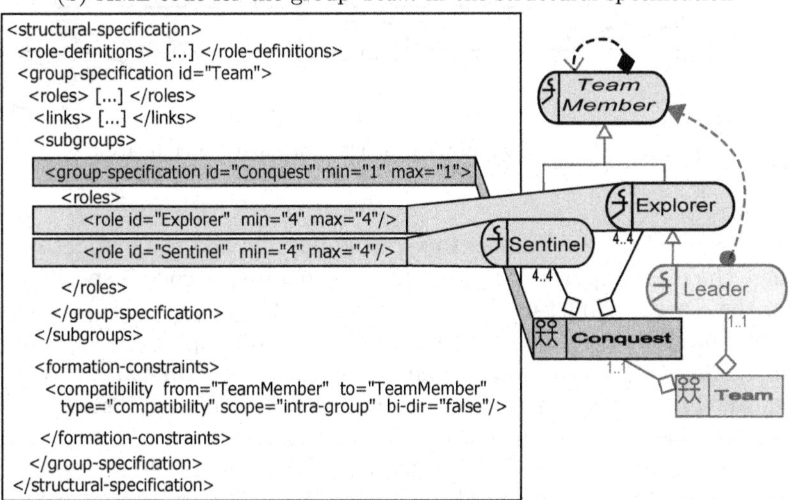

(c) XML code for the subgroup *Conquest* in the structural specification

Fig. 13. XML Code generated for the structural specification

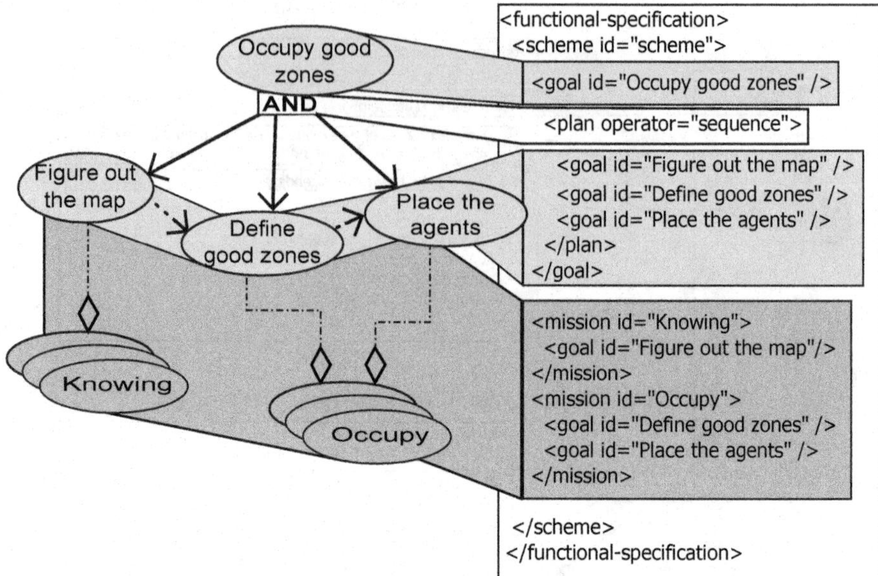

Fig. 14. XML code generated for the functional specification

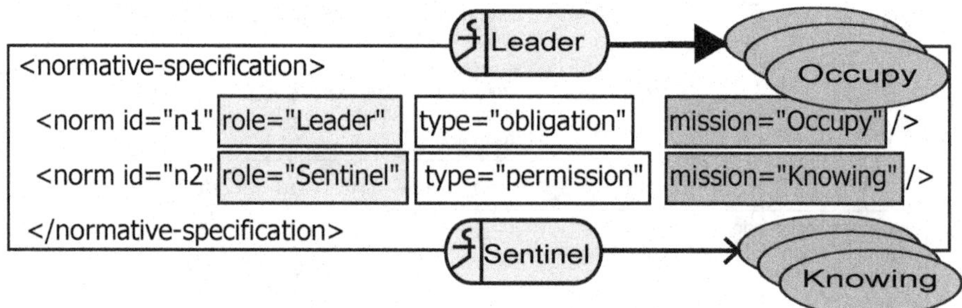

Fig. 15. XML code generated for the normative specification

this class, we used the *environment overview* diagram and the *artifact descriptor*, where the most important information to generate the code is specified. The class for the *Server* artifact used in the *Agents on Mars* example is presented in Figure 16. For each operation defined in the artifact descriptor one *void* method is created. These methods should be annotated with *@OPERATION*. A special method called *init* is used to specify how this artifact is created. If some parameters are defined in the descriptor, these parameters are used in this *init* method. The primitive *defineObsProperty()* is used to define the observable properties for this artifact. For each observable property its name and initial values are defined.

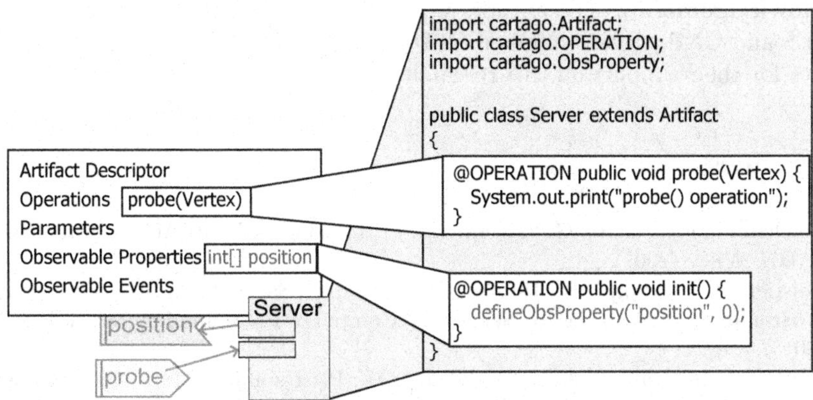

Fig. 16. Java class generated for the environment dimension

7 Conclusions

The Prometheus AEOlus method aims at allowing the MAS analysis and implementation integrating the agent, organization, and environment dimensions. Each dimension is analysed and implemented as first class entity, using specific concepts and abstractions. To minimize the conceptual gap between the analysis and programming phases, we used the same concepts in both phases. The approach main advantage is a straightforward translation from the work products used during the analysis phase into code. Nevertheless, the Prometheus AEOlus method is platform dependent, since it was developed based on the JaCaMo framework, and uses mainly concepts from this framework. Although the proposed method aims at a specific platform, the approach we used to achieve this method (metamodels alignment and an existing method extension) could be followed using other platforms and methods.

We also conducted a preliminary evaluation with a group of 30 undergraduate and graduate students. This primary test aimed to evaluate the method and its modelling language, including aspects like understandability, acceptability, expressiveness and efficiency. The students who took the evaluation had no previous knowledge in the agent oriented field. They used the method to design and analyse a simple example. Then, they answered a ten question survey about the evaluation aspects. The result allowed us to improve the method, changing some diagrams and notations. However, due to the limited time and the limited users knowledge, this preliminary evaluation did not include all method aspects.

The next step in the Prometheus AEOlus development is to implement a tool that supports all Prometheus AEOlus phases and the automatic code generation. We are planning to describe the Prometheus AEOlus method using the SPEM 2.0[14] specification. Also, a formal verification to the final metamodel and a comparison evaluation to other methods is necessary to further improve the method.

Acknowledgements. The authors would like to thank the Brazilian agencies CAPES and CNPq (grant number 140261/2013-3), Prof. Lin Padghan and colleagues for their support on this research.

References

1. Bellifemine, F.L., Caire, G., Greenwood, D.: Developing Multi-Agent Systems with JADE. Wiley (2007)
2. Boissier, O., Bordini, R.H., Hübner, J.F., Ricci, A., Santi, A.: Multi-agent oriented programming with JaCaMo. Science of Computer Programming 78(6), 747–761 (2013)
3. Bordini, R.H., Hübner, J.F., Wooldridge, M.: Programming Multi-Agent Systems in AgentSpeak using Jason. John Wiley & Sons (2007)
4. Braubach, L., Lamersdorf, W., Pokahr, A.: Jadex: Implementing a bdi-infrastructure for jade agents (2003)
5. Brinkkemper, S.: Method engineering: Engineering of information systems development methods and tools. Information and Software Technology 38(4), 275–280 (1996)
6. Cossentino, M., Gaud, N., Hilaire, V., Galland, S., Koukam, A.: ASPECS: An agent-oriented software process for engineering complex systems. JAAMAS 20(2), 260–304 (2010)
7. Cossentino, M., Potts, C.: PASSI: A process for specifying and implementing multi-agent systems using UML (2002)
8. Dam, K.H.: Supporting Software Evolution in Agent Systems. Doctor thesis, RMIT University (2008)
9. DeLoach, S.A., García-Ojeda, J.C.: O-mase: A customisable approach to designing and building complex, adaptive multi-agent systems. Int. J. Agent-Oriented Softw. Eng. 4(3), 244–280 (2010)
10. Demazeau, Y.: From interactions to collective behaviour in agent-based systems. In: 1st. ECCS, pp. 117–132 (1995)
11. Gaud, N., Galland, S., Hilaire, V., Koukam, A.: An organizational platform for holonic and multiagent systems. In: Hindriks, K.V., Pokahr, A., Sardina, S. (eds.) ProMAS 2008. LNCS (LNAI), vol. 5442, pp. 104–119. Springer, Heidelberg (2009)
12. Hübner, J.F., Sichman, J.S., Boissier, O.: Developing organised multiagent systems using the MOISE+ model: Programming issues at the system and agent levels. Int. J. Agent-Oriented Softw. Eng. 1(3/4), 370–395 (2007)
13. Mylopoulos, J., Kolp, M., Castro, J.: UML for agent-oriented software development: The tropos proposal. In: Gogolla, M., Kobryn, C. (eds.) UML 2001. LNCS, vol. 2185, pp. 422–441. Springer, Heidelberg (2001)
14. Object Management Group, Inc. Software & Systems Process Engineering Metamodel Specification v2.0, OMG edition (October 2007)
15. Padgham, L., Winikoff, M.: Developing Intelligent Agent Systems: A Practical Guide. Halsted Press, New York (2004)
16. Pavón, J., Gómez-Sanz, J.: Agent oriented software engineering with INGENIAS. In: Mařík, V., Pěchouček, M., Müller, J. (eds.) CEEMAS 2003. LNCS (LNAI), vol. 2691, pp. 394–403. Springer, Heidelberg (2003)
17. Ricci, A., Piunti, M., Viroli, M.: Environment programming in multi-agent systems: An artifact-based perspective. AAMAS 23, 158–192 (2011)

18. Ricci, A., Viroli, M., Omicini, A.: The A&A programming model and technology for developing agent environments in MAS. In: Dastani, M., El Fallah Seghrouchni, A., Ricci, A., Winikoff, M. (eds.) ProMAS 2007. LNCS (LNAI), vol. 4908, pp. 89–106. Springer, Heidelberg (2008)
19. Winikoff, M., Padgham, L.: The prometheus methodology. In: Bergenti, F., Gleizes, M.-P., Zambonelli, F. (eds.) The Agent-Oriented Software Engineering Handbook, ch. 11, pp. 273–296. Kluwer (2004)

From Multi-Agent Programming to Object Oriented Design Patterns

Mehdi Dastani and Bas Testerink

Intelligent Systems Group
Utrecht University, The Netherlands
{m.m.dastani,b.j.g.testerink}@uu.nl

Abstract. Various agent-based programming languages and frameworks have been proposed to support the development of multi-agent systems. They have contributed to the identification and operationalisation of multi-agent system concepts, features and abstractions by proposing specific programming constructs. Unfortunately, these contributions have not yet been widely adopted by industry. In this paper, we follow the argument that multi-agent programming technology can find its way to industry by introducing design patterns for the existing agent constructs in standard software technology. We provide some object-oriented design patterns based on the programming constructs that have been developed in agent-based programming languages.

1 Introduction

Multi-agent systems (MAS) technology aims at improving solutions for industry problems related to distributed autonomous systems. The MAS community, in particular the agent oriented engineering side, provides high-level (social/cognitive) concepts and abstractions to conceptualize, model, analyse, implement, and test intelligent distributed systems. The development of a multi-agent system boils down to the development of a set of individual agents, their organisation, and the environment with which they interact. Individual agents are required to be autonomous in the sense that they are able to make their own decisions to either achieve their objectives (proactive behaviour) or to respond to their received events (reactive behaviour). The organisation is supposed to coordinate the agents' behaviours in order to ensure the overall objectives of the multi-agent system. Finally, the environment encapsulates shared resources and services that can be used by the agents.

In the past decades, various programming languages and frameworks have been proposed to support the development of multi-agent systems. These programming languages have provided dedicated programming constructs (either in a declarative, imperative, or hybrid style) to support the development of specific features of multi-agent systems. While some programming languages extend standard programming technologies such as Java (e.g. Jade [2] and Jack [4]), other agent-based programming languages are specified from scratch (e.g. 2APL [8],

F. Dalpiaz et al. (Eds.): EMAS 2014, LNAI 8758, pp. 204–226, 2014.

GOAL [13] and Jason [3]). These programming languages and frameworks focus on specific sets of concepts and abstractions for some of which operational semantics and execution platforms are provided.

Without doubt a merit of these programming languages is the plethora of programming constructs that support the implementation of various features of multi-agent systems. For example, BDI-based agent-oriented programming languages such as 2APL, Goal and Jason can be seen as technologies that demonstrate how autonomous agents can be developed by means of a set of conditional plans and a decision procedure that continuously senses the environment to update its state, reasons about its state to select conditional plans, and executes the selected plans. Other programming proposals focus on the implementation of specific features concerning organisations or environments of multi-agent systems by proposing programming constructs to implement norms and sanctions, mobility, services, resources or artefacts.

Although these programming languages and frameworks have contributed to the identification and operationalisation of multi-agents systems concepts, features and abstractions, they have not been widely adopted as standard technologies to develop large-scale industry applications. This may sound disappointing, in particular because technology transfer has been identified as a main challenge and a milestone for the multi-agent programming community. There are various reasons for why these programming languages and frameworks fell short of expectations [6]. First of all, the adoption of new technologies by the industry is generally assumed to be a slow process as the industry often tends to be conservative, employing known and proven technologies. Moreover, industry adopts new technologies when they can be integrated in their existing technologies, and more importantly, when they reduce their production costs, which is in this case the costs of the software development process. Finally, the industry tends to see the contribution of multi-agent programming community as AI technology. The main problems with such technologies are thought to be their theoretical purpose, scalability, and performance.

The aim of this paper is to stimulate the transfer of multi-agent programming technology to industry. We start by the following three observations. First, object-oriented programming languages and development frameworks have already found their ways to industry. Second, it is common practice to use design patterns for often reoccurring problems in object oriented programs. Third, multi-agent programming technology provides solutions to a variety of reoccurring problems in large-scale distributed applications by means of dedicated programming constructs. Based on these observations and as argued in [27], we believe that multi-agent programming technology may find its way to industry by introducing object oriented design patterns that describe multi-agent programming constructs.

The starting point of our approach is to identify multi-agent concepts and abstractions for which language level constructs have been developed and integrated in the existing multi-agent programming languages. The identified concepts and abstractions, together with their developed programming proposals, can then be used to introduce corresponding design patterns in standard object-oriented technology. We thus consider language level constructs, which are proposed and agreed by the multi-agent programming community, as being based and motivated by the best practices used in the development of multi-agent systems. Hence we do not aim at showing how these ideas improve upon industry practices. This consideration justifies our proposed design patterns as formalizing the best practices in the multi-agent programming community. We first explain the multi-agent concepts and abstractions that form the main concern of existing multi-agent programming languages and for which dedicated programming constructs have been proposed. Subsequently we present object-oriented design patterns that support the implementation of these concepts and abstractions in standard object-oriented technology. Finally, we explain that the idea of design patterns for multi-agent concepts is not controversial and provide an overview of the related work and compare them with our proposal.

We would like to emphasize that we consider multi-agent programming technology as domain independent and general purpose technology that aims at supporting the development of distributed intelligent applications in general. We are aware that the use of special purpose programming technologies is growing and constitutes an essential part of the programming practice in companies such as Google, Amazon and IBM. However, we see multi-agent programming technology as being concerned with specific data structures and processes that can support the implementation of multi-agent system concepts such as knowledge, goals, plans, deliberation and decision making, norm, sanctions, monitoring and control. These data structures and processes can be introduced and supported by standard programming technologies such as Java, C++ and C# in order to build distributed intelligent applications.

The structure of this paper is as follows. In Section 2 we identify some concepts for which language level constructs have been proposed in the design of various multi-agent programming languages. In Section 3 and 4 the identified concepts are used to define related design patterns at the individual agent and multi-agent levels, respectively. In Section 5, we discuss our approach and compare it with some existing work.

2 Autonomous Behaviour and Normative Mechanisms

Multi-agent concepts and abstractions are defined with respect to individual agents, multi-agent organisations and multi-agent environments. For example, an individual agent is conceived as a process that continuously senses its environment, reasons about its states, and decides to act by selecting some plans to execute. The agents can thus have autonomous behaviour in the sense that they have the ability to decide on their own which actions or plans to select and perform. Autonomous behaviour can be either proactive (i.e., agents behave to achieve their objectives) or reactive (i.e., agents behave to respond to their received events). These characteristic behaviours of individual agents, for which language level constructs are introduced and integrated in the existing agent-oriented programming languages, are supposed to meet reoccurring challenges in the design and development of software agents. We conceive these characteristics as the best practices for which we aim at presenting design patterns in object-oriented technology.

At the level of multi-agent organisation, concepts and abstractions have been proposed in order to cope with coordination and regulation challenges involved in distributed software systems. Again, we conceive these concepts and abstractions as identifying the best practices suggested by the multi-agent programming community to solve coordination and regulation challenges. We aim at formalizing these best practices as design patterns. In this paper, we focus on norm-based regulation mechanisms that coordinate the agents' behaviour by means of norms being enforced through sanctions. Such mechanisms continuously monitor the agents' behaviour and impose sanctions when norms are violated. In this approach, a norm is considered as a description of good behaviour and a sanction is seen as a system response to norm violations. Norms can be state-based, specifying that certain states are obliged or prohibited. Norms can also be conditional and have a deadline. When the norm condition is satisfied, certain states are obliged or prohibited before the given deadline.

In order to describe the design patterns we shall use the common format from [11]. The proposed design patterns are presented with terminology that is common to object oriented programming, rather than agent technology jargon. We would like to emphasize that we are aware that design patterns should formalize the best practices that have originated from the industry practices. However, although we do not have access to the industry practices regarding the development of intelligent distributed systems, we assume that the commonly agreed upon concepts and abstractions within the multi-agent programming community do reflect proper solutions to reoccurring problems in distributed intelligent systems. These concepts and abstractions are established based on a peer reviewed approach and are believed to facilitate the development of multi-agent systems. Also, in line with [11], the examples throughout the paper illustrate how an application of the patterns might look. They are not meant to compare the solutions resulting from the patterns with other possible solutions such as actor technology.

2.1 Example Reactive Behaviour in Agent Programming

We shall draw our examples from a multi-agent system that we aim at developing in the context of smart roads. We will implement traffic simulation software using SUMO [18] to investigate future traffic scenarios with autonomous cars and intelligent infrastructures. Heterogeneous agents are used to operate cars in SUMO. Every agent has an interface to the simulation platform with which they can accelerate, decelerate, switch lanes, change routes and send messages (to each other or to the infrastructure). For our scenario we use Java to implement agents. We use AspectJ to implement traffic norms and laws. We show how the design patterns can be used to implement the agents and norms. Autonomous cars are made aware of the obligations/prohibitions that apply to them by the infrastructure. As a norm example we take the rule that it is forbidden for a car to move faster than 50km/h after entering an urban area until it leaves the area.

We first discuss the way agent languages allow the programmer to specify which actions to do when. For instance in 2APL, Goal and Jason we have the notion of conditional plans/actions. These are plans that are only applied if they are relevant to the agent's current situation and if they are applicable. As an example, we shall show how in 2APL, Goal and Jason an agent can react to the perception of a new speed limit. In section 3 it is show how this is implemented with the proposed design pattern. We assume that an agent receives an event/percept upon entering an urban area, that states the new speed limit. The agent adopts this speed limit as its own target speed if the speed limit is above its own maximum speed capability, and if it is not in an emergency. But modifying the target speed is only applicable if the agent is capable of adjusting its own speed.

For the 2APL example we have a PC-Rule:

```
1 event(speedLimit(Limit)) <- speedIsAdjustable | {
2     B(maxSpeedCapability(Max));
3     if B(not(inEmergency)){
4         -targetSpeed(_);
5         if(Max > Limit){ +targetSpeed(Limit); }
6         else { +targetSpeed(Max); }
7     }
8 }
```

```
Line 1: Head and guard of the rule. If the head matches the event then the guard
    is checked. If the guard is true (i.e. the agent can determine its own speed)
    then the plan is applied.
Lines 2-7: Maximum speed capability is retrieved and the target speed is adapted.
```

For the Goal example we have two conditional actions:

```
1 if bel( percept(speedLimit(Limit)), speedIsAdjustable,
2         maxSpeedCapability(Max), Max > Limit,
3         not inEmergency, targetSpeed(Current) )
4 then delete(targetSpeed(Current) ) + insert( targetSpeed(Limit)).
5
6 if bel( percept(speedLimit(Limit)), speedIsAdjustable,
7         maxSpeedCapability(Max), Max <= Limit,
8         targetSpeed(Current) )
9 then delete(targetSpeed(Current) ) + insert( targetSpeed(Max)).
```

```
Lines 1-4: The case where the limit is below the maximum attainable speed.
Lines 6-9: The case where the limit is higher than the maximum attainable speed.
```

For the Jason example we have a highly similar plan rule as for 2APL[1]:

```
+!speedLimit(Limit) : speedIsAdjustable <-
    ?maxSpeedCapability(Max);
    if (not(inEmergency)){
        -targetSpeed(_);
        if(Max > Limit){ +targetSpeed(Limit); }
        else { +targetSpeed(Max); };
    }.
```

`Identical comments as the 2APL fragment.`

We can see that for all three languages there is a triggering part (`event(speedLimit(Limit))`, `+!speedLimit(Limit)` and `percept(speedLimit(Limit))`). Aside from that we have a check to see if the plan is applicable (`speedIsAdjustable`), and the plan itself (change of `targetSpeed`). The autonomous behaviour pattern that we propose reflects the structure and application of this type of plan constructs, as they have been proven to be useful and universally supported over the years within the agent programming community. In particular it captures the reactivity to events such as the new speed limit. With a slight difference in implementation it also captures proactivity such as the pursuit of goals in for instance 2APL.

Our autonomous behaviour pattern consists of a scheduler, a context, a collection of strategies and a proxy. The strategies can be seen as the plan constructs from 2APL, Goal or Jason. The context is the data that is required for determining whether a strategy is relevant and applicable. In agent jargon it reflects the beliefs of an agent. The proxy is the interface to agent for the system in which an agent is embedded. The scheduler determines how strategies are selected for execution and how triggers (e.g. events, percepts, goals) are treated. We do not envision an agent to be equal to a single autonomous behaviour. Rather, it can be a complex of heterogeneous behaviours.

2.2 Example Norm in Organisational Programming

As an example norm we shall take that agents in urban zones should not drive faster than 50 km/h. When a car passes a sensor with a higher speed, then it is immediately fined. Its implementation using the proposed patterns is given in section 4. In 2OPL[7] this norm could be implemented with the following norm/sanction constructs:

```
urban_zone(Car):
    <zone(Car,urban),
     F(passing_sensor(Car),speed>50(Car)),
     not zone(Car,urban)>

viol(urban_zone(Car)) => fine(Car,50).
```

[1] The main differences between 2APL and Jason originate from persistent goals in 2APL.

```
Line 1: Norm label.
Lines 2-4: The condition, deontic content (F for forbidden) and deadline
    respectively.
Line 6: The sanction rule for violations of the norm. The agent gets a fine.
```

In NPL[14] we could program the norm as follows:

```
1 norm urban_zone1: zone(Car,urban) ->
2     obligation(Car, urban_zone1, speed<50(Car), 'now').
3 norm urban_zone2: zone(Car,urban) & passing_sensor(Car) &
4     speed>50(Car) ->
5     obligation(Car, urban_zone2, pay_fine(100), 'now').
```

```
Lines 1-2: The obligation to limit the speed to 50 km/h.
Lines 3-5: The obligation to pay the fine when the norm is violated.
```

In the proposed language from [24] we could program the norm as follows:

```
1 Norm condition: FORBIDDEN(speed>50(car)) IF zone(car,urban)
2 Violation condition: passing(car,sensor) AND zone(car,urban)
3                                            AND speed>50(car)
4 Detection mechanism: (omitted)
5 Sanction: (omitted)
6 Repairs: fine(car,50)
```

```
Line 1: Speed of 50 km/h is forbidden if the current zone is urban.
Line 2: The violation condition is when a sensor is passed with more than 50 km/h.
Line 4-5: Omitted fields
Line 6: The car is fined.
```

Normative constructs are prevalent among organisational coordination frameworks for multi-agent systems. Norm based regulation mechanisms can be introduced using existing technologies such as aspect-oriented programming. Aspects allow crosscutting concerns to be programmed separately from the system's core business logic. Norm based regulation mechanisms can be presented as design patterns based on aspects. The key correspondence is to use pointcuts from aspect oriented programming to specify where a norm applies (norm condition), and pointcut advices to check if a norm is violated and how to react to this violation (deadlines and sanctions). The use of aspects may raise concerns about the open nature of multi-agent systems because the source code of the target processes is required in order to program aspects and weave them in the processes at compile time. However, various works promote the use of organisational interfaces for the interaction between agents and the environment, or between agents themselves (cf. controllers in [19] and OrgBoxes in [15]). In such methods it is feasible that the norms are separately developed and maintained from the business logic of the interfaces to the system and the agents that use them.

3 Agent Pattern: Autonomous Behaviour

The behaviour of agents is generally described by beliefs, goals, events and plans. The beliefs of an agent can be seen as a system view (the agent's context information) that the agent uses in its deliberation. We will capture this as a separate class that contains all the necessary data which is needed for selecting plans. A plan is coined a strategy, which is in line with the *strategy* design pattern from [11]. A strategy is selected and executed if it is both relevant and applicable. The relevancy of a strategy depends on the trigger (e.g. a specific goal or event) to which it responds, and whether that trigger occurred. The applicability of a strategy is determined by checking with the context information whether it is possible to execute the strategy.

Name and Classification. The *autonomous behaviour* pattern is a concurrency pattern. This design pattern has no other known names.

Intent. The design pattern's intent is to provide a solution structure for problems where triggers are processed autonomously. This is required for programs where the processes causing those triggers are not responsible for the processing. Design-wise it separates the core logic of the trigger causing processes, from the trigger handling. Aside from this, the pattern also provides structure to make the trigger processing context sensitive. The basic idea is that the behaviour is triggered by the system either through a notification or a direct method call. Then, after being triggered, the behaviour tries to apply an execution strategy to process the trigger.

Motivation and Applicability. The natural scenarios for autonomous behaviours are those where many autonomous processes are already present. The structure of typical scenarios is that independent processes work alongside each other. Examples are multi-agent systems, service oriented architectures and actor based systems.

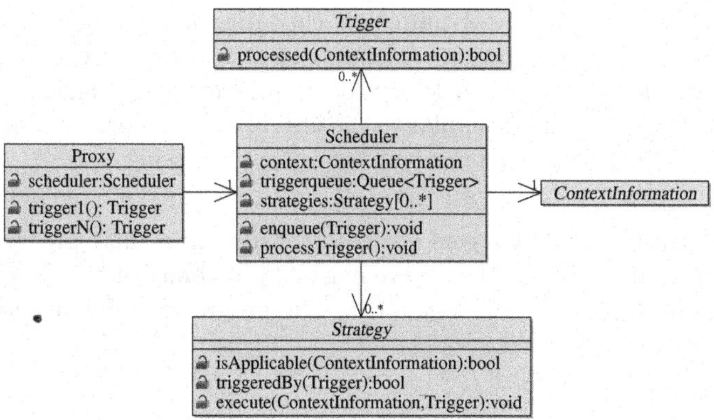

Fig. 1. UML structure of autonomous behaviour

Structure. Figure 1 shows the UML representation of the structure of the design pattern.

Participants

- **Proxy.** Interface to the behaviour. Either clients call the triggering methods (as in the *active object* pattern) or the proxy is subscribed to triggers in the system.
- **Trigger.** Trigger instantiations are tokens indicating which triggers occurred.
- **ContextInformation.** The behaviour's interface to the rest of the system. Also contains all the necessary data that is needed for the application of a strategy.
- **Strategy.** Strategies are used to process triggers. But for different circumstances (determined by the context) there can be different strategies for the same triggers. Also, one strategy might be able to handle several triggers.
- **Scheduler.** The scheduler schedules the triggers for processing. It loops through the trigger queue and applies applicable (by context) strategies for relevant triggers.

Collaborations. The proxy is the interface to the autonomous behaviour. Either client processes can call the trigger methods or the behaviour catches them through a subscribe/notify relation. If a triggering method is called in the proxy, then a trigger instantiation is created and sent to the scheduler. The scheduler schedules the trigger in a queue for processing. It also continuously tries to process triggers by using strategies. A strategy has to be relevant for a trigger, but also applicable given the context of the system. To get information from the rest of the system, the strategy uses the context information instantiation of the behaviour.

Consequences. The pattern decouples trigger from handling, by separating the triggers from the strategies that process them. The behaviour can be expanded with other capabilities such as dynamically changing the strategies. This enables self-healing and self-optimisation. An important design choice is to make the behaviour proactive or reactive. In a proactive behaviour, triggers stay in the queue until processed. This is similar to the idea of a persistent goal. In a reactive behaviour the trigger is considered only once for processing.

Implementation. If the triggers stream in faster than their processing, then memory issues can happen. Also, there exists a possibility that a trigger has no relevant and/or applicable strategy for it. The programmer has to decide what should happen in such cases.

Example Reactive Behaviour Code. An agent in our scenario is composed of an interface to the traffic simulator, a route planner, and various autonomous behaviours. As an example reactive behaviour we will illustrate how an autonomous car can react to a new speed limit. We assume that the example agent is subscribed to various events such as new messages, status updates from the simulation and new obligations/prohibitions. This particular behaviour is designed to deal with new obligations and prohibitions. After the car enters an urban area, it receives an event that states that the car is now prohibited from driving faster than 50 km/h. The agent reacts to this by applying an appropriate strategy to comply with this prohibition. Other strategies can be used to for instance deal with communication obligations, lane position and route prohibitions for blocked roads. The UML schema for this behaviour is shown in Figure 2.

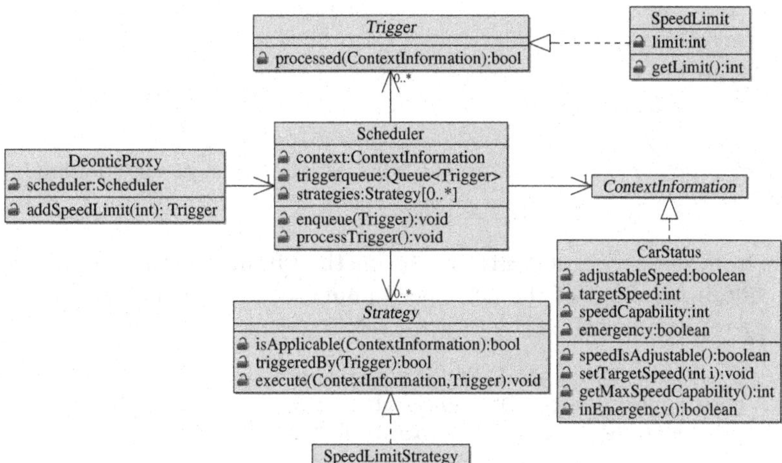

Fig. 2. Example UML structure of a reactive behaviour

An autonomous behaviour becomes reactive if it only considers a trigger once. If no strategy is currently relevant and applicable for a trigger, then it is dropped. For a reactive behaviour the `processTrigger` method could be implemented like this:

```
1  public void processTrigger() {
2      Trigger trigger = triggerqueue.remove();
3      for(Strategy strategy : strategies) {
4          if(!trigger.processed(context)&&
5              strategy.triggeredBy(trigger)&&
6              strategy.isApplicable(context)){
7                  strategy.execute(context, trigger);
8          }
9      }
10     if(!trigger.processed(context)) {
11         // initiate processing error handling
12     }
13 }
```

```
Line 2: The trigger is permanently removed from the queue.
Line 3: All strategies are tried.
```

Lines 4-8: If a strategy is applicable and relevant, then it is executed.
Lines 10-12: If the trigger is still not processed, then an error procedure can take place.

Agents in our scenario have an internal state. To allow strategies to access relevant parts of this state we have a `CarStatus` class that is the context information. This class contains various methods of which the following occur in the example code below:

- `speedIsAdjustable()::`**boolean** returns whether the car can determine its own target speed.
- `setTargetSpeed(`**int** `i)::`**int** set a new target speed.
- `getMaxSpeedCapability()::`**int** returns the maximum speed that the car can reach.
- `inEmergency()::`**boolean** returns whether the car is in an emergency situation.

Aside from these the `getLimit()::`**int** method from the class `SpeedLimit` is used to obtain the limit of the new speed limit. An example implementation of a strategy is given below:

```
1  public class SpeedLimitStrategy implements Strategy {
2      public boolean isTriggeredBy(Trigger trigger) {
3          return trigger instanceof SpeedLimit;
4      }
5
6      public boolean isApplicable(ContextInformation context) {
7          return ((CarStatus)context).speedIsAdjustable();
8      }
9
10     public void execute(ContextInformation context,
11                                                 Trigger trigger) {
12         SpeedLimit sl = (SpeedLimit)trigger;
13         CarStatus cs = (CarStatus)context;
14         if(!cs.inEmergency()){
15             if(cs.getMaxSpeedCapability() > sl.getLimit()){
16                 cs.setTargetSpeed(sl.getLimit());
17             } else {
18                 cs.setTargetSpeed(cs.getMaxSpeedCapability());
19             }
20         }
21         sl.setProcessed(true);
22     }
23 }
```

Line 3: The strategy is triggered by speed limits.
Line 7: The strategy is only applicable if the speed is adjustable by the car.
Line 14: The car ignores speed limits if it is in an emergency.
Lines 15-19: If the limit is lower than the maximum capable speed, then the car's target speed is the limit. Otherwise it can drive as fast as possible.

Example Proactive Behaviour Code. To illustrate proactive behaviour, we will show how an autonomous car commits itself to a goal destination. In this example the car has a set goal destination which is an instance of a trigger. The car has different strategies for getting to the goal. E.g. it can go there as quick as possible, via a dining place or with maximal driving comfort.

The UML for the trigger and strategy interfaces remains the same, as does the UML for the scheduler class. However, we do have different strategies and a different proxy and trigger realization. The UML of the proactive behaviour is shown in Figure 3. Additional strategies are omitted.

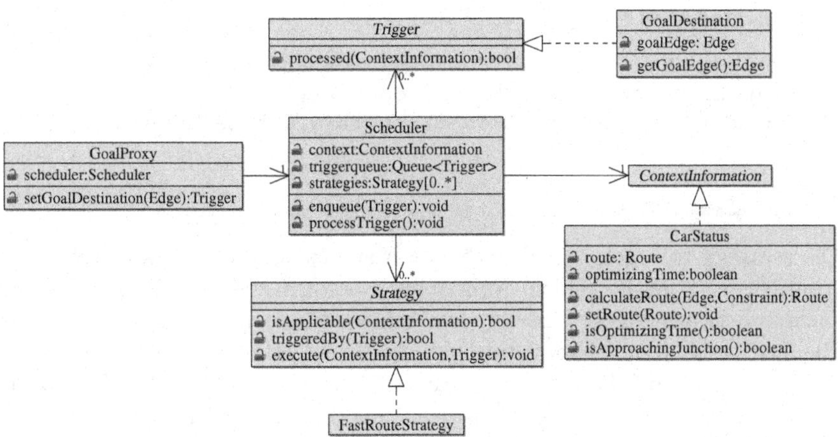

Fig. 3. Example UML structure of a proactive behaviour

An autonomous behaviour becomes proactive if it keeps trying to process a trigger, until it is successfully processed. If no strategy is currently relevant and applicable for a trigger, then it is re-inserted in the queue. Example Java code for the proactive `processTrigger` method is given below.

```
public void processTrigger() {
    for(Strategy strategy : strategies){
        for(int i = 0; i < triggerqueue.size(); i++){
            Trigger trigger = triggerqueue.remove();
            if(!trigger.processed(context)&&
                strategy.triggeredBy(trigger)&&
                strategy.isApplicable(context)){
                    strategy.execute(context, trigger);
            }
            if(!trigger.processed(context)){
                enqueue(trigger);
            }
        }
    }
}
```

Lines 2-3: Per strategy every trigger is checked to see whether the strategy is triggered.
Lines 4 and 10-12: Initially a trigger is removed. When the strategy did not process the trigger it is put back in the queue. This ensures that the trigger is persistent until processed.
Lines 5-8: If the strategy is triggered by the trigger, applicable given the context and still relevant (trigger not already processed) then the strategy is executed.

Triggers in a proactive behaviour are similar to agent goals. The processed method is used to see whether the goal is achieved. For the example destination goal we can check whether the goal is achieved by checking whether the agent has reached the goal edge. An example of how the goal's `processed` method can be implemented is as follows:

```
1 public boolean processed(ContextInformation context) {
2     CarStatus cs = (CarStatus) context;
3     return cs.getCurrentEdge() == this.getGoalEdge();
4 }
```

Line 3: The goal is achieved if the car has reached the goal edge.

The strategy to reach a goal destination as fast as possible is to recalculate the route every time the vehicle approaches a point in the road network where it can switch between edges. This way new information concerning traffic jams etc. can be incorporated in the rerouting process. The destination goal is represented by an instance of the class `DestinationGoal`. It contains a method to get the goal edge. Aside from the aforementioned functionality of the `CarStatus` class we have the following methods in the example code below:

- `isOptimizingTime()::`**boolean** returns whether the car is optimizing its time spent in the simulation.
- `isApproachingJunction()::`**boolean** returns whether the car is approaching a choice between network edges.
- `setRoute(Route)::`**void** changes the route of the car.
- `calculateRoute(Edge,Constraint)::Route` returns a route to the argument edge under the given constraint.

The constant `CarStatus.FASTEST` is a constraint that the route has to be the expected fastest available route. Example code for a route selection strategy is as follows:

```
public class FastRouteStrategy implements Strategy {
    public boolean isTriggeredBy(Trigger trigger) {
        return trigger instanceof GoalDestination;
    }

    public boolean isApplicable(ContextInformation context) {
        CarStatus cs = (CarStatus) context;
        return cs.isOptimizingTime() && cs.isApproachingJunction();
    }

    public void execute(ContextInformation context,
```

```
12                                                       Trigger trigger) {
13           GoalDestination goal = (GoalDestination)trigger;
14           CarStatus cs = (CarStatus)context;
15           cs.setRoute(cs.calculateRoute(goal.getGoalEdge(),
16                                         CarStatus.FASTEST));
17       }
18   }
```

```
Line 3: This strategy triggers for destination goals.
Line 8: This strategy is applicable if the agent is optimizing on travel times and
     is approaching a junction.
Lines 15-16: Calculate the fastest route and set it as the current route.
```

Known Uses. The pattern is visible in Jade where behaviours are used to construct agents. Also actor based programming has similar structures, but with less sophisticated handling of the messages (usually the processing is a big switch/if-else statement). The application of strategies based on the context of the agent is common across various agent programming languages such as 2APL, Goal and Jason. In those languages the reactive variant of the pattern is present and in 2APL and Goal the proactive variant can be found.

Related Patterns. The most related is the *active object* pattern [11]. It too has this structure where calls are made through a proxy and are processed independently. However, it does not contain strategies, nor is the proactive version described for this pattern. Another important related pattern is the *strategy* pattern. It contains the solution to problems where a different execution strategy is needed under different circumstances. One could see the *autonomous behaviour* pattern as an *active object*, combined with the *strategy* pattern.

In the *reactor* pattern [23] applications can register event handlers in an initiation dispatcher. Clients can then send events to the initiation dispatcher which notifies the correct handlers when they can process the events without a block. This is related to our reactive behaviour, due to its similar overall architecture. However, the selected strategies do not solely depend on the type of events. The *proactor* pattern is a variant of the *reactor* pattern. But the *proactor* pattern is very different from our proactive variant. In the *proactor* pattern the handling of the completion of asynchronous events is supported. In contrast, our proactive variant introduces proactiveness by pursuing goals until their achievement.

Notes. In the example code the chosen strategy is fully executed as is the case in for instance the GOAL agent programming language where plans are executed at once. However, this is not the only way to implement this pattern. The pattern can be expanded to instantiate strategies and have the strategy execute one step at a time as in 2APL or Jason (e.g., to prevent the execution of one strategy from blocking the execution of other strategies). It is also possible that the strategies include tests on the (belief) states so that the execution of strategies can be blocked and interleaved. Note that in some cases it is desirable that one strategy or a part of the strategy is executed at once without interleaving its execution with the execution of other strategies. This is for example done in 2APL by introducing atomic plans. In general, we believe that these issues should be decided by the programmer and may not be generic enough to introduce as part of the design pattern.

The same holds for a specification of how beliefs and goals can be managed. An integral part of agent programming languages is a specification of how an agent deals with its beliefs and goals. E.g. how they may change over time. A management system for goals and beliefs would be part of the context of the autonomous behaviour.

4 Organisation Pattern: Normative Constraint

Norms are related to constraints. But the term constraint already has a set meaning in design patterns (from the *constraint* pattern). Hence we refer to the counterpart of norms as normative constraints; constraints that can be violated albeit with consequences.

Name and Classification. The *normative constraint* pattern is a behaviour pattern. This design pattern has no other known names.

Intent. Aspect oriented programming allows to disentangle crosscutting concerns from business logic. Exogenous norm-based regulation mechanisms [9] similarly have the separation of concerns between agents' autonomous behaviour and the norms to which that behaviour must comply. A natural correspondence exists between certain types of norms and aspects.

On the one hand we have a specification of norm violating behaviour, and on the other hand we have the compensation for this violation. The intent of this design pattern is to catch this norm functionality. It allows to exogenously specify the norm from its subjected processes/classes/objects. We achieve this by using aspect oriented programming. In an aspect the pointcuts identify when an obligation/prohibition starts to hold, when the obligation/prohibition is fulfilled, and when the deadline has arrived. The advices are used to detach an obligation/prohibition and to execute the sanction in case of a norm violation.

Motivation and Applicability. Just like the *autonomous behaviour* pattern, the *normative constraint* pattern naturally applies in scenarios where there are many autonomous processes. If multiple processes use the same resource then it is easy to build in constraints in the resource itself (such as in a database). However, sometimes this is not so straightforward. For instance in the traffic scenario we do not want to alter the simulator to facilitate our agents. But we also do not want to force certain pieces of code in agents (we might not have the agent's source). We therefore enforce the norms based on the interface that the agents use. However, we do not want to clutter the interface code with all the code concerning norms, as these are not part of the interface's business logic.

The kind of scenarios where normative constraints are applicable are those where the constraints are mostly on interaction between components, rather than on the usage of a single resource. Typically the norm can change independently of the rest of the system. Also important is that the constraint is violable, it is not a hard constraint which cannot be transgressed.

Structure. In Figure 4 the UML for this pattern is depicted.

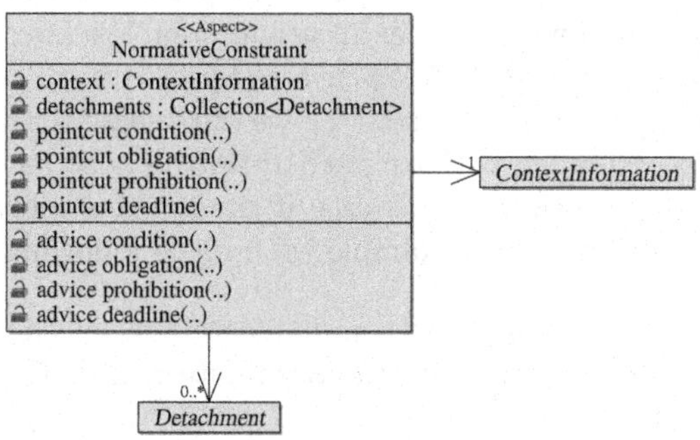

Fig. 4. UML structure of a normative constraint

Participants

- **NormativeConstraint.** The aspect that contains the norm's functionality and is responsible for detaching the norm when applicable, checking for violations of detachments, and removing detachments if necessary.
- **Detachment.** A detachment of the normative constraint. It contains relevant data from when the detachment occurred, which can be used to check whether the constraint is violated or not.
- **ContextInformation.** The context is the interface for information and data gathering of the system.

Collaborations. The normative constraint creates a detachment if the condition holds. It can be the case that there are multiple detachments, but with different data. If the obligation/prohibition holds then the detachment can be removed[2]. If the deadline holds, then the sanction is executed, after which the detachment is also removed.

Consequences The main objective is to separate the norm from the subjects of it. This is inherently the case because of the usage of an aspect. The separation between condition, obligation/prohibition and deadline provides a clear specification of the temporal aspect of a detachable norm. With this pattern a system designer has the possibility to independently design complex violable rule structures for different use cases. The trade off is that the flow of control is harder to grasp because of the use of aspects.

[2] Not necessarily, depending on the use case.

Implementation. Care has to be taken that the norm is not detached extremely often, because each detachment requires memory. If the detachments can somehow be ordered, then a heap or other sorted data structure is preferable to an iterable due to run time complexities. Memory issues can occur easily if the deadlines, obligations and prohibitions are met in a slower pace than that the norm is detached.

Example Code. The following code is the example where a car is forbidden to drive faster than 50 km/h when it is in an urban area. We have sensors that are being called whenever a car passes. When a car passes it is checked whether it is violating a speed limit norm. In this case we only show the urban zone limit, but the norm can be extended with extra conditions to also include speed limits for other situations. Note that in this case if the norm is violated, it does not take away the prohibition. In the example we use the following classes:

- `Car`: Contains a deontic proxy to communicate new speed limits.
- `Organisation`: The organisation to coordinate traffic. Contains a method to make fines.
- `OrganisationInterface`: The interface between the simulation environment and the organisation that is called when cars enter new zone types and pass sensors.
- `SNDetachment`: Speed limit norm detachment. Contains the zone type, the car for which the limit holds, the limit and the fine for violating the norm.

```
public aspect SpeedNorm {
    private ArrayList<SNDetachment> detachments;
    private Organisation organisation;
    // (omitted initialization code)

    pointcut condition(Car c, String type) :
        call(public * OrganisationInterface.enterZone(..)) &&
        args(c,type);

    pointcut prohibition(Car c, Sensor s) :
        call(* OrganisationInterface.passSensor(..)) &&
        args(c, s);

    pointcut deadline(Car c, String type) :
        call(public * OrganisationInterface.enterZone(..)) &&
        args(c,type);

    after() returning(Car c, String type) : condition(c, type){
        if(type.equals("urban")){
            detachments.add(new SNDetachment("urban",c, 50, 50));
            c.getDeonticProxy().addSpeedLimit(50);
        }
    }

    after(Car c, Sensor s) : prohibition(c, s){
        for(SNDetachment d : detachments){
```

```
27                if(d.getCar().equals(c)){
28                    if(s.getVelocity(c)>d.getLimit()){
29                        organisation.makeFine(c,d.getFine());
30                    }
31                }
32            }
33        }
34
35        after(Car c, String type) : deadline(c, type){
36            ArrayList<SNDetachment> toRemove =
37           new ArrayList<SNDetachment>();
38            for(SNDetachment d : detachments){
39                if(d.getCar().equals(c) && !d.getZone().equals(type)){
40                    toRemove.add(d);
41                }
42            }
43            detachments.removeAll(toRemove);
44        }
45    }
```

Lines 6-8: If a car switches from zone type then the condition must be checked.
Lines 10-12: The prohibition must be checked if a car passes a sensor.
Lines 14-16: The deadline must also be checked if a car switches from zone type.
Lines 18-23: Detachment of the norm upon entering an urban zone.
Lines 25-33: If a car violates a limit, then it is fined by the organisation.
Lines 35-44: If a car enters a new zone, then all detachments of the previous zone are removed.

Known Uses. There is quite a lot of work on norms with a condition, obligation/prohibition and deadline, e.g. 2OPL and NPL. In OO programming you typically see some boolean flag in code that signals whether some condition was met before and that is being used to steer execution at a later point.

Related Patterns. Patterns with contracts among objects are also used to ensure behaviour over time. A related work is for instance Contract4J [25]. In design by contract for programs, contracts consist of preconditions, postconditions and invariants. A client must fulfill the precondition so that a server can perform an operation which fulfills the postcondition. Invariant constraints must hold at all times. If a contract is violated, then the program halts (in contrast to normative constraints).

Another related concept, though no pattern, is the Object Constraint Language (OCL), which is a part of UML. OCL is a design tool that allows a designer to specify very specific constraints such as the range of an integer attribute of an object. However, these constraints are also meant as non-violable constraints.

Notes. The presented pattern captures conditional norms in a very generic and basic form. We did not go into details on various topics in normative system research such as different types of norms, the dynamics of norms, norm conflicts and norm awareness. Future efforts will be focused to these topics. We also did not address many synchronization and related issues for distributed systems. Depending on how the normative pattern is used, it can be combined with patterns for decentralized computation. We would like to reemphasize that our approach may suggest that the source code of various distributed components must be available, which may not always be the case, e.g., in open systems. We do assume that the components interact through interfaces that are under the control of the system designer. The system designer can therefore introduce the pointcuts in the interface source code and thereby control the execution of the components.

5 Related Work

The idea of agent-based design patterns has grabbed the attention of many researchers in the field. There have been several proposals focusing on various categories of design patterns (for an overview see [16]). Some of the earliest agent oriented design patterns are proposed by Aridor and Lange [1]. They proposed agent design patterns for mobile agent applications and classified them into traveling patterns, task patterns and interaction patterns. The mobility patterns can be used to enforce encapsulation of mobility management. An example of traveling patterns is the *itinerary* pattern that defines routing schemes for multiple destinations and handles special cases such as non existent destination. The task patterns are concerned with decomposing tasks and their delegation. An example is the *master-slave* pattern that allows task delegation from master to slave. Finally, the interaction patterns are concerned with agents' communication and cooperation. For example, the *meeting* pattern allows agents to dispatch themselves to a specific destination (a meeting place) and engage in local interaction. Our proposed design patterns are complementary as we are not concerned with mobile agent applications, but with the internal design of autonomous agents and how such agents can be controlled and coordinated by means of norms.

Sauvage presents different classes of patterns such as Meta patterns, Methaphoric patterns and Architectural patterns [22]. Examples of meta patterns are *organisation* and *protocols* which are defined in terms of roles, their relations, and messages. An example of metaphoric patterns is the *marks* pattern, which describes an indirect communication model via environment. Examples of architectural patterns are *BDI architecture* consisting of knowledge bases and *horizontal architecture* consisting of parallel modules (e.g., deliberation and act modules). Our proposed design patterns for autonomous behaviour and norm-based coordination are related to the *BDI architecture* pattern and *organisation* pattern. Although Sauvage provides only a two lines description of *BDI architecture* pattern, we provide an extensive description and possible refinements of it. Moreover, Sauvage conceives an *organisation* pattern as being defined in terms roles and their interactions while our organisation is defined in terms of norms being monitored and norm violations being sanctioned.

Separating coordination among processes as a concern has been argued in for instance [12]. In [12] the case is made for special coordination frameworks such as Linda. A coordination framework manages coordination separately from the business logic, which is programmed in a different language. With the use of aspects we can make reusable coordination oriented norms, while staying very close to the computational language of the business logic. Though the use of a separate coordination framework will often remain the preferred choice for distributed systems where processes are made with different implementation languages.

In order to organise interacting intentional software entities in multi-agent systems, social patterns are introduced in [10]. Two specific categories of patterns introduced here are pair patterns and mediation patterns. The pair patterns describe direct interaction between intentional agents while mediation patterns describe intermediate agents that aim at reaching agreement between other agents. An example of pair patterns is the *booking* pattern for booking resources from a service provider, and an example of mediation patterns is the *monitor* pattern that allows receiving notification of changes of state. Our proposed design patterns for autonomous behaviour are complementary to the patterns proposed in [10] and describe the internal design of individual agents. Moreover, our norm based design patterns differ from patterns proposed in [10] as ours are not concerned with explicit interaction between agents.

In [26] a pattern language is presented to capture various patterns in the design of multi-agent systems. The language consists of five interrelated patterns that together capture the different aspects of agent systems. The *virtual environment* pattern captures the design of an environment in which agents are situated. Those agents are captured with the *situated agent* pattern. It is very common that agents have a limited view on the system, which is documented as the *selective perception* pattern. For the coordination of agents the language contains two patterns: *protocol-based communication* and *roles & situated commitments*. The patterns are described in a architectural design language whereas we focused on object-oriented programming. That is less general, but easier to adopt.

Probably the closest agent oriented design patterns to ours are those proposed in [20], which aim at supporting the development of BDI agent-based systems. They use the PRACTIONIST framework, which allows the development of goal oriented agents based on BDI models, to introduce various BDI agent patterns. In particular, they propose four agent design patterns called *dynamic strategy selection* pattern, *intention decomposition* pattern, *mutually exclusive intentions* pattern, and *necessary intention* pattern. For example, the *dynamic strategy selection* pattern describes how an agent's intention can be achieved by the best strategy from a set of strategies at run time. Our design patterns for autonomous behaviour are similar to *dynamic strategy selection* pattern. But, in contrast to this pattern, we distinguish two different refinements for both reactive and proactive behaviours. In our view this distinction is crucial as they generate two important types of behaviour, i.e., reactive behaviour generates only one single response to an event while proactive behaviour maintains a response until the goal is achieved. Moreover, our norm based design pattern are complementary to the patterns introduced in [20].

Another article that introduces similar agent design patterns is [17]. In this article, reactive and deliberative agent patterns are presented as instances of sensory, beliefs, reasoning patterns. These patterns are described briefly and informally in terms of the problem, forces, solution and known uses of the patterns. The problem of a pattern is merely an informal description of the agent type. For example, the problem of a deliberative agent is described as how an agent can select a capability to proactively achieve a goal. The forces represent some requirements and properties of the pattern. For example, the forces of a reactive agents consists of the requirement that an agent needs to be able to respond to a stimulus or a request. The solution explains how the problem should be solved. For example, for a reactive agent patterns it is indicated that the agent acts using a stimulus/response type of behaviour. Finally, the known uses refer to other work that use similar agent types. For example, the authors refer to the work of Cohen and Levesque [5] as a use of deliberative agents.

Finally, Oluyomi et al. [21] presents a two dimensional classification in order to analyse, classify, and describe some existing agent-oriented patterns. The vertical dimension is based on the stages of agent-oriented software engineering and distinguishes seven stages from requirement analysis to implementation and testing phases. The horizontal dimension is based on tasks and activities that are relevant at each stage of software development. For example, at the multi-agent system architectural level, the tasks are to design the system, the involved agents, and their interaction. The vertical and horizontal dimensions identify categories of agent oriented design patterns. For example, the category defined by the multi-agent system architectural level (vertical dimension) and system design activity (horizontal dimension) is identified as a structural patterns which describe the structure of agent organisations in terms of architectural components including knowledge component and environment. An example of an agent oriented pattern that belongs to this category is the *embassy* pattern. This pattern introduces an agent responsible for the interaction between a multi-agent system and other heterogeneous domains. Our design patterns for autonomous behaviour can be seen as a member of the category Agent Internal Architecture - Interaction patterns and our design pattern for norms as a member of the category Agent Oriented Analysis - Organizational patterns.

6 Future Work

The design patterns in this paper are only scratching the surface of all the contributions of the multi-agent programming community. The goal of this paper is to take part in the discussion of how we can engineer multi-agent systems with object oriented technology, so that we can promote the agent paradigm to a wider audience. We will further develop design patterns to deal with for instance concurrency issues, repair strategies and interaction among behaviours and agents. With the input from the multi-agent community we shall reach out to other platforms where object oriented technology is discussed. We shall also release open-source example code to illustrate what projects look like when they are implemented according to the proposed design patterns.

7 Conclusion

The adoption of multi-agent programming tools and technologies by the industry is a major challenge that still needs to be met by the multi-agent programming community. One possible way to meet this challenge is by transferring multi-agent programming technologies to the standard software technologies. An idea is to start with the high-level concepts and abstractions for which the multi-agent programming research field has provided computational models and programming constructs, and propose either corresponding language level supports in the standard programming languages (e.g., C++ or Java), or alternatively propose corresponding design patterns, i.e., general reusable solutions to problems such as proactivity, reactivity, adaptivity, monitoring and control. The language level support can either be realized by standard programming approaches such as meta-programming or aspect-oriented programming, where concepts such as deliberation and control can be considered as different concerns that can be programmed either by meta-programs or aspects. Although these suggestions are not mature and need to be worked out both in details and in practice, attempts along these lines can bring the multi-agent community closer to the industry.

References

1. Aridor, Y., Lange, D.B.: Agent design patterns: Elements of agent application design. In: AGENTS 1998, pp. 108–115 (1998)
2. Bellifemine, F.L., Caire, G., Greenwood, D.: Developing Multi-Agent Systems with JADE. Wiley (2007)
3. Bordini, R.H., Wooldridge, M., Hübner, J.F.: Programming Multi-Agent Systems in AgentSpeak using Jason. John Wiley & Sons (2007)
4. Busetta, P., Ronnquist, R., Hodgson, A., Lucas, A.: Jack intelligent agents - components for intelligent agents in java (1999)
5. Cohen, P.R., Levesque, H.J.: Intention is choice with commitment. Artificial Intelligence 42(2-3), 213–261 (1990)
6. Dastani, M., Gomez-Sanz, J.: Programming multi-agent systems. The Knowledge Engineering Review 20(2), 151–164 (2006)
7. Dastani, M., Grossi, D., Meyer, J.-J.C., Tinnemeier, N.: Normative multi-agent programs and their logics. In: KRAMAS, pp. 16–31 (2008)
8. Dastani, M.: 2apl: A practical agent programming language. Autonomous Agents and Multi-Agent Systems 16, 214–248 (2008)
9. Dastani, M., Grossi, D., Meyer, J.-J.: A logic for normative multi-agent programs. International Journal of Logic and Computation (2011)
10. Do, T.T., Kolp, M., Faulkner, S., Pirotte, A.: Agent-oriented design patterns. In: ICEIS, pp. 48–53 (2004)
11. Gamma, E., Helm, R., Johnson, R., Vlissides, J.: Design Patterns: Elements of Reusable Object-Oriented Software. Addison-Wesley Longman Publishing Co., Inc. (1994)
12. Gelernter, D., Carriero, N.: Coordination languages and their significance. Commun. ACM 35(2), 97–107 (1992)
13. Hindriks, K.V., de Boer, F.S., van der Hoek, W., Meyer, J.-J.C.: Agent programming with declarative goals. In: ATAL 2000, pp. 228–243 (2001)

14. Hübner, J., Boissier, O., Bordini, R.: A normative programming language for multi-agent organisations. Annals of Mathematics and Artificial Intelligence 62, 27–53 (2011)
15. Hübner, J., Sichman, J., Boissier, O.: $\mathcal{S} - \mathcal{M}oise^{+}$: A middleware for developing organised multi-agent systems. In: Boissier, O., et al. (eds.) ANIREM 2005 and OOOP 2005. LNCS (LNAI), vol. 3913, pp. 64–78. Springer, Heidelberg (2006)
16. Juziuk, J., Weyns, D., Holvoet, T.: Design patterns for multi-agent systems: A systematic literature review. In: Shehory, O., Sturm, A. (eds.) Agent-Oriented Software Engineering, pp. 79–99. Springer, Heidelberg (2014)
17. Kendall, E.A., Krishna, P.V.M., Pathak, C.V.: CB Suresh. Patterns of intelligent and mobile agents. In: Proceedings of the Second International Conference on Autonomous Agents, pp. 92–99. ACM Press, New York (1998)
18. Krajzewicz, D., Erdmann, J., Behrisch, M., Bieker, L.: Recent development and applications of SUMO - Simulation of Urban MObility. International Journal on Advances in Systems and Measurements 5(3&4), 128–138 (2012)
19. Minsky, N.H., Ungureanu, V.: Law-governed interaction: A coordination and control mechanism for heterogeneous distributed systems. TOSEM, ACM Transactions on Software Engineering and Methodology 9, 273–305 (2000)
20. Morreale, V., Francaviglia, G., Centineo, F., Puccio, M., Cossentino Bc, M.: Goal-oriented agent patterns with the practionist framework. In: EUMAS 2006 (2006)
21. Oluyomi, A., Karunasekera, S., Sterling, L.: A comprehensive view of agent-oriented patterns. Autonomous Agents and Multi-Agent Systems 15(3), 337–377 (2007)
22. Sauvage, S.: Design patterns for multiagent systems design. In: Monroy, R., Arroyo-Figueroa, G., Sucar, L.E., Sossa, H. (eds.) MICAI 2004. LNCS (LNAI), vol. 2972, pp. 352–361. Springer, Heidelberg (2004)
23. Schmidt, D., Stal, M., Rohnert, H., Buschmann, F.: Pattern-Oriented Software Architecture. Patterns for Concurrent and Networked Objects, vol. 2. Wiley (2000)
24. Vázquez-Salceda, J., Aldewereld, H., Dignum, F.P.M.: Implementing norms in multiagent systems. In: Lindemann, G., Denzinger, J., Timm, I.J., Unland, R. (eds.) MATES 2004. LNCS (LNAI), vol. 3187, pp. 313–327. Springer, Heidelberg (2004)
25. Wampler, D.: Contract4j for design by contract in java: Design pattern like protocols and aspect interfaces. In: Proceedings of the Fifth AOSD Workshop on Aspects, Components, and Patterns for Infrastructure Software, pp. 27–30 (2006)
26. Weyns, D.: A pattern language for multi-agent systems. In: European Conference on Software Architecture, pp. 191–200 (September 2009)
27. Weyns, D., Helleboogh, A., Holvoet, T.: How to get multi-agent systems accepted in industry? Int. J. Agent-Oriented Softw. Eng. 3(4), 383–390 (2009)

CaFé: A Group Process to Rationalize Technologies in Hybrid AAMAS Systems

H. Van Dyke Parunak, Marcus Huber, Randolph Jones, Michael Quist, and Jack Zaientz

Soar Technology, Inc., USA
3600 Green Court, Suite 600
Ann Arbor, MI 48105
{van.parunak,marc.huber,rjones,quist,jzaientz}@soartech.com

Abstract. Most agent research seeks insights about a single technology, and problems are chosen to allow this focus. In contrast, many real-world applications do not lend themselves to a single technology, but require multiple tools. In an applied AI company, each tool often has its own advocate, whose specialized knowledge may lead her to overestimate her tool's contribution and diminish that of other tools. To form an effective team, the various members must have a shared understanding of how their tools complement one another. This paper describes CaFé ("**Ca**ses-**Fe**atures"), a group process that we have prototyped for building a consensus mapping between tools and real-world problems. The five AI technologies encompassed in our prototype are cognitive architectures, intelligent user interfaces, classic multi-agent system paradigms, statistics and machine learning, and swarming. Structured group discussion identifies the dimensions of a feature space in which the technologies are distinct. The scheme that emerged from our exercise does not pretend to be an exhaustive characterization of the techniques, but it is a jointly owned map of our technology capabilities that has proven useful in design of new use cases.

1 Introduction

A recurring topic at AAMAS is how to move the results of research into real-world applications. Our company, Soar Technology (SoarTech), provides applied AI solutions to a range of customers. We find that real applications often do not align well with disciplinary boundaries that guide basic research.

Research progress requires focusing the researcher's attention on a particular approach, tool, or technology, so that it can be characterized theoretically, implemented elegantly, and examined with a thorough experimental design.[1] In this setting, it is appropriate to choose problems that are tailored to the features of the being studied.

Customers in the real world usually do not start with a particular method they wish to exercise. Their pressing problems do not respect the convenient categories according to which we structure research and train students. As a result, organizations that

[1] For our purposes, we use the terms "approach," "tool," and "technology" interchangeably.

F. Dalpiaz et al. (Eds.): EMAS 2014, LNAI 8758, pp. 227–245, 2014.

address real-world needs often assemble a toolbox of capabilities. In our case, we started with a single flagship technology (the Soar cognitive architecture [13]), but over the years have recruited a staff with capabilities quite different from our original focus. In the process, we have encountered a challenge.

Our researchers understand their own approaches very well, and tend to view every problem through a perspective that is appropriate to their own tools. Companies like SoarTech often dissolve into disjoint "centers of excellence," each focused on a single technology, and each marketing to customer problems that align more or less with a center's capabilities. Such a structure under-serves customers in two ways.

First, it may not fully address the needs of the problems to which it does respond. It is not uncommon for a multi-disciplinary company to end up competing with itself on some opportunities, when different technologists want to bring different tools to bear. In such cases, the different facets of the problem might be more thoroughly and robustly addressed if multiple tools could be applied in tandem.

Second, some large and gnarly problems are too complex for a single technical perspective, even for the most optimistic advocate of a single technology. Such problems are typically left to large "system integrators" who may not bring the depth of technical understanding offered by expert researchers. In overcoming the narrowness of academic researchers, system integrators often fall victim to technical shallowness.

As a company, we seek to avoid both the narrow stove-piping of the academy and the shallow technical depth of a large integrator. We want our technical experts to share an understanding of our set of technologies that will enable them to deploy the full strength of their capabilities in synergy with one another. This paper reports on the form and initial results of a group process that we have implemented for this purpose. We expect it to be of value to the AAMAS community in two ways.

First, as a contribution to the software engineering of agent-based systems, it offers a process to enable multi-disciplinary teams to address complex problems that require the hybridization of multiple agent technologies.

Second, though preliminary, the joint feature space that we derived in our initial deployment of the CaFé method may be of interest in its own right.

Section 2 outlines the CaFé process, which draws its name from two information artifacts contributed by each technical advocate: a *Case study* of a problem that is particularly appropriate for her technology, and a list of *Features* of problems for which her technology is appropriate. Section 3 summarizes the specific Cases and Features in our prototype exercise of the methodology. Section 4 reports on the case discussions that form the heart of the process. Section 5 describes the feature space that results from our process. Section 6 demonstrates the use of this feature space in a series of new design patterns. Section 7 offers a concluding discussion.

2 The CaFé Process and Its Context

The CaFé process (Section 2.1) contributes to numerous areas within software engineering (Section 2.2), and brings some discipline to the *de facto* integration of different technologies that other researchers have already identified (Section 2.3).

2.1 Description of the Process

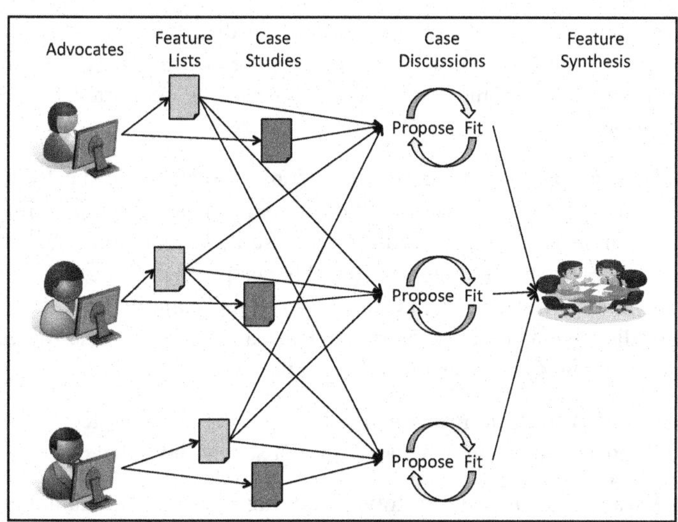

Fig. 1. The CaFé Process

CaFé is a structured group process among advocates for different technologies that encourages them to compare their approaches in the context of several example applications, and helps them to generalize these comparisons as a set of features that make a problem (or part of a problem) appropriate for one or another tool (Fig. 1). Each technology or tool is represented by an advocate who is expert in its use. Each advocate produces two artifacts representing her technology: a *feature list* describing the characteristics of a problem that would recommend the use of her technology, and a *use case* or example problem that she would consider an ideal candidate for deploying her technology. The process of preparing these artifacts before the group begins interaction encourages each advocate to recognize that her technology is better suited to some problems than to others, and to articulate what those problems might look like.

The entire group of advocates then discusses each use case. The discussion includes *proposals* by each advocate of how each technology might contribute to the case, and *fitting* the different technologies into an overall pattern based on the case.

Finally, after discussing all of the individual use cases, the advocates review the features from the individual cases and seek an overall *synthesis* that discriminates among the individual approaches.

The features that result from this process are not as detailed as those initially proposed by the advocates. They do not characterize each technology by itself, but situate it with respect to the other technologies. Most important, they are jointly owned by the advocates as a group, and so can guide collaborative design on new projects.

2.2 CaFé and Conventional Software Engineering

Software engineering is a large and complex discipline, and we view CaFé as a complement to traditional tools rather than a replacement for any of them. To situate the reader, we comment on how CaFé is related to each of the major thrusts of software engineering, as defined in SWEBOK 3.0 [2].

Software Requirements: The various features proposed by technology advocates resemble the characteristics commonly elicited as requirements for a software system (e.g., need for rapid reactivity; support for distributed decentralized operation). However, we found that these characteristics are not sufficient to distinguish the technologies from one another, since the requirements supported by different technologies often overlap.

Software Design: The case discussions typically take the form of proposing high-level designs for the case under discussion, mapping out a high-level architecture for a system to address the needs of the case and nominating the most appropriate technology for each component. From this perspective, CaFé can be viewed as a tool for high-level software design. In fact, the joint feature space that we derived from our case discussions (Section 5) functions as a high-level guide for outlining the architecture of a new system (as illustrated in the examples of Section 6).

Software Construction: Each technology has its own techniques and processes for software construction, which we did not seek to integrate.

Software Testing: Our prototype does not include evaluation, but we discuss possible directions for evaluation in Section 7, and any such process would draw on standard practice in software testing.

Software Maintenance: Good practice in software maintenance cuts across all of our technologies, and we did not explore the contribution of our technologies to it. However, see discussion of "Software Quality" below.

Software Configuration Management: All of our technologies draw on the same supporting systems for configuration management.

Software Engineering Management: We view CaFé as an important contribution to software project management, particularly in the design phase, enabling the integration of insights from different stakeholders.

Software Engineering Process: CaFé is a particular software engineering process that is most valuable in the design phase of a project.

Software Engineering Models and Methods: Each of our technologies has its own distinctive models and methods. We did not explore the interaction among these in this prototype.

Software Quality: ISO/IEC 25010 [12] defines eight product quality characteristics for software (functional suitability, reliability, performance efficiency, operability, security, compatibility, maintainability, and portability), of which CISQ has selected four (reliabililty, performance efficiency, security, and maintainability) that its members ranked as most important [3]. One delegate to EMAS 2014 suggested that these characteristics might provide an alternative set of features with which to distinguish technologies, but it is questionable whether one of our technologies is intrinsically more reliable (respectively, efficient, secure, or maintainable) than another. Quality attributes and our features are related at a deeper level: *in the context of a given* *application*, a feature may contribute to one or another quality attribute, and these relations could be identified through an analysis such as the house of quality [9]. This exercise would be a natural and useful extension of our prototype.

Software Engineering Professional Practice: The accepted professional standards for software engineers cut across all of our technologies.

Software Engineering Economics: As discussed in "Software Quality" (above), in the context of a specific application, the choice of technology will make a difference in the economic viability of a solution. Our exercise suggests that heterogeneous designs, which combine different technologies in a single application, will often be more competitive than designs that draw on a single technology throughout.

Computing Foundations, Mathematical Foundations, Engineering Foundations: Each of our technologies draws on distinctive foundations. We did not explore the relations among these in this prototype.

2.3 Other Work in Hybrid Architectures

CaFé is not the first effort to address the question of combining different technologies to solve a single application problem. We have given examples of such hybrids from our own work before [16]. Others have also suggested such approaches. To name only a few: Ferguson's TouringMachines architecture [7] showed the benefits of layering reaction, planning, and modeling horizontally in a single agent, InteRRaP [8] demonstrated vertical layering of different reasoning modalities, and a combination of neural and cognitive methods was the best performer for event recognition in the DARPA Minds' Eye program [4].

Examples of such combinations are valuable as existence proofs showing that hybrid systems are feasible. These examples demonstrate that fundamentally different reasoning modalities and agent architectures can be interfaced with one another. But they were generated *ad hoc*, and provide little guidance to developers seeking to find appropriate hybrid approaches to other problems. CaFé seeks to offer a disciplined approach to hybrid systems. Building on insight from past experiences ([14,16]), it offers a process for designing hybrid systems from the ground up.

3 The Artifacts

We considered five technologies, all familiar to the AAMAS community, in our initial foray with CaFé. Each has a strong advocate on SoarTech's current technical staff, some of whose publications in each area are referenced below.

- Cognitive Architectures (CA) are reasoning frameworks, such as Soar [13,22] or ACT-R [1], that are derived from high-level cognitive models of human reasoning and problem solving, and are intended to produce realistic human-like results. For example, the Soar cognitive architecture explicitly models different facets of human memory (procedural, semantic, episodic) and learning mechanisms

(reinforcement learning, chunking, experience) motivated by experimental results in cognitive psychology
- Intelligent User Interfaces (IUI) are technologies intended to mediate between human users and machine reasoners (e.g., [21,23]). Like cognitive architectures, they are inspired by insights from experimental psychology, but in this case the focus is on insights into the functioning of the human perceptual system rather than internal reasoning mechanisms.
- Multi-Agent Systems (MAS) is a collection of conventional MAS techniques that focus on inter-agent coordination, including BDI models, joint intention theory, theories of trust and norms, and agent communication languages (e.g., [10,11]). These methods are largely inspired by sociological models.
- Statistics and Machine Learning (SML) uses formal statistical methods to characterize data and detect patterns [17,19]. These techniques include cluster analysis, probabilistic graphical models (such as Bayesian belief networks, hidden Markov models, and Markov networks), neural and kernel-based methods, and generative models such as Latent Dirichlet Analysis, as well as a range of techniques for combining multiple statistical methods.
- Swarming harnesses self-organizing methods inspired by natural systems, with many simple agents interacting locally in a shared environment ("stigmergy") [15], usually through scalar fields over the environment that they both generate and sense. Drawing on insights from statistical physics and complexity theory, these methods can yield system-level behavior that is qualitatively more complex than the behavior of the individual agents, a phenomenon known as "emergent behavior."

For each of these approaches, we summarize the features and the case study proposed by its advocate. The purpose of these summaries is not to attempt a definitive statement of each approach, but to illustrate the flavor and level of detail involved in these artifacts. While these descriptions are abbreviations of the documents prepared by our advocates, each of those documents is still only one or two pages long.

3.1 Cognitive Architectures (CA)

Feature List: Cognitive architectures fit problems with these characteristics:

- Multiple simultaneous, interleaving tasks that frustrate the development of linear procedural code, but can be managed by pattern recognition
- Ability to handle and categorize special cases with pattern-driven processing
- Need to execute in real time (not much slower, but also not much faster), using least commitment to support rapid computation of an acceptable answer that can be refined if time is available
- Need for rapid reactivity to changed circumstances
- Need to support explanation of behavior to human stakeholders
- Real-time learning as the agent executes in the domain.

They are a poor choice for problems that involve

- Rapid processing of large amounts of data (more than 10k items per second)
- Sequential batch processing
- Number crunching
- Execution much faster than real time (as in constructive forecasting)
- Offline learning

Case Study: CA would be a good choice for a chef's decision-support assistant. Recipes are declarative representations of "how to cook" something. But having a great cookbook doesn't make someone a great chef. A great chef has extensive procedural knowledge and the ability to substitute, adapt, and handle interruptions and opportunities. Recipes are inherently serial, but cooking a meal requires opportunistic parallelism. A complete system would require situation interpretation and human-system interaction. The chef domain reflects the need for learning in a number of ways.

- Recipes are forms of declarative knowledge.
- Recipes can be taught/demonstrated.
- There is also "book knowledge" about ingredients, cooking techniques, etc.
- Recipes can be generalized and decomposed in goal-based fashion.
- Chefs acquire expertise by practicing cooking.
- Chefs learn about substitutions, short cuts, and handling unexpected events.
- Cooking knowledge can be "recomposed" to create new recipes and techniques.
- Chefs need to communicate with fellow chefs, servers, and suppliers.

3.2 Intelligent User Interfaces (IUI)

Feature List: Systems for which development of an IUI is appropriate tend to have one or more of the following features:

- Human-centric: Humans need to control, understand, and trust the system and its outputs.
- Incorporate human knowledge: The operator (or operators) have knowledge, including long term domain knowledge and short term situation awareness, that can improve system performance and/or outputs.
- Incorporate human decision-making: The operator(s) can make detections or decisions beyond the system's capability or authorization.
- Adaptive / Mixed Initiative: The system needs to adjust its operating characteristics to take into account changing operator (or actor) beliefs, desires, and intentions, both between and within system execution cycles; alternatively, the system needs to prompt the operator (or actor) to adjust their behavior.
- Representation boundaries: The system needs to mediate between two or more frames (typically, a user representation such as a doctrinal air traffic control grammar and a software engineered representation such as an AI planner structure).
- Naturalistic (multi-modal) usage environment: The system needs to interpret multiple streams of user input (mouse, voice, text, pointing) and/or coordinate multiple streams of output (video, audio, haptic).

- Supporting human constraints: The system needs to act for the user in a domain that exceeds human scale (either long time intervals, large data sets, fast reaction time) or that exceeds the specific operator's ability to act effectively (e.g. expert support for novice users, problems of high complexity or very high cost of error).
- Personalization: The system should be tuned to the specific preferences of a particular user or user group (or actor/actor group).

Case Study: It quickly became apparent that any realistic system we discussed would need to interact with human stakeholders, and in the end we did not consider a separate case for IUI, since we were comfortable that the cases proposed by other advocates would serve well to explore its complementarity with the other technologies.

3.3 Multi-Agent Systems (MAS)

AAMAS is accustomed to a broad use of the acronym "MAS" as including any system (including, for example, a swarming system) with many interacting agents. For our purposes, we focused on coarse-grained MAS techniques that rely on symbolic representations. The advocate for this area is expert in agent communication languages, joint intention theory, and related high-level coordination techniques.

Feature List: Problems that are suggest the need for multi-agent systems exhibit some of the following features.

- Teaming: More than one agent is required to solve a problem.
- Distributed: Computational solution needs to be divided (e.g., complexity, location, incomplete information, role, function, computational space/power).
- Synergistic: Using multiple agents gives a better solution that using a single one.
- Robustness: Reduces/removes single point of failure.
- Decentralized: Advantageous for distinct agents to make independent local decisions, processing (e.g. parallelism), or actions.
- Asynchronous: computation and interaction aren't tightly coupled.
- Organization: Structure (interaction, control) between agents important and/or advantageous (e.g., societal, problem structure, communications requirement).
- Heterogeneous: Distinct agents with differing capabilities.
- Dynamic teaming: Components (agents) motivated but not required to coordinate.
- Competitive: agents can work against each other.
- Flexibility: Independent contributors to portions of distributed solution.
- Complexity/Scalability: Multiple agents with localized modeling and reasoning can address larger problems.
- Semantic: Disparate localized representations and meanings.
- Perspective: Modeling and interpreting other components behavior/state.
- Opacity/Compartmentalized: Certain aspects of solution need to be hidden.

Case Study: An MAS approach would be ideal for a mixed team of soldiers and heterogeneous robots. The robots could include ground, air, surface, and subsurface vehicles, each with potentially different types of sensors, effectors, communication modes, and levels of local computation. Special attention needs to be paid to the changing roles of each entity in the team. Communications are dynamic, because of adversarial jamming, complex terrain that limits propagation, and the need for tight coordination. Relations among the units change constantly as the mission unfolds.

3.4 Statistics and Machine Learning (SML)

Feature list: Problems that are suitable for SML exhibit some of these features:

- The availability of large amounts of sensor data (video/audio capture, etc.) to yield useful levels of significance;
- Difficult to reduce data down to a manageable amount of symbolic information, whether because
  - the correct feature set is not known and must be discovered,
  - the data is intrinsically complex (e.g., speech data), or
  - different symbolic reductions are appropriate in different contexts;
- The availability of clear metrics for correctness of data handling to guide learning;
- Training and testing data available or easy to generate at will;
- Black-box with correct output is sufficient; no requirement to explain the interpretation of the raw data;
- Need to handle uncertain inputs, or to produce multiple results with varying levels of numerical confidence

Case Study: Consider the problem of commanding one or many autonomous (or partially autonomous) assets using multiple modalities in a naturalistic way. Such a system would need to integrate speech recognition, gesture recognition (whether visual or by smartphone or smartwatch with gyro and accelerometer), and sketching, as well as traditional computer or mobile device UIs. For user acceptance, the system would need to match existing protocols. For example, in a military context, gestures should be those already used to command infantry, and structured speech forms such as the SALUTE report [6] or the nine-line brief [5] should be followed, so that a mix of human and robotic assets can be commanded simultaneously.

3.5 Swarming (SW)

Feature List: The advocate for swarming characterized appropriate problems as

- consisting of *discrete* parts, such as robotic platforms, people, units of information, or events; if the natural decomposition of a problem is functional or assertional, rather than in terms of a set of entities, another technology may be preferred;
- consisting of *diverse* entities, performing diverse functions, and dealing with diverse information sources (since individual agents can preserve distinctions that would be lost in the mean-field approach of many equation-based formalisms);
- favoring *distribution* of computation across multiple platforms, whether because of communication limits that hinder centralizing data, or because of the need to parallelize computation in combinatorially large problems.
- allowing *decentralized* decision making by individual members of the swarm, within bounds established by the operator;

- subject to *deprivation* of computational resources, since swarming coordination through shared scalar fields is less demanding than symbolic manipulations;
- subject to rapid *dynamic* change that requires constant self-reorganization.

Case Study: SoarTech has several projects in autonomous systems, such as ground robots and UAVs, and our sponsors are interested in assessing the trustworthiness of their autonomy software. Conventional assessments of the trustworthiness of an engineered system are based on statistical analysis of a fault tree describing the structure of the system [20]. Once we endow a system with autonomy, we must also consider different trajectories through mission space and the demands they put on various platform subsystems. We have developed a representation of an extended fault tree that combines a conventional fault tree of the platform with a hierarchical task network representing mission space, but the resulting structure is too complex to explore exhaustively. We propose using swarming agents to compute a probability distribution over alternative mission instantiations, and thus compute the probability of mission failure, analogous to the Top Undesirable Event in a conventional fault tree analysis.

3.6 An Observation

These feature lists and case study nominations were prepared by the advocates independently of one another. Not surprisingly, they are difficult to compare directly. Some of the features do not distinguish between technologies (for example, the ability to respond to dynamic changes in the world). Others have no counterparts across approaches that would allow direct comparison.

This incommensurability of features is not surprising. In fact, it reflects the challenge of designing a hybrid AAMAS system, starting just with a set of technologies. The trade-offs among them emerge only when we consider them in the context of specific problems, motivating the series of case study discussions that we conducted.

4 Case Discussions

After advocates have circulated feature lists, we discuss each proposed case study. As suggested in Section 3, each discussion has two phases (though in our experience the thread of conversation often switches multiple times between the phases). In the proposal phase, advocates suggest how their technologies could be applied to the case, or to extensions of it that might realistically be required. In the fitting phase, the group seeks to fit the various technologies into the specific use case, exploring how to rationalize the role of each technology. This rationalization frequently draws from the feature lists originally prepared by the advocates, but instead of being unilaterally proposed by the advocates, it is the result of a group consensus. Each of these phases yields important insights about the relations among the technologies.

Each case was suggested by an advocate as ideally suited to one specific technology, but the *proposal* phase of each discussion never lacked for contributions from other advocates. As different advocates envisioned how their tools could be applied to a case, the problem tended to expand in scope. Sometimes different tools addressed the same facet of the problem from a different perspective, but more often the viewpoint prompted by a given tool encouraged us to consider a richer, more complex version of the use case, one that looked less like a toy laboratory problem and more like a real-world system. This experience reflects the insight about real-world problems that motivated CaFé in the first place. We hypothesized that such problems would benefit by synergy among multiple approaches, and in fact the more approaches we considered alongside a problem, the more realistic the problem itself became.

In the *fitting* phase of the discussions, we tried to rationalize the complementary contributions of each technology to the (sometimes expanded) case. This rationalization usually took the form of identifying some feature that distinguished alternative technologies *in the context of the case under discussion.* Sometimes these features were already articulated in the feature lists submitted by the advocates in advance, but often they became clear only through discussion of a concrete case.

For example, <<insert case discussion>>

A central insight resulting from our work on CaFé is the difficulty of comparing technologies directly with one another, and the relative ease of comparing them in the context of a specific problem. The individual features lists often claim the same problem characteristics for different technologies, but discussion of a concrete example serves as a catalyst to highlight the differences that matter among the various approaches. Of course, different cases may yield different points of comparison among technologies, but in practice, after we had gone through three cases, we began to see recurring problem features that repeatedly distinguished between tools. We summarized these features in the final feature synthesis discussion (right-hand side of Fig. 1) to define the joint feature space discussed in the next section.

5 The Joint Feature Space

Two dimensions distinguish four of our technologies: CA, MAS, SML, and SW. These dimensions are a) high and low data integration, and b) high and low decomposability (the face of Fig. 2, and Table 1). We were unable to localize IUI in this space in a way that would distinguish it from the other four. Recall that one motive for CaFé is to understand what portions of a complex problem we should address with which technology. To achieve this objective, we seek a joint feature space that distinguishes all of our technologies. To meet this criterion for IUI, we propose a third dimension, c) high vs. low human involvement (Table 2). Fig. 2 shows the resulting overall feature space. This joint feature space is not a definitive characterization of any of our methods, but instead focuses on features that distinguish them from each other.

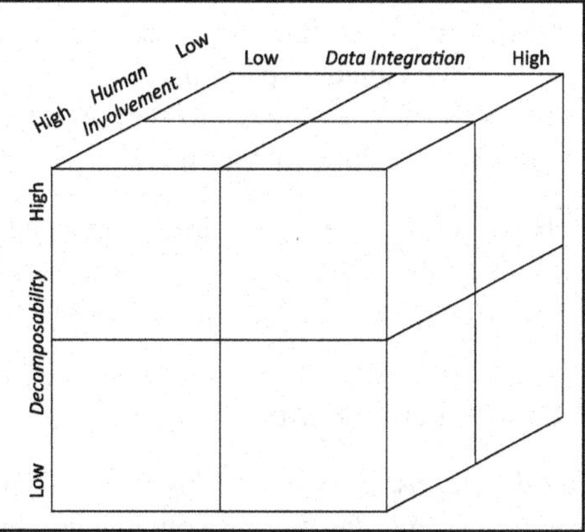

Fig. 2. Joint Feature Space resulting from our execution of the CaFé process

5.1 Data Integration

The Data Integration dimension reflects the degree of linkage among the data items that the problem presents. High data linkage corresponds to a knowledge-rich domain, in which information includes a representation of the semantic relations among data items. In a domain with low data linkage, the relationships among data items are yet to be discovered. Often, problems with low data linkages present a larger amount of data ("data rich" problems), while the knowledge captured in spaces at the high end of the dimension allows the system to work with smaller amounts of data. From a systems perspective, the low integration, data-rich end of the dimension is associated with sensors that access the world directly, while the high integration, knowledge-rich end deals with analysis of data that has been subject to a fair amount of preprocessing. Some aspects of this dimension correspond to the JDL Data Fusion hierarchy [18], in which Level 0 deals with raw signal data, Level 1 identifies objects, Level 2 detects situations among multiple objects, and Level 3 identifies threats.

MAS and CA rely on symbolic knowledge representations, and so are most naturally applied to knowledge-rich problems. SW and SML can use data without such a knowledge overlay and suggest relations among data items that might later be represented explicitly. They can use a knowledge structure as a template against which to compare raw data (for example, using SML with a symbolic grammar), but they do not require this knowledge to be embedded in the data at the outset.

Several of the features suggested by the advocates for individual approaches align with this dimension.

- CA identified the need to explain its reasoning to humans, which requires high semantic content in its representations.
- SML recognized that it is most appropriate when the problem needs a "black box" solver that cannot explain itself.
- SW's use of scalar fields to support deprived applications reflects its focus on data with low semantic integration.

However, by themselves these independent features are not nearly as useful in deconflicting the technologies as is the data integration dimension that emerged as we discussed the application of these tools to common problems.

5.2 Decomposability

The decomposability dimension reflects the degree to which the problem invites solution by multiple interacting components. For problems with high decomposability, it is natural to distribute the solution process across multiple platforms. The most natural processing approach for problems with low decomposability presumes that all information is available on a single platform.

Where the data integration dimension grouped MAS and CA against SML and SW, the decomposability dimension groups MAS and SW against CA and SML. Both MAS and SW use multiple computational entities, but differ in how they coordinate these entities: the stigmergic coordination common with SW agents is subsymbolic, relying on scalar fields over the environment, while MAS agents exchange symbolic information. But in both cases, the information available to individual agents is limited, and differs from agent to agent. CA and SML assume low decomposability. Most examples of CA assume a monolithic reasoner (like the human whose cognition these architectures are intended to imitate). While some clever methods for distributing SML computations have been explored, the fundamental model on which SML rests is the development of a single joint distribution over the variables of interest, which can then be marginalized as required, a computation that is most readily done with all the data in one place.

Again, this dimension reflects some features identified initially by tool advocates:

- SW is applicable to distributed, decentralized problems.
- MAS similarly recognized Teaming, Decentralized, and Distributed as problem characteristics that favor its application.

The case discussion, unlike the individual feature lists, showed the need for low decomposability for most effective application of SML and CA.

These two dimensions effectively distinguish four of our approaches (Table 1). However, IUI did not fit neatly into this taxonomy, leading to a third dimension.

Table 1. Feature Space (without IUI)

Decomposability	Data Integration: Low (Data-Rich)	Data Integration: High (Knowledge-Rich)
High (multiple agents)	Swarming	Multi-Agent Systems
Low (single agents)	Statistics & Machine Learning	Cognitive Architectures

5.3 Human Involvement

By definition, IUI technologies facilitate interaction of a human user with an automated system. One can envision a system drawing on our other approaches that does not interact with a human (for example, a closed-loop control system). But when the system as a whole requires human involvement, a user interface is required, and increasingly these interfaces use some degree of AI to facilitate the interaction. So we distinguish IUI from the other four technologies along a "Human Involvement" dimension on which the others are low and IUI is high.

Though IUI is applicable across the entire space spanned by the two dimensions of Table 1, it takes different forms in different areas of this space, depending on the other processes with whi-ch it interacts, as shown in Table 2.

Table 2. IUI Variants for High Human Involvement

Decomposability	Data Integration: Low (Data-Rich)	Data Integration: High (Knowledge-Rich)
High (multiple agents)	Data Visualizer	Peer Decision-Maker
Low (single agents)		Cognitive State Inspector

- In data-rich domains, IUI predominantly supports data retrieval and visualization. It allows humans to guide automated reasoners (whether SW or SML) (for example, by identifying information requirements, or presenting knowledge templates to which data should be fit), and it presents to the user the structures discovered by underlying SW or SML processing. It naturally supports an interactive approach to data exploration
- In knowledge-rich, highly decomposable domains, IUI naturally allows humans to function as peers alongside computational agents. IUI presents the user with information that is sent to her from other agents, and translates human input into messages that are exchanged with other agents.
- In knowledge-rich domains with low decomposability, IUI enables the user to interact with a single CA agent (e.g., to inspect or modify the agent's state).

The Human Interaction dimension directly reflects the multiple references to people in the original IUI feature list, including "Human centric," "Incorporate human knowledge," and "Incorporate human decision-making."

6 Some New Design Schemata

One of our motives in developing CaFé was facilitating the design of systems to address large, complex problems that require synergy among multiple AI approaches. In this section, we sketch a series of design patterns that illustrate the value of the feature space that we have developed. We could simply present hybrid designs for the case studies that we discussed, but to demonstrate the extensibility of our results, we instead describe a series of concepts distinct from the original case studies, but drawing on the same joint feature space.

It is legitimate to ask how feasible it is to tie these different methods together in a single architecture, as these designs suggest. While we have not explored interface mechanisms explicitly in CaFé, our experience, shared by others who have built previous hybrid systems (Section 2.3), is that interfacing components based on different technologies is a matter of engineering rather than a major hurdle requiring research.

6.1 Data Fusion and Shared Situational Assessment

A common problem in many domains, both military and industrial, is gathering data from many sensors monitoring the physical world, discovering patterns to develop a knowledge-rich characterization of the current situation, and then assuring that all decision-makers share a common view of that situation. Fig. 3 shows how our technologies might interact in such a system.

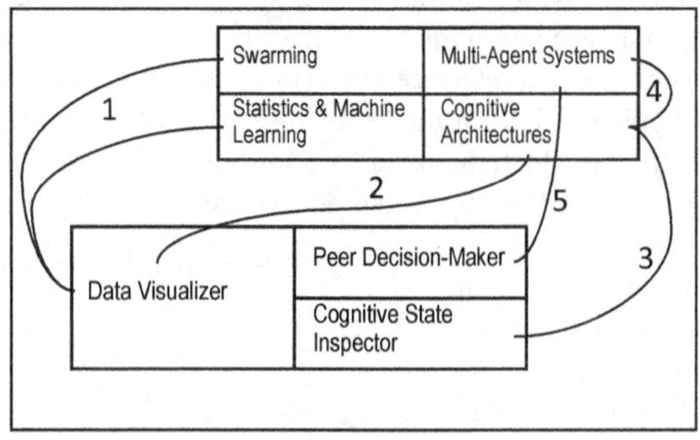

Fig. 3. Schema for Data Fusion and Shared SA

1. Both SW and SML deal with the raw data and detect regularities and patterns, which they expose to a human through a data visualizer IUI. The human in turn can guide the SW and SML agents to refine her view of the world, and refine and enhance the structures that are discovered.
2. Enriched with explicit knowledge through the actions of the human operating the data visualizer, the data can now be consumed by a CA agent that reasons over it in the light of other knowledge (including previous states of the world, mission plans and objectives, and hypotheses). The CA agent can also identify linkages that the human should further explore through the data visualizer IUI.
3. A cognitive state inspector IUI allows the human to monitor the reasoning of the CA agent and perhaps adjust it.
4. The CA agent shares its conclusions with other agents via MAS interfaces, achieving shared situational assessment across the team.
5. Some of these agents may be humans, who participate in the team via a peer decision-maker IUI.

We intentionally leave the links between components in this and the following schemata undirected. In general, we believe that information will flow in both directions; a more refined design would distinguish the nature of the flows in each direction.

6.2 Complex Pattern Detection in Data

Modern data analytics faces a tension between data that are too atomic to be diagnostic and knowledge that is too complex to guide search. For example, a single negative Tweet about US policy might be an isolated comment, part of an emerging viral propaganda campaign, or motivation for an invitation to a public demonstration. These alternatives require different responses, and detecting them depends on patterns involving multiple Tweets. Yet traditional methods of matching an overall pattern against high-volume, high-velocity data do not scale with the complexity of the pattern, particularly if the pattern encompasses several alternative possibilities, only one of which may match. Such patterns are too complex for efficient single-item queries, but the processing to match complete patterns is combinatorially infeasible.

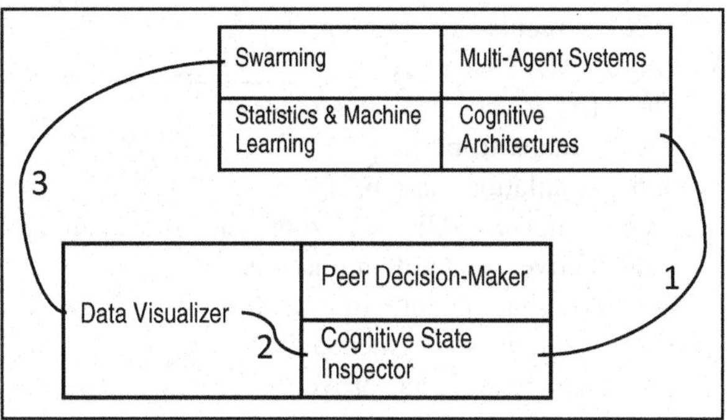

Fig. 4. Schema for Complex Pattern Detection

We are developing an approach to such problems that fits the schema in Fig. 4.

1. A major challenge in knowledge-based systems is authoring the knowledge that drives the system. Currently, complex queries are assembled manually, but our schema anticipates the role of a CA agent in helping a human develop these

patterns, perhaps on the basis of learning from past experience (not shown in the figure). A cognitive state inspector IUI facilitates this interaction.
2. This link indicates interaction between two different human roles: the pattern author (via a cognitive state inspector IUI) and the person using the pattern to interact with the data (via a data visualizer IUI). These may be the same person, or different specialists.
3. To avoid the combinatorial complexity of matching the entire pattern at once to massive data, we use swarming to evaluate the probability that different portions of the pattern are supported by the data, then estimate the value of alternative atomic queries in sharpening these distributions, and execute those queries, all under the supervision of a human via a data visualizer IUI.

6.3 Multi-unit Combat Simulator

A major application area for MAS is in constructive combat simulations. Fig. 5 shows a schema that supports the development of a simulator for a multi-component force.

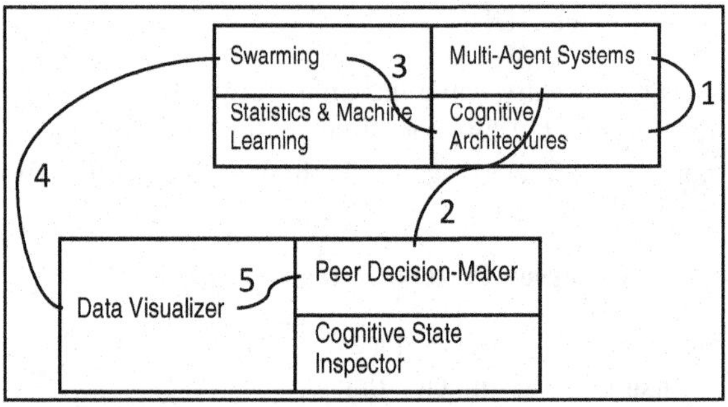

Fig. 5. Schema for Multi-Unit Combat Simulator

1. The simulator's core is a set of CA agents, interacting through MAS interfaces.
2. The MAS organization allows humans to participate in the simulation via a peer decision-maker IUI, realizing the increasingly popular LVC (Live-Virtual-Constructive) mode of simulation.
3. One important feature of cognitive reasoning is anticipating future events. CA agents include some mechanisms for anticipation, but in anticipating geospatial motions, swarming has proven to be a powerful tool.
4. Human players can also benefit from the anticipatory view provided by swarming, via a data visualizer IUI.
5. The data visualizer and peer decision-maker IUIs in this case may be integrated to support a single human player.

6.4 Model Fitting

A recent project gathered opinions from humans via a (non-intelligent) interface to fit weights to knowledge models that let us estimate the similarity behind the human judgments informing the elicited opinions. Fig. 6 shows an expanded version of this system.

1. A CA agent, directed by a human via a cognitive state inspector IUI, develops the knowledge model that is to be fitted to the elicited opinions.

2. Swarming over the model develops the weights on individual edges in the model.
3. The differences between the spectra of weights from different informants are evaluated statistically.
4. The resulting measures of informant similarity then enable a CA agent (which may or may not be the same one involved in the original model authoring) to make more intelligent use of the opinions elicited from the different informants.

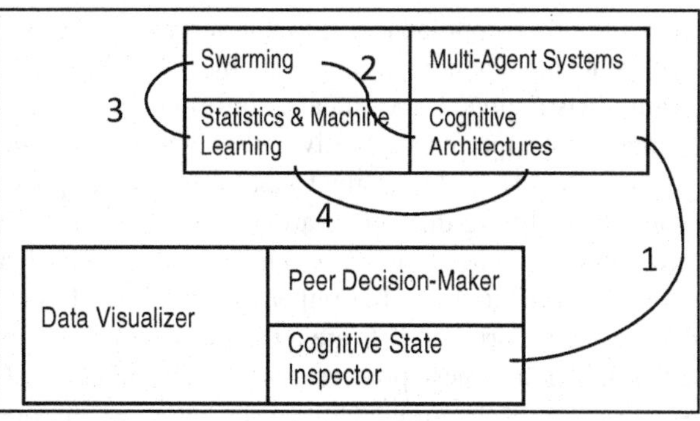

Fig. 6. Schema for Model Fitting

7 Discussion and Conclusion

The method described in this paper enabled experts in different AI specialties to develop a shared feature space showing how their tools complement each other. In turn, this feature space was effective in initial design of new systems beyond the case studies that drove the CaFé process itself.

Our exercise was a prototype of CaFé. We discuss its extensibility and alignment, and how this technique might be evaluated.

By *extensibility*, we mean the behavior of the feature space as new technologies are added to the collection, and as we consider new problems.

We begin with extensibility to new technologies. The five we considered in this exercise do not by any means exhaust the repertoire that we have currently in house, not to mention others that we may acquire. One can imagine game theory in its many variations, distributed constraint optimization, and logic programming, to name only a few. Will adding others require redoing the whole process, yielding a feature space that is radically different from what we discovered for our initial five approaches?

Our experience with IUI is evidence that we can expand the feature space incrementally rather than having to redo it each time we add new technologies with new advocates. IUI did not fit cleanly into the two-dimensional space that the other four approaches suggested. However, adding the Human Involvement dimension allows us to disambiguate it from the other approaches, and careful attention to the nature of the original two-dimensional space allows us to tease apart different techniques within IUI that do exploit the insights of the two-dimensional space.

A related aspect of extensibility concerns the robustness of the joint feature space as we consider new problems. We developed the design schemata in Section 6 to test whether the feature space could be applied to problems other than those that stimulated its definition in our case discussions, and the results encourage us that the space is in fact robust across a wide range of problems.

By *alignment*, we call attention to the fairly minimal overlap between the original feature lists submitted by the advocates, and the dimensions of the resulting feature space. Because the Human Interaction dimension was introduced to distinguish IUI from the other approaches, it is not surprising that this dimension corresponds very closely to the features enumerated by the IUI advocate. However, other individual feature lists include a great deal of information and insight about individual approaches that is not captured explicitly in the dimensions of the joint space.

Some details of the original feature lists do align with the dimensions of the joint space. In addition, this observation about alignment reminds us again of the distinctive purpose of the joint space. Unlike the original feature lists, it is not intended to define each technology, but rather to show how they complement each other. Unused features in the original lists are a reservoir on which we may draw as we consider new technologies and new problems, to refine our understanding, not of technologies in isolation, but of the joint technical space that we are positioned to exploit.

An important but complex question is how one might *evaluate* CaFé. Framing such an evaluation would require identifying a) competing approaches, and b) some figure of merit. Conceptually, software quality attributes [3,12] provide a disciplined approach to measuring the merit of a finished system, but in spite of the existence of numerous hybrid systems (Section 2.3), we know of no other methodology with which one might compare CaFé. We hope that by exhibiting one approach to the problem, we will stimulate others to suggest modifications or competing approaches, that eventually could support a disciplined evaluation. For now, the performance of CaFé can only be evaluated by comparing its products with systems whose technical composition is driven by the informal politics of the developing organization.

Perhaps the most powerful insight from the CaFé experience is the ability of concrete problems to facilitate comparison of different technologies. The usefulness of a third object for clarifying mappings between two other objects suggests that a category theoretic model might be a useful way to formalize the CaFé process and lead to automated tools to support it, a direction that we hope to pursue in future work.

References

[1] Anderson, J.R., Bothell, D., Byrne, M.D., Douglass, S., Lebiere, C., Qin, Y.: An integrated theory of the mind. Psychological Review 111(4), 1036–1060 (2004)

[2] Bourque, P., Fairley, R.E. (eds.): SWEBOK 3.0: Guide to the Software Engineering Body of Knowledge, 3rd edn. IEEE, Piscataway (2014)

[3] CISQ: CISQ Specifications for Automated Quality Characteristic Measures. Object Management Group (2012), `http://it-cisq.org/wp-content/uploads/2012/09/CISQ-Specification-for-Automated-Quality-Characteristic-Measures.pdf`

[4] de Penning, L., d'Avila Garcez, A.S., Lamb, L.C., Meyer, J.-J.C.: Neural-Symbolic Cognitive Agents: Architecture, Theory and Application. In: Lomuscio, A., Scerri, P. (eds.) The 13th International Conference on Autonomous Agents and Multiagent Systems (AAMAS 2014), pp. 1621–1622. IFAAMAS, Paris (2014)

[5] Department of Defense: JP 3-09.3, Close Air Support. Washington, DC, Department of Defense (2009)

[6] Department of the Army: FM 2-22.3 (FM 34-52), Human Intelligence Collector Operations. Washington, DC, Department of the Army (2006)

[7] Ferguson, I.A.: Touring Machines: Autonomous Agents with Attitudes. Computer 25(5), 51–55 (1992)
[8] Fischer, K., Muller, J.P., Pischel, M.: InteRRaP: Unifying Control in a Layered Agent Architecture. German Research Center for Artificial Intelligence, Saarbrucken (1995), http://www.dfki.uni-sb.de/~pischel/interrap.html
[9] Hauser, R., Clausing, D.: The House of Quality. Harvard Business Review 66, 63–73 (1988)
[10] Huber, M.J., Kumar, S., Lisse, S.A., McGee, D.: Integrating Authority, Deontics, and Deontics and Communications within a Joint Intention Framework. In: Huhns, M., Shehory, O. (eds.) The 2007 International Conference on Autonomous Agents and Multiagent Systems (AAMAS 2007). IFAAMAS, Honolulu (2007)
[11] Huber, M.J., Kumar, S., McGee, D.: Toward a Suite of Performatives based upon Joint Intention Theory. In: The AAMAS 2004 Workshop on Agent Communication (AC 2004), New York, NY (2004)
[12] ISO: ISO/IEC 25010:2011: Systems and software engineering – Systems and software Quality Requirements and Evaluation (SQuaRE) – System and software quality models ISO (2011)
[13] Laird, J.E.: The Soar Cognitive Architecture. MIT Press, Cambridge (2012)
[14] Lesser, V., Corkill, D.: Challenges for Multi-Agent Coordination Theory Based on Empirical Observations. In: Lomuscio, A., Scerri, P. (eds.) The 13th International Conference on Autonomous Agents and Multiagent Systems (AAMAS 2014), pp. 1157–1160. IFAAMAS, Paris (2014)
[15] Parunak, H.V.D.: 'Go to the Ant': Engineering Principles from Natural Agent Systems. Annals of Operations Research 75, 69–101 (1997)
[16] Van Dyke Parunak, H., Nielsen, P., Brueckner, S., Alonso, R.: Hybrid Multi-agent Systems: Integrating Swarming and BDI Agents. In: Brueckner, S.A., Hassas, S., Jelasity, M., Yamins, D. (eds.) ESOA 2006. LNCS (LNAI), vol. 4335, pp. 1–14. Springer, Heidelberg (2007)
[17] Quist, M., Yona, G.: A novel robust algorithm for structure-preserving embedding of metric and nonmetric spaces. Journal of Machine Learning Research 5, 399–430 (2004)
[18] Steinberg, A.N., Bowman, C.L.: Revisions to the JDL Data Fusion Model. In: Hall, D.L., Llinas, J. (eds.) Handbook of Multisensor Data Fusion, pp. 2.1–2.19. CRC Press, Boca Raton (2001)
[19] Taylor, G., Quist, M., Hicken, A.: Acquiring Agent-based Models of Conflict from Event Data. In: IJCAI 2009. AAAI Press, Pasadena (2009)
[20] Vesely, W., Stamatelatos, M., Dugan, J., Fragola, J., Minarick, J., Railsback III, J.: Fault Tree Handbook with Aerospace Applications. NASA, Washington, DC (2002), http://www.hq.nasa.gov/office/codeq/doctree/fthb.pdf
[21] Wood, S.D., Zaientz, J.D., Beard, J., Fredriksen, R., Huber, M.: An Intelligent Interface-Agent Framework for Robotic Command and Control. In: The 2004 Command and Control Research and Technology Symposium, San Diego, CA (2004)
[22] Wray, R.E., Jones, R.M.: An introduction to Soar as an agent architecture. In: Sun, R. (ed.) Cognition and Multi-agent Interaction: From Cognitive Modeling to Social Simulation, pp. 53–78. Cambridge University Press, Cambridge (2005)
[23] Zaientz, J.D., Beard, J.: Using Knowledge-Based Interface Design Techniques to Support Visual Analytics. In: Workshop on Intelligent User Interfaces for Intelligence Analysis at IUI 2006, Sydney, Australia (2006)

Efficient Verification of MASs with Projections

Davide Ancona, Daniela Briola, Amal El Fallah Seghrouchni, Viviana Mascardi, and Patrick Taillibert

[1] DIBRIS, University of Genova, Italy
{Davide.Ancona,Daniela.Briola,Viviana.Mascardi}@unige.it
[2] LIP6, University Pierre and Marie Curie, Paris, France
{Amal.Elfallah,Patrick.Taillibert}@lip6.fr

Abstract. Constrained global types are a powerful means to represent agent interaction protocols. In our recent research we used them to represent complex protocols in a very compact way, and we exploited them to dynamically verify actual agents' interactions with respect to different protocols in both Jason and JADE. The main drawback of our previous approach is the full centralization of the monitoring activity, which is delegated to a unique monitor agent in charge of verifying that the messages exchanged among all the agents are compliant with the protocol. This approach works well for MASs with few agents, but could become unsuitable in communication-intensive and highly-distributed MASs where hundreds of agents should be monitored.

In this paper we define an algorithm for projecting a constrained global type onto a set of agents *Ags*, by restricting it to the interactions involving agents in *Ags*, so that the outcome of the algorithm is another constrained global type where interactions involve only agents in *Ags*. The projection mechanism is the first step towards distributing the monitoring activity, making it safer and more efficient: the compliance of a MAS to a protocol could be dynamically verified by suitably partitioning the agents of the MAS into small sets of agents, and by assigning to each partition *Ags* a local monitor agent which checks all interactions involving *Ags* against the projected constrained global type.

Although the projection of well formed constrained global types can be always performed, the resulting projected protocol does not always model all the constraints as the original one. We describe a generate and test algorithm that provides hints on the correctness of the protocol distribution, leaving for further investigation the formal characterization of which protocols can be distributed onto which agents' subsets.

Keywords: Constrained Global Type, Projection, Dynamic Verification, Agent Interaction Protocol.

1 Introduction and Motivation

Distributed monitoring of agent interaction protocols is interesting for various reasons. First, the distribution of monitoring reduces the bottleneck issue due to the potentially high number of communications between the central monitor

F. Dalpiaz et al. (Eds.): EMAS 2014, LNAI 8758, pp. 246–270, 2014.

and the agents of the system. Consequently, the communications are localized according to the distribution topology (how many local monitors are available and where they are localized in the system), improving the efficiency of the monitoring. As usual, distribution increases the robustness of the whole system and prevents for a breakdown, crash or failure of the system. In particular, in the context of distributed environments, having a robust monitoring system requires to distribute the monitoring on several agents which ensure their prompt reaction to events. In addition, the distributed approach is more suitable than the centralized one for asynchronous and/or distributed contexts. Hence, we can mention at least three classes of applications where the distribution of monitoring is relevant.

1. MASs dealing with huge number of agents, for example applications in the context of supervising networks (e.g. [28]). The distribution becomes mandatory to deal with the complexity of the system and to guarantee its scalability.

2. Distributed MASs dealing with distributed agents because of the intrinsic geographical distribution of the system. This often happens in the context of industrial projects.

3. Pervasive MASs: in ambient intelligent systems for instance, agents are mobile (they move from one locality to another one) and their communication depends on their location. In such open environments, agents enter and leave the system and this requires a distributed monitoring of communication (e.g. local registration, etc.).

Usually, in systems related to the above three classes of applications, an overlay of agents is deployed above the real system. Agents are distributed over the system according to the topology distribution which has to satisfy several criteria (logical, physical or temporal, etc.) of communication in order to meet the target application requirements. The induced topology leads the agents to communicate with their local monitor or with their neighboring agents in order to exchange information.

In order to distribute the monitoring activity, the first step to face is to design and implement an algorithm for *projecting the protocol specification onto subsets of agents*, and then allow interactions taking place within these subsets to be monitored by local monitors. This step is the main subject of this paper.

Automatically identifying these subsets of agents in order to guarantee that the distributed monitoring behaves like the centralized one is the second step to face. The current solution to this issue is a generate and test algorithm which may detect the impossibility to distribute the monitoring activity, without however guaranteeing the possibility to distribute it. We leave for further investigation the problem of finding suitable partitions of agents in a MAS which provide formal guarantees that verification through projected types and distributed agents is equivalent to verification performed by a single centralized monitor with a "centralized" global type.

A third interesting issue concerns dynamic redistribution of monitoring agents; even if not explored in this work, projected types could be recomputed dynamically to balance the load among local monitors depending on the currently available resources, and according to some "meta-protocol". Self-adaptation of local monitors along the lines of [13] raises similar issues as dynamic redistribution.

We exploit the formalism of constrained global types [2] for specifying and dynamically verifying agent interaction protocols. In our recent research we demonstrated that they can be used to represent complex protocols in a very compact way, and we exploited them to detect deviations from the protocol in both Jason[1] [3] and JADE[2] [8]. Extensions of the original formalism with attributes have been described [20] and exploited to model a complex, real protocol in the railway domain [21]. This paper shows how a constrained global type can be projected onto a set of agents Ags, obtaining another constrained global type which contains only interactions involving agents in Ags. Although the projection of a well formed global type is always possible, this does not mean that it is always meaningful: as an example, the Alternating Bit Protocol (ABP) that will be introduced later on in this paper can be projected onto any subset of agents in the MAS, but needs to be monitored in a centralized way to verify all its constraints. Our generate and test algorithm detects the impossibility to distribute the monitoring of the ABP, hence providing a useful, although partial, support to the protocol and MAS developers.

The paper is organized in the following way: the sequel of this section describes one motivating scenario for our research; Section 2 overviews the state of the art in runtime monitoring of distributed systems; Section 3 gives the technical background needed for presenting the projection algorithm in Section 4, Section 5 describes the implementation of the algorithm in SWI Prolog and the projection at work, and Section 6 concludes.

Motivating scenario. In order to better understand the impact of distributed monitoring of complex and open systems, let us consider the following scenario: a humanitarian convoy in charge of food transportation is traversing a potentially hostile country. In order to ensure the convoy safety, a set of autonomous unmanned aerial vehicles (UAV) is deployed. The goals assigned to the UAVs are as diverse as: 1. maintaining the convoy within sight of a distant control center thanks to an embedded camera and data transmission; 2. transmitting images of the situation ahead of the convoy (to the convoy itself and to the control center); 3. ensuring data transmission from the convoy to the external world and conversely; 4. detecting potential hazards and informing the convoy and the control center; 5. localizing suspicious vehicles; 6. identifying a designated mobile entity, etc.

Several UAVs are required to achieve some of these goals since they require being at different locations at the same time (goals 1, 2). On the contrary, some goals can be assigned to the same UAV, providing the UAV traveling from one specific location to another one (goals 4, 5, 6). Moreover, some goals can be shared between UAVs (goal 3). When some UAV becomes unavailable, its goals must be allocated to another one or a new UAV must take-off depending on the

[1] `http://jason.sourceforge.net/wp/`

[2] `http://jade.tilab.com/`

resources availability. It is the case when communication failures occur, which might be temporary or permanent. It is also the case of instrument failure on-board UAVs, of meteorological events, etc. Due to situation-related hazards, the convoy might (autonomously or by a decision coming from the control center) decide to change its route. This change has to be taken into account by all the UAVs, which implies at the same time a re-planning of UAVs trajectories but also re-planning of the tasks they have been allocated to since their feasibility is not anymore ensured (fuel resources, communication network, etc.). It is of a major importance that the protocols implemented in the system are monitored for two reasons: 1. possible errors in protocols might generate confusion among agents and generate bad decisions whose consequences might be dramatic; 2. malevolent actors might try to penetrate the system since humanitarian operations almost often occur in a tense political context.

Unfortunately, a centralized monitoring is difficult to carry out in such a system since it forces every agent to communicate with a unique control agent, which is not always possible due to the physical dispersion of the agents. For example, a low altitude UAV can only communicate with a distant control center in gaining altitude, which is incompatible with a permanent monitoring of its communications since most of the UAV mission takes place close to the ground. Hence, in an application such as the humanitarian convoy the distribution of protocol monitoring and the ability of any agent to monitor part of the protocol, if needed, is a problem that must be addressed. It is not a surprise since the functions of the application themselves have to be implemented as autonomous goal-directed agents to be able to tackle the complexity inherent to this kind of systems. Adding a centralized monitoring is then hopeless.

2 State of the Art

In this section we review the literature on runtime monitoring of interaction protocols, on the distribution of monitoring among subsets of components with a specific attention to how decentralized monitoring can ensure global protocol compliance, and on projections that move from global types to global types in order to lighten them.

Runtime monitoring of interaction protocols. Many frameworks and formalisms for monitoring the runtime execution of a distributed system have been proposed in the last years.

One of the most recent and relevant work in this area is SPY (Session Python) [24], a tool chain for runtime verification of distributed Python programs against protocol specifications expressed in Scribble[3]. Given a Scribble specification of a global protocol, the tool chain validates consistency properties, such as race-free branch paths, and generates Scribble (i.e. syntactic) local protocol specifications for each participant (role) defined in the protocol. At runtime, an independent monitor (internal or external) is assigned to each Python endpoint and verifies

[3] `http://www.scribble.org`

the local trace of communication actions executed during the session. That work shares motivations similar to ours. The main differences lie in the expressive power of the two languages, which is higher for our formalism of constrained global types due to the constrained shuffle operator which is missing in Scribble, and in the availability of tools for statically verifying properties of Scribble specifications, which are not available for constrained global types.

Many other approaches for runtime monitoring of distributed systems and MASs exist like those mentioned in the sequel, but with no emphasis on the projection from global to local monitors. This represents the main difference between those proposals and ours.

In [17], aspect-oriented development techniques are used to enhance existing code of runtime monitors, checking the interaction behavior of applications against their specifications. Message Sequence Charts (MSCs) are exploited to specify the interaction behavior of distributed systems and as a basis for automatic runtime monitor generation. An explanation of the monitor generation procedure and tool set is presented using a case study from the embedded automotive systems domain. Addressing the need for formal specification and runtime verification of system-level requirements of distributed reactive systems, [14] presents a formalism for specifying global system behaviors in terms of MSCs assertions, with a technique for the evaluation of the likelihood of success of a distributed protocol under non-trivial communication conditions via discrete event simulation and runtime execution monitoring.

Moving to the MAS field, a great attention has been recently devoted to monitoring norms and commitments: formalizing the entities participating to a protocol and the rules regulating their interaction is in fact an inherent aspect of normative systems. In [23] a generic architecture for observing agent behaviors and recognizing those which comply to or violate the predefined norms is described. The architecture deploys monitors that receive inputs from observers and process these inputs together with transition network representations of individual norms. In this way, monitors determine the fulfillment or violation status of norms. As far as commitments are concerned, one of the first contributions were Commitment Machines [29], a formalism modeling communication protocols supplying a content to protocol states and actions in terms of the social commitments of the participants. The content can be reasoned about by the agents, thereby enabling flexible execution of the given protocol. In [27] Distributed Commitment Machines are defined and the properties of Commitment Machines, both distributed and centralized, are explored. A recent work on relationship between agents and commitment-based protocols is [12], where the authors specify agents in terms of goal models and protocols in terms of commitments among agents. The semantic relationship between agents and protocols is formalized exploiting the relationship between goals and commitments. Given an agent specification and a protocol, it is possible to verify whether the protocol allows the achievement of particular agent goals, and whether the agent's specification supports the satisfaction of particular commitments. In [4] commitments are exploited again in normative MASs: the authors focus on JADE and show that it is possible to account for interactions by exploiting commitment-based protocols, by modifying the Jade Methodology so as to include the new features in a seamless way, and by relying on the notion of artifact.

In [15] a framework for automatic processing of interactions generated using FIPA-ACL[4] is presented. This framework includes three elements: i) an agent interaction architecture to systematize interaction processing tasks, ii) interaction models to build re-usable validated code used to check different phases of interaction processing associated with message semantics, and iii) components and control structures implementing interaction architecture for a particular agent platform. The paper describes the implementation details of the proposed approach developed within the CAPNET agent platform.

Finally, [22] describes an architecture for verifying properties of a multiagent system during its execution. Considering that a correct system is a system verifying the properties specified by the designer, the authors focus on the "property" notion. The architecture, a MAS itself, is based on a set of agents whose goals are to check at runtime the whole system's properties.

Compliance of distributed and centralized monitoring. The problem of distributed monitoring has been faced by many researchers in MASs, web services, sensor networks and other distributed systems, but often the proposed solutions either directly describe a distributed protocol without any central point of control, or dynamically create groups of entities (agents, services, components) for monitoring different areas with no central representation of the global protocol, making these approaches and their theoretical foundations not comparable with ours.

Also, some proposals are similar to ours, but no formal justification of the projection and its coherence with the global protocol is provided. For example, the idea of "splitting" a global protocol into subprotocols has been proposed thirty years ago in the area of network communication protocols [18] and more recently in the one of Web Services choreography [25], but without a theoretical basis.

The formalization and analysis of the relation between a global description of a distributed system and a more machine-oriented description of a set of components that implements it is a problem that has been studied in several contexts and by different communities, as widely discussed for example in the related work section of [10]. Projecting a global protocol into a stub of an executable piece of code, or - on the other way round - verifying at design time that an executable piece of code respects the global protocol specification are problems different from what we face: we do not need to know the implementation of the agents in order to perform a runtime verification of their observable behavior with respect to the global protocol, and we project global protocols involving many agents into sub-protocols involving less, and not global protocols into "implementations".

Although different from ours, contributions dealing with global types projected onto session types and their declination as choreographies projected onto contracts, can be a source of inspiration for identifying the syntactic and semantic conditions which make the projection of a constrained global type feasible.

[4] `http://www.fipa.org/specs/fipa00061/SC00061G.html`

Global types [9,10,16] are behavioral types, whose aim is the specification and verification of multiparty interactions between distributed components. As suggested by the term "global", they describe the overall communication behavior of a distributed system, whereas session types specify the behavior of the single components of a system.

In [10] Castagna et al. tackle the problem of projecting global to session types; in particular, projection is well-defined only if well-formedness conditions are satisfied by global types. Such non trivial conditions are expressed in terms of the semantics of global types, which corresponds to sets of traces. The defined projection algorithm is not complete, since it is not defined for all global types that satisfy the semantic conditions for projectability.

Global types can be seen as web service choreographies[5] describing the interaction of some distributed processes connected through a private multi-party session. Therefore, there is a close relationship between the work of Castagna et al., and those by Zavattaro et al. [6,19] which concern the projection of choreographies into the contracts of their participants. The projection procedure is basically an homomorphism from choreographies to the behavior of their participants. While [7] gives no conditions to establish which choreographies produce correct projections, [19] defines three connectedness conditions that guarantee correctness of the projection for various (synchronous and asynchronous) semantics, solely stated on the syntax of the choreography.

The problem of analyzing choreographies and characterizing their properties has been addressed also by the MAS community. In particular, Baldoni et al. [5] propose a notion of interoperable choreography which basically coincides with Castagna et al.'s notion of liveness: the interaction between the parties must preserve the ability to reach a state in which every party has successfully completed its task. Also the notion of conformance between parties defined by Baldoni et al. may be a basis for proposing methods and algorithms for devising whether a set of projected protocols expressed in our formalism for constrained global types can be used to verify the same properties as the global one.

Lightening global types. As seen in the previous paragraph, projection of global types (resp. choreographies) usually moves from global to session types (resp. from choreographies to contracts). A very recent proposal by T-C. Chen [11] shares with ours the purpose of moving from global types to global types, in order to "lighten" the original global type.

The motivation for Chen's work is that some interactions in global types take place just for the purpose of informing receivers that some message will never arrive or the session is terminated. By decomposing a big global type into several simpler global types, one can avoid such kind of redundant interactions. Chen proposes a framework for easily decomposing global types into light global types, preserving the interaction sequences of the original ones but for redundant interactions.

[5] `http://www.w3.org/TR/ws-cdl-10/`

Although the rationale for our "lightening" function is to remove interactions not involving some agents rather than removing redundant interactions as in Chen's work, her proposal is the only one, to the best of our knowledge, where projection moves from global types to global types. While Chen demonstrates the correctness of her lightening function, she did not implement it yet. Conversely, our projection function is implemented and usable by both JADE and Jason agents, although we did not formally demonstrate its properties yet.

3 Backgroud

This section briefly recaps on constrained global types, omitting their extension with attributes [20] because the projection algorithm discussed in Section 4 is currently defined on "plain" constrained global types only.

Constrained global types (also named "types" in the sequel, when no ambiguity arises) are defined starting from the following entities:

Interactions[6]. An interaction a is a communicative event taking place between two agents. For example, `msg(right_robot, right_monitor, tell, put_sock)` is an interaction involving the sender `right_robot` and the receiver `right_monitor`, with performative `tell` and content `put_sock`.

Interaction types. Interaction types model the message pattern expected at a certain point of the conversation. An interaction type α is a predicate on interactions. For example, `msg(right_robot, right_monitor, tell, put_sock)` $\in$ `put_right_sock` means that interaction `msg(right_robot, right_monitor, tell, put_sock)` has type `put_right_sock`.

Producers and consumers. In order to model constraints across different branches of a constrained fork, we introduce two different kinds of interaction types, called *producers* and *consumers*, respectively. Each occurrence of a producer interaction type must correspond to the occurrence of a new interaction; in contrast, consumer interaction types correspond to the same interaction specified by a certain producer interaction type. The purpose of consumer interaction types is to impose constraints on interaction traces, *without introducing new events.* A consumer is an interaction type, whereas a producer is an interaction type α equipped with a natural superscript n specifying the exact number of consumer interactions which are expected to coincide with it.

Constrained global types. A constrained global type τ represents a set of possibly infinite traces of interactions, and is a possibly cyclic term defined on top of the following type constructors:

- λ (empty trace), representing the singleton set $\{\epsilon\}$ containing the empty trace ϵ.
- $\alpha^n{:}\tau$ (*seq-prod*), representing the set of all traces whose first element is an interaction a matching type α ($a \in \alpha$), and the remaining part is a trace

[6] "Interactions" were named "sending actions" in our previous work. We changed terminology to be consistent with the one used in the choreography community.

in the set represented by τ. The superscript[7] n specifies the number n of corresponding consumers that coincide with the same interaction type α; hence, n is the least required number of times $a \in \alpha$ has to be "consumed" to allow a transition labeled by a.
- $\alpha{:}\tau$ (*seq-cons*), representing a consumer of interaction a matching type α ($a \in \alpha$).
- $\tau_1 + \tau_2$ (*choice*), representing the union of the traces of τ_1 and τ_2.
- $\tau_1|\tau_2$ (*fork*), representing the set obtained by shuffling the traces in τ_1 with the traces in τ_2.
- $\tau_1 \cdot \tau_2$ (*concat*), representing the set of traces obtained by concatenating the traces of τ_1 with those of τ_2.

Since constrained global types are interpreted coinductively [1], it is possible to specify protocols that are not allowed to terminate like for example the `PingPong` protocol defined by the equation

```
PingPong = (ping,0):(pong,0):PingPong
```

where `PingPong` is a logical variable which is unified with a recursive (or cyclic, or infinite) term consisting of the producer interaction type `ping`, followed by the producer interaction type `pong` (both requiring 0 consumers), followed by the term itself. The coinductive interpretation (that is, the greatest fixed point of the function F corresponding to the recursive definition of `PingPong`) is the singleton containing the only valid and infinite interaction trace `ping pong ping pong ping pong` .... The inductive interpretation (that is, the least fixed point of F) of `PingPong` is the empty set, since there is no base for the induction; hence, coinduction [26] is required for correctly dealing with infinite traces.

The valid traces for the type

```
PingPong = ((ping,0):(pong,0):PingPong) + lambda
```

instead, are $\{\epsilon$, `ping pong`, `ping pong ping pong`, ...$\}$, namely all the traces consisting of an arbitrary number (even none or infinite) of `ping pong`.

Let us consider the following simple example where there are two robots (right and left), two monitors (right and left) associated with each robot, and a plan monitor which supervises them (Figure 1). The goal of the MAS is to help mothers in speeding up dressing their kids by putting their shoes on: robots must put a sock and a shoe on the right (resp. left) foot of the kid they help. As robots are autonomous, they could perform the two actions in the wrong order, making the life of the mothers even crazier... Monitors are there to ensure that wrong actions are immediately rolled back. Robots communicate their actions to their corresponding monitors, which, in turn, notify the plan monitor when the robots accomplish their goal. Each robot can start by putting the sock, which is the correct action to do, or by putting the shoe, which requires a recovery by the (right or left, resp.) robot monitor.

[7] In the examples throughout the paper we use the concrete syntax of Prolog where producer interaction types are represented by pairs (α,n).

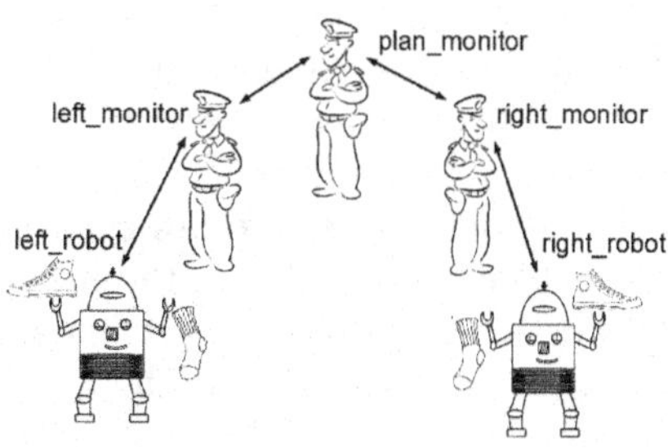

Fig. 1. The "socks and shoes" MAS

As we will see, the left and right monitors play two different roles: they interact with robots to detect wrong actions and recover them, and they also verify part of the protocol, notifying the user of protocol violations. In this MAS, *monitors are part of the protocol itself.* In the MASs described in our previous papers, monitors performed a runtime verification of all the other agents but themselves, and their sole goal was to detect and signal violations. Extending monitors with other capabilities (or, taking another perspective, extending "normal" agents with the capability to monitor part of the protocol) does not represent an extension of the language or framework. The possibility of having agents that can monitor, can be monitored, and can perform whatever other action, was already there, but we did not exploit it before.

The interactions involved in the socks and shoes protocol and their types are as follows:

```
msg(right_robot, right_monitor, tell, put_sock) ∈ put_right_sock
msg(right_robot, right_monitor, tell, put_shoe) ∈ put_right_shoe
msg(right_robot, right_monitor, tell, removed_shoe) ∈ rem_right_shoe
msg(right_monitor, right_robot, tell, obl_remove_shoe) ∈ obl_rem_right_shoe
msg(right_monitor, plan_monitor, tell, ok) ∈ ok_right
msg(left_robot, left_monitor, tell, put_sock) ∈ put_left_sock
msg(left_robot, left_monitor, tell, put_shoe) ∈ put_left_shoe
msg(left_robot, left_monitor, tell, removed_shoe) ∈ rem_left_shoe
msg(left_monitor, left_robot, tell, obl_remove_shoe) ∈ obl_rem_left_shoe
msg(left_monitor, plan_monitor, tell, ok) ∈ ok_left
```

The protocol can be specified by the following types, where SOCKS corresponds to the whole protocol.

```
RIGHT = ((put_right_sock,0):(put_right_shoe,0):(ok_right,0):lambda) +
((put_right_shoe,0):(obl_rem_right_shoe,0):(rem_right_shoe,0):RIGHT),
LEFT = ((put_left_sock,0):(put_left_shoe,0):(ok_left,0):lambda) +
((put_left_shoe,0):(obl_rem_left_shoe,0):(rem_left_shoe,0):LEFT),
SOCKS = (RIGHT | LEFT)
```

The type SOCKS specifies the shuffle (symbol "|") of two sets of traces of interactions, corresponding to RIGHT and LEFT, respectively. The shuffle expresses the fact that interactions in RIGHT are independent (no causality) from interactions in LEFT, and hence traces can be mixed in any order.

Types RIGHT and LEFT are defined recursively, that is, they correspond to cyclic terms. RIGHT consists of a choice (symbol "+") between the finite trace (the constructor for trace is ":") of interaction types (put_right_sock,0), (put_right_shoe,0), (ok_right,0) corresponding to the correct actions of the right robot, and the trace of interaction types (put_right_shoe,0), (obl_rem_right_shoe,0), (rem_right_shoe,0) corresponding to the wrong initial action of the robot, followed by an attempt to perform the RIGHT branch again. Basically, either the right robot tells the right monitor that it put the sock on first, and then it can go on by putting the shoe, or it tells that it started its execution by putting the shoe on. In this case, the right monitor forces the robot to remove the shoe, the robot acknowledges that it removed the shoe, and then starts again. The LEFT branch is the same as the RIGHT one, but involves the left robot and the left node monitor.

An example where sets of traces could be expressed with a fork, but are not completely independent, is given by the Alternating Bit Protocol ABP. We

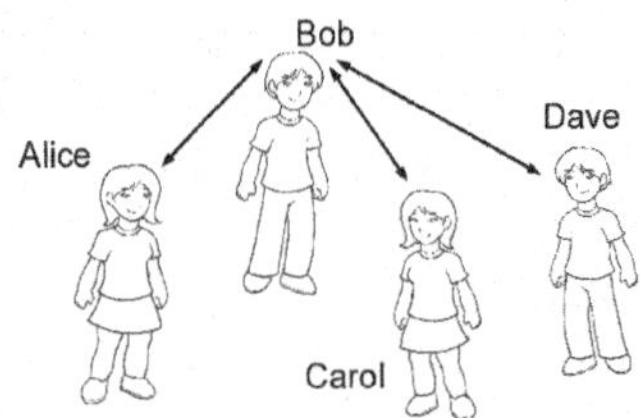

Fig. 2. The ABP3 MAS

consider the instance of ABP where six different sending actions may occur (Figure 2): Bob sends msg1 to Alice (interaction type m1), Alice sends ack1 to Bob (sending action type a1), Bob sends msg2 to Carol (interaction type m2), Carol sends ack2 to Bob (sending action type a2), Bob sends msg3 to Dave (interaction type m3), Dave sends ack3 to Bob (interaction type a3). The ABP is an infinite iteration, where the following constraints have to be satisfied for all occurrences of the sending actions:

– The n-th occurrence of an interaction of type m1 must precede the n-th occurrence of an interaction of type m2 which in turn must precede the n-th occurrence of an interaction of type m3.

– For $k \in \{1, 2, 3\}$, the n-th occurrence of msg$k$ must precede the n-th occurrence of the acknowledge ack$k$, which, in turn, must precede the $(n + 1)$-th occurrence of msg$k$.

The ABP cannot be specified with forks of independent interactions, hence a possible solution requires to take all the combinations of interactions into account in an explicit way. However with this solution the size of the type grows exponentially with the number of the different interaction types involved in the protocol.

With producer and consumer interaction types it is possible to express the shuffle of non independent interactions which have to verify certain constraints. In this way the ABP can be specified in a very compact and readable way. The whole protocol is specified by the following constrained global type ABP3:

```
M1M2M3=m1:m2:m3:M1M2M3,
M1A1=(m1,1):(a1,0):M1A1,
M2A2=(m2,1):(a2,0):M2A2,
M3A3=(m3,1):(a3,0):M3A3,
ABP3=((M1M2M3|M1A1)|(M2A2|M3A3))
```

Fork is associative and the way we put brackets in ABP3 does not matter: ((M1M2M3|M1A1)|(M2A2|M3A3)) has the same meaning as (M1M2M3|(M1A1|M2A2)|M3A3), and as any other association.

4 Projection Algorithm

In the "socks and shoes" example the monitors, besides checking that the robots accomplish their goal, verify also the compliance of the system to the specification of the protocol, given by the type SOCKS. If we assume that the right robot and the right monitor reside on the same node, then it is reasonable that the right monitor verifies only the interactions which are local to its node; to do that, we must project the type SOCKS onto the agents of the node, that is, the right robot and the right monitor.

What we would like to obtain is the type

```
RIGHT_P = ((put_right_sock,0):(put_right_shoe,0):(ok_right,0):lambda) +
((put_right_shoe,0):(obl_rem_right_shoe,0):(rem_right_shoe,0):RIGHT_P),
SOCKS_P = (RIGHT_P|lambda)
```

which only contains interactions where the right robot and the right monitor are involved, either as sender or as receiver.

We can project any protocol onto any set of agents (although it is not necessarily meaningful or useful). For example, projecting the ABP3 on Dave should result into

```
ABP3_P_compact = (m3,0):(a3,0):ABP3_P_compact
```

which just states that Dave must ensure to respect the order between messages of type m3 and acknowledges of type a3 between him and Bob. That projected type can be represented in an equivalent way, even if less compact, as

```
M1M2M3_P = m3:M1M2M3_P,
M3A3_P = (m3,1):(a3,0):M3A3_P,
ABP3_P =((M1M2M3_P|lambda)|(lambda|M3A3_P))
```

Projecting the ABP3 on Bob, instead, should result into the ABP3 itself as Bob is involved in all communications and hence no interaction will be removed from the projection.

Since Dave cannot be aware of the order among messages from other agents to Bob, he can only monitor a part of the protocol. Therefore, distributing the ABP among Alice, Carol and Dave would result in a partial verification of the protocol not able to detect all possible errors; indeed, Bob is necessary for checking the constraints involving `m1`, `m2`, `m3`, and, hence, is the only agent that can monitor the protocol.

In order to allow agents to verify only a sub-protocol of the global interaction protocol, we designed a projection algorithm that takes a constrained global type and a set of agents Ags as input, and returns a constrained global type which contains only interactions involving agents in Ags. The intuition besides the algorithm is that interactions that do not involve agents in Ags are removed from the projected constrained global type. Given the finite set AGS of all the agents that could play a role in the MAS and an interaction type α, $senders(\alpha)$ is the set of all the agents in AGS that could play the role of sender in actual interactions having type α and $receivers(\alpha)$ is the set of all the agents in AGS that could play the role of receiver in interactions of type α. The *involves* predicate holds on one interaction type α and one set of agents Ags, $involves(\alpha, Ags)$, iff $(senders(\alpha) \subseteq Ags) \vee (receivers(\alpha) \subseteq Ags)$.

Projection can be described as a function $\Pi : \mathcal{CT} \times \mathcal{P}(AGS) \rightarrow \mathcal{CT}$ where $\mathcal{CT}$ is the set of constrained global types. Π is driven by the syntax of the type to project[8]; since Π is defined on cyclic terms, the simplest way to define it would be by coinduction as follows:

(i) $\Pi(\lambda, Ags) = \lambda$
(ii) $\Pi(\alpha : \tau, Ags) = \alpha : \Pi(\tau, Ags)$ if $involves(\alpha, Ags)$
(iii) $\Pi(\alpha : \tau, Ags) = \Pi(\tau, Ags)$ if $\neg involves(\alpha, Ags)$
(iv) $\Pi(\tau' \; op \; \tau'', Ags) = \Pi(\tau', Ags) \; op \; \Pi(\tau'', Ags)$, where $op \in \{+, |, \cdot\}$.

However, this definition is not fully correct: it works properly on non cyclic terms (example 1) and on some cyclic terms (example 2), but does not behave correctly with other kinds of cyclic terms as shown in examples 3 and 4.

Example 1 (non cyclic terms). Let us consider a simple non cyclic term T defined by $T = a : b : \lambda$. We want to project T on Ags. Suppose that $involves(a, Ags)$ holds, whereas $involves(b, Ags)$ does not (this assumption will hold for the following examples too), meaning that interaction type a must be kept in the projection and b must be removed. From (ii) we get $\Pi(a : b : \lambda, Ags) = a : \Pi(b : \lambda, Ags)$ (a is kept in the projection), from (iii) we have $\Pi(b : \lambda, Ags) = \Pi(\lambda)$ (b is discarded from the projection), and finally, from (i) we know that $\Pi(\lambda) = \lambda$, therefore $\Pi(T, Ags) = a : \lambda$.

Example 2 (cyclic terms without problems). Let us now consider the cyclic term T s.t. $T = a : T'$ and $T' = b : T$.

[8] In the sequel of this section we will use "type" and "term" interchangeably, as a constrained global type (or just type) is represented by a term.

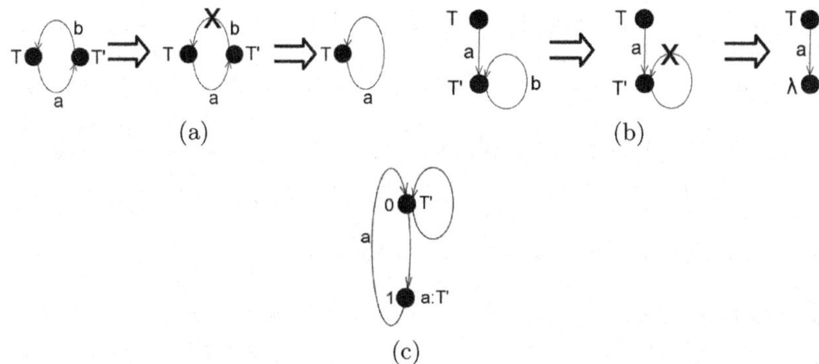

Fig. 3. Correct projection of a cyclic term

Again, the projection is driven by the syntax of T; by applying the definition of Π we have given before, we have $\Pi(a : T', Ags) = a : \Pi(T', Ags) = a : \Pi(b : T, Ags) = a : \Pi(T) = a : \Pi(a : T', Ags)$; while in the previous, non recursive example we could conclude by applying the definition $\Pi(\lambda, Ags) = \lambda$ corresponding to the λ type, in this case we do not have any basis. However, by coinduction we can conclude that $\Pi(a : T', Ags)$ has to return the unique cyclic term T'' s.t. $T'' = a : T''$ (see Figure 3(a)), which corresponds to the correct projection.

Example 3 (cyclic terms with problems - non uniqueness). The definition of Π needs to be refined because it does not always specify a unique result; to see that, let us consider the cyclic term T s.t. $T = a : T'$ and $T' = b : T'$ with the same definition of *involves* as before. Now from the definitions above we get $\Pi(a : T', Ags) = a : \Pi(T', Ags)$, $\Pi(T', Ags) = \Pi(b : T', Ags) = \Pi(T', Ags)$; since $\Pi(T', Ags) = \Pi(T', Ags)$ is an identity, Π is allowed to return any type when applied to T'[9], while the expected correct type should be λ, so that $\Pi(a : T', Ags) = a : \lambda$ (see Figure 3(b)). This example demonstrates that the definition of Π as given before must be reconsidered for coping with cases like this one correctly (see the paragraph "Projection function refined" below).

Example 4 (cyclic term with problems - non contractiveness). Finally, let us consider the cyclic term T s.t. $T = (a : T) + (b : T)$; by (iv) $\Pi(T, Ags) = \Pi(a : T, Ags) + \Pi(b : T, Ags)$, by (ii) $\Pi(a : T, Ags) = a : \Pi(T, Ags)$, and by (iii) $\Pi(b : T, Ags) = \Pi(T, Ags)$, therefore by coinduction the returned type is T' s.t. $T' = (a : T') + T'$; although in this case there exists a unique type that can be returned by Π, such a type is not *contractive.* A type is contractive if all possible cycles in it contain an occurrence of the sequence constructor ":"; Figure 3(c) shows that type T' s.t. $T' = (a : T') + T'$ is not contractive, since the rhs cycle contains only the "+" operator.

Contractive types ensure that runtime verification always terminates and we want that contractive constrained global types like T s.t. $T = (a : T) + (b : T)$ are always projected into contractive constrained global types. The refinement of Π discussed below copes with this requirement as well.

[9] In the same way as the equation $X = X$ is satisfied for any value associated with X.

Projection function refined. To guarantee that the projection function always returns a contractive type and that the correct coinductive definition is implemented, we need to keep track of all types visited by Π along a path[10]; each type is associated with its depth in the path, and with a fresh variable which will be unified with the corresponding computed projection. During the visit, the depth *DeepestSeq* of the deepest visited sequence operator is kept. If a type τ has been already visited (and we can detect this situation because we keep track of all the already visited types, together with their depth and projection), then a cycle is detected: if its depth is less than *DeepestSeq* then the cycle contains an occurrence of the sequence constructor, therefore the projected type associated with τ is contractive and, hence, is returned; otherwise, the projection would not be contractive, therefore λ is returned.

Let us consider again the type $T = (a : T) + (b : T)$ from example 4; when computing its projection, the depth of T is 0, and initially we set the value of *DeepestSeq* to -1. When visiting the lhs path starting from the "+" operator, the type $a : T$ is visited at depth 1, and *DeepestSeq* is set to 1, since the root of $a : T$ is the sequence constructor. Then T is revisited, and since its depth 0 is less than *DeepestSeq*, the projection of the lhs is $T' = a : T'$. When visiting the rhs path starting from the "+" operator, *DeepestSeq* contains again the value -1, and the type $b : T$ is visited at depth 1, but because $involves(b, Ags)$ does not hold, b is discarded with the corresponding sequence constructor, hence *DeepestSeq* is not updated. Then T is revisited, and since its depth 0 is not less than *DeepestSeq*, the projection of the rhs is λ. The next section provides a detailed description of the implementation of the correct projection algorithm.

5 Implementation and Use

In this section, we show Π's implementation and we frame it into our framework for distributed runtime verification of MASs. The framework, depicted in Figure 4, consists of four layers: **(1)** a formalism for describing agent interaction protocols (AIPs) based on constrained global types, along with an algorithm to validate at design time that the described protocol models the expected traces of interaction; **(2)** the projection algorithm, along with a generate and test algorithm for validating at design time that the projection on a given agents' subset can be safely used for dynamic verification; **(3)** a mechanism for verifying at runtime that interactions are compliant with the AIP; and **(4)** a mechanism for intercepting at runtime actual messages involving the agents under monitoring, be them JADE or Jason ones, in a way as transparent as possible.

Whereas the design time validation algorithms supporting layers 1 and 2 can only generate and test traces of finite length, the runtime verification of layer 3 could in principle go on forever, if the protocol is an infinite one: the runtime verification mechanism checks the compliance of each actual interaction taking

[10] By "path" we mean the path in the tree associated with the type; for example, if the type is T s.t. $T = (a : T) + (b : T)$, Π will first visit the path associated with $(a : T)$ and then that associated with $(b : T)$.

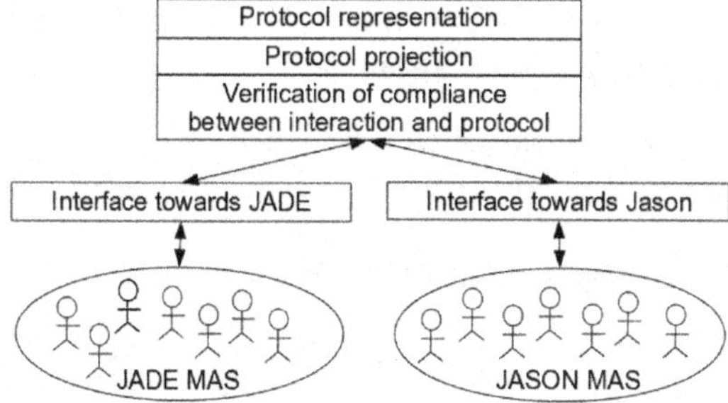

Fig. 4. Our modular framework for distributed runtime verification of MASs

place in the MAS w.r.t. the constrained global time and stops only when a violation is detected.

The choice of JADE and Jason as the two frameworks that we are able to monitor is due to their widespread adoption in the agent community.

Implementation. The projection algorithm has been implemented in SWI Prolog, `http://www.swi-prolog.org/`, which manages infinite terms in an efficient way. Since we need to record the association between any type and its projection in order to correctly detect and maage cycles, we exploited the SWI Prolog library `assoc` for association lists, `http://www.swi-prolog.org/pldoc/man?section=assoc`. The three predicates of the library `assoc` that we use for our implementation are

- `empty_assoc`(*-Assoc*): *Assoc* is unified with an empty association list.
- `get_assoc`(*+Key, +Assoc, ?Value*): *Value* is the value associated with *Key* in the association list *Assoc*.
- `put_assoc`(*+Key, +Assoc, +Value, ?NewAssoc*): *NewAssoc* is an association list identical to *Assoc* except that *Key* is associated with *Value*. This can be used to insert and change associations.

The projection is implemented by a predicate `project(T, ProjAgs, ProjT)` where `T` is the constrained global type to be projected, `ProjT` is the result, and `ProjAgs` is the set of agents onto which the projection is performed. The algorithm exploits the predicate `involves(IntType, ProjAgs)` succeeding if `IntType` may involve one agent, as a sender or a receiver, in `ProjAgs`.

Currently `involves` looks for actual interactions `ActInt` whose type is `IntType` and assumes that senders and receivers in `ActInt` are ground terms, but it could be extended to take agents' roles into account or in other more complex ways. It uses the "or" Prolog operator `;` and the `member` predicate offered by the library `lists`. It exploits the predicate `has_type(ActInt, IntType)` implementing the definition of the type `IntType` of an actual interaction `ActInt`.

```
involves(IntType, List) :-
has_type(msg(Sender, Receiver, _, _), IntType),
(member(Sender, List);member(Receiver, List)).
```

For the implementation of `project/3` we use an auxiliary predicate `project/6` with the following three additional arguments:

- an initially empty association `A` to keep track of cycles;
- the current depth of the constrained global type under projection, initially set to `0`;
- the depth of the deepest sequence operator belonging to the projected type, initially set to `-1`.

```
project(T, ProjAgs, ProjT) :-
empty_assoc(A), project(A, 0, -1, T, ProjAgs, ProjT).
```

The predicate is defined by cases.

1. `lambda` is projected into `lambda`.

   ```
   project(_Assoc, _Depth, _DeepestSeq, lambda, _ProjAgs, lambda):- !.
   ```

2. If `Type` has been already met while projecting the global type (`get_assoc (Type, Assoc, (AssocProjType,LoopDepth))` succeeds), then its projection `ProjT` is `AssocProjType` if `LoopDepth =< DeepestSeq` and is `lambda` otherwise. The "if-then-else" construct is implemented in Prolog as `Condition -> ThenBranch ; ElseBranch`.

   ```
   project(Assoc, _Depth, DeepestSeq, Type, _ProjAgs, ProjT) :-
   get_assoc(Type,Assoc,(AssocProjType,LoopDepth)),!,
   (LoopDepth =< DeepestSeq -> ProjT=AssocProjType; ProjT=lambda).
   ```

3. `T = (IntType:T1)`. `IntType` is a consumer since it has no integer number associated with it. `ProjT` is recorded in the association `A` along with the current depth `Depth` (`put_assoc((IntType:T1),Assoc,(ProjT,Depth), NewAssoc)`). If `IntType` involves `ProjAgs`, `ProjT=(IntType:ProjT1)` where `ProjT1` is obtained by projecting `T1` onto `ProjAgs`, with association `NewAssoc`, depth of the type under projection increased by one, and depth of the deepest sequence operator equal to `Depth`. If `IntType` does not involve `ProjAgs`, then the projection on `T` is the same as `T1` with association `NewAssoc`, depth of the type under projection equal to `Depth`, and depth of the deepest sequence operator equal to `DeepestSeq`.

   ```
   project(Assoc, Depth, DeepestSeq, (IntType:T1), ProjAgs, ProjT) :- !,
   put_assoc((IntType:T1),Assoc,(ProjT,Depth),NewAssoc),
   (involves(AMsg, ProjAgs) ->
   IncDepth is Depth+1,
   project(NewAssoc,IncDepth,Depth,T1,ProjAgs,ProjT1),
   ProjT=(IntType:ProjT1);
   project(NewAssoc,Depth,DeepestSeq,T1,ProjAgs,ProjT)).
   ```

4. `T = ((IntType,N):T1)`. `(IntType,N)` is a producer since it has an integer number `N` associated with it. The clause for projection is identical to the previous case, except for the atom `ProjT=(IntType:ProjT1)` in the first branch of the condition which becomes `ProjT=((IntType,N):ProjT1)`.

5. `T = T1 op T2`, where `op` ∈ {`+`, `|`, `*`}: the association between `T1 op T2` and the projected type `ProjT` is recorded in the association `Assoc` along with the current depth `Depth`, `T1` and `T2` are projected into `ProjT1` and `ProjT2` respectively, with association equal to `NewAssoc`, depth of the type under projection increased by one and depth of the deepest sequence operator equal to `DeepestSeq`. The result of the projection is `ProjT=(ProjT1 op ProjT2)`. For example, if `op` is `+`, the Prolog clause is:

```
project(Assoc, Depth, DeepestSeq, (T1+T2), ProjAgs, ProjT) :- !,
put_assoc((T1+T2),Assoc,(ProjT,Depth),NewAssoc),
IncDepth is Depth+1,
project(NewAssoc, IncDepth, DeepestSeq, T1, ProjAgs, ProjT1),
project(NewAssoc, IncDepth, DeepestSeq, T2, ProjAgs, ProjT2),
ProjT=(ProjT1+ProjT2).
```

Types `SOCKS_P` and `AP3_P` shown at the beginning of Section 4 have been obtained by applying the projection algorithm to types `SOCKS` and `ABP3` respectively. The reason why they are not as compact as possible, which is mainly evident in `AP3_P`, is that the projection algorithm does not implement a further simplification step and hence some types which have been projected into `lambda` could have been safely removed.

The result of the projection may be a type equivalent to `lambda`. For example, if we project `ABP` to the set {`eric`}, no interaction involves it and the result is `(lambda|lambda)|lambda|lambda`. Optimizing the algorithm to perform this simplification step is a forthcoming improvement, easy to face in Prolog. On the other hand, we have already observed that the projection may be the same as the projected type. This happens for example if we project `ABP` to the set {`bob`}, which interacts with all the agents in the MAS.

Design time validation that centralized protocol behaves as expected. In SWI Prolog we have implemented a mechanism for generating all the different traces (sequences of interactions) with length N, where N can be set by the user, that respect a given protocol. This mechanism is necessary during the design of the protocol and allows the protocol designer to make an empirical assessment of the conversations that will be recognized as valid ones during the runtime verification. We used this mechanism for validating the "centralized" protocols.

For example, Table 1 (left) shows one of the 16380 different traces with length 12 of the SOCKS protocol (for sake of presentation, we abbreviate `right_robot` in `right_r`, `right_monitor` in `right_m`, `left_robot` in `left_r`, `left_monitor` in `left_m`, `msg` in `m`, and we drop the `tell` performative from interactions). The trace corresponds to an execution where the protocol reached a final state and no other interactions could be accepted after the last one. In the output produced by the SWI Prolog algorithm, this information is given by means of an asterisk after the last interaction. Traces that are prefixes of longer (maybe infinite) ones have no asterisk at their end. Table 1 (right) shows one of the 30713 different traces with length 16 of the ABP3 protocol. Since the ABP3 is an infinite protocol, all its traces are prefixes of infinite ones.

Table 1. Traces of the SOCKS and ABP "centralized" protocols

SOCKS protocol	ABP protocol
m(right_r, right_m, put_sock)	msg(bob, alice, tell, m1)
m(left_r, left_m, put_shoe)	msg(bob, carol, tell, m2)
m(left_m, left_r, oblige_remove_shoe)	msg(carol, bob, tell, a2)
m(left_robot, left_m, removed_shoe)	msg(alice, bob, tell, a1)
m(right_r, right_m, put_shoe)	msg(bob, dave, tell, m3)
m(right_m, plan_monitor, ok)	msg(dave, bob, tell, a3)
m(left_robot, left_m, put_shoe)	msg(bob, alice, tell, m1)
m(left_m, left_r, oblige_remove_shoe)	msg(bob, carol, tell, m2)
m(left_r, left_m, removed_shoe)	msg(alice, bob, tell, a1)
m(left_r, left_m, put_sock)	msg(bob, dave, tell, m3)
m(left_r, left_m, put_shoe)	msg(bob, alice, tell, m1)
m(left_m, plan_monitor, ok)	msg(carol, bob, tell, a2)
*	msg(dave, bob, tell, a3)
	msg(bob, carol, tell, m2)
	msg(alice, bob, tell, a1)
	msg(carol, bob, tell, a2)

By generating traces of different length and inspecting some of them, the protocol designer can get a clear picture of whether the protocol he/she designed behaves in the expected way. Of course this manual inspection gives no guarantees of the correctness of the protocol specification, but in our experience it was enough to early detect flaws.

Design time validation that the projected protocol makes sense. This step was devised for giving hints on whether the decentralized monitoring can ensure global protocol compliance. In fact, although all well-formed deterministic and contractive constrained global types can be projected, not all possible partitions of a subset of all agents of the system to be verified allows a full distributed monitoring of the protocol's properties.

For example, in the case of the SOCKS protocol, deciding which were the subsets of agents onto which projecting the global protocol in order to distribute the monitoring activity was easy: interactions induce a graph connecting pairs of agents that interact at some point, and in this case the graph is a tree as shown in Figure 1. By projecting onto {`left_monitor`} and allowing `left_monitor` to monitor its own interactions, we make a complete check of the left branch of the tree. In the same way, by projecting onto {`right_monitor`} and allowing `right_monitor` to monitor its own interactions, we make a complete check of the right branch. Projecting onto {`plan_monitor`} in this case would be useless, as interactions with this agent are already checked by the left and right monitors and the `plan_monitor` does not perform further checks; in particular, it does not check that messages from the left and right monitor arrive in some specific order. However, projecting onto {`plan_monitor`} would make sense if the MAS were a "sub-MAS" of a larger system, where more couples of robots exist. In that case, we might expect that each plan monitor would report the outcome of activities of its couple of robots to an agent higher in the hierarchy. Interactions with this top-level agent should be monitored by the plan monitor (or vice-versa) and should be transparent to the agents monitoring the robots.

In the MAS implementing the ABP3 protocol shown in Figure 2, things are different due to the constraints in the fork. Although interactions induce a tree like in the SOCKS case, projecting onto Alice, Carol and Dave and allowing these three agents to check their own interactions would not be enough to verify all the protocol's constraints, as already observed in Section 4. The ABP3 cannot be distributed, hence we need a centralized monitor (which might be an external monitor or Bob himself, as it is involved in all the interactions) that "sniffs" the interactions among all the agents and verifies their compliance to the ABP3. None prevents us from projecting ABP3 also onto Alice, Carol and Dave and asking them to monitor the part of the protocol where they are involved, but this would be a useless redundancy, as Bob (or the external monitor) would already verify their part.

In order to detect the fact that, for example, projecting the ABP3 onto Dave gives no complete information on the protocol properties, we implemented an empirical method based on a "generate and test" brute force algorithm, consisting in generating all the traces of a given length of the projected protocol, and verifying if they are compliant with the global protocol. This method works only on finite traces; furthermore, while all detected positives are true, negatives may be false.

For example, Table 2 (left) shows one of the 2 different traces with length 12 of the SOCKS protocol projected onto {`right_robot, right_monitor`}. All the traces of length from 1 to 12 of the projected SOCK protocol are compliant with the global one, hence our compliance algorithms answers "maybe".

Table 2. Traces of projections of the SOCKS and ABP protocols

`SOCKS` protocol projected onto {`right_robot, right_monitor`}	`ABP3` protocol projected onto {`dave`}
m(right_r, right_m, put_shoe)	msg(bob, dave, tell, m3)
m(right_m, right_r, oblige_remove_shoe)	msg(dave, bob, tell, a3)
m(right_r, right_m, removed_shoe)	msg(bob, dave, tell, m3)
m(right_r, right_m, put_shoe)	msg(dave, bob, tell, a3)
m(right_m, right_r, oblige_remove_shoe)	msg(bob, dave, tell, m3)
m(right_r, right_m, removed_shoe)	msg(dave, bob, tell, a3)
m(right_r, right_m, put_shoe)	msg(bob, dave, tell, m3)
m(right_m, right_r, oblige_remove_shoe)	msg(dave, bob, tell, a3)
m(right_r, right_m, removed_shoe)	msg(bob, dave, tell, m3)
m(right_r, right_m, put_sock)	msg(dave, bob, tell, a3)
m(right_r, right_m, put_shoe)	msg(bob, dave, tell, m3)
m(right_m, plan_monitor, ok)	msg(dave, bob, tell, a3)
	msg(bob, dave, tell, m3)
	msg(dave, bob, tell, a3)
	msg(bob, dave, tell, m3)
	msg(dave, bob, tell, a3)

Table 2 (right) shows the only trace with length 16 of the ABP3 protocol projected onto {dave}. This trace, as well as the shorter ones, is not compliant with the global ABP3 protocol because it does not respect the constraint that m3 must follow m1 and m2. The compliance algorithm answers "no", meaning that when projecting the ABP3 onto Dave we are no longer able to check the verification of some constraints in the global protocol.

As we have seen in Section 2, tackling the compliance problem in a formal way is a complex task, which can be faced following different approaches and heavily depends on the formalism employed for specifying protocols. Despite this interesting theoretical open problem, the compliance algorithm we have developed has proved to work well in practice in the case studies we considered.

Runtime verification of actual interactions in Jason and JADE. In our previous papers we discussed many experiments of the verification mechanism carried out on both in Jason [3] and JADE [8]. Although those experiments did not deal with projected types since projection had not been implemented yet, verifying the compliance of a set of agents w.r.t. a constrained global type works in the same way whether the type is a centralized or projected. In this paragraph we limit ourselves to briefly discussing the "socks and shoes" MAS in Jason.

The MAS is represented in Figure 1. We projected the SOCKS constrained global type shown in Section 3 onto the three sets of agents {left_monitor}, {right_monitor} and {plan_monitor}. The three resulting constrained global types are used by agents left_monitor, right_monitor and plan_monitor respectively. Each of these agents monitors all the messages that it either receives or sends, using the "message sniffing" mechanism described in [3]. We run different experiments by changing the actual messages sent by the agents in the MAS, in order to obtain both correct and wrong executions. As an example, Figure 5 shows the output of an interaction where the right_monitor sends a message with content very_good to the plan_monitor, instead of the ok content foreseen by the protocol. The plan_monitor correctly detects a dynamic type checking error (last lines of the messages in the screenshot).

Similar experiments have been carried out with JADE; the outcome of the monitoring activity in both Jason and JADE were the expected ones, both in case of correct and wrong executions.

6 Conclusions and Future Work

In this paper we have defined an algorithm for projecting a constrained global type onto a set of agents *Ags*, to allow distributed dynamic verification of the compliance of a MAS to a protocol. Besides describing the algorithm and its SWI Prolog implementation, we have framed it into the context of a full monitoring framework for agent systems, currently interfaced with Jason and JADE.

For what concerns future work, we are planning to extend the projection algorithm in order to be able to properly deal with the more general notion of attribute global type.

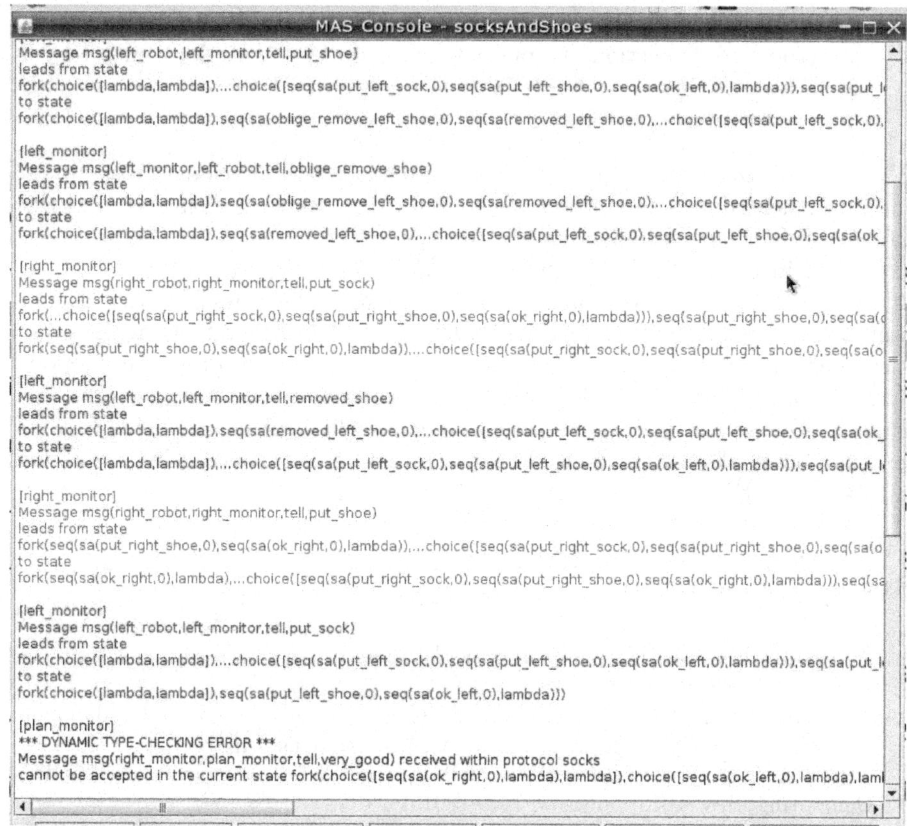

Fig. 5. Projected SOCKS protocol in Jason: the `right_monitor` violates the protocol

Also, we are investigating the possible ways to partition the set of agents for projecting types, to minimize the number of monitors, while ensuring safety of dynamic verification. In Section 2 we analyzed many different research areas, looking for solutions to the problem and for formal demonstrations that the distribution of the protocol allows monitoring the same properties as the centralized version, but even the works which seem closer to ours, namely those related with global and session types, and with choreographies, cannot be directly adopted to guarantee the correctness of the projection in our context, for four main reasons:

1. we may project on subsets of agents, if needed, and non necessarily onto individual agents;
2. we project constrained global types into constrained global types, not into "implementations": the implementation of the agents is relevant neither for the projection stage, nor for the monitoring one;
3. the expressive power of our formalism is different from other approaches: a compliance analysis must take the specific features of the formalism into account;

4. all the proposals found in literature to solve the problem of checking the correctness of projection, simply enforce syntactic restrictions on protocol specifications (as done in Scribble), whereas we would like to come out with a less restrictive approach.

While taking inspiration from these approaches will be extremely useful, we will nevertheless need to develop a new approach, taking the features and the intended use of our formalism into account.

Finally, in the examples considered in this paper, types are projected statically (that is, before the system is started) because we have assumed that agents cannot move among nodes, but monitoring would be also possible in the presence of agent mobility, as described in the scenario outlined in the introduction. However, in this case the implementation of a self-monitoring MAS is more challenging, because monitor agents have to dynamically project the global type in reaction to any change involving the set of monitored agents. Tackling scenarios of this kind is the final long term goal of our research.

References

1. Ancona, D.: Regular corecursion in Prolog. Computer Languages, Systems & Structures 39(4), 142–162 (2013)
2. Ancona, D., Barbieri, M., Mascardi, V.: Constrained global types for dynamic checking of protocol conformance in multi-agent systems. In: Shin, S.Y., Maldonado, J.C. (eds.) Proceedings of the 28th Annual ACM Symposium on Applied Computing, SAC 2013, pp. 1377–1379 (2013)
3. Ancona, D., Drossopoulou, S., Mascardi, V.: Automatic Generation of Self-monitoring MASs from Multiparty Global Session Types in Jason. In: Baldoni, M., Dennis, L., Mascardi, V., Vasconcelos, W. (eds.) DALT 2012. LNCS, vol. 7784, pp. 76–95. Springer, Heidelberg (2013)
4. Baldoni, M., Baroglio, C., Capuzzimati, F.: 2COMM: A commitment-based MAS architecture. In: Cossentino, M., El Fallah Seghrouchni, A., Winikoff, M. (eds.) EMAS 2013. LNCS (LNAI), vol. 8245, pp. 38–57. Springer, Heidelberg (2013)
5. Baldoni, M., Baroglio, C., Chopra, A.K., Desai, N., Patti, V., Singh, M.P.: Choice, interoperability, and conformance in interaction protocols and service choreographies. In: Sierra, C., Castelfranchi, C., Decker, K.S., Sichman, J.S. (eds.) 8th International Joint Conference on Autonomous Agents and Multiagent Systems, AAMAS 2009, vol. 2, pp. 843–850. IFAAMAS (2009)
6. Bravetti, M., Zavattaro, G.: Towards a unifying theory for choreography conformance and contract compliance. In: Lumpe, M., Vanderperren, W. (eds.) SC 2007. LNCS, vol. 4829, pp. 34–50. Springer, Heidelberg (2007)
7. Bravetti, M., Zavattaro, G.: Contract compliance and choreography conformance in the presence of message queues. In: Bruni, R., Wolf, K. (eds.) WS-FM 2008. LNCS, vol. 5387, pp. 37–54. Springer, Heidelberg (2009)
8. Briola, D., Mascardi, V., Ancona, D.: Distributed runtime verification of JADE multiagent systems. In: Camacho, D., Braubach, L., Venticinque, S., Badica, C. (eds.) Intelligent Distributed Computing VIII. SCI, vol. 570, pp. 81–92. Springer, Heidelberg (2014)

9. Carbone, M., Honda, K., Yoshida, N.: Structured communication-centred programming for web services. In: De Nicola, R. (ed.) ESOP 2007. LNCS, vol. 4421, pp. 2–17. Springer, Heidelberg (2007)
10. Castagna, G., Dezani-Ciancaglini, M., Padovani, L.: On global types and multiparty session. Logical Methods in Computer Science 8(1) (2012)
11. Chen, T.: Lightening global types. In: Donaldson, A.F., Vasconcelos, V.T. (eds.) Proceedings 7th Workshop on Programming Language Approaches to Concurrency and Communication-cEntric Software, PLACES 2014. EPTCS, vol. 155, pp. 38–46 (2014)
12. Chopra, A.K., Dalpiaz, F., Giorgini, P., Mylopoulos, J.: Reasoning about agents and protocols via goals and commitments. In: Proceedings of the 9th International Conference on Autonomous Agents and Multiagent Systems, AAMAS 2010, vol. 1, pp. 457–464. IFAAMAS, Richland (2010)
13. Coppo, M., Dezani-Ciancaglini, M., Venneri, B.: Self-adaptive monitors for multiparty sessions. In: 22nd Euromicro International Conference on Parallel, Distributed, and Network-Based Processing, PDP 2014, pp. 688–696. IEEE (2014)
14. Drusinsky, D., Shing, M.-T.: Verifying distributed protocols using MSC-assertions, run-time monitoring, and automatic test generation. In: Proceedings of the 18th IEEE/IFIP International Workshop on Rapid System Prototyping, RSP 2007, pp. 82–88 (May 2007)
15. German, E., Sheremetov, L.B.: An agent framework for processing FIPA-ACL messages based on interaction models. In: Luck, M., Padgham, L. (eds.) AOSE 2007. LNCS, vol. 4951, pp. 88–102. Springer, Heidelberg (2008)
16. Honda, K., Yoshida, N., Carbone, M.: Multiparty asynchronous session types. In: POPL 2008, pp. 273–284. ACM (2008)
17. Krüger, I.H., Meisinger, M., Menarini, M.: Runtime verification of interactions: From MSCs to aspects. In: Sokolsky, O., Taşıran, S. (eds.) RV 2007. LNCS, vol. 4839, pp. 63–74. Springer, Heidelberg (2007)
18. Lam, S., Shankar, A.U.: Protocol verification via projections. IEEE Transactions on Software Engineering SE-10(4), 325–342 (1984)
19. Lanese, I., Guidi, C., Montesi, F., Zavattaro, G.: Bridging the gap between interaction- and process-oriented choreographies. In: Cerone, A., Gruner, S. (eds.) Sixth IEEE International Conference on Software Engineering and Formal Methods, SEFM 2008, pp. 323–332. IEEE Computer Society (2008)
20. Mascardi, V., Ancona, D.: Attribute global types for dynamic checking of protocols in logic-based multiagent systems. Theory and Practice of Logic Programming, 13(4-5-Online-Supplement) (2013)
21. Mascardi, V., Briola, D., Ancona, D.: On the expressiveness of attribute global types: The formalization of a real multiagent system protocol. In: Baldoni, M., Baroglio, C., Boella, G., Micalizio, R. (eds.) AI*IA 2013. LNCS (LNAI), vol. 8249, pp. 300–311. Springer, Heidelberg (2013)
22. Meron, D., Mermet, B.: A tool architecture to verify properties of multiagent system at runtime. In: Bordini, R.H., Dastani, M., Dix, J., El Fallah Seghrouchni, A. (eds.) PROMAS 2006. LNCS (LNAI), vol. 4411, pp. 201–216. Springer, Heidelberg (2007)
23. Modgil, S., Faci, N., Meneguzzi, F., Oren, N., Miles, S., Luck, M.: A framework for monitoring agent-based normative systems. In: Proceedings of the 8th International Conference on Autonomous Agents and Multiagent Systems, AAMAS 2009, vol. 1, pp. 153–160. IFAAMAS, Richland (2009)

24. Neykova, R., Yoshida, N., Hu, R.: SPY: Local verification of global protocols. In: Legay, A., Bensalem, S. (eds.) RV 2013. LNCS, vol. 8174, pp. 358–363. Springer, Heidelberg (2013)
25. Qiu, Z., Zhao, X., Cai, C., Yang, H.: Towards the theoretical foundation of choreography. In: Proceedings of the 16th International Conference on World Wide Web, WWW 2007, pp. 973–982. ACM, New York (2007)
26. Sangiorgi, D.: On the origins of bisimulation and coinduction. ACM Trans. Program. Lang. Syst. (2009)
27. Winikoff, M.: Implementing flexible and robust agent interactions using distributed commitment machines. Multiagent and Grid Systems 2(4), 365–381 (2006)
28. Wörn, H., Längle, T., Albert, M., Kazi, A., Brighenti, A., Seijo, S.R., Senior, C., Bobi, M.A.S., Collado, J.: DIAMOND: Distributed multi-agent architecture for monitoring and diagnosis. Production Planning & Control 15(2), 189–200 (2004)
29. Yolum, P., Singh, M.P.: Commitment machines. In: Meyer, J.-J.C., Tambe, M. (eds.) ATAL 2001. LNCS (LNAI), vol. 2333, pp. 235–247. Springer, Heidelberg (2002)

Infinite States Verification in Game-Theoretic Logics: Case Studies and Implementation

Slawomir Kmiec and Yves Lespérance

Dept. of Electrical Engineering and Computer Science, York University, Toronto, ON, Canada
{skmiec,lesperan}@cse.yorku.ca

Abstract. Many practical problems where the environment is not in the system's control can be modelled in game-theoretic logics (e.g., ATL). But most work on verification methods for such logics is restricted to finite state cases. De Giacomo, Lespérance, and Pearce have proposed a situation calculus-based logical framework for representing such infinite state game-type problems together with a verification method based on fixpoint approximates and regression. Here, we extend this line of work. Firstly, we describe some case studies to evaluate the method. We specify some example domains and show that the method does allow us to verify various properties. We also find some examples where the method must be extended to exploit information about the initial state and state constraints in order to work. Secondly, we describe an evaluation-based Prolog implementation of a version of the method for complete initial state theories with the closed world assumption. It generates successive approximates and checks if they hold in the situation of interest. We describe some preliminary experiments with this tool and discuss its limitations.

1 Introduction

Many practical problems where the environment is not completely under the system's control, such as service orchestration, contingent planning, and multi-agent planning, can be modeled as games and specified in game-theoretic logics. There has been much work to define such logics (e.g., Alternating-Time Temporal Logic (ATL)) and develop verification methods for them, mainly model checking techniques [1]. However, most such work is restricted to finite state settings. De Giacomo, Lespérance, and Pearce [8] (hereafter DLP) have developed an expressive logical framework for specifying such problems within the situation calculus [16]. In their approach, a game-like problem/setting is represented as a *situation calculus game structure*, a special kind of action theory that specifies who the players are, what the legal moves are, etc. They also define a logic that combines the μ-calculus, game-theoretic path quantifiers (as in ATL), and first-order quantification, for specifying properties about such game settings. Additionally, they propose a procedural language for defining game settings, GameGolog, which is based on ConGolog [9]. Finally, they propose a method for verifying temporal properties over infinite state game structures that is based on fixpoint approximates and regression.

While DLP give examples to illustrate the expressiveness and convenience of their formalism, they recognize that their work is essentially theoretical and call for experimental studies to understand whether these techniques actually work in practice. This is

F. Dalpiaz et al. (Eds.): EMAS 2014, LNAI 8758, pp. 271–290, 2014.

what we begin to address in this paper. We develop several example problems involving infinite state domains and represent them as situation calculus game structures. We then examine whether the DLP fixpoint approximates verification method works to verify common temporal properties. In many cases, it does indeed work. So to some extent, our work validates the DLP proposal.

We do however find other examples where the DLP method does not converge in a finite number of steps. We note that the method uses only the simplest part of the action theory, the unique name and domain closure axioms, to try to show that successive approximates are equivalent (after performing regression). Clearly, using the whole action theory is problematic as it includes a second-order axiom to specify the domain of situations. We show that in some cases, adding a few key facts that are entailed by the entire theory (from simple axioms about the initial state to state constraints proven by induction) is sufficient to get convergence in a finite number of steps. This means that the method can be used successfully in a wider range of problems if we can rely on the modeler to identify such facts. Thus, our case studies show that the kind of method proposed by DLP (and related approaches like [5,6]) often does work for infinite domains, where very few verification methods are available, and allows reasoning about a range of game problems.

Note that in our case studies, the fixpoint approximation method was performed manually. We also describe an evaluation-based Prolog implementation of a version of the method for complete initial state theories with the closed world assumption. It generates successive approximates and checks if they hold in the situation of interest. We describe some experiments with this tool and discuss its limitations.

The paper is organized as follows. In the sext section, we review the situation calculus and the DLP framework for representing infinite state game problems and their verification method. In Section 3, we present our three case studies and discuss the results. In Section 4, we discuss our implementation of the method and how it handles the problems in two of our case studies. In the last section, we review the contributions of this work, discuss related work, and mention some issues for future work.

2 Situation Calculus Game Structures

The situation calculus (SitCalc) is a many-sorted predicate logic language for representing dynamically changing worlds in which all changes are the result of named actions [16,18]. Actions are terms in the language, e.g., $pickup(R, X)$ could represent an action where a robot R picks up an object X. Action terms are denoted by α possibly with subscripts to differentiate different action terms. Action variables are denoted by lower case letters a possibly with subscripts. Action types, i.e., actions functions, which may require parameters, are denoted by upper case letters A possibly with subscripts. Situations represent possible world histories and are terms in the language. The distinguished constant S_0 denotes the initial situation where no action has yet been performed. The distinguished function symbol do is used to build sequences of actions such that $do(a, s)$ denotes the successor situation that results from performing action a in situation s. Fluents are predicates or functions whose values may vary from situation to situation. They are denoted by symbols that take a situation term as their last argument. A distinguished predicate symbol $Poss(a, s)$ is used to state that an action a is physically possible (i.e. executable) in a situation s.

Given this language, one can specify action theories that describe how the world changes as the result of the available actions. We focus on *basic action theories* as proposed in [18]. We assume that there is a *finite number of action types* in the domains we consider. Thus, a basic action theory $\mathcal{D}$ is the union of the following disjoint sets: the foundational, domain independent axioms of the situation calculus (Σ); precondition axioms stating when actions are executable ($\mathcal{D}_{poss}$); successor state axioms describing how fluents change between situations ($\mathcal{D}_{ssa}$); unique name axioms for actions and domain closure on action types ($\mathcal{D}_{ca}$); and axioms describing the initial configuration of the world ($\mathcal{D}_{S_0}$). Successor state axioms specify the value of fluents in situation $do(a, s)$ in terms of the action a and the value of fluents in situation s; they encode the causal laws of the world and provide a solution to the frame problem.

Situation calculus game structures, proposed by DLP, are a specialization of basic action theories that allow multi-agent game-like settings to be modeled. In SitCalc game structures, every action a has an agent parameter and the distinguished function $agent(a)$ returns the agent of the action. Axioms for the $agent$ function are specified for every action type and by convention the agent parameter is the first argument of any action type. It is assumed that there is a finite set $Agents$ of agents who are denoted by unique names. Actions are divided into two groups: choice actions and standard actions. Choice actions model the decisions of agents and they are assumed to have no effect on any fluent other than $Poss$, $Legal$, and $Control$. Standard actions are the other non-choice actions. Choice actions are always physically possible, i.e., for all choice actions a and situations s, $Poss(a, s)$. DLP introduce a distinguished predicate $Legal(s)$ that is a stronger version of possibility/legality and models the game structure of interest. It specifies what actions an agent may execute and what choices can be made according to the rules of the game. The axioms provided for $Legal$ specify the game of interest. It is required that the axioms for $Legal$ entail three properties: (1) $Legal$ implies physically possible ($Poss$), (2) legal situations are the result of an action performed in legal situations, and (3) only one agent can act in a legal situation, i.e., the game is a turn-taking game. $Control(agt, s)$ holds if agent agt is the one that is in control and can act in a legal situation s; it is defined as follows:

$$Control(agt, s) \doteq \exists a.Legal(do(a, s)) \wedge agent(a) = agt.$$

As a result of the above constraints on $Legal$, it follows that the predicate $Control$ holds for only one agent in any given legal situation. As explained in DLP, games where several agents act simultaneously can often be modeled using a round-robin of choice actions. If the result of such simultaneous choices is non-deterministic, a "game master" agent that makes the decision can be introduced. Note however that the framework assumes that the agents all have complete information and that actions are fully observable. Note also that the state of the game in situation s is captured by the fluents. Finally, DLP define a SitCalc game structure to be an action theory $\mathcal{D}_{GS} = \Sigma \cup \mathcal{D}_{poss} \cup \mathcal{D}_{ssa} \cup \mathcal{D}_{ca} \cup \mathcal{D}_{S_0} \cup \mathcal{D}_{legal}$, where $\mathcal{D}_{legal}$ contains the axioms for $Legal$ and $Control$ and for the function $agent()$, and the other components are as for standard basic action theories [18]. Note that here, a game structure is a type of situation calculus theory and not a single game model as is often the case.

DLP introduce a logical language $\mathcal{L}$ for expressing temporal properties of game structures. It is inspired by ATL [1] and based on the μ-calculus [17], as used over game structures as in [4]. The key element of the $\mathcal{L}$-logic is the $\langle\langle G\rangle\rangle \bigcirc \varphi$ operator defined as follows:

$$\begin{array}{l}\langle\langle G\rangle\rangle \bigcirc \varphi \doteq \\ \quad (\exists agt \in G.\, Control(agt, now) \wedge \\ \quad\quad \exists a.\, agent(a) = agt \wedge Legal(do(a, now)) \wedge \varphi[do(a, now)]) \vee \\ \quad (\exists agt \notin G.\, Control(agt, now) \wedge \\ \quad\quad \forall a.\, agent(a) = agt \wedge Legal(do(a, now)) \supset \varphi[do(a, now)])\end{array}$$

This operator, in essence, specifies that a coalition G of agents can ensure that φ holds next, i.e., after one more action, as follows. If an agent from the coalition G is in control in the current situation, then all we need is that there be some legal action that this agent can perform to make the formula φ hold. If the agent in control is not in coalition G, then what we need is that regardless of the action taken by the in-control agent (for all) the formula φ holds after the action. The whole logic $\mathcal{L}$ is defined as follows:

$$\begin{array}{l}\Psi ::= \varphi \mid Z(\boldsymbol{x}) \mid \Psi_1 \wedge \Psi_2 \mid \Psi_1 \vee \Psi_2 \mid \exists x.\Psi \mid \forall x.\Psi \mid \\ \quad \langle\langle G\rangle\rangle \bigcirc \Psi \mid [[G]] \bigcirc \Psi \mid \mu Z(\boldsymbol{x}).\Psi(Z(\boldsymbol{x})) \mid \nu Z(\boldsymbol{x}).\Psi(Z(\boldsymbol{x})).\end{array}$$

In the above, φ is an arbitrary, possibly open, situation-suppressed situation calculus uniform formula, Z is a predicate variable of a given arity, $\langle\langle G\rangle\rangle \bigcirc \Psi$ is as defined above, $[[G]] \bigcirc \Psi$ is the dual of $\langle\langle G\rangle\rangle \bigcirc \Psi$ (i.e., $[[G]] \bigcirc \Psi \equiv \neg\langle\langle G\rangle\rangle \bigcirc \neg\Psi$[1]), and μ (resp. ν) is the least (resp. greatest) fixpoint operator from the μ-calculus, where the argument is written as $\Psi(Z(\boldsymbol{x}))$ to emphasize that $Z(\boldsymbol{x})$ may occur free, i.e., not quantified by μ or ν, in Ψ.

The language $\mathcal{L}$ allows one to express arbitrary temporal/dynamic properties. For example, the property that group G can ensure that eventually $\varphi(\boldsymbol{x})$ (or has a strategy to achieve $\varphi(\boldsymbol{x})$), where $\varphi(\boldsymbol{x})$ is a situation suppressed formula with free variables $\boldsymbol{x}$, may be expressed by the following least fixpoint construction:

$$\langle\langle G\rangle\rangle\Diamond\varphi(\boldsymbol{x}) \doteq \mu Z(\boldsymbol{x}).\, \varphi(\boldsymbol{x}) \vee \langle\langle G\rangle\rangle \bigcirc Z(\boldsymbol{x})$$

Similarly, group G's ability to maintain a property $\varphi(\boldsymbol{x})$ can be expressed by the following greatest fixpoint construction:

$$\langle\langle G\rangle\rangle\Box\varphi(\boldsymbol{x}) \doteq \nu Z(\boldsymbol{x}).\varphi(\boldsymbol{x}) \wedge \langle\langle G\rangle\rangle \bigcirc Z(\boldsymbol{x})$$

We say that there is a path where $\varphi(\boldsymbol{x})$ holds next if the set of all agents can ensure that $\varphi(\boldsymbol{x})$ holds next: $\exists \bigcirc \varphi(\boldsymbol{x}) \doteq \langle\langle Agents\rangle\rangle \bigcirc \varphi(\boldsymbol{x})$. Similarly there is a path where $\varphi(\boldsymbol{x})$ eventually holds if the set of all agents has a strategy to achieve $\varphi(\boldsymbol{x})$: $\exists\Diamond\varphi(\boldsymbol{x}) \doteq \langle\langle Agents\rangle\rangle\Diamond\varphi(\boldsymbol{x})$.

DLP propose a procedure based on regression and fixpoint approximation to verify formulas of logic $\mathcal{L}$ given a SitCalc game structure theory. This recursive procedure

[1] Although $\neg\langle\langle G\rangle\rangle \bigcirc \neg\Psi$ is not in $\mathcal{L}$ according to the syntax, the equivalent formula in negation normal form is.

$\tau(\Psi)$ tries to compute a first-order formula uniform in current situation now that is equivalent to Ψ:

$$\begin{aligned}
&\tau(\varphi) = \varphi\\
&\tau(Z) = Z\\
&\tau(\Psi_1 \wedge \Psi_2) = \tau(\Psi_1) \wedge\ \tau(\Psi_2)\\
&\tau(\Psi_1 \vee \Psi_2) = \tau(\Psi_1) \vee \tau(\Psi_2)\\
&\tau(\exists x.\Psi) = \exists x.\tau(\Psi)\\
&\tau(\forall x.\Psi) = \forall x.\tau(\Psi)\\
&\tau(\langle\langle G\rangle\rangle \bigcirc \Psi) = \mathcal{R}(\langle\langle G\rangle\rangle \bigcirc \tau(\Psi))\\
&\tau([[G]] \bigcirc \Psi) = \neg\mathcal{R}(\langle\langle G\rangle\rangle \bigcirc \tau(\text{NNF}(\neg\Psi)))\\
&\tau(\mu Z.\Psi) = \mathit{lfp} Z.\tau(\Psi)\\
&\tau(\nu Z.\Psi) = \mathit{gfp} Z.\tau(\Psi)
\end{aligned}$$

In the above, $\mathcal{R}$ represents the regression operator and $\langle\langle G\rangle\rangle \bigcirc \Psi$ is regressable if Ψ is regressable, NNF$(\neg\Psi)$ denotes the negation normal form of $\neg\Psi$, and $\mathit{lfp}Z.\Psi$ and $\mathit{gfp}Z.\Psi$ are formulas resulting from the following least and greatest fixpoint procedures:

$$\begin{array}{ll}
\mathit{lfp}Z.\Psi = & \mathit{gfp}Z.\Psi = \\
\quad R := False; & \quad R := True; \\
\quad R_{new} := \Psi(False); & \quad R_{new} := \Psi(True); \\
\quad \textbf{while } (\mathcal{D}_{ca} \not\models R \equiv R_{new})\{ & \quad \textbf{while } (\mathcal{D}_{ca} \not\models R \equiv R_{new})\{ \\
\qquad R := R_{new}; & \qquad R := R_{new}; \\
\qquad R_{new} := \Psi(R)\ \} & \qquad R_{new} := \Psi(R)\ \}
\end{array}$$

The fixpoint procedures test if $R \equiv R_{new}$ is entailed given only the unique name and domain closure for actions axioms $\mathcal{D}_{ca}$. In general, there is no guarantee that such procedures will ever terminate i.e., that for some i $\mathcal{D}_{ca} \models R_i \equiv R_{i+1}$. But if the *lfp* procedure does terminate, then $\mathcal{D}_{GS} \models R_i[S] \equiv \mu Z.\Psi(Z)[S]$ and R_i is first-order and uniform in now (and similarly for *gfp*). In such cases, the task of verifying a fixpoint formula in the situation calculus is reduced to that of verifying a first-order formula. We have the following result:

Theorem 1. of DLP [8]: *Let $\mathcal{D}_{GS}$ be a situation calculus game structure and let Ψ be an $\mathcal{L}$-formula. If the algorithm above terminates, then $\mathcal{D}_{GS} \models \Psi[S_0]$ if and only if $\mathcal{D}_{S_o} \cup \mathcal{D}_{ca} \models \tau(\Psi)[S_0]$.*

3 Case Studies

3.1 Light World (LW)

Our first example domain is the Light World (LW), a simple game we designed that involves an infinite row of lights, one for each integer. A light can be on or off. Each light has a switch that can be flipped, which will turn the light on (resp., off) if it was off (resp., on). There are 2 players, X and O. Players take turns and initially it is X's turn. The goal of player X is to have lights 1 and 2 on in which case player X wins the game. Initially, lights 1 and 2 are known to be off and light 5 is known to be on. Note that this is clearly an infinite state domain as the set of lights that can be turned on or off is infinite. Note also that the game may go on forever without the goal being reached (e.g., if player O keeps turning light 1 or 2 off whenever X turns them on).

We will show that the DLP method can be used to verify some interesting properties in this domain. We apply the method with one small modification: when checking whether the two successive approximates are equivalent, we use an axiomatization of the integers D_Z in addition to the unique names and domain closure axioms for actions D_{ca}^{LW}, as our game domain involves one light for every integer.[2] The game structure axiomatization for this domain is:

$$\mathcal{D}_{GS}^{LW} = \Sigma \cup \mathcal{D}_{poss}^{LW} \cup \mathcal{D}_{ssa}^{LW} \cup \mathcal{D}_{ca}^{LW} \cup \mathcal{D}_{S_0}^{LW} \cup \mathcal{D}_{Legal}^{LW} \cup \mathcal{D}_{Z}.$$

We have only one action $flip(p, t)$, meaning that player p flips light t, with the precondition axiom (in $\mathcal{D}_{poss}^{LW}$): $Poss(flip(p, t), s) \equiv Agent(p)$. We have the fluents $On(t, s)$, meaning that light t is on in situation s, and $turn(s)$, a function that denotes the agent whose turn it is in s. The successor state axioms (in $\mathcal{D}_{ssa}^{LW}$) are as follows:

$$On(t, do(a, s)) \equiv \exists p\, a = flip(p, t) \wedge \neg On(t, s) \vee On(t, s) \wedge \forall p.a \neq flip(p, t)$$
$$turn(do(a, s)) = p \equiv p = O \wedge turn(s) = X \vee p = X \wedge turn(s) = O$$

The rules of the game are specified using the $Legal$ predicate. We have the following axioms in $\mathcal{D}_{legal}^{LW}$:

$$Legal(do(a, s)) \equiv Legal(s) \wedge \exists p, t.\ Agent(p) \wedge turn(s) = p \wedge a = flip(p, t)$$
$$Control(p, s) \doteq \exists a.Legal(do(a, s)) \wedge agent(a) = p$$
$$agent(flip(p, t)) = p, \qquad \forall p.\{Agent(p) \equiv (p = X \vee p = O)\}, \qquad X \neq O$$

Thus legal moves involve the player whose turn it is flipping any switch. We have the following unique name and domain closure axioms for actions in $\mathcal{D}_{ca}^{LW}$:

$$\forall a.\ \{\ \exists p, t.\ a = flip(p, t)\}$$
$$\forall p, p', t, t'.\ \{\ flip(p, t) = flip(p', t') \supset p = p' \wedge t = t'\ \}$$

Finally, the initial state axioms in $\mathcal{D}_{S_0}^{LW}$ are: $turn(S_0) = X, \neg On(1, S_0), \neg On(2, S_0)$, $On(5, S_0)$, and $Legal(S_0)$.

For our first verification example, we consider the property that it is possible for X to eventually win assuming O cooperates, which can be represented by the following formula:

$$\exists\Diamond Wins(X) \doteq \mu Z.Wins(X)\ \vee\ \exists \bigcirc Z,$$

where $Wins(X, s) \doteq Legal(s) \wedge On(1, s) \wedge On(2, s)$. We apply the DLP method to this example. We can show that the regressed approximations simplify as follows (see

[2] Our axioms and the properties we attempt to verify only use a very simple part of integer arithmetic. It should be possible to generate the proofs using the decidable theory of Presburger arithmetic [11] after encoding integers as pairs of natural numbers in the standard way [12]. Most theorem proving systems include sophisticated solvers for dealing with formulas involving integer constraints and it should be possible to use these to perform the reasoning about integers that we require.

[14] for more detailed versions of all proofs in this paper):

$\mathcal{D}_{ca}^{LW} \models R_0(s) \doteq Wins(X,s) \vee \mathcal{R}(\exists \bigcirc False) \equiv$
$\quad Legal(s) \wedge On(1,s) \wedge On(2,s)$

This approximation evaluates to true if s is such that X is winning in s already (in no steps), i.e., if light 1 and light 2 are on in s.

$\mathcal{D}_{ca}^{LW} \cup D_Z \models R_1(s) \doteq Wins(X,s) \vee \mathcal{R}(\exists \bigcirc R_0) \equiv$
$\quad Legal(s) \wedge On(1,s) \wedge On(2,s) \vee$
$\quad Legal(s) \wedge (turn(s) = X \vee turn(s) = O) \wedge On(1,s) \vee$
$\quad Legal(s) \wedge (turn(s) = X \vee turn(s) = O) \wedge On(2,s)$

This approximation evaluates to true if s is such that X can win in at most 1 step; these are legal situations where player X is already winning or where one of lights 1 or 2 is on, as X or O can turn the other light on at the next step.

$\mathcal{D}_{ca}^{LW} \cup D_Z \models R_2(s) \doteq Wins(X,s) \vee \mathcal{R}(\exists \bigcirc R_1) \equiv$
$\quad Legal(s) \wedge On(1,s) \wedge On(2,s) \vee$
$\quad Legal(s) \wedge (turn(s) = X \vee turn(s) = O)$

This approximation evaluates to true if s is such that X can win in at most 2 steps; this is the case if X is winning already or if s is any legal situation where it is X or O's turn, as the controlling player can turn light 1 on at the next step and the other player can and light 2 on at the second step.

$\mathcal{D}_{ca}^{LW} \cup D_Z \models R_3(s) \equiv Wins(X,s) \vee \mathcal{R}(\exists \bigcirc R_2) \equiv$
$\quad Legal(s) \wedge On(1,s) \wedge On(2,s) \vee$
$\quad Legal(s) \wedge (turn(s) = X \vee turn(s) = O)$

The fixpoint iteration procedure converges at the 4th step as we have: $\mathcal{D}_{ca}^{LW} \cup D_Z \models R_2(s) \equiv R_3(s)$. Note that it can be shown using the entire theory (by induction on situations) that $\mathcal{D}_{GS}^{LW} \models R_2(s) \equiv Legal(s)$, as it is always either X's or O's turn. Thus, it is possible for X to eventually win in any legal situation. It then follows by Theorem 1 of DLP that: $\mathcal{D}_{GS}^{LW} \models \exists \Diamond Wins(X)[S_0]$ if and only if $\mathcal{D}_{GS}^{LW} \models Legal(S_0) \wedge \{On(1,S_0) \wedge On(2,S_0) \vee turn(S_0) = X \vee turn(S_0) = O\}$. By the initial state axioms, the latter holds so $\mathcal{D}_{GS}^{LW} \models \exists \Diamond Wins(X)[S_0]$, i.e., player X can eventually win in the initial situation.

For our second example, we look at the property that X can ensure that he/she eventually wins no matter what O does, i.e., the existence of a strategy that ensures $Wins(X)$. This can be represented by the following formula:

$$\langle\langle\{X\}\rangle\rangle \Diamond Wins(X) \doteq \mu Z.\, Wins(X) \vee \langle\langle\{X\}\rangle\rangle \bigcirc Z$$

We apply the DLP method to try to verify this property. We can show that the regressed approximations simplify as follows:

$\mathcal{D}_{ca}^{LW} \cup \mathcal{D}_Z \models R_0(s) \doteq Wins(X,s) \vee \mathcal{R}(\langle\langle\{X\}\rangle\rangle \bigcirc False) \equiv$
$\quad Legal(s) \wedge On(1,s) \wedge On(2,s)$

This approximation evaluates to true if s is such that X is already winning in s (in no steps); these are situations where lights 1 and 2 are already on.

$\mathcal{D}_{ca}^{LW} \cup \mathcal{D}_Z \models R_1(s) \doteq Wins(X,s) \vee \mathcal{R}(\langle\langle\{X\}\rangle\rangle \bigcirc R_0) \equiv$
$\quad Legal(s) \wedge On(1,s) \wedge On(2,s) \vee$

$Legal(s) \wedge turn(s) = X \wedge On(1, s) \vee$
$Legal(s) \wedge turn(s) = X \wedge On(2, s)$

This approximation evaluates to true if s is such that X can ensure it wins in at most 1 step. This holds if lights 1 and 2 are already on or if either light 1 or 2 is on and it is X's turn, as X can then turn the other light on at the next step.

The next approximate R_2 simplifies to the same formula as R_1 and $\mathcal{D}_{ca}^{LW} \cup \mathcal{D}_Z \models R_1(s) \equiv R_2(s)$, so the fixpoint iteration procedure converges in the 3rd step. Therefore by Theorem 1 of DLP: $\mathcal{D}_{GS}^{LW} \models \langle\langle\{X\}\rangle\rangle\Diamond Wins(X)[S_0] \equiv R_1(S_0)$ Since both lights 1 and 2 are off initially, it follows by the initial state axioms that $\mathcal{D}_{GS}^{LW} \models \neg\langle\langle\{X\}\rangle\rangle\Diamond Wins(X)[S_0]$, i.e., there is no winning strategy for X in S_0. However, we also have that $\mathcal{D}_{GS}^{LW} \models \langle\langle\{X\}\rangle\rangle\Diamond Wins(X)[S_1]$, where $S_1 = do(flip(O, 3), do(flip(X, 1), S_0))$, i.e., X has a winning strategy in the situation S_1 where X first turned light 1 on and then O flipped light 3, as X can turn on light 2 next.

Note that when the fixpoint approximation method is able to show that a coalition can ensure that a property holds eventually, the theory is complete, and we have domain closure, we can always extract a strategy that the coalition can follow to achieve the property: a strategy works if it always selects actions for the coalition that get it from one approximate to a lower approximate (R_i to R_{i-1}).

3.2 Oil Lamp World (OLW)

The DLP method tries to detect convergence by checking if the i-th approximate is equivalent to the $(i+1)$-th approximate using only the unique name and domain closure axioms for actions D_{ca} (to which we have added the axiomatization of the integers). We now give an example where this method does not converge in a finite number of steps. However, we also show that if we use some additional facts that are entailed by the entire theory D_{GS}^{OLW}, including the initial state axioms, when checking if successive approximates are equivalent, then we do get convergence in a finite number of steps.

Consider the Oil Lamp World (OLW), a variant of the Light World (LW) domain discussed earlier. It also involves an infinite row of lamps, one for each integer, which can be on or off. A lamp has an igniter that can be flipped. When this happens, the lamp will go on provided that the lamp immediately to the right is already on, i.e., flipping the igniter for lamp t will turn it on if lamp $t+1$ is already on. There is only one agent, X. The goal of X is to have lamp 1 on, in which case X wins. Observe that the game may go on indefinitely without the goal being reached, e.g., if X keeps flipping a lamp other than lamp 1 repeatedly.

The game structure axiomatization for this domain is: $\mathcal{D}_{GS}^{OLW} = \Sigma \cup \mathcal{D}_{poss}^{OLW} \cup \mathcal{D}_{ssa}^{OLW} \cup \mathcal{D}_{ca}^{OLW} \cup \mathcal{D}_{S_0}^{OLW} \cup \mathcal{D}_{Legal}^{OLW} \cup \mathcal{D}_Z$. As in the previous example, we have only one action, $flip(p, t)$, meaning that p flips the igniter on light t, with the following precondition axiom (in $\mathcal{D}_{poss}^{OLW}$): $Poss(flip(p, t), s) \equiv Agent(p)$. But there is no turn taking in this game as there is only one agent X. We have the successor state axiom (in $\mathcal{D}_{ssa}^{OLW}$):

$$On(t, do(a, s)) \equiv \exists p\, a = flip(p, t) \wedge On(t+1, s) \vee On(t, s).$$

Note that once a lamp is turned on it remains on. The axioms in $\mathcal{D}_{legal}^{OLW}$ specifying the rules of the game are similar to the ones given earlier for the Light World domain, and include:

$$Legal(do(a, s)) \equiv Legal(s) \wedge \exists p, t.\ Agent(p) \wedge a = flip(p, t).$$

Thus legal moves involve X flipping any igniter. The unique name and domain closure axioms for actions and the initial state axioms are exactly as in the Light World example.

We are interested in verifying the property that it is possible for X to eventually win, which is represented by the following formula:

$$\exists\Diamond Wins(X) \doteq \mu Z.\{\ Wins(X) \vee \exists \bigcirc Z\ \}$$

where $Wins(X, s) \doteq Legal(s) \wedge On(1, s)$. We begin by applying the DLP method and try to show that successive approximates are equivalent using only the unique name and domain closure axioms for actions $\mathcal{D}_{ca}^{OLW}$ and the axiomatization of the integers $\mathcal{D}_Z$. We can show that the regressed approximations simplify as follows:

$\mathcal{D}_{ca}^{OLW} \cup \mathcal{D}_Z \models R_0(s) \doteq Wins(X, s) \vee \mathcal{R}(\exists \bigcirc False) \equiv Legal(s) \wedge On(1, s)$
This approximation evaluates to true if s is such that X is already winning (in no steps); these are situations where lamp 1 is on.

$\mathcal{D}_{ca}^{OLW} \cup \mathcal{D}_Z \models R_1(s) \doteq Wins(X, s) \vee \mathcal{R}(\exists \bigcirc R_0) \equiv$
$\quad Legal(s) \wedge (On(1, s) \vee On(2, s))$
This approximation evaluates to true if s is such that X can win in at most 1 step; these are legal situations where either lamp 1 is on or where lamp 2 is on, and then X can turn lamp 1 on at the next step.

$\mathcal{D}_{ca}^{OLW} \cup \mathcal{D}_Z \models R_2(s) \doteq Wins(X, s) \vee \mathcal{R}(\exists \bigcirc R_1) \equiv$
$\quad Legal(s) \wedge (On(1, s) \vee On(2, s) \vee On(3, s))$
This approximation evaluates to true if s is such that X can win in at most 2 steps; these are legal situations where either lamp 1 is on, or where lamp 2 is on (and then X can turn lamp 1 on at the next step), or where lamp 3 is on (and then X can turn on lamps 2 and 1 at the next steps).

We can generalize and show that for all natural numbers i,

$$D_{ca}^{OLW} \cup D_Z \models R_i \equiv Legal(s) \wedge \bigvee_{1 \leq j \leq i+1} On(j, s).$$

That is, X can win in at most i steps if some lamp between 1 and $i + 1$ is on. It follows that for all i, $D_{ca}^{OLW} \cup D_Z \not\models R_i \equiv R_{i+1}$, since one can always construct a model of $D_{ca}^{OLW} \cup D_Z$ where every light except $i + 2$ is off. Thus, the plain DLP method fails to converge in a finite number of steps.

Nonetheless, there is a way to strengthen the DLP method to get convergence in a finite number of steps. The idea is to use some facts that are entailed by the entire theory in addition to the unique name and domain closure axioms for actions D_{ca}^{OLW} and the integer axioms D_Z. First, we can show by induction on situations that any lamp that is on in the initial situation will remain on forever, i.e.,

$$\mathcal{D}_{GS}^{OLW} \models \forall k(On(k, S_0) \supset \forall s\, On(k, s)).$$

Then, it follows that for any natural numbers $i, j, i \leq j$,

$$\mathcal{D}_{ca}^{OLW} \cup \mathcal{D}_Z \cup \{On(i + 1, S_0), \forall k(On(k, S_0) \supset \forall s\, On(k, s))\} \models R_j \equiv Legal(s).$$

In essence, X can eventually win in any legal situation where some lamp n is known to be on. It follows that:

$$\mathcal{D}_{ca}^{OLW} \cup \mathcal{D}_Z \cup \{On(i+1, S_0), \forall k(On(k, S_0) \supset \forall s\, On(k, s))\} \models R_i \equiv R_{i+1}.$$

Thus, the method converges in a finite number of steps if we use the facts that some lamp n is known to be on initially and that a lamp that is on initially remains on forever. Moreover, our initial state axioms include $On(5, S_0)$. Thus, $\mathcal{D}_{GS}^{OLW} \models \exists\Diamond Wins(X)[S_0]$, i.e., X can eventually win in the initial situation, as it is legal and lamp 5 is on.

We can also show by induction on situations that if all lamps are off initially, they will remain so forever:

$$\mathcal{D}_{GS}^{OLW} \setminus \mathcal{D}_{S_0}^{OLW} \models (\forall k\, \neg On(k, S_0)) \supset (\forall s \forall k\, \neg On(k, s)).$$

Then, we can show by a similar argument as above that the fixpoint approximation method converges in a finite number of steps if we use the facts that all lamp are off initially and that if all lamps are off initially, they remain off forever.

3.3 In-Line Tic-Tac-Toe (TTT1D)

Our final example domain is more like a traditional game. It involves a one-dimensional version of the well-known Tic-Tac-Toe game that is played on an infinite vector of cells, one for each integer. We show that the DLP method does work to verify both the possibility of winning and the existence of a winning strategy in this game, although in the former case the proof is long and tedious. There are two players, X and O, that take turns, with X playing first. All cells are initially blank, i.e., marked B. Players can only put their mark at the left or right edge of the already marked area. The functional fluent $curn$ denotes the marking position on the left (negative) side of the marked area and similarly $curp$ denotes the marking position on the right (positive) side of the marked area. Initially, $curn$ refers to cell 0 and $curp$ to cell 1. Player p can put its mark in the cell on the left (negative) side of the marked area, i.e., the cell referred to by $curn$, by doing the action $markn(p)$. This also decreases the value $curn$ by 1 so that afterwards, it points to the next cell on the left. There is an analogous action $markp(p)$ for marking the cell on the right (positive) side of the marked area denoted by $curp$. A player wins if it succeeds in putting its mark in 3 consecutive cells. E.g., if initially we have the following sequence of moves: $[markp(X), markn(O), markp(X), markn(O), markp(X)]$, then in the resulting situation the board is as follows:

$$\ldots, B_{-3}, B_{-2}, O_{-1}, O_0, X_1, X_2, X_3, B_4, B_5, \ldots$$

(with the subscript indicating the cell number) and X wins. Note that the game may go on indefinitely without either player winning, for instance if player O always mimics the last move of player X.

The game structure axiomatization for this domain is: $\mathcal{D}_{GS}^{T^31D} = \Sigma \cup \mathcal{D}_{poss}^{T^31D} \cup \mathcal{D}_{ssa}^{T^31D} \cup \mathcal{D}_{ca}^{T^31D} \cup \mathcal{D}_{S_0}^{T^31D} \cup \mathcal{D}_{Legal}^{T^31D} \cup \mathcal{D}_Z$. The precondition axioms (in $\mathcal{D}_{poss}^{T^31D}$) state that the actions $markn(p)$ and $markp(p)$ are always possible if p is an agent. The successor state axioms (in $\mathcal{D}_{ssa}^{LW}$) are as follows:

$$\begin{aligned}
&curn(do(a,s)) = k \equiv \\
&\quad \exists p.\{a = markn(p)\} \wedge curn(s) = k+1 \vee curn(s) = k \wedge \forall p.\{a \neq markn(p)\} \\
&curp(do(a,s)) = k \equiv \\
&\quad \exists p.\{a = markp(p)\} \wedge curp(s) = k-1 \vee curp(s) = k \wedge \forall p.\{a \neq markn(p)\} \\
&cell(k, do(a,s)) = p \equiv \\
&\quad a = markp(p) \wedge curp(s) = k \ \vee a = markn(p) \wedge curn(s) = k \vee \\
&\quad cell(k,s) = p \wedge \neg\exists p'.\{a = markp(p') \wedge curp(s) = k\} \\
&\qquad \wedge \neg\exists p'.\{a = markn(p') \wedge curn(s) = k\} \\
&turn(do(a,s)) = p \equiv agent(a) = X \wedge p = O \wedge turn(s) = X \\
&\quad \vee agent(a) = O \wedge p = X \wedge turn(s) = O
\end{aligned}$$

The rules of the game are specified (in $\mathcal{D}_{legal}^{T^3 1D}$) as follows:

$$\begin{aligned}
&Legal(do(a,s)) \equiv Legal(s) \wedge \\
&\quad \exists p.\{\ turn(s) = p \wedge agent(a) = p \wedge (a = markn(p) \ \vee a = markp(p))\ \} \\
&Control(p,s) \doteq \exists a.Legal(do(a,s)) \wedge agent(a) = p \\
&agent(markn(p)) = p, \qquad agent(markp(p)) = p \\
&\forall p.\ \{Agent(p) \equiv (p = X \vee p = O)\}, \qquad X \neq O
\end{aligned}$$

The unique name and domain closure axioms for actions are specified in the usual way. Finally, we have the following initial state axioms in $\mathcal{D}_{S_0}^{T^3 1D}$: $curn(S_0) = 0$, $curp(S_0) = 1$, $turn(S_0) = X$, and $Legal(S_0)$.

We first consider whether it is possible for X to eventually win $\exists\Diamond Wins(X)$, where

$$\begin{aligned}
&Wins(p,s) \doteq \exists k(Legal(s) \wedge \\
&\quad ((curn(s) = k-2 \wedge cell(k-1,s) = p \wedge cell(k,s) = p \wedge cell(k+1,s) = p) \vee \\
&\quad (curp(s) = k+2 \wedge cell(k+1,s) = p \wedge cell(k,s) = p \wedge cell(k-1,s) = p)))
\end{aligned}$$

(Note that this simple definition allows both players to win.) If we apply the original DLP method to this property (using only the unique name and domain closure axioms for actions $\mathcal{D}_{ca}^{T^3 1D}$ and the axiomatization of the integers $\mathcal{D}_Z$ to show that successive approximates are equivalent), the fixpoint approximation procedure does eventually converge, but only after 11 steps. The proof is very long and tedious and there are numerous cases to deal with. The reason for this is that we cannot use the fact that $curn$ is always less than $curp$ and that the cells that are between them are non-blank and that the other cells are blank; these state constraints are consequences of the initial state axioms and successor state axioms. So our proof has to deal with numerous cases where there are non-blank cells to the left of $curn$ or to the right of $curp$ (if we use these state constraints, the proof becomes much simpler). We omit the detailed proof (which appears in [14]). But we have that:

$$\mathcal{D}_{ca}^{T^3 1D} \cup \mathcal{D}_Z \models R_{10}(s) \doteq Wins(X,s) \vee \mathcal{R}(\exists \bigcirc R_9) \equiv Legal(s)$$

Thus, it is possible for X to win in at most 10 steps in all legal situations. Moreover we have that $\mathcal{D}_{ca}^{T^3 1D} \cup \mathcal{D}_Z \models R_{10}(s) \equiv R_{11}(s)$, and thus the fixpoint approximation procedure converges in the 11th step. There are situations where it does take at least 10 steps/moves for X to win, for instance if we have $curp < curn$ with two blank cells in between, i.e., $\uparrow_p BB \uparrow_n$, where $\uparrow_n$ represents the position of $curn$ and similarly for $\uparrow_p$ and $curp$, and it is O's turn. The fact that $curp < curn$ means that the initial marks that are made will later be overwritten. It is straightforward to check that it takes at least 10 moves for X to have 3 X's in a row and win (O wins as well), for instance if O keeps playing $markn$ and X keeps playing $markp$. It follows from our convergence result by Theorem 1 of DLP that: $\mathcal{D}_{GS}^{T^3 1D} \models \exists\Diamond Wins(X)[S_0] \equiv R_{10}(S_0) \equiv Legal(S_0)$. Since we have $Legal(S_0)$ in the initial state axioms, it follows that $\mathcal{D}_{GS}^{T^3 1D} \models \exists\Diamond Wins(X)[S_0]$, i.e., it is possible for X to win in the initial situation.

Finally, we consider the property that X can ensure that it eventually wins $\langle\langle\{X\}\rangle\rangle\Diamond Wins(X)$. We can apply the original DLP method to this property (using only the unique name and domain closure axioms for actions $\mathcal{D}_{ca}^{T^3 1D}$ and the axiomatization of the integers $\mathcal{D}_Z$ to show that successive approximates are equivalent). We can show that the regressed approximations simplify as follows:

$$\mathcal{D}_{ca}^{T^3 1D} \cup \mathcal{D}_Z \models R_0(s) \doteq Wins(X,s) \vee \mathcal{R}(\langle\langle\{X\}\rangle\rangle \bigcirc False) \equiv Wins(X,s)$$

$$\begin{aligned}\mathcal{D}_{ca}^{T^3 1D} \cup \mathcal{D}_Z \models\ & R_1(s) \doteq Wins(X,s) \vee \mathcal{R}(\langle\langle\{X\}\rangle\rangle \bigcirc R_0)\\ &\equiv R_0(s) \vee XCanPlayToWinNext(s)\end{aligned}$$

where $XCanPlayToWinNext(s) \doteq Legal(s) \wedge turn(s) = X \wedge$

$$\begin{aligned}&(\exists k.(curn(s) = k-1 \wedge cell(k,s) = X \wedge cell(k+1,s) = X) \vee\\ &\exists k.(cell(k-2,s) = X \wedge cell(k-1,s) = X \wedge curp(s) = k) \vee\\ &\exists k.(cell(k-2,s) = X \wedge cell(k-1,s) = X \wedge curn(s) = k \wedge curp(s) = k+1) \vee\\ &\exists k.(curn(s) = k-2 \wedge curp(s) = k-1 \wedge cell(k,s) = X \wedge cell(k+1,s) = X) \vee\\ &\exists k.(cell(k-2,s) = X \wedge curn(s) = k-1 \wedge cell(k,s) = X \wedge curp(s) = k+1) \vee\\ &\exists k.(curn(s) = k-2 \wedge cell(k-1,s) = X) \wedge curp(s) = k \wedge cell(k+1,s) = X))\end{aligned}$$

This approximation evaluates to true if s is such that X can ensure to win in at most 1 step. These are legal situations where there are 3 X marks in a row on either side, i.e. $\uparrow_n XXX$ or $XXX \uparrow_p$, or where it is X's turn and there are 2 X marks already and X can fill in the missing cell to get 3 in a row, i.e. $\uparrow_n XX$ or $XX \uparrow_p$ or $\uparrow_n \uparrow_p XX$ or $XX \uparrow_n \uparrow_p$ or $\uparrow_n X \uparrow_p X$ or $X \uparrow_n X \uparrow_p$.

$$\begin{aligned}\mathcal{D}_{ca}^{T^3 1D} \cup \mathcal{D}_Z \models\ & R_2(s) \doteq Wins(X,s) \vee \mathcal{R}(\langle\langle\{X\}\rangle\rangle \bigcirc R_1) \equiv\\ & R_1(s) \vee Legal(s) \wedge turn(s) = O \wedge\\ & \exists m.(curn(s) < m-2 \wedge cell(m-2,s) = X \wedge cell(m-1,s) = X \wedge curp(s) = m) \wedge\\ & \exists n.(curn(s) = n-1 \wedge cell(n,s) = X \wedge cell(n+1,s) = X \wedge n+1 < curp(s))\end{aligned}$$

This approximation evaluates to true if s is such that X can ensure to win in at most 2 steps. These are legal situations where X can ensure to win in at most 1 step as above, or where it is O's turn and we have both $X_k X \uparrow_p$ with $\uparrow_n < k$ and $\uparrow_n XX_k$ with $\uparrow_p > k$; then if O plays $markn$ then X can play $markp$ to win afterwards, and if O plays $markp$ then X can play $markn$ to win afterwards. The next approximation $R_3(s)$ simplifies to exactly the same formula as $R_2(s)$. Thus the procedure converges in the 4th step as we have: $\mathcal{D}_{GS}^{T^3 1D} \cup \mathcal{D}_Z \models R_2(s) \equiv R_3(s)$. Therefore by Theorem 1 of DLP: $\mathcal{D}_{GS}^{T^3 1D} \models \langle\langle\{X\}\rangle\rangle\Diamond Wins(X)[S_0] \equiv R_2(S_0)$. It follows by the initial state axioms that $\mathcal{D}_{GS}^{T^3 1D} \models \neg\langle\langle\{X\}\rangle\rangle\Diamond Wins(X)[S_0]$ i.e., there is no winning strategy for X in S_0. But $\mathcal{D}_{GS}^{T^3 1D} \models \langle\langle\{X\}\rangle\rangle\Diamond Wins(X)[S_1]$, where $S_1 = do([markp(X), markn(O), markp(X), markn(O)], S_0)$, i.e., there is a winning strategy for X in a situation where X has marked twice on the right and O has marked twice on the left. We have also developed two other examples of games played on an infinite vector of cells to evaluate the DLP method; see [14] for details.

4 An Evaluation-Based Verification Tool

To further examine the feasibility of automating the DLP method, we have developed an evaluation-based Prolog implementation of a version of the method for complete initial state theories with the closed world assumption. The system can correctly verify many properties in infinite state game structures. The method is completely automated, unlike most theorem proving-based approaches. Here "evaluation-based" refers to the use of evaluation instead of entailment to check state properties under the condition of complete information (i.e., single model) and the closed-world assumption. The verifier is domain-independent. One major limitation of the current prototype is that it does not actually check for convergence of the fixpoint approximation, and thus may not terminate when the DLP method does, as we discuss later.

Our verifier builds on the logic programming evaluator for situation calculus projection queries developed by Reiter [18] for complete initial state theories with the closed world assumption. That approach uses a Prolog encoding of the domain's basic action theory as defined in [18]. For example, for the In-Line Tic-Tac-Toe domain, we have:

```
% Precondition Axioms
poss(markn(P),S)  :- agent(P).
poss(markp(P),S)  :- agent(P).
% Successor State Axioms
curn(K,do(A,S))  :- A=markn(_), curn(KX,S), K is KX - 1;
   not(A=markn(_)), curn(K,S).
curp(K,do(A,S))  :- A=markp(_), curp(KX,S), K is KX + 1;
   not(A=markp(_)), curp(K,S).
cell(K,M,do(A,S)) :- A=markp(M), curp(K,S); A=markn(M), curn(K,S);
   (not(A=markn(M)); not(curn(K,S))),
   (not(A=markp(M)); not(curp(K,S))), cell(K,M,S).
turn(P,do(A,S))  :- turn(x,S), P = o; turn(o,S), P = x.
legal(do(A,S))  :- turn(P,S), (A=markn(P) ; A=markp(P)), legal(S).
% Initial State Axioms
cell(_,b,s0). % all cells are initially blank
curn(0,s0). curp(1,s0). turn(x,s0). legal(s0).
```

One can evaluate projection queries using such a program, e.g., check whether `cell(2,b,do(markp(x),s0))`, i.e., that cell 2 is still blank after agent X marks right in the initial situation. The program works essentially by regressing the query to the initial situation and evaluating it against the initial state axioms. Regression involves replacing fluent atoms by the instantiated right-hand side of their successor state axiom, thus transforming a query about a situation into an equivalent one about the previous situation. For example, `cell(2,b,do(markp(x),s0))` is regressed into

```
markp(x)=markp(b), curp(2,s0);
markp(x)=markn(b), curn(2,s0);
(not(markp(x)=markn(b)); not(curn(2,s0))),
(not(markp(x)=markp(b)); not(curp(2,s0))), cell(2,b,s0)
```

which succeeds because the last disjunct holds according to the encoded initial state axioms and the unique name assumption.

Reiter [18] shows how to define an evaluator for a rich set of first-order queries on top of such an encoding of the basic action theory. Here is some of the evaluator code:

```
holds(P & Q,S) :-!, holds(P,S), holds(Q,S). % conjunction
holds(P v Q,S) :-!, (holds(P,S); holds(Q,S)). % disjunction
holds(some(V,P),S) :-!, subst(V,_,P,P1), holds(P1,S). %existential
% handled by replacing the variable by a fresh Prolog variable
holds(all(V,P),S) :-!, holds(-some(V,-P),S). % universal
...
% handling negation
holds(-P,S) :- ll_atom(P), !, not(holds(P,S)).
holds(-(-P),S) :- !, holds(P,S).
holds(-(P & Q),S) :- !, holds(-P v -Q,S).
holds(-(P v Q),S) :- !, holds(-P & -Q,S).
...
holds(-all(V,P),S) :- !, holds(some(V,-P),S).
holds(-P,S) :- not(holds(P,S)).
% handling atoms
holds(Pred,S) :- restoreSitArg(Pred,S,PredEx), !, PredEx.
```

The evaluator recursively evaluates the arguments of conjunctions and disjunctions. Existential quantification is left for Prolog to handle. Universal quantification is rewritten using negation and existential quantification. Negation is distributed over conjunction and disjunction. Finally, atomic fluents are regressed and evaluated using the Prolog encoding of the basic action theory.

Our verifier checks if a given temporal property expressed in the $\mathcal{L}$-Logic holds for a given situation. It is defined by extending Reiter's evaluator. We handle the key temporal operator $\langle\langle G\rangle\rangle \bigcirc \Psi[S]$ essentially by translating it into its situation calculus definition, and then checking the result in the usual way using a combination of regression and evaluation:

```
holds(canEnsureNext(G,F),S) :- !, (
   incontrol(G,S), holds(exists_successor(G,F),S);
   incontrol(-G,S), holds(forall_successors2(-G,F),S)).
holds(exists_successor(G,F),S) :- !, member(P,G),
   agent_action(P, A), S1=do(A,S), legal(S1), holds(F,S1), !.
holds(forall_successors2(-G,F),S) :- !,
   not(holds(exists_successor2(-G,-F),S)).
holds(exists_successor2(-G,F),S) :- !, agent(P), not(member(P,G)),
   agent_action(P, A), S1=do(A,S), legal(S1), holds(F,S1), !.
```

The $[[G]] \bigcirc \Psi[S]$ case is handled as $\neg\langle\langle G\rangle\rangle \bigcirc \neg\Psi[S]$.

The μ and ν operators are handled by generating successive fixpoint approximates R_i as in the DLP method, except that we bound the number of approximates generated and we do not check for convergence, we simply check if the successive approximates hold in the situation of interest S:

```
holds(mu(z,F),S) :- !, mu_approx(z,F,false,1,S).
holds(nu(z,F),S) :- !, mu_approx(z,F,true,1,S).
mu_approx(Z,F,Int,N,S) :- binding_diameter(Max), N>Max, !,
   write('binding diameter '), write(N),
   write(' reached - stop'), nl, !, fail.
mu_approx(Z,F,Int,N,S) :- subst(Z,Int,F,Fx), holds(Fx,S), !,
   output1(N,Fx).
mu_approx(Z,F,Int,N,S) :- M is N+1, subst(Z,Int,F,Int2), !,
   mu_approx(Z,F,Int2,M,S).
```

By not checking for convergence, i.e. whether $\mathcal{D} \models R_{i+1} \equiv R_i$, we avoid the need for complex logical reasoning requiring theorem proving techniques. The downside is that the verifier will never terminate on $\mu Z.\Psi$ queries that are false even if the fixpoint approximation converges, as it does not detect this. To ensure termination, the user may impose a bound on the number of approximates that are generated and evaluated. The idea is similar to the binding diameter concept in bounded model checking [3]. In some cases, the bound can be a number of moves that is reasonable in the game modeled. The formula $\langle\langle G\rangle\rangle\Diamond\Psi$ is defined in terms of the μ operator as $\mu Z.\Psi \vee \langle\langle G\rangle\rangle \bigcirc Z$:

```
holds(canEnsureEventually(G,F),S):-
   !,holds(mu(z,F v canEnsureNext(G,z)),S).
```

For this, our verifier generates fixpoint approximates and evaluates them in the given situation S, stopping as soon as one of the approximates evaluates to true:

> let $R_0 := \Psi \vee \langle\langle G\rangle\rangle \bigcirc False$ and evaluate $R_0[S]$; if it succeeds, return success;
> else let $R_1 := \Psi \vee \langle\langle G\rangle\rangle \bigcirc R_0$ and evaluate $R_1[S]$; if it succeeds, return success;
> ...
> else let $R_{limit} := \Psi \vee \langle\langle G\rangle\rangle \bigcirc R_{limit-1}$ and evaluate $R_{limit}[S]$; if it succeeds, return success;
> else return failure.

We have tested our verifier on some of our infinite state game structure examples. On the In-Line Tic-Tac-Toe domain, the verifier can confirm that both agents can cooperate to ensure that X wins (in 5 steps) in the initial situation, i.e., the following query succeeds after generating and evaluating 6 approximates:

```
?- holds(canEnsureEventually([x,o],wins(x)),s0).
trying ##### approximation 1 ---> wins(x) v next([x, o], false)
[...]
trying ##### approximation 6 ---> wins(x) v
   next([x, o], wins(x) v
      next([x, o], wins(x) v
         next([x, o], wins(x) v
            next([x, o], wins(x) v
               next([x, o], wins(x) v next([x, o], false))))))
[...]
> successor EXISTS for G --->
     next([x, o], wins(x) v next([x, o], false)) ---> for
```

```
      do(markn(o), do(markp(x), do(markn(o), do(markn(x), s0))))
[...]
> ##### approximation 6 holds --->
[...]
wins(x) v
   next([x, o], wins(x) v
      next([x, o], wins(x) v
         next([x, o], wins(x) v
            next([x, o], wins(x) v
               next([x, o], wins(x) v next([x, o], false))))))
yes
```

As part of doing the verification, the system finds a sequence of actions by the two cooperating agents that allows X to win.

The verifier can also confirm that agent X can ensure that it wins (in 1 step) in the situation $do(markn(o), do(markp(x), do(markn(o), do(markp(x), s0))))$, where X has already put 2 marks on the right and O had already put 2 marks on the left. However, if we try to check if X can ensure that it wins in the situation $do(markp(x), do(markn(o), do(markp(x), s0)))$, where X has already put 2 marks on the right and O had already put 1 mark on the left, the verifier cannot confirm that the query is in fact false; it keeps generating successive approximates and eventually gives up after reaching the binding diameter. The problem is that O can always prevent X from winning at the next step and the verifier is not checking whether it has converged to a fixpoint in the approximation.

We have also tested our verifier on the Light World domain. This is more challenging because there are infinitely many legal actions at every state, as any switch can be flipped. The verifier succeeds in confirming that X can ensure that it wins in the situation where it flipped light 2 on initially and then O flipped light 4 on, as X can win in one step by flipping light 1 on next. But it cannot confirm that the two agents can cooperate to ensure that X eventually wins in the initial situation S_0. The problem is that this requires two steps (where X first flips light 1 or 2 on and then O flips the other one on) and there is an infinite number of flipping actions that can be performed at the first step, all of which must be considered before concluding that X cannot win in one step in S_0. If we bound the set of switches that are considered (e.g., only allow flipping the first 10 switches), then the verifier will be able to successfully verify that the query holds. It first establishes that X cannot win in one step (e.g., by flipping any of the 10 available switches) and then succeeds in finding a sequence of two actions that allows X to win. However, bounding the set of switches essentially makes the game finite state and changes what temporal properties hold. A better approach would be to modify the game to allow the set of switches considered to be progressively expanded, perhaps by a neutral agent. The important thing is to allow more actions/branches in a state only as longer sequences of actions are considered.

Additionally, the verifier cannot show that X cannot ensure that it eventually wins in the situation where it has already flipped light 2 on (as O can flip it off next and continue undoing any progress that X makes towards the goal). The verifier succeeds in showing that O can prevent X from winning at the next step (O can flip any switch except 1). It then generates the third approximate and tries to show that X can win in one step after every action that O makes next. If we bound the set of switches that are considered, the verifier can confirm that X cannot win in two steps as O can flip light 2 off next. The verifier keeps generating and evaluating successive approximates and eventually gives up after reaching the binding diameter. It does not check whether successive approximates are equivalent, and thus fails to detect that the fixpoint approximation has converged after generating the fourth approximate.

We have also tested our verifier on a formalization of the standard 2D Tic-Tac-Toe game (used as an example in [8]), a finite state domain. In this case the verifier can do a complete search and correctly answers queries about the existence of a winning strategy. For example, it can confirm that X cannot ensure that it eventually wins in the initial situation with a blank board; it can also confirm that X can ensure that it eventually wins in a situation where X has marked the center square and O has then marked a non-corner square.

To summarize, in finite state domains the verifier correctly answers queries as it can do a complete search. In infinite state domains, our verifier can often show that least fixpoint queries are true but cannot show that least fixpoint queries are false (and greatest fixpoint queries are true), because it does not check whether successive approximates are equivalent. We hope to address this in future work.

In many cases, we would like to verify properties assuming that agents are following certain strategies, or have certain strategic preferences. For example, in standard 2D Tic-Tac-Toe, one might know that a player always tries to mark corners first. This would allow modelling more realistic types of agents. It can also cut down significantly on the number of alternative actions that must be considered and speed up verification. Knowing that the opponent follows certain strategic preferences may provide the player with a way to ensure it eventually wins when it could not otherwise.

We have extended the DLP formalization to support this. There are many ways to model strategic preferences. A simple approach is to assume that the modeler defines a predicate $\mathit{Preferred}(p, a, s)$ that holds if and only if action a is a preferred action for player p in situation s. Note that there may be several alternative preferred actions in a situation. Other specifications of strategic preferences can be mapped to this form.

It is straightforward to modify the logic to only consider paths where all players select actions according to their preferences. We change the semantics of the $\langle\langle G\rangle\rangle \bigcirc \Psi$ operator as follows. If a player in G is in control in the current situation, Ψ must hold after some preferred action for him if there is one; if there is no preferred action, Ψ must hold after some legal action. If a player not in G is in control, Ψ must hold after all preferred actions for him if there is some preferred action, and after all legal actions if there is none. This means that $\mathit{Preferred}(p, a, s)$ represents soft constraints. If there are no preferred actions in a situation, we revert to considering all legal actions. Our implementation supports this type of specification of player action preferences and we have tested it on some standard 2D Tic-Tac-Toe examples.

Our verifier also supports the use of the GameGolog language proposed in DLP to specify the game structure procedurally. See [14] for more details. The current prototype implemented in SWI Prolog (`www.swi-prolog.org`), together with some examples, is available at `www.cse.yorku.ca/~skmiec/SCGSverifier/`. We believe that our verifier implementation is sound (assuming a "proper" Prolog interpreter is used, i.e., one that flounders on negative queries with free variables). It is not complete, in part for the same reasons that Prolog is not a complete reasoner for first order logic. We leave the proof of soundness for future work.

5 Discussion and Related and Future Work

In this paper, we described the results of some case studies to evaluate whether the DLP verification method actually works. We developed various infinite state game-type domains and applied the method to them. Our example domains are rather simple, but have features present in practical examples (e.g., the $T^3 1D$ domain is 1D version of Tic-Tac-Toe on an infinite board). Our experiments do confirm that the method does work on several non-trivial verification problems with infinite state space. We also identify some examples where the method, which only uses the simplest part of the domain theory, the unique names and domain closure for action axioms, fails to converge in a finite number of steps. We show that in some of these cases, extending the method to use some selected facts about the initial situation and some state constraints does allow us to get convergence in a finite number of steps. Our example domains and properties should be useful for evaluating other approaches to infinite state verification and synthesis.

We also described an evaluation-based Prolog implementation of a version of the DLP method for complete initial state theories with the closed world assumption. It generates successive approximates and checks if they hold in the situation of interest, but does not check if the sequence of approximates converges. Our verifier is fully automatic, unlike most theorem proving-based tools. We have also extended the framework to allow agents' strategic preferences to be represented and used in verification. See [14] for more details about our verification experiments, proofs, and implemented verifier.

Among related work that deals with verification in infinite-states domains, let us mention [5,6], which also uses methods based on fixpoint approximation. There, characteristic graphs are introduced to finitely represent the possible configurations that a Golog program representing a multi-agent interaction may visit. Their specification language is rich modal variant of the situation calculus with first and second order quantifiers, temporal operators and path quantifiers as in CTL*, and dynamic logic operators labeled with Golog programs. However, the language does not include fixpoint operators or alternating-time quantifiers, and is not a game structure logic. In their verification procedure, like DLP, they check for convergence using only the unique name axioms for actions part of the action theory. Also closely related is [19], which uses a fixpoint approximation method to compose a target process expressed as a ConGolog program out of a library of available ConGolog programs. Earlier, [13] proposed a fixpoint approximation method to verify a class of temporal properties in the situation calculus, called property persistence formulas. [20] shows how a theorem proving tool can be used to verify properties of multi-agent systems specified in ConGolog and an extended situation calculus with mental states. A leading example of a symbolic model checker for multi-agent systems is MCMAS [15]. [2] shows that model checking of an expressive temporal language on infinite state systems is decidable if the active domain in all states remains bounded. As well, [10] shows that verification of temporal properties in bounded situation calculus theories where there is a bound on the number of fluent atoms that are true in any situation is decidable. [7] identifies an interesting class of Golog programs and action theories for which verification is decidable.

In future work, we would like to further develop our evaluation-based verifier. We plan to extend it to perform limited symbolic reasoning to detect if successive approximates are equivalent. We will also do more experimental evaluation. We would also like to implement an open-world symbolic version of the DLP method, perhaps by writing proof tactics in a theorem proving environment. It would also be desirable to develop techniques for identifying initial state properties and state constraints that can be used to show finite convergence in cases where these are needed. More generally, we need a better characterization of when this kind of method can be used successfully. The DLP framework assumes that only one agent can act in any situation, and that all agents have complete knowledge of the situation and that actions are fully observable. As a first step, it would be interesting to extend it to support synchronous moves by multiple agents. Going further, the framework should be generalized to deal with private knowledge and partial observability. Finally, the approach should be evaluated on real practical problems.

References

1. Alur, R., Henzinger, T.A., Kupferman, O.: Alternating-time temporal logic. J. ACM 49(5), 672–713 (2002)
2. Belardinelli, F., Lomuscio, A., Patrizi, F.: An abstraction technique for the verification of artifact-centric systems. In: Brewka, G., Eiter, T., McIlraith, S.A. (eds.) Principles of Knowledge Representation and Reasoning: Proceedings of the Thirteenth International Conference, KR 2012, Rome, Italy, June 10-14, pp. 319–328. AAAI Press (2012)
3. Biere, A.: Bounded model checking. In: Biere, A., Heule, M., van Maaren, H., Walsh, T. (eds.) Handbook of Satisfiability, pp. 457–481. IOS Press (2009)
4. Bradfield, J., Stirling, C.: Modal mu-calculi. In: Handbook of Modal Logic, vol. 3, pp. 721–756. Elsevier (2007)
5. Claßen, J., Lakemeyer, G.: A logic for non-terminating Golog programs. In: Brewka, G., Lang, J. (eds.) Principles of Knowledge Representation and Reasoning: Proceedings of the Eleventh International Conference, KR 2008, Sydney, Australia, September 16-19, pp. 589–599. AAAI Press (2008)
6. Claßen, J., Lakemeyer, G.: On the verification of very expressive temporal properties of non-terminating Golog programs. In: Coelho, H., Studer, R., Wooldridge, M. (eds.) Proceedings of 19th European Conference on Artificial Intelligence, ECAI 2010, Lisbon, Portugal, August 16-20, pp. 887–892. IOS Press (2010)
7. Claßen, J., Liebenberg, M., Lakemeyer, G.: On decidable verification of non-terminating Golog programs. In: Proceedings of the 10th International Workshop on Nonmonotonic Reasoning, Action and Change (NRAC 2013), Beijing, China, pp. 13–20 (2013)
8. De Giacomo, G., Lesperance, Y., Pearce, A.R.: Situation calculus-based programs for representing and reasoning about game structures. In: Lin, F., Sattler, U., Truszczynski, M. (eds.) Principles of Knowledge Representation and Reasoning: Proceedings of the Twelfth International Conference, KR 2010, Toronto, Ontario, Canada, May 9-13, pp. 445–455 (2010)
9. De Giacomo, G., Lespérance, Y., Levesque, H.J.: ConGolog, a concurrent programming language based on the situation calculus. Artificial Intelligence 121(1–2), 109–169 (2000)

10. De Giacomo, G., Lespérance, Y., Patrizi, F.: Bounded Situation Calculus Action Theories and Decidable Verification. In: Brewka, G., Eiter, T., McIlraith, S.A. (eds.) Principles of Knowledge Representation and Reasoning: Proceedings of the Thirteenth International Conference, KR 2012, Rome, Italy, June 10-14, pp. 467–477. AAAI Press (2012)
11. Enderton, H.B.: A mathematical introduction to logic. Academic Press (1972)
12. Hamilton, A.G.: Numbers, Sets and Axioms: The Apparatus of Mathematics. Cambridge University Press (1982)
13. Kelly, R.F., Pearce, A.R.: Property persistence in the situation calculus. Artif. Intell. 174(12-13), 865–888 (2010)
14. Kmiec, S.: Infinite States Verification in Game-Theoretic Logics. Master's thesis, Dept. of Electrical Engineering and Computer Science, York University, Toronto, Canada (2013)
15. Lomuscio, A., Qu, H., Raimondi, F.: MCMAS: A model checker for the verification of multi-agent systems. In: Bouajjani, A., Maler, O. (eds.) CAV 2009. LNCS, vol. 5643, pp. 682–688. Springer, Heidelberg (2009)
16. McCarthy, J., Hayes, P.: Some philosophical problems from the standpoint of artificial intelligence. In: Machine Intelligence, vol. 4, pp. 463–502. Edinburgh University Press (1969)
17. Park, D.: Finiteness is mu-ineffable. Theor. Comput. Sci. 3(2), 173–181 (1976)
18. Reiter, R.: Knowledge in Action. Logical Foundations for Specifying and Implementing Dynamical Systems. MIT Press (2001)
19. Sardina, S., De Giacomo, G.: Composition of ConGolog programs. In: Boutilier, C. (ed.) IJCAI 2009, Proceedings of the 21st International Joint Conference on Artificial Intelligence, Pasadena, California, USA, July 11-17, pp. 904–910 (2009)
20. Shapiro, S., Lespérance, Y., Levesque, H.J.: The cognitive agents specification language and verification environment for multiagent systems. In: The First International Joint Conference on Autonomous Agents & Multiagent Systems, AAMAS 2002, Bologna, Italy, July 15-19, pp. 19–26. ACM Press (2002)

Side Effects of Agents Are Not Just Random

Bruno Mermet and Gaële Simon

Greyc – CNRS UMR 6072
Bruno.Mermet@univ-lehavre.fr

Abstract. Side effects are an important characteristic of MAS, and proving them is an interesting issue. They often can be expressed as liveness properties. But there is no system dedicated to this kind of proof. The GDT4MAS framework allows to specify and prove the correctness of multiagent systems. This framework is mainly dedicated to prove safety properties about the system and to prove that agents achieve their goal(s). However, there is no proof principle to prove that agents satisfy liveness properties that are not part of their goal(s). In this article, we propose a proof mechanism that addresses this kind of problem: we show how we can add to GDT4MAS a proof mechanism adapted to prove leads-to properties, a subclass of liveness properties.

1 Introduction

During the execution of a MAS, unexpected system properties are often observed. These properties can either be useful (they can be for example called *emergent properties*) or harmful. In both cases, it may be interesting to prove that such properties will eventually happen in order to understand how they happen. However, to our knowledge, there is no system suitable to prove such properties.

Proving the correctness of multiagent systems is a hard problem that has been tackled for several years. Most of the works on the subject have established that a new formal specification and proof system, dedicated to multiagent systems, should be developed. Among them, GDT4MAS [1] proposes interesting characteristics. Especially, the proof obligation generation process is fully automatisable and it can be applied to very large systems, essentially because it relies on theorem proving and first-order logic rather than on model-checking and propositional logic.

However, if this system is well-suited to prove invariant properties (also called safety properties) and to guarantee that agents satisfy their main goal, it does not propose any proof system to guarantee that an agent establishes liveness properties that are not part of its main goal, which is necessary when considering side effects.

So, in this article, we propose to add a new proof system to GDT4MAS dedicated to the verification of a well-known kind of liveness properties: *leads-to* properties.

F. Dalpiaz et al. (Eds.): EMAS 2014, LNAI 8758, pp. 291–308, 2014.

Of course, there are techniques to verify leads-to properties in distributed systems [2,3,4], but these techniques are dedicated to systems where all the processes are globally taken into account for each proof that must be performed.

Most of these techniques are dedicated to systems where processes work on independant variables, and synchronize occasionnaly to exchange information (This for instance the case of the π-calculus [4]).

On the contrary, in a method such as TLA$^+$ [3], shared variables can be specified, but the proof process requires to consider, for each step of the system trace, all the actions that may be considered. This is not suitable for multi-agents systems, because the number of possible actions is very large and thus, the property to prove would be to complicated to be performed by an automatic (or human) prover.

To perform efficient proofs on multi-agents systems, a compositional proof system is required. This is the case of the GDT4MAS proof system, and this is a property we require for a proof system dedicated to leads-to properties in multi-agents systems.

In the next section, we briefly introduce the notion of liveness property. In section 3, we recall the main concepts of the GDT4MAS framework. The new proof system we propose is described in section 4, and its application is examplified in section 5. Finally, a comparison with other works is proposed in section 6.

2 Invariant and Liveness Properties

When dealing with formal verification of software, many kinds of properties may be considered. In this section, we present two kinds of them: invariant properties and liveness properties.

2.1 Invariant Properties

Invariant properties specify a set of states the system must satisfy at every moment. They are often presented as properties specifying that "nothing bad happens". Theses properties are mainly safety properties. Indeed, when specifying safety critical systems (as, for instance, a train control system), a first critial step is to verify that the system does not reach an unsafe state. In a formal verification system such as the B method, used by corporates developing safety critical systems, this kind of property is the only one that is formally proven.

Using temporal logic, an invariant property IP is specified as:

$$\Box(IP)$$

However, a system doing nothing may trivially verify such invariant properties. Indeed, these properties do not specify anything about the task of the system.

2.2 Liveness Properties

Contrary to invariant properties, liveness properties specify how the system should modify its state. They are often presented as properties specifying that "something good will happen". There are many kinds of liveness properties. Here are a small presentation of some of them. More details can be found for instance in [2,3].

- **One-day**: a given property OD will eventually become true:

$$\Diamond(OD)$$

- **Leads-to**: a given property LT will eventually become true every time another property P is true:

$$\Box(P \rightarrow \Diamond LT)$$

- **Until**: a given property UP remains true until another property becomes true (and P will eventually become true):

$$\Box(UP \rightarrow (\Box(UP \vee P) \wedge \Diamond P)$$

In the rest of this article, we will only consider *leads-to* properties. Indeed, a *one-day* property is a subtype of a *leads-to* property (with $P \triangleq true$ and $LT \triangleq OD$), and an *until* property is also a special kind of *leads-to* property.

3 The GDT4MAS Framework and the GDT Model

3.1 Main Concepts

In the GDT4MAS framework, the MAS is described by an environment, mainly specified by variables, an invariant (denoted $i_{\mathcal{E}}$ in the sequel) and a population of agents evolving in this environment. Each agent is described as an instance of an agent type. As a consequence, in the following, after a short description of the notations we use, the notions of agent type and of agent behaviour are described.

3.2 Notation

Notation 1 (primed and unprimed variable)
When the value of a variable v in two execution states is considered, the value of v in the first state, called the current state, is written v, and its value in the second state is written v'. For instance, the action consisting in increasing the value of v by 1 is specified by the postcondition $v' = v + 1$.

3.3 Agent Type Specification

Simplified Definition 2 (Agent Type) *An agent type t is mainly described by a name ($name_t$), a set of variables ($VarI_t$), an invariant (i_A), and a behaviour (b_t) defined by a GDT.*

Definition 3 (Goal Decomposition Tree (GDT)). *A Goal Decomposition Tree describes the behaviour of the agents of a given type. Each node of this tree is a GDT goal. The tree structure is defined thanks to the decomposition of each GDT goal into subgoals using decomposition operators. A predicate called Triggering Context (TC) is associated to each GDT: an agent begins the execution of its behaviour every time its TC is true.*

Simplified Definition 4 (GDT goal) *A GDT goal g is described by a name ($name_g$), a satisfaction condition (sc_g), a gpf (gpf_g), a decomposition or an action and an ns flag (ns_g). The satisfaction condition is a predicate specifying the property the goal must establish when it succeeds, whereas the gpf (*Guaranted Property in case of Failure*) is a predicate specifying the property the goal must establish when its execution fails. The ns flag specifies whether the goal always succeeds (*Necessarily Satsfiable or NS*) or not (NNS).*

Please notice that when the execution of a node fails, the invariant must still remain true. The failure of a node represents the fact that, in a real world, an agent is not always guaranted to succeed in realizing a task dealing with the environment. For instance, a robot that must move its arm may be blocked by an object, or its arm may be rusty, reducing the amplitude of its move. However, even when the execution of a goal fails, the invariant must be preserved, because the safety of the system must still be ensured.

Simplified Definition 5 (Action) *An action α is specified by a name ($name_\alpha$), a precondition (pre_α), a postcondition ($post_\alpha$), an ns flag (ns_α) and a gpf (gpf_α). The precondition is a predicate specifying when the action is enabled, the postcondition specifies what that action does ($x' = x - 1$ for instance expresses that the action decreases the value of x by 1), the ns flag has the value NS if the action is guaranteed to always succeed, and NNS if the action may fail. The gpf is a predicate specifying what is however guaranteed to be true if the action fails.*

Definition 6 (Goal decomposition). *A GDT goal is either a leaf goal or an intermediate goal. An action is attached to a leaf goal, whereas an intermediate goal is decomposed into several subgoals, thanks to a decomposition operator. A list of decomposition operators can be found in [5].*

Among others, we can introduce the following decomposition operators:

- **SeqOr**: Sequential Or. It decomposes the parent goal N into several subgoals N_i. Subgoals are executed from the left to the right. If the considered subgoal succeeds, N is achieved and the execution of the decomposition ends. But if it fails, the next subgoal is considered. If the last subgoal is executed and fails, the satisfaction condition of N must be evaluated to know if N is however achieved or not.
- **SeqAnd**: Sequential And. It decomposes the parent goal N into several subgoals N_i. Subgoals are executed from the left to the right. If the considered subgoal succeeds, the next one is executed. If the last subgoal is executed and succeeds, N is achieved. But if a subgoal fails, the satisfaction condition of N must be evaluated to determine whether N is achieved or not.

- **SyncSeqOr** and **SyncSeqAnd**: These operators are similar to the SeqOr and SeqAnd operator, but a subset of environment variables can be locked during the whole execution of the parent goal decomposition.

An example of GDT is given in figure 1. In this figure, goals are described by their satisfaction condition. Moreover, NS goals are surrounded by a double ellipse. In satisfaction conditions, x and x' respectively represent the value of the variable x before and after the goal execution.

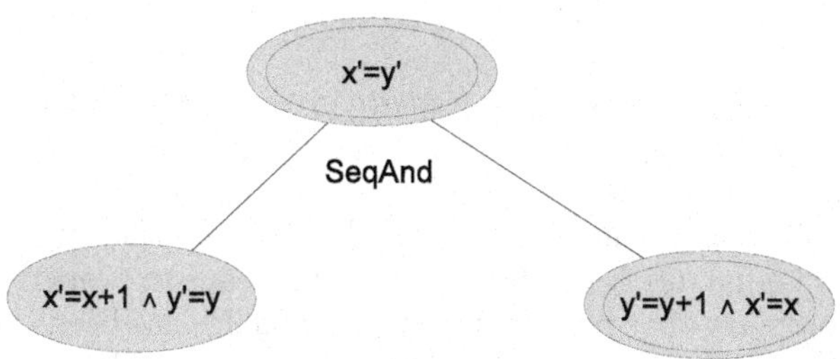

Fig. 1. Simple GDT

3.4 Proof System: General Principles

The proof system for GDT4MAS relies on *Proof Schemas* (PS). Applying a proof schema generates *Proof Obligations* (PO), that may be proven by an automatic prover, such as PVS [6]. At the moment, PS allow us to prove several kinds of properties. We first prove invariants at the agent-type level and at the system-level. Moreover, the proof system of the method verifies that goal decompositions are valid. Most PS rely on goal contexts. These contexts are computed automatically starting from the root goal. Intuitively, the context C_G of a goal G is a predicate summarizing the state in which goal G will be executed.

3.5 Notations

In this section, we present two notations of GDT4MAS that will be used in the sequel.

Notation 7 (Priming) *Let f be a predicate/expression. If f contains at least one primed variable, then $pr(f) = f$. Otherwise, $pr(f)$ is the predicate/expression derived from f where each unsubscripted variable is primed.*

Examples: $pr((x = x_0)) \equiv (x' = x_0)$ and $pr((x = x')) \equiv (x = x')$.

Notation 8 (Invariant) *Let A an agent situated in an environment $\mathcal{E}$. We write:*

- *i_A the invariant regarding variables of the agent;*
- *$i_{\mathcal{E}}$ the invariant associated to the environment variables;*
- *$i_{\mathcal{E}A}$ the conjunction of i_A and $i_{\mathcal{E}}$.*

4 A New Proof Mechanism Dedicated to Leads-to Properties

This section presents the proof mechanism we propose to verify that some leads-to properties are established by an agent. Here, we only consider leads-to properties that are associated to an agent; no other agent is required to establish this property.

In this section, we consider a *leads-to* property L defined so:

$$L \equiv \Box(P_L \rightarrow \Diamond Q_L)$$

A classical way to establish that a *leads-to* property is verified by a specification consists in associating a *variant* and a *witness* to this property [2].

Informally, a variant expresses the progress towards the establishment of Q_L. If it is proven that an agent makes a variant decrease and that when this variant reaches its lower bound, Q_L is established, then the leads-to property L is proven. A witness is a property that represents the fact that P_L has been true, and thus, that Q_L must be established. In this article we propose to adapt this mechanism to verify leads-to properties of agents.

4.1 Definitions and Notations

We begin by a formal definition of a variant:

Definition 9 (Variant). *A variant is a decreasing sequence defined in a well-founded structure.*

Of course, this definition requires to define what a well-founded stucture is.

Definition 10 (Well-founded Structure). *A well-founded structure* $(S, <)$ *is a set* S *with an order relation* $<$ *such that every decreasing sequence in* S *has a lower bound. For instance,* $(\mathbb{N}, <)$ *is a well-founded structure.*

Corollary 11 *A variant has a lower bound. We write* ${V_0}_L$ *the lower bound of a variant* V_L.

In this article, we will only consider variants defined on $(\mathbb{N}, <)$. This property must be added to the invariant of the agent.

Definition 12 (Witness). *Let* $L \equiv \Box(P_L \rightarrow \Diamond Q_L)$ *a leads-to property. A witness is a property that must be true when* P_L *is true, and remains true until* Q_L *is true.*

Notation 13 (Variant and Witness) *Let* L *a leads-to property associated to an agent* A. *We write:*

- V_L *the variant we associate to* L *to prove it;*
- ${V_0}_L$ *the lower bound of the variant* V_L*;*
- W_L *the witness we associate to* L *to prove it.*

4.2 Sketch of the Proof Process

Thanks to the variant and witness we associate to a leads-to property, proving that an agent establishes a leads-to property L consists in proving that:

1. The chosen variant is a variant:
   - when it has reached its lower bound, Q_L is established;
   - once P_L has been true and until Q_L becomes true, the agent must execute its gdt.
   - there is no other agent that increases the variant;
2. The chosen witness is a witness;
   - it is true when P_L is true;
   - when W_L is true, it remains true until Q_L becomes true.
3. The agent progresses: when the agent executes its gdt, it makes the variant decrease or it establishes Q_L.

In the next parts of this section, we detail each of these steps.

4.3 The Chosen Variant Is... a Variant!

To prove that V_L is a variant, we have to prove that, when it has reached its lower bound, the desired property is satisfied. So, we have to add the following proof obligation:

$$i_{\mathcal{E}A} \wedge (V_L = V_{0_L}) \rightarrow Q_L \tag{1}$$

Moreover, we also have to prove that once P_L has been true, and until Q_L becomes true, the agent is activated, and thus executes its GDT. This is established by proving the following property, where TC_A is the triggering context of the agent:

$$i_{\mathcal{E}A} \wedge W_L \wedge \neg Q_L \rightarrow TC_A \tag{2}$$

Finally, we also have to prove that no other agent makes the variant increase once P_L has been established until Q_L is established. So, for each other agent A in the system, we have to check for every action α used in a leaf goal G (we recall that *post* and *gpf* of actions contain primed variables):

$$i_{\mathcal{E}A} \wedge C_G \wedge W_L \wedge (post_\alpha \vee gpf_\alpha) \rightarrow pr(V_L) \leq V_L \tag{3}$$

4.4 The Witness Property... Is a Witness!

As explained before, we associate to our *leads-to* property L a witness property W_L that verify both following properties:

- **Initialisation** : W_L must be true when P_L is true;
  The property that must be verified is the following:

$$i_{\mathcal{E}A} \wedge P_L \rightarrow W_L \tag{4}$$

- **Finalization** : W_L remains true until Q_L becomes true.
  For each agent, we have to establish that, when it modifies the environment (that is to say, when it performs an action, whether it succeeds or not), if the witness is true before the action, then it is still true after the action has been performed, unless Q_L has become true. So, for each action α associated to a leaf goal G of each agent A, we have to verify:

$$i_{\mathcal{E}A} \wedge C_G \wedge W_L \wedge (post_\alpha \vee gpf_\alpha) \rightarrow pr(W_L \vee Q_L) \tag{5}$$

4.5 The Agent Progresses

In order to prove that each execution of the GDT of an agent defines a progress towards the establishment of property Q_L, we have to prove that the execution of the main goal performs such a progress, that is to say, the main goal of the agent is a *progress goal*.

Definition 14 (Progress goal (pg)). *We call* Progress Goal *a goal that either makes the variant decrease or establishes property Q_L. For a leads-to property L, we associate to each goal G a boolean pg_{L_G} that is true if and only if G is a progress goal.*

Determining that a goal is a progress goal can be done by inference rules relying on the structure of the gdt, once we know which leaf goals make progress. Moreover, as the gdt execution depends on the success status of goals, we must determine, for each goal, if it is a *success progress goal* and if it is a *failure progress goal*.

Definition 15 (Success Progress Goal (spg)). *We call* Success Progress Goal *a goal that either makes the variant decrease or establishes property Q_L when it is executed and succeeds. For a leads-to property L, we associate to each goal G a boolean spg_{L_G} that is true if and only if G is a success progress goal.*

Definition 16 (Failure Progress Goal (fpg)). *We call* Failure Progress Goal *a goal that either makes the variant decrease or establishes property Q_L when it is executed and fails. For a leads-to property L, we associate to each goal G a boolean fpg_{L_G} that is true if and only if G is a failure progress goal.*

Corollary 17 *A goal is a progress goal if and only if it is a success progress goal and a failure progress goal. So, for every goal G, we have $pg_{L_G} = spg_{L_G} \wedge fpg_{L_G}$.*

In the following paragraphs, we first present how we determine spg and fpg leaf goals, and then, we show how we infer these properties for non-leaf goals. Finally, we give proof schemas that we have to associate to non-spg and non-fpg leaf goals.

Determining the Set of spg and fpg Leaf Goals. To determine if a goal is a spg goal, we have to check that when this goal succeeds (and so, establishes its satisfaction condition), it either makes the variant decrease or establishes Q_L. Of course, we must only consider executions of this goal performed when P_L has been true, which is specified by the fact that W_L is true. Hence the following property that must be established by each non lazy[1] spg leaf goal G:

$$(i_{\mathcal{E}A} \wedge W_L \wedge C_G \wedge pr(sc_G)) \rightarrow ((pr(V_L) < V_L \vee pr(Q_L)) \qquad (6)$$

In the same way, a goal G is a fpg leaf goal if and only if it verifies the following property:

$$(i_{\mathcal{E}A} \wedge W_L \wedge C_G \wedge pr(gpf_G)) \rightarrow ((pr(V_L) < V_L \vee pr(Q_L)) \qquad (7)$$

Please notice that, the gpf of an NS goal being $false$, such goals are *fpg* goals.

Inference of spg and fpg Properties. A first way to ensure that a non-leaf goal is spg or fpg consists in demonstrating that it is a consequence of the decomposition. In this article, we only detail this process for the SeqAnd/SyncSeqAnd and SeqOr/SyncSeqOr operators.

SeqAnd and SyncSeqAnd : Let G a goal decomposed into G_1 *SeqAnd* G_2.

G is a spg goal, if, in all the cases where G may succeed, the variant decreases. Goal G may succeed in three cases, detailed below:

- Of course, G succeeds when G_1 then G_2 succeed. In this case, if either G_1 or G_2 are spg goals, goal G makes the variant decrease.
- Because of side effects, G may also succeed even if G_1 has failed. Then, G_1 must be fpg.
- Finally, G may also succeed when G_1 has succeeded, leading to the execution of G_2, which has failed. In this case, if G_1 is spg or G_2 is fpg, then the variant decreases.

So, we are guaranted that goal G is spg if:

$$\begin{cases} spg_{L_{G_1}} \wedge spg_{L_{G_2}} \\ fpg_{L_{G_1}} \\ spg_{L_{G_1}} \wedge fpg_{L_{G_2}} \end{cases}$$

As a consequence, here is a sufficient condition to determine that a goal is a spg goal:

$$fpg_{L_{G_1}} \wedge (spg_{L_{G_1}} \vee pg_{LG_2}) \rightarrow spg_{L_G} \qquad (8)$$

[1] In this article, we only focus on non lazy goals, that is to say goals that are always executed even if their satisfaction condition is already true when the goal is considered.

Now, to determine if G is a fpg goal, we consider both cases where it can fail, that is to say when its first subgoal fails or when its second subgoal fails after the first one has succeded. Hence:

$$fpg_{L_{G_1}} \wedge (spg_{L_{G_1}} \vee fpg_{L_{G_2}}) \rightarrow fpg_{L_G} \tag{9}$$

SeqOr and SyncSeqOr : Let G a goal decomposed into G_1 *SeqOr* G_2.
Goal G may succeed in the three following cases:

- goal G_1 succeeds;
- goal G_1 fails, and then, goal G_2 succeeds.
- goal G_1 fails, and then, goal G_2 fails but, because of side effects, goal G succeeds anyway.

So, we have:

$$spg_{L_{G_1}} \wedge (fpg_{L_{G_1}} \vee pg_{L_{G_2}}) \rightarrow spg_{L_G} \tag{10}$$

The only case where Goal G may fail is when G_1 and G_2 fail. So, the fact that one of theses goals is spg ensure that G is spg. Hence:

$$fpg_{L_{G_1}} \vee fpg_{L_{G_2}} \rightarrow fpg_{L_G} \tag{11}$$

Using Satisfaction Conditions to Determine spg Goals Inference rules 8 and 10 to determine if a goal is spg give sufficient properties, but theses properties are not always necessary. A typical example is when the satisfaction condition of a non-leaf goal directly establishes either Q_L or makes the variant decrease. So, for every non leaf goal G that has not been characterized as a spg goal by the inference rules described above, we will also verify if property 6 is true. If this is the case, goal G can be identified as an spg goal. An example of such a case is given in the case study, section 5.2.

Non-fpg and Non-spg Leaf Goals. When a leaf goal G is not a spg goal, we however must prove that this goal does not make the variant increase when it succeeds. So, for each non-spg goal, we have to prove the following formula:

$$i_{\mathcal{E}A} \wedge W_L \wedge C_G \wedge pr(sc_G) \rightarrow pr(V_L) \leq V_L \tag{12}$$

In the same way, for each goal G that is not a fpg goal, we must prove:

$$i_{\mathcal{E}A} \wedge W_L \wedge C_G \wedge gpf_G \rightarrow pr(V_L) \leq V_L \tag{13}$$

Indeed, this is necessary to guarantee that between two steps during which the agent makes the variant decrease, it is not increased in another way.

5 Application on a Small Example

We choose here of course a very simple example, in order to be able to present all the principles of the proof. We consider a "multiagent system" with only one agent modifying the variant.

Please notice that the system may contain several other agents. In this case, as explained in section 4.3, it has to be proven that their actions do not increase the variant. Taking into account the dynamicity of the environment relies on the same principle, because, as explained in previous articles, the dynamicity of the environment can be modeled by an agent modifiying the state of the environment.

The environment contains two variables, x and d, and is specified by the following invariant:

$$i_{\mathcal{E}} = \begin{cases} x \in \mathbb{N} \\ d \in \mathbb{B} \\ d \leftrightarrow (x > 0 \wedge x \leq 10) \end{cases} \tag{14}$$

Our agent has a behaviour described by the GDT given in figure 2. In this figure, goals names (from A to E) and their *simplified* satisfaction conditions are given. By *simplified* SC, we mean that we did not write the part specifying that the value of other variables are not modified. For instance, the full SC of node D is $y' = 2 \wedge x' = x \wedge d' = d$.

Informally, the goal of this agent is to decrease the value of the environment variable x, by 2 if possible, and otherwise by 1.

Moreover, the triggering context of the agent, its invariant and the gpf of node E are defined so:

$$TC_a \triangleq d \tag{15}$$

$$I_a \triangleq (y \in \mathbb{N}) \tag{16}$$

$$gpf_E \triangleq x' = x \wedge d' = d \tag{17}$$

$$gpf_B \triangleq x' = x \tag{18}$$

We want to prove that this agent establishes the following leads-to property:

$$\Box(x = 10 \rightarrow \Diamond x = 0) \tag{19}$$

As you can see, this is not directly a goal of the agent, whose behaviour only specifies that it reduces the value of variable x when variable d is true.

We will use x as the variant and d as the witness. To conform to the notation used in the previous section, we have:

$$P_L \triangleq (x = 10) \tag{20}$$

$$Q_L \triangleq (x = 0) \tag{21}$$

$$V_L \triangleq (x) \tag{22}$$

$$V_{0_L} \triangleq (0) \tag{23}$$

$$W_L \triangleq (d) \tag{24}$$

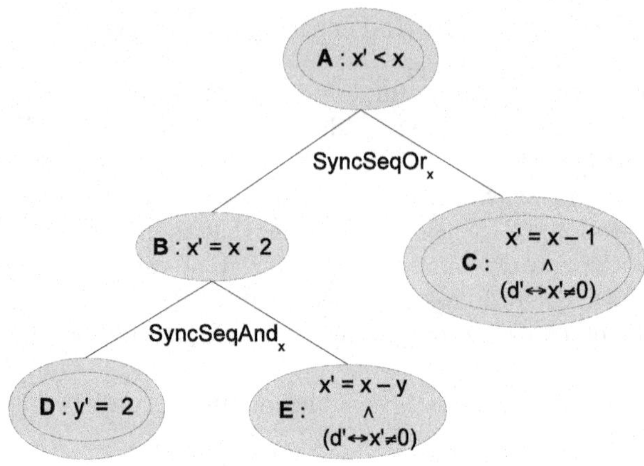

Fig. 2. GDT of the example

This article beeing focused on the proof of liveness properties, we do not present other proofs that must be performed to guarantee the correctness of this specification.

Moreover, in order to give readable formulae, we do not give full contexts of nodes and thus, hypotheses in theorems to prove are simplified.

5.1 Determining Leaf Progress Goals

goal *D* As goal D is a NS goal, it is a fpg goal.

To determine if it is spg, we must establish property 6 for this goal. Thus, we have:

$$W_L \triangleq d$$
$$C_D \triangleq d$$
$$pr(sc_D) \triangleq (y' = 2)$$

Of course, the conjunction of these properties with the invariant does not imply $x' < x$ or $x' = 0$. So, D is not an spg goal. So:

$$spg_D = false \tag{25}$$
$$fpg_D = true \tag{26}$$

goal *E* When goal E is considered, we have:

$$W_L \triangleq d$$
$$C_E \triangleq \begin{cases} d_{-2} \wedge y_{-1} = 2 \wedge x_{-1} = x_{-2} \\ d_{-1} = d_{-2} \wedge y = y_{-1} \wedge x = x_{-1} \end{cases}$$
$$pr(sc_E) \triangleq x' = x - y \wedge (d' \leftrightarrow x' \neq 0)$$

The context of goal E given above is calculated by the context inference rules of the GDT4MAS method. It expresses the fact that goal E is considered only after goal D has succeeded when it has been executed in its context.

To establish that E is a spg goal, according to 6, we must demonstrate that the conjunction of these properties imply that the variant decreases, that is to say $x' < x$. This is obvious because, from C_E, we can deduce $y = 2$ and from $pr(sc_E)$, we can deduce $x' = x - y$. So, E is a spg goal.

We also have to determing if E is a fpg goal, thanks to rule 7. Among the hypotheses of this rule, we have gpf_E (which implies $x' = x$, see 17) and requires as conclusion either $x' < x$ (which cannot be true!) or $x' = 0$ which cannot be guaranted because the context does not provide any knowledge about the value of x. So, goal E is not a fpg goal.

So, we have:

$$spg_E = true \tag{27}$$

$$fpg_E = false \tag{28}$$

Goal C. About goal C, we have the following properties:

$$\begin{array}{l} W_L \triangleq d \\ C_C \triangleq (d_{-2} \wedge x_{-1} = x_{-2} \wedge x = x_{-1}) \\ pr(sc_C) \triangleq (x' = x - 1 \wedge (d' \leftrightarrow x' \neq 0)) \end{array}$$

To establish that goal C is a spg goal, we must try to establish rule 6. This rule requires to prove, from the conjunction of the above properties, that the variant decreases ($x' < x$) or that property Q_L is true. This is obvious because, from sc_C, we deduce that $x' = x - 1$, which implies $x' < x$. So, goal C is a spg goal. Moreover, as this goal is a NS goal, this is also a fpg goal. So we have:

$$spg_C = true \tag{29}$$

$$fpg_C = true \tag{30}$$

Conclusion. As a conclusion, we know that no leaf goal make the variant increase. Moreover, spg goals and fpg goals are respectively the following:

$$SPG = \{C, E\} \tag{31}$$

$$FPG = \{C, D\} \tag{32}$$

$$PG = \{C\} \tag{33}$$

5.2 Inference of the Progress Property

Goal B. To determine if goal B is a spg goal, we apply rule 8 that provides the following sufficient condition to guarantee that goal B is spg:

$$fpg_D \wedge (spg_D \vee pg_E)$$

However, D is not a spg goal and E is not a pg goal. Thus, with this rule, we cannot determine that goal B is spg. So, we try to apply rule 6. Considering goal B, we have:

$$W_L \triangleq d$$
$$C_B \triangleq d$$
$$pr(sc_B) \triangleq x' = x - 2$$

And we have to establish that the conjunction of these formulae implies either $x' < x$ of $x' = 0$. As sc_B implies $x' = x - 2$, we obviously have $x' < x$. So, B is a spg goal.

We now have to determine if goal B is a fpg goal, applying rule 9:

$$fpg_D \wedge (spg_D \vee fpg_E)$$

As goal E is not a fpg goal and D is not a spg goal, we can deduce that goal B is not a fpg goal. So we have:

$$spg_B = true \qquad (34)$$
$$fpg_B = false \qquad (35)$$

Goal A To determine if goal A is a spg goal, we apply rule 10, which gives:

$$spg_B \wedge (fpg_B \vee pg_C)) \rightarrow spg_A$$

As we have established before that goal B is spg (34) and that goal C is pg (33), we can establish that goal A is a spg goal.

Conclusion. Goal A being a NS goal and a spg goal, we now know that each execution of the GDT of the agent makes the variant decrease.

5.3 The Chosen Variant Is a Variant

Correctness. According to equation 1, to prove that the chosen variant is effectively a variant, we have to prove:

$$i_{\mathcal{E}A} \wedge x = 0 \rightarrow x = 0$$

This is obviously true !

Activation. According to equation 2, we have to prove:

$$i_{\mathcal{E}A} \wedge d \wedge \neg(x = 0) \rightarrow (x = 10 \vee d)$$

Once again, this formula is obviously true.

5.4 The Witness Is a Witness

Initialisation. From formula 4, weh have to verify:

$$x = 10 \wedge (d \leftrightarrow (x > 0 \wedge x \leq 10)) \rightarrow d$$

This is still an obviously true formula.

Finalization. We have to apply proof schema 5 for every leaf goal (and we recall here that, according to GDT4MAS principles, the gpf of an NS action is $false$).

Goal D. The NS action δ associated to goal D is defined by:

$$\begin{array}{l} post_\delta \triangleq y' = 2 \wedge d' = d \\ gpf_\delta \triangleq false \end{array}$$

So, with the context of goal D given above, we must establish:

$$i_{\mathcal{E}A} \wedge d \wedge d \wedge ((d' = d \wedge y' = 2) \vee false) \rightarrow pr(d \vee x = 0)$$

That can be simplified into:

$$i_{\mathcal{E}A} \wedge d \wedge d' = d \wedge y' = 2 \rightarrow d' \vee x' = 0$$

This property is obviously true (as d and $d' = d$ can be found among the hypotheses).

Goal E The action η associated to goal E is defined by:

$$\begin{array}{l} post_\eta \triangleq x' = x - y \wedge (d' \leftrightarrow x' \neq 0) \\ gpf_\eta \triangleq x' = x \wedge d' = d \end{array}$$

Using C_E given above, applying proof schema 5, we obtain the following proof obligation:

$$\begin{array}{l} i_{\mathcal{E}A} \wedge d_{-2} \wedge y_{-1} = 2 \wedge x_{-1} = x_{-2} \\ d_{-1} = d_{-2} \wedge y = y_{-1} \wedge x = x_{-1} \wedge d \\ ((x' = x - y \wedge (d' \leftrightarrow x' \neq 0)) \vee (x' = x \wedge d' = d)) \\ \rightarrow pr(d \vee x = 0) \end{array}$$

In order to simplify the explanation of the demonstration (that can be however easily performed by an automatic prover), we remove useless hypotheses. So, we have to prove:

$$\begin{array}{l} (d \wedge x' = x - y \wedge (d' \leftrightarrow x' \neq 0)) \vee (d \wedge x' = x \wedge d' = d) \\ \rightarrow d' \vee x' = 0 \end{array}$$

The structure of this formula being $a \vee b \rightarrow c$, we will successively demonstrate $a \rightarrow c$ and $b \rightarrow c$.

- $(d \wedge x' = x - y \wedge (d' \leftrightarrow x' \neq 0)) \rightarrow d' \vee x' = 0$
  We use a proof-by-case on the value of d'. Either d' is true, and so, the goal is true, or d' is false. In the latter case, according hypothesis 2, $x' = 0$, and so the goal is true. QED.
- $(d \wedge x' = x \wedge d' = d) \rightarrow d' \vee x' = 0$
  As d and $d' = d$ are hypotheses, we obviously deduce d'. QED.

So the proof obligation generated by applying proof schema 5 to goal E is true.

Goal C The action associated to goal C is defined by:

$$\begin{aligned} &post_\gamma \triangleq x' = x - 1 \wedge (d' \leftrightarrow x' \neq 0) \\ &gpf_\gamma \triangleq false \end{aligned}$$

Using C_C and applying proof schema 5 to goal C, we have to prove:

$$\left.\begin{array}{r} i_{\mathcal{E}A} \wedge d_{-2} \wedge x_{-1} = x_{-2} \wedge x = x_{-1} \wedge d \\ ((x' = x - 1 \wedge (d' \leftrightarrow x' \neq 0)) \vee false) \end{array}\right\} \rightarrow pr(d \vee x = 0)$$

In order to simplify the explanation of the demonstration (that can be however easily performed by an automatic prover), we remove useless hypotheses. So, we have to prove:

$$(d' \leftrightarrow x' \neq 0) \rightarrow (d' \vee x' = 0)$$

The proof is obvious: either d' is true, and so, the goal is true, or d' is false and so, from hypotheses, $x' \neq 0$ is false, and so, $x' = 0$. QED.

5.5 Conclusion

Following the proof system described in section 4, we have been able to establish that an agent whose behaviour is described by the gdt given in figure 2 satisfies a liveness property that is not a part of its main goal.

6 Comparison with other Works

Several formal specification languages dedicated to multiagent systems exist. However, they are often not suited to proof mechanisms. This is for instance the case of 2APL [7], that is finally more a programming language than a specification language suited to proof. MetateM [8] gives the developer a way to specify properties, and the system controls that the execution does not violate these properties. However, this is a proof-by-construction process; this means that the proof is performed only at the execution time, and if the initial conditions change, a new proof (consisting in an execution of this new initial state) must be performed.

Finally, most works dealing with the verification of multiagent systems rely on model-checking principles. One of the most recent work in this area is the definition of AJPF [9], a model-checker relying on JPF [10] and the *Agent Infrastructure Layer AIL*. This is, as far as we know, the only system that proposes a way to verify leads-to properties on multi-agent systems. However, a first drawback of the method is the time taken by the system to establish the property (several hours for a very simple system). Of course, a more optimized model-checker such as SPIN [11], may greatly reduce the time required. However, such systems remain dedicated to small-size systems. Moreover, such systems have a more serious drawback: although they can be used to prove a property such as the property we have proven in section 5: $\Box(x = 10 \to \Diamond x = 0)$, they cannot be applied when the left-hand side property (here, $x = 10$) characterize an infinite number of states. For instance, if we would be interested in proving the following leads-to property: $\Box(x \geq 10 \to \Diamond x = 0)$, a model-checking-based method would fail, whereas the process we propose would be as efficient as it is in the given example.

The same problem can be found with MCMAS [12], which moreover does not provide a way to verify leads-to properties. This model-checking technique tries to verify formulae specified in propositionnal logic, as AJPF. The main disadvantage of this technique is that, relying on propositionnal logic, proofs cannot be generalized on systems of any size. For instance, in the cited article, it is shown that the verification of the dinning cryptographers must be performed for each number of cryptographers we are interested in. Moreover, even if the time taken for 10 cryptographers is quite good, performances decrease dramatically when the number of cryptographers increase. Finally, with such a technique, to prove that the MAS work with any number of cryprgrapher, an infinite number of verifications must be performed, requiring, of course, an infinite time.

Indeed, as model checking techniques may be applided on systems with several millions of states, their complexity is a critical aspect that must be taken into consideration. But with theorem proving techniques, this criterion is somewhat less important. Indeed, each proof requires a very short time, and the number of proofs is very low, compared to the number of states generated in model checking techniques (for instance, even on a very large industrial system, less that 50,000 proofs had to be verified [13]). For instance, with the GDT4MAS model, if we call $n(t)$ the number of nodes of an agent type t and T the set of agent types, the number of proofs to perform is approximately $2\Sigma_{t \in T} n(t)$.

7 Conclusion and Perspectives

In this article, we have shown that the GDT4MAS model, that was mainly dedicated to the proof of invariant properties, can be extended to prove liveness properties such as lead-to properties. As other proof obligations of the GDT4MAS framework, the new proof obligations generated are easily proven by an automatic theorem prover such as PVS.

This kind of proof can help in analyzing the behaviour of a MAS. In the work presented here, we have only considered liveness properties associated to a single agent. Of course, more general liveness properties at the system level will have to be considered, especially properties that are established not only by a single agent, but by a subset of the agents in the system. This is a short-term perspective. Moreover, at it is classically performed in standard verification systems, our proof system can only prove leads-to properties $P\ leads-to\ Q$ for which there is a continuous progress to Q once P has been true. In a multiagent system where agents are fully autonomous, we also have to consider properties for which this progress is not continuous. This is a long-term perspective for us.

References

1. Mermet, B., Simon, G.: GDT4MAS: An extension of the GDT model to specify and to verify MultiAgent Systems. In: Decker, et al. (eds.) Proc. of AAMAS 2009, pp. 505–512 (2009)
2. Chandy, K.M., Misra, J.: Parallel Program Design: A Foundation. Addison-Wesley (1988)
3. Lamport, L.: The syntax and semantics of TLA$^{?+?}$. Part 1: Definitions and Modules (June 1996)
4. Milner, R., Parrow, J., Wlaker, D.: A calculus of mobile processes. Journal of Information and Computation 100 (1992)
5. Mermet, B., Simon, G., Zanuttini, B., Saval, A.: Specifying and verifying a MAS:The *robots on mars* case study. In: Dastani, M., El Fallah Seghrouchni, A., Ricci, A., Winikoff, M. (eds.) ProMAS 2007. LNCS (LNAI), vol. 4908, pp. 172–189. Springer, Heidelberg (2008)
6. SRI International: PVS, `http://pvs.csl.sri.com`
7. Dastani, M.: 2APL: A practical agent programming language. Journal of Autonomous Agents and Multi-Agent Systems 16, 214–248 (2008)
8. Fisher, M.: A survey of concurrent METATEM – The language and its applications. In: Gabbay, D.M., Ohlbach, H.J. (eds.) ICTL 1994. LNCS, vol. 827, pp. 480–505. Springer, Heidelberg (1994)
9. Dennis, L., Fisher, M., Webster, M., Bordini, R.: Model checking agent programming languages. Automated Software Engineering 19(1), 5–63 (2012)
10. NASA: Java Path Finder, `http://babelfish.arc.nasa.gov/trac/jpf`
11. Holzmann, G.J.: The Model Checker SPIN. IEEE Trans. Softw. Eng. 23, 279–295 (1997)
12. Lomuscio, A., Qu, H., Raimondi, F.: MCMAS: A model checker for the verification of multi-agent systems. In: Bouajjani, A., Maler, O. (eds.) CAV 2009. LNCS, vol. 5643, pp. 682–688. Springer, Heidelberg (2009)
13. Abrial, J.R.: Formal methods in industry: achievements, problems, future. In: International Conference on Software Engineering, pp. 761–768 (2006)

Mutation Testing for Jason Agents

Zhan Huang, Rob Alexander, and John Clark

Department of Computer Science, University of York, York, United Kingdom
{zhan.huang,robert.alexander,john.clark}@cs.york.ac.uk

Abstract. Most multi-agent system (MAS) testing techniques lack empirical evidence of their effectiveness. Since finding tests that can reveal a large proportion of possible faults is a key goal in testing, we need techniques to assess the fault detection ability of test sets for MAS. Mutation testing offers a direct and powerful way to do this: it generates modified versions of the program ("mutants") following a set of rules ("mutation operators") then checks if a test set can distinguish the original program from the (functionally non-equivalent) mutants. In this paper, we propose a set of mutation operators for the agent-oriented programming language Jason, and then introduce a mutation testing system for individual Jason agents that implements a subset of our proposed mutation operators. We use this subset to assess a test set for a Jason agent that meets a combination of existing agent-based coverage criteria. The assessment shows that this test set is not adequate to kill all mutants.

Keywords: Test Evaluation, Mutation Testing, Agent-Oriented Programming, Jason.

1 Introduction

Multi-agent systems (MAS) are a promising paradigm for engineering autonomous and distributed systems. Testing MAS is a challenging activity, however, because of the increased complexity, large amount of data, irreproducibility, non-determinism and other characteristics involved in MAS [9]. Although many techniques have been proposed to address the difficulties in MAS testing, most of them lack empirical evidence of their effectiveness [10].

Effective testing requires tests that are capable of revealing a high proportion of faults in the system under test (SUT). It can be difficult to find real faulty projects to verify the real fault detection ability of a test set; instead, we can use coverage-based and fault-based testing techniques.

For coverage based techniques, the tests or their executions are measured against some coverage criteria based on some model of the SUT (or other relevant model); if they cover all model elements defined in the coverage criteria, the tests are said to be adequate for the coverage criteria – in other words, they examine the involved model elements thoroughly. Existing coverage criteria for MAS testing include Low et al.'s plan and node based coverage criteria for BDI agents [1], Zhang et al.'s plan and event based coverage criteria for Prometheus agents [2], and Miller et al.'s protocol and plan based coverage criteria for agent interaction testing [3].

F. Dalpiaz et al. (Eds.): EMAS 2014, LNAI 8758, pp. 309–327, 2014.

Fault based techniques offer a more direct way to assess the fault detection ability of the tests than coverage based ones: faults are seeded into the SUT by some means, typically by hand or by *mutation* [12]. After seeding faults (i.e. producing faulty versions of the SUT), each test is executed against first the original SUT then each faulty version. For each faulty version, if its behaviour differs from the original SUT in at least one test, it will be marked as "killed" to indicate that the fault(s) seeded in it can be detected by the tests. Therefore, the fault detection ability of the tests can be assessed by the "kill rate" – the ratio of the killed faulty versions to all faulty versions: higher the ratio is, more effective the tests are. Those non-killed faulty versions reveal the weaknesses of the existing tests so that testers can enhance these tests (in order to kill those versions) by improving some of them or adding new ones.

Mutation is a systematic and automatic way of generating modified versions of the SUT ("mutants") following a set of rules ("mutation operators"). The process of using mutation to assess tests is called mutation testing. Mutation is more commonly used to seed faults than the hand-seeded way because many theories and empirical evidences support it; for instance [13] shows that it provides an efficient way to seed faults that are more representative of realistic faults than hand-seeded ones. However, the mutation operators used to guide mutant generation may lead to a large number of mutants so that comparing the behaviour of each mutant with that of the original SUT in each test is computationally costly. Another problem is that mutation unpredictably produces *equivalent mutants* – alternate implementations of the SUT that are not actually faulty (as the result, no tests can differentiate the original SUT from them), and thus which must be excluded from test evaluation. Although the process of detecting equivalent mutants may be partially automated, much manual work is still required.

Many studies show that mutation testing provides a more rigorous test evaluation than coverage-based techniques [11], so it is usually used to evaluate or compare other testing techniques (e.g. that are based on some coverage criteria). The key to successful mutation testing is to select an appropriate set of mutation operators. Here we define "appropriate" in terms of two criteria: effectiveness and efficiency. Effectiveness is the value of the individual operators for assessing tests, it requires *representativeness*, which means a mutation operator should be able to guide seeding faults that are representative of realistic ones, and *power*, which means an operator should be able to guide generating hard-to-kill non-equivalent mutants. Efficiency is concerned with the computational cost due to the operator set, it requires that the operator set generate a reasonable (computationally tractable) number of non-equivalent mutants.

There is some preliminary work on mutation testing for MAS. Nguyen et al. [4] use standard mutation operators for Java to assess tests for JADE agents (which are implemented in Java). As to the work on MAS model/language specific mutation operators, Adra and McMinn [5] propose a set of mutation operator classes for agent-based models. Saifan and Wahsheh [6] propose and classify a set of mutation operators for JADE mobile agents. Savarimuthu and Winikoff [7, 8] systematically derive a set of mutation operators for the AgentSpeak agent language and another set for the GOAL agent language. Most existing work focuses on deriving mutation operators from agent models/languages, a recent paper [8] evaluates the representativeness of the mutation operators for the agent language GOAL by comparison with realistic bugs.

In our work, we aim to explore the use of mutation testing for MAS, with the intention that our work can be used to assess and enhance the tests derived from existing testing techniques (e.g. that are based on some coverage criteria) for MAS. This paper presents our preliminary work – in Section 2 we propose a set of mutation operators for Jason [14], which is an implementation of the AgentSpeak language; in Section 3 we introduce a mutation testing system for individual Jason agents that implements a subset of our proposed mutation operators; in Section 4 we show the use of our implemented mutation operators in assessing and enhancing a test set (for a Jason agent) satisfying some existing agent-based coverage criteria, and the evaluation of the power of these operators by observing which one(s) lead to hard-to-kill non-equivalent mutants; in Section 5 we discuss the relationships between our work and previous related work; in Section 6 we summarise our work and make some suggestions for where this work could go in the future.

2 Mutation Operators for Jason

Mutation operators are rules to guide mutant generation by making changes to the description (syntax) of the program[1]. For instance, a mutation operator for procedural programs called *Relational Operator Replacement (ROR)* requires that *each occurrence of one of the relational operators (<, ≤, >, ≥, =, ≠) is replaced by each of the other operators* [11]. A mutant usually only contains a simple, unary fault (e.g., in the above example, each generated mutant only replaces a single relational operator by another), because of the two underlying theories [12] in mutation testing: the *Competent Programmer Hypothesis* states that programmers create programs that are close to being correct; the *Coupling Effect* states that tests that can detect a set of simple faults can also find complex faults.

Since mutation is typically performed at program level, a set of mutation operators is specific to a given programming language. To design mutation operators for a programming language, it is common to start by proposing an initial set based on the syntax and features of the language, and then to refine an effective set through evaluation.

The language we chose is Jason, which is a multi-agent system programming language that uses the extended AgentSpeak to specify agents in terms of beliefs, initial goals and plans, uses Java to customize agent architectures, define agent environments and implement various extensions. We chose to mutate the extended AgentSpeak code at first because it directs the behaviour of Jason agents.

Savarimuthu and Winikoff [7] apply the guidewords of HAZOP (Hazard and Operability Study) into the syntax of AgentSpeak to systematically derive a set of mutation operators. In contrast to their work, firstly we explicitly describe each of our derived operators while they do not give and describe their actual full operator set. Secondly we mutate the Jason-extended version of AgentSpeak, so some of our operators are specific to Jason. Finally, we borrow some ideas from other existing mutation opera-

[1] This paper only concerns conventional mutation testing, i.e. syntactic mutation testing, although some recent work applies mutation testing to program semantics.

tors (for both conventional programs and MAS) when deriving ours, in the hope of preliminarily refining our set, e.g., by excluding ones that are not sensible.

We base our work on Jason's Extended Backus–Naur Form (EBNF), where a list of production rules is defined that describe Jason's grammar. The EBNF we use is a simplified version in [14] that does not include some advanced features such as *directives* and conditional/loop statements in the plan body. We divide these production rules into high-level and low-level ones – the high-level production rules specify the main syntactical concepts that are closely related to how Jason agents generally work, while the low-level ones specify the basic logical representations forming the Jason syntactical concepts. Accordingly our mutation operators for Jason can also be described as high- or low-level. In the following two subsections we present these mutation operators according to which production rules they are derived from.

2.1 High-Level Mutation Operators for Jason

Fig. 1 shows the high-level production rules in Jason's EBNF; from this, we have derived 13 high-level mutation operators.

```
1:   agent ::= (belief)* (init_goal)* (plan)*
2:   belief ::= literal [":-" log_expr] "."
3:   init_goal ::= "!" literal "."
4:   plan ::= [label] triggering_event [":" context] ["<-" body] "."
5:   label ::= "@" atomic_formula
6:   triggering_event ::= ("+" | "-") ["!" | "?"] literal
7:   context ::= log_expr | true
8:   body ::= body_formula (";" body_formula)* | true
9:   body_formula ::= ("!" | "!!" | "?" | "+" | "-" | "-+") literal |
             action | internal_action | rel_expr
10:  action ::= atomic_formula
11:  internal_action ::= "." (atomic_formula | formula_for_comm)
-----------------------------------------------------------------
12:  formula_for_comm ::=
             "send(" receiver "," illocutionary_force "," message_content
                   ["," reply] ["," timeout] ")" |
             "broadcast(" illocutionary_force "," message_content ")"
13:  receiver ::= agent_id | "[" agent_id ("," agent_id)* "]"
14:  illocutionary_force ::= tell | untell | achieve | unachieve | askOne |
             askAll | tellHow | untellHow | askHow
15:  message_content ::= propositional_content |
             "[" propositional_content ("," propositional_content)* "]"
16:  propositional_content ::= belief | triggering_event | plan | label
```

Fig. 1. High-level production rules in Jason's EBNF (Rule 1–11 are slightly adapted from [14], 12–16 are the ones we added for specifying Jason agent communication)

Production rule 1 states that an agent is specified in terms of beliefs, initial goals and plans. From this rule we derive the following three mutation operators:

- **Belief Deletion (BD):** *A single belief in the agent is deleted.*
- **Initial Goal Deletion (IGD):** *A single initial goal in the agent is deleted.*
- **Plan Deletion (PD):** *A single plan in the agent is deleted.*

Production rule 2 states that a belief can be a literal representing some fact, or a rule representing some fact will be derived if some conditions get satisfied. The introduction of rules enables Jason to perform *theoretical reasoning* [15]. From this production rule we derive the following mutation operator:

- **Rule Condition Deletion (RCD):** *The condition part of a rule is deleted.*

A rule that RCD is applied to will only have its conclusion part – a literal – left, as a belief held by the agent regardless of whether the (now deleted) conditions get satisfied.

Production rule 6 states that the triggering event of a plan consists of a literal following one of the six types: belief addition (+), belief deletion (–), achievement goal addition (+!), achievement goal deletion (–!), test goal addition (+?) and test goal deletion (–?). It can be seen that an event that can be handled by Jason plans represents a change – addition or deletion (represented using + or – operator respectively) – to the agent's beliefs or goals. From this rule we derive the following mutation operator:

- **Triggering Event Operator Replacement (TEOR):** *The triggering event operator (+ or –) of a plan is replaced by the other operator.*

We don't have an operator that changes the trigger type i.e. one of achievement goal, test goal and belief to another. This is because as learned from [8], this type of change doesn't make sense, and because in the case no events can match the modified trigger it will be equivalent to PD (Plan Deletion) anyway.

Production rule 7 states that the context of a plan can be a logical expression, or be always true (the latter is equivalent to the context not being specified at all). The plan context defines the condition under which the plan that has been triggered becomes a candidate for commitment to execution. From this production rule we derive the following mutation operator:

- **Plan Context Deletion (PCD)**: *The context of a plan is deleted if it is non-empty and not set true.*

Production rule 8 states that the body of a plan can be a sequence of formulae, each of which will be executed in order, or set *true* (the latter is equivalent to the body not being specified at all). From this rule we derive the following three mutation operators:

- **Plan Body Deletion (PBD)**: *The body of a plan is deleted if it is non-empty or not set true.*
- **Formula Deletion (FD)**: *A single formula in the body of a non-empty plan is deleted.*
- **Formulae Order Swap (FOS)**: *The order of any two adjacent formulae in the body of a plan that contains more than one formula is swapped.*

FOS comes from an idea behind some existing mutation operators that the order of elements in a sequence is changed. Although elements can be arranged in many ways, we choose to only swap two adjacent elements (i.e. formulae) because as suggested in [8], it can avoid generating a large number of mutants.

In many cases, PBD is equivalent to PD (Plan Deletion). However, since the plan context can contain internal actions that may cause changes in the agent's internal state, the plan that PBD is applied to may still have an effect on the agent although its body has been deleted, in this case PBD is not equivalent to PD.

Production rule 9–11 states that a body formula can be one of the six types: achievement goal (!literal or !!literal), test goal (?literal), mental note (+literal, –literal, –+literal), action (atomic_formula), internal action (.atomic_formula or .formula_for_comm[2]) and relational expression. The former three types are involved in generating *internal events* that correspond to changes in achievement goals, test goals and beliefs respectively. Similar to how we derived the Triggering Event Operator Replacement (TEOR) operator, from this production rule we derive the following mutation operator:

- **Formula Operator Replacement (FOR):** *The operator of an achievement goal formula (! or !!) is replaced by the other operator, so is that of a mental note formula (+, –, –+).*

It is worth noting that the achievement goal formula has two types: "!" is used to post a goal that must be achieved before the rest of the plan body can continue execution, "!!" allows the plan containing the goal to run alongside the plan for achieving the goal. In the latter case, the two plans can compete for execution due to the normal intention selection mechanism.

We don't consider changing the formula type i.e. one of achievement goal, test goal and belief to another because as noted in [8], this type of change doesn't make sense; neither do we consider the formula type of action, internal action or relational expression for the similar reason.

Production rules 12–16 are the ones we added for specifying Jason agent communication. It can be seen that two internal actions: *.send* and *.broadcast*, are used by Jason agents to send messages. The main parameters in these actions include the message receiver(s) (only used in *.send* action) that can be a single or a list of agents identified by the agent ID(s), the illocutionary force (*tell*, *untell*, *achieve*, etc.) representing the intention of sending the message and the message content that can be one or a list of propositional contents. From these production rules we derive the following three mutation operators:

- **Message Receiver Replacement (MRR):** *The receiver or the list of receivers in a .send action is replaced by another agent ID (or some subset of all the agent IDs in the MAS). If the action is .broadcast, it will be first converted to its equivalent .send action and then applied this mutation operator.*
- **Illocutionary Force Replacement (IFR):** *The illocutionary force in an action for sending messages is replaced by another illocutionary force.*
- **Propositional Content Deletion (PCD2):** *A single propositional content in the message content is deleted.*

---

[2] *formula_for_comm* actually belongs to *atomic_formula*. We separate it in order to specify rules for agent communication.

It is worth noting that a propositional content is some component of another type (e.g., belief, plan, etc.). Therefore, the mutation operators for these components can also be applied for mutating agent communication.

2.2 Low-Level Mutation Operators for Jason

Fig. 2 shows the low-level production rules in Jason's EBNF; from this, we have derived 11 low-level mutation operators, most of which are borrowed from existing operators for conventional programs.

```
1:  literal ::= ["~"] atomic_formula
2:  atomic_formula ::= (<ATOM> | <VAR>) ["(" term ("," term)* ")"] ["[" term
        ("," term)* "]"]
3:  term ::= literal | list | arithm_expr | <VAR> | <STRING>
4:  log_expr ::= simple_log_expr | "not" log_expr | log_expr "&" log_expr |
        log_expr "|" log_expr | "(" log_expr ")"
5:  simple_log_expr ::= (literal | rel_expr | <VAR>)
6:  rel_expr ::= rel_term [("<" | "<=" | ">" | ">=" | "==" | "\==" | "=" | "=..")
        rel_term]+
7:  rel_term ::= literal | arithm_expr
8:  arithm_expr ::= arithm_term [("+" | "-" | "*" | "**" | "/" | "div" | "mod")
        arithm_term]*
9:  arithm_term ::= <NUMBER> | <VAR> | "-" arithm_term |
        "(" arithm_expr ")"
```

Fig. 2. Low-level production rules in Jason's EBNF (Source: [14])

Production rule 1 states that a literal is an atomic formula or its strong negation (~*l*). Strong negation is introduced to overcome the limitation of default negation in logic programming: an agent can explicitly express that something is *false* by using strong negation, or express that it cannot conclude whether something is *true* or *false* using default negation (i.e. by the simple absence of a belief on the matter). From this production rule we derive the following mutation operator:

- **Strong Negation Insertion/Deletion (SNID):** *The form of a literal (affirmative or strong negative) is transformed to the other form.*

Production rule 2 and 3 state that an atomic formula consists of a relation followed by a list of annotations. Annotations can be used to provide further information about the relation. *source* is an important annotation that is appended to some atomic formulae automatically by Jason is used to represent where the atomic formulae (or the component it represents) come from by taking one of the three parameters: *percept*, *self* or an agent ID. For instance, belief *likes(rob, apples)[source(tom)]* implies the information that *rob* likes apples comes from agent *tom*. From these production rules we derive the following two mutation operators:

- **Annotation Deletion (AD):** *A single annotation of an atomic formula is deleted, if one exists.*
- **Source Replacement (SR):** *The source of an atomic formula is replaced by another source, if it exists.*

Production rule 4 and 5 define logical expressions; rule 6 and 7 define relational expressions; rule 8 and 9 define arithmetic expressions. Since some mutation operators for conventional programs have been designed for these concepts [11], we can just slightly adapt so as to use them in the context of Jason:

- **Logical Operator Replacement (LOR):** *A single logical operator (& or |) is replaced by the other operator.*
- **Negation Operator Insertion (NOI):** *The negation operator ("not") is inserted before a (sub) logical expression.*
- **Logical Expression Deletion (LED):** *A single sub logical expression is deleted.*
- **Relational Operator Replacement (ROR):** *A single relational operator ("<", "<=", ">", ">=", "==", "\==", "=", "=..") is replaced by another operator.*
- **Relational Term Deletion (RTD):** *A single relational term in a relational expression is deleted.*
- **Arithmetic Operator Replacement (AOR):** *A single arithmetic operator ("+", "–", "*", "**", "/", "div", "mod") is replaced by another operator.*
- **Arithmetic Term Deletion (ATD):** *A single arithmetic term in an arithmetic expression is deleted.*
- **Minus Insertion (MI):** *A minus (–) is inserted before an arithmetic term.*

3 muJason: A Mutation Testing System for Jason Agents

We have developed a mutation testing system for individual Jason agents called muJason[3], where we have implemented the 13 high-level mutation operators via Jason APIs and Java reflection, both of which can be used to access and modify the architectural components of the agents and the state of the MAS at runtime. The class diagram and the user interface of muJason are shown in Fig. 3 and Fig. 4 respectively.

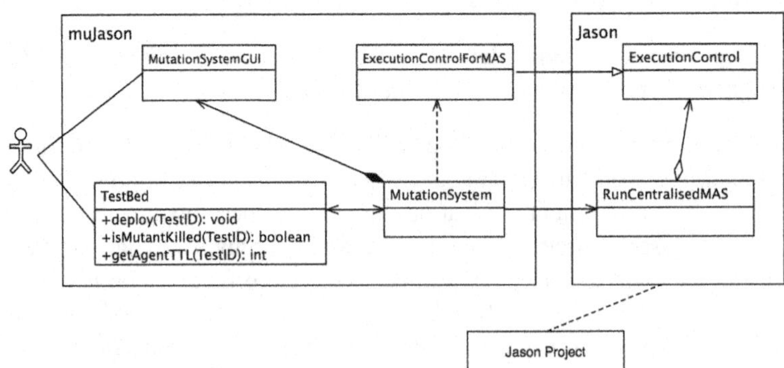

Fig. 3. The class diagram of muJason

[3] http://mujason.wordpress.com

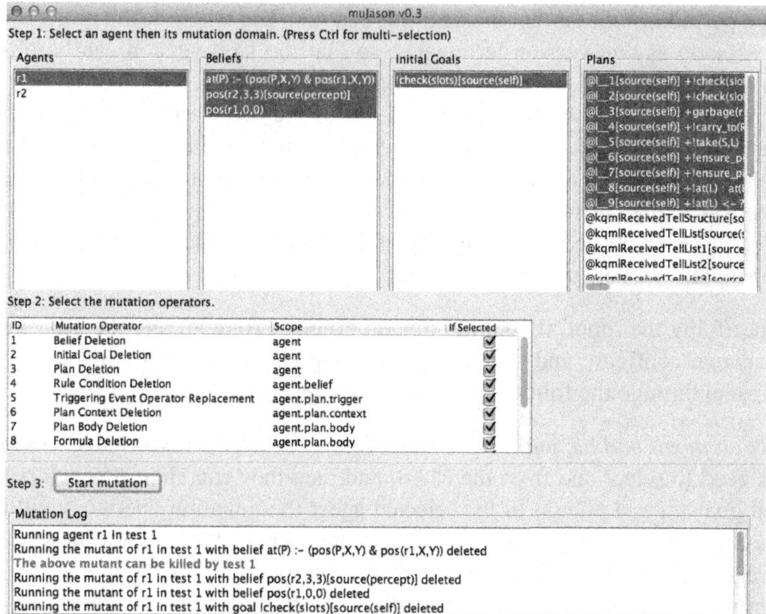

Fig. 4. The user interface of muJason

muJason can be launched by running the *MutationSystem* class and passing the name of the Jason project configuration file (postfixed with ".mas2j") as the parameter. Then muJason will load the Jason project and display the mutation testing control panel (as shown in Fig. 4), where users can configure, start and observe mutation testing processes.

Before initiating a mutation testing process, users need to specify the input of each test, the killing mutant criterion (or the oracle) for each test and the TTL (Time to Live) of the original/mutated agent under each test in the *deploy(testID)*, *isMutantKilled(testID)* and *getAgentTTL(testID)* methods provided by the *TestBed* class (as shown in Fig. 3), respectively. Each of these methods is described as follows:

- *deploy(testID)*: this method sets up the initial configuration of the Jason system prior to each test run. It is called each time by taking an ID identifying one of the tests, so users can write code to specify the starting configuration as the input of each test.
- *isMutantKilled(testID)*: this method is used to determine whether a mutant under some test is killed (as indicated by the Boolean return value). It is called as soon as each mutant terminates, and is passed the ID of the current test. Therefore, in this method users can write code to check whether the mutated agent has been killed by each individual test, in other words, in there users can implement the oracle for each test.
- *getAgentTTL(TestID)*: this method is used to specify the lifetime of the original/mutated agent (as the return value) under each test. Since agents usually run indefinitely, an original/mutated version of the agent can only be allowed to run for a

certain period of time so that the next one can run. The whole Jason project will restart as soon as one version terminates, so that the next version can be observed from (and mutated at) the same starting point of the MAS. The lifetime or TTL of an agent is measured by the number of cycles the agent can perform; it must be enough for the agent to expose all the behaviour involved in the process of killing mutants. The TTL for a test is actually part of the killing mutant criterion/oracle for that test. Although there may be ways to automatically terminate the mutant once it is observed being killed, for simplicity in the beginning, the TTL for a test is fixed and manually set depending on the users' experience.

After specifying the input, the killing mutant criterion (oracle) and the TTL for each test, users can configure and start a mutation testing process in the mutation testing control panel through the following steps (as shown in Fig. 4):

1. *Select an agent and its mutation domain.* Since muJason aims at individual agents, users need to select one from the MAS, and then they can choose which belief(s), initial goals(s) and plan(s) of the selected agent the mutation operators will be applied into. They can ignore the agents/components unnecessary for testing, e.g., the GUI agents and the built-in plans for enabling agent communication.
2. *Select the mutation operators.* After specifying the mutation domain of an agent, users can select the mutation operators that will be applied into the mutation domain.
3. *Start the mutation testing process.* After the above steps, users can start the mutation testing, observe its process in the mutation testing control panel and wait for its result. The mutation testing process can be described using the following pseudo-code:

```
For each test identified by a testID:
    Set up the starting config as the input of the
      test
    Get the specified TTL for the test
    Run the original Jason project for the TTL
    Restart the Jason project
    Create a mutant generator taking the selected
      agent, mutation domain and mutation operators
    While the generator can generate another mutant:
        Generate the next mutant
        Run the modified Jason project for the TTL
        Check if the mutant is killed under the
          current test, if so mark it "killed"
        Restart the Jason project
```

4 Evaluation

To perform a preliminary evaluation of the power of our implemented mutation operators, we use them to guide generating mutants of an agent in a Jason project, then examine whether a test set designed using a combination of existing agent-based coverage criteria can kill all the non-equivalent mutants. We think the operators that can guide generating the hard-to-kill non-equivalent mutants are powerful to reveal the weaknesses of this test set.

4.1 Experimental Setup

The Jason project we chose is available on the Jason website[4], and is called *Cleaning Robots*. It involves a cleaner agent, an agent besides an incinerator (we call it incinerator agent later for convenience) and several pieces of garbage located in a gridded area as shown in Fig. 5 (*R1* represents the cleaner agent, *R2* represents the incinerator agent, *G* represents the garbage). When this project is launched, the cleaner agent will move along a fixed path that covers all grid squares (move from the leftmost square to the rightmost one in the first row, then "jump" to the leftmost square in the second row and move to the rightmost one in the same row, and so on). If it perceives that the square it is in contains garbage, it will pick it up, carry it and then move to the square where the incinerator agent is along a shortest path (diagonal movement is allowed). The cleaner agent will drop the garbage after arriving so that the incinerator agent can take it to burn. After dropping garbage the cleaner agent will return to the square where it just found the garbage along a shortest path (diagonal movement allowed), and then continue moving along the fixed path until it reaches the last square.

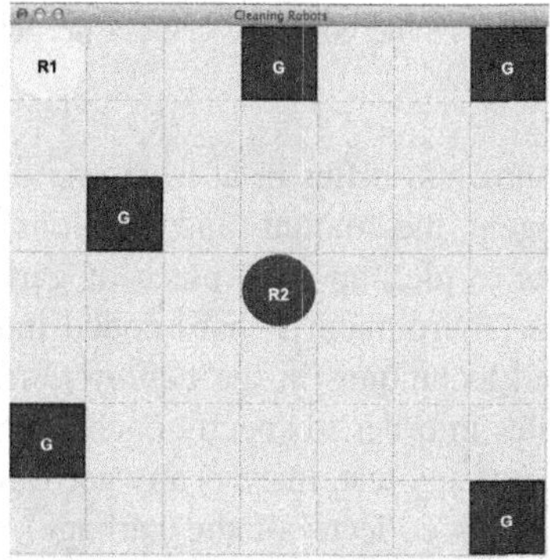

Fig. 5. The *Cleaning Robots* example

In order to test the cleaner agent, we specify test inputs that each describe a different environment in which the agent is located. We design test inputs according to the test coverage criteria proposed by Low et al. [1]. Their criteria are based on plans and nodes (formulae) in BDI agents, so they are suitable for the Jason agent paradigm. Fig. 6 shows the subsumption hierarchy of their criteria – the criterion at the starting point of an arrow subsumes the one at the end of the arrow, e.g., for any agent, a test set satisfying node path coverage criterion also satisfies node coverage criterion. This Jason project is simple and doesn't concern plan and node failure, so we ignore the

4 `http://jason.sourceforge.net/wp/examples/`

related criteria, i.e. node with success and failure coverage criterion and plan with success and failure coverage criterion (that is to say, for this project they are equivalent to node coverage criterion and plan coverage criterion respectively). After manual analysis of the AgentSpeak program of the cleaner agent we design ten test inputs (different environments) that collectively meet node path coverage criterion, plan context coverage criterion and plan path coverage criterion, and for the involved cyclic paths we apply the *0-1-many* rule. We think this combination forms the most rigorous one among Low et al.'s criteria (as can be seen in Fig. 6) and is viable for testing the cleaner agent.

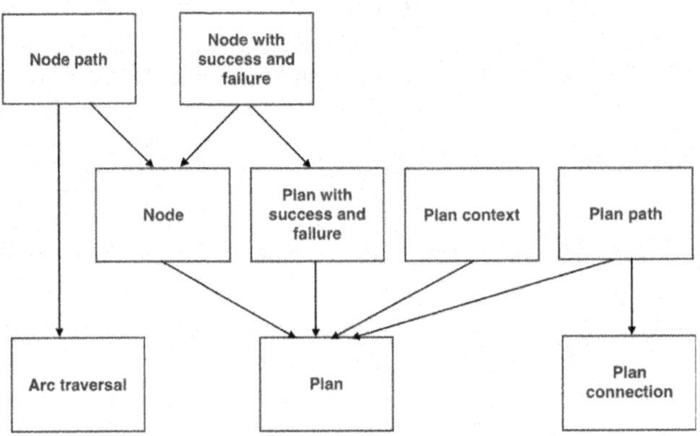

Fig. 6. The subsumption hierarchy of the coverage criteria proposed by Low et al. (Redrawn from [1])

These test inputs (environments) differ in at least one of the three variables – the location of the incinerator agent, the amount (and locations) of garbage and the probability the cleaner agent has to pick up each piece of garbage successfully when it attempts to. Since the agent environment is hard-coded into a java file, we use text replacement and class reload techniques in the *deploy(testID)* method to modify the values of these three variables in order to specify each test input. We consider a mutant to be killed if, at the end of any test, there is any garbage uncollected (in contrast, the non-mutated version always collects all the garbage). To implement this criterion/oracle, we use Jason APIs and Java reflection in the *ifMutantKilled(testID)* method to check whether all the squares in the environment are empty except the two taken by the cleaner agent and the incinerator agent respectively. In the *getAgentTTL(testID)* method, for each individual test, we set the lifetime of the original/mutated agent to a value that is enough to collect all garbage. This value equals the exact time taken by the original agent to finish its work (we observe this by giving the original agent a normal run under that test) plus a modest tolerance value.

Next we configure a mutation testing process for the cleaner agent as shown in Fig. 4: first we choose *r1* which is the name of the cleaner agent, and then all of its three beliefs, one initial goal and nine plans excluding those built-in ones for enabling agent communication. Next we check all the implemented operators. After these we start and observe the mutation testing itself.

4.2 Results

After the mutation testing, muJason displays the results as shown in the first three columns of the table in Fig. 7: the first column lists the mutation operators we selected, the second column lists the total number of mutants generated by each selected operator and the third column lists the number of the killed mutants that corresponds to each selected operator. From the displayed results we can see that the three operators for agent communication – Message Receiver Replacement (MRR), Illocutionary Force Replacement (IFR) and Propositional Content Deletion (PCD2) – are not useful because this Jason project doesn't involve agent communication. We also observe that our implemented operators (excepts the ones for agent communication) have resulted in a manageable number of mutants, i.e. 70 mutants, among which 60 have been killed while 10 not killed. We track these non-killed mutants in the log of the mutation testing process and analyse their corresponding changes in the code. We present our analysis results in the last two columns, and discuss each non-killed mutant below.

Mutation Operator	No. of Generated Mutants	No. of Killed Mutants	No. of Non-Killed Equivalent Mutants	No. of Non-Killed Non-Equivalent Mutants
BD	3	1	2	0
IGD	1	1	0	0
PD	9	8	1	0
RCD	1	1	0	0
TEOR	9	8	1	0
PCD	4	4	0	0
PBD	6	6	0	0
FD	16	15	0	1
FOS	10	9	1	0
FOR	11	7	3	1
MRR	0	0	0	0
IFR	0	0	0	0
PCD2	0	0	0	0
Total	70	60	8	2

Fig. 7. The results of the mutation testing

Equivalent Mutants

The Belief Deletion (BD) operator generates three mutants, in each of which an initial belief in the belief base of the agent is deleted. Two mutants are equivalent, however, they should not have been generated. Recall that muJason provides access to and makes changes to the initial state of the MAS rather than the agent code. This implementation is equivalent to mutating the code directly because the code will be interpreted to the initial state that subsequently affects the MAS behaviour. However, two of the three beliefs we choose – *pos(r2, 3, 3)* and *pos(r1, 0, 0)* representing the initial positions of the incinerator agent and the cleaner agent respectively, are not defined in the agent (AgentSpeak) code – they are from the environment (Java) code, which is not our mutation target. Like beliefs from the agent code, they have been automatically added into the belief base by the Jason engine before the initial state of the MAS becomes accessible, so they appear as mutation options, which have been selected by us. Also, deleting them before the MAS runs will not change the agent behaviour because they will be automatically added again soon due to the mechanism of how Jason handle beliefs from environments.

The Plan Deletion (PD) operator generates one equivalent mutant, in which a plan that has empty context and empty body is deleted. This plan only exists in the first place to prevent a certain source of spurious runtime errors; when it is deleted, the agent will throw error messages at runtime, but there is no other effect on the agent behaviour. It could be suggested that this is in fact a non-equivalent mutant, but the runtime of the system is variable and the difference here is tiny. This mutant is not killed because our killing mutant criteria or test oracles don't check for this source of errors.

The Triggering Event Operator Replacement (TEOR) operator generates one equivalent mutant, in which the triggering event of the empty plan (discussed above for the PD operator) is changed from addition to deletion of some goal. This will just prevent the error messages discussed above from being thrown, so there is no change at all to the agent behaviour.

The Formula Operator Swap (FOS) operator generates one equivalent mutant, in which two formulae whose executions are completely independent (their order doesn't matter) are swapped. Specifically, the original order is first to remember the location where the agent just picked up the garbage, and then to move to the incinerator agent; reversing the order makes no difference to the agent behavior because this location will be used only after both formulae completes (more precisely, after the agent drops the garbage), although the original order seems more rational.

The Formula Operator Replacement (FOR) operator generates three equivalent mutants, in each of which a goal formula type "!" is replaced by "!!" or vice versa. As discussed in Section 2, a "!" goal pursuit stops the current plan until completed, while a "!!" goal pursuit can carry on in parallel with the rest of the plan. It is not difficult to see that in some cases they can be replaced by each other with no changes in the agent behaviour (only with semantic difference).

Non-equivalent Mutants

The Formula Deletion (FD) operator generates one non-equivalent mutant, in which the formula that is used to drop the carried garbage is deleted. It is not killed because our killing mutant criteria or test oracles are incomplete: they don't check whether the cleaner agent drops the carried garbage – it can pick up all the garbage without dropping any and still pass the tests.

The Formula Operator Replacement (FOR) operator produces one non-equivalent mutant, in which the formula *–+pos(last,X,Y)* in plan *+!carry_to(R)* is replaced by

+pos(last,X,Y). The former formula is used to update the belief that keeps last location where garbage was found, so that the agent can retrieve then return to this location after it drops garbage at the incinerator agent, so as to continue checking the remaining squares along the fixed path. However, when the formula is changed to the new version, each time the cleaner agent finds garbage, it will add a new belief representing the location of this garbage into the belief base rather than replacing the old one.

The above mutation introduces a fault, because it means that the agent will end up with several versions of "last location at which I found garbage" stored in its memory. In many cases, this is not a problem. When the cleaner agent has finished at the incinerator agent, it will try to take a shortest route back to last location where it found garbage. To do this, it queries for its belief about the last location, and it will always retrieve the correct one because Jason's default belief selection mechanism will always select the matching one that is added to the belief base most recently.

After each movement step, however, the agent will query "does my current location correspond to the last location I found garbage" i.e. should it cease its fast movement and go back to its slow side-to-side sweep of the map? If the agent is at any location where it previously found garbage, Jason's belief query mechanism will cause the answer to that question to be "yes" – all of the "last garbage location" beliefs will be checked for a match. At that point, it will go back into its slow sweep, even though (in this simple world) there's no chance of finding new garbage before it reaches the actual last garbage location. As a consequence, the whole collection process will take longer and the agent may not collect all the garbage within its specified time-to-live.

This fault cannot be detected by any of our tests designed for the cleaner agent, because in our tests (by chance) it never passes through a previous garbage location when returning to last collected garbage location (Fig. 5 shows an example where it would happen). In order to detect this fault, we add a test input that satisfies the following three conditions:

- A piece of garbage, *G1*, is located in a shortest path between the incinerator agent and another piece of garbage *G2*.
- *G1* is found prior to *G2*. This requires that *G1* and *G2* be located after where the incinerator agent is along the fixed side-to-side path that the agent uses to check all the squares.
- *G1 and G2* are not in the same row. This enables us to observe that the agent does indeed return to where *G1* was found after dropping either garbage for burning.

Fig. 8 shows a test that will detect this fault and thus kill this mutant. Under this test, the cleaner agent (*R1*) will always return to the location where *G1* was found after dropping either *G1* or *G2* at the incinerator agent (*R2*). It will then continue moving along the fixed side-to-side path from this location, and the second time it does this, this wastes time (there is guaranteed to be no further garbage on the way to the G2 location, since it's already swept that area). The additional time it spends doing this takes it over its time-to-live so the agent fails the test.

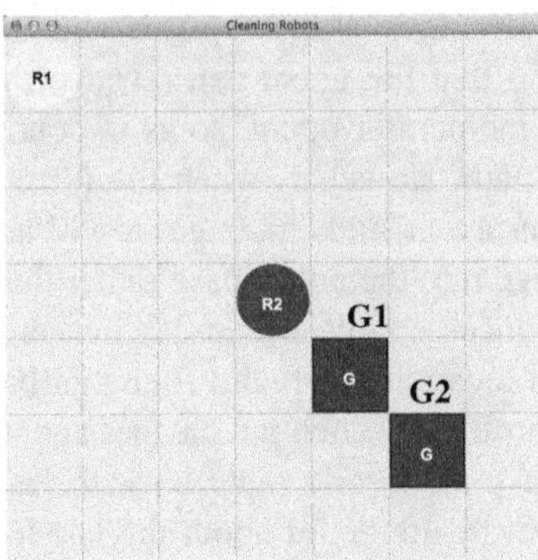

Fig. 8. A test that can detect the fault of multiple last locations

4.3 Discussion

In order to evaluate the power of our implemented high-level mutation operators, we used them to assess a test set for a simple Jason agent. We designed the test inputs according to what we thought as the most rigorous and viable criterion (a combination of three criteria) among those proposed by Low et al. Then we analysed the generated mutants that were not killed by the test set. To find out the hard-to-kill non-equivalent ones from these mutants, we took the following steps:

Firstly, we excluded two sources of mutants – those that should not have been generated and those non-equivalent but non-killed because of the incomplete test oracles (see 4.2 for the details). Those two sources are due to weaknesses in our implementation so they can be avoided.

Secondly, we excluded the equivalent mutants. Although they are of little interest to our current work, the details of them may be of some interest for future studies on how to reduce the relevant equivalent mutants. For instance, in some cases changing the formula operator "!!" to "!" only affects the agent behaviour in efficiency, so this rule can be ignored if this source of difference is not considered when killing mutants. Similarly, the Triggering Event Operator Replacement (TEOR) operator should not be applied to the empty plans that are only used to prevent spurious runtime messages.

Finally, we found a non-equivalent mutant that was not killed (regardless of how the test oracles are specified). From this, we deduce that Formula Operator Replacement (FOR) that generates this mutant is probably a powerful operator, more precisely, the rule of changing the formula operator "–+" to "+" is powerful.

5 Comparison with Related Work

Savarimuthu and Winikoff [7] systematically derive a set of mutation operators from the syntax of the AgentSpeak language (except that they derive those for agent communication from the Jason-style code). In contrast to their work, firstly we explicitly describe each of our derived operators while they do not give and describe the actual full operator set. Secondly we mutate the Jason-extended version of AgentSpeak, so some of our operators are specific to Jason while others are also applicable to AgentSpeak.

Jason-specific examples are the Rule Condition Deletion (RCD) operator that involves rules (introduced by Jason to enable theoretical reasoning), the Formula Operator Replacement (FOR) operator that involves some Jason specific operators (!! and –+), the Strong Negation Insertion/Deletion (SNID) operator that involves strong negation (introduced by Jason to increase the expressive power), and the Annotation Deletion (AD) and Source Replacement (SR) operator that involves annotations (specific to Jason).

Finally, we borrow some ideas from other existing mutation operators (for both conventional programs and MAS) when deriving ours, in the hope of preliminarily refining our set. For instance, changing a belief type to a goal type or vice versa doesn't make much sense (as learned from [8]), so it is not considered; there have been some well-defined mutation operators for some traditional concepts that are also used in Jason grammar (e.g., arithmetic expression), so we can directly borrow them after small adjustments.

Savarimuthu and Winikoff [8] systematically derive another set of mutation operators for the GOAL agent language (like AgentSpeak, GOAL is another language for programming cognitive agents), and then evaluate the representativeness of their set by comparison with some realistic bugs. In contrast, we evaluate the power of our set by comparison with some existing coverage criteria. Since an effective operator set requires ones that are both representative of realistic faults and powerful to guide generation of hard-to-kill mutants, our evaluation approach is complementary to theirs.

We have attempted to compare our evaluation results with theirs and found that our Formula Operator Replacement (FOR) operator (which is powerful in our experiment) is similar to one of their mutation rules – A:op1 (changing an operator), which doesn't involve any realistic bug observed in their experiment. However, considering our hard-to-kill mutant is generated by changing the mental note formula "–+bel", which is actually a composition of two adjacent formulae "–bel; +bel", to "+bel", while A:op1 doesn't involve any composite operator, our mutant is actually the result of their another rule – AC:drop (dropping an action), which involves the 4th most realistic bugs (i.e. 14 bugs, while the most representative rule involves 31 bugs) observed in their experiment. This comparison is not very convincing since the two studies are based on different agent languages, and both are quite preliminary, but it shows a way to evaluate the effectiveness of mutation operators, i.e. examining both the representativeness and the power of each operator.

Another related work is Adra and McMinn's [5]. Although they use a rather different agent model, some of their ideas are relevant to our work. They propose four mutation operator classes, among which their class for agent communication (Miscommunication, Message Corruption) corresponds to our operators for agent communication (Message Receiver Replacement, Illocutionary Force Replacement, Proposition Content Deletion and other involved high- and low-level operators), and their class for an agent's memory corresponds to our operators for beliefs (Belief Deletion, Rule Deletion and other involved low-level operators). Their mutation operator class for agent's function execution does not directly correspond to our operators since our agent model adopts the BDI reasoning mechanism, while their model does not. As to their mutation operator class for the environment, it is not relevant to our operators for agents, although environment is an important dimension of MAS.

6 Conclusions

In this paper we presented our preliminary work on mutation testing for Jason agents. We proposed a set of mutation operators for the Jason-extended AgentSpeak language and we described a mutation testing system called muJason, which implements the high-level subset of our operators. We then used our implemented operators to assess a test set (for an example agent) that satisfies some coverage criteria proposed by Low et al. [1]. We found a mutation operator – Formula Operator Replacement (FOR) – that guided generation of a non-equivalent mutant that is hard to kill. We are hence able to add a test into the test set for killing this mutant (and, probably, similar mutants or faults).

Our work extends Savarimuthu and Winikoff's work [7, 8] mainly in two respects: first, we extend the mutation operators for AgentSpeak by some operators specific to Jason; second, we propose an approach for assessing the power of operators, which is complementary to their approach for assessing the representativeness of operators.

Our work is preliminary and has a number of weaknesses. In terms of deriving mutation operators, we may miss some that may be of interest to our experiment since we did not consider the complete syntax of Jason and systematic ways to derive them (instead we intended to start with an initial set then implement and evaluate them in an incremental way). As to our evaluation, our results are limited as we only considered a single simple agent and a single source of coverage criteria, and because our finding is specific to Jason (the hard-to-kill mutant we found is the result of changing the Jason-specific formula operator "−+").

Our work also has some scalability issues. Firstly, we did not adopt an appropriate testing technique to specify test inputs and oracles; instead we used inefficient approaches such as manual specification via Java reflection, which are very difficult to use to specify a number of tests that are required by complex systems and tests that are able to detect small differences to the system behavior (mutants often only lead to such small differences). Secondly, in deriving test inputs that satisfies a specific coverage criterion, we did not use any technique for auto-measuring test coverage to guide our derivation work; instead we derived them by manual analysis of the program, which is impractical for complex programs.

Future work will first address the above issues. Before further evaluation of the power of our mutation operators, we will develop a unit testing technique for Jason agents (unit testing provides a flexible way to specify tests that are able to detect small differences in behavior) and techniques for auto-measuring test coverage. We will then be able to apply our approach to more complex Jason systems and to a range of coverage criteria. In the mean time, we will derive more mutation operators for Jason agents, then implement and evaluate them, along with the low-level ones that we proposed in this paper but did not implement in muJason so far.

Other potentially valuable studies include evaluating the representativeness of mutation operators for Jason (or other agent languages), improving the efficiency of mutation testing for multi-agent systems (e.g. by auto-reduction of equivalent mutants) and mutation of other aspects of multi-agent systems (e.g., environments, organizations and semantics).

References

1. Low, C.K., Chen, T.Y., Rönnquist, R.: Automated test case generation for BDI agents. Autonomous Agents and Multi-Agent Systems 2, 311–332 (1999)
2. Zhang, Z., Thangarajah, J., Padgham, L.: Automated unit testing for agent systems. In: 2nd International Working Conference on Evaluation of Novel Approaches to Software Engineering (ENASE 2007), pp. 10–18 (2007)
3. Miller, T., Padgham, L., Thangarajah, J.: Test coverage criteria for agent interaction testing. In: Weyns, D., Gleizes, M.P. (eds.) Proceedings of the 11th International Workshop on Agent Oriented Software Engineering, pp. 1–12 (2010)
4. Nguyen, C.D., Perini, A., Tonella, P.: Automated continuous testing of multi-agent systems. In: The Fifth European Workshop on Multi-Agent Systems (2007)
5. Adra, S.F., McMinn, P.: Mutation operators for agent-based models. In: Proceedings of 5th International Workshop on Mutation Analysis. IEEE Computer Society (2010)
6. Saifan, A.A., Wahsheh, H.A.: Mutation operators for JADE mobile agent systems. In: Proceedings of the 3rd International Conference on Information and Communication Systems, ICICS (2012)
7. Savarimuthu, S., Winikoff, M.: Mutation operators for cognitive agent programs. In: Proceedings of the 2013 International Conference on Autonomous Agents and Multi-Agent Systems (AAMAS 2013), pp. 1137–1138 (2013)
8. Savarimuthu, S., Winikoff, M.: Mutation Operators for the GOAL Agent Language. In: Winikoff, M., El Fallah Seghrouchni, A., Winikoff, M. (eds.) EMAS 2013. LNCS (LNAI), vol. 8245, pp. 255–273. Springer, Heidelberg (2013)
9. Houhamdi, Z.: Multi-agent system testing: A survey. International Journal of Advanced Computer Science and Applications (IJACSA) 2(6), 135–141 (2011)
10. Nguyen, C.D., Perini, A., Bernon, C., Pavón, J., Thangarajah, J.: Testing in multi-agent systems. In: Gleizes, M.-P., Gomez-Sanz, J.J. (eds.) AOSE 2009. LNCS, vol. 6038, pp. 180–190. Springer, Heidelberg (2011)
11. Ammann, P., Offutt, J.: Introduction to Software Testing. Cambridge University Press (2008)
12. Mathur, A.P.: Foundations of Software Testing. Pearson (2008)
13. Andrews, J.H., Briand, L.C., Labiche, Y.: Is mutation an appropriate tool for testing experiments? In: International Conference on Software Engineering (2005)
14. Bordini, R.H., Hübner, J.F., Wooldridge, M.: Programming Multi-Agent Systems in AgentSpeak using Jason. John Wiley & Sons (2007)
15. Wooldridge, M.: An Introduction to MultiAgent Systems, 2nd edn. John Wiley & Sons (2009)

Tractable Reasoning about Group Beliefs*

Barbara Dunin-Kęplicz[1], Andrzej Szałas[1,2], and Rineke Verbrugge[3]

[1] Institute of Informatics, Warsaw University, Poland
keplicz@mimuw.edu.pl

[2] Dept. of Computer and Information Science, Linköping University, Sweden
andrzej.szalas@mimuw.edu.pl

[3] Institute of Artificial Intelligence, University of Groningen, The Netherlands
L.C.Verbrugge@rug.nl

Abstract. In contemporary autonomous systems, like robotics, the need to apply group knowledge has been growing consistently with the increasing complexity of applications, especially those involving teamwork. However, classical notions of common knowledge and common belief, as well as their weaker versions, are too complex. Also, when modeling real-world situations, lack of knowledge and inconsistency of information naturally appear. Therefore, we propose a shift in perspective from reasoning in multi-modal logics to querying paraconsistent knowledge bases. This opens the possibility for exploring a new approach to group beliefs. To demonstrate expressiveness of our approach, examples of social procedures leading to complex belief structures are constructed via the use of epistemic profiles. To achieve tractability without compromising the expressiveness, as an implementation tool we choose 4QL, a four-valued rule-based query language. This permits both to tame inconsistency in individual and group beliefs and to execute the social procedures in polynomial time. Therefore, a marked improvement in efficiency has been achieved over systems such as (dynamic) epistemic logics with common knowledge and ATL, for which problems like model checking and satisfiability are PSPACE- or even EXPTIME-hard.

Keywords: Cooperation, reasoning for robotic agents, formal models of agency, knowledge representation, tractability.

1 A New Perspective on Beliefs

Classical approaches to common knowledge capture the essence of the mutuality involved in what it means to deal with common knowledge, as contrasted with distributed knowledge. According to the usual understanding, the essence of these notions is *consensus* between group participants. This is clearly visible in the notion of general knowledge $\text{E-K}{\small\text{NOW}}_G$ (every agent in group G knows), and propagation of consensus, through iterations $\text{E-K}{\small\text{NOW}}_G^k$ up to common knowledge $\text{C-K}{\small\text{NOW}}_G$, which informally can be seen as an infinitely iterated stack of general knowledge operators. This manner of building common knowledge, originating from epistemology and modal logic, captures "what every fool knows" [28, 44], [23, Chapter 2]. Indeed common knowledge is

* This work was partially supported by Polish National Science Centre grants 2011/01/B/ST6/02769, 2012/05/B/ST6/03094 and Vici grant NWO 227-80-001.

F. Dalpiaz et al. (Eds.): EMAS 2014, LNAI 8758, pp. 328–350, 2014.

helpful in drawing common consequences from commonly known premises, which is invaluable in creating models of others. But this comes at the price of super-polynomial complexity, causing grave problems when engineering multi-agent systems for use in time-critical situations [5, 24].

Theories dealing with various notions of knowledge and teamwork in multi-agent systems have been developed, among them the multi-modal logic TEAMLOG [23]. TEAMLOG allows to precisely model notions motivating agents to cooperate, such as collective intention, which integrates a strictly cooperative team together into a whole, and collective commitment, leading directly to team action based on a social plan that delineates how subgoals have been delegated to agents that have committed to perform them. Since teamwork occurs in various very diverse forms, it would not suffice to introduce one iron-clad notion of collective intention or collective commitment. Instead, using the expressive power of TEAMLOG, both notions should be calibrated to fit a variety of circumstances. The elements that vary from context to context are the levels of agents' awareness about the agent itself, other agents and the environment. Various forms of knowledge and beliefs constitute a fundamental layer of TEAMLOG.

As the role of group knowledge has recently evolved, it may instead be useful for participants to preserve their individual beliefs, while at the same time being a member of a larger group structure with group beliefs that govern the group's behavior. Instead of "what every fool knows", group knowledge would then tend to express synthetic information extracted from the information delivered by individuals. Thus, more so than in classical epistemic and doxastic logical approaches, there should be a clear distinction between agents' individual informational stances and the groups' ones. Consensus is not a requirement anymore, as group members do not necessarily adopt group conclusions. It suffices that during the group's lifetime they obey them.

In autonomous systems, the need to apply group knowledge has been growing with the increasing complexity of real-world applications, especially those involving cooperation or teamwork. A field that particularly expanded recently is robotics. In fact, contemporary robotics has now advanced so far that it has become necessary to investigate performance issues. Since more and more intelligent robots are able to autonomously perform sophisticated and precise maneuvers, we inevitably approach the era of strict cooperation among robots, software agents and people. Typical examples of such cooperation are emergency situations or catastrophes [2, 17, 24, 37, 47].

During robots' cooperation, an attempt to create consensus seems to be superfluous. Instead, in time-critical situations it is essential to *reduce the complexity* of both communication and reasoning. It is often too computationally costly to establish and reason about common beliefs and common knowledge. Especially when the information derives from different sources and is *imprecise*, problems arise due to the properties discussed in [21], including limited accuracy of sensors and other devices, restrictions on time and other resources, unfortunate combinations of environmental conditions, and limited reliability of physical devices. This combination of properties inevitably introduces *inconsistencies* on many different levels: in the information available to individual agents, between different agents, as well as between agents and groups and between groups and groups.

Even though in classical logical approaches, inconsistency immediately trivializes reasoning — "Ex falso sequitur quodlibet" — we intend to avoid such an effect. Robots are often sent to unknown terrains and face a need to sensibly proceed regardless of their ignorance and/or inconsistent information. This leads us to a paraconsistent approach, i.e., an approach that tolerates inconsistencies.[1] Thus, instead of fighting with inconsistencies, we treat them as first-class citizens. Typically, they need to be resolved sooner or later, depending on the situation in question, but in some reasonable cases they can even remain unresolved (see, e.g., [29]).

How to formally model such complicated situations? First of all, Dunin-Kęplicz and Szałas [19,21] have proposed a shift in perspective: from reasoning in multi-modal systems of high complexity to querying (paraconsistent) knowledge bases. This has led to a novel formalization of complex beliefs. In order to bridge the gap between idealized logical approaches and their actual implementations, the novel notion of *epistemic profile* serves as a tool for transforming preliminary beliefs into final ones.

An epistemic profile reflects an agent's individual reasoning capabilities: it defines a schema in which an agent reasons and deals with conflicting information and ignorance. These skills are achievable by combining various forms of reasoning, including belief fusion, disambiguation of conflicting beliefs, and completion of lacking information. More formally, an epistemic profile corresponds to a function mapping finite sets of ground literals to ground literals (see Definition 3.3). As epistemic profiles can be devised analogously both on an individual and a group level, we achieve a uniform treatment of individual and group beliefs.

Various challenges occurring when building epistemic profiles can be solved with the use of 4QL, a four-valued rule-based query language designed by Małuszyński and Szałas [40, 42, 53].[2] Our approach builds on ideas underlying 4QL, which allows for negation in premises and conclusions of rules. It provides simple, yet powerful constructs (modules and external literals) [40, 41] and more general multisource formulas [53] for expressing non-monotonic rules reflecting, among others, lightweight forms of default reasoning [51], auto-epistemic reasoning [45], defeasible reasoning [49], and the local closed world assumption [27]. Importantly, 4QL enjoys tractable query computation and captures all tractable queries; this means that 4QL can express exactly those properties which can be checked in deterministic polynomial time with respect to the size of the database domain (see [41] for details). Therefore, 4QL is a natural implementation tool opening the space for a diversity of applications by providing firm foundations for paraconsistent knowledge bases used by external applications. This paper is part of a larger research program started in [18–21, 25]. The main contributions of this article are (see also Table 1):

- Providing a tractable methodology for modeling *group beliefs* that ensures a proper treatment of inconsistent or lacking information, while avoiding unwanted effects like logical omniscience;
- Implementing examples of *social procedures*, leading to complex belief structures, via the use of epistemic profiles and 4QL;

[1] Paraconsistency has a long tradition and is intensively investigated (see, e.g., [4]).

[2] See also `http://4ql.org`, which provides an open source experimental interpreter of 4QL.

Table 1. Shift in perspective on group beliefs

Traditional approaches	The new approach
"What every fool knows"	Synthetic information extracted from individuals or other groups
Holistic knowledge	Selected aspects only
Consensus	Group members not forced to adopt group conclusions: only required to obey them during the group's lifetime
Logical omniscience	Incomplete/inconsistent beliefs allowed
Monotonicity	Non-monotonic resolution of incomplete/inconsistent beliefs offered
Homogeneity (typically)	Heterogeneity: reasoning is individualized; heterogeneous information sources allowed
Reasoning intractable	Tractability: reasoning in deterministic polynomial time

- Showing how to *tame inconsistency and incompleteness* in individual and group beliefs;
- Showing that social procedures for creating group beliefs, expressed in 4QL and using lightweight forms of non-monotonic reasoning, can be executed in *deterministic polynomial time.*

In this paper we focus on belief formation rather than belief maintenance and revision. Such dynamic aspects, for which 4QL is eminently suitable, will be presented in future work.

The rest of the paper is structured as follows. Section 2 presents a robot rescue scenario to be used as running example, while Section 3 presents the logical background on belief structures, epistemic profiles and 4QL. The heart of the paper includes Section 4, which introduces methods for creating group beliefs in 4QL according to agents' and groups' epistemic profiles. Section 5 focuses on solving the problem of conflicting information at the group level. Section 6 provides a formalization of the robot rescue scenario. Section 7 discusses the influence of group beliefs on members' individual beliefs. In Section 8, we show that social procedures expressible in 4QL are in fact tractable. We end with a discussion and topics for future research in Section 9.

2 Running Example: Robot Rescue Scenario

Consider a group of robots, each equipped with a temperature sensor. In our running example, their beliefs, as hardwired by the robots' manufacturer, are expressed by the following rules:

– if $\big(\textit{temperature} \leq 65^oC\big)$ then operating is safe; (1)

– if $\big(65^oC < \textit{temperature} \leq 80^oC\big)$ then risk of damage is serious; (2)

– if $\big(80^oC < \textit{temperature}\big)$ then it is certain that operating is impossible. (3)

Assume that there is fire in certain regions, resulting in a high temperature in these regions and their neighborhoods. Let a surveillance team $team = \{r_1, \ldots, r_k\}$ $(k > 1)$ of robots be formed, whose group beliefs include the one that searching for victims is more important than preserving robots. An example of a group belief can be:

– enter the affected region and search for victims unless it is certain that operating in the region is impossible. (4)

To formalize these and related rules we shall use the following relations, where R represents regions:

- $temp(R, T)$: temperature in R is T;
- $risk(R)$: situation in R is risky;
- $allowed(R)$: entering R is allowed (perhaps also in a risky situation);
- $search(R)$: search for victims in R.

Let us emphasize that each agent (robot) is equipped with its individual knowledge base, so it has individual beliefs about these relations. We also assume that geographic information system (GIS)-based information about subregions and robots' locations is available via the following relations:

- $close(P, R)$: robot P is close to R;
- $subreg(S, R)$: S is a subregion of R.

We use this robot rescue scenario throughout the paper.

3 Preliminaries

In what follows we assume that domains of objects are finite and that agents' reasoning is grounded in knowledge bases rather than in arbitrary theories. That is, in reasoning we allow rules and facts and consider well-supported models only.

3.1 Language, Belief Structures and Epistemic Profiles

We view *epistemic profiles* as the general means to express a variety of strategies for belief acquisition and formation. In order to apply them here, we present a summary of some of the most important definitions from [19–21, 40, 42]. The semantical structures *constituents* and *consequents* reflect the processes of agents' belief acquisition and formation. An agent starts with *constituents*, i.e., sets of beliefs acquired by perception, expert-supplied knowledge, communication with other agents, and many other ways. Next, the constituents are transformed into *consequents* according to the agent's *individual epistemic profile*. Consequents contain final, "mature" beliefs.

In a multi-agent system, for each group, the *group epistemic profile* is set up, where consequents of group members become constituents at the group level and such constituents are further transformed into group consequents. Observe that in this way, various perspectives of agents involved are taken into consideration and merged. Similarly, groups may be members of larger groups, perhaps containing individuals, too, etc.

Table 2. Truth tables for $\wedge$, $\vee$, $\rightarrow$ and $\neg$ (see [40, 54])

$\wedge$	f	u	i	t
f	f	f	f	f
u	f	u	u	u
i	f	u	i	i
t	f	u	i	t

$\vee$	f	u	i	t
f	f	u	i	t
u	u	u	i	t
i	i	i	i	t
t	t	t	t	t

$\rightarrow$	f	u	i	t
f	t	t	t	t
u	t	t	t	t
i	f	f	t	f
t	f	f	t	t

	$\neg$
f	t
u	u
i	i
t	f

As to the language, we use the classical first-order language over a given vocabulary without function symbols, presented in [21, 40, 53]. We assume that *Const* is a fixed set of constants, *Var* is a fixed set of variables and *Rel* is a fixed set of relation symbols.

Definition 3.1. A *literal* is an expression of the form $R(\bar{\tau})$ or $\neg R(\bar{\tau})$, with $\bar{\tau}$ being a sequence of arguments, $\bar{\tau} \in (Const \cup Var)^k$, where k is the arity of R. *Ground literals over Const*, denoted by $\mathcal{G}(Const)$, are literals without variables, with all constants in *Const*. If $\ell = \neg R(\bar{\tau})$ then $\neg \ell \stackrel{\text{def}}{=} R(\bar{\tau})$. ◁

Though we use classical first-order syntax, the semantics substantially differs from the classical one as truth values $\mathbf{t}, \mathbf{i}, \mathbf{u}, \mathbf{f}$ (true, inconsistent, unknown, false) are explicitly present; the semantics is based on sets of ground literals rather than on relational structures. This allows one to deal with lack of information as well as inconsistencies. Because 4QL is based on the same principles, it can directly be used as implementation tool.

The semantics of propositional connectives is summarized in Table 2. Observe that definitions of $\wedge$ and $\vee$ reflect minimum and maximum with respect to the ordering:

$$\mathbf{f} < \mathbf{u} < \mathbf{i} < \mathbf{t}, \tag{5}$$

as argued in [1, 40, 54]. Similarly, the semantics of quantifiers in formulas $\forall x A(x)/\exists x A(x)$ is defined using ordering (5), by taking the minimum (respectively, maximum) of the truth values of $A(a)$ for $a \in \Delta$, where Δ is the domain of x.

As a reminder from [40, 54], the truth tables for conjunction $\wedge$ and disjunction $\vee$ are defined as minimum and maximum with respect to the truth ordering, respectively. The implication $\rightarrow$ is a four-valued extension of classical implication, and is used to interpret 4QL-clauses. Whenever the body of a clause has value $\mathbf{f}$ or $\mathbf{u}$, the truth value of the whole clause is defined to be $\mathbf{t}$. This reflects our intention not to draw conclusions from false or unknown information: a clause with a body that is $\mathbf{f}$ or $\mathbf{u}$ is always satisfied, so one does not need to update its head. On the other hand, from an inconsistent body, we want to conclude that the head is also inconsistent. Thus, for a body with value $\mathbf{i}$, the implication is $\mathbf{t}$ if the head is $\mathbf{i}$, and $\mathbf{f}$ otherwise. If the body takes value $\mathbf{t}$ and the head takes value $\mathbf{t}$ or $\mathbf{i}$, the implication as a whole is $\mathbf{t}$. Note that, in contrast to classical two-valued logic, it is not the case that $\varphi \rightarrow \psi$ is equivalent to $\neg\varphi \vee \psi$, so the classical abbreviations cannot be used.

Let $v : Var \longrightarrow Const$ be a *valuation of variables*. For a literal ℓ, by $\ell(v)$ we understand the ground literal obtained from ℓ by substituting each variable x occurring in ℓ by constant $v(x)$.

Definition 3.2. The *truth value* $\ell(L, v)$ of a literal ℓ with respect to a set of ground literals L and valuation v, is defined by:

$$\ell(L,v) \stackrel{\text{def}}{=} \begin{cases} \mathfrak{t} \text{ if } \ell(v) \in L \text{ and } (\neg\ell(v)) \notin L; \\ \mathfrak{i} \text{ if } \ell(v) \in L \text{ and } (\neg\ell(v)) \in L; \\ \mathfrak{u} \text{ if } \ell(v) \notin L \text{ and } (\neg\ell(v)) \notin L; \\ \mathfrak{f} \text{ if } \ell(v) \notin L \text{ and } (\neg\ell(v)) \in L. \end{cases}$$
◁

Belief structures can now be defined as in [19,21].[3] Here, the concept of an *epistemic profile* is the key abstraction involved in belief formation. If S is a set, then $\text{FIN}(S)$ represents the set of all finite subsets of S.

Definition 3.3. Let $\mathbb{C} \stackrel{\text{def}}{=} \text{FIN}(\mathcal{G}(Const))$ be the set of all finite sets of ground literals over constants in *Const*. Then:

- an *epistemic profile* is any function $\mathcal{E} : \text{FIN}(\mathbb{C}) \longrightarrow \mathbb{C}$;
- by a *belief structure over epistemic profile* $\mathcal{E}$ is meant a structure $\mathcal{B}^{\mathcal{E}} = \langle \mathcal{C}, F \rangle$ with $\mathcal{C} \subseteq \mathbb{C}$ being a nonempty finite set of *constituents*,[4] and $F \stackrel{\text{def}}{=} \mathcal{E}(\mathcal{C})$ being the *consequent* of $\mathcal{B}^{\mathcal{E}}$. ◁

Importantly, final beliefs are represented as consequents.

3.2 The 4QL Rule Language

The rule language 4QL has been introduced in [40] and further developed in [42,53]. Beliefs in 4QL are distributed among *modules*, illustrated by the following example.

Example 3.4. Consider the scenario specified in Section 2. With each robot we associate a module containing relations '*temp*', '*risk*', '*search*'. With the group '*team*' we associate a module containing relations '*risk*', '*search*', '*allowed*'. The geographic information system module '*gis*' contains relations '*subreg*' and '*close*'. ◁

The 4QL language allows for negation in premises and conclusions of rules. It is based on the four-valued logic described in Section 3.1. The semantics of 4QL is defined by *well-supported models* [40–42,53], i.e., models consisting of (positive or negative) ground literals, where each literal is a conclusion of a derivation starting from facts. For any set of rules, such a model is uniquely determined:

> "Each module can be treated as a finite set of literals and this set can be computed in deterministic polynomial time with respect to the number of constants occurring in the module" [40,42].

Thanks to this correspondence and the fact that 4QL captures PTIME, the constituents and consequents of Definition 3.3, being PTIME-computable, can be directly implemented as 4QL modules (see also Theorem 8.1).

[3] Their indeterministic version is introduced and discussed in [22].

[4] That is, a constituent is any set $C \in \mathbb{C}$.

Remark 3.5. Note that this prevents the unfortunate effects of the *logical omniscience problem* (for a survey of the problem, see, e.g., [28, 38, 44, 52]): to check whether a formula A belongs to a set of beliefs of an individual or a group, one only has to determine what is its truth value in the respective consequent. Formula A can be considered as a query to a corresponding 4QL module, so tractability is preserved. As 4QL allows to express PTIME-computable queries only, intractable/uncomputable classes of valid formulas (e.g., expressing the consequences of the Peano axioms for first-order arithmetic) cannot be expressed as valid beliefs unless explicitly added to knowledge bases. $\lhd$

For specifying rules and querying modules, we adapt the language of [53]. To define the language, we need the notion of multisource formulas defined as follows.

Definition 3.6. A *multisource formula* is an expression of the form: $m.A$ or $m.A \in T$, where:

- m is a module name;
- A is a first-order or a multisource formula;
- $T \subseteq \{\mathfrak{t}, \mathfrak{i}, \mathfrak{u}, \mathfrak{f}\}$.

We write $m.A = v$ (respectively, $m.A \neq v$) to stand for $m.A \in \{v\}$ (respectively, $m.A \notin \{v\}$). $\lhd$

The intuitive meaning of a multisource formula $m.A$ is:

> "return the answer to query expressed by formula A, computed within the context of module m".

The value of '$m.A \in T$' is:

$$\begin{cases} \mathfrak{t} \text{ when the truth value of } A \text{ in } m \text{ is in the set } T; \\ \mathfrak{f} \; otherwise. \end{cases}$$

Let $A(X_1, \ldots, X_k)$ be a multisource formula with $X_1, \ldots, X_k$ being all its free variables and let D be a finite set of literals (a belief base). Then A, understood as a query, returns tuples $\langle d_1, \ldots, d_k, v \rangle$, where $d_1, \ldots, d_k$ are database domain elements and the value of $A(d_1, \ldots, d_k)$ in D is v.

Example 3.7. The following formula:

$$\exists S(gis.subreg(S, R) \wedge temp(S, T) \wedge T > 65) \quad (6)$$

states that there is a subregion of R with the temperature T exceeding 65. The 'gis' module stores information about subregions; the part '$gis.subreg(S, R)$' of (6) uses this module.[5] More precisely, formula (6), understood as a query, returns triples $\langle region, temperature, value \rangle$ such that the truth value of formula (6) is *value* when $R = region$ and $T = temperature$.

The formula:

$$\big(\exists S(gis.subreg(S, R) \wedge temp(S, T) \wedge T > 65)\big) \in \{\mathfrak{t}, \mathfrak{i}, \mathfrak{u}\}. \quad (7)$$

is true when the value of formula (6) is $\mathfrak{t}$, $\mathfrak{i}$ or $\mathfrak{u}$, and is false otherwise. $\lhd$

[5] It is assumed that formulas without a module label refer to the current module.

Definition 3.8.

- *Rules* are expressions of the form:

$$conclusion \text{ :– } premises. \tag{8}$$

  where *conclusion* is a positive or negative literal and *premises* are expressed by a multisource formula.
- A *fact* is a rule with empty premises (such premises are evaluated to $\mathbf{t}$).
- A *module* is a syntactic entity encapsulating a finite number of facts and rules.
- A 4QL *program* is a set of modules, where it is assumed that there are no cyclic references to modules involving multisource formulas of the form $m.A \in T$. ◁

Openness of the world is assumed, but rules can be used to close it locally or globally. Rules may be distributed among modules. Here follows an example, using the robot rescue scenario of Section 2.

Example 3.9. Consider the following rules within a module, say m, of a given robot:

$$risk(R) \text{ :– } close(R) \wedge [\text{formula (7)} = \mathbf{t}]. \tag{9}$$

$$\neg allowed(R) \text{ :– } temp(R, T) \wedge T > 80. \tag{10}$$

Rule (9) expresses the fact that region R is risky for the robot if it is close to R and formula (7) is true. Rule (10) states that the robot is not allowed to enter regions where the temperature exceeds 80°C.

One can query module m using multisource formulas like $m.risk(R)$, $m.allowed(R)$, $m.risk(R) \in \{\mathbf{t}, \mathbf{i}\}$, etc. ◁

4 Between Individual and Group Beliefs

Group beliefs gather conclusions of reasoning processes of the agents involved. Therefore, they are generally more synthetic than beliefs of group members, and deal with selected aspects only. If not stated differently, group beliefs prevail over individual ones. If a group belief about some aspect is missing or is inconsistent, an agent should be able to grab adequate information from its individual belief base or possibly complete it non-monotonically. These features should be reflected in the *epistemic profiles* (as discussed in Section 3.1).

4.1 Adjusting 4QL to Epistemic Profiles

To simplify formalization of epistemic profiles in 4QL, we shall identify consequents of robot r (or group of robots G) with a 4QL module having the same name r (respectively, G). For a truth value w, we write:

- $m.A = w$ to stand for $m.A \in \{w\}$;
- $m.A \neq w$ to stand for $m.A \in \{\mathbf{t}, \mathbf{i}, \mathbf{u}, \mathbf{f}\} - \{w\}$.

Although all phenomena presented in this paper are expressible in 4QL, we shall also use notation extending 4QL, yet simplifying the formalizations we need. For a group of robots $G = \{r_1, \ldots, r_k\}$ ($k \geq 1$), we introduce the following notation:

- $\exists r \in G[A(r)] \stackrel{\text{def}}{=} A(r_1) \vee \ldots \vee A(r_k)$;
- $\forall r \in G[A(r)] \stackrel{\text{def}}{=} A(r_1) \wedge \ldots \wedge A(r_k)$;
- $\#\{r \in G \mid A(r)\}$ is the number of members of G making A true (A is assumed here not to have free variables other than r); we shall also use the abbreviation $\#G \stackrel{\text{def}}{=} \#\{r \in G \mid \mathbf{t}\}$ (the number of members of G).

Example 4.1. Consider the robot rescue scenario. Typical rules for the robots can be:

$$search(R) \text{ :– } team.search(R) = \mathbf{t}. \tag{11}$$

$$\neg search(R) \text{ :– } temp(R, T) \wedge T > 80. \tag{12}$$

The first rule states that the robot should start searching for victims in region R if $search(R) = \mathbf{t}$ is a *team*'s belief. If the temperature excludes the possibility of robots' operation (see rule (3)), then the conclusion is $\neg search(R)$. Of course, rules (11)–(12) may lead to inconsistency when the temperature in a given region is over 80^oC and *team* still believes that searching that region is in order. This inconsistency can easily be resolved. If rules (11)–(12) are in a module, say m, then the robot may use a rule like:

$$\neg search(R) \text{ :– } m.search(R) = \mathfrak{i}. \tag{13}$$

Of course, one can define more refined solutions than *(13)*. ◁

4.2 Establishing Group Belief

Common knowledge and its weaker approximations, such as iterated general knowledge, can be viewed as a paradigmatic form of group knowledge. However, for many applications this is too much to ask for. After all, when using standard modal logics, such as in [23,44], the levels of iterated general beliefs harbor the risk of combinatorial explosion. Even for a group as small as three agents, $G = \{1, 2, 3\}$, we have:

$$\text{E-BEL}_G(p) \Leftrightarrow \text{BEL}(1, p) \wedge \text{BEL}(2, p) \wedge \text{BEL}(3, p); \tag{14}$$

$$\text{for } k \geq 1\text{: E-BEL}_G^{k+1}(p) \Leftrightarrow \text{E-BEL}_G(\text{E-BEL}_G^k(p)). \tag{15}$$

Observe that (15), when written in full, has 3^{k+1} conjuncts, so the complexity of building levels of general belief is exponential in the number of required levels, therefore not computable in polynomial time. Thus, for time-critical applications, one should completely change the approach to group belief.

Actually, full-fledged general and common belief is not needed for many real-world applications. The necessary shared belief state may result from agreement, some example methods of which will be listed in Section 4.3. On the other hand, the notion of *distributed knowledge* is sometimes referred to as "what a wise person would know".

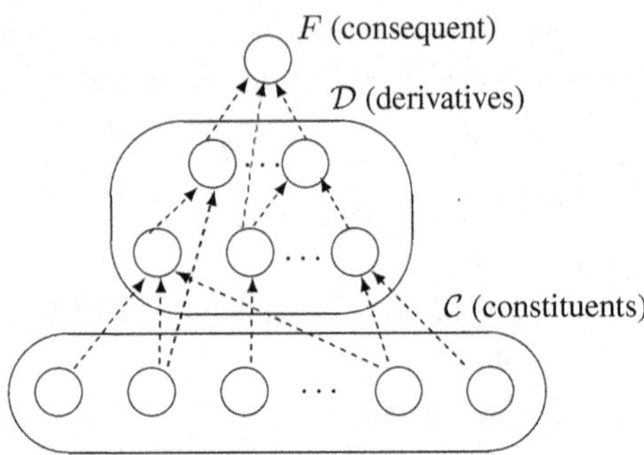

Fig. 1. Implementation framework for belief structures and epistemic profiles. Arrows indicate belief fusion processes.

This wise person would pull together the individual knowledge of group members, and would draw only classical conclusions from the combined information [44]. Distribution of reasoning is also an important feature of our approach, but why should we limit ourselves to classical reasoning only? Group knowledge may go even further than traditional distributed knowledge or belief: when starting from the same individual beliefs of the group members, a variety of reasoning methods and other techniques may lead to much more far-reaching conclusions. Epistemic profiles are introduced to encapsulate the variety of techniques used.

4.3 Building Epistemic Profiles

Creation of group beliefs takes place in the broader context of producing *derivatives*, understood as a complex process of drawing conclusions by different, temporarily existing, virtual subgroups or intermediate views [20, 21].[6] When the final *consequent* has been reached, the virtual subgroups involved may (but do not have to) disintegrate, while the consequent itself is spread among initial group members. This whole process, reflected in Figure 1 (from [20] with permission), can take place at any level of group aggregation.[7]

Using well-known heuristics, agents and groups have the possibility to complete their knowledge. Several reasoning methods can be used in the context of 4QL, as discussed in [18, 20, 25]:

- non-monotonic reasoning including the local closed-world assumption;
- default reasoning, circumscription, etc.;
- defeasible reasoning;
- methods inspired by argumentation theory.

A variety of social procedures, in combination with the reasoning methods above, may be used to establish different types of group knowledge or belief:

[6] Note that derivatives do not occur in the definition of belief structures. They are used to define epistemic profiles in a better structured and more readable manner.

[7] Though epistemic profiles may, in general, be of arbitrary complexity, in the current paper we only allow 4QL-based reasoning guaranteeing tractability.

- public announcements [16];
- different voting methods [48];
- methods involving power relations [11,35].

Example 4.2. Assume that agents in group G vote about the truth value of the formula:

$$temp(R,T) \wedge T > 65. \tag{16}$$

A simple way to encode such majority voting is:

$$risk(R) :- \#\{r \in G \mid r.[(16)] = \mathsf{t}\} > \#\{r \in G \mid r.[(16)] = \mathsf{f}\}.$$

The above rule can be made more subtle, e.g., by setting:

$$risk(R) :- \#\{r \in G \mid r.[(16)] \in \{\mathsf{t}, \mathfrak{i}\}\} > \#\{r \in G \mid r.[(16)] \in \{\mathsf{f}, \mathsf{u}\}\}.$$

Of course, such voting may be made more context-dependent by using relations other than those occurring in (16). ◁

It may be profitable to investigate the consequences of making group decisions based on voting rather than, for example, lengthy persuasion dialogues, such as those needed to establish collective intentions [13].

In appropriate circumstances, one may choose *seeing* rather than *communicating* as a method to create group belief. This can be seen as an analogy to "co-presence" [12]: by joint attention, the information is seen by everybody and everybody knows that the others in the group see this, and so on. Formally, this is more restrictive than the majority voting of the above example; for the robot rescue example such "co-presence" could follow the rule:

$$risk(R) :- \#\{r \in G \mid r.[(16)] = \mathsf{t}\} = \#G.$$

The relevant combination of social procedures and reasoning techniques is to be implemented as individual and group epistemic profiles by means of multisource formulas and 4QL modules.

4.4 Creating Virtual Groups

Sometimes a *virtual group* is created (among other reasons) in order to establish appropriate group beliefs. Whenever this happens, the virtual group's reasoning method has to be fixed, either implicitly or explicitly, and then represented in the virtual group's epistemic profile.

However complex the process of drawing a consequent from the constituents may be in terms of subgroups involved, at the end, the resulting consequent is seen by members of the initial group only. Analogously, in order to answer a question in daily life, you may look at Wikipedia, ask experts, and ask friends what they think about the issue. When you have finally drawn your conclusion, you often forget about the details of this process and do not necessarily communicate your final conclusion to all people involved, but only to those who need to know. This makes the process less complex and safer from the perspective of information security and, not to forget, also more relaxed.

The next important issue is a proper organization of reasoning processes and information sharing between different groups and/or agents belonging to different groups at the same time. As in everyday life, during an agent's reasoning and activities as a member of one group, the beliefs of other groups to which the agent belongs are temporarily suspended or hidden. In this situation, the agent sees only its individual and the current group beliefs. This way, switching between groups becomes simple and computationally efficient.[8] When a group belief is formed, this does not force each member to change its individual informational stance (Section 7). Relaxing this postulate creates an important difference from the attainment of common knowledge in the modal logic framework.

5 Conflicting Information

Whenever conflicting information appears, it may be resolved on the individual or group level in a similar way. If there is no means to resolve it within a given time and other constraints, the group can resort to less resource-demanding kinds of heuristics. As to timing, there are at least three strategies:

- "Killing inconsistency at the root": to solve them as soon as possible;
- On the other extreme, "living with inconsistency": to postpone disambiguation to the last possible moment (or even forever);
- Intermediate: to solve inconsistency each time new relevant information appears.

In the sequel, we focus on techniques for resolving inconsistencies, as those are generally independent of timing strategies.

5.1 Examples of Techniques

The context of the following simple examples is a group of robots in the rescue scenario deciding on the truth value of *search*(X), which is crucial in their decision making about whether action is needed.

Example 5.1. One can resolve potential inconsistencies using one of the following example policies.

- Search if at least one group member is convinced to do this:
$$\mathit{search}(R) \text{ :- } \exists r \in \mathit{team}[r.\mathit{search}(R) = \mathbf{t}]. \tag{17}$$
- Search if no group member opposes:
$$\mathit{search}(R) \text{ :- } \forall r \in \mathit{team}[r.\mathit{search}(R) \neq \mathsf{f}]. \tag{18}$$

[8] See also the discussion in Section 7, in particular Figure 2.

- Search if at least one group member is convinced to do this and no group member opposes:

$$search(R) :- (17) \wedge (18). \tag{19}$$

Of course, there are many other reasonable ways for resolving inconsistencies, some of them discussed below. ◁

In more complex scenarios, techniques for resolving inconsistency may reflect knowledge about the application domain involving legal regulations, argumentation, or other accepted strategies, such as the social procedures on which we focus next.

5.2 Social Procedures Solving Inconsistencies

In the subsequent example cases, the robots use different procedures to resolve inconsistent information about whether an area is risky, *risk(reg)*.

Case A: peer-to-peer Solving inconsistencies among peers may not be immediately possible. A possibility is to ignore the $\mathfrak{i}$-values and decide that on the group level, $risk(reg)$ is true. This solution takes the majority vote among the $\mathfrak{t}$ and $\mathfrak{f}$ votes only and is computationally very simple, as the following example solutions indicate.

Example 5.2. Suppose $G = \{r_1, r_2, r_3\}$ and one agent assigns value $\mathfrak{i}$ to $risk(reg)$ while two other agents assign $\mathfrak{t}$. It seems reasonable that the group then considers $risk(reg)$ to be true. The following rule formalizes this approach.

$$risk(reg) :- \exists r \in G(r.risk(reg) = \mathfrak{i}) \ \wedge \#\{r \in G \mid r.risk(reg) = \mathfrak{t}\} = 2.$$

Of course, this solution may be modified in particular cases, for example, when the agent voting for $\mathfrak{i}$ is much more reliable in estimating risk than other team members. A rule like the above can be generalized to arbitrary numbers of agents, for example "the majority among the agents who are voting $\mathfrak{t}$ or $\mathfrak{f}$, assigns $\mathfrak{t}$ to $risk(reg)$" can be formalized as

$$risk(reg) :- \#\{r \in G \mid r.risk(reg) = \mathfrak{f}\} < \#\{r \in G \mid r.risk(reg) = \mathfrak{t}\}. \quad \triangleleft$$

Example 5.3. Let again $G = \{r_1, r_2, r_3\}$. Now suppose two agents assign value $\mathfrak{u}$ to $risk(reg)$, while one agent assigns $\mathfrak{t}$ to it. What should be done with this lack of information? In case of majority voting, it seems fine to ignore the $\mathfrak{u}$ votes and restrict to taking the majority among the $\mathfrak{t}$ and $\mathfrak{f}$ votes. Also for larger groups, even if there are many agents assigning $\mathfrak{u}$ to the formula, it still makes sense to compute the majority among the $\mathfrak{t}$ and $\mathfrak{f}$ votes only, as done in Example 4.2. ◁

Case B: with authority or outside expert Let us describe several possible procedures using the framework of 4QL, in the context of the robot rescue scenario.

Procedure B1: *A group belief identified with the leader's or an expert's belief*

Suppose $expLead$ is a consequent of an expert or leader knowledge base, deciding whether certain regions R are risky. If the expert's or leader's value of $risk(R) = \mathbf{t}$, then the group value corresponds. The following rules can then be used to express *team*'s consequents as to the risk:

$$risk(R) :- expLead.risk(R) = \mathbf{t}.$$

$$\neg risk(R) :- expLead.risk(R) \in \{\mathbf{u}, \mathbf{i}, \mathbf{f}\}.$$

Procedure B2: *Conditional choice between leader, expert, and majority*

A safer choice is to use all information about $risk(R)$ based on trustworthiness:

> "If there is an outside expert on $risk(R)$, then we take his decision that $risk(R) = \mathbf{t}$ as the group decision; else, if the leader's evaluation of $risk(R)$ is $\mathbf{t}$, then we take on the leader's decision as group belief; else, we cast a majority vote."

This is reflected in the following rules, where exp is a group of outside experts and $lead$ is the leader:

$$risk(R) :- \exists e \in exp[e.risk(R) = \mathbf{t}]. \tag{20}$$

$$risk(R) :- \forall e \in exp[e.risk(R) \neq \mathbf{t}] \wedge lead.risk(R) = \mathbf{t}. \tag{21}$$

$$risk(R) :- \forall e \in exp[e.risk(R) \neq \mathbf{t}] \wedge lead.risk(R) \neq \mathbf{t} \wedge \text{`}risk(R) = \mathbf{t} \text{ wins voting'}. \tag{22}$$

Note that the voting in the last line can be formalized along the lines of Example 4.2.

To infer negative conclusions as to $risk(R)$, one can add rules negating conclusions and premises of (20)–(22). For example, adding such negations in rule (20), we obtain:

$$\neg risk(R) :- \neg \exists e \in exp[e.risk(R) = \mathbf{t}].$$

One could also close the relation *risk* in various ways. If rules (20)–(22) are defined in module m, then the simplest closure can be obtained using the following rule (in a module other than m):

$$\neg risk(R) :- m.risk(R) \neq \mathbf{t}.$$

6 A Formalization of the Robot Rescue Scenario

Let us now formalize an illustrative example of an epistemic profile for the module *team* using the robot rescue scenario of Section 2. Recall that 4QL modules can be identified with sets of literals. In what follows we use this identification.

The *team*'s belief structure consists of constituents:

- consequents of each robot $r_1, \ldots, r_k$ in *team*;
- the gis module.

To define *team*'s epistemic profile, we use the following derivatives:

- *allClose*, containing the relation *risk*, calculated according to votes of all agents close to a given region;
- *safe*, containing the relation *allowed*, stating that searching a given region is allowed (no certainty of damaging robots there).

The above derivatives are used for illustration purposes only.
The module *allClose* contains, among others, the following rules:

$$\begin{aligned} risk(R) \text{ :- } & \#\{r \in team \mid gis.close(r,R) = \mathsf{t} \wedge r.risk(R) = \mathsf{t}\} > \\ & \#\{r \in team \mid gis.close(r,R) = \mathsf{t} \wedge r.risk(R) \neq \mathsf{t}\}. \\ \neg risk(R) \text{ :- } & \#\{r \in team \mid gis.close(r,R) = \mathsf{t} \wedge r.risk(R) = \mathsf{t}\} \leq \\ & \#\{r \in team \mid gis.close(r,R) = \mathsf{t} \wedge r.risk(R) \neq \mathsf{t}\}. \end{aligned}$$

The module *safe* contains the rule:

$$\neg allowed(R) \text{:- } \exists r \in team \big(gis.close(r,R) = \mathsf{t} \wedge r.temp(R,T) = \mathsf{t} \wedge T > 80\big).$$

The *team*'s consequent can be defined, for example, by the following rules:

$$risk(R) \text{ :- } allClose.risk(R). \tag{23}$$

$$\neg risk(R) \text{ :- } allClose.(\neg risk(R)) \wedge safe.allowed(R) \neq \mathfrak{f}. \tag{24}$$

$$search(R) \text{ :- } safe.allowed(R) \neq \mathfrak{f}. \tag{25}$$

Of course, robots may have individual beliefs about *risk* and *search*(R) contradicting (23)–(25). These inconsistencies can be resolved by a rule similar to (13), concluding that a robot cannot search regions where it cannot operate without being damaged.

7 From Groups Down to Agents

Group belief may be naturally used to clarify agents' individual beliefs. For example, if for some agent r the value of P is $\mathfrak{u}$ or $\mathfrak{i}$, and for group G the value became one of $\mathfrak{t}, \mathfrak{f}$, then generally it makes sense for r to adopt this latter truth value. Formally, this could be handled by a default rule in the agent's epistemic profile, where we distinguish between a constituent of r, denoted by c, and its consequent, denoted by r:

> if $c.P \in \{\mathfrak{i}, \mathfrak{u}\}$ and $G.P \in \{\mathfrak{t}, \mathfrak{f}\}$ (prerequisite) and it is consistent that "special situation (S) does not occur" (justification), then $r.P$ becomes $G.P$.

This is achieved in 4QL by placing the following rules in the module implementing consequent r:

$$P \text{ :- } c.P \in \{\mathfrak{i}, \mathfrak{u}\} \wedge G.P = \mathfrak{t} \wedge S \in \{\mathfrak{f}, \mathfrak{u}\}.$$

$$\neg P \text{ :- } c.P \in \{\mathfrak{i}, \mathfrak{u}\} \wedge G.P = \mathfrak{f} \wedge S \in \{\mathfrak{f}, \mathfrak{u}\}.$$

This way, coherence of knowledge can be maintained. The process does call for calculating a new well-supported model. Such downward reflection is useful when the group decides about critical situations. Then each individual should follow this.

When a decision is not life-critical, different opinions remain possible. For example, when a jury decides that the Best Paper Prize should be given to A while an individual jury member would have preferred B, (s)he can keep her/his opinion while the group decision stands. Similarly when a program chair decides that a certain paper is acceptable for the proceedings, individual program committee members do not need to agree to the group decision. The mode of adaptation to group beliefs needs to be included in everyone's epistemic profile. This real-world model of the information flow between a group and its individual members fits to many contexts better than common knowledge.

While 4QL does not allow for circular dependencies between modules, it is important to note that there may be loops in managing beliefs when circular dependencies among individuals and groups occur in applications, for example, due to the used updating policies. However, it is the responsibility of application designers to avoid such loops. The following example illustrates this issue.

Example 7.1. Consider a module m being a constituent of a group belief structure with consequent G. Let m consist only of facts of the form:

$$s(a), \neg s(b), s(c), \ldots,$$

and let G consist of the rule:

$$r(X) :\!-\ m.s(X) = \mathbf{t}. \tag{26}$$

Suppose further that an external application implements the following policy of updates:

$$m.s(X) \text{ becomes false whenever } G.r(X) \text{ becomes true;} \tag{27}$$

$$m.s(X) \text{ becomes true whenever } G.r(X) \text{ becomes unknown.} \tag{28}$$

If, at some point, a fact $s(d)$ becomes true in m then rule (26) makes $G.r(d)$ true. However, when $G.r(d)$ becomes true, the update (27) makes $m.s(d)$ false which, in turn, makes $G.r(d)$ unknown (the premise of rule (26) becomes false). According to (28), whenever $G.r(d)$ becomes unknown, $m.s(d)$ becomes true, and a loop occurs. However, this loop is caused by the design of the update policy, being out of the scope of 4QL itself. $\lhd$

To avoid loops, no circularity should be allowed. To achieve non-circularity, one may equip each agent with several belief structures:

- the main one modeling the agent's beliefs;
- a separate belief structure associated with each group the agent belongs to;
- other structures, when needed.

Figure 2 shows an example of such an architecture. Agent A has its "main" belief structure B with consequent F, which becomes a constituent of belief structures $G_1, \ldots, G_k$

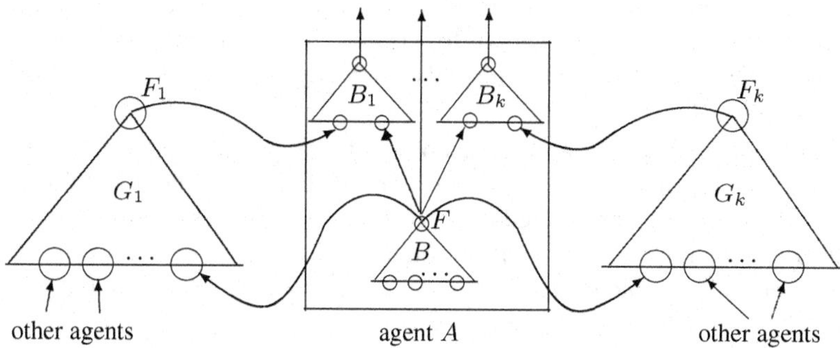

Fig. 2. Architecture of groups and agents. Arrows indicate the use of consequents of belief structures as constituents of other belief structures.

of groups A belongs to. For every group belief structure G_i $(1 \leq i \leq k)$ there is an associated belief structure B_i within A, with constituents F and F_i. Each belief structure B_i exists as long as A is a member of group G_i. This way agent A can easily switch between belief structures according to the role it plays at a given moment. When B_i is being deleted, belief structure B may be updated using information from B_i, but circularity is avoided.

8 Complexity

Consider a static situation without knowledge base updates. Thus, we have a snapshot of a system consisting of, say, k individuals and n groups, each of them computing its consequents according to its epistemic profile (Definition 3.3). Since data complexity of 4QL is PTIME and 4QL captures PTIME (see [41,42]), we have the following result, where, as usually, finite domains are assumed.

Theorem 8.1. *Assume that the number of constituents of each individual as well as the number of belief structures associated with each individual/group is bounded by a constant. Let k be the number of agents and let n be the number of groups under consideration.*

- *If each constituent and epistemic profile involved is implemented in 4QL, then the complexity of computing them all is $O\big((k+n)*p(|Const|)\big)$, where p is a polynomial and Const is the set of constants occurring in constituents and epistemic profiles.*
- *Every epistemic profile/belief structure computable in deterministic polynomial time (PTIME with respect to data complexity) can be expressed in 4QL (assuming linear ordering on Const is given).* ◁

Note that in this way, tractability is achieved. Though complexity depends on k and n, these parameters reflect the numbers of individuals and groups involved in a given mission. Such individuals and groups must have been generated somehow, so we can safely assume the existence of computational capacity to handle them.

If system dynamics is considered, Theorem 8.1 guarantees that every time updates need to be performed, they can be done in deterministic polynomial time. In fact, the role of 4QL is to provide firm foundations for knowledge bases used by applications external to 4QL. The application's behavior and complexity are controlled by its designers (see also Example 7.1).

Note that there is a price to pay for tractability of our approach. Namely, we neither allow disjunctive facts nor disjunctive conclusions of rules, so without additional constructs we cannot express unrestricted disjunctive reasoning unless PTIME =NPTIME. On the other hand, all tractable reasoning schemata are captured by our framework, so all tractable forms of disjunctive reasoning are expressible, too, though not necessarily directly.

9 Discussion and Conclusions

In the current literature on knowledge and beliefs, modal logic-based approaches are dominant. Even though they suit very well to idealized epistemic theories, they are hardly applicable to real-world complex scenarios. In order to apply them one needs to use some restricted versions of modal logics, like in [36, 46]. However, neither of these approaches deals with *inconsistent* knowledge bases and [36] deals solely with limited forms of *incomplete* multi-agent knowledge. In contrast, in the current paper we offer a novel approach to group beliefs, intended to bridge the gap between theory and applications.

We also introduce a variety of social procedures for creating group beliefs within a paraconsistent four-valued framework offered by 4QL, allowing for tractable reasoning. Importantly, our approach does not share unwanted omniscience effects like closure under logical consequence or irrelevant belief handling.

To the best of our knowledge, a paraconsistent approach to beliefs has so far mainly been pursued in the context of belief revision [43, 50], not the creation of group beliefs. These other approaches substantially differ from ours. Their models are based on criteria and rationality indexes [50] or on relevant logic [43].

Accepting four rather than two logical values considerably simplifies our approach where one is not forced to find general embeddings of $\{\mathsf{t}, \mathfrak{i}, \mathsf{u}, \mathsf{f}\}$ into $\{\mathsf{t}, \mathsf{f}\}$ that would work in all considered contexts. Instead, we offer a framework in which such embeddings can much more easily be obtained either totally or partially, or even avoided altogether, in a highly context- and user-dependent manner. To our knowledge, such flexibility, expressiveness and at the same time tractability has not been achieved before.

We have taken into account that agents are heterogeneous in the ways that they reason; this in contrast to classical epistemic logics, which view agents as if they were homogeneous; a recent exception is the work by Liu [39]. Agents' reasoning patterns may differ significantly, which is reflected in the epistemic profiles of individual agents as well as of different (sub-)groups. Another approach to heterogeneity of information sources is proposed in [6, 10, 31, 32], where multi-context systems are considered. Inconsistencies in multi-context systems are addressed, e.g., in [7,26]. To fuse knowledge from various contexts, bridge rules are used. However, the associated reasoning problems are typically of high complexity [7].

Developed from logic programming, answer set programming has been used to formalize qualitative decision making in individual agents [9, 30]. However, to decide whether a given program has some answer set is NP-complete already in the propositional case while non-grounded programs have exponentially higher complexity [8]. In a multi-agent epistemic context Baral et al. [3] provide an answer set programming approach to group beliefs; in their approach, reasoning problems such as the muddy children puzzle, however, inherit their high complexity from modal logic. In addition, like the modal approaches discussed above, the above-mentioned answer set programming approaches allow only consistent models and do not provide means for disambiguating inconsistencies.

There are also many techniques for resolving inconsistencies other than those presented and discussed in our paper. In particular, one could apply techniques known from defeasible reasoning [49]. One could also think of applying Boolean games in which control over specific literals is assigned to different agents. For some examples from the extensive literature, we refer to [11, 33, 35, 48].

We have also proposed some extensions to 4QL, allowing one to express a rich repertoire of combinations of social procedures with non-monotonic reasoning techniques and inconsistency disambiguation, based on the possibilities of 4QL. Although these extensions can be expressed in "pure" 4QL, we have achieved their substantial simplification here, which also is a novel contribution.

We have represented epistemic profiles, belief structures and social procedures for creating group belief in 4QL, discussing a number of example procedures of increasing intricacy. Theorem 8.1 then shows that all these aspects can be executed in polynomial time. This is a marked improvement over some of the most well-known logics for multi-agent systems. More precisely, for modal logics incorporating common knowledge or common belief, model checking is PSPACE-complete, while the satisfiability problem is EXPTIME-complete [16, 23, 44]. For logics of propositional control and coalition logics, both model checking and satisfiability are PSPACE-complete [35]. Finally, for alternating-time temporal logic (ATL), both model checking and satisfiability are even EXPTIME-complete [34, 55]. In real-time applications like time-critical teamwork, the advantages of using a tractable approach such as the one advocated here are essential.

In future work, we will also apply our approach to finding tractable solutions for classical puzzles in epistemic logic, such as the wise men, the muddy children, and the sum and product puzzle. These are classically formalized and solved by constructing (dynamic) epistemic models, which are often huge in terms of the input [14, 15, 28, 44].

This paper is part of a larger research program. Here, we focus on belief formation in heterogeneous groups, while dynamical aspects, such as maintenance of group beliefs and belief revision, are left to future research. A general problem in robotics is how the activities of different groups dovetail and interleave together. This needs to be smartly organized to allow agents to smoothly switch between activities in different groups. While the focus of this paper is agents' *reasoning* via individual and group epistemic profiles, in future work we will discuss the organizational part of group activities.

References

1. de Amo, S., Pais, M.: A paraconsistent logic approach for querying inconsistent databases. International Journal of Approximate Reasoning 46, 366–386 (2007)
2. Balakirsky, S., et al.: Towards heterogeneous robot teams for disaster mitigation: Results and performance metrics from RoboCup Rescue. Journal of Field Robotics 24(11-12), 943–967 (2007)
3. Baral, C., Gelfond, G., Son, T.C., Pontelli, E.: Using answer set programming to model multi-agent scenarios involving agents' knowledge about other's knowledge. In: Proceedings of the 9th International Conference on Autonomous Agents and Multiagent Systems, vol. 1, pp. 259–266. International Foundation for Autonomous Agents and Multiagent Systems (2010)
4. Bézieau, J.J., Carnielli, W., Gabbay, D. (eds.): Handbook of Paraconsistency. College Publications (2007)
5. Bordini, R., Dastani, M., Dix, J., El Fallah-Seghrouchni, A. (eds.): Multi-Agent Programming: Languages, Platforms and Applications. Springer (2009)
6. Brewka, G., Eiter, T.: Equilibria in heterogeneous nonmonotonic multi-context systems. In: Proc. of the 22nd AAAI Conf. on Artificial Intelligence, pp. 385–390. AAAI Press (2007)
7. Brewka, G., Eiter, T., Fink, M., Weinzierl, A.: Managed multi-context systems. In: Walsh, T. (ed.) Proc. of the 22nd International Joint Conference on Artificial Intelligence, IJCAI 2011, pp. 786–791. IJCAI/AAAI (2011)
8. Brewka, G., Eiter, T., Truszczynski, M.: Answer set programming at a glance. Commun. ACM 54(12), 92–103 (2011)
9. Brewka, G.: Answer sets and qualitative decision making. Synthese 146(1-2), 171–187 (2005)
10. Casali, A., Godo, L., Sierra, C.: A language for the execution of graded BDI agents. Logic Journal of the IGPL 21(3), 332–354 (2013)
11. Chalkiadakis, G., Elkind, E., Wooldridge, M.: Computational Aspects of Cooperative Game Theory. Morgan & Claypool Publishers (2011)
12. Clark, H., Marshall, C.: Definite reference and mutual knowledge. In: Joshi, A., Webber, B., Sag, I. (eds.) Elements of Discourse Understanding, pp. 10–63. Cambridge University Press (1981)
13. Dignum, F., Dunin-Kęplicz, B., Verbrugge, R.: Creating collective intention through dialogue. Logic Journal of the IGPL 9, 145–158 (2001)
14. Ditmarsch, H.P.v., Ruan, J., Verbrugge, L.C.: Model checking sum and product. In: Zhang, S., Jarvis, R.A. (eds.) AI 2005. LNCS (LNAI), vol. 3809, pp. 790–795. Springer, Heidelberg (2005)
15. van Ditmarsch, H.P., Ruan, J., Verbrugge, R.: Sum and product in dynamic epistemic logic. Journal of Logic and Computation 18(4), 563–588 (2008)
16. van Ditmarsch, H., van der Hoek, W., Kooi, B.: Dynamic Epistemic Logic, vol. 337. Springer (2007)
17. Doherty, P., Heintz, F., Kvarnström, J.: High-level mission specification and planning for collaborative unmanned aircraft systems using delegation. Unmanned Systems 1(1), 75–119 (2013)
18. Dunin-Kęplicz, B., Strachocka, A., Szałas, A., Verbrugge, R.: A paraconsistent approach to speech acts. In: Proc. Workshop on Argumentation in Multi-Agent Systems, pp. 59–78. IFAAMAS (2012)
19. Dunin-Kęplicz, B., Szałas, A.: Epistemic profiles and belief structures. In: Jezic, G., Kusek, M., Nguyen, N.-T., Howlett, R.J., Jain, L.C. (eds.) KES-AMSTA 2012. LNCS, vol. 7327, pp. 360–369. Springer, Heidelberg (2012)

20. Dunin-Kęplicz, B., Szałas, A.: Paraconsistent distributed belief fusion. In: Fortino, G., Badica, C., Malgeri, M., Unland, R. (eds.) Intelligent Distributed Computing VI. SCI, vol. 446, pp. 56–69. Springer, Heidelberg (2013)
21. Dunin-Kęplicz, B., Szałas, A.: Taming complex beliefs. In: Nguyen, N.T. (ed.) Transactions on CCI XI. LNCS, vol. 8065, pp. 1–21. Springer, Heidelberg (2013)
22. Dunin-Kęplicz, B., Szałas, A.: Indeterministic belief structures. In: Jezic, G., Kusek, M., Lovrek, I., Howlett, R. J., Jain, L.C. (eds.) Agent and Multi-Agent Systems: Technologies and Applications. AISC, vol. 296, pp. 57–66. Springer, Heidelberg (2014)
23. Dunin-Kęplicz, B., Verbrugge, R.: Teamwork in Multi-Agent Systems: A Formal Approach. Wiley (2010)
24. Dunin-Kęplicz, B., Verbrugge, R., Slizak, M.: TEAMLOG in action: A case study in teamwork. Comput. Sci. Inf. Syst. 7(3), 569–595 (2010)
25. Dunin-Kęplicz, B., Strachocka, A.: Perceiving rules under incomplete and inconsistent information. In: Leite, J., Son, T.C., Torroni, P., van der Torre, L., Woltran, S. (eds.) CLIMA XIV 2013. LNCS (LNAI), vol. 8143, pp. 256–272. Springer, Heidelberg (2013)
26. Eiter, T., Fink, M., Schüller, P.: Approximations for explanations of inconsistency in partially known multi-context systems. In: Delgrande, J.P., Faber, W. (eds.) LPNMR 2011. LNCS (LNAI), vol. 6645, pp. 107–119. Springer, Heidelberg (2011)
27. Etzioni, O., Golden, K., Weld, D.: Sound and efficient closed-world reasoning for planning. Artificial Intelligence 89, 113–148 (1997)
28. Fagin, R., Halpern, J., Moses, Y., Vardi, M.: Reasoning About Knowledge. MIT Press (1995)
29. Gabbay, D., Hunter, A.: Making inconsistency respectable: A logical framework for inconsistency in reasoning. In: Jorrand, P., Kelemen, J. (eds.) FAIR 1991. LNCS, vol. 535, pp. 19–32. Springer, Heidelberg (1991)
30. Gelfond, M., Kahl, Y.: Knowledge Representation, Reasoning, and the Design of Intelligent Agents - The Answer-Set Programming Approach. Cambridge University Press (2014)
31. Giunchiglia, F., Serafini, L.: Multilanguage hierarchical logics, or: How we can do without modal logics. Artificial Intelligence 65(1), 29–70 (1994)
32. Giunchiglia, F., Serafini, L., Giunchiglia, E., Frixione, M.: Non-omniscient belief as context-based reasoning. In: IJCAI, vol. 93, pp. 9206–9203 (1993)
33. Harrenstein, P., van der Hoek, W., Meyer, J.J., Witteveen, C.: Boolean games. In: van Benthem, J. (ed.) Proc. of the 8th Conference on Theoretical Aspects of Rationality and Knowledge, pp. 287–298. Morgan Kaufmann Publishers Inc. (2001)
34. van der Hoek, W., Lomuscio, A., Wooldridge, M.: On the complexity of practical ATL model checking. In: Proc. of the 5th AAMAS, pp. 201–208. ACM (2006)
35. van der Hoek, W., Wooldridge, M.: On the logic of cooperation and propositional control. Artificial Intelligence 164(1-2), 81–119 (2005)
36. Lakemeyer, G., Lespérance, Y.: Efficient reasoning in multiagent epistemic logics. In: De Raedt, L., Bessière, C., Dubois, D., Doherty, P., Frasconi, P., Heintz, F., Lucas, P. (eds.) Proc. of ECAI 2012 - 20th European Conference on Artificial Intelligence. Frontiers in Artificial Intelligence and Applications, vol. 242, pp. 498–503. IOS Press (2012)
37. Landén, D., Heintz, F., Doherty, P.: Complex task allocation in mixed-initiative delegation: A UAV case study. In: Desai, N., Liu, A., Winikoff, M. (eds.) PRIMA 2010. LNCS, vol. 7057, pp. 288–303. Springer, Heidelberg (2012)
38. Levesque, H.J.: A logic of implicit and explicit belief. In: Proceedings of the Fourth National Conference on Artificial Intelligence (AAAI 1984), pp. 198–202 (1984)
39. Liu, F.: Diversity of agents. In: Agotnes, T., Alechina, N. (eds.) Proc. of the ESSLLI Workshop on Resource-bounded Agents, pp. 88–98 (2006)
40. Małuszyński, J., Szałas, A.: Living with inconsistency and taming nonmonotonicity. In: de Moor, O., Gottlob, G., Furche, T., Sellers, A. (eds.) Datalog 2010. LNCS, vol. 6702, pp. 384–398. Springer, Heidelberg (2011)

41. Małuszyński, J., Szałas, A.: Logical foundations and complexity of 4QL, a query language with unrestricted negation. Journal of Applied Non-Classical Logics 21(2), 211–232 (2011)
42. Małuszyński, J., Szałas, A.: Partiality and inconsistency in agents' belief bases. In: Barbucha, D., et al. (eds.) Proc. KES-AMSTA. Frontiers of Artificial Intelligence and Applications, vol. 252, pp. 3–17. IOS Press (2011)
43. Mares, E.: A paraconsistent theory of belief revision. Erkenntnis 56, 229–246 (2002)
44. Meyer, J.J.C., van der Hoek, W.: Epistemic Logic for Computer Science and Artificial Intelligence. Cambridge University Press (1995)
45. Moore, R.: Possible-world semantics for autoepistemic logic. In: Proc. 1st Nonmonotonic Reasoning Workshop, pp. 344–354 (1984)
46. Nguyen, L.A.: On modal deductive databases. In: Eder, J., Haav, H.-M., Kalja, A., Penjam, J. (eds.) ADBIS 2005. LNCS, vol. 3631, pp. 43–57. Springer, Heidelberg (2005)
47. Nourbakhsh, I., Sycara, K., Koes, M., Yong, M., Lewis, M., Burion, S.: Human-robot teaming for search and rescue. IEEE Pervasive Computing 4(1), 72–79 (2005)
48. Nurmi, H.: Voting Procedures under Uncertainty. Springer (2002)
49. Nute, D.: Defeasible logic. In: Handbook of Logic in Artificial Intelligence and Logic Programming, pp. 353–395. Oxford University Press (1994)
50. Priest, G.: Paraconsistent belief revision. Theoria 67, 214–228 (2001)
51. Reiter, R.: A logic for default reasoning. Artificial Intelligence Journal 13, 81–132 (1980)
52. Sim, K.: Epistemic logic and logical omniscience: A survey. International Journal of Intelligent Systems 12, 57–81 (1997)
53. Szałas, A.: How an agent might think. Logic Journal of the IGPL 21(3), 515–535 (2013)
54. Vitória, A., Małuszyński, J., Szałas, A.: Modeling and reasoning with paraconsistent rough sets. Fundamenta Informaticae 97(4), 405–438 (2009)
55. Walther, D., Lutz, C., Wolter, F., Wooldridge, M.: ATL satisfiability is indeed EXPTIME-complete. Journal of Logic and Computation 16(6), 765–787 (2006)

Semantic Representations of Agent Plans and Planning Problem Domains

Artur Freitas, Daniela Schmidt, Alison Panisson,
Felipe Meneguzzi, Renata Vieira, and Rafael H. Bordini

Pontifical Catholic University of Rio Grande do Sul - PUCRS
Postgraduate Programme in Computer Science, School of Informatics (FACIN)
Porto Alegre - RS - Brazil
{artur.freitas,daniela.schmidt,alison.panisson}@acad.pucrs.br,
{felipe.meneguzzi,renata.vieira,rafael.bordini}@pucrs.br

Abstract. Integrating knowledge representation approaches with agent programming and automated planning is still an open research challenge. To explore the combination of those techniques, we present a semantic model of planning domains that can be converted to both agent programming plans as well as planning problem definitions. Our approach allows the representation of agent plans using ontologies, enabling the integration of different formalisms since the knowledge in the ontology can be reused by several systems and applications. Ontologies enable the use of semantic reasoning in planning and agent systems, and such semantic web technologies are significant current research trends. This paper presents our planning ontology, exemplify its use with an instantiation, and shows how to translate between ontology, agent code, and planning specifications. Algorithms to convert between these formalisms are shown, and we also discuss future directions towards the integration of semantic representation, automated planning, and agent programming.

Keywords: ontology, knowledge representation, agent plan, automated planning.

1 Introduction

Knowledge representation approaches using ontologies are being studied as promising techniques to enable semantic reasoning, knowledge reuse, interoperability, and so on. However, the use of ontologies integrated with agent systems and planning formalisms is still a research path at its initial steps. To investigate this issue, we present a semantic model to represent the knowledge about planning domains.

More specifically, we developed an ontology encoded in OWL (Web Ontology Language) [1] to model planning domains based on the HTN (Hierarchical Task Network) paradigm [2]. This conceptualisation was instantiated in the Protégé[1] ontology editor to model a classical problem, known as "Gold Miners". This example demonstrates how planning domains can be modelled in our ontology, and we also show the equivalent agent plans and planning specifications generated from this scenario.

[1] `http://protege.stanford.edu/`

F. Dalpiaz et al. (Eds.): EMAS 2014, LNAI 8758, pp. 351–366, 2014.

Furthermore, we propose algorithms to convert the OWL planning ontology to different formalisms, such as agent programming plans in AgentSpeak [3] and planning problem domain specifications in SHOP (Simple Hierarchical Ordered Planner) [4]. These algorithms to automatically translate from OWL to other formalisms (and vice-versa) were implemented in Java using the OWL API [5]. Therefore, planning domains instantiated in the ontology can be automatically converted to AgentSpeak [3] or SHOP [4] code (and the other way around) using the aforementioned methods. This work aligns the fields of knowledge representation and reasoning with the domain of automated planning, and this opens the path to interesting research directions that are still beginning to emerge in the relevant communities.

For instance, our approach enables to derive planning domain models and agent programming plans from existing ontological knowledge, and also to convert again from these formalisms to ontology representations. In other words, this work investigates the integration of ontologies with agent programming and other planning formalisms in order to explore semantic representations of planning domains. Thus, our goal is to explore and demonstrate the utilisation of ontologies more expressively than previous work in automated planning and agent-oriented development.

This paper is organised as follows. Next section provides a comprehensive background on ontologies, focusing on preparing the reader to relate ontologies with agent-oriented programming and planning formalisms. A section of related work is presented afterwards to map the state of the art on using ontologies in planning systems. Then, a section explaining our conceptualisation (TBox, *i.e.*, Terminological Box) is presented. This conceptualisation is composed of classes and properties to represent planning domains. Next, we show an instantiation (ABox, *i.e.*, Assertion Box) of this TBox in order to demonstrate how to use the proposed ontology to model a corresponding planning problem. We explain how to convert from our planning ontology to AgentSpeak [3] plans; and also from the ontology to SHOP [4] domain definitions. Algorithms coded in Java with the OWL API [5] to make these conversions are discussed afterwards. Then, we conclude this paper and point out other possible investigations and research directions towards the integration of ontology, planning and agent development.

2 Ontologies and OWL

Ontology is defined as an "explicit specification of a conceptualisation" [6]. A conceptualisation stands for an abstract model of some aspect of the world, therefore an ontology is a knowledge representation structure composed of concepts, properties, individuals, relationships and axioms [7], as described in sequence. A **concept** is an abstract group, set, class or collection of objects that share common properties. A **property** is used to express relationships between concepts in a given domain. More specifically, it describes the relationship between the first concept (*i.e.*, the domain), and the second, which represents that property range. An **individual** (also called instance, object or fact) is the "ground-level" component of an ontology which represents a specific element of a concept or class. A **relationship** is an instance of a property, which relates two individuals: one in the relationship domain, and one in its range. An **axiom** is used to impose constraints on the values of classes or individuals, so axioms are generally expressed using logic-based languages, such as first-order logic. Axioms, also called rules, are used to verify the consistency of the ontology and to perform inferences.

The use of ontology empowers the execution of some interesting features, such as semantic reasoners and semantic queries. Semantic reasoners, for example Pellet [8], provide the functionalities of *consistency checking*, *concept satisfiability*, *classification* and *realisation*. *Consistency checking* ensures that an ontology does not contain contradictory facts; *concept satisfiability* checks if it is possible for a concept to have instances; *classification* computes the subclass relations between every named class to create the complete class hierarchy; and *realisation* finds the most specific classes that an individual belongs to [8]. In other words, semantic reasoners are able to infer logical consequences from a set of axioms. Reasoners are also used to apply rules such as the ones coded in SWRL (Semantic Web Rule Language) [9]. Moreover, ontologies can be semantically queried through SQWRL (Semantic Query-enhanced Web Rule Language) [10], which is a simple and expressive language for implementing semantic queries in OWL. OWL is a semantic web standard formalism intended to explicitly represent the meaning of terms in vocabularies and the relationships between those terms [1].

OWL is based on Description Logics (DL), which formed the basis of several ontology languages [7]. The name DL is motivated by the fact that the important notions of the domain are specified by concept descriptions, *i.e.*, expressions that are built from atomic concepts (unary predicates) and atomic roles (binary predicates) using the concept and role constructors provided by the particular DL. DL systems provide various inference capabilities to deduce implicit knowledge from the explicitly represented knowledge [7]. For example, the *subsumption algorithm* determines subconcept-superconcept relationships; the *instance algorithm* infers instance relationships; and the *consistency algorithm* identifies whether a knowledge base (consisting of a set of assertions and a set of terminological axioms) is non-contradictory.

Given this technological development, it is natural to think that there would be many advantages in using it more expressively in agent-oriented software engineering. The work reported in [11] pointed out to the following advantages of such integration: (*i*) more expressive queries in the belief base, since its results can be inferred from the ontology and thus are not limited to explicit knowledge; (*ii*) refined belief update given that ontological consistency of a belief addition can be checked; (*iii*) the search for a plan to deal with an event is more flexible because it is not limited to unification, *i.e.*, it is also possible to consider subsumption relationships between concepts; and (*iv*) agents can share knowledge using ontology languages, such as the case of OWL.

This section presented a background on ontologies, where we can observe that several advantages can emerge by using them more expressively in agent-oriented software engineering and planning. Next section investigates the state of the art regarding related studies integrating ontologies with artificial intelligence planning approaches.

3 Related Work

The work in [12] explains how an OWL reasoner can be integrated with an artificial intelligence planner. Investigations on the efficiency of such integrated system and how OWL reasoning can be optimized for this context were also presented. In their approach, the reasoner is used to store the world state, answer the planner's queries regarding the evaluation of preconditions, and update the state when the planner simulates the effects of operators. Also, they described the challenges of modelling service preconditions, effects and the world state in OWL, examining the impact of this in the planning process. Specifically, the SHOP2 HTN planning system was integrated with the OWL DL reasoner Pellet to explore the use of semantic reasoning over the ontology [12].

A generic task ontology to formalise the space of planning problems was proposed in [13]. According with its authors, this task ontology formalises the nature of the planning task independently of any planning paradigm, specific domains, or applications and provides a fine-grained, precise and comprehensive characterization of the space of planning problems. The OCML (Operational Conceptual Modelling Language) was used to formalise the task ontology proposed in [13], since it was argued that this language provides both support for producing sophisticated specifications, as well as mechanisms for operationalising definitions to provide a concrete reusable resource to support knowledge acquisition and system development.

Another related work [14] defines a series of translations from ontologies to planning formalisms: one from OWL-S process models to SHOP2 domains; and another from OWL-S composition tasks to SHOP2 planning problems. They describe an implemented system which performs these translations using an extended SHOP2 implementation to plan with over the translated domain, and then executing the resulting plans. In summary, the work of [14] explored how to use the SHOP2 HTN planning system to do automatic composition in the context of Web Services described in OWL-S ontologies.

Reference [15] proposes a planning and knowledge engineering framework based on OWL ontologies that facilitates the development of domains and uses Description Logic (DL) reasoning during the planning steps. In their model, the state of the world is represented as a set of OWL facts (*i.e.*, assertions on OWL individuals), represented in an RDF (Resource Description Framework) graph; actions are described as RDF graph transformations; and planning goals are described as RDF graph patterns. Their planner integrates DL reasoning by using a two-phase planning approach that performs DL reasoning in an off-line manner, and builds plans on-line, without doing any reasoning. Their planner uses a subset of DL known as DLP (Description Logic Programs) that has polynomial time complexity and can be evaluated using a set of logic rules.

Several authors are proposing semantic representation of planning domains in ontologies. Also, approaches to translate among planning formalisms and ontologies are usually explored. These approaches can involve the use of semantic reasoners before or during the planning steps. However, to the best of our knowledge, our work is the first to address the integration of ontologies in OWL [1] with both the HTN [2] formalism and with agent programming plans.

Next section explains the proposed planning ontology coded in OWL [1], which is explored to generate both agent plans in AgentSpeak [3] and SHOP [4] specifications of planning problem domains.

4 The Planning Ontology Conceptualisation

In classical planning, the main aim of the planning task is to attain a goal-state, which is usually specified in terms of a number of desired properties of the world. To model this domain, we developed an ontology, encoded in OWL [1] and built with Protégé, to represent HTN planning domains. Protégé is an open source ontology editor which also enables the visualisation of ontologies in different ways, the execution of semantic reasoners, and several other interesting features. The concepts and properties formalized in our proposed HTN planning ontology can be visualised in Figure 1. The conceptualisation was created based on the definitions of [2], [16] and [17], and a description of these concepts can be found next:

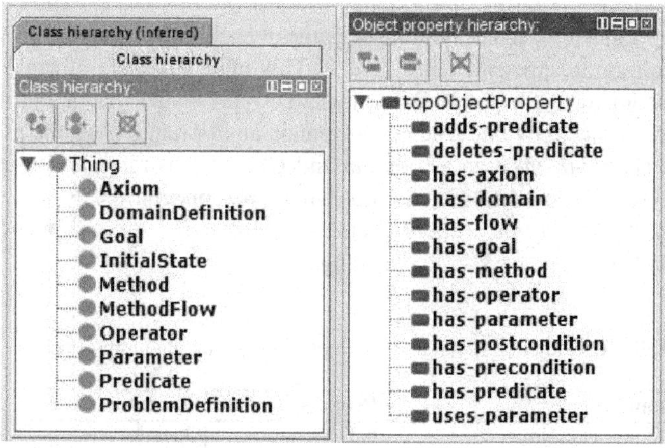

Fig. 1. Concepts and properties of the planning ontology

- **DomainDefinition:** A domain definition is a description of a planning domain, consisting of a set of methods, operators, and axioms.
- **Operator:** Each operator indicates how a primitive task can be performed. It is composed of: name, parameters, preconditions, a delete list and an add list giving the operator's negative and positive effects.
- **Method:** Each method indicates how to decompose a compound task into a partially ordered set of subtasks, each of which can be compound or primitive. The simplest version of a method has three parts: the task for which it is to be used, the preconditions, and the subtasks that need to be done in order to accomplish it.
- **Axiom:** Axioms can infer preconditions that are not explicitly asserted in the current state. The preconditions of methods or operators may use conjunctions, disjunctions, negations, universals and existential quantifiers, implications, numerical computations and external function calls.
- **Predicate:** A predicate has a name and it contains any number of parameters. Predicates are used to represent the preconditions and postconditions of actions, as well as the state of the world (*i.e.*, the state of affairs).

- **Parameter:** A parameter is a variable symbol whose name begins with a question mark (*e.g.*, as ?x or ?agent), and it is used by operators, methods and predicates.
- **MethodFlow:** The flows of a method specify how it can be decomposed based on the current state of the world (which is represented in predicates). Thus, each method flow contains an ordered list of preconditions and an ordered list of methods or operators invocations. Each method must contain at least one flow.
- **ProblemDefinition:** Planning problems are composed of logical atoms (*i.e*, initial state) and task lists (high-level actions to perform), which means, a set of goals.
- **Goal:** Goals in HTN are method invocations with specific parameters that the planner will have to decompose in a sequence of operators (*i.e.*, a plan).
- **InitialState:** An instance of initial state models the problem by means of predicates that represent the state of the world at the beginning of the simulation.

The concepts that are used as domain or range of each property in the proposed HTN planning ontology are presented in Table 1. This table illustrates formal definitions that were developed to formalize the knowledge represented in our ontology. Some object properties have only one concept as domain and/or range (*e.g.*, the property *has-operator* has *DomainDefinition* as domain and *Operator* as range). However, logical expressions were also used to include more than one concept in this slot, such as the case of the *has-postcondition* property that has the *MethodFlow* concept as domain and the expression "*Operator or Method*" as range.

Table 1. Domain and range of each property in the planning ontology

Domain	**Property**	**Range**
DomainDefinition	has-operator	Operator
DomainDefinition	has-method	Method
DomainDefinition	has-axiom	Axiom
InitialState	has-predicate	Predicate
Method	has-flow	MethodFlow
Operator	adds-predicate	Predicate
Operator	deletes-predicate	Predicate
Predicate	uses-parameter	Parameter
ProblemDefinition	has-domain	DomainDefinition
ProblemDefinition	has-goal	Goal
Method, Operator or Predicate	has-parameter	Parameter
MethodFlow or Operator	has-precondition	Predicate
MethodFlow	has-postcondition	Operator or Method

Besides the classes and properties, OWL annotations were used to represent additional information in the relationships of this ontology instantiations. When representing relationships with predicates or parameters, the order in which they have to appear must be known, which is annotated when a property targeting one of them is instantiated. Annotations are also the best choice to model logical expressions among predicates and which parameters are required when a method or operator instance relates with a predicate. Three new annotations were designed with this purpose: *position*, *logicalExpression* and *parameters*. The *position* annotation stores the location where that element must be written in the corresponding files, and it can be used in the following properties: *has-flow, has-precondition, adds-predicate, deletes-predicate, uses-parameter* and *has-parameter*. The *logicalExpression* annotation was created to be used only in relationships involving the *has-precondition* property. Finally, the *parameters* annotation must be used only within the properties *has-precondition, adds-predicate* and *deletes-predicate*. This annotation was employed in order to relate instances of predicates used to define specific operators and methods with instances of parameters.

Figure 2 illustrates the concepts and properties (with their domain and range) in a more intuitive way using the OntoGraf[2] plug-in, which can be found in Protégé. In this representation, the ontology is viewed as a graph, where the nodes are concepts and the edges represent object properties relating the concepts. This section presented how we modelled the concepts and properties of our HTN planning ontology using OWL. The next sections show an instantiation (ABox) of this previously explained ontology conceptualisation (TBox) to model a specific scenario. Then, we show the equivalent agent programming plans in AgentSpeak [3] and planning domain specifications in SHOP [4] derived from our ontology representation.

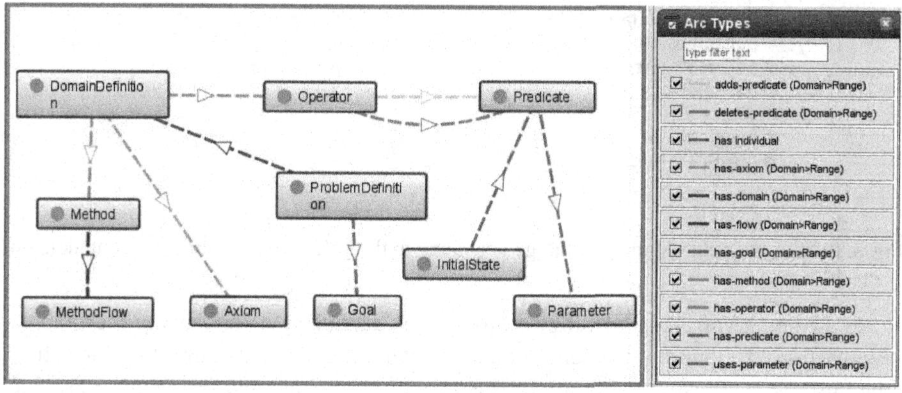

Fig. 2. Visual representation of our planning ontology in Protégé (OntoGraf plug-in)

5 Instantiating the Planning Ontology

To investigate the feasibility of defining a planning domain as an instantiation of our OWL ontology, we also used the Protégé ontology editor to create a simple definition of a planning problem domain scenario. We modelled a well-known multi-agent scenario known as *gold miners*[3], where agents playing the role of miners have to move in an environment, and search specific positions. Our scenario includes only one instance of the *Operator* concept (named *move*) and one instance of *Method* (named *pursuitPosition*).

[2] http://protegewiki.stanford.edu/wiki/OntoGraf

[3] http://multiagentcontest.org/2006

The operator *move* has two preconditions, one negative effect and one positive effect, all represented as predicates. The method *pursuitPosition* has two different flows, each one with its corresponding preconditions and effects. A snapshot of the instantiation using this scenario (*gold miners*) can be seen in Figure 3. It is important to highlight that Figure 3 illustrates the ontology instantiation in Protégé that corresponds exactly to the previously explained specification. Next we demonstrate that it is possible to convert from our ontology formalism both to planning specifications and to agent plans. In fact, this paper explains methods for converting among these different formalisms.

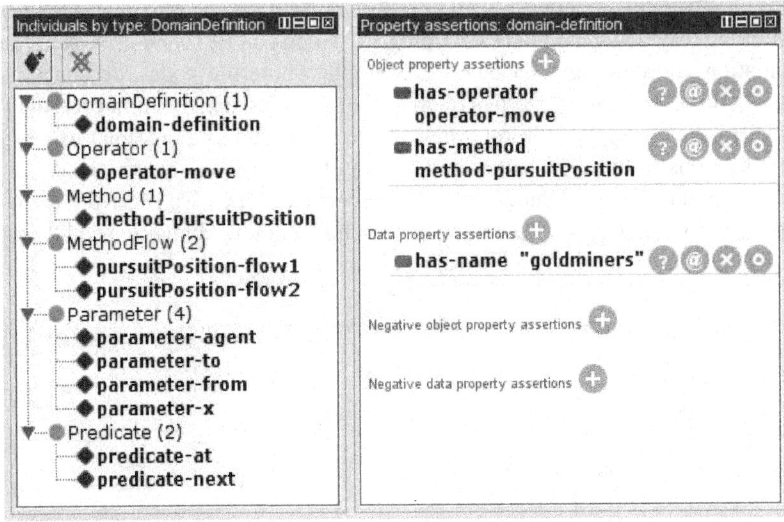

Fig. 3. Instantiating our planning ontology according to the goldminers specific planning domain

An advantage of using ontology editors is the capability of enhancing the graphic visualisation of planning problem domains instances as well as agent plans and their relationships, as illustrates Figure 4. This visualisation was obtained using a Protégé plug-in known as OntoGraf, however it is possible to explore the ontologies using different editors. In this example, the user can visualize domain features such as how the instances are related, and the visualization can be customized to show only the desired characteristics of the corresponding instantiation. Moreover, an ontology representation makes possible to explore features such as rules coded in SWRL [9] and inferences empowered by semantic reasoners [8]. The next sections show how to convert from our planning ontology in OWL both to agent programming plans in AgentSpeak [3] and to artificial intelligence planners specifications in SHOP [4].

The list of instances and their relationships is presented below, where "a : C" denotes that the instance 'a' is a type of 'C', and "(a,b) : R" indicates that the instance 'a' is related to instance 'b' through the property 'R'. This list is a full description of the example used in this paper, which corresponds to Figures 3 and 4. This example was instantiated in the ontology to be converted both to a planning specification in SHOP and agent plans in AgentSpeak.

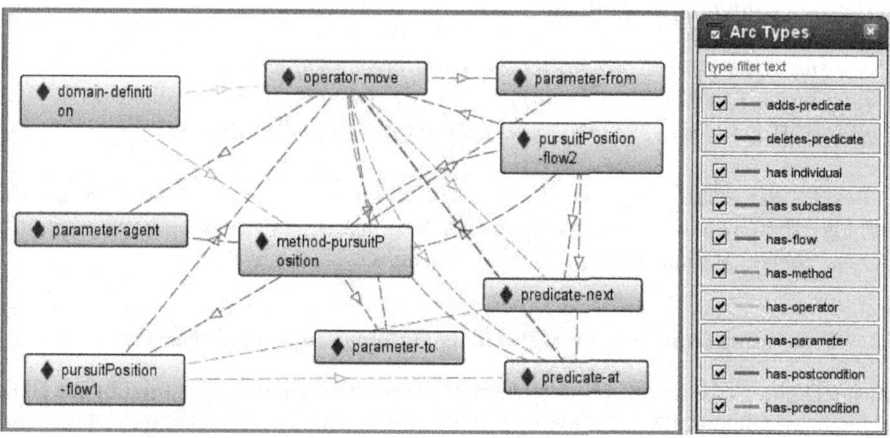

Fig. 4. Visualising the instances of our planning ontology in Protégé (OntoGraf plug-in)

domain-definition : DomainDefinition
operator-move : Operator
method-pursuitPosition : Method
pursuitPosition-flow1 : MethodFlow
pursuitPosition-flow2 : MethodFlow
parameter-agent : Parameter
parameter-to : Parameter
parameter-from : Parameter
parameter-x : Parameter
predicate-at : Predicate
predicate-next : Predicate
(domain-definition, operator-move) : has-operator
(domain-definition, method-pursuitPosition) : has-method
(operator-move, parameter-agent) : has-parameter
(operator-move, parameter-from) : has-parameter
(operator-move, parameter-to) : has-parameter
(operator-move, predicate-at) : has-precondition
(operator-move, predicate-next) : has-precondition
(operator-move, predicate-at) : deletes-predicate
(operator-move, predicate-at) : adds-predicate
(method-pursuitPosition, pursuitPosition-flow1) : has-flow
(method-pursuitPosition, pursuitPosition-flow2) : has-flow
(method-pursuitPosition, parameter-agent) : has-parameter
(method-pursuitPosition, parameter-from) : has-parameter
(method-pursuitPosition, parameter-to) : has-parameter
(pursuitPosition-flow1, predicate-at) : has-precondition
(pursuitPosition-flow1, predicate-next) : has-precondition

(pursuitPosition-flow1, operator-move) : has-postcondition
(pursuitPosition-flow2, predicate-at) : has-precondition
(pursuitPosition-flow2, predicate-next) : has-precondition
(pursuitPosition-flow2, operator-move) : has-postcondition
(pursuitPosition-flow2, method-pursuitPosition) : has-postcondition

Besides the relationships listed above to describe the example instantiated in our ontology, there is a data property *has-name*. Also, our instantiation represent *positions* and *parameters* as annotation in these relationships.

5.1 Converting from our OWL Planning Ontology to AgentSpeak Plans

Most techniques for Multi-Agent System development are heavily inspired by the BDI architecture (Beliefs, Desires and Intentions). For example, the AgentSpeak [18] language was introduced in 1996 as a formalisation of BDI agents to enable agent programs to be written using a notation similar to (guarded) Horn clauses. Agents achieve their goals through the use of plans that can be composed of sub-plans and that are ultimately converted into actions. This approach is similar to the one used in the HTN planning formalism, where methods are decomposed into operators. A plan body coded in AgentSpeak [3] is typically a sequence of actions to be executed and further goals to be achieved. AgentSpeak plans have three distinct parts [3]: the *triggering event*, the *context*, and the *body*. Together, the *triggering event* and the *context* are called the head of the plan. The three plan parts are syntactically separated by ':' and '<–' as follows:

Syntax of AgentSpeak Plans

```
triggering_event : context <- body.
```

The following code (*miner.asl*) corresponds to a plan in AgentSpeak generated from our planning ontology instantiation. The scenario is the *gold miners* previously explained, and this example respects the presented AgentSpeak plan syntax [3]. Every instance of the *Operator* concept is mapped to an agent plan: its name becomes the *triggering event*, its preconditions form the *context* and its effects becomes the *body*. Similarly, each instance of *Method* is also translated to an AgentSpeak plan, with its corresponding preconditions and decomposition scheme. Both the operators and methods mantain their parameters when being converted from the ontology to agent code.

Our *gold miners* scenario instantiated in the ontology generates the *miner.asl* code which is depicted below. It can be noted that the *move Operator* becomes a plan with the *triggering event +!move(Agent, From, To)*. The *context* of this plan is composed of a conjunction of two instances of *Predicate*: *at(Agent, From)* and *next(From, To)*. The body (or effect) of this plan is to execute the external action *move(Agent, From, To)* in the environment, to remove the belief *at(Agent, From)*, and to add the belief *at(Agent, To)*. Similarly, our scenario depicts how a *Method* in our ontology is converted to an AgentSpeak plan. The main difference from the *Operator* previously explained is that the plan *body* is composed of goals to be achieved by the agent.

`miner.asl (AgentSpeak code generated from our planning ontology)`

```
+!move(Agent, From, To) :
    at(Agent, From) & next(From, To) <-
        move(Agent, From, To);
        -at(Agent, From);
        +at(Agent, To).

+!pursuitPosition(Agent, From, To) :
    at(Agent, From) & next(From, To) <-
        !move(Agent, From, To).

+!pursuitPosition(Agent, From, To) :
    at(Agent, From) & next(From, X) <-
        !move(Agent, From, X);
        !pursuitPosition(Agent, X, To).
```

The contribution of this section is to sketch how an HTN domain in our ontology can be mapped into an AgentSpeak program (however, detailed translation algorithms and implementation are future work).

5.2 Converting from our OWL Planning Ontology to SHOP Domain Definitions

SHOP is a HTN planning system based on *ordered task decomposition* whose syntax and semantics are given in [4]. In other words, SHOP is a HTN-planner implementation which enables domain-independent automated planning. In HTN planning, the objective is to create a plan to perform a set of tasks (abstract representations of things that need to be done), starting with an initial state-of-the-world. HTN planning is done by problem reduction: planners recursively decompose tasks into subtasks until they reach primitive tasks that can be performed directly by planning operators. A set of methods is required in order to tell the planner how to decompose nonprimitive tasks into subtasks, where each method is a schema for decomposing a particular kind of task into a set of subtasks (provided that the preconditions are satisfied).

We briefly highlight SHOP syntax in the code below to facilitate the understanding of how an instantiation can be converted from our ontology to SHOP specifications. Similarly to our ontology, the SHOP formalism is composed of operators and methods, which can contain preconditions and effects.

Syntax of SHOP Planning Domain Definitions

```
(defdomain domain_name (
   (  :operator (!operator_name ?parameters)
   ((preconditions ?parameters))
   ((negative_effects ?parameters))
   ((positive_effects ?parameters)))

   (  :method (method_name ?parameters)
   ((preconditions ?parameters))
   ((method_or_operator ?parameters)))
   )
```

The following code illustrates the corresponding SHOP domain definition (named *gold miners*) which corresponds to the previous explained scenario instantantied in our ontology as example. We can observe that the instances of *Operator* and *Method* (and its corresponding relationships) are converted in the generated *miner.jshop* specification depicted below. More details about the algorithms to convert from our planning ontology to the SHOP planning domain specifications (and vice-versa) can be found in the next section of this paper.

miner.jshop (SHOP code generated from our planning ontology)

```
(defdomain goldminers (
   (  :operator (!move ?agent ?from ?to)
   ((at ?agent ?from) (next ?from ?to))
   ((at ?agent ?from))
   ((at ?agent ?to)))

   (  :method (pursuitPosition ?agent ?from ?to)
   ((at ?agent ?from) (next ?from ?to))
   ((!move ?agent ?from ?to)))

   (  :method (pursuitPosition ?agent ?from ?to)
   ((at ?agent ?from) (next ?from ?x))
   ((!move ?agent ?from ?x) (pursuitPosition ?agent ?x ?to)))
   )
```

6 Planning and Ontology Conversions

This section demonstrates, in a high level of abstraction, the algorithms implemented in Java to convert OWL ontologies to SHOP specification files, and vice-versa, which is from SHOP domain definitions to the corresponding OWL ontology instances. Thus, we established a bidirectional mapping among the elements of our OWL planning ontology and the elements represented in the SHOP domain specifications. The same principle might be applied to convert among our ontology and AgentSpeak code, such as previously demonstrated with an example in this paper, however algorithms for doing that are not presented in this work.

6.1 Converting from the OWL Ontology to SHOP

The OWL API [5] was used to read the ontology elements and parse each one of them, and Java was used to write them in a corresponding jshop file. OWL API is an open source Java API (Application Programming Interface) for creating, manipulating and serialising OWL ontologies.

The instances, concepts, properties and annotations in the ontology previously presented are queried and the corresponding SHOP component is generated to that specific ontology element to construct the corresponding jshop file. For example, *Operator*'s instances might be related with *Parameter*'s instances through the *has-parameter* property, and with instances of *Predicate* by means of the properties *has-precondition*, *adds-predicate* and *deletes-predicate*. The algorithm for converting the OWL to a jshop file is the following:

for each instance *df* of DomainDefinition concept **do**
  create the jshop corresponding file
  operators ← has-operator relationships of *df*
  for each Operator *op* in *operators* **do**
    extract *op* information from the ontology
    write *op* parameters, conditions and effects in order
  end for
  methods ← has-method relationships of *df*
  for each Method *met* in *methods* **do**
    extract *met* information from the ontology
    write *met* parameters and flows in order
  end for
end for

6.2 Converting from SHOP to the OWL Ontology

Previous section demonstrated how one example is converted from our ontology both to SHOP specifications and AgentSpeak code. This section shows the algorithms to convert both from the ontology to SHOP domain, and vice-versa, which are already implemented. However, the algorithms to convert between ontology and agent plans are currently being developed, but we already exemplified how this conversion can be made in this paper.

The OWL API [5] was also used to write the ontology elements, after implementing a parser in Java to read and interpret the jshop file. This approach makes the opposite direction from the previous one, which converted from the OWL planning ontology to a specification in SHOP.

In this algorithm, for each component found when parsing the jshop file, such as a new operator or method, then the equivalent OWL individual is created with the OWL API and included in the ontology instantiation being created (which can be instances, object properties, data properties or annotations). For example, when reading an *Operator*, it is required to extract its parameters, preconditions and effects; however while reading a *Method*, the information to be extracted concerns about its parameters and flows. The algorithm to convert a jshop file to a corresponding instantation of our OWL planning ontology is the following:

```
while there are tokens remaining in the jshop file do
    token ← nextToken()
    if token = defdomain then
        create corresponding DomainDefinition instance
    end if
    if token = operator then
        create corresponding Operator instance
        read its parameters, preconditions and effects
        create the corresponding ontology elements
    end if
    if token = method then
        create corresponding Method instance
        read its parameters and flows
        create the corresponding ontology elements
    end if
end while
```

7 Final Remarks

We presented an investigation towards the integration of agent-oriented programming and automated planning with semantic technologies. More specifically, this paper proposed an ontology to represent planning formalisms. Our ontology was developed in OWL [1] to represent HTN [2] domains and problems in the context of automated planning and agent-oriented programming. The proposed ontology was instantiated to exemplify its use and to demonstrate its feasibility. Also, we presented algorithms to convert specifications between different formalisms such as OWL [1] and SHOP [4]. The algorithms have been coded in Java using the OWL API [5].

Given the similarities among planning formalisms and agent programming plans, we also explored how to generate a corresponding AgentSpeak [3] code, which is a logical language to program agent plans. As examples of relations between concepts in these two formalisms we can currently highlight: method & plan; precondition & context; and operator & external action. Thus, we also explored how to convert from our OWL [1] planning ontology to AgentSpeak [3] plans, and vice-versa. In other words, our approach enables new ways to derive both planning specifications and agent code.

As pointed out in [15], the use of OWL ontologies as a basis for modelling domains allows the reuse of knowledge in the semantic web. However, research in this direction is still in their initial steps. We have briefly discussed the state of the art of approaches that integrate ontologies with planning and agent-oriented programming, commenting on their findings and contributions.

As future work, we plan to investigate ontology reasoning mechanisms and semantic technologies features within the scope of our planning ontology. One example would be creating rules (*e.g.*, in SWRL [9]) to infer knowledge such as inconsistencies in ontology instantiations. The ability to use ontologies to infer and generate knowledge over a domain is a motivation to investigate how ontology representations can be integrated with planning and agent-oriented programming. Thus, as next step in this direction, we will explore advantages of using the semantic reasoning enabled by ontologies.

Another interesting area to explore is extending the planning ontology to address further planning characteristics, such as non-deterministic HTN planning formalisms. However, if the conceptualisation changes, the parsers may have to be adjusted accordingly to handle new concepts and properties in the ontology. Currently, we plan to continue assessing the correctness of our algorithms (for converting between OWL [1] to SHOP [4]) by testing them with more examples. Moreover, we are currently coding the algorithms to convert beween the ontology and AgentSpeak [3].

This work investigated the conversion from OWL [1] ontologies to both SHOP [4] and AgentSpeak [3], since these languages are used in our research project, but in a similar way different planning systems and agent programming languages could also be explored. The inclusion of ontology-based semantic technologies in such complex multi-agent platforms is expected to bring together the power of knowledge-rich approaches and complex distributed systems.

Acknowledgements. Part of the results presented in this paper were obtained through research on a project titled "Semantic and Multi-Agent Technologies for Group Interaction", sponsored by Samsung Eletrônica da Amazônia Ltda. under the terms of Brazilian federal law No. 8.248/91.

References

1. Bechhofer, S., van Harmelen, F., Hendler, J., Horrocks, I., McGuinness, D.L., Patel-Schneider, P.F., Stein, L.A.: OWL Web Ontology Language Reference. Technical report, W3C (February 2004)
2. Erol, K., Hendler, J.A., Nau, D.S.: HTN planning: Complexity and expressivity. In: Hayes-Roth, B., Korf, R.E. (eds.) AAAI, pp. 1123–1128. AAI Press/The MIT Press (1994)
3. Bordini, R.H., Hübner, J.F., Wooldridge, M.: Programming multi-agent systems in AgentSpeak using Jason. John Wiley & Sons (2007)
4. Nau, D., Cao, Y., Lotem, A., Avila, H.M.: SHOP: Simple hierarchical ordered planner. In: Proceedings of the 16th International Joint Conference on Artificial Intelligence, vol. 2, pp. 968–973. Morgan Kaufmann Publishers Inc., San Francisco (1999)
5. Horridge, M., Bechhofer, S.: The OWL API: A Java API for OWL ontologies. Semant. Web 2(1), 11–21 (2011)

6. Gruber, T.R.: Toward principles for the design of ontologies used for knowledge sharing. Int. J. Hum.-Comput. Stud. 43(5-6), 907–928 (1995)
7. Baader, F., Horrocks, I., Sattler, U.: Description logics. In: Staab, S., Studer, R. (eds.) Handbook on Ontologies, pp. 3–28. Springer (2009)
8. Sirin, E., Parsia, B., Grau, B.C., Kalyanpur, A., Katz, Y.: Pellet: a practical OWL-DL reasoner. Web Semant. 5(2), 51–53 (2007)
9. Horrocks, I., Patel-Schneider, P.F., Boley, H., Tabet, S., Grosof, B., Dean, M.: SWRL: A Semantic Web Rule Language combining OWL and RuleML. In: W3C Member Submission, World Wide Web Consortium (2004)
10. O'Connor, M.J., Das, A.K.: SQWRL: A query language for OWL. In: Hoekstra, R., Patel-Schneider, P.F. (eds.) OWLED. CEUR Workshop Proceedings, vol. 529, CEUR-WS.org (2008)
11. Moreira, Á.F., Vieira, R., Bordini, R.H., Hübner, J.F.: Agent-oriented programming with underlying ontological reasoning. In: Baldoni, M., Endriss, U., Omicini, A., Torroni, P. (eds.) DALT 2005. LNCS (LNAI), vol. 3904, pp. 155–170. Springer, Heidelberg (2006)
12. Sirin, E., Parsia, B.: Planning for semantic web services. In: Semantic Web Services Workshop at 3rd International Semantic Web Conference, ISWC 2004 (2004)
13. Rajpathak, D., Motta, E.: An ontological formalization of the planning task. In: International Conference on Formal Ontology in Information Systems (FOIS 2004), pp. 305–316 (2004)
14. Sirin, E., Parsia, B., Wu, D., Hendler, J., Nau, D.: HTN planning for web service composition using SHOP2. Web Semant. 1(4), 377–396 (2004)
15. Bouillet, E., Feblowitz, M., Liu, Z., Ranganathan, A., Riabov, A.: A knowledge engineering and planning framework based on OWL ontologies. In: Proceedings of the Second International Competition on Knowledge Engineering (2007)
16. Ilghami, O.: Documentation for JSHOP2. Technical report, University of Maryland, Department of Computer Science, College Park, MD 20742, USA (May 2006)
17. Nau, D., Au, T.C., Ilghami, O., Kuter, U., Murdock, J.W., Wu, D., Yaman, F.: SHOP2: an HTN planning system. J. Artif. Int. Res. 20(1), 379–404 (2003)
18. Rao, A.S.: AgentSpeak(L): BDI agents speak out in a logical computable language. In: Perram, J., Van de Velde, W. (eds.) MAAMAW 1996. LNCS, vol. 1038, pp. 42–55. Springer, Heidelberg (1996)

N-Jason: Run-Time Norm Compliance in AgentSpeak(L)

JeeHang Lee[1], Julian Padget[1],
Brian Logan[2], Daniela Dybalova[2], and Natasha Alechina[2]

[1] Department of Computer Science,
University of Bath,
Bath, BA2 7AY, UK
{j.lee,j.a.padget}@bath.ac.uk
[2] School of Computer Science,
University of Nottingham,
Nottingham, NG8 1BB, UK
{bsl,dxd,nza}@cs.nott.ac.uk

Abstract. Normative systems offer a means to govern agent behaviour in dynamic open environments. Under the governance, agents themselves must be able to reason about compliance with state- or event-based norms (or both) depending upon the formalism used. This paper describes how norm awareness enables a BDI agent to exhibit norm compliant behaviour at run-time taking into account normative factors. To this end, we propose ***N-Jason***, a run-time norm compliant BDI agent framework supporting norm-aware deliberation as well as run-time norm execution mechanism, through which new unknown norms are recognised and bring about the triggering of plans. To be able to process a norm such as an obligation, the agent architecture must be able to deal with deadlines and priorities, and choose among the plans triggered by a particular norm. Consequently, we extend the syntax and the scheduling algorithm of AgentSpeak(RT) to operate in the context of ***Jason***/AgentSpeak(L) and provide 'real-time agency', which we explain through a detailed examination of the operational semantics of a single reasoning cycle.

Keywords: Norms, BDI, Agent Programming Language, Normative System.

1 Introduction

In conventional development of BDI agents, norm compliance is typically achieved by design. That is, by specifying plans that are triggered by detached norms, because the agent programmer knows which norms the agent shall adopt, and then prioritising those rules so that the supporting norms are chosen over those preferred by the agent's mental attitudes, in order to suppress conflicts between the normative and the agent's existing goals. This creates an undesirable dependence between the agent implementation and the norm implementation, which creates two issues:

1. When an agent encounters new and unknown norms, which were not taken into account at design time, there is typically no plan to deal with those norms in the

F. Dalpiaz et al. (Eds.): EMAS 2014, LNAI 8758, pp. 367–387, 2014.

plan library at run-time. Hence, norm compliant behaviour cannot normally be exhibited because the norms are unavoidably ignored. Yet worse, agents may suffer a punishment from the enforcement of the normative system as a result of a violation caused by their incapacity to process the normative event.
2. The hierarchical prioritisation of normative over ordinary plans deprives an agent of its autonomy, since the norms in effect are treated as hard constraints, whose violation is not possible.

We believe that such tensions can be resolved by the use of an extended model of norm awareness. In the literature on BDI agents, norm awareness, which is a precursor to norm compliance, is typically manifested in two places: (i) at the *perception* level, by taking new unknown norms into account as part of the generic execution mechanism [13,14] and (ii) at the *deliberation* level, by attempts to resolve the conflict between normative factors and agents' mental attitudes [1,9]. We propose to coalesce these approaches into one 'sense–think–act' reasoning cycle informed by the concept of awareness, which Charlton [4] describes as the capacity *"to select and integrate relevant inputs from a complex environment to enable humans or animals to choose between a large repertoire of behavioural responses"*. This definition reminds us that, in order to be norm aware, agents should have knowledge (or understanding) about norms in respect of: (i) what (state) the norms intend to reach or to achieve, (ii) which action plans are appropriate to execute norms and (iii) which behaviour agents should prefer between normative goals and the agent's own interests.

Thus, this paper addresses the convergence of these approaches in the context of the BDI agent architecture, in order to be able to ground the discussion of how the extended model of norm awareness enables a BDI agent to exhibit norm compliant behaviour at run-time. To do so, we propose ***N-Jason***, a run-time norm-compliant BDI agent framework supporting a run-time norm execution mechanism, under which new and unknown norms are recognised and enable the triggering of an appropriate plan (if present), in conjunction with norm-aware deliberation [1]. To be able to process a norm such as an obligation, the agent architecture should be able to deal with deadlines and priorities, and choose among plans triggered by a particular norm. Consequently, we extend the syntax and the scheduling algorithm of AgentSpeak(RT) [15] to operate in the context of ***Jason***/AgentSpeak(L) [3] and provide 'real-time agency', which we explain through a detailed examination of the operational semantics of a single reasoning cycle.

The paper is organised as follows. In §2 an institutional framework and semantics of norms considered in ***N-Jason*** are introduced. It is followed by §3, where we present a run-time norm compliant BDI agent framework including programming language and interpreter. After the operational semantics in §4, related work and the contribution of this work are contrasted in §5. The conclusion and future work are discussed in §6.

2 Institutional Framework

Normative frameworks can be viewed as a kind of external repositories of (normative) knowledge from which (normative) guidance may be delivered to agents. Usually, a normative framework is composed of a set of rules whose purpose is to model the normative positions established by the actions of agents and hence realise the governance of individual agents in the society. These rules are not hard-coded recipes presenting reactive behaviours, such as those in the static expert systems, but rather describe consequences arising from observations for the purpose of reasoning about the current context, resulting in situation-specific norms. The framework identifies not only correct and incorrect actions but also norms such as obligations, permissions and prohibitions through the institutional trace that records its evolving internal state, subject to observed external events representing actions in the external world.

Depending on the formalism of the normative system, norms can be categorised as state- or event-based. State-based norms usually express higher level norms that impose desirable or required states on the system (or an environment), often as a logical combination of institutional facts, which should be brought about by the actions of agents [8]. In contrast, event-based norms generally represent relatively lower level activities addressing possibly executable events (or actions) at the individual agent level [7]. In this paper, we use Cliffe's institutional model [5] for the purpose of providing detached event-based norms, upon which we develop the run-time norm compliance model presented here.

The institutional framework provides a formal action language Inst*AL* to specify norms, describing coordinations and interactions between agents and (or) environments in the context of an institution. The normative specification is translated to a computational model that utilises Answer Set Programming (ASP) [10], which enables reasoning about the current context described in the institution. The institution is composed of a set of *institutional states*, evolving over time triggered by the occurrence of both internal and external *events*. An institutional state is a set of *fluents* which are present (denoting true) or absent (denoting false) at a given time instant. In addition, such institutional fluents are divided into *domain fluents* and *normative fluents* which are further partitioned into: (i) *power* ($\mathcal{W}$) – indicates events that are empowered to bring about institutional change (ii) *permission* ($\mathcal{P}$) – indicates events that can occur without violation, and (iii) *obligations* ($\mathcal{O}$) – specifies events that are obliged to happen before the occurrence of a deadline (e.g. a timeout), or else a violation occurs.

These normative fluents represent the normative consequences of particular behaviours which should be achieved by agents in a certain context. For example, if an agent *X* is obliged to carry out an action *act* by deadline *deadline* otherwise the violation event *violation* is generated, the form of the normative information is represented as:

```
obl(act, deadline, violation)
```
(*obligation*)

Also if an agent *X* is permitted to perform an action *act*, then the representation is:

```
perm(act)
```
(*permission*)

The determination of those normative consequences is carried out using an answer set solver driven by a rule-based specification (Inst*AL*) which explores all possible outcomes derivable from the institutional state arising from the occurrence of a single

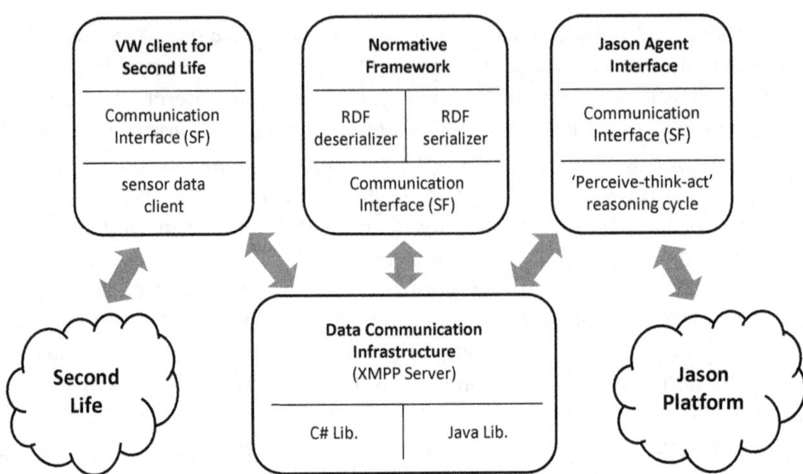

Fig. 1. Governing virtual characters behaviour with Insitutions

event[1] as determined by the generation and consequence rules that comprise the institutional model.

Lee *et al.* [12] demonstrate a governance mechanism using this institutional model that shows how the normative consequences of particular actions can be delivered to agents' minds as percepts (to conventional ***Jason*** agents rather than the variety described here) either on request or by subscription, making them available for the agent reasoning process. The components in this case comprise: (i) the virtual agents (VA) in Second Life, (ii) an institutional model for social norm reasoning, and (iii) BDI agents that are responsible for individual reasoning, as illustrated in Figure 1. The virtual agents (VA) in the virtual world appear as sensors to the rest of the system: as soon as virtual world events are detected in *Second Life* (*SL*), the VA turns them into symbolic representations and publishes them, while both the BDI agent and the institution subscribe to that topic. When the institution receives this information, it triggers the social norm reasoning process, which determines the new normative positions of the actors and identifies appropriate behaviours for the current (social) situation. This information is then published as `perm(act)` or `obl(act, deadline, violation)` for the BDI agent to incorporate into its reasoning process, following the principles set out in [1]. When the decision making process (for norm compliance) is completed, the action plans are published, which are then interpreted by the VA using the atomic actions available in the virtual world – because the virtual agent actions are typically more primitive that those of the intelligent agent.

With regards to the norm compliance in BDI agents, as described in Figure 1, van Riemsdijk *et al.* suggest in [14] that one feasible approach for run-time norm execution is the use of *"pre-existing capabilities"* in the agent program when an agent encounters

[1] Note: the institutional model can also function as a normative oracle for an agent, if presented with a sequence of events, in which case it derives all the possible outcomes from all possible orderings of those events, subject to whatever constraints are specified on the ordering.

new and unknown norms. This assumes that event-based norms can identify the associated necessary actions, since event-based norms typically refer to relatively low-level activities that address possibly executable events (or actions) at the individual agent level [7]. If appropriate information can be extracted from the detached norm, such that it is recognisable to an agent, in this way an agent presumably may execute unknown norms and so exhibit a form of norm compliance at run-time.

For example, the `act` term in an obligation represents a similar level of knowledge to plans or events in a BDI agent program. If an agent can retrieve and recognise what action (or event) is required to be achieved, then it can trigger certain plans and attempt to carry out such behaviour even though the norm is not handled explicitly in the agent specification. With regard to the norm-aware reasoning, an agent may deduce a preference, if it is able to know the relative priorities, and critical impact or the deadline of normative factors by extracting `deadline` and `violation` information. This norm-aware reasoning may allow an agent to pursue its own preferences between its own goals, norms and sanctions by measuring feasibility, as proposed by Alechina *et al.* [1]. In this paper, we only use obligations for such purpose, in order to focus on the essential aspects of the agent's internal reasoning process. Additionally, we consider the handling of prohibitions for the compatibility with other normative systems, however they are not explicit in the institution mechanism employed here.

3 The *N-Jason* BDI Agent Framework

In this section we outline ***N-Jason***, a norm aware BDI agent interpreter and its programming language for run-time norm compliant agent behaviour. In principle, it extends ***Jason***/AgentSpeak(L) syntactically, semantically and in the reasoning process of the interpreter. In practice, ***N-Jason*** is conceptually similar to AgentSpeak(RT) [15], which is capable of dealing with deadlines and priorities and scheduling intentions with the aim of providing real-time agency. ***N-Jason*** is conceptually a superset of AgentSpeak(RT), to which it adds normative concepts (i.e. obligations, permissions, prohibitions, deadlines, priorities and durations) and norm aware deliberation.

We firstly examine work to date with regards to the programming language aspect. This is followed by an informal explanation of the ***N-Jason*** reasoning cycle. Subsequently, we show how the extended model of norm awareness in BDI agents is established by the combination of the run-time norm execution mechanism and norm-aware deliberation.

3.1 The *N-Jason* Agent Programming Language

A ***N-Jason*** agent consists of four main components: beliefs, goals, events and a set of plans. Beliefs and goals are identical to those in standard ***Jason***, while events and plans are extended. We now give a brief summary of the extended features of the basic elements in the agent specification. We take advantage of ***Jason***'s plan annotation mechanism to provide deadline, duration and priority information, so that each feature is simply a term, such as `deadline(X)`, `duration(Y)` or `priority(Z)`, where the parameters are (positive) integer literals. The interpretation of these annotations and examples are covered in the following.

Belief: A *belief* represents agent's information (e.g. initial states of an agent, internal knowledge established through the reasoning cycle) and its knowledge about the environments wherein agents are situated (e.g. percepts observed by agents, messages containing the information about other agents and norms delivered from normative frameworks). Typically, a belief is represented as a grounded atomic formula. The collection of beliefs is referred to as a belief base, which contains belief literals in the form of belief atoms and negations.

Goal: A *goal* is one of two basic types: an achievement goal or a test goal. The former are usually specified as predicates prefixed by the '!' operator. This specifies a certain state of the environment that the agent wants to achieve, which is indicated when the predicate associated with its achievement goal is true. The latter test goal, for which the prefix is the '?' operator, indicates that agents want to know whether the associated predicate is a true belief.

Event: An *event* is the main component for triggering agent's plans. In principle, changes in agent's mental attitudes (i.e. beliefs, goals and intentions) give rise to events. There are two types of events: one is an addition event denoted by '+', which means the addition of a belief or an achievement goal. The other is a deletion event denoted by '–', referring to a recantation of a base belief.

As in ***Jason***, an addition event is categorised by a belief addition event denoted by '+' and a goal addition event jointly denoted by '+' and '!'. All external belief changes bring about belief addition events, so as to initiate the execution of corresponding plans. In contrast, the goal addition event results from both internal and external changes in goals. In other words, explicit goals from the users or other agents result in a goal addition event, but also a goal addition event can be generated by internal operations affecting the agent's mental attitude, such as the execution of subgoals triggered in response to an external event.

Support for normative concepts is provided by an extension of the syntax for an event by the addition of *deadline* and *priority* information. The deadline is a real time value indicating a deadline by which an intention should be achieved. It is expressed in a some adequate unit of real world time. When the deadline is passed, it is no longer feasible to achieve an intention or to give a response with a belief change. The priority is a positive integer value that expresses the relative importance between the achievement of an intention and responding to changes in a belief. A larger value reflects a higher priority. Both can optionally be specified in the annotation (a list of terms in between square brackets "[" and "]") at the end of an event. For example the event:

```
+!at(X, Y)[deadline(900), priority(10)]
```

specifies the goal adoption that an agent moves to the coordinate (X, Y), by the deadline 900, with priority 10. By default, the deadline is taken as infinity and the priority as zero. Note that the deadline and priority annotations do not play a part in unification at plan selection stage.

Plan: A *plan* is a sequence of actions (and subgoals) which is a means to achieve a (main) goal or a means to respond to changes in beliefs by agents. The plan typically consists of a head and a body, but sometimes an optional plan label, which defines an index, a name and other information, can be specified. The head is composed of a triggering event, which specifies an event for which the plan is to be used and a context specifying the condition which must be true for the plan to be a candidate for execution. The body is a series of actions and subgoals to achieve a main goal.

The plan is extended to support normative concepts. Given the three main elements, a duration is proposed in ***N-Jason***, specifically in order to enable assessment of the *feasibility* of the plan associated with the deadline (see §3.4). The duration is a non-negative integer value representing a required time to execute the plan. In principle, the duration may be determined by the summation of an execution time of each external action in the plan body. For simplicity, we follow the assumption described in [1], that the estimated time for each external action is fixed and already known. Like deadline and priority, a duration can be optionally specified in the plan label in the form of an annotation (a list of terms in between square brackets "[" and "]"). For example, the plan:

```
@plan[duration(50)]
+!at(X, Y) : req(ag)
<- move_toward(X, Y); !ack(ag).
```

is triggered by the request from the agent *ag* to move to the coordinate (X, Y), and then to send back an acknowledgement to *ag*. The required (or estimated) execution time of the plan is 50.

3.2 The *N-Jason* Interpreter

The interpreter plays an important role in the operationalisation of agent programs. The agent's belief base, intentions and events are manipulated by the interpreter, and practical reasoning consisting of deliberation and means-ends reasoning is performed to achieve a goal or to respond to environmental changes.

During a single reasoning cycle, run-time norm compliance is accomplished by an extended model of norm awareness that has three steps:

1. *Event Reconsideration*, to find out what the norm is intended to achieve or to reach,
2. *Option Reconsideration*, to identify which plan is the most appropriate in response to the norm,
3. *Intention Scheduling*, to confirm the decision about which behaviour agent would prefer between goals, norms and sanctions.

The interpreter code of ***N-Jason*** is shown in Algorithm 1. B is the belief base, E is the event base, G is a set of goals and I is a set of intentions of an agent. The function *create-tevent* encodes a percept as a triggering event and returns it. The function *add-event* updates the agent's event base with an event which is a pair of a triggering event and an intention. The function *update-belief* updates the agent's belief base with a percept p. The function *type* returns a type of p, either *obligation* or *prohibition*, if p is a norm. The function *edp* constructs a triggering event using the terms in the event-based norm, if the type of p is a norm (e.g. obligations). The functions EVENT- and OPTION-RECONSIDERATION accomplish the run-time norm execution mechanism described in §3.3. The main algorithm of the SCHEDULE function which carries

Algorithm 1. ***N-Jason*** **Interpreter Reasoning Cycle**

```
1: B :=B0 /* B0 are initial beliefs */
2: G :=G0 /* G0 are initial goals */
3: E :=E ∪ G
4: P :=P ∪ N /* P are percepts and N are norms */
5: for all p ∈ P and p ∉ B do
6:     te_p = create-tevent(p)
7:     R_te_p := {πθ | θ is a mgu for te_p and plan π}
8:     if R_te_p ≠ ∅ then
9:         E :=add-event(E, te_p)
10:    else if R_te_p = ∅ and type(p) = (obl | proh) then
11:        E :=EVENT-RECONSIDERATION(p)
12:    end if
13:    B :=update-belief(B, p)
14: end for
15: for all ⟨te, τ⟩ ∈ E do
16:    O_te := {πθ | θ is an applicable unifier for te and plan π}
17:    πθθ' := S_O(O_te) where θ' is a context unifier for te and plan π
18:    if πθθ' = nil then
19:        πθθ' := OPTION-RECONSIDERATION(te)
20:    end if
21:    if πθθ' ≠ nil and τ ∉ I then
22:        I := I ∪ πθθ'
23:    else if πθθ' ≠ nil and τ ∈ I then
24:        I := (I\τ) ∪ push (πθθ'σ, τ) where σ is an mgu for πθθ' and τ
25:    else if πθθ' = nil and τ ∈ I then
26:        I := (I\τ)
27:    end if
28:    I :=SCHEDULE(I)
29:    if I ≠ ∅ then
30:        I :=EXECUTE(I)
31:    end if
32: end for
```

out norm-aware intention scheduling is shown in §3.4. The internal operation of the ***N-Jason*** interpreter is extended from [15]. We use the same notations as in [15] for consistency and comparability.

We now give an informal explanation of one reasoning cycle in the interpreter. At the start (lines 1–4), we assume that an agent perceives knowledge (P) from its environment and about its normative positions (N) (e.g. obligations) from one or more institutional frameworks. N is treated just like P, that is a form of percept at this stage, by the interpreter (line 4).

The belief base (B) and the event base (E) are updated by P in the belief update process (*belief-update-function (buf)* more precisely) (see lines 6–13). This belief update involves the creation/addition of events in response to each new percept. Once a percept (p) is encoded as a triggering event (te_p) by the function *create-tevent*, the interpreter checks whether te_p has a set of relevant plans R_{te_p}[2] in the plan library Π. If R_{te_p} is retrieved, then E is updated with the event, a pair of te_p and its intention, by the function *add-event*. If no relevant plan is retrieved, te_p is ignored but B is updated in any case with p by the function *update-belief*. The same approach is taken for norms when the norms and its relevant plans are already specified in the agent program. Otherwise, the event reconsideration process (line 11) starts to find out what the norms are intended to achieve, as the first step in run-time norm execution.

Next, the interpreter starts the reasoning process in order to determine an applicable plan[3] in the selected set of applicable plans (O_{te}). The selection function S_O chooses a single option from O_{te} as a result of the unification of event and context. If S_O retrieves nothing (denoted by nil), then the interpreter follows exactly the same path as described above. The option reconsideration process (line 19) tries to find out which action plans are appropriate to execute unknown norms, as the second step in run-time norm execution. See lines 17–20.

If one single applicable plan is successfully retrieved by S_O, then the means-ends reasoning adds the applicable plan (π) as an intended means (IM) on top of an intention (I). If te of π is an internal event then π added in the existing I, otherwise a new I is created with π to be added in there (line 21–27). This is followed by the intention scheduling process which returns a *preference maximal set* of intentions in deadline order (line 28). Afterwards, one intention selected by the intention selection function S_I is finally executed (line 30). The details of the remainder are exactly the same as in [3] or [15].

3.3 Run-Time Norm Execution

In §3.2, we explained that run-time norm execution is realised by two steps: (i) event reconsideration and (ii) option reconsideration. Prior to defining those reconsideration processes, we firstly define a property of the *executability* of norms at run-time. We say that a norm such as `obl(evt, deadline, violation)`, is *executable* at run-time iff:

1. $p \in P$ and $type(p) = (obligation \mid prohibition)$, where p is a percept, formed from a list of terms such as $term(``,'' \ term)^*$, in a set of newly observed percepts P at run-time;
2. $te_p \notin E$, where te_p is a triggering event generated from the percept p, and E is an event base, which is a set of events $\{(te, \tau), (te', \tau'), \ldots\}$, where an event is a pair of a triggering event and an intention (te, τ);
3. $edp(p) \neq nil$ and $\{(te_{edp(p)}, \tau_{edp(p)})\} \cap E \neq \varnothing$, where $edp(p)$ is a function extracting the obliged event together with its deadline and priority from p, $te_{edp(p)}$ is a triggering event of the $edp(p)$, an event term in the norm, and $\tau_{edp(p)}$ is an intention of $te_{edp(p)}$ and
4. $R_{te_{edp(p)}} \neq \varnothing$, where $R_{te_{edp(p)}}$ is a set of relevant plans.

[2] A relevant plan for a particular event is a plan whose triggering event matches the particular event. There can be many relevant plans for each triggering event in general [3].

[3] An applicable plan is a candidate plan for execution, which has a context that evaluates to true given the agent's current beliefs [3].

Algorithm 2. Event Reconsideration

Require: $P := P \cup N$
Require: $te_p = \mathit{create\text{-}tevent}(p)$
1: **if** $p \in P$ **and** $type(p) = obligation$ **then**
2: $te_{edp(p)} = \mathit{create\text{-}tevent}(edp(p))$
3: $R_{te_{edp(p)}} := \{\pi\theta \mid \theta$ is a mgu for $te_{edp(p)}$ and plan $\pi\}$
4: **if** $R_{te_{edp(p)}} \neq \varnothing$ **then**
5: $E := \mathit{add\text{-}event}(E, te_p)$
6: **end if**
7: **else if** $p \in P$ **and** $type(p) = prohibition$ **then**
8: $\Xi := \mathit{add\text{-}prohibition}(\Xi, edp(p))$
9: **end if**

The executability determines the necessity of further reconsideration for the new and unknown norms. If those norms are judged executable at the perception stage, the event-reconsideration process starts for the addition of such norms to the event base as triggering events. Similarly, the executability also enables the option-reconsideration in order to execute an applicable plan in relation to the triggering events derived from the norms.

Event Reconsideration aims to verify that a norm perceived at run-time is executable although no corresponding plan exists in the agent program. If an event extracted from a detached norm has a relevance to a certain set of plans, it thus has potential to trigger specific ones, and it is then concluded that the norm is executable. If the norm is proven to be executable, the interpreter adds the norm to the event base E as an achievement goal addition event. The procedure for event reconsideration is as follows (see Algorithm 2):

1. Extract the terms representing an obliged event, a deadline and its priority[4] from the obligation by the function *edp*, whose practical implementation may vary, depending on norm representations in various systems (line 2),
2. Construct a new triggering event (an achievement goal addition event in this case) from the combination of extracted terms (line 2),
3. Query the existence of a set of relevant plans with such a constructed triggering event (line 3),
4. Add such triggering event to E, if relevant plans are successfully retrieved (line 5) and
5. If the norm is a prohibition, then the extracted event is added into the prohibition base (Ξ) (line 7 - 8) and will be revisited at the norm deliberation stage [5].

For example, suppose there is a detached obligation `obl(at(X, Y), 1030, 10)`. If relevant plans are not found in the agent program (plan library of an agent, to be

[4] In principle, the last term is an event which arises when a violation occurs. This value normally indicates the criticality of such a violation. Higher values represents a higher priority.

[5] ***N-Jason*** supports prohibitions as described above, and is therefore compatible with normative systems supporting prohibitions, but we note that the institutional model described in §2 does not have an explicit representation of prohibition, but only the absence of permission.

precise) in response to the obligation, the function *edp* firstly extracts the event (`at(X, Y)`), deadline (`1030`) and priority (`10`) from the obligation. Next, the interpreter constructs a new triggering event (an achievement goal addition event as described above) such as `+!at(X,Y)[deadline(1030), priority(10)]` using the extracted information. Subsequently, the interpreter queries the existence of relevant plans to S_R once again with a new triggering event, `+!at(X,Y)[deadline(1030), priority(10)]`. If the retrieval of relevant plans is successful, then the original event, `+!obl(at(X, Y), 1030, 10)`, is added to E.

One exceptional aspect in event-reconsideration is the addition of a deontic event te_p (which is a detached norm) instead of a normal event $te_{edp(p)}$ (which is a newly constructed triggering event) into the event base E. In so doing, we intend to distinguish norm-triggered intentions from ordinary intentions that normal events trigger, so as to facilitate norm-aware deliberation (see §3.4) in ***N-Jason***. In principle, ***Jason*** creates different intentions in response to different triggering events. Given this characteristic, both a deontic and a normal event create a deontic and a normal intention in ***N-Jason***, respectively. The intended means included in both intentions are identical since a deontic and a normal event trigger exactly the same plan in an agent program. However, the properties (e.g. deadline and priority) of each intention are different. The normal intention follows the original deadline and priority specified in the plan. In contrast, the deontic intention has different deadline and priority, which are inherited from those in the detached norm. As a result, these intentions are the main source of norm-aware deliberation. An agent is able to deliberate on norms and agent's private goals through the evaluation of the relative importance and urgency using norm-triggered (i.e. deontic) intentions and ordinary event-triggered (i.e. normal) intentions.

Suppose a plan whose label is `example`, is specified in an agent program:

```
@example[duration(50)]
+!at(X, Y)[deadline(1000), priority(5)]
<- move_toward(X, Y); !ack(ag).
```

Assuming that a normal event triggering `example` is added to event base E. Then it creates a normal intention using a pair of normal event and its associated plan `plan_-example`, whose deadline and priority are 1000 and 5, respectively. Later, a detached obligation `obl(at(X, Y), 1030, 10)` is received. Following Algorithm 2, the deontic event `+!obl(at(X, Y), 1030, 10)` is added to E, since a relevant plan `example` is found. Consequently a deontic intention is created using a pair of a deontic event and its associated plan `example`. Its deadline and priority are 1030 and 10, respectively, which are different from those in the normal intention. Obviously, we have two intentions whose properties are different, although the intended means are absolutely same. Hence, ***N-Jason*** is able to carry out norm-aware deliberation on norms and the agent's own goals using those intentions. If ***N-Jason*** simply adds a normal event instead of a deontic event when an obligation is detached, then norm-aware deliberation may not be feasible since there must be only one normal intention.

Option-Reconsideration is a central element in the practical reasoning process whereas the event reconsideration happens at the perception stage. The main objective of option reconsideration is the determination of an applicable plan corresponding to the new and unknown norm – whose executability is already verified – and is thus

Algorithm 3. Option Reconsideration

Require: $\langle te_p, \tau \rangle \in E$ where te_p is an event and τ is an intention
Ensure: $\pi\theta\theta'$ where θ' is a context unifier for $te_{edp(p)}$ and plan π
1: **if** $type(p) = obligation$ **then**
2: $\quad te_{edp(p)} = create\text{-}tevent(edp(p))$
3: $\quad R_{te_{edp(p)}} := \{\pi\theta \mid \theta$ is a mgu for $te_{edp(p)}$ and plan $\pi\}$
4: $\quad$ **if** $R_{te_{edp(p)}} \neq \varnothing$ **then**
5: $\quad\quad O_{te_{edp(p)}} := \{\pi\theta \mid \theta$ is an applicable unifier for $te_{edp(p)}$ and plan $\pi\}$
6: $\quad\quad \pi\theta\theta' := S_O(O_{te_{edp(p)}})$ where θ' is a context unifier for $te_{edp(p)}$ and plan π
7: $\quad$ **end if**
8: **end if**

added to E as an achievement goal addition event. If the applicable plan is chosen, then it will probably be used to enact a norm-compliant behaviour, unless it is infeasible as judged by intention scheduling (described in §3.4). The procedure is shown in Algorithm 3.

Like *Event-Reconsideration*, te_p is generated by a new and unknown norm that does not have any relevant plans R_{te_p} at this moment. Thus at the beginning of the option reconsideration, the interpreter carries out the same process for event reconsideration:

1. Extract the event term $edp(p)$ of the norm in order to retrieve relevant plans $R_{te_{edp(p)}}$ (as before), if the type of p is a norm (i.e. an obligation) (line 1 - 2),
2. Retrieve the relevant plans corresponding to the $te_{edp(p)}$ by the unification of an atomic-formula in a triggering event and each plan in an agent (line 3),
3. Determine a set of applicable plans with the constructed triggering event (line 5) and
4. Select a single applicable plan as an intended means to which to commit, through the extended unification of a triggering event, a plan and a context (line 6).

3.4 Norm Awareness in Deliberation

Norm awareness in the deliberation process is achieved by the scheduling of intentions with deadlines and priorities. We extend the algorithm proposed in [15] with the consideration of prohibitions in order to establish a conflict-free *preference maximal set* of intentions. In effect, this is like [1] who proposes a scheduling algorithm that brings about a *preference maximal set* of intentions, but that depends upon (N-)2APL's parallel execution of plans, whereas here the scheduling algorithm for *(**N-**)**Jason*** has to take account of the single-threaded plan execution model in ***Jason***.

The scheduling algorithm is introduced in Algorithm 4. A set of candidate intentions $I_C = \{\tau, \tau', \dots\}$, which is sorted in descending order of a priority, is inserted into a scheduling process. If each intention is *feasible*, i.e. a plan on top of the intention can be executed before the deadline and is not prohibited by a set of prohibition $\Xi = \{\xi, \xi', \dots\}$, then the intention is added to the *preference maximal set* (Γ) whose criteria are defined as follows:

Algorithm 4. Scheduling of Intentions

$\Gamma := \varnothing, \Xi' := \varnothing$
for all $\tau \in I$ in descending order of priority **do**
    if $\{\tau\} \cup \Gamma$ is feasible **then**
        if $\tau \notin \Xi$ **then**
            $\Gamma := \{\tau\} \cup \Gamma$
        else
            for all $\xi \in \Xi$ **do**
                $\Xi' := \{\tau\theta \mid \theta \text{ is a mgu for } \xi \text{ and intention } \tau\}$
            end for
            if $priority(\tau) > max\{priority(\xi), \forall \xi \in \Xi'\}$ **then**
                $\Gamma := \{\tau\} \cup \Gamma$
            end if
        end if
    end if
end for
sort Γ in order of increasing deadline
return Γ

1. An intention is feasible *iff* the execution of the intention is completed before its deadline, that is, for τ,

$$ne(\tau) + et(\tau) - ex(\tau) \leq dl(\tau)$$

   where τ denotes an intention, $ne(\tau)$ is the time at which τ will next execute, $et(\tau)$ is the time required to execute τ, denoted in the plan label, $ex(\tau)$ is the elapsed time to execute τ to this point, and $dl(\tau)$ is the deadline for τ specified in the plan [1].

2. The intention should not be prohibited, that is, for τ
   - $\tau \notin \Xi$ or
   - $\tau \in \Xi$, then $\forall \xi \in \Xi, \tau = \xi$ and $priority(\tau) > max\{priority(\xi), \forall \xi \in \Xi\}$

   where τ is an intention, ξ is a prohibited event in the prohibition base Ξ and *priority* is a priority retrieval function.

Scheduling in ***N-Jason*** is also pre-emptive in that the adoption of a new intention τ may prevent scheduled intentions with lower priority than τ (including currently executing intentions) being added to the new schedule just as in N-2APL and AgentSpeak(RT). Intentions that cannot meet their deadline are dropped.

3.5 Implementation

We have implemented ***N-Jason*** on top of the existing code base for ***Jason*** version 1.3.6. The latest prototype[6] of ***N-Jason*** implements the core language extensions (i.e. syntax, semantics) described in §3.1 and the extensions (e.g. run-time norm execution, norm-aware deliberation) described in §3.3 and §3.4. In addition, we implement a norm

[6] ***N-Jason*** is available via `http://bsf.googlecode.com/svn/tags/njason-0.0.1/`

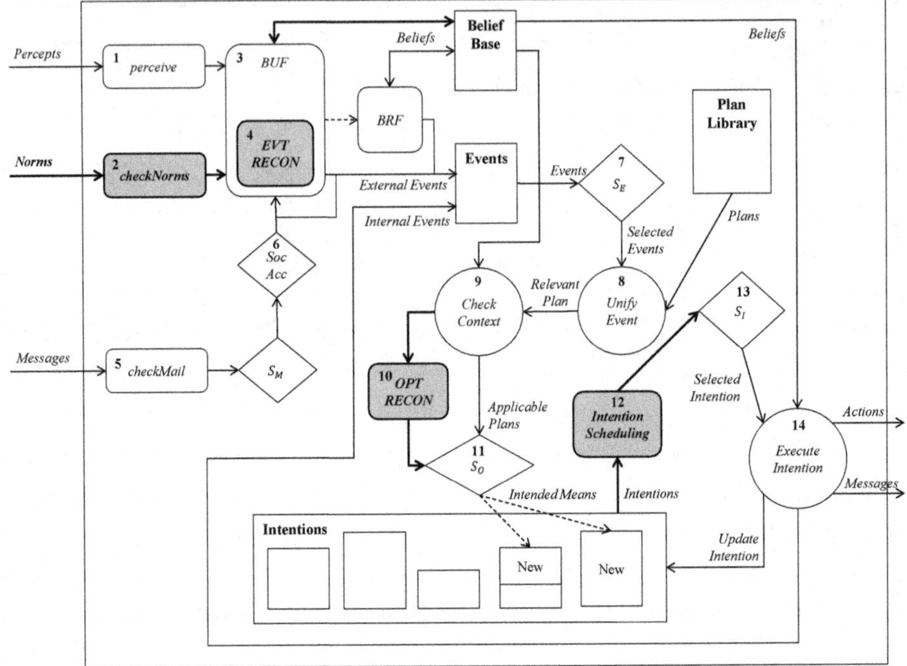

Fig. 2. Extended Features of ***N-Jason*** on ***Jason***/AgentSpeak(L)

adoption mechanism in ***N-Jason***, so that an agent under the governance of institutional frameworks is able to receive situationally appropriate norms and subsequently add them as percepts for processing by the reasoning cycle.

Figure 2 shows the extended features[7] and how they fit into the ***Jason*** interpreter. The language extensions, run-time norm execution and norm-aware deliberation are implemented as part of the reasoning cycle of the ***Jason*** interpreter. The norm adoption mechanism is implemented as an extension of the `AgArch` class.

In brief, one reasoning cycle of ***Jason*** is modelled as a transition system over states. The configuration of a ***Jason*** agent [3], contains the current state, denoted s, where $s \in$ {ProcMsg, SelEv, RelPl, ApplPl, AddIM, SelInt, ExecInt, ClrInt}. Each state has a corresponding procedure – `applyProcMsg()`, `applySelEv()`, `applyRelPl()`, `applySelAppl()`, `applyFindOp()`, `applyAddIM()`, `applyProcAct()`, `applySelInt()`, `applyExecInt()` – which are internal to the `reasoningCycle()` method in the transition system. To this transition system, we add the states RcvNorm and `schInt` and customise the procedures `reasoningCycle()`, `applyRelPl()`, `applyFindOp()`, `applySelInt()`. The complete states are detailed in §4.1.

We now sketch some details of the implementation. To begin with, we extend the ***Jason*** agent reasoning architecture class (`AgArch`) by subclassing in order to facilitate the norm adoption mechanism ($^{2}checkNorms$). Run-time norm execution is achieved

[7] Grey boxes with numbers 2, 4, 10, 12 in Figure 2 are new features. For more explanation about other white boxes see Chapter 4 of [3].

by *Event-* and *Option-Reconsideration* as described in Algorithms 2 and 3 above. The former, $^4EVTRECON$ in Figure 2, is implemented by customising the native belief update function (`buf()`) which is a subroutine of `reasoningCycle()` to implement Algorithm 2. For the latter, $^{10}OPTRECON$ in Figure 2, we customise the native option selection function (`applyFindOp()`) to implement Algorithm 3. Norm-aware deliberation, $^{12}IntentionScheduling$ in Figure 2, is accomplished by an intention scheduler with deadlines and priorities implemented in a newly created `IntentionScheduler` class. The scheduling (`schedule()`) method in this class is inserted just before the intention selection function (`selectIntention()`) which is a part of the `applySelInt()` procedure.

Apart from the above changes to the interpreter, the language syntax extensions are implemented by the customisation of the annotation processing routine (`setLabel()` and `setTEvent()`) in the `Plan` class.

3.6 Example

As an example, we consider robots serving beer in a pub, whose main role is to get an order and to deliver a beer to the customer. We assume the existence of some institutions delivering desirable social norms, subject to the observations of participants, and that all agents are governed by such systems. A part of the agent program is shown below:

```
@P1[duration(5)]
+!at(X, Y) : not at(X, Y) <- moveToward(X, Y).

@P2[duration(10)]
+!order(X, Y) <- get(beer); moveToward(X, Y).

// A request from customer seated at (X, Y).
// The deadline is D and the priority is P.
+request(X, Y)[deadline(D), priority(P)]
<- !order(X, Y)[deadline(D), priority(P)].
```

At time 100, the robot receives the following events:

E1: `+!request(2, 3)[deadline(130), priority(20)]`
A request from customer seated at (2, 3).
The deadline is 130 and the customer is important so the priority is 20.

E2: `+!request(1, 1)[deadline(115), priority(10)]`
A request from customer seated at (1, 1).
The deadline is 115 and the the priority is 10.

E3: `+!request(3, 3)[deadline(130), priority(10)]`
A request from customer seated at (3, 3).
The deadline is 130 and the the priority is 10.

These three events trigger the plan P2, and give rise to three possible intentions τ_1 (P2 triggered by (2, 3)), τ_2 (P2 triggered by (1, 1)) and τ_3 (P2 triggered by (3, 3)). τ_2 is not feasible, thus it is dropped, whereas τ_1 and τ_3 are feasible, so scheduled in deadline order: τ_1 is scheduled first between 100 and 110 since it has an earlier deadline followed by τ_3 between 110 and 120. Now the agent starts the execution of τ_1.

Let consider an announcement of a fire alarm by one of the normative frameworks. It broadcasts an obligation containing the coordinates of an exit to all participants so they may escape from the building. Suppose the norm is `obl(at(0, 0), 115, 100)`. Although the obligation is not stated in the agent's program, it is executable since the agent has a *pre-existing* moving ability `!at(X, Y)`, which is enough to satisfy the obligation. With the event- and option-reconsideration, the event :

E4: `+!at(0, 0)[deadline(115), priority(100)]` is generated from the obligation, thus adoption the plan P1, bringing about an intention τ_4 (P1 triggered by (0, 0)). During the execution of τ_1, τ_3 and τ_4 are inserted into a new schedule in deadline order: since the priority of τ_4 is greater than τ_3 and τ_4 has a more urgent deadline, the agent starts to execute τ_4, triggered by the obligation, before the execution of τ_3.

Notwithstanding, that this example is extremely simple, it provides a useful in-principle illustration of norm-aware deliberation – as performed by intention scheduling – as well as the run-time norm execution mechanism in ***N-Jason***.

4 Operational Semantics

In this section, we present a theoretical foundation for the ***N-Jason*** programming language with semantics based upon an extension of the operational semantics for ***Jason***/AgentSpeak(L). Given the formal semantics of ***Jason*** we extend the transition rules which transform one extended configuration into another. To begin with, we show a configuration of individual ***N-Jason*** agents which is almost unchanged except for norm configuration. In the following section, we describe the transition rules that give rise to a configuration change at each state in a single reasoning cycle. For consistency and comparability, we follow exactly the same notations as those in published ***Jason*** descriptions excepting the normative aspects.

4.1 *N-Jason* Configuration

The configuration of ***N-Jason*** is a tuple $\langle ag, C, N, T, s\rangle$ where:

- ag is an agent program consisting of a set of beliefs bs and a set of plans ps, as defined by the EBNF in [3].
- An agent's circumstance C is a tuple $\langle I, E, A\rangle$, where I is a set of *intention* $\{i, i', \ldots\}$, E is a set of *events* $\{(te, i), (te', i'), \ldots\}$, in which event is a pair of a triggering event and an intention (te, i) and A is a set of actions an agent performs in the external environment.
- N is a tuple $\langle \Gamma, \Xi\rangle$ denoting normative consequences delivered from normative systems, where Γ is a set of obligations $\{\gamma, \gamma', \ldots\}$ and Ξ is a set of prohibition $\{\xi, \xi', \ldots\}$.
- T is a tuple $\langle R, A_p, \iota, \varepsilon, \rho\ \rangle$ defining a trace of provisional information required for subsequent steps within a single reasoning cycle, where R is the set of *relevant plans*, A_p the sets of applicable plans, and ι, ε and ρ record an intention, event, and applicable plan (respectively) at a specific moment under consideration within the execution of a single reasoning cycle.

– The current state s within an agent's reasoning cycle is denoted by $s \in \{$RcvNorm, ProcMsg, SelEv, RelPl, ApplPl, AddIM, SchInt, SelInt, ExecInt, ClrInt$\}$.

4.2 Transition Rules

The execution of the ***N-Jason*** program leads the modification of the initial configuration of an agent via transition rules given below. For the sake of brevity, we do not repeat the communication semantics, since these are unaffected by the changes in relation to norms.

In general, the transition would normally start from the state ProcMsg, but we propose a preceding step RcvNorm, as described in §2 because this provides the hook for the consideration of the norm as part of the reasoning cycle. Thus, note that the initial configuration of this model is $\langle ag, C, N, T, \mathsf{RcvNorm}\rangle$, where ag is specified by the agent program and other all components are empty, and the reasoning cycle starts from RcvNorm with the transition rules given below.

Receiving Detached Norms: As described in §2, institutional frameworks may distribute norms via broadcasting when a norm is activated by the fulfilment of institutional states triggered by external events in the environment. As soon as the event-based norms are received, the norms effectively act like an ordinary event thus trigger the transition of the agent's mental state. Rule **RcvNorm** (see Figure 3) updates the agent belief base and an event base component C_E associated with adding new norms, specifically in case of obligations in an obligation base N_Γ. Otherwise, only a prohibition is added into the prohibition base and there are no updates to other components.

Relevant Plans: (see Figure 4) If the transition of states (RcvNorm $\mapsto$ SelEv) is successful after RcvNorm and the state SelEv selects one event from the component E of which event is either $\langle te, i\rangle$ or $\langle \gamma, i\rangle$, rule **Rel_1** starts to assign the set of relevant plans to component T_R in the state RelPl. Rule **Rel_2** indicates the reconsideration situation where a new triggering event extracted from the obligation is assigned to the component C_E, where $\mathsf{Evt}(\gamma)$ is a function constructing a triggering event by the retrieval of information from γ. Rule **Rel_3** assigns a set of relevant plans to T_R in respect of the reconsidered event. Rule **Rel_4** and **Rel_5** cope with the situation where no relevant plan is retrieved. In those cases, events (both ordinary event and reconsidered event) are simply ignored and the state returns to SelEv.

Since transition rules between (AppPl $\mapsto$ AddIM) are almost same as those in ***Jason*** we give a brief description of each rule at each state from here. If T'_R is successfully assigned then it is followed by: (i) AppPl which assigns a set of applicable plans to T_{A_P} by retrieving those relevant plans whose contexts are believed to be true, (ii) SelAppl which assigns a particular intended means selected by an option selection function S_O to T_ρ, and (iii) AddIM which adds a selected intended means to C_I which is an existing intention or a newly created one. If transitions fail between (AppPl $\mapsto$ AddIM), then the state SelInt becomes the next step. For more information, see [3].

Scheduling of Intentions: Rule **SchInt** (see Figure 5) updates the component C'_I by the function SCHEDULE(C_I). Note that the scheduling function, SCHEDULE(C_I), sorts

$$\frac{N \neq \{\}}{\langle ag, C, N, T, \mathsf{RcvNorm}\rangle \rightarrow \langle ag', C, N', T, \mathsf{SelEv}\rangle} \qquad \textbf{(RcvNorm)}$$

where: $ag'_{bs} = ag_{bs} \cup \{\gamma\}$
$N'_{\Gamma} = N_{\Gamma} \cup \{\gamma\} \vee N'_{\Xi} = N_{\Xi} \cup \{\xi\}$

Fig. 3. Transition Rule for Receiving a Norm

$$\frac{T_{\varepsilon} = \langle te, i\rangle \quad \mathsf{RelPlans}(ag_{ps}, te) \neq \{\}}{\langle ag, C, N, T, \mathsf{RelPl}\rangle \rightarrow \langle ag, C, N, T', \mathsf{ApplPl}\rangle} \qquad \textbf{(Rel\_1)}$$

where: $T'_R = \mathsf{RelPlans}(ag_{ps}, te)$

$$\frac{T_{\varepsilon} = \langle \gamma, i\rangle \quad \mathsf{RelPlans}(ag_{ps}, \gamma) = \{\}}{\langle ag, C, N, T, \mathsf{RelPl}\rangle \rightarrow \langle ag, C', N, T, \mathsf{RelPl}\rangle} \qquad \textbf{(Rel\_2)}$$

where: $C'_E = \{\langle \mathsf{Evt}(\gamma), i\rangle\}$

$$\frac{T_{\varepsilon} = \langle \mathsf{Evt}(\gamma), i\rangle \mathsf{RelPlans}(ag_{ps}, \mathsf{Evt}(\gamma)) \neq \{\}}{\langle ag, C, N, T, \mathsf{RelPl}\rangle \rightarrow \langle ag, C, N, T', \mathsf{ApplPl}\rangle} \qquad \textbf{(Rel\_3)}$$

where: $T'_R = \mathsf{RelPlans}(ag_{ps}, \mathsf{Evt}(\gamma))$

$$\frac{\mathsf{RelPlans}(ag_{ps}, te) = \{\}}{\langle ag, C, N, T, \mathsf{RelPl}\rangle \rightarrow \langle ag, C, N, T, \mathsf{SelEv}\rangle} \qquad \textbf{(Rel\_4)}$$

$$\frac{\mathsf{RelPlans}(ag_{ps}, \mathsf{Evt}(\gamma)) = \{\}}{\langle ag, C, N, T, \mathsf{RelPl}\rangle \rightarrow \langle ag, C, N, T, \mathsf{SelEv}\rangle} \qquad \textbf{(Rel\_5)}$$

Fig. 4. Transition Rules for Relevant Plans

$$\frac{T_{\rho} = \{\}}{\langle ag, C, N, T, \mathsf{SchInt}\rangle \rightarrow \langle ag, C', N, T, \mathsf{SelInt}\rangle} \qquad \textbf{(SchInt)}$$

where: $C'_I = \text{SCHEDULE}(C_I)$

Fig. 5. Transition Rule for Scheduling Intentions

intentions in order of priority and deadline so as to determine the *preference maximal set* of intentions discussed in §3.4.

After this step, the transition system follows the same rules as presented in [3] in order to execute an intended means in an particular intention selected by S_I in between SelInt, ExecInt and ClrInt.

5 Related Works

There has been much research over a number of years on the matter of norm compliance through the combination of normative frameworks and classical (BDI-type) cognitive agents [2,11]. However, research on compliance of norms at the individual agent level has received less attention. As discussed in §1, this problem can be decomposed into two perspectives: to facilitate a generic norm execution mechanism at run-time, and to focus on the rational decision making between norms and existing goals.

Alechina *et al.* [1] introduce N-2APL, a norm-aware BDI agent architecture and its programming language. It is able to carry out norm-aware deliberation, which aims to permit agents to resolve the conflicts between an agent's own goals, normative goals and sanctions. This is accomplished by a deadline- and priority-based intention scheduling algorithm, which weighs the feasibility for all intentions that may bring about conflicts. The (potential) sanctions may affect agent decision making, but violations are possible in this approach. Given N-2APL, Dybalova *et al.* [9] demonstrate norm-compliant agents in location-based gaming environments in conjunction with the organisational framework, 2OPL [6]. There, once organisations have broadcast state-based norms to all participants, the individual agents achieve a state of the environment described in the norms using a design-based approach. ***N-Jason*** is also able to support norm-aware deliberation in conjunction with an institutional model, which is similar to the combination of N-2APL and 2OPL, but extends the concept of norm awareness to the whole reasoning cycle. As a result, it supports agents in being design-based norm compliant, but can additionally deliver run-time compliance through norm execution.

Meneguzzi *et al.* [13] focuses on norm awareness at the perception level, by extending the AgentSpeak(L) BDI architecture with a run-time plan modification technique. It enables agents to behave appropriately in response to newly accepted norms at run-time. However, it assumes that the norms are non-conflicting, so it does not consider scheduling of plans with regards to their deadlines or possible sanctions in accordance with existing goals in agents. Whereas [13] takes a rather practical perspective, van Riemsdijk *et al.* [14] introduce a formal framework for generic norm execution, which allows agents to be norm compliant by triggering or preventing actions in new and unknown norms at design time. However the agent in [14] works at the level of individual actions (its decision mechanism chooses actions rather than plans) and the norms are specified in terms of actions, making in effect a norm-reactive agent, and it is unclear how the decision mechanism can combine actions to achieve goals and thereby the objective of a norm-deliberative agent. In ***N-Jason***, run-time norm execution is in practice accomplished at the level of plans to achieve goals, and norms indicate a sort of event that triggers plans. Moreover, in ***N-Jason*** run-time norm compliance is achieved on top of the norm aware decision making and in conjunction with the execution mechanism.

Notwithstanding the benefits of ***N-Jason***, there are some issues to highlight in respect of the mechanism for run-time norms. The norm compliance strategy is hard-coded in the semantics of the language, leaving only a capacity for configuration via the plan annotations, whereas the strategy is programmable through agent plans (i.e. supporting the design of strategy by an agent programmer) in JaCaMo [2] and N-2APL [1]. Thus, the proposal presented here provides a pre-packaged approach to normative reasoning, since it deprives the agent of the scope to change plans dynamically or mis-behave intentionally, based on rules the agent programmer designs. However, the mechanism put forward here does enable legacy agents, which have no compliance rule or strategy in their specification, to become norm-aware automatically. Thus, those agents' behaviour can be coordinated through the governance of normative frameworks without further engineering effort.

Another issue lies in the simple mechanism for the operationalisation of norms in run-time norm execution. The approach described here means the ontology and syntax of norms that can be executed are limited to those present in the plan library of an agent. In consequence, some detached norms, that may correspond semantically to one of an agent's plans, but which are ontologically different from the plan, will be ignored or violated. We are considering how to generalise the execution mechanism with the analysis of semantics of norms, following [14], in conjunction with plan synthesis.

6 Conclusion and Future Works

In this paper, we have presented a design for a norm-aware BDI agent, ***N-Jason***, that enables the exhibition of norm compliance at run-time. Basically ***N-Jason*** offers a generic norm execution mechanism on top of norm-aware deliberation to contribute to the exploitation of run-time norm compliance. Run-time norm execution specifically focuses on the operationalisation of new and unknown (event-based) norms not stated in the agent program at run-time. By judging the executability of them, ***N-Jason*** agents executes those norms following an extended model of norm awareness consisting of: (i) *event reconsideration*, to find out what the norm is intended to achieve or to reach, and (ii) *option reconsideration*, to identify which plan is the most appropriate in response to the norm. The selection of norm compliant behaviour is achieved in the norm-aware deliberation process by *intention scheduling* with deadlines, priorities and prohibitions which confirms the decision about which behaviour agent would prefer between goals, norms and sanctions. It brings about a *preference maximal set* of intentions in order to realise the norm compliance. ***N-Jason*** is implemented in ***Jason***/AgentSpeak(L) and extends its syntax and semantics to create ***N-Jason***.

We believe that run-time norm compliance model is beneficial for the enhancement of both a norm compliance capability and agent autonomy from the agent's perspective. However, we note that the behaviour triggered by run-time norm execution may look like unpredictable/unwanted behaviour from the agent programmer's perspective.

Although this paper particularly considers the execution of event-based norms at run-time in conjunction with the institutional model, the extension to support state-based norms and its normative systems can easily be incorporated into ***N-Jason*** agents and will be as future work. We also plan to detect violations which are generated in the norm aware deliberation, particularly when the normative goals are dropped during scheduling. This offers a potentially useful link for enforcement in the context of normative system implementation. In addition, both empirical and analytical evaluation of the performance of ***N-Jason*** requires proper investigation.

References

1. Alechina, N., Dastani, M., Logan, B.: Programming norm-aware agents. In: Proceedings of the 11th International Conference on Autonomous Agents and Multiagent Systems, Richland, SC, pp. 1057–1064 (2012)
2. Boissier, O., Bordini, R.H., Hübner, J.F., Ricci, A., Santi, A.: Multi-agent oriented programming with jacamo. Sci. Comput. Program. 78(6), 747–761 (2013)
3. Bordini, R., Hübner, J., Wooldridge, M.: Programming Multi-Agent Systems in AgentSpeak using Jason. Wiley Series in Agent Technology. John Wiley & Sons (2007)
4. Charlton, B.: Evolution and the cognitive neuroscience of awareness, consciousness and language. Cognition 50, 7–15 (2000)
5. Cliffe, O., De Vos, M., Padget, J.: Specifying and reasoning about multiple institutions. In: Noriega, P., Vázquez-Salceda, J., Boella, G., Boissier, O., Dignum, V., Fornara, N., Matson, E. (eds.) COIN 2006 Workshops. LNCS (LNAI), vol. 4386, pp. 67–85. Springer, Heidelberg (2007)
6. Dastani, M., Tinnemeier, N.A., Meyer, J.-J.C.: A programming language for normative multi-agent systems. In: Multi-Agent Systems: Semantics and Dynamics of Organizational Models, pp. 397–417 (2009)
7. De Vos, M., Balke, T., Satoh, K.: Combining event-and state-based norms. In: Proceedings of the 2013 International Conference on Autonomous Agents and Multi-agent Systems, AAMAS 2013, pp. 1157–1158. International Foundation for Autonomous Agents and Multiagent Systems, Richland (2013)
8. Dignum, V.: A Model for Organizational Interaction. PhD thesis, Utrecht University (2004)
9. Dybalova, D., Testerink, B., Dastani, M., Logan, B.: A framework for programming norm-aware multi-agent systems. In: Dignum, F., Chopra, A. (eds.) Proceedings of the 15th International Workshop on Coordination, Organisations, Institutions and Norms, COIN 2013 (2013)
10. Gelfond, M., Lifschitz, V.: Classical negation in logic programs and disjunctive databases. New Generation Comput. 9(3/4), 365–386 (1991)
11. Hubner, J.F., Sichman, J.S., Boissier, O.: Developing organised multiagent systems using the moise+ model: programming issues at the system and agent levels. Int. J. Agent-Oriented Softw. Eng. 1(3/4), 370–395 (2007)
12. Lee, J., Li, T., Padget, J.: Towards polite virtual agents using social reasoning techniques. Computer Animation and Virtual Worlds 24(3-4), 335–343 (2013)
13. Meneguzzi, F., Luck, M.: Norm-based behaviour modification in bdi agents. In: Proceedings of The 8th International Conference on Autonomous Agents and Multiagent Systems, AAMAS 2009, vol. 1, pp. 177–184. International Foundation for Autonomous Agents and Multiagent Systems, Richland (2009)
14. van Riemsdijk, M.B., Dennis, L.A., Fisher, M., Hindriks, K.V.: Agent reasoning for norm compliance: A semantic approach. In: Proceedings of the 2013 International Conference on Autonomous Agents and Multi-agent Systems, AAMAS 2013, pp. 499–506. International Foundation for Autonomous Agents and Multiagent Systems, Richland (2013)
15. Vikhorev, K., Alechina, N., Logan, B.: Agent programming with priorities and deadlines. In: The 10th International Conference on Autonomous Agents and Multiagent Systems, Richland, SC, pp. 397–404 (2011)

Typing Multi-Agent Systems via Commitments

Matteo Baldoni, Cristina Baroglio, and Federico Capuzzimati

Università degli Studi di Torino — Dipartimento di Informatica
c.so Svizzera 185, I-10149 Torino, Italy
{matteo.baldoni,cristina.baroglio,federico.capuzzimati}@unito.it

Abstract. This work presents an agent typing system, that differently than most of other proposals relies on notions that are typical of agent systems instead of relying on a functional approach. Specifically, we use commitments to define types. The proposed typing includes a notion of compatibility, based on subtyping, which allows for the safe substitution of agents to roles along an interaction that is ruled by a commitment-based protocol. Type checking can be done dynamically when an agent enacts a role. The proposal is implemented in the 2COMM framework and exploits Java annotations. 2COMM is based on the Agent & Artifact meta-model, exploit JADE and CArtAgO, by using CArtAgO artifacts in order to reify commitment protocols.

Keywords: Commitments, Static and dynamic type checking, Agents and Artifacts, JADE, Implementation.

1 Introduction

Software infrastructures are quickly changing, becoming more and more global, pervasive and autonomic. Computing is becoming ubiquitous, with embedded and distributed devices interacting with each other. Multi-Agent Systems (MAS) have been recognized to be a promising paradigm for this kind of scenarios, however, as the complexity of programming these systems increases, the need for effective tools for reasoning on properties of programs becomes stronger and stronger. This is particularly true in the case of open systems, where heterogeneous and autonomously developed agents may need to interact. MAS usually rely on interaction protocols (or other kinds of "contract") to specify the interacting behavior that is expected of the agents. How can, then, an agent, a designer, the system verify that the agent has the the means for carrying on the encoded interaction? How to decide whether the agent is capable of behaving in a certain way or whether it shows specific skills/properties?

One way is to rely on some *typing of agents*, in a way that is similar to the typing of objects. Typing provides abstractions to perform sophisticated forms of program analysis and verifications: it helps performing compile-time/run-time error checking, modeling, documentation, verification of conformance and of compliance, reasoning about programs and components. It also allows a simple form of (a priori/runtime) verification. To the best of our knowledge, Zapf and Geihs

F. Dalpiaz et al. (Eds.): EMAS 2014, LNAI 8758, pp. 388–405, 2014.

[34] were the first to propose the use of a type system for (mobile) agents, and they also introduced the idea of using sub-typing for the substitution of more specific subclasses in places where more general classes are expected, thus supporting safe extension and program re-use. More recent examples include [18,19,1,26]. In particular, [26] describes an agent-oriented programming language with a type checking that is inspired by mainstream object-oriented languages, and [1] uses global session types for realizing monitors of the interaction.

Differently than [18,19,26], we believe that, since types are abstraction tools for easily programming and modeling, for typing MAS it is necessary to rely on concepts that are typical abstractions of MAS, rather than relying on abstractions from other programming paradigms. Similarly to [1], our proposal is centered around *interaction*, which we believe to be one essential aspect of MAS. Differently than [1], we rely on commitments rather than on global session types. *Commitments* [13,28] are one of the fundamental abstractions for ruling agent interaction while preserving agent autonomy. For this reason, we discuss how commitments can be used for typing MAS and why it is interesting to rely on them. Specifically, we report the first steps towards a definition of a behavioral-based typing system for autonomous agents. The proposal is not bound to a specific agent programming language but, rather, it can be implemented in different frameworks. In the paper we describe an implementation in 2COMM [2]. The paper is organized as follows. Section 2 reports and comments the relevant literature motivating our proposal. Section 3 describes the 2COMM system that we used for the implemantation. Section 4 introduces the type system, while Section 5 describes its implementation. Conclusions end the paper.

2 Background and Motivation

The notion of "typing an agent" requires a precise, crisp definition. In programming languages, type systems are used to help designers and developers in avoiding code errors, bugs, that can entail unpredictable results. Type systems can be weak or strong, static or dynamic, but at the end they all share the same goal: support the development of error-free and human-readable code.

Most agent system implementations (JADE [9], Jack [20], A-Globe [29]) are based on programming languages like Java and do not supply agent type support but rather rely on the typing system of the language used for developing the system. Zapf and Geihs [34] underlined the importance of using a type system which allows dynamic type checking and proposed to base agent typing (1) on the externally visible actions of the agents, that they identify as being the messages agents accept and send, (2) on the meaning of the messages agents can exchange which includes, through the special symbol *self*, a characterization of the agent itself, (3) on the used communication protocol. They structure an agent type as a triple. The first component is the *syntactic type*, which is stateless and consists of the set of the input messages and of the set of output messages. The second is a *transition type*, i.e. a finite state automaton capturing a communication protocol similarly to regular types [22]. The third and last component is the *semantic type*, an annotation aimed at checking behavior-compatibility, based on J. F. Sowa's conceptual graphs.

We agree on the importance of dynamic type checking for verifying that an agent fits the requirements for interacting in an open MAS in the moment the agent decides to enter the interaction, because it may have the required properties only when it enters the system; on the importance of relying only on externally visible actions, because the agents' internal states are not inspectable; on the importance of accounting for the interaction protocol, because it captures the rules of encounter of the agents, ruling their interaction. What we disagree with is the solution adopted by the authors of relying on finite state automata for describing the interaction as well as for describing the agents' behavior. This hinders the agent's autonomy in two ways. The first reason is that agents must supply a description of their behavior. Secondly, this description concerns how to do things, rather than what to do: it is prescriptive. An agent may have the possibility (and the capability) of doing something in different ways. We think that the typing system should be capable of featuring a more flexible representation of the behavior, with the possibility of leaving the choice of how to act up to the agent.

The main claim of [1] is the importance of using interaction protocols for representing the functioning of a system. To this aim, they use global session types as an abstraction tool, which allows automatically generating monitors that are aimed at verifying the correctness of on-going, multi-party interactions. In particular, the global session type is used to automatically generate a monitor agent, which intercepts all the exchanged messages and verifies whether the protocol is respected. This proposal is implemented in Jason [12]; a global session type is represented by a cyclic Prolog term, which is consumed as messages are sniffed. Along the line of the previous proposal, [1] focuses on externally visible actions (message exchanges) and on the use of interaction protocols. It differs from the previous one in that there is no actual type system, but rather global session types are used for specifying the interaction of a system from a global perspective. Since agents are not typed, when they enter a system, it is not possible to verify whether their behavior is compatible with the protocol nor it is possible to search for agents showing characteristics which allow them to successfully take part to the system. It is up to the monitor agent to check the exchanged messages. This is surely an important functionality but it is not type checking. In other words, the representation does not clearly express what an agent can do nor what is expected of an agent. Moreover, we disagree with the choice of realizing the monitor as an agent. In order for the system to be transparent, the monitor should be inspectable by the interacting agents, and the infrastructure should guarantee that the monitor is notified of all the exchanged messages. We believe that the environment should supply proper monitoring services, or an artifact, but not another autonomous agent.

Ricci and Santi [25,26] defined the SimpAL language, where types are seen as useful for realizing integrated development environments, and they implemented an Eclipse plugin [27]. The approach to typing is a classic one, grounded on *interfaces*. This is the way in which most programming languages assure coherence, and prevent (statically) or detect (dynamically) logical errors. SimpAL extends the notion of interface to the agent abstraction level, introducing the notion of *role* as a collection of *tasks*, that an agent is capable to perform. A role will be implemented by an agent script, containing the behavioural logic of the agent. Specifically, a SimpAL *role* is an interface, while a role *task* is a method signature, which includes a list of formal parameters needed for its completion, that are expressed as pairs $\langle name : Type \rangle$. SimpAL provides environment typing and organizational typing too, used for programming coordination, resources and interactions between agents.

A typing of agents merely based on syntactic interfaces is criticized in [34], where the authors explain how conventional typing does not suffice the context of agent systems. The critic bases upon work by Nierstrasz [22] on active objects, that showed how the enumeration of the possible input and output messages is not sufficient to guarantee the interoperability. It is advisable to rely, instead, on some sort of behavioral type, including semantic information. Moreover, in SimpAL agent type checking is static. This is not a major concern in a homogeneous, single application environment. However, in an open MAS, where agents may be composed dynamically, static type checking is not enough; instead, it is necessary to rely on dynamic type checking and on monitoring. In this setting, agents themselves may verify their conformance to a role in order to decide whether to enter an interaction as well as to decide whether adopting new behaviors. As a consequence, the notion of type not only is a tool that supports the programmer's work but it becomes an programming element, that is used by agents in order to take decisions.

The proposal that we present in this paper concerns an agent typing system, which is characterized by (1) being based on typical agent society abstractions (social relationships), (2) being based on the agents' observable behavior, (3) dynamically checking if agents satisfy role requirements, (4) supplying a runtime monitoring environment. The implementation is provided in 2COMM, a middleware for developing open MAS whose interaction is commitment-based [2], which combines the well-known JADE [9] and CArtAgO [24] platforms. JADE agents interact based on commitment protocols. Each interaction protocol is realized as a CArtAgO artifact. Such an artifact provides social relationships as environmental resources. Dynamic checks are realized based on Java annotations.

3 Reference Framework

This proposal relies on the 2COMM middleware [2,3] for developing Multi-Agent Systems. In 2COMM, the MAS is specified as a set of *social relationships*, that govern the behavior of the agents taking part into the system. In a system made of autonomous and heterogeneous actors, social relationships cannot but concern the observable behavior [17]: for this reason, and in order to give them that normative value which allows them to create social expectations, we realize social relationships by means of *commitments* [28].

On the other hand, we need social relationships to be *accepted* explicitly by the participants to the interaction, and possibly to be *inspected* by the agents, in order to decide whether conforming to them. To this aim, we need to explicitly model social relationships as resources, that are available to the interacting peers. Given that agents and social relationships are both first-class entities, that interact in a bi-directional manner, we adopt the Agents and Artifacts (A&A) meta-model [32,23], that extends the agent paradigm with another primitive abstraction, the artifact. A&A provides abstractions for environments and artifacts, that can be acted upon, observed, perceived, notified, and so on. When embodied inside artifacts, social relationships can be examined by the agents (to take decisions about their behavior), as advised in [14], used (which entails that agents accept the corresponding regulations), constructed, e.g., by negotiation, specialized, composed, and so forth.

2COMM[1] [2] provides a middleware for programming social relationships, by exploiting a declarative, interaction-centric approach. It is based on a combination of JADE [9] and CArtAgO [24]. JADE provides the agent platform, characterized by a FIPA compliant communication framework, and an agent-developing middleware. CArtAgO is a framework based on the A&A meta-model which extends the agent programming paradigm with the first-class entity of *artifact*: a resource that an agent can use. CArtAgO provides a way to define and organize *workspaces*, that are logical groups of artifacts, and that can be joined by agents at runtime. The environment is itself programmable and encapsulates services and functionalities. CArtAgO provides an API to program *artifacts* that agents can use, regardless of the agent programming language or the agent framework used. CArtAgO artifacts reify communication and interaction, represented in terms of commitment-based protocols. From an organizational perspective, a protocol is structured into a set of roles. A role represents a way of manipulating the social state and belongs to the artifact which reifies a protocol. Roles and agents are different entities, and we assume that roles cannot live autonomously: they exist in the system in view of the interaction, because agents, for interacting, use artifacts and execute actions on them [8]. Agents will use an interaction artifact to establish a channel of normed, mediated communication. The roles of such an artifact specify how agents can manipulate it: by enacting a role, an agent receives social powers by the artifact. Social powers have different and public social consequences, that we express in terms of commitments.

In 2COMM interaction is ruled by *commitment-based protocols*. A *commitment* $C(x, y, r, p)$ represents a directed obligation between a debtor x and a creditor y to bring about the consequent condition p when the antecedent condition r holds. A commitment may be manipulated by means of a set of primitives: delegate, assign, release [30]. They represents contractual relationships between agents, thus agents have the social expectation that an agent involved in a commitment as a debtor will realize the consequent condition; the debtor is responsible for the violation of a commitment. A *commitment protocol* defines a collection of actions,

[1] The source files of the system and examples are available at the URL `http://di.unito.it/2COMM`

whose social effects are expressed in terms of commitment primitives, e.g., adding a new commitment, releasing another agent from some commitment, satisfying a commitment, see [33]. We assume that commitment conditions are yielded by the execution of artifact operations. For example, having a commitment C1 $= C(x, y, r, p \wedge q)$, a protocol artifact needs to supply at least an operation that makes r true, at least an operation that makes p true and at least an operation that makes q become true. The use of commitments gives a normative characterization to agent coordination [13,28]. When an agent uses a protocol artifact it accepts the regulations it contains and, in particular, that by executing certain actions it will be the debtor of some commitments. Public acceptance of the regulations is extremely important because it allows reasoning about the agents' behavior [15].

Figure 1 shows an excerpt of the 2COMM UML diagram. Overall the middleware is organized as follows: JADE supplies standard agent services (message passing, distributed containers, naming and yellow pages services, agent mobility); when needed, an agent can enact a protocol role, thus using a *communication artifact* – implemented by exploiting CArtAgO, which provides a set of operations by means of which agents participate in a mediated interaction session. Each communication artifact corresponds to a specific protocol enactment and maintains an own social state and an own communication state.

Class *CommunicationArtifact* (CA for short) provides the basic communication operations *in* and *out* for allowing mediated communication. by means of which agents respectively ask to play or to give up playing a role. CA extends an abstract version of the *TupleSpace* CArtAgO artifact: briefly, a blackboard that agents use as a tuple-based coordination means. In and out are, then, operations on the tuple space. CA also traces who is playing which role by using the property *enactedRoles*.

Class *Role* extends the CArtAgO class *Agent*, and contains the basic manipulation logic of CArtAgO artifacts. Thus, any specific role, extending this super-type, will be able to perform operations on artifacts, whenever its player will decide to do so. Role provides static methods for creating artifacts and for *enacting/deacting* roles. This is done by passing a reference to the JADE agent behavior that will actually play the role. The class *CARole* is an inner class of CA and extends the Role class. It provides the *send* and *receive* primitives, by which agents can exchange messages. Send and receive are implemented based on the *in* and *out* primitives provided by CA.

ProtocolArtifact (PA for short) extends CA and allows modeling the social layer with the help of commitments. It maintains the state of the on-going protocol interaction, via the property *socialState*, a store of social facts and commitments, that is managed only by its container artifact. This artifact implements the operations needed to manage commitments (create, discharge, cancel, release, assign, delegate). PA realizes the commitment life-cycle and for the assertion/retraction of facts. Operations on commitments are realized as *internal operations*, that is, they are not invokable directly: the protocol social actions will use them as primitives to modify the social state. Being an

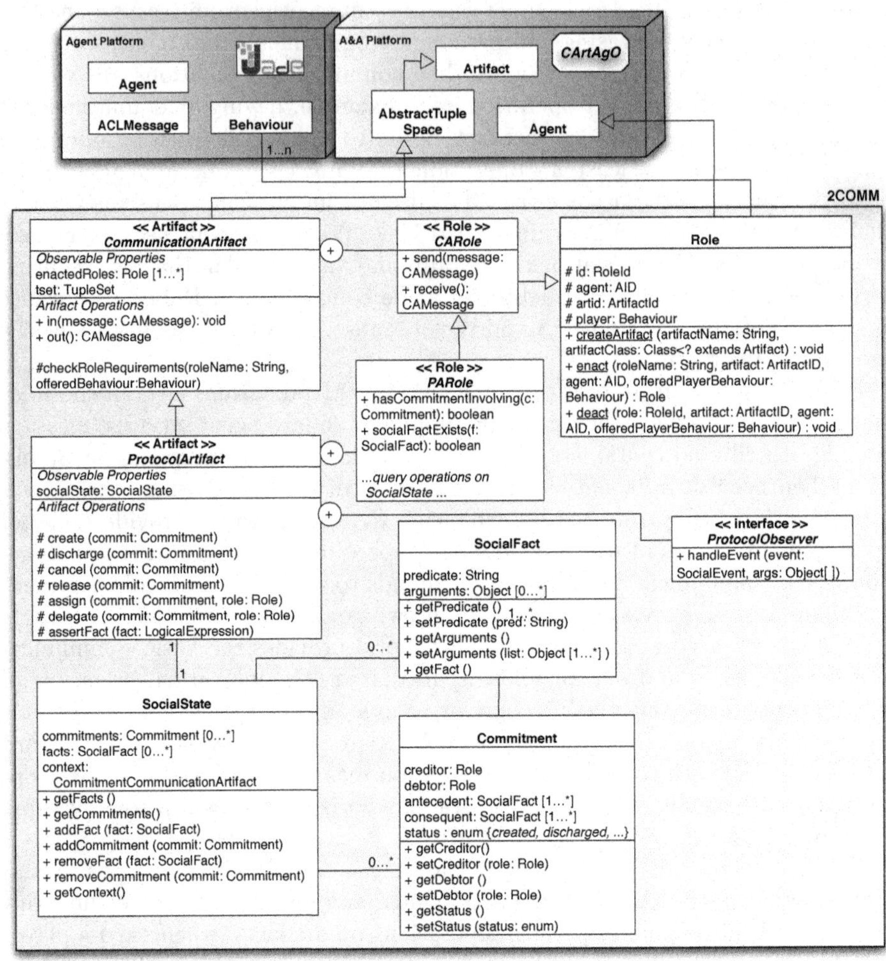

Fig. 1. UML Architecture of 2COMM

extension of CA, PA maintains two levels of interaction: the social one (based on commitments), and the communication one (based on message exchange). The class *PARole* is an inner class of PA and extends the CARole class. It provides the primitives for *querying the social state*, e.g. for asking the commitments in which a certain agent is involved, and the primitives that allow an agent to become, through its role, an *observer of the events* occurring in the social state. For example, an agent can query the social state to verify if it contains a commitment with a specific condition as consequent, via the method `existsCommitmentWithConsequent(InteractionStateElement el)`. Alternatively, an agent can be notified about the occurrence of a social event, provided that it implements the inner interface *ProtocolObserver*. Afterwards, it can start observing the social state. PARole also inherits the communication primitives defined in CARole.

In order to specify a *commitment-based interaction protocol*, it is necessary to extend PA by defining the proper social and communicative actions as operations on the artifact itself. Actions can have guards that correspond to *context preconditions*: each such condition specifies the context in which the respective action produces the described social effect. Since we want agents to act on artifacts only through their respective roles, when defining a protocol it is also necessary to create the roles. We do so by creating as many extensions of PARole as protocol roles. These extensions are realized as inner classes of the protocol: each such class will specify, as methods, the powers of a role. Powers allow agents who play roles to actually execute artifact operations. The reification of commitment protocols by way of artifacts has many advantages: by exploiting the distributed nature of artifacts it is possible to naturally rely on a modularization that helps the re-use of software, it is possible to implement run-time monitoring functionalities, and it is possible to provide a normative characterization of interaction thanks to commitments.

4 Typing MAS

To the aim of defining an agent typing system, we assume each agent a to be characterized by a set of behaviors $\{b_1, \ldots, b_m\}$, enabling a to perform various activities. Along the lines of [22], we view types as partial specifications of behavior, which support in using agents to play protocol roles safely. A type τ is a set of commitments $\{c_1, c_2, \ldots, c_n\}$, defined inside a collection of definitions of artifacts, that represents the environmental setting. The debtor, creditor, conditions of each commitment are defined as roles and actions inside some artifact, i.e. artifact definitions provide name spaces. Commitments, by having a normative value, can be seen as specifications of behavior because the debtor agents are expected to behave so as to satisfy them. A behavior b has type τ, denoted as $b : \tau$, if it is capable of satisfying the commitments in the type. This means that it allows to make the consequent conditions in the commitments become true.

Definition 1 (Type). *Given an agent a, with a set of behaviors $b_1 : \tau_1$, ..., $b_m : \tau_m$, we say that a has type $\tau = \bigcup_{i=1}^{m} \tau_i$, denoted as $a : \tau$.*

Let $P = r_1 \circ \ldots \circ r_n$ be an interaction protocol, where r_i are all the protocol roles. Let p be a protocol action, whose execution creates the commitments c_1, ..., c_n, (conditionally) binding the executor to achieve some conditions. This represents the fact that p *requires* the executor can satisfy (directly or indirectly – i.e. by way of other agents) c_1, ..., c_n. So, we say that p has type $\tau = \{c_1, \ldots, c_n\}$, denoted as $p : \tau$.

Definition 2 (Role and Protocol Types). *Let $p_1 : \tau_1$, ..., $p_m : \tau_m$ be the actions of P that the role r_j allows to execute together with their respective types. The type of role r_j is $\tau_j = \bigcup_{i=1}^{m} \tau_i$. Finally, the type of P is $\{r_1 : \tau_1, \ldots, r_n : \tau_n\}$.*

We, now, introduce a notion of *subtype*, that is inspired to the width subtyping used for records. Given two types τ_1 and τ_2, we say that τ_1 is a *subtype* of τ_2, denoted by $\tau_1 \leq \tau_2$, when the set of commitments of τ_2 is included in the one of τ_1, i.e. $\tau_2 \subseteq \tau_1$. A subtype is a stronger specification which guarantees that the set of values satisfying it is a subset of the set of values of the supertype. What kinds of properties should types specify? According to the principle of substitutability [31] an instance of a subtype can always be used in any context in which an instance of the supertype is expected. A subtype at least guarantees the "promises" of the supertype, at least the same commitments, and possibly more, are satisfiable.

Since our subtyping relationship is defined based on subset inclusion, it is easy to see that subtyping is a *partial order*, and thus shows the properties of *reflexivity*, *antisimmetry*, and *transitivity*. More interestingly, the *subsumption* property also holds: consider an agent $a : \tau$ and suppose $\tau \leq \tau'$, then $a : \tau'$.

The rationale of the proposed subtyping relationship is that we mean to support the substitution of an actual agent and its behaviors to the specification of requirements that is given by a role: any behavior which is capable of achieving a superset of the required commitments will fit our case. Any operation feasible on the supertype will be supported by the subtype. This definition makes it possible to introduce a notion of *compatibility* of agents with roles.

Definition 3 (Compatibility). *An agent $a : \tau$ is* compatible with *a protocol role $r : \tau'$ if $\tau \leq \tau'$.*

In fact, since $a : \tau$ and $\tau \leq \tau'$, by subsumption $a : \tau'$. So, we are guaranteed that a can achieve the commitments it could get engaged into, when playing r, directly or by relying on other agents. Generally, a will have a more specialized behavior w.r.t. what the role demands.

We, now, show that subtyping guarantees substitutability: namely, that substituting a role by an agent that is compatible with it preserves the type of the protocol. Such a verification should be performed dynamically during the enactment of the protocol role.

Property 1 (Substitutability). Let $P = r_1 \circ \ldots \circ r_n$ be an interaction protocol of type τ. The system obtained by the enactment of the protocol, performed by the set of agents $a_1, \ldots, a_n$, each compatible with its respective P role, preserves the type τ.

The proof is trivially obtained by considering the above definitions.

Besides the behavioural-oriented notion of typing described above, we rely on Java to perform event (action) type checking. In fact, since they are implemented as artifact operations, when an agent uses an operation, through a role, the Java compiler checks the correctness of the parameters.

By adopting classical depth and width subtyping rules for records, i.e. $\{r_1 : \tau_1, \ldots, r_n : \tau_n\} \leq \{r_1 : \tau'_1, \ldots, r_m : \tau'_m\}$ if $m \leq n$ and $\tau_i \leq \tau'_i$, for all i from 1 to m, it is possible to introduce also a notion of protocol specialization.

Definition 4 (Specialization). *Let $P : \tau$ and $P' : \tau'$ be two interaction protocols with their respective types. We say that P' is a specialization of P if $\tau' \leq \tau$.*

5 Implementing the typing in 2COMM

Let us, now, introduce the way in which we implemented the proposed typing system in 2COMM. The implementation relies on *Java annotations*[2]. These are commonly used to provide meta-data about a program which can be used by the compiler, or be used at deploy time or, as in our case, at run-time.

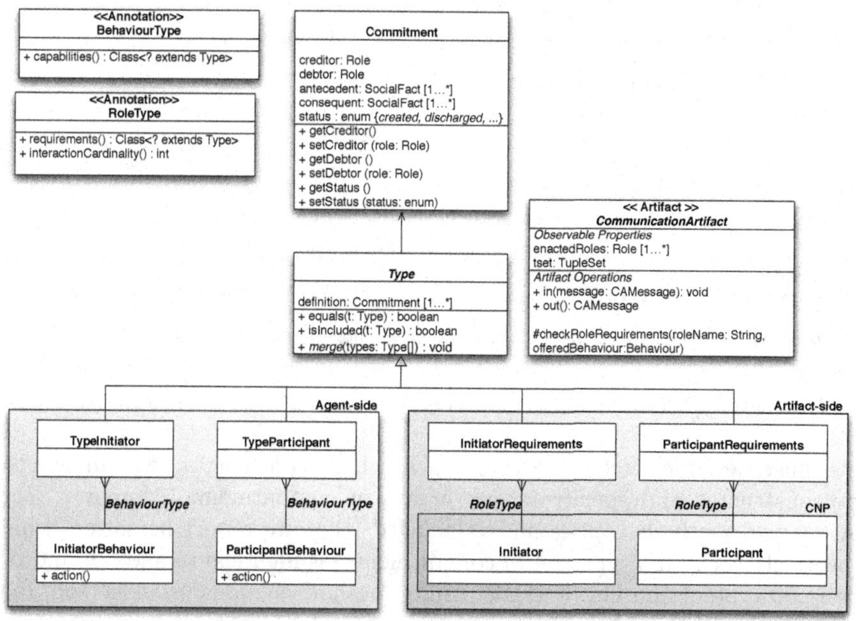

Fig. 2. UML Architecture of the typing system

With reference to Figure 2, we introduced two annotations, one for interaction protocol roles, the other for agent behaviors. They are respectively *@RoleType* and *@BehaviourType*. They both represent commitment sets. The former via the annotation property *requirements*, the latter via the annotation property *capabilities*. *@RoleType* also contains a property *interactionCardinality*, specifying whether a role can be concurrently played by many agents – as it is, for instance, the case of the Contract Net Protocol role Participant.

In our implementation, a type (Definition 1) is specified as an object of sort *Type*, which is an abstract class which contains the field *definition* (an array of commitments).

[2] More information about Java annotations can be retrieved at `http://docs.oracle.com/javase/tutorial/java/annotations/`

```
public abstract class Type {
  final private ArrayList<Commitment> definition;
  protected Type(Commitment[] commitsDefinition) {
    definition = new ArrayList<Commitment>();
    for (Commitment c : commitsDefinition) {
      definition.add(c);
    }
  }
  public boolean isIncluded(Type includerType) {
    boolean included = true;
    for (Commitment c : this.definition) {
      if (included) {
        included = false;
        for (Commitment d : includerType.definition) {
          if (c.equals(d)) {
            included = true;
            break;
          }
        }
      }
      else break;
    }
    return included;
  }
  public boolean equals(Type t) {
    return this.isIncluded(t) && t.isIncluded(this);
  }
  public static Type merge(ArrayList<Type> typesToMerge) {
  ...
  }
  ...
}
```

Type must be subclassed by actual types, whose constructors will invoke the superconstructor and specify proper arrays of commitments. Moreover, *Type* specifies two methods, *equals* and *isIncluded* (that we report hereafter) which respectively verify if a type (set of commitments) is identical to another and if a type is subtype of another. A static, utility method *merge* is provided too, that creates a new Type object from the union of commitments of types passed as parameters.

The *equals* method considers two commitments equal if all their components are respectively equal.

```
public boolean equals(SocialStateElement el) {
  if (el.getElType() != SocialStateElementType.COMMITMENT)
    return false;
  Commitment c = (Commitment)el;
  return (this.getCreditor().equals(c.getCreditor()) &&
    this.getDebtor().equals(c.getDebtor()) &&
    this.getAntecedent().equals(c.getAntecedent()) &&
    this.getConsequent().equals(c.getConsequent())
  );
}
```

Antecedent and consequent formulas have to match exactly, while the identities of creditors and debtors are checked as follows:

```
public boolean equals(RoleId otherRoleId) {
  if (this.type == otherRoleId.type && this.type == PARTICULAR_ROLE)
    return this.id == otherRoleId.id;
  else
    return this.getRoleName().equals(otherRoleId.getRoleName());
}
```

The implementation can compare commitments that are instantiated and involve specific agents or that are "generic", in that they involve protocol roles. To separate the two cases, in the former the debtor and creditor of a commitment are associated to the case *PARTICULAR_ROLE* while in the latter they are associated to the case *GENERIC_ROLE*. This information is used by the method *equals*: A debtor/creditor identity is considered equal to that of another in two cases: (1) when the two refer to the very same enactment of a certain role (i.e. they refer to the same agent); (2) when one or both identities refer to a role type (e.g. the initiator) and the respective role names are equal.

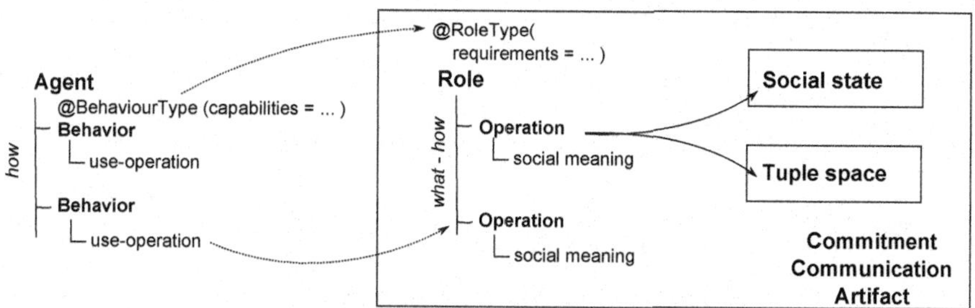

Fig. 3. Agent typing and roles definition

With reference to Figure 3, type checking amounts to verifying if the commitments specified in the *capabilities* property of annotation @BehaviourType include the commitments specified in the *requirements* of the annotation @RoleType. The check is performed by the method *checkRoleRequirements* which is included in the class *CommunicationArtifact*. This method, which is executed in the context of *enactRole*, uses the set of behaviors of an agent and the role this means to play, and computes an answer by extracting at run-time the information contained in the involved annotations. An agent can successfully enact a role only if it is compatible with it (Definition 3), i.e. only if its type is a subtype of that of the role. For the property of substitutability, the enactment preserves the type of the protocol, thereby assuring safety.

```
public abstract class CommunicationArtifact extends AbstractTupleSpace {
  ...
  protected boolean checkRoleRequirements(String roleName,
      Behaviour[] offeredPlayerBehaviours) {
  // check the requested Role Name
  if (!enabledRoles.containsKey(roleName)) {
    logger.debug("Role "+roleName+" not found among enabled roles.");
    return false;
  }
  // control is excluded for role "CA_Role"
  if (roleName.equals(CA_ROLE))
    return true;
  Class<? extends Behaviour> behClass;
  ArrayList<Annotation> behaviourTypeAnnotations
              = new ArrayList<Annotation>();
  Annotation behaviourSatisfyAnnotation;
  for (Behaviour beh : offeredPlayerBehaviours) {
    behClass = beh.getClass();
    behaviourTypeAnnotation
```

```
                = behClass.getAnnotation(BehaviourType.class);
            if (behaviourTypeAnnotation == null)
              // if null, correct annotation is missing
              return false;
          Class<?> roleClass;
          try {
            String roleClassName = (this.getClass().getName())
                + "$" + roleName;
            roleClass = Class.forName(roleClassName);
          } catch (ClassNotFoundException e) {
            return false;
          }
          Annotation roleAnnotation =
              roleClass.getAnnotation(RoleType.class);
          if (roleAnnotation == null) {
            return false;
          }
          // Both annotations retrieved
          // Getting instances for retrieved types
          ArrayList<Type> typesToMerge = new ArrayList<Type>();
          Type behaviourType;
          Type roleType;
          Type mergedType;
          for (Annotation ann : behaviourTypeAnnotations) {
            behaviourType = ((BehaviourType)ann).capabilities()
                        .getDeclaredConstructor().newInstance();
            typesToMerge.add(behaviourType);
          }
          roleType = ((RoleType)roleAnnotation).requirements()
                        .getDeclaredConstructor().newInstance();
          mergedType = Type.merge(typesToMerge);

          return roleType.isIncluded(mergedType);
          }
}
```

When an agent tries to enact a role, the artifact, whose role is being enacted, is in charge for checking the compliance between the agent's behaviour and the role requirements. The method *checkRoleRequirements* of the class *CommitmentArtifact* performs these controls. This implementation realizes the principle of *compatibility*: an agent can enact a role provided it has a (set of) behaviour(s) that are compatible with the type of the role.

The *Type* abstract class, together with the *@RoleAnnotation* and *@BehaviourType* annotation classes, allows constructing types as Java structures, an approach similar to the one proposed in [34], where each agent carries an object representing its type.

Let us, now, show an example of annotation added on top of an implementation of the Contract Net Protocol presented in [3]. We will focus on the role Initiator and on an agent willing to play that role.

```
public class CNPArtifact extends ProtocolArtifact {
...
  @RoleType(requirements = InitiatorRequirements.class)
  public class Initiator extends PARole {
    public Initiator(Behaviour player, AID agent) {
      super(INITIATOR_ROLE, player, agent);
    }
    ...
  }
}
```

The role Initiator is tagged by the *@RoleType* annotation, whose value for the property *requirements* is set to *InitiatorRequirements.class*, a class that builds the set of commitments that defines the type of the role. *InitiatorRequirements* is specified in this way:

```
public class InitiatorRequirements extends Type {
   public InitiatorRequirements() throws MissingOperandException,
                                          WrongOperandsNumberException {
      super(new Commitment[]{
         new Commitment(CNPArtifact.INITIATOR_ROLE,
            CNPArtifact.PARTICIPANT_ROLE, "propose",
            new CompositeExpression(LogicalOperatorType.OR,
            new Fact("accept"), new Fact("reject")))
      });
   }
   ...
}
```

Specifically, this class contains the commitment $C(CNPArtifact.INITIATOR\_ROLE,\ CNPArtifact.PARTICIPANT\_ROLE,\ propose,\ accept \vee reject)$, where $CNPArtifact$ is the CommitmentArtifact which realizes the Contract Net Protocol.

On the agent's side, an agent willing to play the role *Initiator* must offer a set of behaviors that are typed accordingly. In our case, we suppose that the agent offers the following behavior:

```
@BehaviourType(capabilities = TypeInitiator.class)
public class InitiatorBehaviour extends OneShotBehaviour implements
         CNPInitiatorObserver {
      ....
}
```

where the class *TypeInitiator* specifies the *capabilities* shown by the agent through the behavior. Once again, this is a set of commitments the behavior can satisfy. *TypeInitiator* is a subclass the *Type*:

```
   public TypeInitiator() throws MissingOperandException,
            WrongOperandsNumberException {
      super(new Commitment[]{
         new Commitment(CNPArtifact.INITIATOR_ROLE,
               CNPArtifact.PARTICIPANT_ROLE, "propose",
               new CompositeExpression(LogicalOperatorType.OR,
               new Fact("accept"), new Fact("reject"))),
         new Commitment(TradeArtifact.BUYER_ROLE,
               TradeArtifact.SELLER_ROLE, "pay", "deliver"
               )
      });
   }
   ...
}
```

It is easy to see that the commitment perfectly matches the requirements, and so the enactment will succeed. Notice that the presented implementation is slightly different w.r.t. the definition of *compatibility* with a role (Definition 3): it uses a collection of behaviours instead of an agent because in JADE there is no reference to the agents that we could exploit. The result is a more restrictive test, which does not necessarily account for the whole agent but considers only the set of behaviors the agent displays.

6 Discussion and Future Work

This paper presented a typing system for MAS. The key characteristic of the proposal is that the typing system is defined based on notions that are typical of agents rather than on a functional approach. Specifically, it relies on the "social capabilities" of the agents. As such, the proposal represents a novelty w.r.t. previous work on agent typing, which applies the functional type theory [18,19,26]. The functional approach benefits of the results of a vast literature, but types should be aimed at providing abstraction/modeling features that help the programmer. Functional typing systems discard the typicalities of agents and, thus, in our view, they do not accomplish their aim.

Besides providing the basic notions of type, subtype, compatibility and substitutability, we implemented the proposal in the context of the 2COMM framework [2]. 2COMM allows programming social relationships by exploiting a declarative, interaction-centric approach, and was developed by relying on existing technologies as far as possible. In particular, the social relationships that arise along the interaction among agents are captured as social commitments – realized as first-class objects –, while interaction is mediated by protocol artifacts.

The choice of relying on commitments is motivated by the desire of typing agents and roles in a way that results minimally prescriptive, so to preserve the autonomy of the agents as far as possible. Indeed, we agree with [22,34] that the typing system should include a representation of the behavior but, differently than in those works – which deal with objects, we are also convinced of the need of a representation which does not hinder the agents' autonomy. For this reason, a prescriptive representation, based on finite state automata – as the one introduced in those works, would not be adequate. Commitments allow specifying the expected behavior of agents without imposing unnecessary restrictions. In case a more expressive language for specifying constraints is needed, it is possible to rely either on proposals like [21], where conditions inside commitments can express temporal regulations, or on proposals like 2CL [6], where commitment protocols are enriched with explicit temporal constraints on the evolution of the social state. This kind of extension is one of our next goals.

Clearly, a type system allows only a light check of the behavior of the involved agents, being more concerned with a safe usage rather than a full behavioral compatibility. It does not imply that an agent which has the same type of another agent will display the same behavior. This does not exclude the possibility to integrate deeper checks, for instance based on model checking such as [10].

The described agent typing system will help realizing both static, compile-time coding support and dynamic, run-time type checking. Inspired by [27], the former can be realized by developing a plugin for an IDE that provides coding support, like smart code completion or type warning or error. The latter, instead, amounts to the development of tools for verifying, at run-time, the compliance between the agent's logics and the role requirements, signalling the occurrence of wrong enactments when needed. Altogether similar tools based on the substitutability property, which guarantees the safe replacement of agents to roles, when they have the same type or the agent has a subtype of the role. In the current proposal such a verification is performed as a syntactic inclusion of commitment sets. This is limitating because it does not consider logical expressions inside commitment antecedent and consequent conditions. To solve the problem we mean to study the applicability of complex typing systems, relying on union and intersection types [16].

Type checking as a light verification adopts notions, e.g. substitutability, that are used also for facing the issues of interoperability and conformance discussed in [7,5]. The conformance verification aims at guaranteeing that when an agent plays a role, or substitutes another agent in an on-going interaction, the interoperability of the system is preserved – in the present paper, when an agent plays a role, the protocol type is preserved. In [7,5], protocols are represented by way of a sort of finite state automata. Thus, the approach suffers from the drawbacks due to a prescriptive description, that, as we explained (Section 2, see the comments to the approach in [1]), does not suit well the autonomy of the agents. Another direction of research that we mean to pursue is to explore how commitment-based types can be adapted to solve the issue of conformance in MAS.

Finally, in [4], we presented an extension of JaCaMo [11] that, analogously to 2COMM, allows reasoning about social relationships in Jason agents. We aim to introduce the use of the proposed typing system also in that setting. This would allow an even deeper comparison to SimpAL, which is built on top of the same platform.

Acknowledgements. We thank the anonymous reviewers for their helpful comments, which gave us important suggestions for future developments.

References

1. Ancona, D., Drossopoulou, S., Mascardi, V.: Automatic generation of self-monitoring mass from multiparty global session types in jason. In: Baldoni, M., Dennis, L., Mascardi, V., Vasconcelos, W. (eds.) DALT 2012. LNCS (LNAI), vol. 7784, pp. 76–95. Springer, Heidelberg (2013)
2. Baldoni, M., Baroglio, C., Capuzzimati, F.: 2COMM: A commitment-based MAS architecture. In: Cossentino, M., El Fallah Seghrouchni, A., Winikoff, M. (eds.) EMAS 2013. LNCS (LNAI), vol. 8245, pp. 38–57. Springer, Heidelberg (2013)
3. Baldoni, M., Baroglio, C., Capuzzimati, F.: A Commitment-based Infrastructure for Programming Socio-Technical Systems. ACM Transactions on Internet Technology, Special Issue on Foundations of Social Computing (to appear, 2014)
4. Baldoni, M., Baroglio, C., Capuzzimati, F.: Reasoning about Social Relationships with Jason. In: Chopra, A., Verhagen, H. (eds.) Proc. of the 1st International Workshop on Multiagent Foundations of Social Computing, SC-AAMAS 2014, Held in Conjuction with AAMAS 2014, Paris, France (May 2014)
5. Baldoni, M., Baroglio, C., Chopra, A.K., Desai, N., Patti, V., Singh, M.P.: Choice, Interoperability, and Conformance in Interaction Protocols and Service Choreographies. In: Proceedings of the 8th International Conference on Autonomous Agents and Multiagent Systems, AAMAS 2009, pp. 843–850. IFAAMAS (2009)

6. Baldoni, M., Baroglio, C., Marengo, E., Patti, V.: Constitutive and Regulative Specifications of Commitment Protocols: A Decoupled Approach. ACM Transactions on Intelligent Systems and Technology, Special Issue on Agent Communication 4(2), 22:1–22:25 (2013)
7. Baldoni, M., Baroglio, C., Martelli, A., Patti, V.: A priori conformance verification for guaranteeing interoperability in open environments. In: Dan, A., Lamersdorf, W. (eds.) ICSOC 2006. LNCS, vol. 4294, pp. 339–351. Springer, Heidelberg (2006)
8. Baldoni, M., Boella, G., van der Torre, L.: Interaction between Objects in `powerjava`. Journal of Object Technology, Special Issue OOPS Track at SAC 2006 6(2) (2007)
9. Bellifemine, F., Bergenti, F., Caire, G., Poggi, A.: JADE - A Java Agent Development Framework. In: Bordini, R.H., Dastani, M., JDix, J., El Fallah-Seghrouchni, A. (eds.) Multi-Agent Programming: Languages, Platforms and Applications. Multiagent Systems, Artificial Societies, and Simulated Organizations, vol. 15, pp. 125–147. Springer (2005)
10. Bentahar, J., Meyer, J.-J.C., Wan, W.: Model Checking Communicative Agent-based Systems. Knowledge-Based Systems 22(3), 142–159 (2009)
11. Boissier, O., Bordini, R.H., Hübner, J.F., Ricci, A., Santi, A.: Multi-agent oriented programming with JaCaMo. Science of Computer Programming 78(6), 747–761 (2013)
12. Bordini, R.H., Hübner, J.F.: BDI agent programming in agentspeak using *Jason*. In: Toni, F., Torroni, P. (eds.) CLIMA 2005. LNCS (LNAI), vol. 3900, pp. 143–164. Springer, Heidelberg (2006)
13. Castelfranchi, C.: Principles of Individual Social Action. In: Holmstrom-Hintikka, G., Tuomela, R. (eds.) Contemporary Action Theory: Social Action. 2, pp. 163–192. Kluwer, Dordrecht (1997)
14. Chopra, A.K., Singh, M.P.: Elements of a business-level architecture for multiagent systems. In: Braubach, L., Briot, J.-P., Thangarajah, J. (eds.) ProMAS 2009. LNCS, vol. 5919, pp. 15–30. Springer, Heidelberg (2010)
15. Conte, R., Castelfranchi, C., Dignum, F.: Autonomous norm acceptance. In: Müller, J.P., Rao, A.S., Singh, M.P. (eds.) ATAL 1998. LNCS (LNAI), vol. 1555, pp. 99–112. Springer, Heidelberg (1999)
16. Coppo, M., Dezani-Ciancaglini, M., Margaria, I., Zacchi, M.: Toward isomorphism of intersection and union types. In: Graham-Lengrand, S., Paolini, L. (eds.) ITRS. EPTCS, vol. 121, pp. 58–80 (2013)
17. Dastani, M., Grossi, D., Meyer, J.-J.C., Tinnemeier, N.: Normative Multi-agent Programs and Their Logics. In: Meyer, J.-J.C., Broersen, J. (eds.) KRAMAS 2008. LNCS (LNAI), vol. 5605, pp. 16–31. Springer, Heidelberg (2009)
18. Grigore, C., Collier, R.: Supporting agent systems in the programming language. In: Hübner, J.F., Petit, J.-M., Suzuki, E. (eds.) Web Intelligence/IAT Workshops, pp. 9–12. IEEE Computer Society (2011)
19. Grigore, C., Collier, R.W.: Af-raf: An agent-oriented programming language with algebraic data types. In: Lopes, C.V. (ed.) SPLASH Workshops, pp. 195–200. ACM (2011)
20. Howden, N., Rönnquist, R., Hodgson, A., Lucas, A.: Intelligent agents - summary of an agent infrastructure. In: Proc. of the 5th International Conference on Autonomous Agents (2001)
21. Marengo, E., Baldoni, M., Baroglio, C., Chopra, A.K., Patti, V., Singh, M.P.: Commitments with Regulations: Reasoning about Safety and Control in REGULA. In: Tumer, K., Yolum, P., Sonenberg, L., Stone, P. (eds.) Proceedings of the 10th International Conference on Autonomous Agents and Multiagent Systems, AAMAS 2011, vol. 2, pp. 467–474. IFAAMAS, Taipei (2011)

22. Nierstrasz, O., Tsichritzis, D. (eds.): Object-Oriented Software Composition, vol. 6, pp. 99–121. Prentice-Hall (1995)
23. Omicini, A., Ricci, A., Viroli, M.: Artifacts in the a&a meta-model for multi-agent systems. Autonomous Agents and Multi-Agent Systems 17(3), 432–456 (2008)
24. Ricci, A., Piunti, M., Viroli, M.: Environment programming in multi-agent systems: An artifact-based perspective. Autonomous Agents and Multi-Agent Systems 23(2), 158–192 (2011)
25. Ricci, A., Santi, A.: From actors to agent-oriented programming abstractions in simpal. In: Leavens, G.T. (ed.) SPLASH, pp. 73–74. ACM (2012)
26. Ricci, A., Santi, A.: Typing Multi-agent Programs in simpAL. In: Dastani, M., Hübner, J.F., Logan, B. (eds.) ProMAS 2012. LNCS (LNAI), vol. 7837, pp. 138–157. Springer, Heidelberg (2013)
27. Santi, A., Ricci, A.: An eclipse-based ide for agent-oriented programming in simpal. In: Proc. of The Seventh Workshop of the Italian Eclipse Community (2012)
28. Singh, M.P.: An ontology for commitments in multiagent systems. Artif. Intell. Law 7(1), 97–113 (1999)
29. Šišlák, D., Rehák, M., Pěchouček, M., Rollo, M., Pavlíček, D.: A-globe: Agent development platform with inaccessibility and mobility support. In: Software Agent-Based Applications, Platforms and Development Kits, pp. 21–46. Birkhäuser Basel (2005)
30. Telang, P.R., Singh, M.P.: Specifying and Verifying Cross-Organizational Business Models: An Agent-Oriented Approach. In: IEEE Transactions on Services Computing, pp. 1–14 (2011)
31. Wegner, P., Zdonik, S.B.: Inheritance as an Incremental Modification Mechanism or What Like Is and Isnt Like. In: Gjessing, S., Nygaard, K. (eds.) ECOOP 1988. LNCS, vol. 322, pp. 55–77. Springer, Heidelberg (1988)
32. Weyns, D., Omicini, A., Odell, J.: Environment as a first class abstraction in multiagent systems. Autonomous Agents and Multi-Agent Systems 14(1), 5–30 (2007)
33. Yolum, p., Singh, M.P.: Commitment machines. In: Meyer, J.-J.C., Tambe, M. (eds.) Intelligent Agents VIII. LNCS (LNAI), vol. 2333, pp. 235–247. Springer, Heidelberg (2002)
34. Zapf, M., Geihs, K.: What type is it? a type system for mobile agents. In: 15th European Meeting on Cybernetics and Systems Research (EMCSR) (2000)

Robust Collaboration: Enriching Decisions with Abstract Preferences

Loïs Vanhée[1,2], Frank Dignum[1], and Jacques Ferber[2]

[1] Utrecht Universiteit, The Netherlands
[2] LIRMM, University of Montpellier II, France

Abstract. Aspects of human societies provide a rich source of inspiration for influencing individual and social behaviors in order to achieve collaboration in a MAS. This article particularly investigates how human cultures and particularly human values can be used as an inspiration for achieving collaboration. Indeed, human values abstractly set what individuals consider as important, driving them towards similar individual and social outcomes, helping them to work together. We want to reproduce the same type of behaviors in MASs, even if we do not aim at faithfully reproducing human behavior.

Preferences are used for modeling values. But, specifically for values, preference functions order abstract yet driving criteria (e.g. "security vs. freedom" instead of "blue vs. red"). Values support abstract decisions, which drive agents to make local decisions that support some coherence at the collective level.

We show that integrating values as a design constraint have many benefits for designing collaborative MAS. In particular, they offer greater flexibility and robustness to the system. Furthermore, values provide a top-down perspective for designing MASs which can be combined with traditional methods (e.g. norms, organizations) for lowering overall design complexity.

Keywords: Agent Oriented Software Engineering, Methodology, Collaboration, Values, Preferences.

1 Introduction

"The firefighter agent is about to enter in the burning house in order to extinguish the fire and rescue victims. Should it immediately enter the house or spend precious seconds in order to first double check that tasks of other colleagues that support the agent's entrance have been completed?"

Current methods for supporting collaboration have troubles for solving such a dilemma, particularly in complex environments (e.g. quick evolution, adversarial agents, numerous interactions between environmental variables, partly visible dynamics, many possible contexts). Current methods for supporting collaboration specify decisions to be taken for concrete and expected choices. But by definition of complex environments, these choices are numerous and there is rarely a single simple rule which determines the best answer for any situation.

F. Dalpiaz et al. (Eds.): EMAS 2014, LNAI 8758, pp. 406–430, 2014.

How many norms have to be created in order to cope with those dilemmas? How large should a protocol be? With cooperation, how many details have to be considered before performing any action? Without mentioning the difficulty, as a system designer, to predict all those possible dilemmas which may lead to collaboration failures.

Looking at humans, they generally manage to cope quite well with such a dilemma. Maybe we can get some inspiration from their reasonings. Our goal consists in building models inspired by the way human solve some problems with the aim of transposing this solution to their artificial counterparts. Plenty of former methods use similar inspirations for designing agents and improving collaboration (e.g. BDI, norms, organizations, protocols). In human societies, norms and protocols[1], despite being particularly extensive in the domain of fire fighting, do not specify how to resolve the dilemma presented in introduction. Norms and protocols are used in human societies for coping with limited and well-expected technical issues (e.g. sensing pain in the hand while watering means electrical hazard. Change watering to "spread" mode in order to limit conductivity; techniques for manipulating the water hose). But, the relative success of human societies given this lack of formal control suggests that humans have other mechanisms for both to making decisions and creating expectations about others. But which ones?

As a possible answer, we propose to investigate at cultures. Cultures can be seen as a set of shared mental attitudes which exist within a society or a group. These mental attitudes have many influences: they can range from *values* which are big abstract principles about how to behave in life (e.g. timeliness, relationship with authority) to *practices* which are more local and concrete (e.g. greeting protocols). Those influences tend to support each other (e.g. if timeliness is important, concrete rules tend to support timeliness). As a rule of thumb, humans tend to use the most concrete rule available when making decisions and rely on values when no rule is available, for more exceptional decisions.

Back to our dilemma from that human perspective, consider that our team of firefighters has a culture which favors a value of timeliness. Assume also that for that specific dilemma, no practice or rule explicitly states how individuals should behave. In such a situation, individuals investigate their values and know that "timeliness" is an important value for the group. In other words, individuals are culturally willing to sacrifice local utility for being in time, considering for instance that group success is more important than individual success. In that case, any agent supporting the firefighter would do his or her best in order to be on time, possibly sacrificing some local utility (e.g. preferring to delay rescuing a victim for making sure that the water hose is operational on time). Thus, culture *influences decisions* of individuals. In addition, cultures also influence *expectations* that individuals can create about others. For instance, the firefighter agent which is about to enter the burning house, knows that timeliness is important. Thus, if he or she do the best to be on time and assumes that the work of

[1] See some documentations for training firefighters at `http://www.udsp34.org/index.php?p=pres&Ctt_Doc_Categorie=4`

others is done. So the firefighter can accurately decide to enter without having to double-check.

Back to the MAS-design perspective, we propose to inspire from cultures in order to solve MAS problems[2]. Practices are already well-handled by existing literature for promoting collaboration (e.g. norms, protocols). To that extent, practices are not further investigated in this article, even if they can be related with techniques for achieving collaboration which are further investigated in this article. Contrarily, values, which importance for driving collaboration has just been illustrated, are relatively new to the design of methods for supporting collaboration. Values are abstract but broadly influential. They offer principled and justifiable answers to dilemmas that agents can encounter. Values drive individuals and societies towards environmental or social outcomes which are culturally preferable without strongly constraining decisions. Values provide offer another possibility for system designers to drive agents, since system designers determine what agents culturally prefer.

Values are complementary with existing solutions for achieving collaboration. Indeed, values support abstract complex decisions that agents have to make (e.g. buying a house). Nevertheless, they are inappropriate for driving simple and more standardized decisions that agents have to make (e.g. moving to the house). Such decisions are more appropriately handled by practices. Thus, values are not an alternative but an additional method for achieving collaboration. Values cope with some problems which are hard to handle with more concrete approaches, while these latter approaches cope with problems hard to handle with values.

From a modeling perspective, we propose to model value systems in using preferences. Indeed, the core property of a value system drive what consider as important by determining the relative importance of their values. Nevertheless, human values are not any preference (e.g. preferring red over blue). Human values encompass abstract aspects which can be related to many decisions (e.g. timeliness, respect of authority). This article provides some principles for determining what values are to be integrated within a value systems and their possible influence of agents.

More technically, value systems are abstract preferences, which raise some technical challenges for designing agents. Indeed, they are inadequate for managing concrete agents decision, because values are abstract (e.g. no need to reason about one's values to determine which foot to start walking with). For those particular decisions, more appropriate tools should be used, such as BDI agents or protocols. Nevertheless, in order to avoid conflicting specifications, these concrete behaviors should support and thus be related with the value system of an agent. This article proposes solutions for bridging the gap in terms of abstraction between abstract preferences to concrete action.

---

[2] *Disclaimer*: this article aims at providing a solution for engineering MASs. Values are just inspirations, we do not aim at faithfully replicating their influence on behavior but instead at finding in which context they are useful. We prefer "incredible" working solutions than credible human-like failures.

The content of this paper is organized as follows. Section 2 describes a running example illustrating our concepts throughout the article. Section 3 describes the related work. Section 4 describes solutions for integrating preferences in agent decision processes. Section 5 describes the use of shared preferences for achieving collaboration. Section 6 describes examples of human cultures that can be used as inspiration for designing shared preference. The main contributions of this article correspond to the content of Section 4 and Section 5.

2 Running Example

A running example is used in order to better illustrate concepts and methods described throughout this article.

Consider a MAS supporting a team of fire fighters. Each fire fighter has his own agent. Each agent keeps track of the information of the fire fighter's situation and can confer with the other agents about which information or action advise to give to its fire fighter. We may also assume that agents can be involved within the system for supporting humans. In the following we identify the agents with the persons they support for ease of reference. The mission (or goal) of the agents consists in extinguishing fires and rescuing people who got injured due to the crisis. In addition to fire fighters, a special agent called the "fire commander" (represented by a_{fc}) located in the firetruck can communicate with the fire fighters using point to point communication.

In this setting, an agent (indicated by a_1) is about to make a decision. The situation of a_1 is as follows: *The fire commander planned for me. I have to be at the fire place at time T. There, I will support agent a_2 for extinguishing the fire. While moving to the fire, I spotted a person nearby.*

a_1 has to chose between three available options:

1. *Rescue*: a_1 delays its action to move towards the fire and rescues the victim instead. The time required to rescue the victim is unpredictable: if the victim is healthy, the action can be very quick (ask the victim to leave), if the victim is injured this action can take much longer (the agent has to stabilize and to carry the victim out of the danger zone). The fire fighter regulations state that a_1 is forbidden to leave a victim if a victim is injured.
2. *Report*: a_1 delays its action to move towards the fire and warns the fire commander about the presence of a person. This action takes some time but is quicker than helping.
3. *Ignore*: the agent stores the information that a person has been spotted and keeps moving towards the fire.

If a_1 has some available time before T, the situation is referred to as d_t. Otherwise (a_1 is short in time), the situation is referred to as $d_{\bar{t}}$.

A warning has to be issued before going further. In order to be easily understandable, we keep that example simple. But simple examples are easily coped by other methods (e.g. a single norm can state: "obliged to report spotted victims"). Nevertheless, we aim at considering complex and dynamic environments.

To that extent, when considering this running example, consider that the decision to be made can be done in many different contexts (e.g. in an isolated house, in a skyscraper, in a warzone). In that case, methods for designing simple constraints require much more design efforts. Indeed, these methods are more appropriate for driving behavior in well-expected scenarii but at less adequate when the context have multiple influences on many decisions (e.g. need three norms just depending on the location: rescuing victims in an isolated house; rushing to the fire in a skyscraper; determining origins of casualties in warzones). Contrarily, we aim at showing that such a complex problem is better handled by values. While this example is purposefully very simple and specific in order to be understandable, desirable solutions for this outcome are expected to be adaptable for a wide variety of contexts.

3 Previous Work

This section introduces two categories of related work. First, Section 3.1 presents existing work for achieving collaboration. This work is encompasses cultural practices that we do not further model in this article. Furthermore, presenting this previous work allows to better display how our work contributes to that field. Second, Section 3.2 presents existing frameworks for modeling preferences which are used in order to model our values.

3.1 Driving Collaboration

Former research in MAS extensively investigated the design of multi-agent solutions for reaching system goals via the collective action of individual agents [10,13,15,27]. Indeed, these methods are particularly useful for solving collective problems or for supporting interactions of self-interested agents, which are the main practical applications of MASs. Since this article aims at driving collective action, these methods require to be introduced. They are introduced from a decreasing order of the influence from system designers on collective action.

Determining which method should be selected highly depends on the problem complexity. As a general rule, the more system designers restrict behaviors of individuals, the more system designers can drive collective action, the more complex is the task of the system designer. To that extent, methods which give the most influence to system designers are also the ones which are the most limited by environmental complexity. In addition, those methods allow to reach the highest efficiency but their closeness to environmental constraints tend to limit their flexibility and robustness.

Methods. From an extreme perspective, system designers can be totalitarian by completely restricting agent behavior. The main frameworks of this perspective can be related to MDP-like approaches (DEC-MDP, DEC-POMDP, POSG [3]) for collaborative agents and Game Theory [5] for selfish agents.

Some methods give further methods by only partly constraining agent behaviors. More pragmatically, these methods aim at being just enough constraining for making sure that agents cannot go against desirable collective outcomes. Some of them are inspired by natural social systems [1], stygmergy [23] or human societies (e.g. norms, organizations, protocols). Norms [6] are rules which forbid collectively harmful behaviors. Organizations [12] allocate roles and create obligations between individuals. Protocols [14] standardize patterns of interactions.

Some other methods offer even further freedom to agents. These methods rely on abstract rules. These abstract rules do not aim at tightly enforcing concrete collective action (e.g. be at the meeting point at time T). Instead they aim at providing abstract and general rules to agent (e.g. forbidden to be late). Agents are free enough to circumvent the rules, but they are expected not to and to be intelligent enough to comply with norms. To our knowledge frameworks for modeling abstract representations are limited to rule-based methods (norms, organizations and protocols) such as OperA[2].

On another extreme, system designers completely hand off direct control on agents. In that case, agents do not have any behavioral restrictions by design. Desirable collective outcomes are expected to be reached by the action of benevolent (namely, being cooperative [9]) agents. In general, these agents are provided with important reasoning capabilities (e.g. explicit representation of the environment, capable of automatically proposing coordination solutions).

Relation with Our Work. There are two relations between these methods and ours. The first relation concerns the integration of some of these methods in our framework of cultures. Indeed, our cultures are composed of two parts: values and practices. The former is explored by this paper but the latter is encompassed by that previous work. Practices correspond to standardized restrictions on behaviors. Practices conceptually directly encompass (abstracted or not) norms and protocols. By extension, practices can contain any other approaches which aim at restraining concrete agent behaviors.

The second relation consists in integrating values within this framework of methods. Values belong to the set of abstract methods. Thus, values should be used in complex in dynamic environments. They aim at promoting flexible and robust collaboration but are not the best tool for achieving efficiency.

3.2 Preferences

Preferences [7] are used for ordering a set of objects $\boldsymbol{\Omega}$. Formally, preferences are a transitive binary relation $\succ$ over $\boldsymbol{\Omega}$. For instance, "I prefer apple over oranges" can be represented by "apple$\succ$orange". In our setting, $\boldsymbol{\Omega}$ is the set of expected outcomes that can result from a decisions made by agents.

Representing preferences can be a difficult task when $\boldsymbol{\Omega}$ is large, because many objects have to be compared with one another. In spite of the cost of time, humans have difficulties to express object-to-object comparisons and prefer instead to use more generic statements (e.g. I prefer blue over red). In order to efficiently designing preference functions in using human-like descriptions, former research [7,25] proposes some core principles and solutions.

Efficient representations generally rely on the existence of criteria[3] which evaluate objects (e.g. cost in time, money or human lives). If criteria are independ, each independent criteria can be internally ordered (e.g. saving 200€ from the flames is preferred than saving 100 € from the flames), allowing to use the *Ceteris Paribus* ordering method (e.g. any outcome which saves 200€ from the flames is better than any other outcome saving 100 € from the flames with all other criteria being equal). Furthermore, ordering outcomes can also be achieved in integrating evaluations of criteria within the order (e.g. saving lives is more important than anything else, saving one hour of activity for an agent is as important as saving the equivalent of 100€ from the fire). These methods for efficiently representing preferences are particularly interesting in our setting, since they offer a more efficient and justifiable representation of desirable outcomes.

Preferences and Self-oriented Reasoning. Preferences can drive self-oriented agents for making complex decisions. Indeed, preferences can provide principle for supporting agent decisions. These principles are particularly relevant for resolving dilemmas (e.g. I have to visit A and B. Shall I start with A or B?). In particular, using criteria for designing preferences can help justifying their decisions made using values (e.g. human victims are more likely to be found in the housing location A there than in the warehouse B which contains many precious items. Since saving human lives is preferred on saving wealth, I go first in A). [25] propose a framework for supporting decisions using user values. [17] propose a.framework for integrating preferences for making decisions in GOAL.

Preferences are inadequate for making very concrete decisions. Indeed, preferences require to *estimate the outcome* of decisions. When evaluating very concrete decisions (e.g. starting to walk using the right or left foot), preferences either have to integrate overly concrete aspects (e.g. I prefer starting walking using the right foot) or to include complex predictions about preference outcomes for these decisions (e.g. starting with the left foot is quicker in order to go to A but may induce extra costs), even if they may be adequate for punctual decisions. In the first case, the complexity of the preference function explodes with environment complexity. In the second case, this is the complexity of the estimation function which explodes.

Instead, preferences are appropriate for making more abstract decisions. These decisions which tend to be less frequent, lowering the number of outcomes to be estimated and the number of preferences this function should encompass. In addition, abstract decisions can be more easily connected with abstract preferences, which allow to keep the preference function simple.

Preferences are to be distinguished with goals. Goals correspond to concrete situations which can be achieved. They are either achieved, failed or ongoing. Preferences, instead, correspond to preferable situations. Preference cannot be "achieved" or "satisfied" but they permanently pursued and optimized against (unlike maintenance goals which are either maintained or failed). The same applies with norms which are either violated or not.

[3] Also known as perspectives.

Making preferences public help agents to create expectations about each other and to use preferences of other agents for adequately interacting with them. As an illustration of the difficulties triggered by hiding preferences, [4] propose a negotiation framework for agreeing on individually preferred outcomes without revealing private preferences. The effort which is deployed in this article in order to efficiently reach an agreement in spite of benevolent agents show the inherent difficulties for working together with private preferences. This inherent difficulty incited us to assume that in our framework preferences are visible by other agents.

Preferences and Collective Reasoning Preferences can be used for making decisions which takes into consideration preferences of other agents. This topic is particularly investigated by Game Theory [5]. Game Theoretical representations model for each agent in a group the desirability of collective outcomes for each possible collective actions of that group. These outcomes are ordered in terms of preferences for each agent. In this setting, agents are assumed to be rational, i.e. they should select an action which allow them to get the best outcome assuming that other agents are also rational. To that extent, Game Theoretical frameworks allow to make decisions while taking other agents into consideration. Nevertheless, Game Theory suffer multiple restrictions in terms of modeling: outcomes, other agents and their preferences should be known. In addition, predicting possible outcomes is intractable in presence of many agents with multiple choices.

Preferences can be used for directly driving collective action. This framework corresponds to mechanism design or implementation theory [19]. These frameworks extensively rely on Game Theory frameworks and thus suffer similar limitations caused by complexity.

Relation with Our Work Our work is tightly connected to these former works in several points. Indeed, our model of values relies on those models of preferences. Furthermore, we also want to use values for driving decisions of individuals but also to create expectations about behaviors of others.

We also aim at contributing to that domain. We propose a method for achieving collaboration in complex environments. We somehow expanding the challenges tackled by mechanism design but for complex problems.

4 Integrating Values in Decisions

This section presents how to integrate values within agent decisions. As a first step, we present as an inspiration how values influence humans decisions. Then, we use this inspiration for proposing a model and a possible implementation of the integration of values within agent decision processes. Next, present some advantages sharing values when designing agents: creating expectations about other agents and better interacting with humans. Finally, we conclude this section by relating the decision process with our running example.

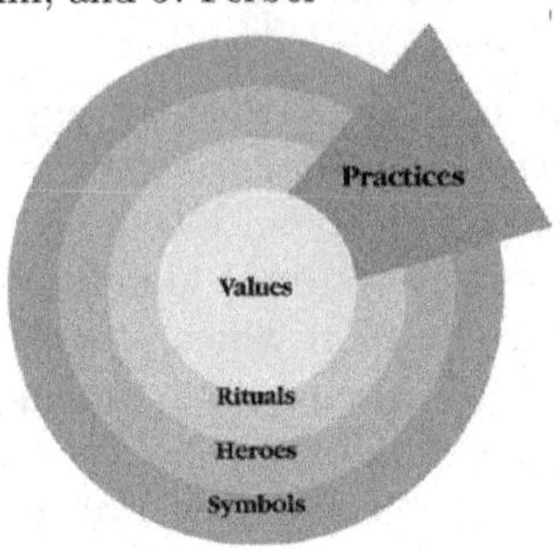

Fig. 1. Onion diagram, abstractly modeling the contents of cultures, from [18]

4.1 Inspiration

Before going into details of modeling values, let us first investigate more in details what human values are about. Values belong to cultures. Cultures are broadly investigated in social sciences [16,18]. These studies acknowledge that cultures are particularly fuzzy and difficult to grasp (unlike emotions which are relatively easier to pinpoint for instance). Nevertheless, these studies propose some simplified models in order to see the main influences of cultures which can be easily used as an inspiration for designing MAS.

These studies model cultures as collectively shared values (representing what individuals consider important, such as being normal or being rational) and practices (e.g. greeting by bowing or shaking hands), as illustrated in Figure 1. Practices are more visible, standardized, easy to change and situation dependent. Values are more internalized, implicit and all encompassing.

In this article, we discard the creation of models for driving practices. Indeed, these models have been extensively studied by the MAS community through norms, protocols, partly organizations and so on. Thus we leave interested readers consulting the rich and available literature about that topic.

Values are the most subtle part of cultures. Let us consider how they impact on decisions in order to model them. Cultural studies state that decisions made by individuals are influenced by human nature and cultures and personality. Human nature can be considered as individual rationality (e.g. selecting options leading to goal achievement). Personality corresponds to an individual variance for considering problems. This aspect does not seem relevant with regard to our goal for supporting collaboration, so it is left out in this article. Cultures are values and practices. As a rule of the thumb, when making a decision, agents consider how to achieve their goals (driven by human nature and possible external constraints such as protocols) while being conform with their practices (e.g. not violating cultural norms). If there are still multiple options available, values influence which option to select. This rule is of course not an absolute truth (e.g. values sometimes drive people to go against their self-interest or against practices, a model of such decisions is proposed in [11]), but it covers the standard decision process while remaining simple enough to model.

The term "values" can introduce some confusion and requires to be further introduced. A value is an abstract and broad perspective for considering a situation (e.g. achievement, self-direction, more examples are given in Section 6). The value*s* of an individual are informally the set of values which are given some importance by an individual. Nevertheless, values of an individual are not binary (e.g. either caring about achievement or discarding it) but relative with each other (e.g. giving relatively more importance to achievement than to self-direction). In the following value*s* are referred to as "value systems".

With that new information in mind, value systems seems to match well with preferences. [17,25] propose to use preferences as soft constraints, which allow to decide when multiple rationally and norm-compliant choices are available. Nevertheless, value systems are more specific than any preference function. Indeed, value systems should order abstract and driving values.

4.2 Integrating Value Systems in Agent Decision Processes

In order to make decisions which are streamlined with their value systems, agents require two capabilities: they have to be capable of *estimating the outcomes* of their decisions and order these outcomes using their *preference function.* These two capabilities are combined in order to make the decision which achieve the preferred estimated outcome according to agent's value system.

Estimating Outcomes Decision outcomes model the estimated effects of making a decision (e.g. performing an action) in a given situation. We talk about estimated effects, because they cannot be predicted for sure (e.g. actions might fail, the environment or other agents can interfere). Several solutions exist for representing and estimating about the consequences of decisions.

[22] uses a planning approach, assuming a bounded search span. The outcome of action corresponds to the expected satisfaction of the final situations which would be reached assuming that the agent selects the most satisfactory actions in the future. This representation implies some assumptions for the model. First, this model discards the presence of other agents. Second, expected outcomes are limited to single-dimensional real numbers in order to limit complexity. Third, a complete environment model is required.

[25, p. 109-136] uses a more logic-based approach, which consists in estimating "by hand" the consequence of a decision using qualitative tags. For instance, the expected effect of performing the "rescue" action is that the victim will be rescued, the agent will probably be late and the agent will be near the victim. Such representation should also describe longer term or uncertain consequences of decisions. For instance, hiding in the fire truck is immediately "safe" but "unsafe" situation if the fire is expected to spread.

Estimating long-term consequences of decisions can be difficult if these decisions are too concrete. This difficulty is caused by possible incompleteness of the environmental model, partial information and collective action. If all these elements would be modeled through some uncertainty factors, one would soon reach a point where the effects of actions are completely unknown.

The representation of [25] allows to cut short the search for all possible effects (which is intractable) by heuristically estimating consequences of decisions.

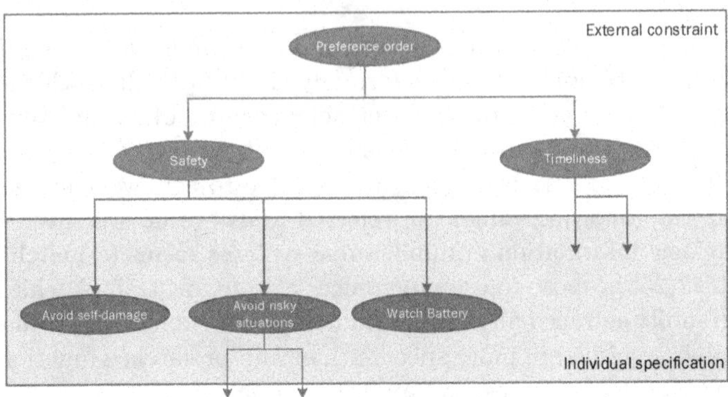

Fig. 2. Preference decomposition of firefighter agents. Each node of the thee is further specified by its children. Leafs are to be directly connected with evaluation outcomes.

However, this approach is more suitable for making strategic actions (e.g. whether to collaborate with a specific agent) rather than low-level decisions (e.g. whether to send a specific message or another the other agent). The reason being that the range of outcomes and of possible situations explodes when being concrete, thus making intractable the design of heuristics.

Ordering Preferences. Preferences are used for modeling the value system of agents. Technically, preferences are used for ordering the values of agents.

Ordering outcomes require to connect the value system to outcomes. Nevertheless but value systems are too abstract to be easily connected with concrete decisions (e.g. evaluating the safeness of the route to take). In order to better evaluate the desirability of an outcome for a given value, we propose to use more concrete criteria for supporting this evaluation. For instance, the evaluation of the safeness of a route can be supported by the three criteria: "avoiding risky situation", "avoiding self-damage" and "watching battery". Of course, these criteria are just a guidance and the decision tree may not be complete. Decisions which badly fulfills these more specific criteria can still be preferred (e.g. going through the fire without recharging is bad for all three options but still better than getting around the fire which would certainly lead to burning the agent).

Similarly, these criteria can be further related with more concrete criteria. Indeed, these criteria can still be abstract and evaluating them can rely on other and more concrete criteria (e.g. relating "avoid risky situations" with "avoid fire" and "avoid collapse risks"). From a more global perspective, value systems can be represented as a generalization tree[4], in which children of a criteria are specific criteria which can be used as a support for evaluating its parent. An illustration of that tree is proposed in Figure 2.

From a collective perspective, this generalization tree is partly shared by agents. More precisely, the highest part of the tree is shared by all agents. Then, this tree can be refined locally by specifying criteria.

[4] Or directed acyclic graph, since multiple criteria can rely on similar more concrete criteria.

From a design perspective, this representation combines a top-down and a bottom-up approach. Indeed, abstract value systems can be connected to more concrete decisions in further specifying them. The other way around, designers can aim at making abstract decisions which outcomes can be connected to more abstract criteria.

Using such a generalization tree has multiple advantages. First, designers of preference functions can connect their abstract decisions in a step-wise way, by adding criteria in an increasing order of concreteness. This decomposition has the advantage of avoiding to connect a value to far too many criteria for making principled decisions. Furthermore, each criteria can be related to sub-criteria which are not too far enough in terms of abstraction, helping to better justify decisions. Third, each criteria can be reused used as a sub-criteria multiple times, lowering the cost of designing criteria (e.g. "avoiding self-damage" can be used as a sub-criterion for both "safety" and "limiting costs" criteria). Last but not least, this representation leaves a lot of freedom about using criteria when designing preferences. For instance, just by changing how a criteria relies on its sub-criteria, agents can be driven to extreme safety ; extreme punctuality ; or a balanced combination of the two.

4.3 Towards Hybrid Agents Using Values

Value systems are adequate for supporting decisions with abstract reasoning, but they are impractical for handling concrete behavior. Concrete behavior is better handled by traditional solutions for designing agents or coordinating them (like plain code, BDI, planning, protocols), but those solutions are less adapted for integrating abstract drives. These two solutions are complementary and there is a clear gain in connecting both together. This section proposes some principles for an implementation model of the influence of value systems on decisions.

A first solution consists in implicitly integrating value systems within decisions, i.e. without explicitly relating a model preferences with decisions. This approach has the advantage of shortcutting the design of a complete value function and avoiding to evaluate outcomes of actions. But, this approach has multiple limitations. First, value systems cannot be changed without having to directly change agent decision process. Second, value-related decisions are less justifiable, introducing subjectivity. This subjectivity can be difficult to handle if preferences are related to multiple criteria and each criteria can encompass a wide range of evaluations (e.g. if timeliness and safety are both relatively important and enter into consideration for a decision, hard to compare each solution). In such a case, it may become difficult to determine which decision to select in a principled way.

Most of these issues can be solved by explicitly integrating value systems within agent decision processes. Multiple solutions can be investigated for achieving that. For instance, [17] proposes to integrate preferences for determining which plan to select when multiple plans can be fired in a given situation.

As an extension, we suggest to use a hybrid model. This model would be composed of three layers. A *tactical* layer would cope with concrete decisions. A *strategical* layer using abstract value systems would manage abstract longer-term decision, as suggested by [25]. These two layers would be connected through an interaction layer. In this layer, strategical decisions can influence tactical decisions, for instance by changing goals, activating a module[8] or executing a protocol. In return, strategical decisions are influenced by tactical outcomes, for instance through belief updates, goal fulfillment, or a specific procedure state is reached. Hybrid agent architectures are not new. The more adequate one for that purpose that we found in the literature is inteRRaP [21]. inteRRaP proposes different reasoning layers with different internal logics (reacting to the environment, planning from a single agent point of view, planning from a group point of view). Nevertheless, such architectures tend to focus on different perspective than ours (social versus individual or system reactivity). They do not seem immediately applicable in our context but propose an interesting inspiration.

As a closing word, the aim of this subsection consists in showing the type of decisions which are adequately connected with value systems. In particular, value systems appear particularly useful for supporting and influencing abstract strategical decisions. This type of decisions show the ease to connect value systems with hybrid models. Nevertheless, the global aim of this article is not to provide a very concrete implementation of one solution for using value systems, even if such an implementation is an immediate follow-up. Instead, we want to show how value systems can be beneficial for designing MAS and this subsection highlights how easily they can be implemented.

4.4 Benefits of Value-Based Agents

Creating Expectations about Other Agents. Since value systems are expected to be shared within the agent community, agents can create expectations about each other drives and resulting behaviors. Furthermore, value systems can be used for creating expectations about the environment and the society. For instance, if timeliness is important, then other agents are assumed to be on time. As a result, agents can create the social assumption that schedules are reliable. Thus agents can plan while tightly optimizing their schedules, leading to overall higher performance. The same can be applied for environmental assumptions (e.g. if timeliness is important, resources are assumed to be available on time).

Expectations can be integrated in several ways. A first solution consists in integrating them by design. Designers can integrate them knowing what is collectively considered as important (e.g. if timeliness is important, then other agents prefer not to accept too many tasks at once). This solution requires human intervention, but it allows to shortcut the need for creating these expectations on the fly. Furthermore, designers can integrate their insights, providing a richer variety of expectations within agents.

A second solution consists in automatically creating expectations about behaviors of other agents. This solution can be achieved in relying on the assumption that value systems are shared. Agents can use these systems for making Game-Theoretical expectations about behaviors of other agents in estimating their preferences, if the setting is simple enough. Agents can also be used for evaluating the responses of other agents. Such an expectation is particularly useful for achieving cooperation. Indeed, preferences can be used for driving the generation and the selection collective plans as well as justifying them to other agents, which is a basic task of cooperation. Nevertheless, agents only share the most abstract part of their value systems and only partly their beliefs. Thus, estimating other's preferred outcomes may be imperfect but should still be relatively close to reality.

Making the comparison with other approaches, expectations created by value systems are more abstract and less certain than those resulting from concrete approaches for collaboration (e.g. norms). Indeed, expectations for value systems are not adequate for sharply predicting concrete behaviors. For instance, "saving humans" does not mean than agents will rescue victims as soon as possible. Instead, agents may believe that more lives can be saved by extinguishing the fire (e.g. as in the running example in a skyscraper). Nevertheless, if some option is clearly better than other, agents are very likely to create adequate expectations about other agents. Furthermore, the more the value tree is shared, the more agents are more likely to create adequate expectations. At the opposite, expectations provided by other methods for achieving collaboration (e.g. norms) are more concrete and specific to a situation or interaction (e.g. protocols). Thus, these expectations tend to be relatively precise and accurate. As a concluding word, both expectations are complementary. Combining them offers useful perspectives.

Value Systems: Towards Human-Agent Interaction? Value systems are particularly useful for supporting interactions between human and agents. Using value systems for linking human and agents is relatively little cumbersome for humans. Indeed, value systems are relatively intuitive to grasp (e.g. efficiency, comfort, timeliness). They avoid the learning curve induced by understanding the possibilities of more concrete approaches which restrict behaviors of agents. Furthermore, humans can intuitively adapt value systems of agents to their needs, without requiring specific programming capabilities. From the agent side, given an allocated value system, agents can determine which expectations human users make about them. They can also use value systems for creating more concrete rules for interacting with humans.

Value-based systems are also appropriate for avoiding systems to be rejected due to their complexity. Indeed, decisions are supported by value systems. Thus, decisions can be explained in terms that humans can understand (e.g. "I extinguished the fire because I think it will save more lives"). Consequently, agent decisions appear less arbiraty to humans, which can then better support collaborative interactions with humans, in human-agent societies.

Finally, value systems provide a simple model of human psychology. Consequently, agents can use value systems of humans in order to create expectations about them, as they would with other agents with value systems. Value systems are abstract enough to create some abstract expectations about human behavior, while not creating expectations about concrete human behavior. These latter expectations are likely to mismatch, unless strong restrictions are imposed to humans behaviors.

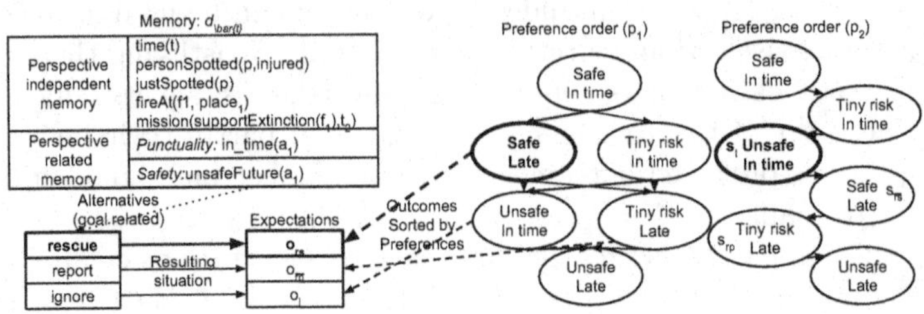

Fig. 3. Decision process for an agent with preference function p_1 in situation $d_{\bar{t}}$ Bold lines and text highlight choices made by the agent. If a_1 uses preference p_2, then the selected action is "ignore".

4.5 Running Example

Perspectives In this example, four preferences are considered: safety p_1, punctuality p_2 and combinations of these two. The whole decision process is illustrated in Figure 3.

Estimating Outcomes. If "rescue" tactical action is performed, a_1 expects o_{rs}: $late(a_1), at(injured\_person)$. If "report" is performed in d_t, a_1 expects o_{rp}: $in\_time(a_1), reported(a_1, person), at(unknown\_position)$. If "report" is performed in $d_{\bar{t}}$, a_1 expects $o_{\bar{rp}}$: $late(a_1), at(unknown\_position)$. If "ignore" is performed, a_1 expects o_i: $in\_time(a_1), unreported(person), at(fire)$.

Preference Functions. Safety is represented by the following order: situations with the property *safe* are better than those with the property *tiny_risk* which are better than those with the property *unsafe*. *safe* is true if the agent is far from fire (e.g. rescuing the injured person, thus $at(injured\_person)$ is true), *tiny_risk* is true the agent may be have to move to the fire (e.g. when $at(unknown\_position)$ is true, for instance when the agent waits for leader instructions) and *unsafe* if the agent is near a fire (thus $at(fire)$ is true). Punctuality is represented by the following order: situations with $in\_time(a_1)$ are better than those with $late(a_1)$.

p_1 and p_2 are combinations of safety and punctuality. p_1 compromises punctuality and safety. p_2 drastically favors punctuality over safety: for two situations s_1 and s_2; s_1 is better than s_2 if, for timeliness s_1 is better than s_2 or they are incomparable with regard to timeliness and for safety s_1 is better than s_2.

5 Integrating Value Systems in Collaboration

This section investigates the benefits of integrating value systems for improving collaboration from a collective perspective. As a first observation, value systems alone insufficient for achieving collaboration alone. First, because values support drives which are not directly related to system goals. Second, because value systems are too abstract for constraining concrete agent behaviors, which are particularly important for conducting concrete interactions with other agents (e.g. value systems are not adequate for determining whether to drive on the left or on the right). These more concrete interactions are better supported by more traditional methods (e.g. norms, organizations, cooperation). In the following, we aim at combining value systems with such methods.

This section investigates first the influence of value systems over collaboration in human societies using concrete methods for supporting collaboration. Then, we use this link as an inspiration for improving collaboration in artificial societies using value systems.

5.1 Inspiration

The relationship between cultures and collective performance has been broadly studied for human societies. These studies focus on generalist influences of cultures on collective behaviors but some studies focus more specifically of this influence in the context of organizations or corporations. Figure 4 illustrates such an observed correlations between some cultural features (power distance and uncertainty avoidance) and preferred organizational patterns. These patterns drive in turn the type of collective performance profiles which can be achieved (e.g. bureaucracies are fitter for simple and static environments while adhocracies are fitter for more complex and dynamic environments [20]). This section aims at replicating such a property, in investigating how value systems can improve collaboration in a MAS.

These studies give high importance to the influence of culture, for the main reason that they drive individuals towards common individual and collective outcomes. This drive helps individuals to understand and create expectations about each other. Furthermore, value systems also highlight what is important for individuals and drive them towards similar outcomes. Thus, individuals decisions tend to be streamlined when having multiple possible choices (e.g. 5 minutes late for a meeting versus gaining 10 minutes for oneself), allowing to support abstract collective properties.

5.2 Combining Values and Former Approaches for Collaboration

Value systems and concrete approaches tackle very different problems. This section aims at considering these differences and how they can be combined with each other.

Abstract Values and Concrete Collaboration The higher is a criteria in the value tree, the more this criteria is abstract and thus the least environment-dependent it is. Value systems are relatively reusable, even if they may require to be locally adapted to specific environments. Nevertheless, they are not perfectly adequate for making very concrete decisions.

Value systems enforce properties which are abstract and relatively independent from a given system (e.g. being in time, not causing others do be delayed). Conversely, traditional methods for achieving collaboration tend to be more related to environmental or interaction properties (e.g. concrete norms, protocols). Thus, these approaches tend to better enforce concrete decisions.

Value systems appear to combine well with other solutions for achieving collaboration. They offer generic and abstract drives which lead to useful system properties (e.g. timeliness, degree of independence of agents) without strictly forbidding any concrete behaviors. In addition, value systems help agents to make abstract actions which influence more concrete decisions (e.g. which goal to select, which abstract method to use in order to tackle a given problem). Nevertheless, collaboration solutions are still crucial for enforcing concrete environmental and interaction properties, which are required for tightly connecting agent actions.

Drives versus Constraints. Value systems determine what agents should consider as important, given some abstract and generic perspectives. Value systems can be seen as drives. In particular, value systems are shared within the community. Thus, agents are all driven towards similar outcomes and all consider the same things as important. This shared drives is crucial for avoiding individuals go against expectations of others. Furthermore, this shared drive helps behaviors to conflict with each other, given value-driven properties. For instance, with timeliness all agents know the importance of deadlines, which drive agents and are used for creating assumptions. Thus, no agent jeopardizes these deadlines without a good reason.

Value systems systems and other approaches complement well with regard to this aspect. Indeed, value systems can be used for determining *what* is important for agents in general. Conversely, other approaches determine *how* to behave in given expectable situations. Value systems help to abstractly and collectively drive agents towards desirable collaborative behavior. Value systems systems provide to agents some high-level guidelines about what agents should pursue when using the more concrete tools for collaborating (e.g. do not circumvent a safety rule by doing something dangerous). This link is particularly relevant for achieving cooperation. Indeed value systems can be used for determining collective goals and plans and for creating expectations about behavior of individuals with regard to that plan (e.g. with timeliness, sub-plans are likely to be assigned deadlines, which are highly used for optimizing global plans).

Furthermore, value systems guide agents in situations where agents are given some freedom. Such a situation can be desired by system designers. But this situation can happen if the agent has to perform an unexpected decision, in which rules do not apply. In that case, supporting agent decision is crucial in order to prevent the agent to go against the system due to a lack of guidance.

Performance. The influence of value systems on collaboration is relatively independent from the environment. To that extent, collaboration promoted by value systems tend to be relatively less sensitive to failures or to unexpected events, supporting robust and flexible collaboration. Nevertheless, this relative independence with the environment makes difficult to tightly optimize interactions of agents, making more difficult to pursue high efficiency.

This influence is relative to other approaches and provided in a general context. Indeed, value systems support a wide variety of behaviors with different performance profiles (e.g. timeliness tend to improve time to completion at the expense of robustness) and other approaches can be particularly robust or flexible.

Value systems are adequate for handling complex and dynamic environments. Indeed, value systems do not restrain agent behavior for resolving complex problems. To that extent agents are not restricted in the way they resolve problems and can thus develop more freely adaptive solutions. Such possibility is crucial for complex and dynamic environments for which restricting concrete behaviors may be hard to determine or can become inadequate.

Designing Collaboration with Value Systems. Integrating value systems raises now perspectives for designing collaboration.

Top Down vs. Bottom Up Concrete approaches restrain local behaviors and generally aim at achieving more abstract properties, using a bottom-up approach. Abstract approaches provide abstract constraints and are made more concrete, in a top-down approach. Value systems expand the latter category, which is at the moment composed of abstract normative and organizational systems (e.g. OperA [2]).

These two approaches can be combined together in order to leverage design costs. Indeed, reaching concreteness with abstract methods and abstraction with concrete methods is particularly expensive. Combining the two allows to use each method for the problems they are is adequate for.

Design Guidelines for Agents Value systems determine what agents consider as important. To that extent, they provide clear guidelines about what agents should focus on and thus the type of mechanisms they should encompass (e.g. time management for timeliness). From a collective perspective, value systems help to determine the set of concepts that agents can use for interacting with each other (e.g. deadlines for timeliness).

Designing Drives Designing value systems differ from former approaches because system designers have to drive agents instead of restricting their behavior. With value systems, system designers can only determine agents preferences and connect these preferences with the environment and decisions to be made. This form of design can appear difficult on first glance because designers cannot directly affect behaviors but instead about drives which would lead to desired behaviors. Idem, when debugging, system designers have to investigate whether agents making undesired decisions wrongly estimated outcomes or whether agents are not inclined enough towards a more adequate value.

Designing the Whole System As a recommendation, value systems and other methods for collaborating should be streamlined by design. For instance, if timeliness important, then time should play a crucial role in norms and organizations. Norms should determine time limitations, such that agents which rely on these norms can integrate them in their schedule in order to be sure they do not miss deadlines. If that is not the case, value systems may conflict with other methods of collaboration, leading to counter-productive behaviors.

As a future work, we consider the integration of value systems with systems including dynamic constraints for supporting collaboration (e.g. dynamic environments and norm base). In such scenario, we may expect agent to adapt the constraints base to the environment but also to value systems (e.g. removing safety rules leading to further danger). If value systems are also assumed to change, we suggest to make the value-base less dynamic than more concrete aspects, since value systems should be less sensitive to the environment.

6 Example of Useful Values for Improving Collaboration

In previous sections, we presented how value systems can be integrated in the design of MASs. This section proposes more concrete examples of what kind of objects can be integrated as a value. In particular, these examples of value systems are inspired by in human cultures. The core aim of showing these examples, in addition to provide immediate solutions, is to give an idea of the level of abstraction that we have in mind when we discuss about value systems. In addition, we want to show that each value has an important impact potential on plenty of individual and collective decisions. This impact has in turn plenty of consequences on design perspective (e.g. which norm to combine with a given preference).

As a disclaimer, these examples should serve as an inspiration of solutions which can be used for improving collaboration. Nevertheless, the model presented in this article does not aim at faithfully replicating human behaviors. Consequently, we kept only examples of cultural influences which are relevant for improving collaboration in MAS. Aspects which are too human oriented (e.g. desire from hedonism, ways to express emotions) are left out in this article.

Value systems are not a new topic and former researchers have empirically established them for human societies. The most used model is the Schwartz value model [24]. Schwartz empirically recognizes 10 value systems: stimulation, self-direction, universalism, benevolence, conformity, tradition, security, power, achievement and hedonism. These value systems can directly be used as criteria for modeling artificial value systems, as proposed in this article.

Cultural dimensions provide another source of inspiration for designing value systems. Each dimension evaluates cultural responses to dilemmas, like "What is more important, rules or relationships?" [16]. These dilemmas highlight some abstract choice which impact plenty of decisions. These choices indicates the influence of underlying value systems which can be integrated in our value-model (even if cultural dimensions are not value systems). On the track of linking culture and collective behavior in MASs, [26] conceptualize links between cultural dimensions, individual behavior, emerging collective behavior and performance.

In the rest of this section, we briefly introduces cultural dimensions from [16,18] which highlight crucial dilemma can be considered when integrating value systems in collaborative MASs.

Fig. 4. Culture and preferred organizational pattern, from [18]

6.1 Power Distance (PDI)

[18] defines Power Distance as the cultural relative importance given to formal and informal statuses.

In high PDI, subordinates prefer to give information and decision power to leaders. Leaders are expected to decide and assign clear orders for subordinates. As a result, in such a culture, leaders tend to have the more information and can thus make well-informed decisions. In addition, leaders can further optimize subordinate schedules because subordinates tend to be expected to wait for and comply with instructions, allowing to increase collective efficiency. From the perspective of system performance, high PDI tends to lower system robustness: leaders are bottlenecks (in particular in information-rich or complex environments). Thus, failing or missing leaders leads to a collapse of the communication and decision structures. In the running example, agents with high PDI value systems are likely to perform the "report" action. Indeed, this action makes sure that leaders possess the adequate information without going against orders given by agents. If agents run out of time or the leader is assumed to already have the information, they can also "ignore" the victim. "Rescue" is unlikely triggered because they are not supported to take that initiative without receiving the authorization.

In low PDI, individuals give less power to statuses. They consider themselves as independent and of equal value with regard to information and decisions. They are likely to take more initiatives and carry their own tasks. As a result, individuals have locally more information but leaders are less informed to technical details, providing with higher-level feedback. Such a culture is likely to increase system robustness, since no agent is critical to the system. Nevertheless, the lack of centralization of information and decisions tends to lower efficiency. In the running example, the lack of strong leadership is likely to let a_1 determine which action to pick, maximizing utility from an individual perspective. To that extent, "rescue" the victim is the most likely option, unless the task to be achieved by the a_1 particularly important. In the latter case, the agent may "report" if given enough time or "ignore" if lacking time.

6.2 Uncertainty Avoidance (UAI)

[18] depicts uncertainty avoidance the cultural sensitivity of individuals towards the certainty of their situations and their decisions.

In high UAI, individuals prefer to can create strong assumptions about their beliefs. To this extent, they either try to lower this uncertainty either by getting more information or by making assumptions about it (e.g. someone will support me when I will enter the burning house). As a result, individuals prefer to behave according to standards, further reducing uncertainties for itself as well as for others. Thus, as a an emerging property, individuals can expect less variability from actions of other agents or environmental states, further enforcing the benefits of making assumptions. High UAI is very efficient for static environment because a lot of assumptions can be made about the environment allowing to optimize collective action. Nonetheless, this preference is not flexible: if the environment is dynamic, either agents constantly update their procedures or they may try to apply mis-adapted procedures leading to failures. In the running example, an agent with high UAI is likely to pick a solution which minimizes generated uncertainty. "Rescue" is the most unlikely option, because it may prevent the agent to be at the fireplace while it should to be there, creating uncertainty for others which is particularly undesirable. "Ignore" may lead to the casualty of the victim which is mixed feelings. "Report" seems the best option, since it would lower uncertainties of the fire commander without creating so many uncertainties for the firefigter.

In low UAI, individuals are less sensitive to uncertainty. Their behavior is more directed by goals than by procedures. To that extent, behaviors are likely to be more adaptive, leading to more variability in environmental situation. In that case, this variability is not problematic because other agents expect the environment to be uncertain. They do not make inappropriate assumptions. This adaptability tends to raise collective flexibility but lowers efficiency due to difficulty for standardizing. In the running example, an agent with a low UAI value system has little incentive for following standards. Such an agent is likely to make similar decisions as a low PDI agent, thus maximizing local utility.

6.3 Sequential versus Synchronous Perception of Time

[16] describes two paradigms to consider time management: sequential and synchronous.

In sequential time, individuals consider time as a sequence of events. Respecting deadlines is very important to not delay this time-line. As consequence, timeliness is expected from other individuals. From a collective perspective deadlines and schedules are expected to be more reliable. Thus, such an APF is likely to improve efficiency and lower time to completion in allowing accurate planning of tight schedules. But, this approach fails when time considerations cannot be estimated accurately (lower flexibility) and is sensitive to failures, missing agents and congestion (lower robustness). In the example agents with sequential value-systems will do their best in order to be on time. In any situation they are likely to "ignore" the victim. Nevertheless, if timeliness is not set to an extreme importance, they are likely to "report" in d_t.

In synchronous time, time is considered as a resource to be planned against. To that extent, individuals prefer to locally maximize their efficiency, for instance by taking opportunities. With this consideration of time, timeliness is less important than lowering efficiency, so individuals tend to be late. Other individuals can expect delays and thus can, for instance, prepare activities for filling waiting time. This form of time management can also lead to high efficiency, if the environment is suitable for "filling in" waiting time. A negative point concerns the unpredictability of time to completion: an agent can continuously delay a task because of getting opportunities to perform other tasks more efficiently. In the example, synchronous agents select which action to perform in comparing the time cost incurred by selecting one of the other option (time for extinguishing a wider fire if "help" and time for getting back and rescuing for "ignore", estimated cost for sending someone else rescuing for "report").

7 Conclusion

With a similar idea than BDI, norms, organizations and protocols, this article proposes to use aspects of human societies, namely cultures, as an inspiration for improving collaboration in problem-solving MAS. Cultures provide a rich inspiration for MAS, by distinguishing two levels of influences: abstract values and concrete practices. The latter being already well studied (e.g. norms, protocols), we focus on the former. We propose solutions for expanding agent design in order to incorporate value systems and we investigate the benefits of integrating value systems on top of practices for driving agent societies.

Value systems are abstract drives shared by agents. Value systems specify uniformly to all agents some abstract aspects that they should consider as important when making decisions. By sharing a similar emphasis on what is important, agents can more easily determine which decisions are streamlined with collaboration. From a collective perspective, this drive allows the emergence of abstract desirable properties (e.g. deadlines tend to be reliable). Value systems can also be used by agents for creating some weak expectations about drives of other agents, their behaviors, the environment and the society (e.g. an agent in a culture promoting safety can expect support from the others).

Value systems offer a complementary perspective to existing approaches for supporting collaboration. Existing methods for supporting collaboration would gain in also integrating value systems. From an individual perspective, value systems are abstract enough for driving decisions in possibly any situation, particularly in unexpected scenarii, which may be above the limits of more concrete methods. From a collective perspective, value systems provide abstract directions about *what* agents shall pursue while practices describe more concretely *how* agents should behave. This complementarity has numerous benefits. The main one being that they provide cross views for tackling problems. This crossed view allows to avoid inherent explosion in terms of design complexity which happens for solving problems with an inappropriate approach. For instance, individual sharp and well expected behavior is relatively captured by norms while abstract collective patterns are more easily driven by abstract value systems. From a performance perspective, concrete approaches are appropriate for achieving high efficiency by providing tight guidance in standard situations. Value systems offer high flexibility and robustness in providing agents core principles for making principled decisions when rules fail to direct them. This decision support makes of value an adequate solution for coping with complex and dynamic environments.

Concerning possible applications of value systems, we identified three categories of applications: *Unknown, evolving environments* (e.g. exploration, building dynamic sensor networks). In such an environment, system designers cannot easily determine beforehand adequate patterns of collaboration. Agents should rather do it on the fly, depending on the situation. Value systems offer an adequate guidance for driving collaboration in these many possible situations.

Adversarial environments (e.g. military applications, game-oriented applications). In such an environment, concrete approaches are risky because they tend to force some behavioral patterns for achieving collaboration. These patterns put the system at risk of being exploited (e.g. trigger an emergency call in order to attract all the drones around, weakening the main entrance). Instead, value systems offer versatile and adaptive behavior which still aims at promoting collaboration.

Human-machine interactions (e.g. health-care robots, serious gaming). As further advocated in this article, value systems are numerous advantages for connecting humans with software agents. Value systems are intuitive, easy to adapt, provide a simple model of human drives and agents can use value systems for justifying their decisions.

For future work, we plan to integrate value systems within an agent. We plan on using the hybrid agent, which combines a value-driven strategical layer with a tactical layer influenced by traditional design tools. The layer for practices should encompass a high-level BDI representation such as $2APL$ or GOAL. Then, we plan to create a society of such hybrid agents and investigate their individual and collective behavior on a concrete problem. This implementation allows us to confront ourselves to technical issues raised by real problems and to investigate how far value systems can be used. From this confrontation, we expect to gain further knowledge about methodologies which are relevant for the designing value-based agents and about the connexion between value-systems with other methods for supporting collaboration.

References

1. Abdallah, H., Emara, H.M., Dorrah, H.T., Bahgat, A.: Using Ant Colony Optimization algorithm for solving project management problems. Expert Systems with Applications 36(6), 10004–10015 (2009)

2. Aldewereld, H., Dignum, V.: OperettA: Organization-Oriented Development Environment. In: Dastani, M., El Fallah Seghrouchni, A., Hübner, J., Leite, J. (eds.) LADS 2010. LNCS (LNAI), vol. 6822, pp. 1–18. Springer, Heidelberg (2011)
3. Amato, C.: Cooperative Decision Making. In: Kochenderfer, M.J. (ed.) Decision Making Under Uncertainty: Theory and Application, ch. 7, pp. 159–187. MIT Press (2014)
4. Baarslag, T., Fujita, K., Gerding, E.H., Hindriks, K., Ito, T., Jennings, N.R., Jonker, C., Kraus, S., Lin, R., Robu, V., Williams, C.R.: Evaluating Practical Negotiating Agents: Results and Analysis of the 2011 International Competition (2012)
5. Binmore, K.: Playing for Real: A Text on Game Theory. Oxford University Press (2008)
6. Boella, G., Torre, L., Verhagen, H.: Introduction to normative multiagent systems (2006)
7. Brafman, R.I., Domshlak, C.: Preference Handling An Introductory Tutorial. AI Magazine 30, 58–86 (2013)
8. Cap, M., Dastani, M., Harbers, M.: Belief/goal sharing modules for BDI languages. In: 2011 CSI International Symposium on Computer Science and Software Engineering (CSSE), pp. 87–94 (2011)
9. Castelfranchi, C.: Formalizing the Informal? In R. Demolombe and R. Hilpinen, editors. In: Proceedings of the 5th International Workshop on Deontic Logic in Computer Science (DEON 2000), Toulouse, France, January 20-22. Informal Proceedings, pp. 3–5. ONERA (2000)
10. Di Marzo Serugendo, G., Gleizes, M.-P., Karageorgos, A. (eds.): Self-organizing Software, from Natural to Artificial Adaptation. Springer (2011)
11. Dignum, F., Dignum, V.: Emergence and enforcement of social behavior. In: Anderssen, R.S., Braddock, R.D., Newham, L.T.H. (eds.) 18th World IMACS Congress and MODSIM 2009 International Congress on Modelling and Simulation, pp. 2942–2948 (2009)
12. Dignum, V., Dignum, F.: A Logic of Agent Organizations. Logic Journal of IGPL 20(1), 220–240 (2011)
13. Durfee, E.H.: Distributed Problem Solving and Planning. In: Luck, M., Mařík, V., Štěpánková, O., Trappl, R. (eds.) ACAI 2001. LNCS (LNAI), vol. 2086, pp. 118–149. Springer, Heidelberg (2001)
14. Durfee, E.H., Lesser, V.R.: Using Partial Global Plans to Coordinate Distributed Problem Solvers. In: Bond, A.H., Gasser, L. (eds.) Proceedings of the Tenth International Joint Conference on Artificial Intelligence IJCAI 1987, pp. 875–883. Morgan Kaufmann Publishers (1987)
15. Ferber, J.: Multi-Agent Systems: An Introduction to Distributed Artificial Intelligence. Addison-Wesley (1999)
16. Hampden-Turner, A., Trompenaars, C.: The seven cultures of capitalism: Value systems for creating wealth in the United States, Japan, Germany, France, Britain, Sweden, and the Netherlands. Currency Doubleday (1993)
17. Hindriks, K.V., van Riemsdijk, M.B.: Using Temporal Logic to Integrate Goals and Qualitative Preferences into Agent Programming. In: Baldoni, M., Son, T.C., van Riemsdijk, M.B., Winikoff, M. (eds.) DALT 2008. LNCS (LNAI), vol. 5397, pp. 215–232. Springer, Heidelberg (2009)
18. Hofstede, G., Hofstede, G.J., Minkov, M.: Cultures and Organizations: Software of the Mind, 3rd edn. McGraw-Hill Professional (2010)
19. Maskin, E.: Implementation theory. In: Aumann, R., Hart, S. (eds.) Science, vol. 1, pp. 237–288. Elsevier (2002)

20. Mintzberg, H.: The structuring of organizations: A synthesis of the research. Prentice-Hall (1979)
21. Müller, J.P., Pischel, M.: The agent architecture inteRRaP: Concept and application, p. 99. Citeseer (1993)
22. Nguyen, T., Do, M., Gerevini, A., Serina, I., Srivastava, B., Kambhampati, S.: Planning with Partial Preference Models. CoRR, abs/1101.2 (2011)
23. Omicini, A., Ricci, A., Viroli, M., Castelfranchi, C., Tummolini, L.: Coordination artifacts: Environment-based coordination for intelligent agents. In: Proceedings of the Third International Joint Conference on Autonomous Agents and Multiagent Systems, AAMAS 2004 (2004)
24. Schwartz, S.H.: A Theory of Cultural Value Orientations: Explication and Applications. Comparative Sociology 5(2), 137–182 (2006)
25. van der Weide, T.: Arguing to motivate decisions. PhD thesis, Utrecht Universiteit (2011)
26. Vanhée, L., Dignum, F., Ferber, J.: Towards Simulating the Impact of National Culture on Organizations. In: Alam, S.J., Van Dyke Parunak, H. (eds.) MABS 2014. LNCS (LNAI), vol. 8235, pp. 151–162. Springer, Heidelberg (2013)
27. Wooldridge, M.: Introduction to Multiagent Systems. John Wiley & Sons, Inc. (2002)

The Interaction as an Integration Component for the JaCaMo Platform

Maicon Rafael Zatelli and Jomi Fred Hübner

Department of Automation and Systems Engineering
Federal University of Santa Catarina (UFSC) – Florianópolis, SC – Brazil
xsplyter@gmail.com, jomi.hubner@ufsc.br

Abstract. Interaction is a subject widely investigated in multi-agent systems (MASs), but some issues are still open. While most of current approaches of interaction in MAS just consider the interaction between agents, some problems are better modeled when the MAS is composed of agents, environment, interaction, and organization. In our approach, we integrate the interaction with the other MAS components, like the organization and the environment, keeping it as a first class abstraction. In this paper we present a conceptual model for the interaction component, a programming language to specify the interaction, and how our approach was integrated in an MAS platform. The main result of this paper is the conception of the interaction as a first class abstraction considering an MAS composed of agents, environment, interaction, and organization.

1 Introduction

It is quite common in MAS that the agents need to interact to achieve their goals. Sometimes an MAS can be composed of *Agent*, *Environment*, *Interaction*, and *Organization* as introduced in [15,23]. In this kind of MAS, the interaction does not concern only the agents, it is strongly related to the environment and the organization of the system. For instance, besides interacting directly with other agents, agents also interact with objects in their environment by means of acting and sensing.

Many works already exist about agents, organization, and environment. There are tools to specify, develop, and execute each of these components. For example, an MAS developer is able to build the environment by means of CArtAgO [40], the organization by means of AGR [21], ISLANDER [20], Moise [27], and so forth, and finally, the agents by means of GOAL [24], JADE [11], 2APL [13], Jason [10], and so on. There are also tools to link these components to work together, such as EIS [5] and JaCaMo [9]. This separation of concerns can improve the maintenance, modularity, organization, reuse of code, etc. It is also easy to see that each of these components can be programmed by different developers, which also facilitates the division of tasks.

In addition, several approaches defend the idea of keeping the interaction as a first class abstraction [14, 32–34, 43, 44]. However, none of current works (Sec. 2) provide us features to specify and execute the interaction considering the existence of the other MAS components, that is, to allow the specification, development, and execution of the interaction not considering only agents, but also considering the environment and the organization.

F. Dalpiaz et al. (Eds.): EMAS 2014, LNAI 8758, pp. 431–450, 2014.

We already introduced a conceptual model and a programming language for the interaction considering the other MAS components in previous works [49, 50]. In this paper we focus on the integration of the interaction with the JaCaMo platform. JaCaMo is a project that allows the developer to consider each one of the MAS components as first class abstraction. Although the agent, environment, and organization components are already considered by this platform, the interaction component was not properly integrated. In this platform, the interaction is not a first class abstraction, it is simply reduced to messages coded inside the agents program. For instance, it is not easy to find in the code how the system interaction is programmed (it is indeed spread in several agent programs).

The aim of our work about interaction (conceptual model (Sec. 3), programming language (Sec. 4), and integration with JaCaMo (Sec. 5)) is to provide a mechanism to institutionalize how the agents may interact with the different elements in an MAS to achieve the organizational goals. We are linking the organization (e.g. its goals) to the agents (that should fulfill them) and to the environment (by defining interaction protocols that could be used as guidelines for the achievement of the goals). By considering the interaction with the environment, we can formalize more general situations in a protocol, where the agents should interact with the environment by means of performing actions and perceiving changes. We are looking for an interaction component that is able to deal with the other three MAS components. It means that we are considering a more complex MAS, composed of *Agent*, *Environment*, *Interaction*, and *Organization*. The main results that we got with our approach are detailed in Sec. 6 while further works and conclusions are presented in Sec. 7.

2 Related Work

In this section, we present the interaction problematic and some related work. We start with the works focused on interaction between agents, followed by those that consider the interaction with the environment, and in the following, the works that regard the interaction with the organization. Finishing this section, we mention some works that have already introduced the interaction problematic considering the integration with the three other components.

2.1 Interaction and Agents

There are several drawbacks of specifying the interaction inside of the agents code [19, 32, 44]. One of them is related to the maintainability of the system. If the interaction specification is modified, it is necessary to update the code of each agent involved. Another one is related to the protocol composition. The protocols could not be composed at run-time in order to allow more complex interactions.

As pointed by some approaches, it is unnecessary to keep the interaction control inside the agents code [31–33, 35, 44]. The separation of the two issues simplifies the development of applications, leading to a modular approach [22]. Consequently, protocols can be used to compose more complex protocols [12, 16, 17, 28, 37, 38]. In [28, 38, 44], other advantages of a modular approach are presented such as the specification of reusable protocols, the improvements in the validation process, and the capacity to share protocols between agents at run-time.

2.2 Interaction and Environment

One of the main limitations in most of works is to consider the interaction only by means of message exchange between agents, not considering the agent interaction with the environment [2, 3, 6]. Some examples that justify this kind of interaction are presented in [2, 3]. One of these examples refers to the election in the human world. When people have to do an election, they do not say the candidate name. They use their hands to interact with the electronic ballot box or simply raise them without saying any word. On the one hand, the electronic ballot box is responsible for computing the votes and notify the winner. On the other hand, by raising their hands, people also may discover the winner of some election only by counting the upper hands. In both cases, the interaction occurs by actions and percepts in the environment and not by speech acts.

There are some works that consider the relation between interaction and environment. In [39] and [42], it is presented a model that allows some different kinds of interaction, called overhearing, or eavesdropping. In this kind of interaction, the agent intercepts messages of others by using the environment. The environment is a way to send and receive messages. In [30], the aim is to conceive an environment as a way to allow indirect interaction. Their focus is on interaction like stigmergy, which is the interaction used by several natural systems such as amoebae and ants. In [35], the environment is considered as a mediator between agents and not a proper first class abstraction. In [31], the environment is also considered by another perspective: the agents could recognize other agents by the concept of neighborhood. The agents are only able to communicate with others depending on how far they are from each other. In both cases [31, 35], it is not considered the actions or percepts performed by the agents in the environment. Moreover, although their approach consider the concept of *roles*, such roles are not related to organizational roles. As a consequence, the specification may lack coherence since different role conceptualization may exist in different components. A role, for example, while existing inside a protocol, may not exist in the organization.

The MERCURIO framework [2, 3], a very similar work to ours, focus on integration of the interaction model regarding agents and environment. The environment considers the actions performed by the agents and the percepts that the agents may sense. However, the main aim of MERCURIO is to deploy the interaction with the environment, thus the interaction is also not strongly connected with the organization. As in [31, 35], the roles in the interaction are not the same roles as in the organization.

Finally, in [4, 41] the authors use artifacts to handle the interaction between the agents. In [41], the aim is to provide a communication infrastructure based on artifacts. The implementation of such infrastructure is done in JaCaMo platform [9] and the authors provide the representation of two kinds of artifacts. The former has the aim to represent the interaction protocol itself and allows the specification of a sequence of messages. The latter defines each speech act individually. In [4], the authors use CArtAgO artifacts to embed commitment-protocols following the model introduced in [46–48]. Their work also enriches the JADE [7] with mechanisms to exploit the use of commitments and protocols based on commitments. Each artifact keeps a social state, which is composed of social facts and commitments. Thus, the agents are able to reason about the interaction by means of observing the social state evolution. In both cases [4,41], instead of the agents exchange messages directly, they use the operations provided by the artifacts. For example, in the contract-net protocol, the operations of the artifact can be `cfp`, `propose`, `refuse`, `accept`, `reject`, `done`, and `failure`. Moreover, the communication artifacts have the aim to notify the receiver about the messages.

2.3 Interaction and Organization

The relation between interaction and organization is also important. The GAIA methodology [45], for instance, has already defined a role as a composition of four main attributes: responsibilities, permissions, activities, and protocols. The protocols are responsible for specifying the interaction between the agents that are playing the organizational roles.

Some works about organization already relate the interaction with the organization by means of a dialogical dimension [8, 18, 20, 21, 25]. In this case, they use several organizational concepts, like goals, roles, and obligations. Each of these concepts is strongly connected with the interaction concepts, which means that, for example, the roles in the interaction are the same roles as in the organization.

2.4 Summary

Although none of the presented works addresses the integration of the interaction with the three other components in order to allow its specification, development, and execution, some works already address this topic in an AOSE perspective. MAS-ML [43] and O-MaSE [14] are a modeling language and methodology, respectively, which consider the interaction integration with the three other components. However, both approaches are conceived for the specification phase and do not consider the implementation and execution phases. In addition, even providing tools to generate code, they do not generate the interaction code.

Thus, even if some authors are concerned with the interaction between agents and some of the other components, none of them integrates the interaction with the three components in a unified perspective and consider the development and execution phases. Moreover, in some of them, the interaction specification is conceived to be handled by humans during the MAS design and does not allow the agents to read it (or eventually to change it) at run-time. By not considering the interaction as a first class entity and by lacking an integration with the other three components, we may have a series of difficulties in the development of some applications: (i) it is difficult to have an overall view of the interaction in the MAS because the interaction code is spread in several parts of the system (e.g. it is only possible to see the interaction if we open the code of each agent involved in the interaction); (ii) the MAS developer is not able to formalize (by means of a programming language) the expectations about the MAS evolution considering the interaction both with the environment and with other agents; (iii) it is not possible to provide a more detailed specification for the agents to help them to achieve organizational goals, especially if the agents need to interact with the environment; and

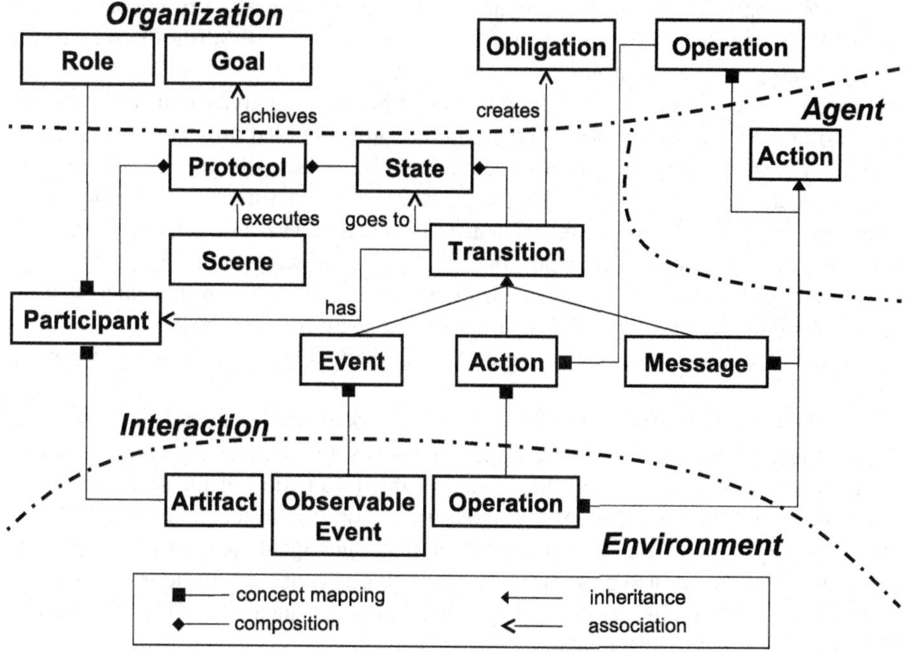

Fig. 1. Conceptual model

(iv) agents in open systems have more difficulties to interact because the interaction protocols are not explicitly specified and available at run-time.

3 Conceptual Model

This section briefly presents how the several MAS components are conceptually integrated with the interaction. Only the core ideas of the model are described here. More details can be found in [49].

Fig. 1 shows the four MAS components and the relations between the interaction and the others. In order to keep the figure clear and clean, we only show the concepts that were directly related to the interaction. The most important concept in our model is the interaction protocol[1], which is basically composed of a set of participants, transitions, states, and goals. Each transition links two states (one source state and one target state) and it can be fired by an event, a message, or an action. When some transition is fired, a new state is achieved and the protocol execution progresses. In order to separate the protocol specification and the protocol execution, we call *scene* an instance of a protocol. It is possible for a protocol to have several scenes executing at the same time.

The organizational concepts used in our model (top of Fig. 1) are based on the organizational models presented in [18, 27]. The interaction is related to organization in

[1] In this paper, we consider the definition of protocol presented in [29].

four points. Firstly, the protocols are related to organizational goals. A protocol specifies a possible interaction scheme to achieve them. When a protocol finishes successfully, the organizational goal is considered achieved. For example, if there is an organizational goal for an agent to contract a company to build a house, such goal can be achieved by the use of a contract-net protocol. The protocol is just *one* (and not the *only* or even a *mandatory*) way for the agents to achieve the organizational goals. It can exists several protocols to achieve the same goal and the agents could also achieve a goal using other means. We could also imagine the existence of protocols without a relation to organizational goals, however, in this work, our main objective with the use of protocols is to help the agents to achieve the organizational goals. Thus, we are not interested in the representation of protocols that do not drive the agent to accomplish organizational goals and neither about what the agents do for achieving their own (not organizational) goals.

The second organizational concept used in our model is obligation. The transitions of a protocol are related to organizational obligations. Obligations are created for the agents to perform the action that fires some enabled transition of the scene and thus evolve its execution. For example, if there is a transition in a protocol that specifies that some agent needs to tell the price of a product to another agent, an obligation with this information will be created as soon as the transition is enabled. Furthermore, the use of obligations does not hinder the agents from trying other means to achieve the goals. The agents are free to violate them.

Thirdly, the participants of a protocol are related to organizational roles. To be a participant in a protocol, an agent must previously play a role in the organization (e.g. the role `baker` or `manager`). Since the organization constraints the role adoption based on the agent skills, the agent will be able to perform the activities required as a participant in the protocol. Finally, the organization also provides operations, which are the actions that some agent can perform in the organization such as adopts or leaves some role, commits to some mission or goal, and achieves some goal.

The environmental concepts used in our model (bottom of Fig. 1) are based on the A&A meta-model introduced in [36]. We map the concept of artifact onto a participant in the interaction component, which constrains the participation of artifacts in the protocol; the operations, which represent the actions that the agents can perform in the environment (for example, the agent can execute actions to regulate the temperature of an oven, such as turns the oven on or off); and finally, the observable events, which agents can perceive in the environment, such as an alarm indicating that the temperature of an oven is too high, the color of something, the sound of a machine, etc. It is important to notice that the artifacts are not an autonomous entity and, in our approach, we are not trying to define what the *artifacts* should do. Rather, the protocol defines which actions the *agents* should do on them. Besides the actions, the use of protocols is a way to handle the observable events that are being produced by the artifacts.

The agent component (right side of Fig. 1) provides the concepts of action, which can be some action performed in the environment or in the organization, and the message exchange, which represents the use of communicative acts (e.g. `tell`, `achieve`) in order to interact with the other agents. The actions that the agents perform in the environment or in the organization are mapped onto their respective concepts in their respective components. An action performed by the agent in the organization is mapped onto the concept of action in the organization component while an action performed by the agent in the environment is mapped onto the concept of action in the environment component. Finally, the concept of message exchange is directly mapped onto the concept of message in the interaction component.

The conceptual model introduced in this section is a generic solution for the integration of the organization, environment, and agents based on the concepts depicted in Fig. 1. For example, if the organization provides concepts like goals, roles, and obligations, it can fit very well in the proposed model. Moreover, the model can also be adapted to other organizations, environments, or agents. One of the core ideas of this paper is to take advantage of using a formal representation for the interaction considering the environment and the organization. A well-detailed protocol (specified by means of messages, actions, and events) can help the development of open systems or help the agents that do not know how to achieve some organizational goal. Thus, protocols are used to define a more general behavior for a *system* and not simply to define the behavior of the agents using message exchange.

4 A Language to Specify Interaction Protocols

In this section, we map the concepts presented in Fig. 1 onto a programming language used to specify interaction protocols.[2] The language is mostly presented by means of two examples. The aim of the first example is to provide a typical sequence of steps used to write a protocol in our approach. For this first example, we consider a simplified situation where an agent must make a cake. The protocol shows especially how an agent interacts with the environment by means of actions and percepts. The second example illustrates more features of the language, such as the specification of message exchanges and timeouts. In both examples, we present very simple situations, however the real advantages of the proposed interaction protocols are better noticed in large MAS, where the system is composed of hundreds of agents with complex tasks and interactions.

The first step to build a protocol with the proposed language is to decide which organizational goals the protocol must achieve. For example, to make a cake for a bakery organization, we can conceive a protocol as a way to achieve the goal "*to make a cake*". When the cake is done, the goal "*to make a cake*" can be set as achieved.

In the following, we need to decide who will be the participants of the protocol. Using the example of the cake, we can assume that in the bakery organization there are the roles *baker* and *cake_decorator*. The *baker* is responsible for the cake production while the *cake_decorator* is responsible for the cake decoration. Therefore we can define `baker` and *cake_decorator* as participants of the protocol. In addition, we may include some environment elements that will participate of this scenario. For example, we will need an *oven*, a *blender*, a *clock*, etc.

Then we specify the states of the protocol and the order that they should be achieved. The states of a protocol can be achieved by means of transitions that can be fired by

[2] We will only briefly present the most important parts of the language, since more details can be found in [50].

Algorithm 1. Making a cake protocol

```
protocol making_a_cake {
  description: "Tell the agent how to make a cake";
  goals: "to_make_a_cake";
  participants:
    agBaker agent "baker";
    agCakeDecorator agent "cake_decorator";
    artBlender artifact "artifacts.Blender";
    artOven artifact "artifacts.Oven";
    artClock artifact "artifacts.Clock";
  states:
    n1 initial; n2; n3; n4; n5; n6 final;
  transitions:
    n1 - n2 # agBaker -- action "mixIngredients" -> artBlender;
    n2 - n3 # agBaker -- action "putCake" -> artOven;
    n3 - n4 # agBaker -- action "setTimer" -> artClock;
    n4 - n5 # artClock -- event "alarm" -> agCakeDecorator;
    n5 - n6 # agCakeDecorator -- action "takeCake" -> artOven;
}
```

actions that the agents perform in the environment, events that the agents can perceive, and messages that the agents can exchange. Back to the *making a cake* scenario we can see some transitions. We can define as a first transition that the agent with the role *baker* needs to mix the ingredients using the *blender*. In the second transition, the *baker* needs to put the cake into the *oven* and finally it needs to set the *clock* with the required time. After the time elapses, the *clock* emits a sound, which can notify the *cake_decorator* that the cake is done. Thus, the *cake_decorator* can take the cake out of the *oven*. In Sec. 5, we give more details about how transitions produce obligations.

Finally, we can define a name, some description, the initial state, and the final states. Notice that we can have several final states, however we can only have one initial state. In the *making a cake* scenario, we can set the initial state as when there is "nothing" of the cake. As a final state, we can set the state after the agent takes the cake out of the oven. Therefore, when this final state is achieved, the goal *to make a cake* is achieved in the organization. A possible implementation of this protocol is presented in Code 1.

The advantage of using protocols in the case of the making a cake scenario is the openness. A new agent, which has never made a cake before, can adopt the role *baker* and follow the protocol specification. The protocol is a way to guide the new agent to make the cake. Therefore, we can replace the agents and if they know how to follow protocols, they can make a cake easily. Another aspect of this example is that we only used actions and events, such as *put the cake into the oven*, *take the cake out of the oven*, *set the time in the clock*, and *the sound emitted by the clock*. Both actions and events are related to environmental concepts. Although the transitions in our example represent macro-tasks, we could detail the protocol as much as we need. For example, the transition `n5 - n6` could be detailed using other actions. Instead of simply taking the cake out of the oven, we could specify that the agent should turn the oven off, open the oven door, take the cake out of the oven, and close the oven door.

Code 2 presents another example of protocol, where the aim is to serve a customer in a store and the sellers do an election in order to decide which one will serve the customer. The participation of the agents is defined in lines 5 and 6, which state that they

Algorithm 2. Attending protocol

```
1. protocol attending {
2.   description: "Serve a customer";
3.   goals: "chooseSeller";
4.   participants:
5.     playerCustomer agent "customer";
6.     playerSeller agent "seller" all;
7.     artBallotBox artifact "artifacts.BallotBox";
8.   states: k1 initial; k2; k3; k4 final;
9.   transitions:
10.    k1 - k2 # playerCustomer -- message[tell] "needSeller" -> playerSeller;
11.    k2 - k3 # playerSeller -- action "vote(X)" -> artBallotBox
                 : ".string(X) & .is_agent(X)";
12.    k2 - k3 # timeout 30000;
13.    k3 - k4 # artBallotBox -- event "winner(Y)" -> playerSeller;
14. }
```

must play the role `customer` (line 5) or the role `seller` (line 6) in the organization. The protocol also includes the participation of a ballot box artifact to help the agents to vote in an anonymous approach (line 7).

The protocol is composed of four states (line 8): `k1`, `k2`, `k3`, and `k4`, where `k1` is the initial state and `k4` is the final state. On the one hand, the available transition from state `k1` is defined in line 10. It defines that the agent who is playing the participant `playerCustomer` must send a message to the agents who are playing the participant `playerSeller` informing them that it needs some seller. On the other hand, the available transitions from state `k2` are those defined in lines 11 and 12. The former can be triggered only by agents participating as `playerSeller` in the protocol by doing the action `vote(X)` on the artifact `artBallotBox` (the ballot box). The latter is defined with a `timeout` statement (line 12). The `timeout` is important in situations where temporal constraints are fundamental, such as the time that an agent must wait for the proposals of the others in an auction.

An important mechanism used in the language is the unification, which is equivalent with the traditional unification mechanism of several agent languages and also Prolog. When an agent performs the action `vote` or the environment produces the event `winner`, it must unify with their respective expressions `vote(X)` and `winner(Y)`, where X and Y are variables. Notice that in transition `k2 - k3` we have specified the test `".string(X) & .is_agent(X)"` which means that the agent performs the action `vote(X)`, the `X` must be both a `String` and an existing agent in the MAS. Moreover, it is important to notice that this test expression is any `String`, which means we can have many ways to evaluate some action. More details about this mechanism is explained afterwards.

Finally, the last transition of the protocol (line 13) defines that the `artBallotBox` counts the votes and emits an observable event named `winner(Y)`, where `Y` is the winner name. With the successful termination of the protocol, the goal `chooseSeller` is achieved in the organization (line 3).

It is also possible to specify different ways to fire transitions. Fig. 2 presents the language grammar with its non-terminal symbols. The non-terminal `duty` defines what must happen to fire the transitions and each transition may have several different

```
protocol           ::= "protocol" <ID> "{" description
                                              goals
                                              participants
                                              states
                                              transitions "}"
description        ::= ("description" ":" <STRING> ";")?
goals              ::= "goals" ":" (goal)+
goal               ::= <STRING> ";"
participants       ::= "participants" ":" (participant)+
participant        ::= participantId partDescription ";"
partDescription    ::= ("agent" role | "artifact" type) partCardinality
partCardinality    ::= ("all" | ("min" <INTEGER>)? ("max" (<INTEGER> | "+"))?)
participantId      ::= <ID>
type               ::= <STRING>
role               ::= <STRING>
states             ::= "states" ":" (state)+
state              ::= stateId ("initial" | "final")? ";"
stateId            ::= <ID>
transitions        ::= "transitions" ":" (transition)+
transition         ::= stateId "-" stateId "#" (occurrence | timeout | import)
timeout            ::= "timeout" <INTEGER> ";"
import             ::= "import" <STRING> mapping ";"
mapping            ::= "mapping" "{" (mapFromTo)+ "}"
mapFromTo          ::= participantId participantId ";"
occurrence         ::= pCardOccur "--" duty "->" pCardOccur ((trigger)+ | ";")
pCardOccur         ::= participantId ("[" <INTEGER> "]")?
duty               ::= dutyType <STRING>
dutyType           ::= ("event" | "action" | "message" "[" <ID> "]")
trigger            ::= ("trigger" pattern (":" content)? | ":" content) ";"
pattern            ::= <STRING>
content            ::= <STRING>
```

Fig. 2. Language grammar [50]

Algorithm 3. Reply to call-for-proposals in the contract-net protocol

```
1. no2 - no3 # seller -- message[tell] "replyCFP(CNPId)" -> client
           trigger "refuse(CNPId)" : ".number(CNPId)";
           trigger "propose(CNPId,Offer)" : ".number(CNPId) & .number(Offer)";
```

verifications (represented by the non-terminal `trigger`) to make sure whether some occurrence is valid to fire it. For example, in Code 3, we specified part of the contract-net protocol. In this part, the agents playing the participant `seller` must answer the call-for-proposals (`replyCFP(CNPId)`) sent by the agent playing the participant `client`. The triggers define the two possible answers that the agents could use to fire the transition `no2 - no3`. The former indicates that the `seller` could refuse to make a proposal (`refuse(CNPId)`), while the latter indicates that the `seller` could send a proposal (`propose(CNPId,Offer)`). In the previous protocols, presented in Code 1 and Code 2, we do not have such kind of situation because for each transition there is only one way to fire it. However, as presented in Code 3, we can represent transitions that could be fired using other ways.

The non-terminal `trigger` is composed of an expression to evaluate the occurrence pattern (represented by the non-terminal `pattern`) and an expression to evaluate the occurrence content (represented by the non-terminal `content`). For example, in Code 3,

Algorithm 4. Protocol composition

```
1. y2 - y3 # import "election.ptl"
                mapping {
                  employee elector;
                };
```

the pattern is represented by "refuse(CNPId)" and "propose(CNPId,Offer)", while the evaluation of the content is represented by ".number(CNPId)" and ".number(CNPId) & .number(Offer)", respectively. If the occurrence satisfies the pattern, then we can evaluate the content of the variables (if there are variables in the pattern).

If the pattern is omitted, the expression defined in the non-terminal duty will be considered as the pattern. For example, the pattern is omitted in the case of the protocols presented in Code 1 and Code 2. Considering the transition k2 - k3 presented in Code 2 (line 11), the expression specified in the duty (vote(X)) is used as the pattern. Next to the symbol : (line 11), it is defined the expression to evaluate the content of the action. Suppose the agent tries to execute something like vote("Ana",22). This action is not valid because it does not unify with the pattern vote(X), then the action is discarded. However, suppose that the agent performs the action vote(22). This action follows the pattern because it unifies the pattern (with X = 22), however the action is invalid because 22 is not a String, as required by the content. Finally, suppose the agent tries to execute the action vote("Ana"). We have X = "Ana" and "Ana" is a String. If Ana is also an agent, the action is valid to fire the transition.

Other features of the language are the composition of protocols and the cardinality. The composition is made by using the import directive. The import directive needs the information about the file of the sub-protocol and a mapping between the participants of the protocol and the sub-protocol. The mapping is necessary because, sometimes, the protocols may not have the same participants. An example of composition is presented in Code 4. In this case, the transition y2 - y3 will be fired after the election protocol be accomplished. The mapping in this protocol is made by defining that the participant employee will be the participant elector in the election protocol. Although the election protocol needs a goal related to it, during the composition its goal will be ignored. Only the goals related to the main protocol will be used at run-time.

The language also provides two different kinds of cardinality: the participant cardinality and the transition cardinality. The former is related to the required number of entities playing some participant in the protocol. The latter is related to the number of entities that are necessary to perform the duty specified in some transition. For example, we can have several attendants in a call-center, however we just need *one* to answer the phone. In an election, we have electors and it is necessary that *all* of them participate. Therefore, with cardinality mechanisms we can define these situations. Such features are presented in more details in [50].

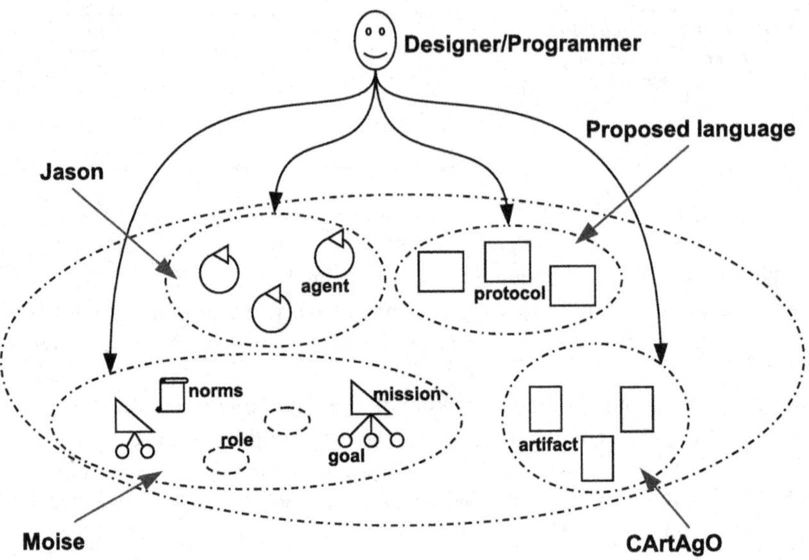

Fig. 3. Concern separation

5 Integrating with JaCaMo

The main aim of the integration of our interaction approach with JaCaMo is to provide an MAS programming platform supporting concerns separation also considering the interaction.[3] Fig. 3 shows a general idea of the integration. In JaCaMo platform, the MAS developer can already program each of the three components separately and each component can be programmed with specific tools and languages. The organization can be programmed using Moise, the agents can be programmed using Jason, and the environment can be programmed by using CArtAgO. In our work, we also enrich the JaCaMo platform with the interaction component, which also has its proper tool and language. The next two sections detail how the integration was made.

5.1 Mapping the Conceptual Model onto JaCaMo Platform

In order to integrate our approach into JaCaMo platform, we map the model presented in Fig. 1 onto the JaCaMo platform. Since the components of agent, organization, and environment in JaCaMo already use the same concepts, we need to integrate the relations between the interaction component and the other ones. As part of the integration, we introduce an interaction artifact (`SceneArtifact`), which allows the agents to work with the interaction component. A similar integration was already done with the organization by means of ORA4MAS artifacts [26].

Basically, when the agent receives an organizational obligation to achieve some organizational goal, it can verify which protocol can be used to help the accomplishment of

[3] The full implementation of our approach can be found at `https://sourceforge.net/projects/intmas/`.

Algorithm 5. Handling the organizational obligations created by the scene artifact.

```
1. +obligation(MyName, _Scene,
             transition(_CurrentState, _GotoState, _TriggerType, _Target, Duty),
             _Deadline):
2.   .my_name(MyName)
3. <-
4.   !Duty.
```

the goal. The agent can instantiate the protocol by informing its specification. Each instance of a protocol is executed in a different instance of the SceneArtifact, which allows the agent to follow the execution of each scene individually. The SceneArtifact reads the protocol specification and convert it in several observable properties to guide the agents during the scene execution.

The relation between the protocol and the organizational goal (Fig. 1) is reified by using a link between the artifact SceneArtifact and the artifact SchemeBoard of the organization. The artifact SchemeBoard is the responsible to deal with the organization goals in the organizational component of JaCaMo. Therefore, when the SceneArtifact achieves the final state of a protocol, it changes the state of the goals related to the protocol in the organization by means of that link.

An important part of our approach is the use of obligations, represented by the relation between transition and obligation (Fig. 1). Everytime the scene achieves a new state, new obligations are created to help the agents to accomplish the protocol. For example, suppose the protocol presented in Code 2. When the state k1 is enabled, an obligation related to the transition k1 - k2 is created. This obligation defines that the agent playing the participant playerCustomer should send a message needSeller, using the performative tell, to the agents playing the participant playerSeller. When the messages are sent, the scene moves from state k1 to k2 and the obligation is accomplished. As a consequence, new obligations will be created. In this case, it will be created an obligation related to the transition k2 - k3 for the agents playing the participant playerSeller to perform the action vote(X) on the artifact artBallotBox. In addition, this new obligation will have a timeout of 30000 milliseconds, as defined in line 12. Although created from a fact in the interaction component, the obligations exist in the organizational component of the MAS.

The agents in JaCaMo already knows how to handle organizational obligations because it is a concept already used in Moise. Thus, it is not necessary to build any new specific mechanism for the agents to work with the obligations created by the interaction component. The main advantage of using obligations is that they are created at run-time, which also means that the protocols can be updated at run-time. For example, if the order of the transitions is modified in the protocol specification, the next obligations will be created respecting the new order of the transitions. Therefore, the agents code usually does not need to be modified all the time that the protocol is modified, since the agents simply follow the obligations.

The Jason code presented in Code 5 illustrates how the agents can deal with the obligations created by the interaction component. In line 1, it is indicated that the agents perceive an obligation to do a duty in a certain moment of the scene execution. That duty

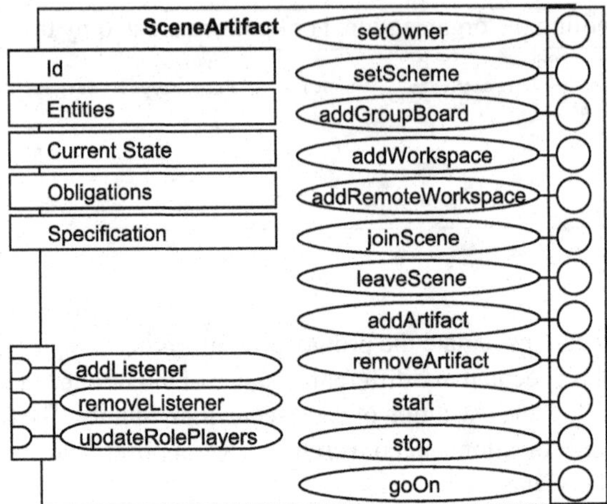

Fig. 4. Scene artifact

must be done in order to fire the enabled transition. As soon as the agents perceive that obligation, they create a new goal to accomplish that duty (line 4). Notice that it is only necessary to add the code presented in Code 5 in the agents program to make the agents able to create their own goals to accomplish the duties of the protocol. If the protocol is modified, other obligations for the agents are created and the agents will be able to continue following the protocol in the same way.

Fig. 4 shows the interface of the `SceneArtifact`, with its operations and observable properties. The operations allow the agents to play some participant of the scene (`joinScene`), to leave the scene (`leaveScene`), add and remove artifacts of the scene (`addArtifact` and `removeArtifact`, respectively), and to start (`start`), stop (`stop`), or continue (`goOn`) the scene execution. Moreover, by means of observable properties, the agents can get some information about the scene. For example, they can see the current state of the scene (`Current State`), the enabled transitions (by means of the `Current State` property), their obligations (`Obligations`), the entities that are playing the participants (`Entities`), the protocol specification (`Specification`), etc.

Since CArtAgO uses the concept of *links* to allow the representation of "operations" that can be accessed by other artifacts, we specify some links to allow the development of tools to monitor the scene execution. In that sense, there are links to add and remove some listener (`addListener` and `removeListener`, respectively). The general idea of these links is to allow other artifacts to receive information about the scene evolution. For example, it is possible to get information about the enabled states and transitions, the fired transitions and the actions, messages, and events that were responsible to fire each transition.

The last link (`updateRolePlayers`) is necessary because the interaction mechanism needs to know which are the agents playing each role in the organization. This information is used to handle the cardinalities and to make sure that certain agent is really playing some role. The Moise `GroupBoard` artifact already provides a link to add listeners and gets such information. In the same way, we need to handle the cardinalities

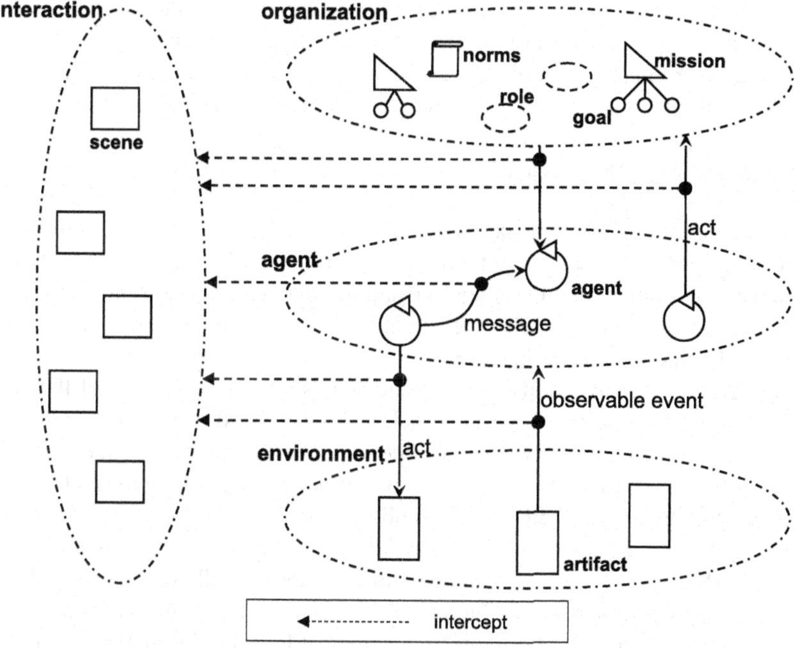

Fig. 5. Interception model

of artifacts and verify if certain artifact is of some kind. Therefore, we created a link (`getArtifactList`) into the `WorkspaceArtifact` in CArtAgO. This link has the aim to return the list of all artifacts and their kinds in some workspace. Such mechanisms are introduced to reify the relations between interaction participant with organizational role and environmental artifact, as presented in the conceptual model (Fig. 1).

5.2 Getting Messages, Actions, and Events

All the messages, actions, and events must be intercepted and sent to the scenes. Fig. 5 shows the interception model. It shows messages, actions, and events being intercepted during their occurrences. The agents do not need to notify the scene artifact about what they are doing explicitly, since they could try to cheat the interaction mechanism. For example, they could notify the interaction about things that they have never done.

Some related work use a mediator agent to get the necessary information [1], however the mediator agent is an autonomous entity and then it is possibly malicious. Our approach to get messages, actions, and events is similar to the approach presented in [3, 35], where the authors define a layer that behaves like a filter to consider only the correct messages to change the interaction state. In order to do that in JaCaMo platform, in a first moment, we modified the agent architecture. The new agent architecture intercepts the messages exchanged between the agents, the events that occurs in the environment, and the actions that the agents perform in the environment. Notice that the agents interact with the organization in JaCaMo by means of organizational artifacts in the environment, therefore it is not necessary to create a specific mechanism to deal with the actions performed in the organization. In the end, the messages, actions, and events that were intercepted are delivered to the scenes that the agents are attending. Then, they will be processed and evaluated in order to fire the enabled transitions.

6 Results and Discussion

Our main contribution in this paper is the integration of the interaction component into the JaCaMo platform. With this integration we have an MAS platform to program the agents, the environment, the organization, and the interaction, all of them as first class abstractions. We can now specify the interaction in a separated component, avoiding specifying the interaction inside the code of agents or other components.

As another result, we can also specify the agents more independent of the application. Before the integration of our approach into JaCaMo, it was necessary to specify how the agents interact with the other MAS components in their own code. With the interaction integrated into JaCaMo by means of artifacts and assuming the fact that agents already know how to deal with artifacts and organization, the agents do not need any specific mechanism to deal with the interaction. Even in the case of open and heterogeneous MAS, a global behavior can be defined for the overall system by means of the interaction. It is possible because the interaction allows the definition of the desired sequence of steps to achieve the organizational goals. Moreover, while the organizational goals provide information about *what* the agents need to do, the interaction protocols provide a more detailed description about *how* to behave to achieve them.

The integration with the JaCaMo platform allowed us to evaluate our interaction proposal and also to provide an example of how to integrate it into an MAS platform composed of agents, environment, and organization. In our experiments, we saw several advantages considering the interaction as a first class abstraction. For example, we can update the interaction without changing the code of the other MAS components. We also got some positive results with the relations that we made between the interaction and the other MAS components. For example, the obligations facilitate the agent programming and allow the agents to reason about them, specially whether the agents already can handle organizational obligations, as in the case of JaCaMo platform. We can change the sequence of transitions of protocols and, because the obligations are created in execution time regarding to transitions, we do not need to update the agents code. Moreover, in future works, norms and obligations will allow us to create punishment and reward mechanisms to prevent malicious behavior and reward the agents with good performances. The relation between participant in the interaction and role in the organization allows the agents to search for partners to cooperate because the protocols specify which roles they must interact with. The relation between interaction and environment by means of artifacts permits the specification of how the agents must proceed to interact with the artifacts by means of actions and observable events.

As some drawbacks of the integration with JaCaMo platform, we noticed a decrease in performance and some negative impact related to scalability. In fact, it was an expected impact because we did not focused on performance and scalability issues in this first moment. The main reason for this negative impact is the interception and management of messages, actions, and events that happen in the MAS execution. Since most of them could be relevant to the scenes, after the interception mechanism catch such occurrences we need to send them to the scenes and process them. So far, we built a centralized solution to process such occurrences in each scene, however it seems not the best solution for an MAS where there are many messages exchanges, actions, and events. The improvement of these issues remains as future work.

Another questionable point of our approach is related to the number of different languages that the developer should learn in order to implement an MAS using JaCaMo platform. With the integration of the interaction component into JaCaMo platform, the MAS developer will have four different languages to learn, each one dedicated to specify one of its components (agents, organization, environment, and interaction). Indeed, learning four languages would require more time and investments from the MAS developers. However, all the four languages are more suitable to implement their own concerns. For example, in order to specify the environment, it is better to use a specific environmental language than to specify the environment by means of an agent language. Naturally, when it is necessary to implement a simple MAS, most of times, the agents themselves are enough to solve the problems. The organization, environment, and interaction are better suitable to implement large and complex systems, where the separation of concerns is underlying.

Finally, our approach is not the only one to deal with interaction and some of the other components. As we presented in Sec. 2, there are several approaches of interaction, however, none of them integrate the interaction with all the other three MAS components in a unified way. Some of them handle the interaction between agents, others deal with the interaction and the environment or organization. Furthermore, our proposal is focused on more complex MAS, composed of agents, environment, and organization. Our aim is to integrate these components by means of the interaction and explore the advantages of this kind of MAS.

7 Conclusions and Future Works

In this paper we presented the integration of an approach of interaction considering agents, environment, and organization into the JaCaMo platform. Although we present the integration with the JaCaMo platform, our approach can also be integrated with other MAS platforms. We also highlighted the interaction model and the programming language. As future works, we intend to evaluate the use of this proposal in the development of large systems and also to verify protocols that are created by some agent, since the agents could create protocols at run-time and execute it. Other interesting subjects to explore are how the agents could reason about a protocol in order to optimize its execution, and a proposal of a mechanism to specify and handle exceptions. Finally, mechanisms of punishment and reward should be studied for the purpose of evaluating the performance of the agents when they are participating of some scene.

Acknowledgments. The authors are grateful for the support given by CNPq, grants 140261/2013-3 and 306301/2012-1. We would also like to thank the reviewers for the useful comments and questions, which helped us to improve this paper.

References

1. Ancona, D., Drossopoulou, S., Mascardi, V.: Automatic generation of self-monitoring MASs from multiparty global session types in jason. In: Baldoni, M., Dennis, L., Mascardi, V., Vasconcelos, W. (eds.) DALT 2012. LNCS, vol. 7784, pp. 76–95. Springer, Heidelberg (2013)
2. Baldoni, M., Baroglio, C., Bergenti, F., Boccalatte, A., Marengo, E., Martelli, M., Mascardi, V., Padovani, L., Patti, V., Ricci, A., Rossi, G., Santi, A.: MERCURIO: An interaction-oriented framework for designing, verifying and programming multi-agent systems. In: Proc. of MALLOW, pp. 134–149 (2010)
3. Baldoni, M., Baroglio, C., Bergenti, F., Marengo, E., Mascardi, V., Patti, V., Ricci, A., Santi, A.: An interaction-oriented agent framework for open environments. In: Pirrone, R., Sorbello, F. (eds.) AI*IA 2011. LNCS (LNAI), vol. 6934, pp. 68–79. Springer, Heidelberg (2011)
4. Baldoni, M., Baroglio, C., Capuzzimati, F.: 2COMM: A commitment-based mas architecture. In: Proc. of the 1st EMAS@AAMAS, pp. 17–32 (2013)
5. Behrens, T.M., Hindriks, K.V., Dix, J.: Towards an environment interface standard for agent platforms. Annals of Mathematics and Artificial Intelligence 61(4), 261–295 (2011)
6. Bel-Enguix, G., Jimenez-Lopez, M.D.: Agent-environment interaction in a multi-agent system: A formal model. In: Proc. of GECCO, pp. 2607–2612. ACM, New York (2007)
7. Bellifemine, F., Bergenti, F., Caire, G., Poggi, A.: JADE - a java agent development framework. In: Bordini, R.H., Dastani, M., Dix, J., Fallah-Seghrouchni, A.E. (eds.) Multi-Agent Programming. Multiagent Systems, Artificial Societies, and Simulated Organizations, vol. 15, pp. 125–147. Springer (2005)
8. Boissier, O., Balbo, F., Badeig, F.: Controlling multi-party interaction within normative multi-agent organizations. In: Proc. of MALLOW, pp. 17–32 (2010)
9. Boissier, O., Bordini, R.H., Hübner, J.F., Ricci, A., Santi, A.: Multi-agent oriented programming with JaCaMo. Science of Computer Programming (2011)
10. Bordini, R.H., Hübner, J.F., Wooldridge, M.: Programming multi-agent systems in AgentSpeak using Jason. Wiley, Liverpool (2007)
11. Braubach, L., Pokahr, E., Lamersdorf, W.: Jadex: A BDI agent system combining middleware and reasoning. In: Software Agent-Based Applications, Platforms and Development Kits, pp. 143–168. Birkhaeuser (2005)
12. Cabac, L., Moldt, D., Rölke, H.: A proposal for structuring Petri net-based agent interaction protocols. In: van der Aalst, W.M.P., Best, E. (eds.) ICATPN 2003. LNCS, vol. 2679, pp. 102–120. Springer, Heidelberg (2003)
13. Dastani, M., Meyer, J.-J.C.: A practical agent programming language. In: Dastani, M., El Fallah Seghrouchni, A., Ricci, A., Winikoff, M. (eds.) ProMAS 2007. LNCS (LNAI), vol. 4908, pp. 107–123. Springer, Heidelberg (2008)
14. DeLoach, S.A., Valenzuela, J.L.: An agent-environment interaction model. In: Padgham, L., Zambonelli, F. (eds.) AOSE 2006. LNCS, vol. 4405, pp. 1–18. Springer, Heidelberg (2007)
15. Demazeau, Y.: From interactions to collective behaviour in agent-based systems. In: Proc. of EuroCogSci, Saint-Malo, pp. 117–132 (1995)
16. Desai, N., Mallya, A.U., Chopra, A.K., Singh, M.P.: OWL-P: A methodology for business process development. In: Kolp, M., Bresciani, P., Henderson-Sellers, B., Winikoff, M. (eds.) AOIS 2005. LNCS (LNAI), vol. 3529, pp. 79–94. Springer, Heidelberg (2006)
17. Desai, N., Singh, M.P.: A modular action description language for protocol composition. In: Proc. of AAAI, pp. 962–967. AAAI Press (2007)
18. Dignum, V., Vázquez-Salceda, J., Dignum, F.P.M.: OMNI: Introducing social structure, norms and ontologies into agent organizations. In: Bordini, R.H., Dastani, M., Dix, J., El Fallah Seghrouchni, A. (eds.) PROMAS 2004. LNCS (LNAI), vol. 3346, pp. 181–198. Springer, Heidelberg (2005)

19. Doi, T., Tahara, Y., Honiden, S.: IOM/T: An interaction description language for multi-agent systems. In: Proc. of AAMAS, pp. 778–785. ACM, New York (2005)
20. Esteva, M., Rosell, B., Rodriguez-Aguilar, J.A., Arcos, J.L.: AMELI: An agent-based middleware for electronic institutions. In: Proc. of the Third International Joint Conference on Autonomous Agents and Multiagent Systems. Proc. of AAMAS, vol. 1, pp. 236–243. IEEE Computer Society, Washington, DC (2004)
21. Ferber, J., Gutknecht, O., Michel, F.: From agents to organizations: An organizational view of multi-agent systems. In: Giorgini, P., Müller, J.P., Odell, J. (eds.) AOSE 2003. LNCS, vol. 2935, pp. 214–230. Springer, Heidelberg (2004)
22. Cabri, G., Leonardi, L., Zambonelli, F.: BRAIN: A framework for flexible role-based interactions in multiagent systems. In: Meersman, R., Schmidt, D.C. (eds.) CoopIS/DOA/ODBASE 2003. LNCS, vol. 2888, pp. 145–161. Springer, Heidelberg (2003)
23. Hammer, F., Derakhshan, A., Demazeau, Y., Lund, H.H.: A multi-agent approach to social human behaviour in children's play. In: Proc. of IAT, Washington, pp. 403–406 (2006)
24. Hindriks, K.V.: Programming rational agents in GOAL. In: Multi-Agent Programming: Languages and Tools and Applications, pp. 119–157 (2009)
25. Hübner, A., Dimuro, G.P., Costa, A.C.R., Mattos, V.L.D.: A dialogic dimension for the Moise+ organization model. In: Proc. of MALLOW, pp. 21–26 (2010)
26. Hübner, J.F., Boissier, O., Kitio, R., Ricci, A.: Instrumenting multi-agent organisations with organisational artifacts and agents. Autonomous Agents and Multi-Agent Systems 20(3), 369–400 (2010)
27. Hübner, J.F., Sichman, J.S., Boissier, O.: A model for the structural, functional, and deontic specification of organizations in multiagent systems. In: Bittencourt, G., Ramalho, G.L. (eds.) SBIA 2002. LNCS (LNAI), vol. 2507, pp. 118–128. Springer, Heidelberg (2002)
28. Vitteau, B., Huget, M.-P.: Modularity in interaction protocols. In: Dignum, F.P.M. (ed.) ACL 2003. LNCS (LNAI), vol. 2922, pp. 291–309. Springer, Heidelberg (2004)
29. Huhns, M.N., Stephens, L.M.: Multiagent systems and societies of agents. In: Weiss, G. (ed.) Multiagent Systems, pp. 79–120. MIT Press, Cambridge (1999)
30. Keil, D., Goldin, D.Q.: Indirect interaction in environments for multi-agent systems. In: Weyns, D., Van Dyke Parunak, H., Michel, F. (eds.) E4MAS 2005. LNCS (LNAI), vol. 3830, pp. 68–87. Springer, Heidelberg (2006)
31. Kubera, Y., Mathieu, P., Picault, S.: Interaction-oriented agent simulations: From theory to implementation. In: Proc. of ECAI, pp. 383–387. IOS Press, Patras (2008)
32. Miller, T., McBurney, P.: Using constraints and process algebra for specification of first-class agent interaction protocols. In: O'Hare, G.M.P., Ricci, A., O'Grady, M.J., Dikenelli, O. (eds.) ESAW 2006. LNCS (LNAI), vol. 4457, pp. 245–264. Springer, Heidelberg (2007)
33. Miller, T., McBurney, P.: On illegal composition of first-class agent interaction protocols. In: Proc. of ACSE, pp. 127–136. Australian Computer Society, Inc., Darlinghurst (2008)
34. Miller, T., McGinnis, J.: Amongst first-class protocols. In: Artikis, A., O'Hare, G.M.P., Stathis, K., Vouros, G.A. (eds.) ESAW 2007. LNCS (LNAI), vol. 4995, pp. 208–223. Springer, Heidelberg (2008)
35. Oliva, E., Viroli, M., Omicini, A., McBurney, P.: Argumentation and artifact for dialogue support. In: Rahwan, I., Moraitis, P. (eds.) ArgMAS 2008. LNCS (LNAI), vol. 5384, pp. 107–121. Springer, Heidelberg (2009)
36. Omicini, A., Ricci, A., Viroli, M.: Artifacts in the A&A meta-model for multi-agent systems. Autonomous Agents and Multi-Agent Systems 17, 432–456 (2008)
37. Paurobally, S., Cunningham, J.: Achieving common interaction protocols in open agent environments. In: Proc. of AAMAS (2002)
38. Paurobally, S., Cunningham, J., Jennings, N.R.: Developing agent interaction protocols using graphical and logical methodologies. In: Dastani, M., Dix, J., El Fallah-Seghrouchni, A. (eds.) PROMAS 2003. LNCS (LNAI), vol. 3067, pp. 149–168. Springer, Heidelberg (2004)

39. Platon, E., Sabouret, N., Honiden, S.: Overhearing and direct interactions: Point of view of an active environment. In: Weyns, D., Van Dyke Parunak, H., Michel, F. (eds.) E4MAS 2005. LNCS (LNAI), vol. 3830, pp. 121–138. Springer, Heidelberg (2006)
40. Ricci, A., Viroli, M., Omicini, A.: CArtAgO: An infrastructure for engineering computational environments in MAS. In: Weyns, D., Parunak, H.V.D., Michel, F. (eds.) Proc. of E4MAS, Hakodate, Japan, pp. 102–119 (2006)
41. Rodrigues, T.F., da Rocha Costa, A.C., Dimuro, G.P.: A communication infrastructure based on artifacts for the JaCaMo platform. In: Proc. of the 1st AAMAS Workshop on Engineering MultiAgent Systems, pp. 97–111 (2013)
42. Saunier, J., Balbo, F.: Regulated multi-party communications and context awareness through the environment. Multiagent Grid Syst, 75–91 (2009)
43. Silva, V.T., Choren, R., de Lucena, C.J.P.: A UML based approach for modeling and implementing multi-agent systems. In: Proc. of AAMAS, pp. 914–921. IEEE Computer Society, Washington, DC (2004)
44. Singh, M.P.: Information-driven interaction-oriented programming: BSPL, the blindingly simple protocol language. In: Proc. of AAMAS, pp. 491–598 (2011)
45. Wooldridge, M., Jennings, N.R., Kinny, D.: The Gaia methodology for agent-oriented analysis and design. Autonomous Agents and Multi-Agent Systems, 285–312 (2000)
46. Yolum, P., Singh, M.P.: Designing and executing protocols using the event calculus. In: Proceedings of the Fifth International Conference on Autonomous Agents, AGENTS 2001, pp. 27–28. ACM (2001)
47. Yolum, p., Singh, M.P.: Commitment machines. In: Meyer, J.-J.C., Tambe, M. (eds.) Intelligent Agents VIII. LNCS (LNAI), vol. 2333, pp. 235–247. Springer, Heidelberg (2002)
48. Yolum, P., Singh, M.P.: Reasoning about commitments in the event calculus: An approach for specifying and executing protocols. Annals of Mathematics and Artificial Intelligence (2004)
49. Zatelli, M.R., Hübner, J.F.: A unified interaction model with agent, organization, and environment. In: Anais do IX ENIA@BRACIS, Curitiba, Brazil (2012)
50. Zatelli, M.R., Hübner, J.F.: A language to specify the interaction considering agents, environment, and organization. In: Anais do VII WESAAC, São Paulo, Brazil (2013)

Author Index

Ahlbrecht, Tobias 81
Albayrak, Sahin 163
Alechina, Natasha 367
Alexander, Rob 309
Alves Franco Brandao, Anarosa 146
Ancona, Davide 246

Baldoni, Matteo 388
Baroglio, Cristina 388
Bordini, Rafael H. 351
Briola, Daniela 246
Brown, Matthew 103

Capuzzimati, Federico 388
Casare, Sara 146
Caval, Costin 15
Clark, John 309

Dastani, Mehdi 204
Delle Fave, Francesco M. 103
Dignum, Frank 406
Dignum, Virginia 127
Dix, Jürgen 81
Dunin-Kęplicz, Barbara 328
Dybalova, Daniela 367

El Fallah Seghrouchni, Amal 15, 246

Ferber, Jacques 406
Freitas, Artur 351

Gleizes, Marie-Pierre 40
Graja, Zeineb 40

Hadj Kacem, Ahmed 40
Heßler, Axel 163
Hindriks, Koen V. 1
Huang, Zhan 309
Huber, Marcus 227
Hübner, Jomi Fred 181, 431

Jensen, Andreas Schmidt 127
Jiang, Albert Xin 103
Jones, Randolph 227

Kmiec, Slawomir 271
Köster, Michael 81
Kraus, Philipp 81
Küster, Tobias 163

Lee, JeeHang 367
Lespérance, Yves 271
Logan, Brian 367

Mascardi, Viviana 246
Maurel, Christine 40
Meneguzzi, Felipe 351
Mermet, Bruno 291
Migeon, Frédéric 40
Müller, Jörg P. 81

Nunes, Ingrid 58

Padget, Julian 367
Panisson, Alison 351
Parunak, H. Van Dyke 227

Quist, Michael 227

Rosoff, Heather 103

Schmidt, Daniela 351
Shieh, Eric 103
Sichman, Jaime 146
Simon, Gaële 291
Sullivan, John P. 103
Szałas, Andrzej 328

Taillibert, Patrick 15, 246
Tambe, Milind 103
Testerink, Bas 204

Uez, Daniela Maria 181

Vanhée, Loïs 406
Verbrugge, Rineke 328
Vieira, Renata 351
Villadsen, Jørgen 127

Zaientz, Jack 227
Zatelli, Maicon Rafael 431
Zhang, Chao 103